STREAMLINED

Richard Manion Architecture

STREAMLINED

Text by Adele Cygelman
Principal Photography by Erhard Pfeiffer

images
Publishing

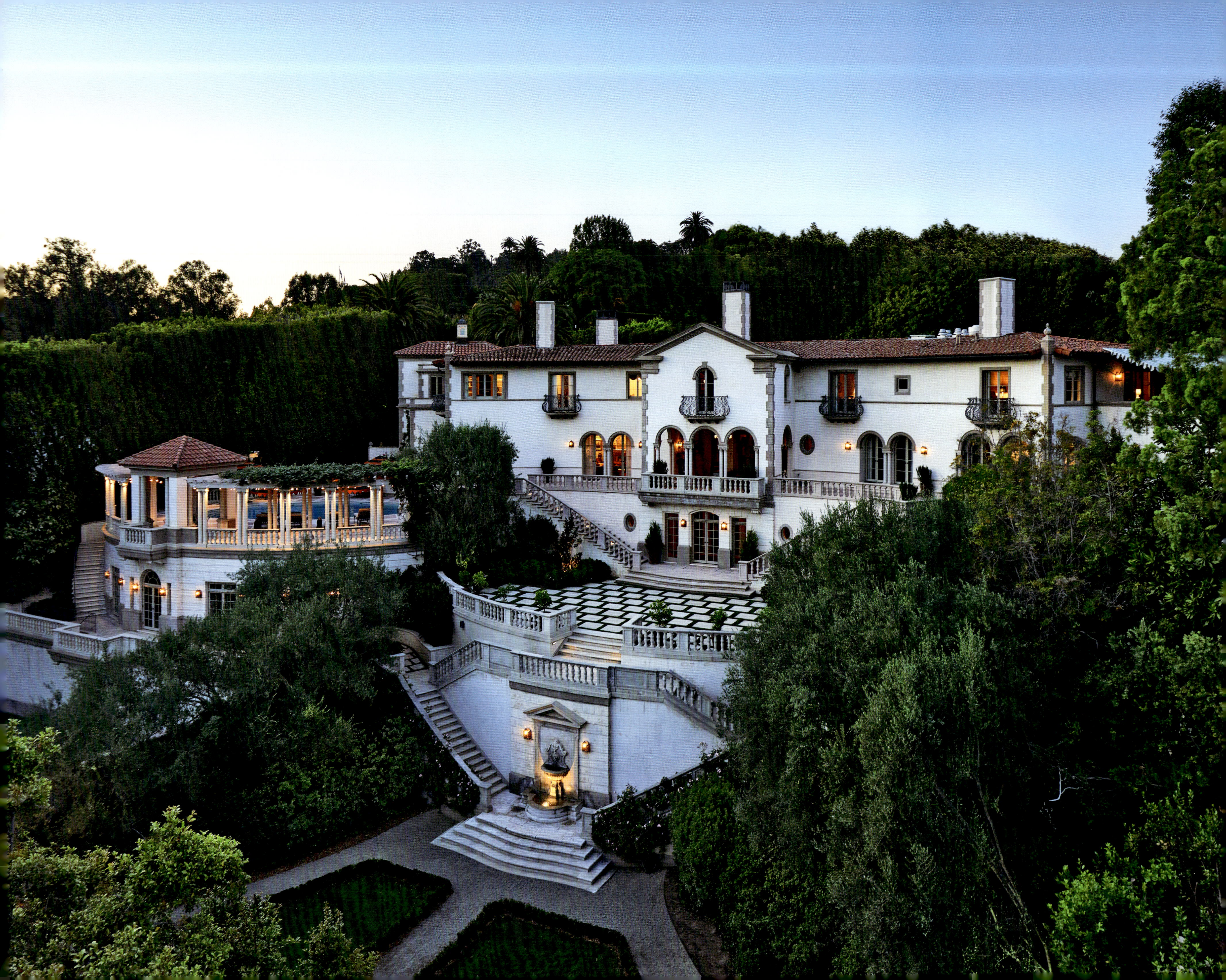

This book is dedicated to the people who made this work possible and to the many great influences that have inspired me over the years. To my trusting clients, it is an honor to create unique environments that reflect your personal lifestyles and serve as elegant backdrops for living. To my dedicated office and team members over the years, your tireless efforts and invaluable contributions show in every facet of the work that we have created together. To my talented colleagues in design, construction and consulting, thank you for what we can achieve when we collaborate as a team. And last, but not least, to my family and friends, thank you for your endless support and sage counsel.

Richard Manion

Los Angeles, 2020

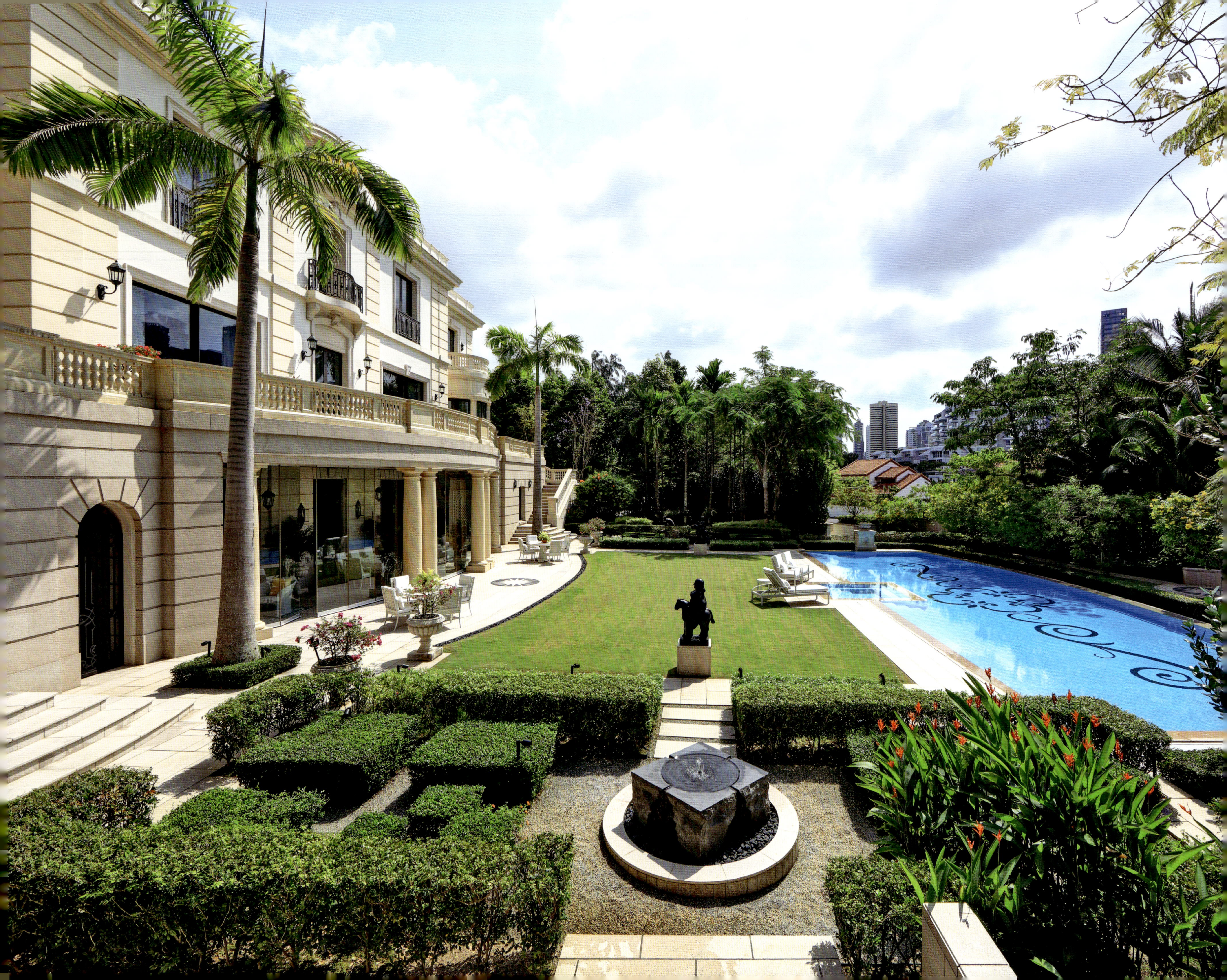

CONTENTS

FOREWORD

"House" is an inadequate word to describe the ground-up construction of Colline d'Or, an estate inspired by eighteenth-century French châteaux, set on an 18-acre plot of land atop a hill overlooking San Francisco Bay. Nonetheless, this house was the first I worked on with Richard Manion.

Starting in 2003, we proceeded to work on this house over the course of six years from start to finish, designing and selecting in tandem the color palettes, cabinetry, fireplaces, fixtures, fittings, hardware, wall finishes, and ironwork. Richard's vision encompassed every detail. The last remaining family-owned silk manufacturer in Lyon provided period textiles from its archives. A venerable French hardware manufacturer with over 17,000 patterns furnished the custom gilt bronze door and window hardware. A French sculptor working in the Italian town where Michelangelo sourced marble 500 years ago carved statuary marble garden sculptures of the Four Seasons based on the ones at Versailles. A team of Florentine artists hand-painted the ceilings with grotesques inspired by Herculaneum and kiln-fired a tile panoramic mural for the indoor swimming pool room. We traveled to France, Italy, and the Far East with our client, fueled by our interest in classicism and exoticism (and tangentially inspired by the Sun King's reception of the ambassadors of Siam at Versailles in 1686). The house demanded a balance between fantasy and historical research, creativity and rigor, attention to detail, and patience. It was a profound experience, one that forged an ironclad friendship between us, and between us and our client (with whom we later worked on another very different house that appears in this book, the Kaiser Estate). To paraphrase Charles Ryder in Evelyn Waugh's *Brideshead Revisited*, we were all drowning in honey, stingless.

Since that time, I have had the privilege of working on a number of other houses with Richard Manion and his team. He approaches every project like an artist with a blank canvas. There are recurrent stylistic elements that make his work recognizable, but originality is the cornerstone, based on his mastery of history and architecture.

His approach is grounded in the Beaux-Arts method; his artistic process is based on quantitative problem solving. He listens to his clients and, in responding to their ideas, pushes his own vision to create houses that are personal and new. He intuits their goals and desires, both stated and unspoken.

In this volume there is a breadth and variety of projects within a framework of simplicity and restraint, discretion and harmony. The story of these houses is also revealed in the team of people working together with a shared vision, as Le Brun, Le Vau and Le Nôtre did at Versailles in the seventeenth century. Richard Manion is not easily satisfied; the difficult solution is often the best, even if in the end it looks natural and inevitable.

Sketching, modeling, and reworking each architectural element until all details are refined and realized. A process of discovery, architecture, landscape and interiors. A reimagination of the past to create something harmonious, something new. Classic. Modern.

David Desmond
Los Angeles, 2020

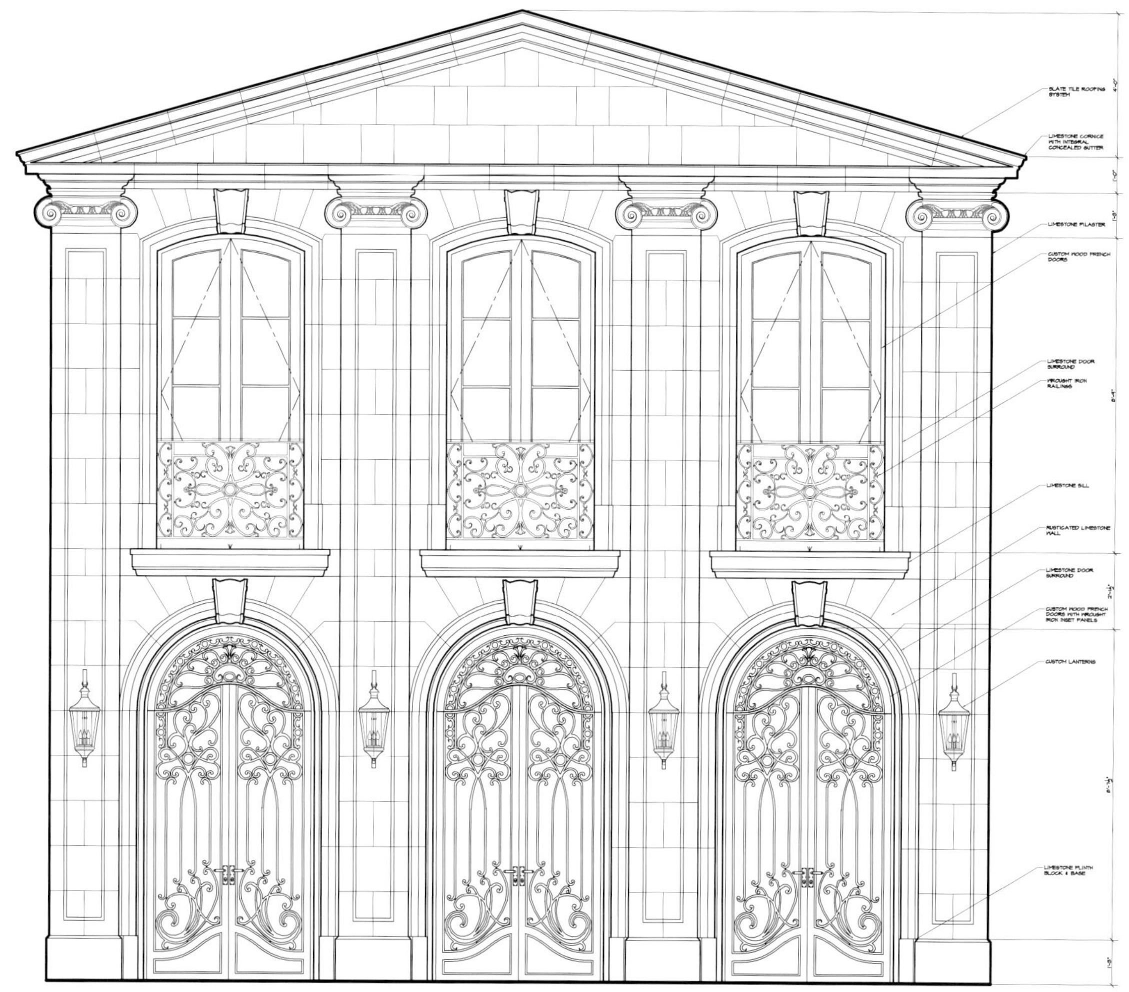

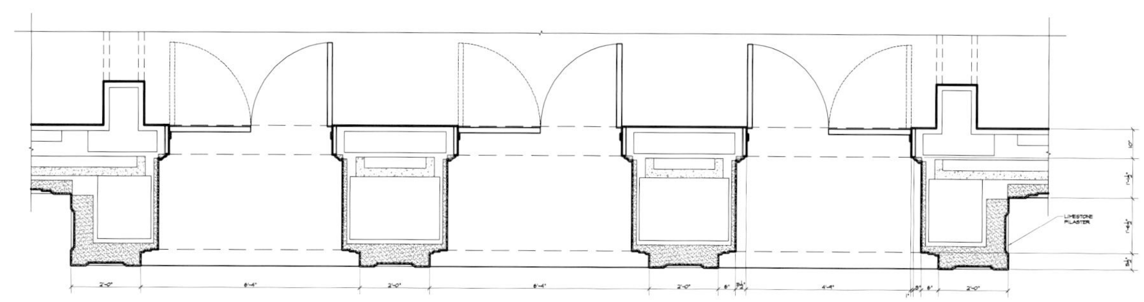

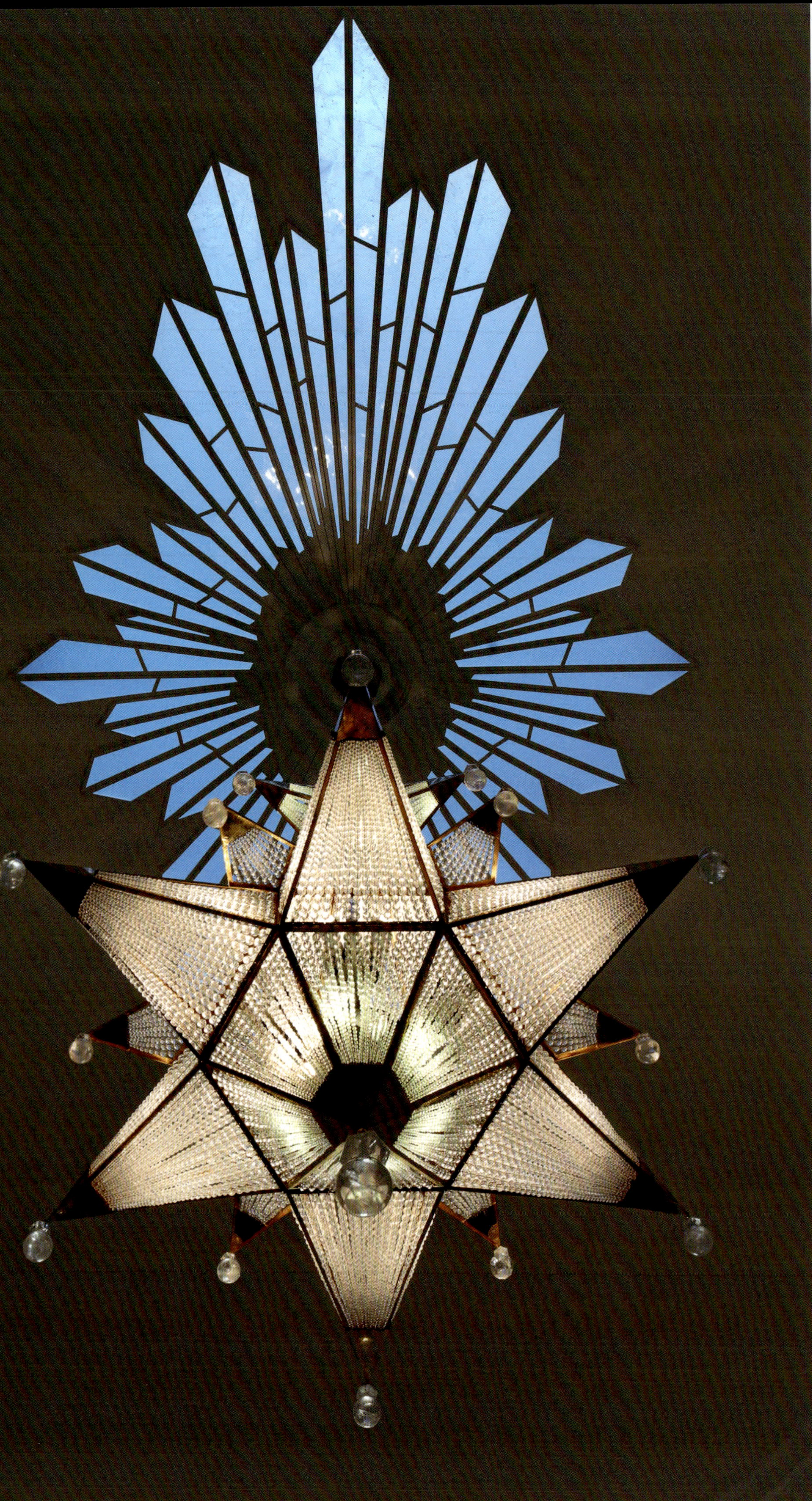

INTRODUCTION

In the great tradition of architects before me, my work has evolved over time. I am at heart an eclectic, drawing inspiration from history, travel, and imagination. This may have its roots in an East Coast childhood that was impressed as much by the sense of permanence and tradition explored during summer vacations among the great houses of Newport, Rhode Island, as it was by studying the wonderful and often fantastical buildings of Frank Lloyd Wright, of which I often built my own versions with LEGO bricks.

An equally powerful influence that impacted me early on was visiting relatives in Southern California during the mid-1970s. Los Angeles held a fascination from film and television, but spending time during several summers offered a different perspective from that of the entertainment world. I was intrigued by the incredibly eclectic architecture that filled its neighborhoods and streets with houses of every imaginable architectural style, inspired as much by the Spanish Colonial history and Mediterranean geography as by an encyclopedia of world design. This experience piqued my interest in exploring architectural history around the world and studying how imagery and its meaning come together in the built environment.

My early design experiences were grounded in tradition when I apprenticed in New York after college, and I brought that direction along when I made the move to establish an architectural career in Los Angeles. Local family connections gave me an opportunity to pursue design in Southern California's unique environment. With an innate curiosity about architectural history, I enjoyed the exploration of numerous architectural styles that appealed to clients and architects alike. While early work often focused upon Mediterranean Revival styles, of which Italian-inspired residences were historical favorites, Colonial Revival works that drew inspiration from local Streamline Moderne and Art Deco–influenced houses from 1930s Los Angeles became a personal devotion. It was during the height of this effort that two major trends were developing that would greatly shape the direction of my current work: exploring streamlined and modern design themes in houses; and the nature of contemporary living to become more and more casual.

The first monograph of my work, which was published under IMAGES' *New Classicists* series, explored early architectural themes that were based upon the evolution of Western classicism and the many lessons that it had to teach about organization, composition, detail, and integration with regional and vernacular traditions, thus bridging the gap between my East Coast roots and making a new home in California.

This second book is about the integration of modernism within an overall framework of tradition and heritage, responding to the evolving nature of my clients' programs and lifestyles and my design ideas. Academic studies of European modernism, with its visionary approach and embodiment of the machine age, came back to inspire, but with the understanding that many of its roots could be traced back to the heritage of classical design principles. My goal is to unite ideas about tradition, history, and modernity in a synergy and explore the meaning of shared architectural imagery and heritage for our time. For me, "Architecture is frozen music," as Goethe wrote.

While it's sure to be a surprise to my clients, and may be so to colleagues as well, the last thing that I could ever do is design a house for myself. It would need to evolve on a continual basis!

Richard Manion
Los Angeles, 2020

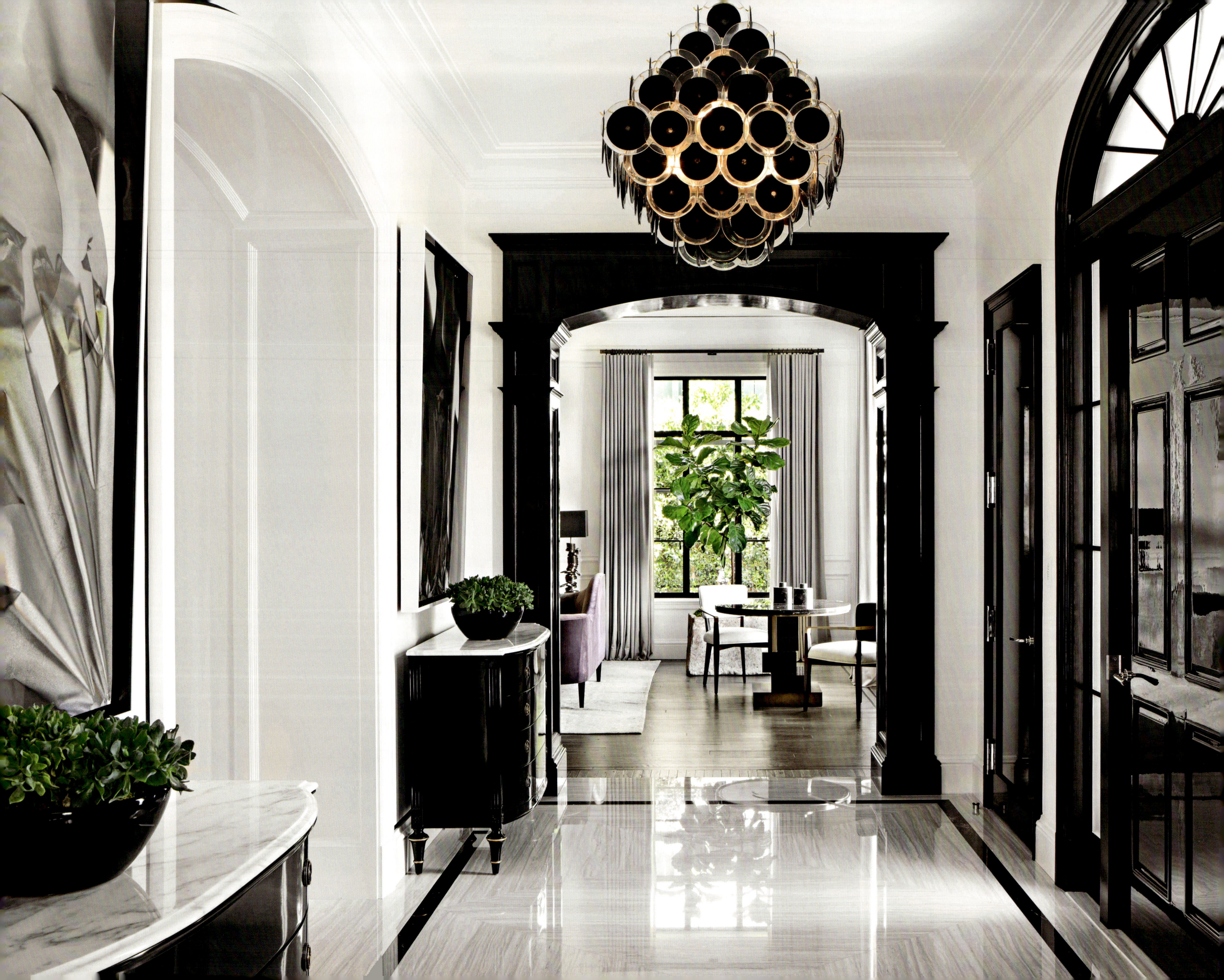

SELECTED WORKS

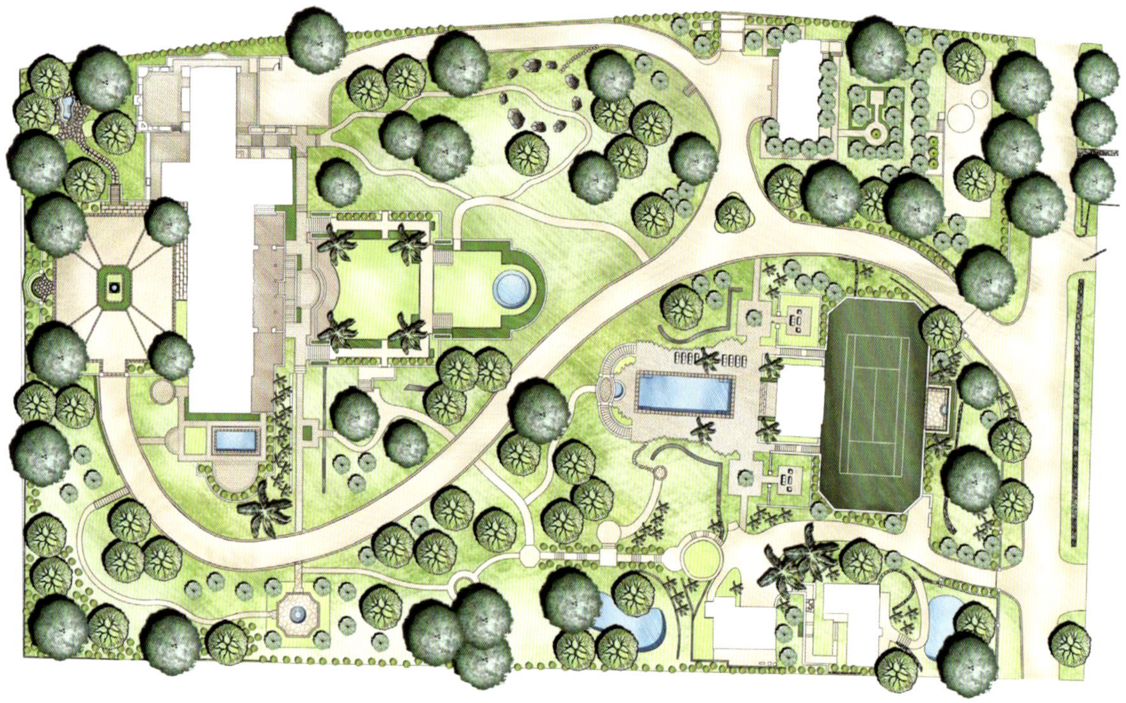

VILLA MONTAGNE AL MARE

Montecito

This grand Mediterranean estate was designed in 1929 by noted California architect Reginald Johnson for a Boston family as their winter retreat. We call it Montagne Al Mare because the views through the house are to the gardens and behind you are the mountains as backdrop that cascade down to the sea.

The house embodies many of the characteristic features of the Mediterranean Revival style of the early twentieth century. It was an interpretation of an Italian country house adapted to Southern California, and it drew its inspiration from the smaller Tuscan villas created during the early Italian Renaissance, with its mottled yellow ocher plaster walls, contrasting gray-toned pietra serena cast stone and plaster surrounds, wide overhanging eaves with carved rafter tails, and tile roof, all features typical of that style.

Our clients needed more casual living spaces, bedroom suites, and places for family fun and enjoyment. To keep the integrity of the central picturesque Italian structure, we integrated a family wing at the east end with a breakfast room, kitchen, family room, and outdoor dining and gathering area around a fireplace and pizza oven. The back of the house underwent the greatest transformation. The rear loggia had been enclosed by the previous owner as an interior sunroom and a new loggia added as a rear garden overlook. We turned the sunroom into a conservatory with changes in materials and the addition of potted palms and plants. A projecting family room was sensibly turned into a formal dining room for hosting large dinners, which had been missing from previous iterations of the house. Interiors by Atelier AM reflect the union of Californian and Italian themes—casual elegance, eclectic furnishings from the present and the past, and our clients' love of all things beautiful and meaningful.

The magnificent grounds included a sloping formal garden originally laid out by Lockwood de Forest that has been reworked into cascading terraced levels, which are more usable, and are reached by a set of double stairs. The gardens and walkways meander down to the pool house, guest cottages, and tennis court.

This painstaking restoration of a historic estate and gardens as a family getaway mirrors Reginald Johnson's original intent and reinforces its foundation for the future.

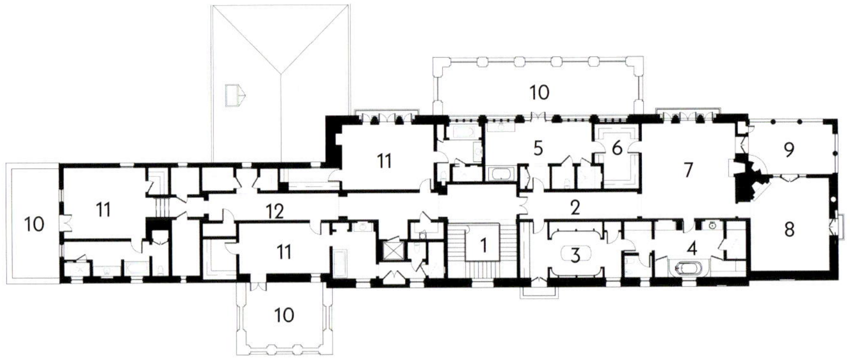

SECOND-FLOOR PLAN

1 Main stair
2 Master hall
3 Her closet
4 Her bath
5 His bath
6 His closet
7 Master sitting room
8 Master bedroom
9 Master terrace
10 Terrace
11 Bedroom
12 East hall

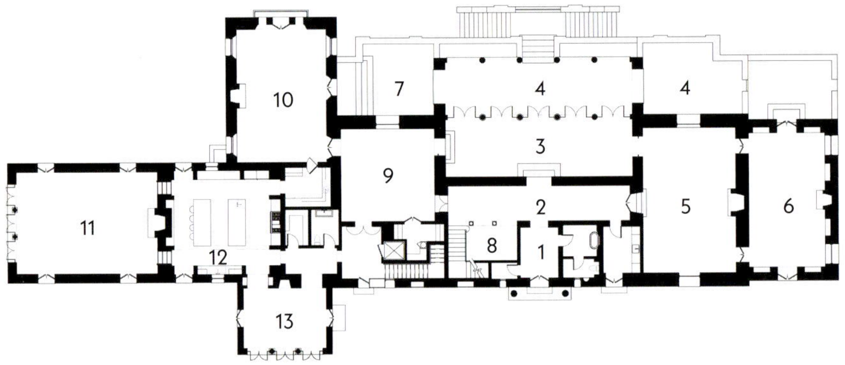

FIRST-FLOOR PLAN

1 Foyer
2 Gallery
3 Sunroom
4 Loggia
5 Living room
6 Library
7 Terrace
8 Stair hall
9 Salon
10 Formal dining
11 Family room
12 Kitchen
13 Breakfast room

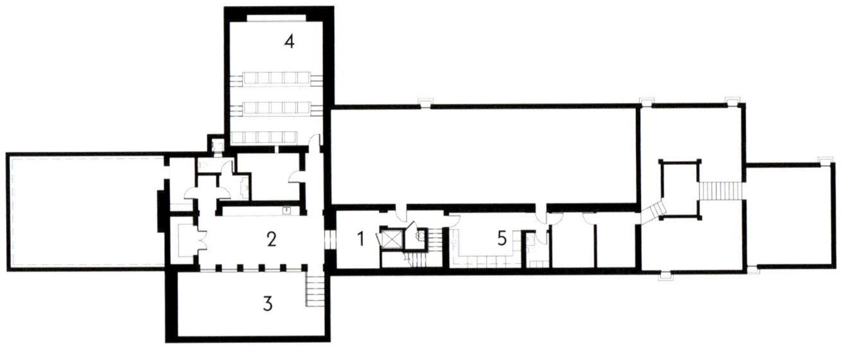

LOWER-LEVEL PLAN

1 Foyer
2 Lounge
3 Billiard room
4 Theater
5 Laundry

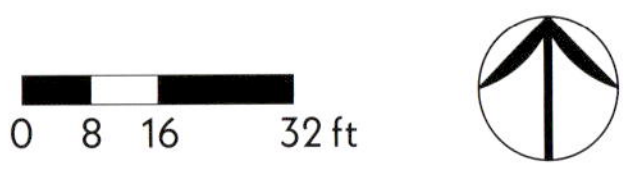

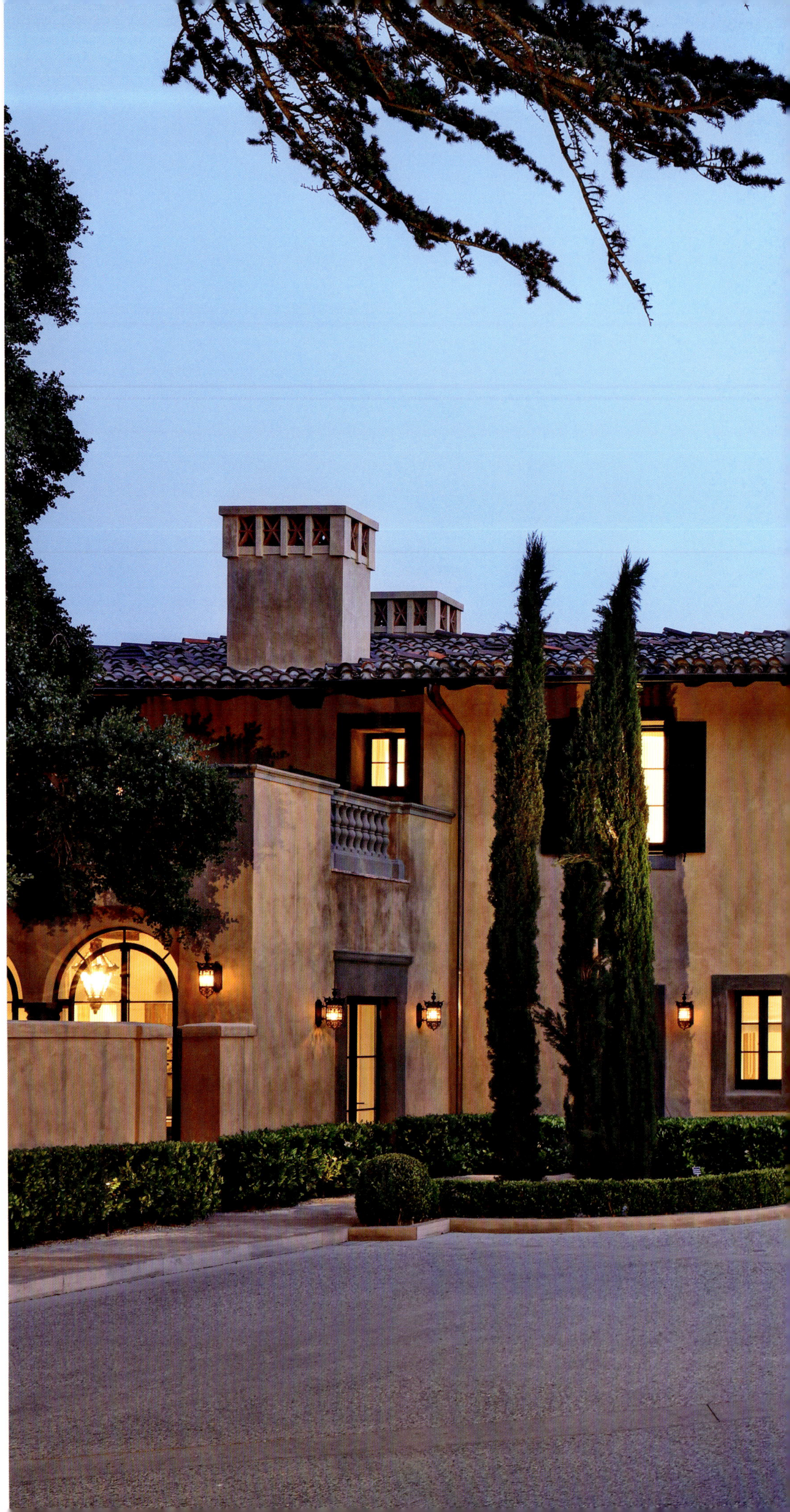

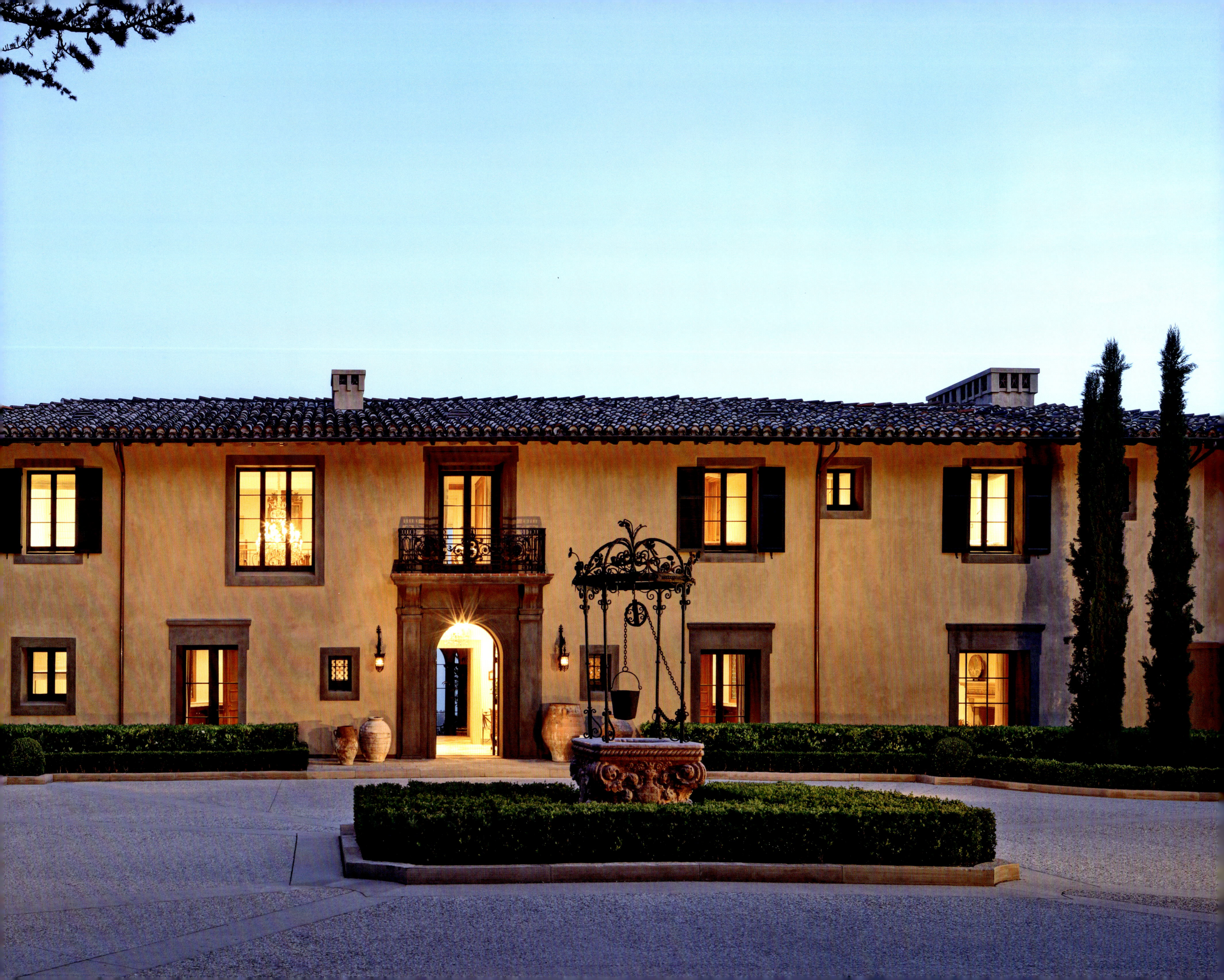

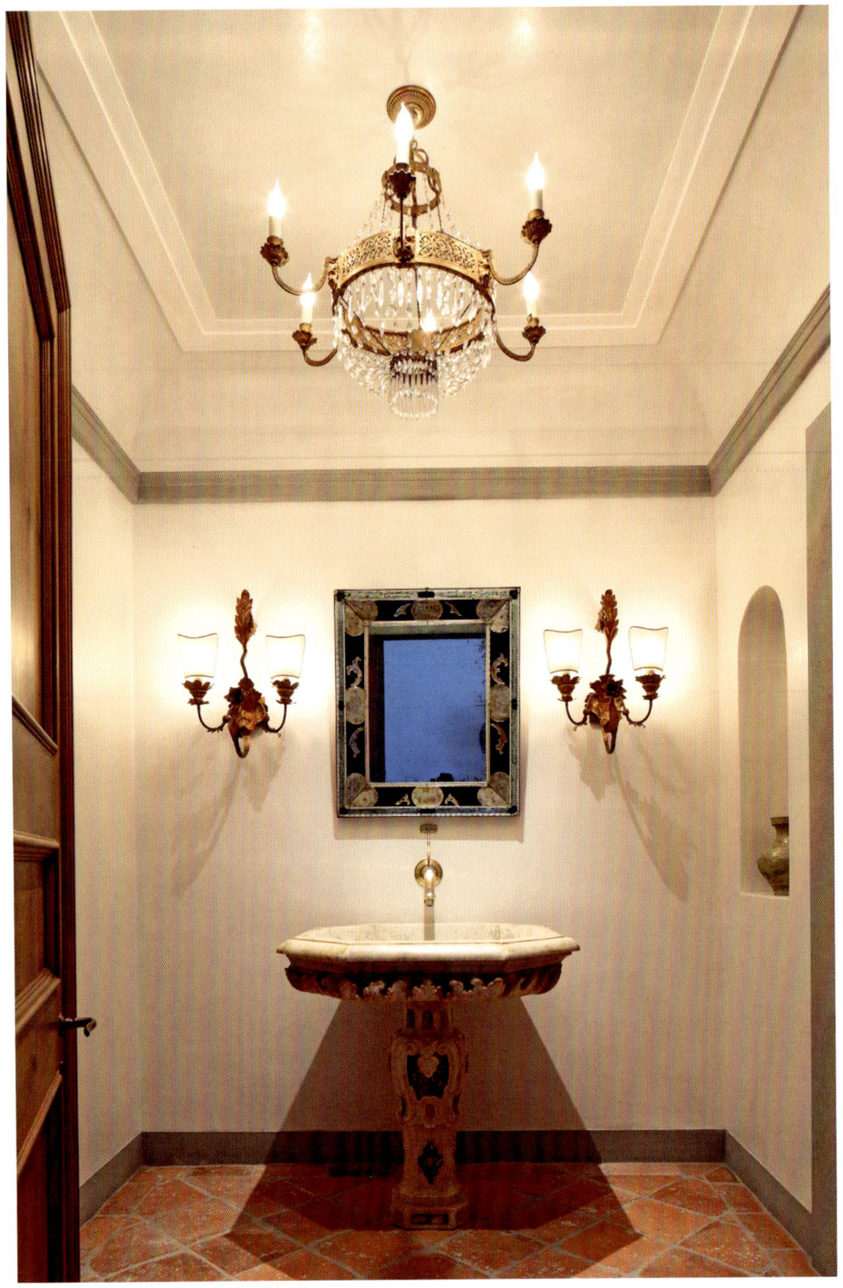

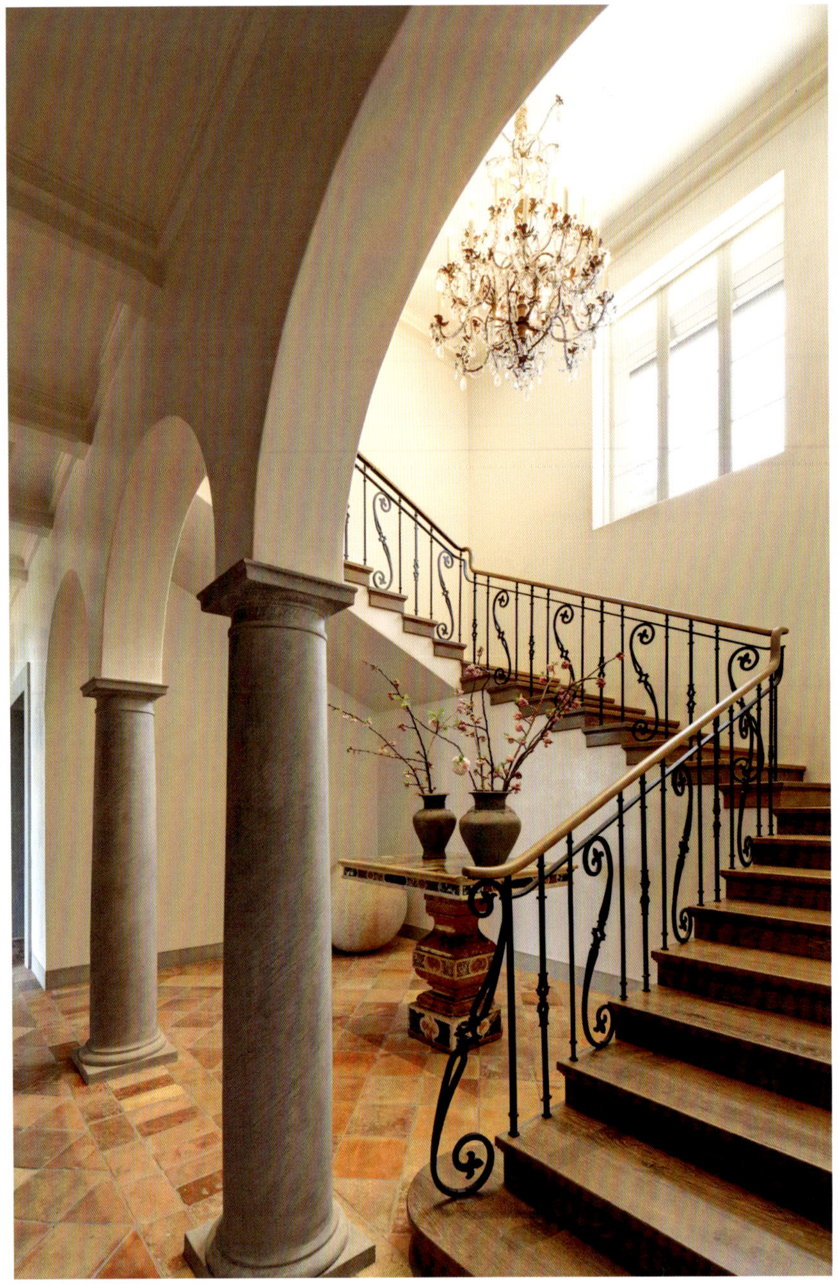

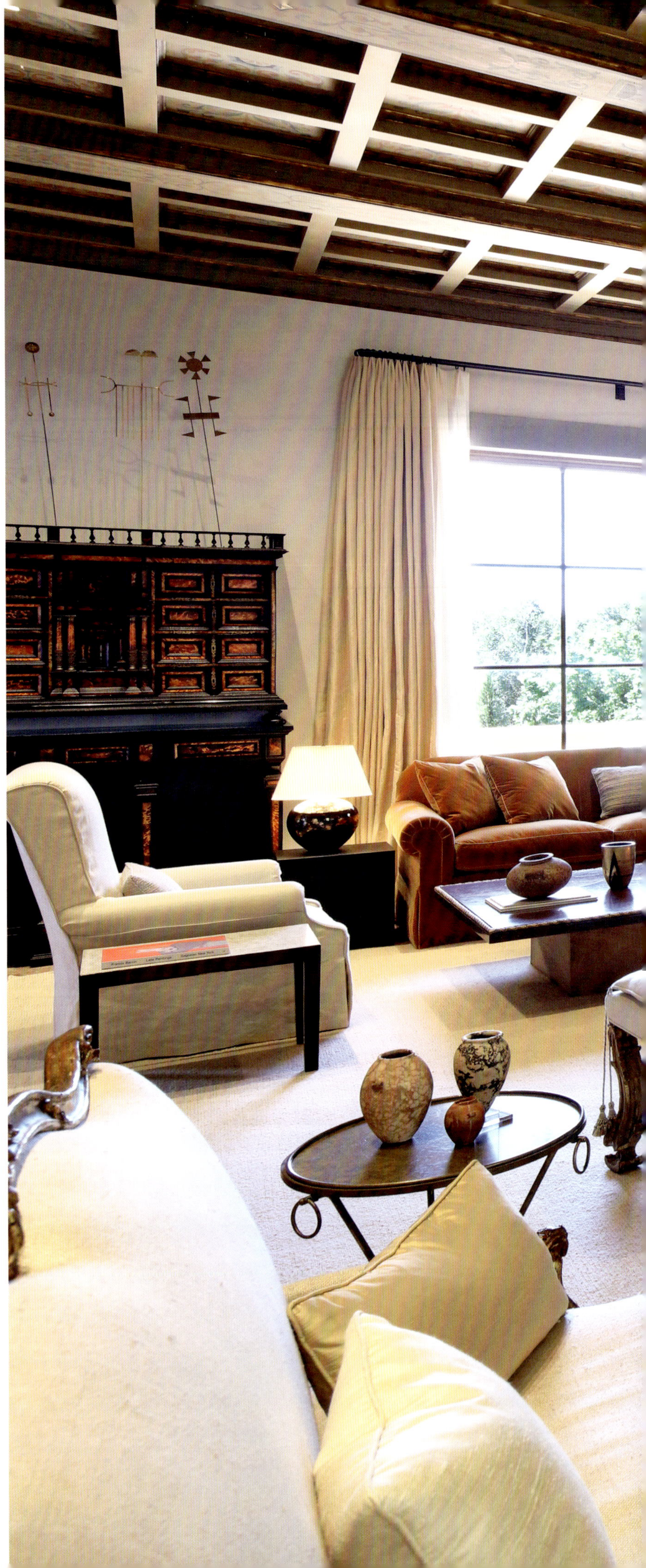

PREVIOUS PAGES: *This grand Mediterranean Revival estate, designed in 1929 by Reginald Johnson with the period's signature tile roof, mottled plaster walls, cast stone surrounds, and antique well head, was given new life as a family retreat, but with elements that tied it more to Italy than California.*

ABOVE LEFT: *A reclaimed baptismal font was turned into a sink in the formal powder room.*

ABOVE RIGHT: *Everything in the entry hall—pietra serena columns, Italian terra cotta floor, walnut stairs—is new except for the original railing.*

RIGHT: *The living room's original coffered wood ceiling was restored and new pietra serena doorways added. The interiors by Atelier AM blend seventeenth- and eighteenth-century Italian furnishings with ancient artifacts and twentieth-century art.*

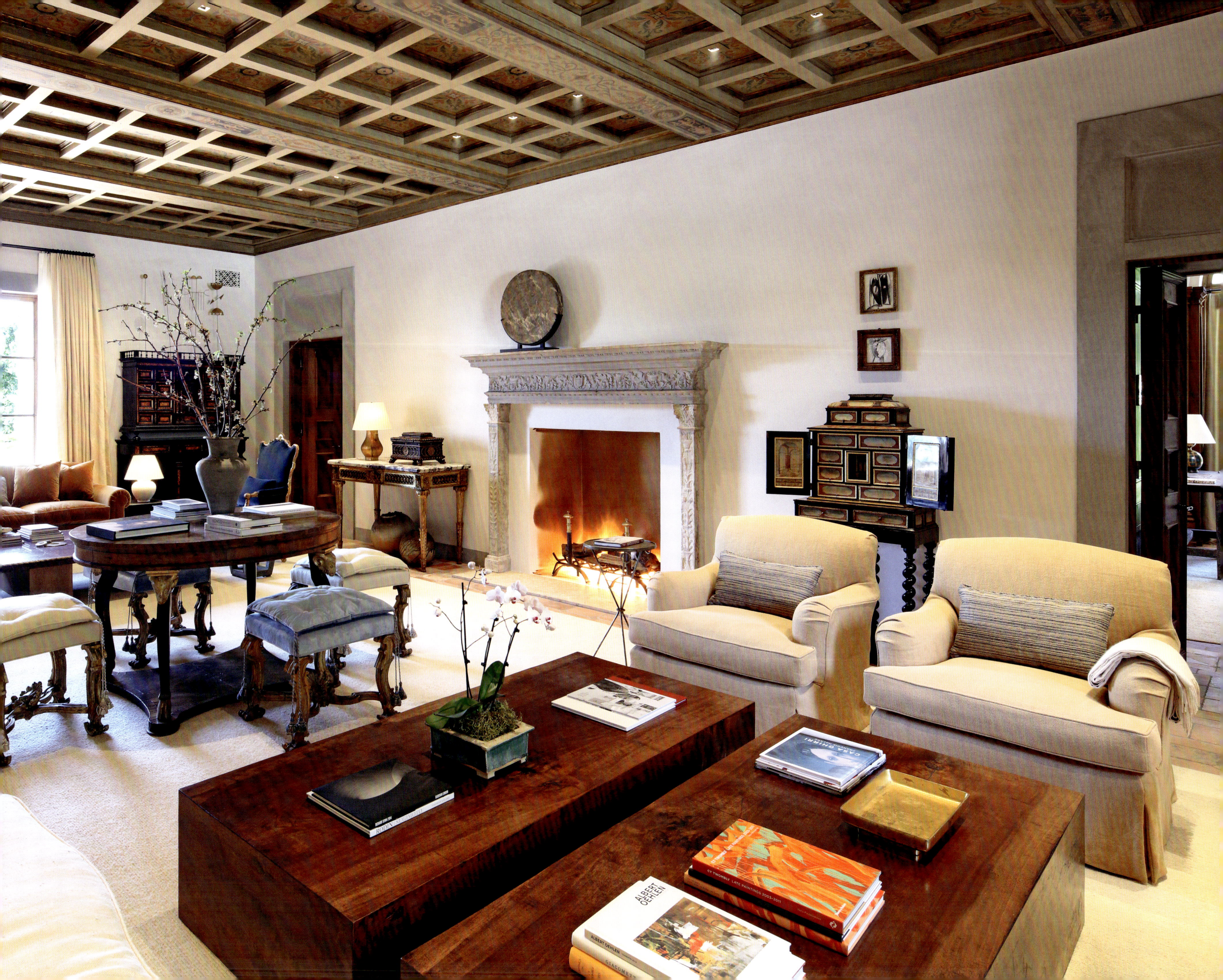
ALBERT OEHLEN

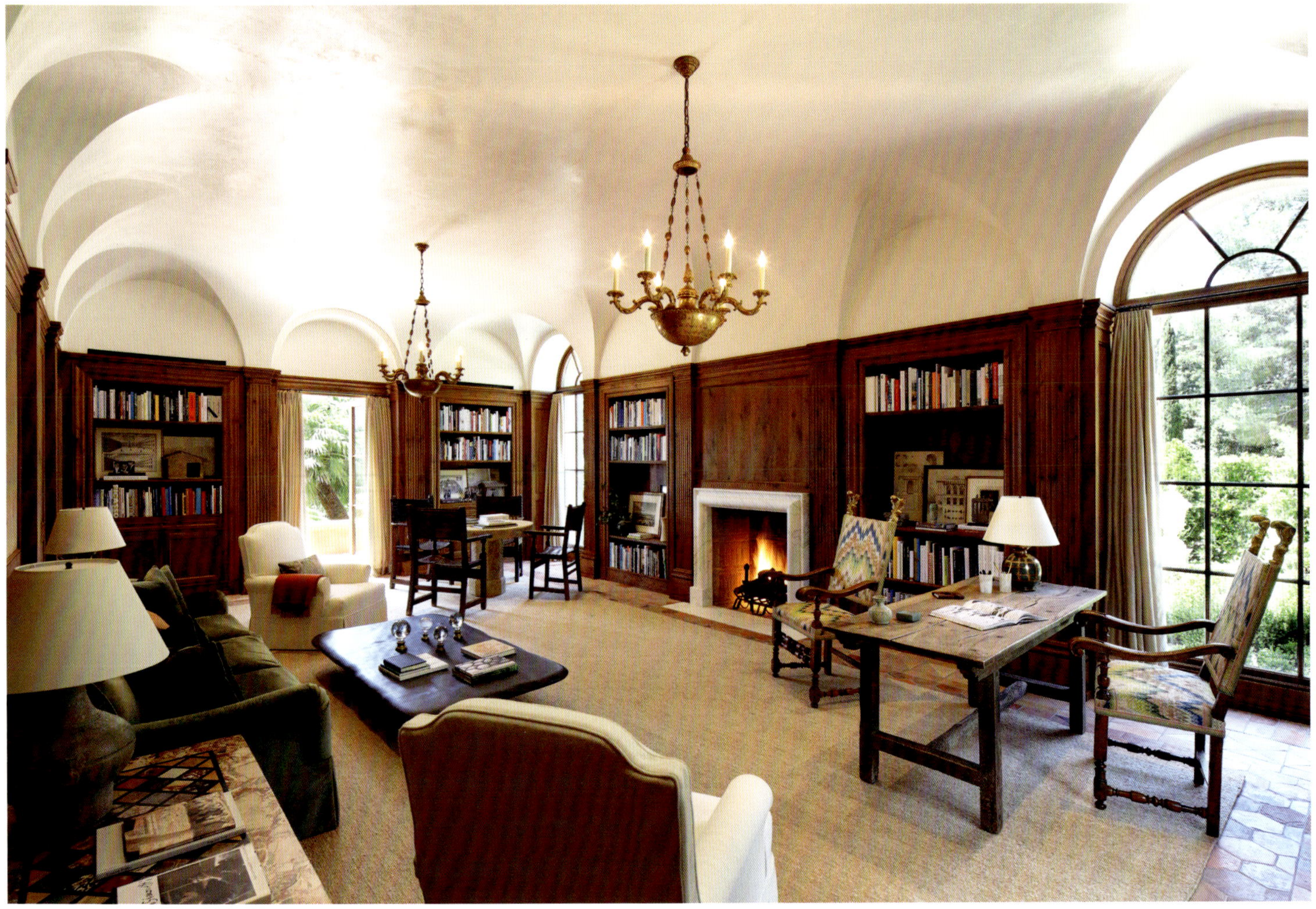

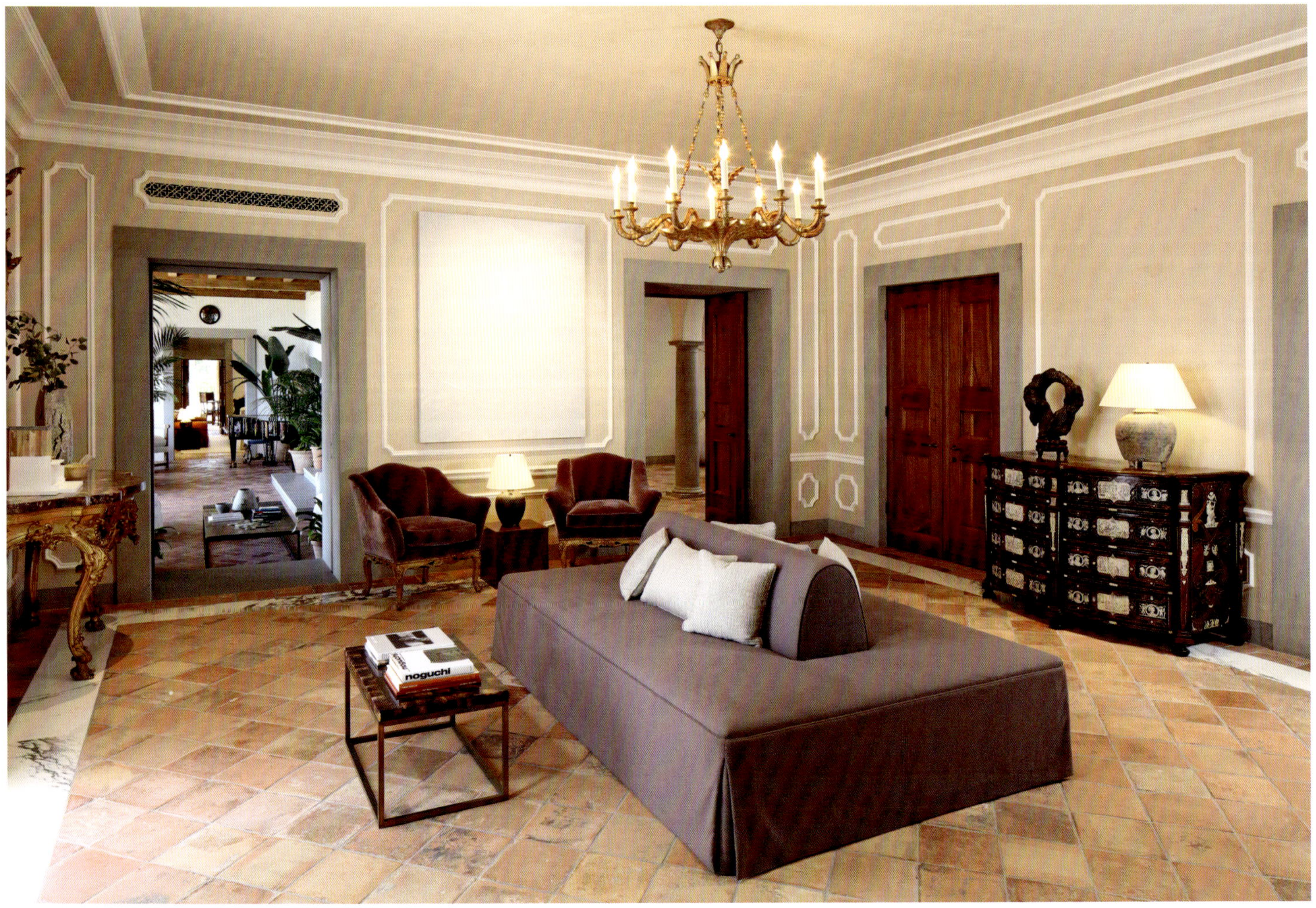

TOP LEFT: *The library has dry matte wax walnut paneling to give it an aged look and was made brighter with vaulting; the plaster is off-white and the windows are arched on one side, flat-topped on the other.*

LEFT: *The salon is the bridge between the living areas and the dining room and acts as a vestibule to the new family wing with the kitchen and breakfast room.*

OPPOSITE: *With a complex geometric parquet floor, matte coffered wood ceiling, and veined marble fire surround, the dining room is a synthesis of intricate patterns.*

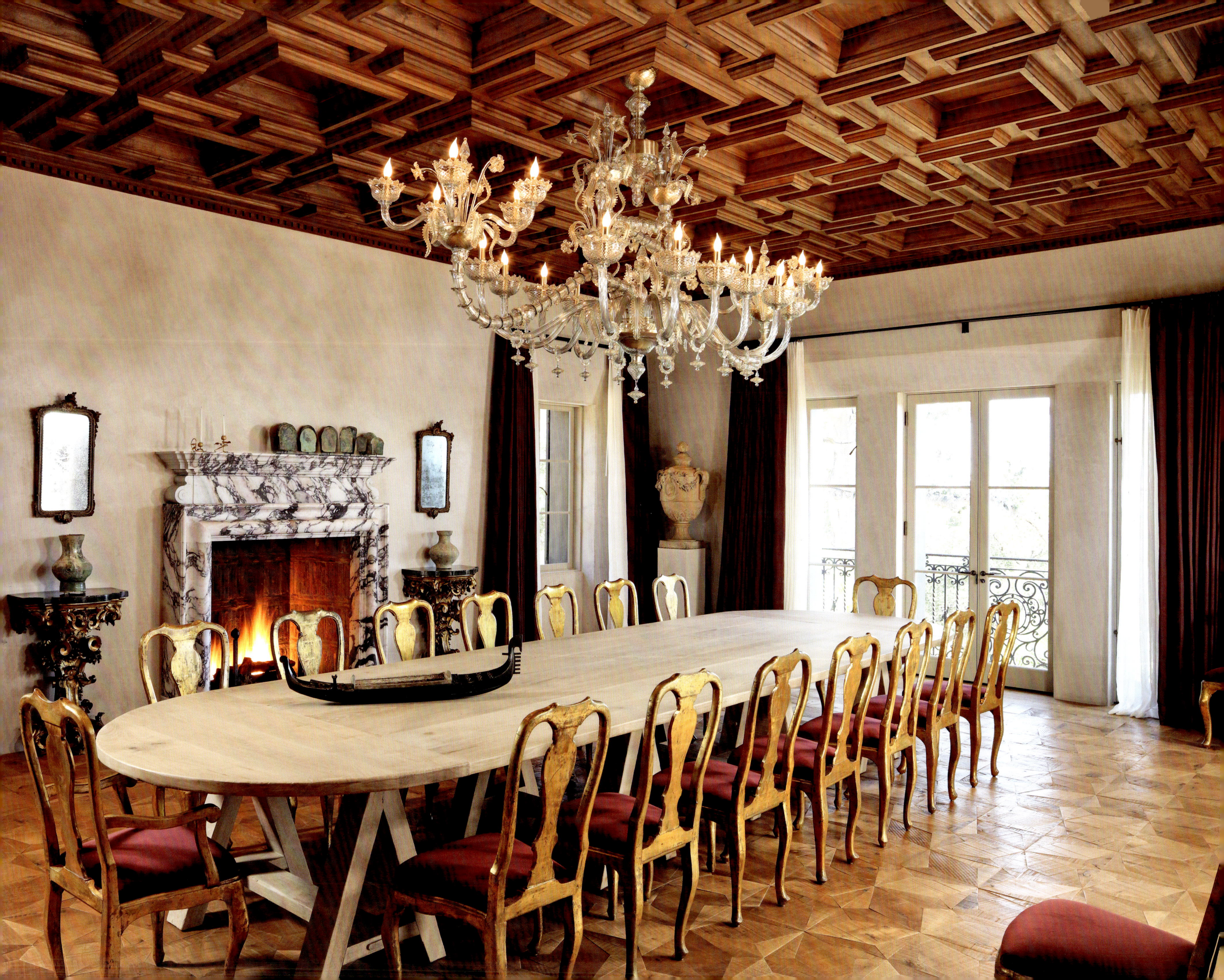

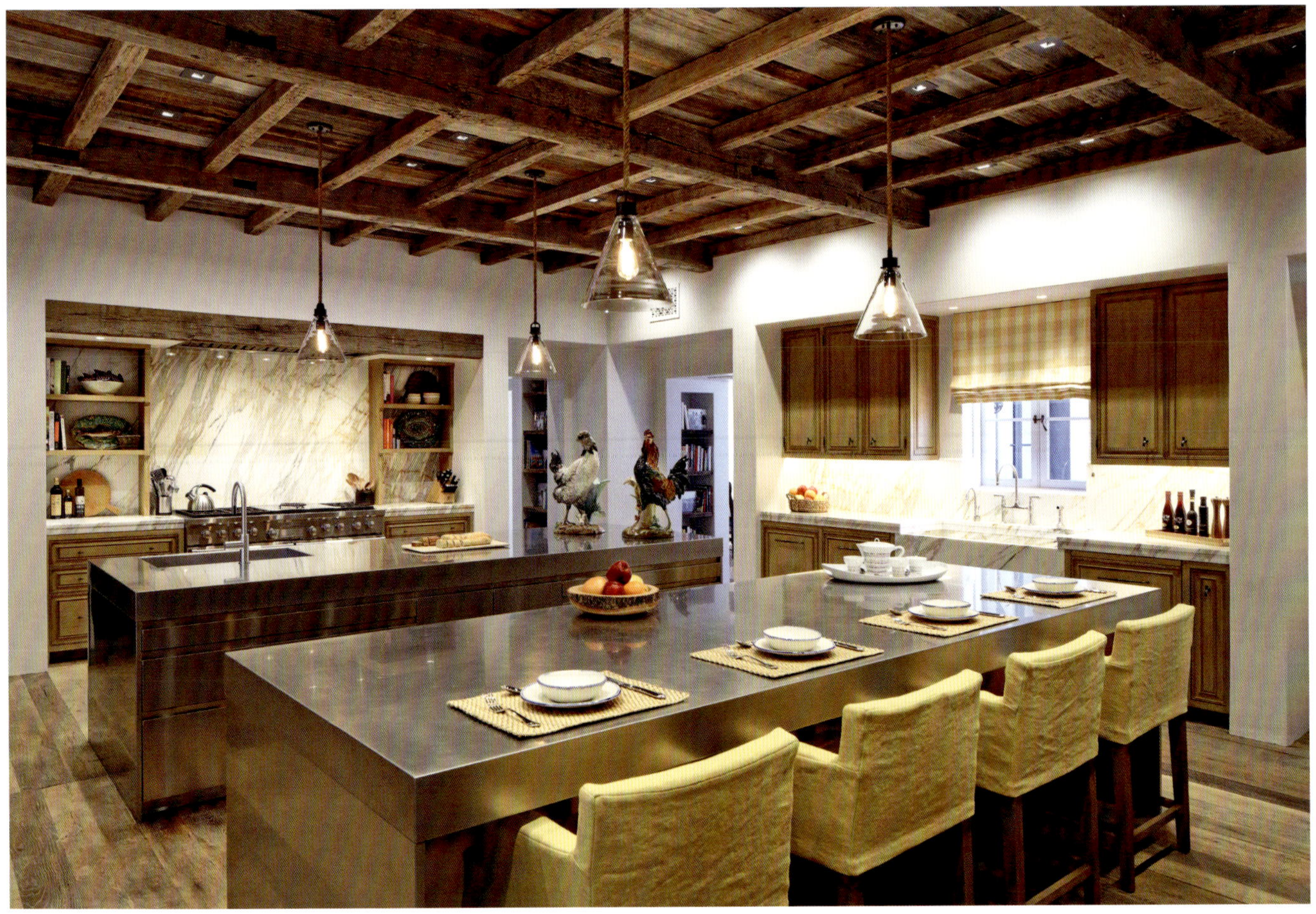

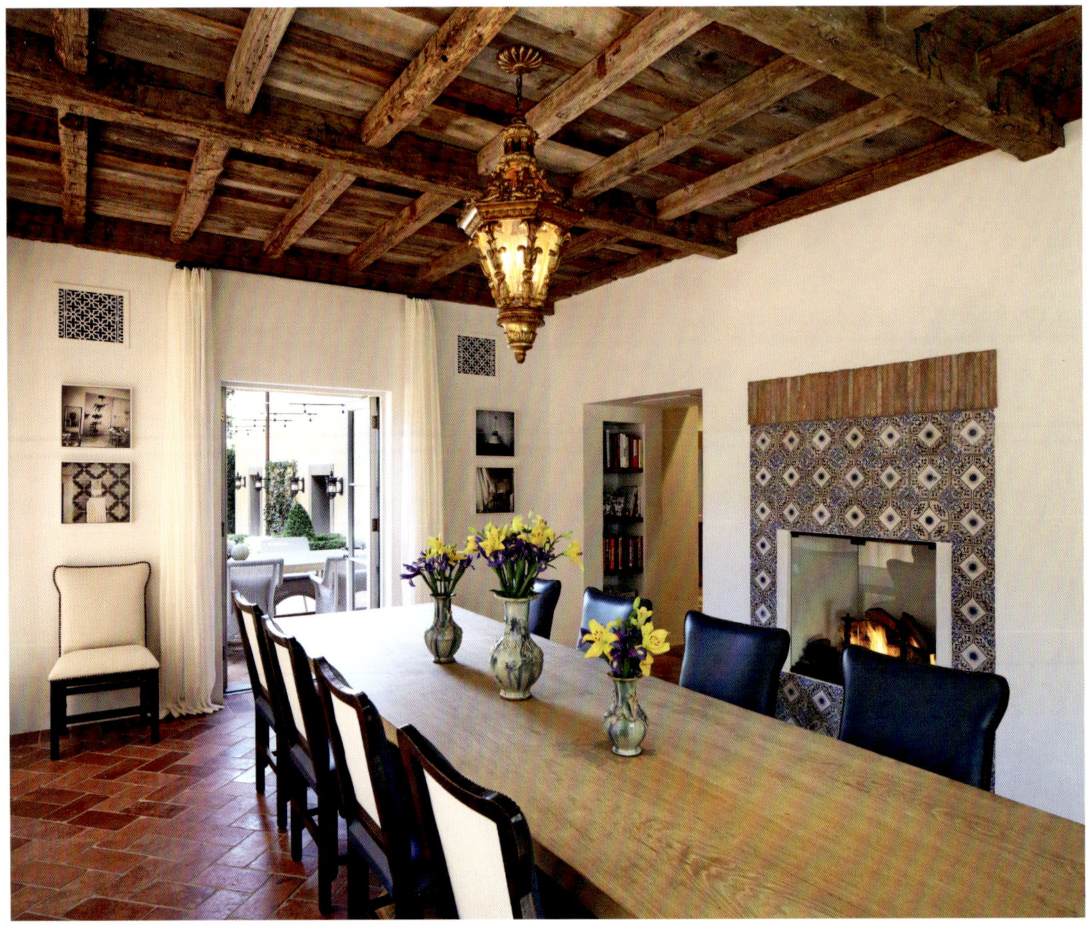

ABOVE LEFT: *The new kitchen was given an antique ceiling and flooring with traditional-looking side cabinetry and finishes, while the islands contrast in modern stainless steel.*

ABOVE RIGHT: *Our clients needed more casual spaces, such as the breakfast room, that weren't part of 1920s living.*

RIGHT: *Located off the breakfast room and kitchen, the family terrace offers outdoor dining, pizza oven, barbecue, and a fireplace illuminated by overhead string lights.*

OPPOSITE: *The family room with arched metal casement French doors. A stone and marble consultant helped us source materials and keep them as authentic as possible.*

FOLLOWING PAGES, TOP LEFT: *A monolith carved out of the earth with geometry and massing in plaster, the basement, which contains the entertainment spaces, is an updated version of a crypt that's been given a more contemporary feel.* BOTTOM LEFT: *To the right of the basement is the tasting room and wine cellar with banquettes tucked in between the arched columns. The tasting room overlooks the vaulted billiard room.* RIGHT: *The other new wing includes the second-floor master suite that was brightened with larger windows and French doors; the master sitting room mixes antiques with early-twentieth-century pieces.*

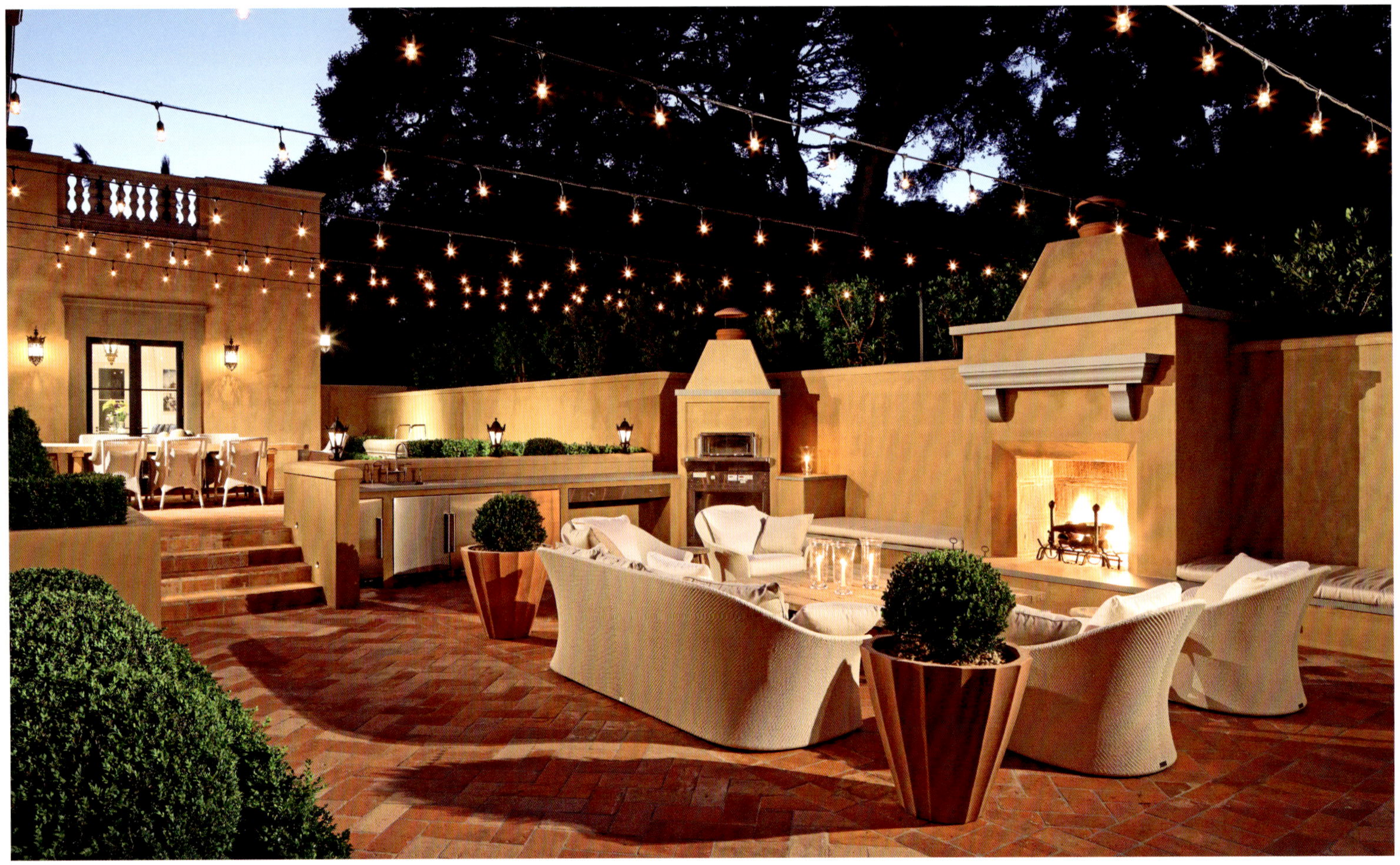

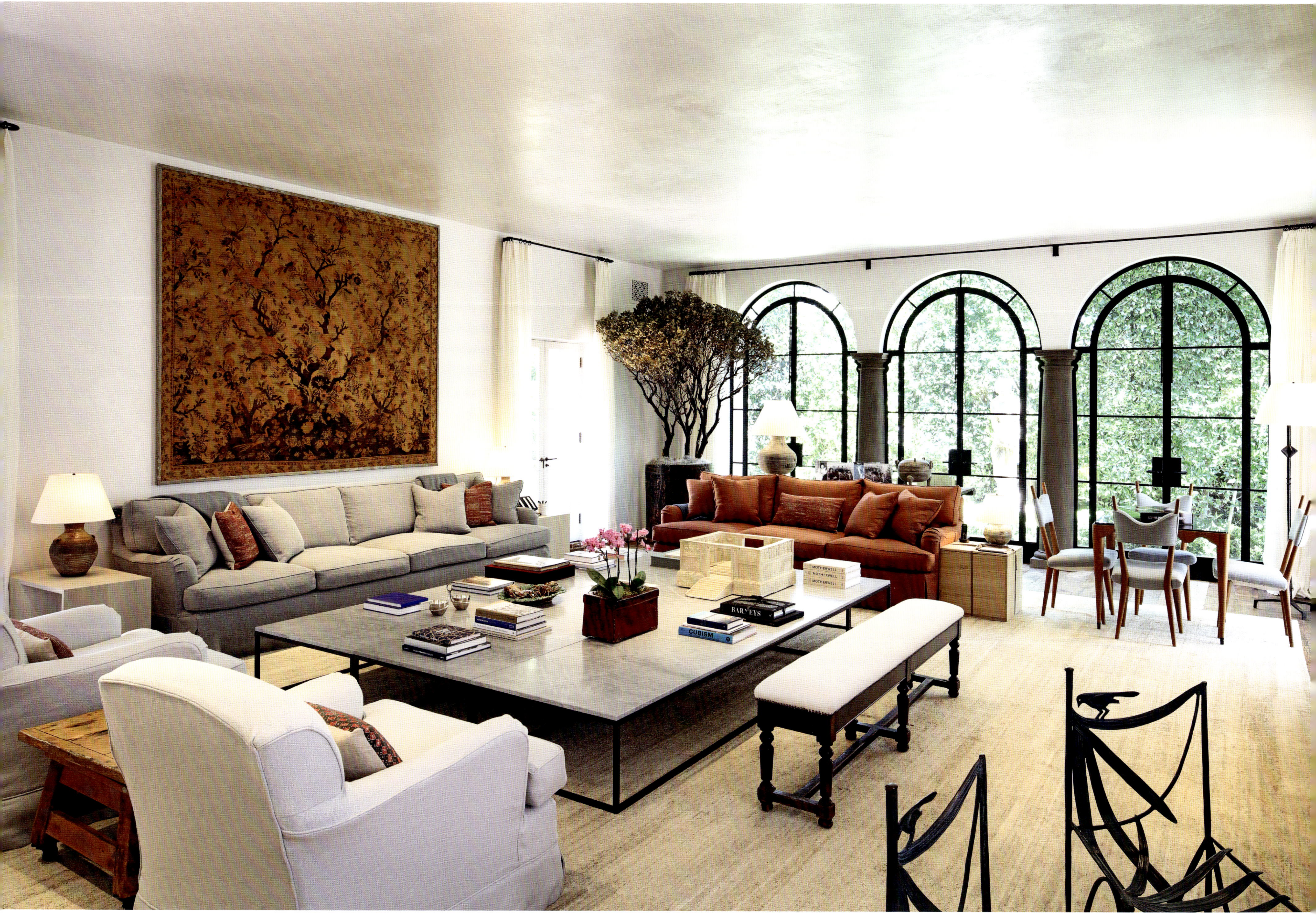

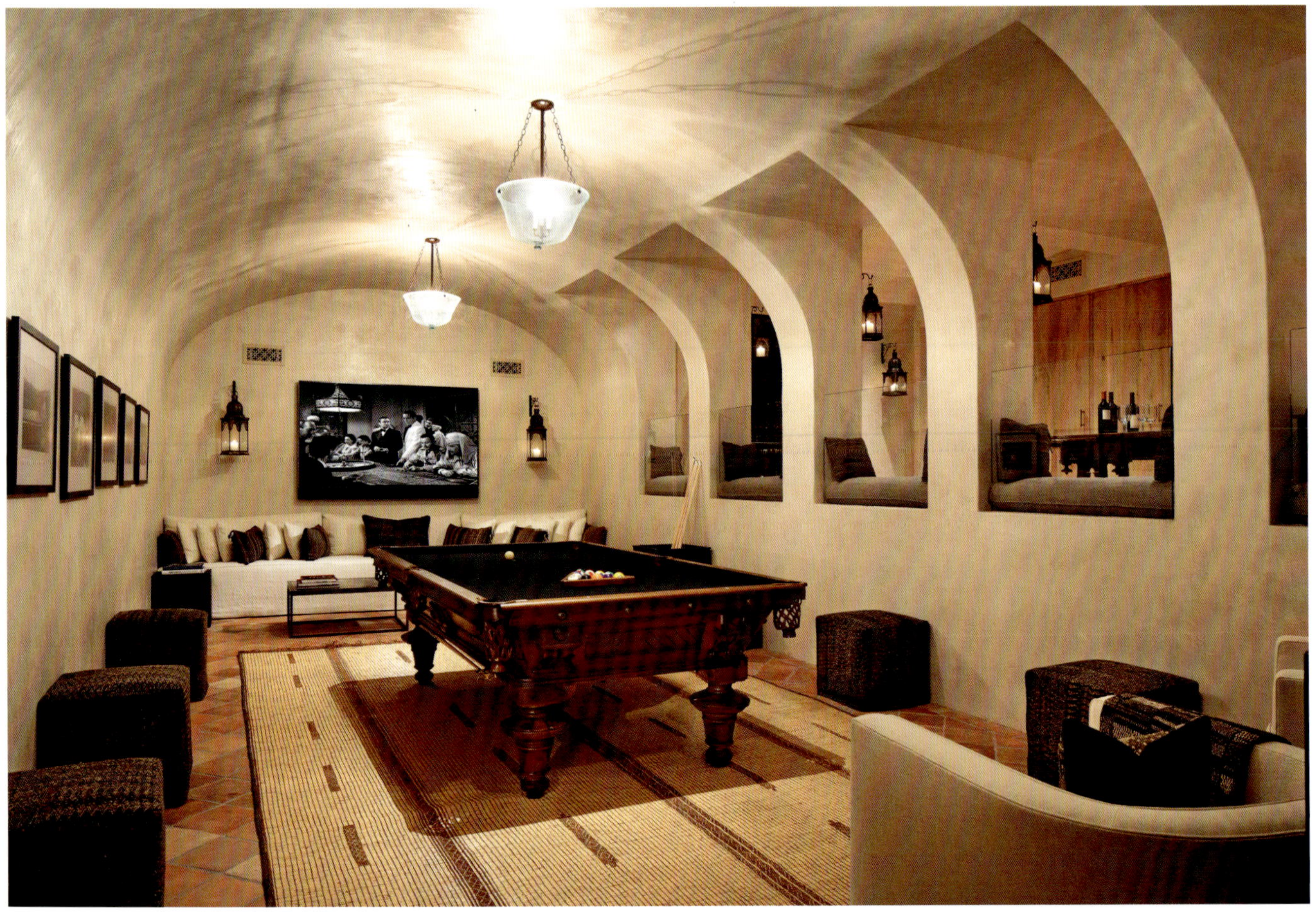

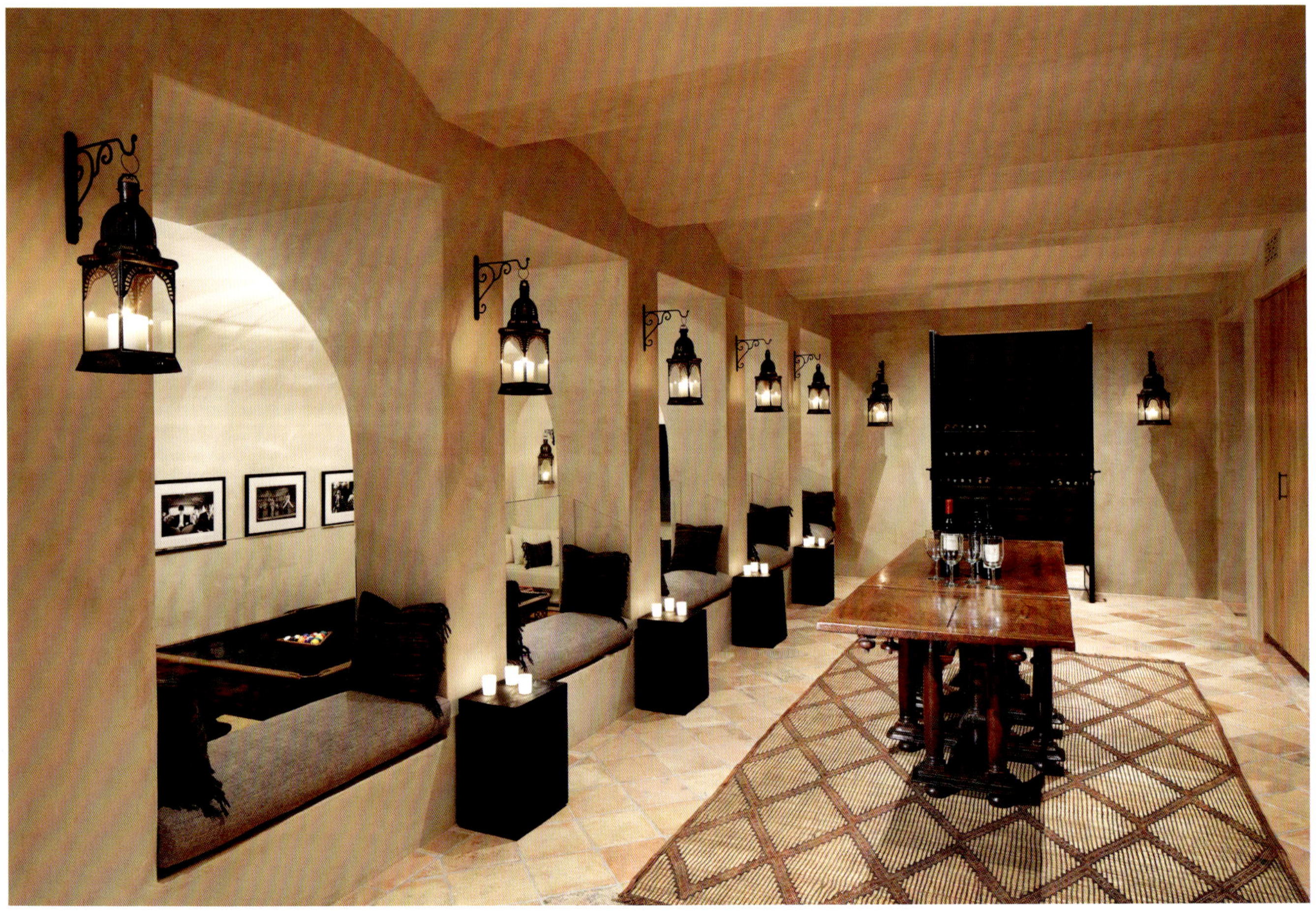

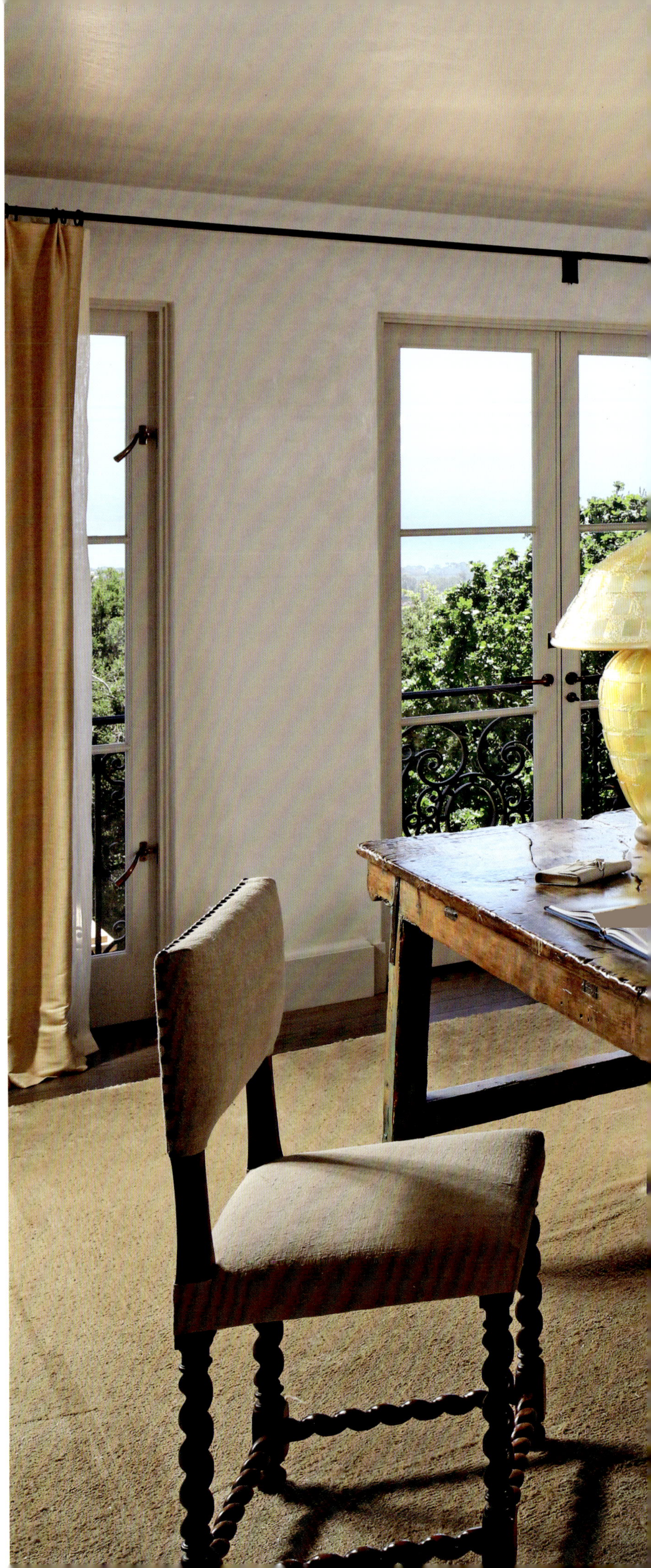

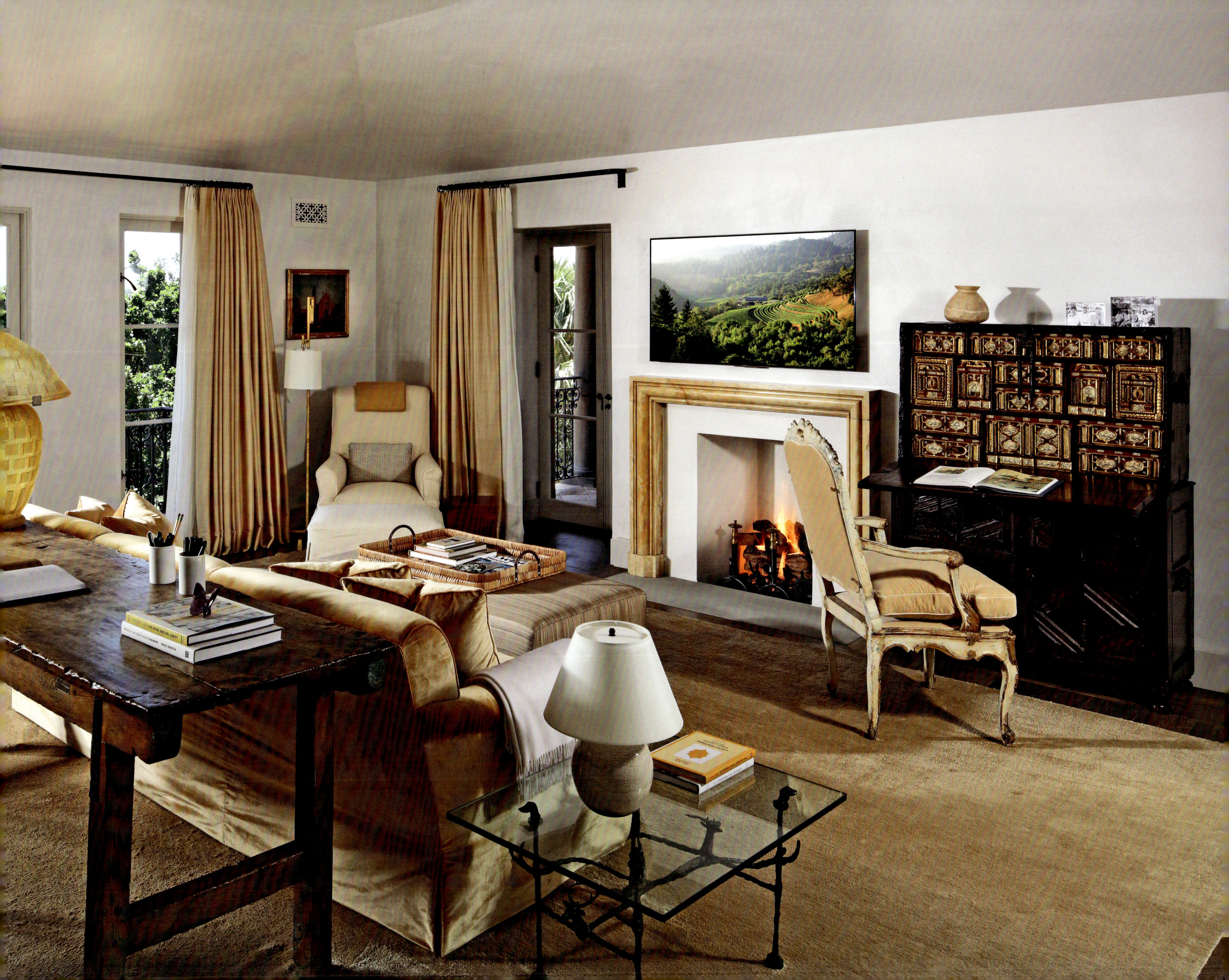

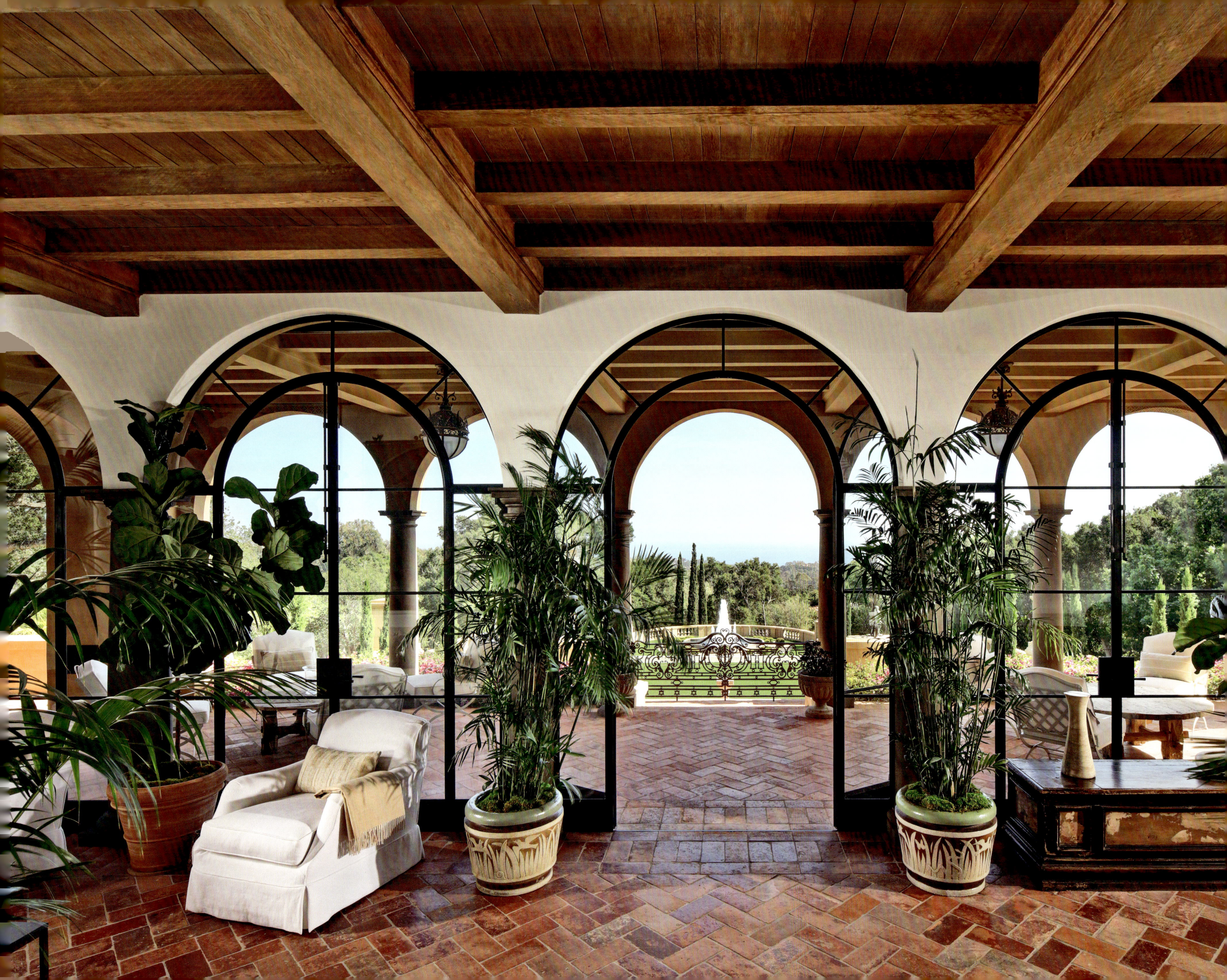

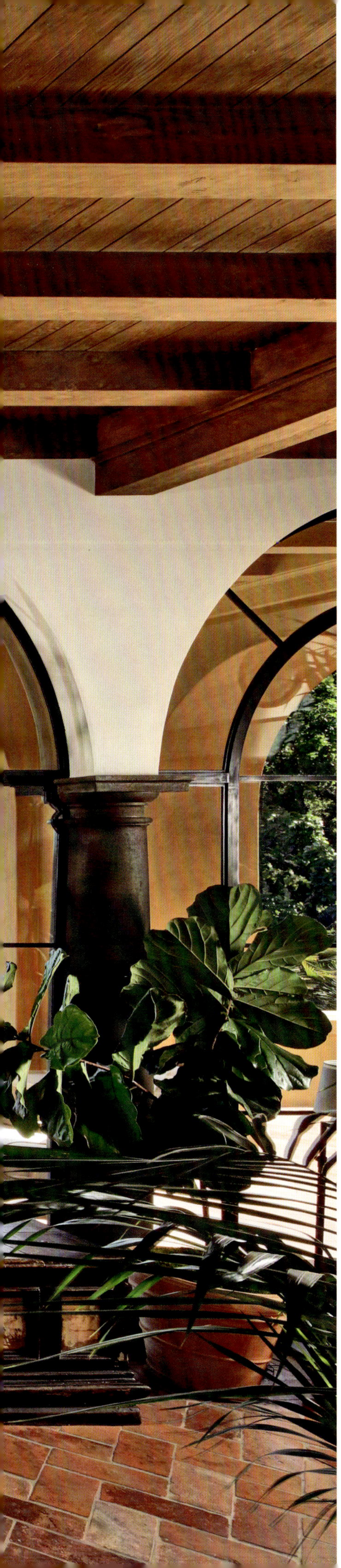

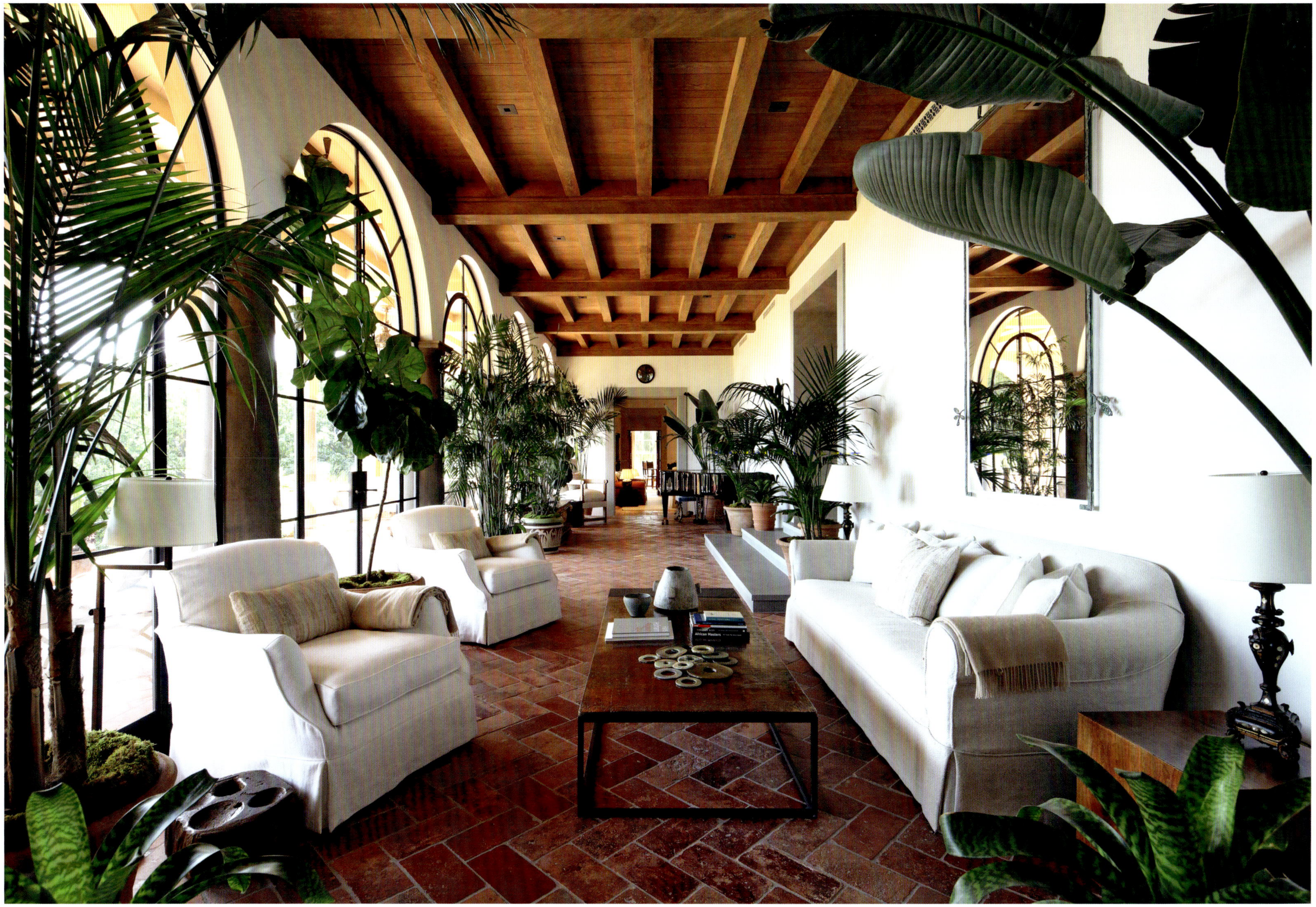

ABOVE: *The greatest transformation was to the back of the house. The long sunroom was originally an open loggia that is now enclosed like a conservatory, with potted palms and plants. The metal windows are a nod to early 1920s Southern California houses that would often have thin windows to blur the distinction between inside and out.*

LEFT: *The sunroom flows out to the outdoor loggia, which was built by the previous owner, with new floors and redone portals.*

FOLLOWING PAGES, LEFT: *The current landscaping by Leyva & Wilde hews to a Mediterranean plant palette.* RIGHT: *The grounds were originally a sloping landscape by Lockwood de Forest, but none of his gardens has survived. A previous owner reworked the slopes into more usable terracing that provides flat areas for gatherings. The great lawn with an ocean view leads down past statuary, classical arched columns, and the Baroque fountain to the pool and pool house.*

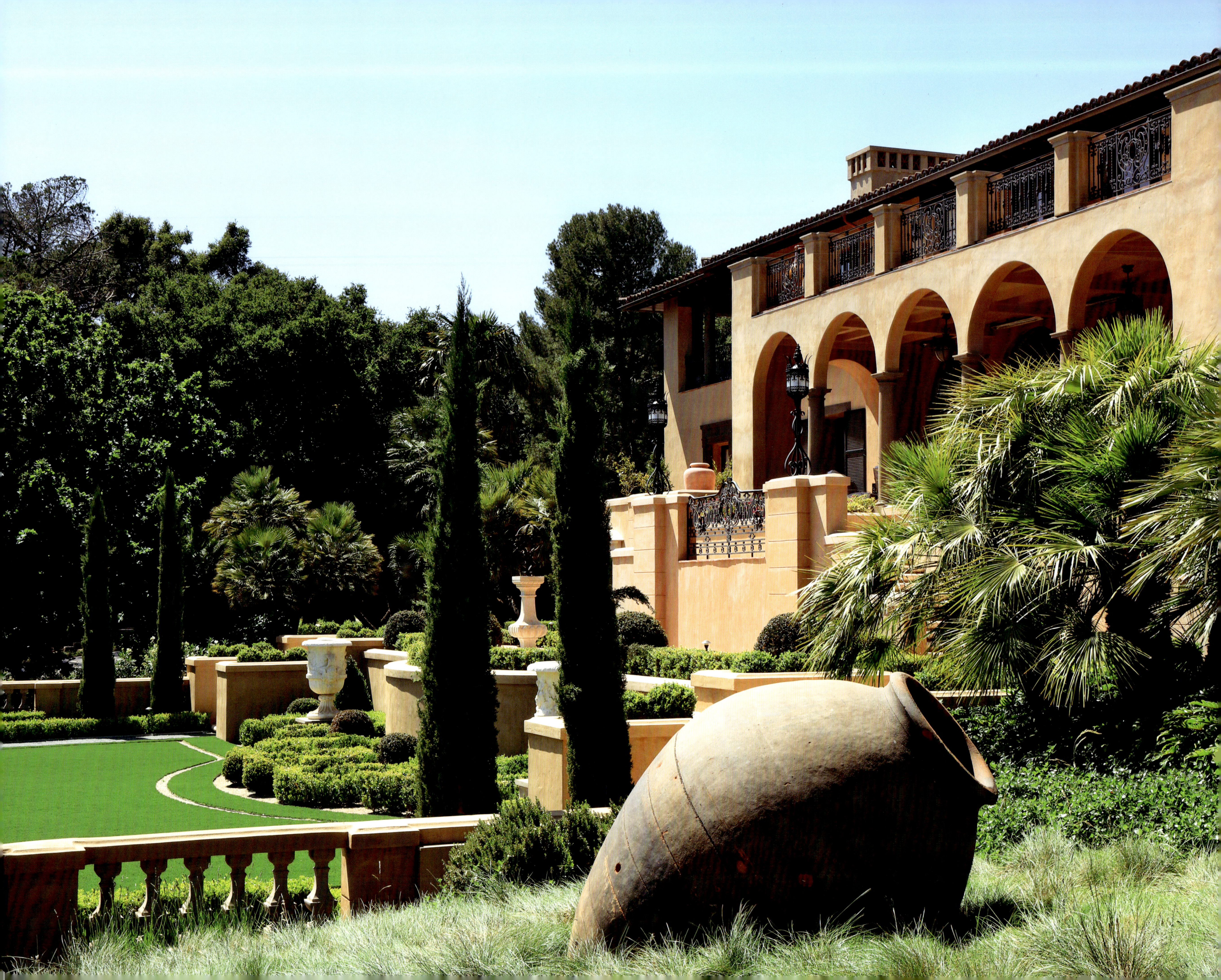

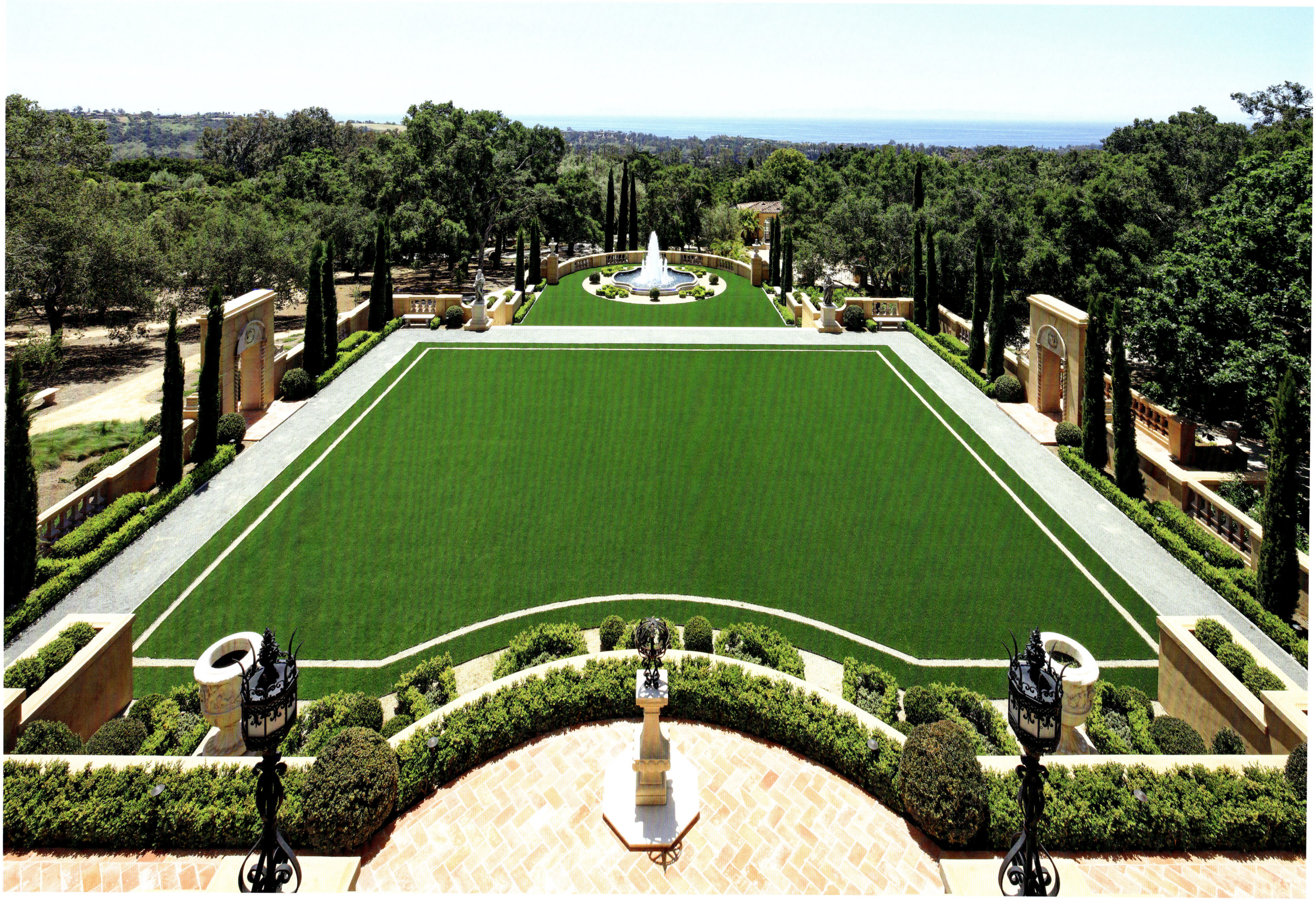

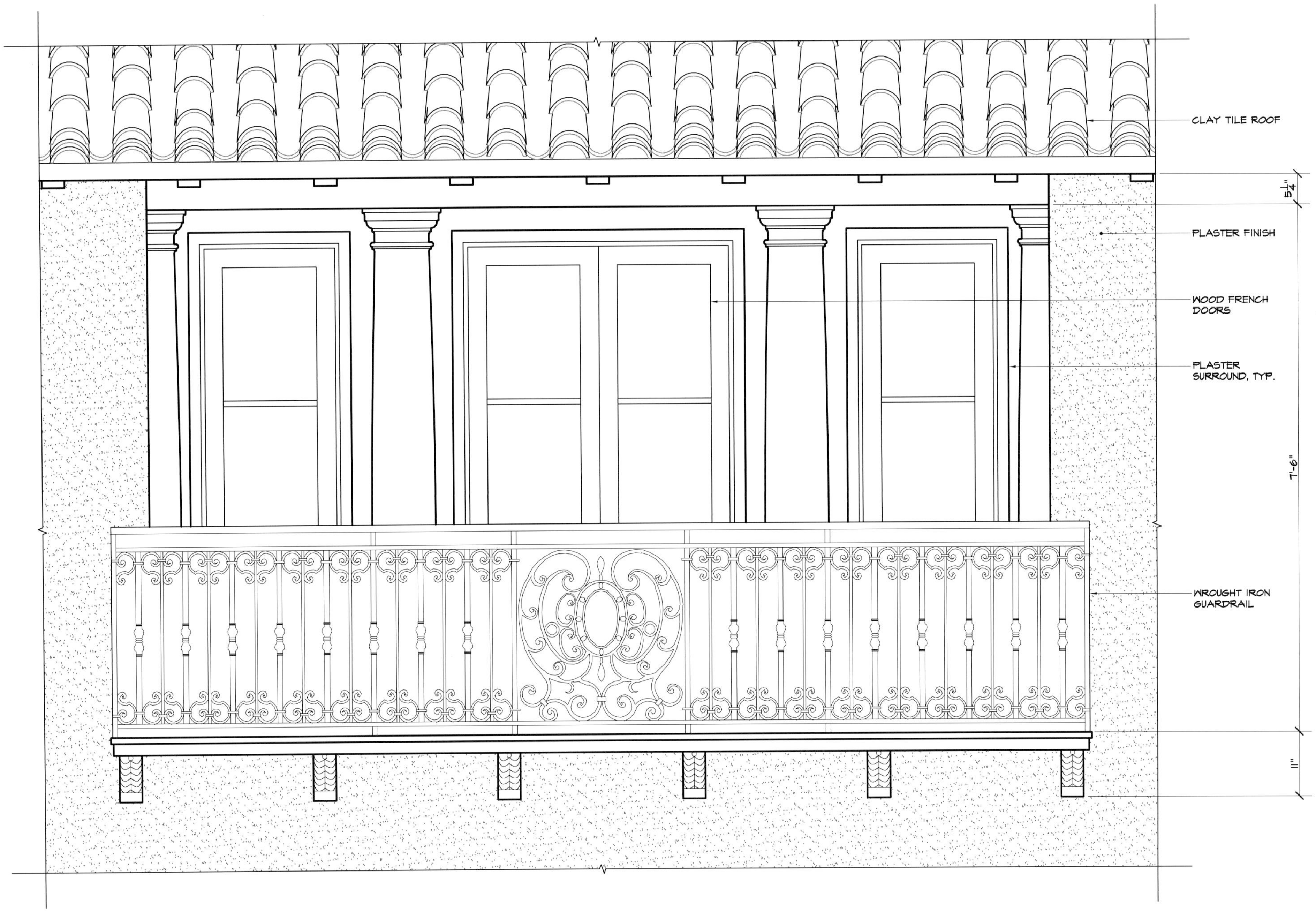

ABOVE: *A detail drawing of the master sitting room's French doors and railing.*

OPPOSITE: *The rear façade reveals the central picturesque Italian structure that was inspired by the smaller, more eclectic Tuscan villas of the early Renaissance. New wings were integrated at the edges so as not to detract from the original building. At right is the family wing that houses the dining room, kitchen, family room, and breakfast room. At left is the study/library with the upstairs master suite.*

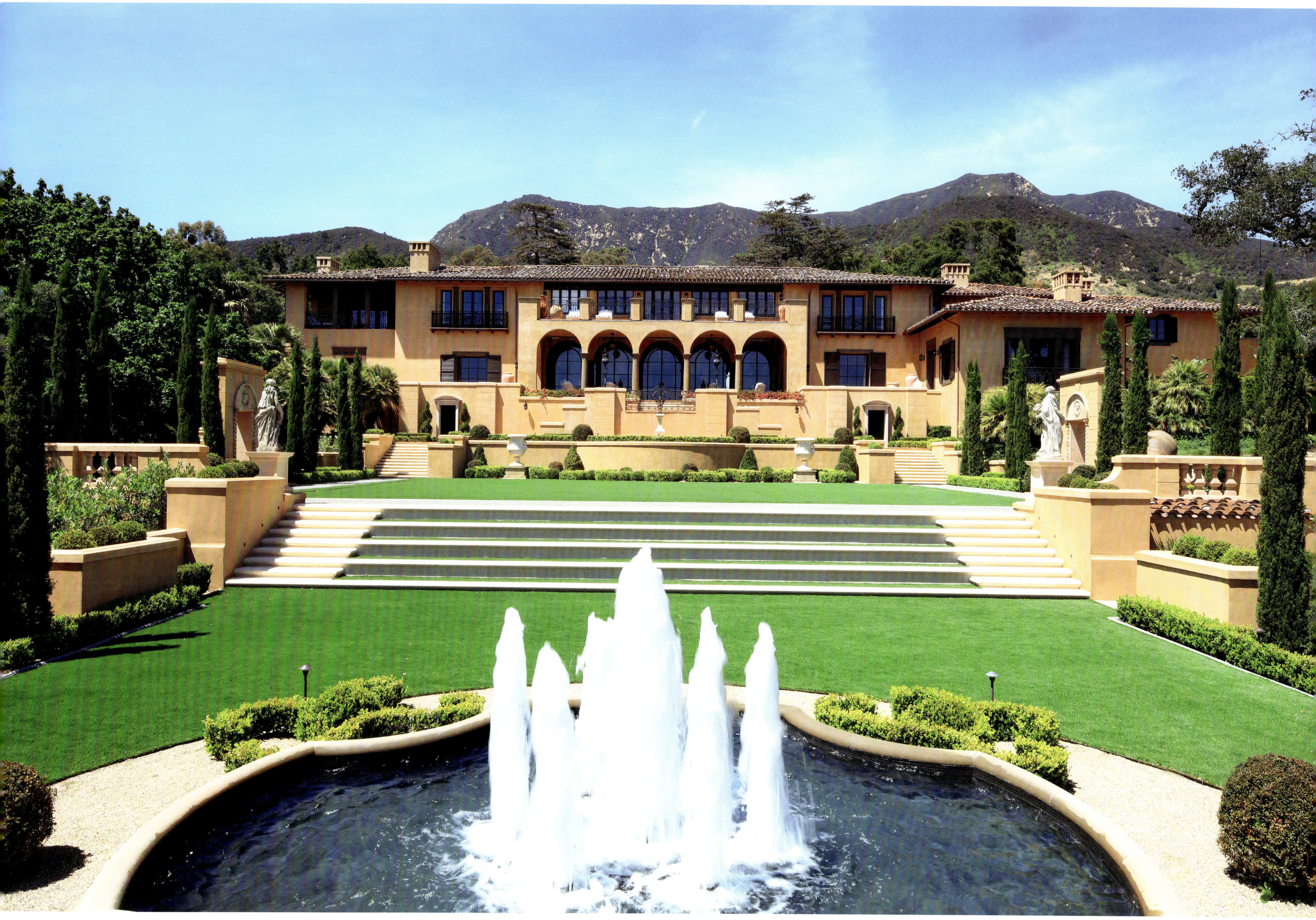

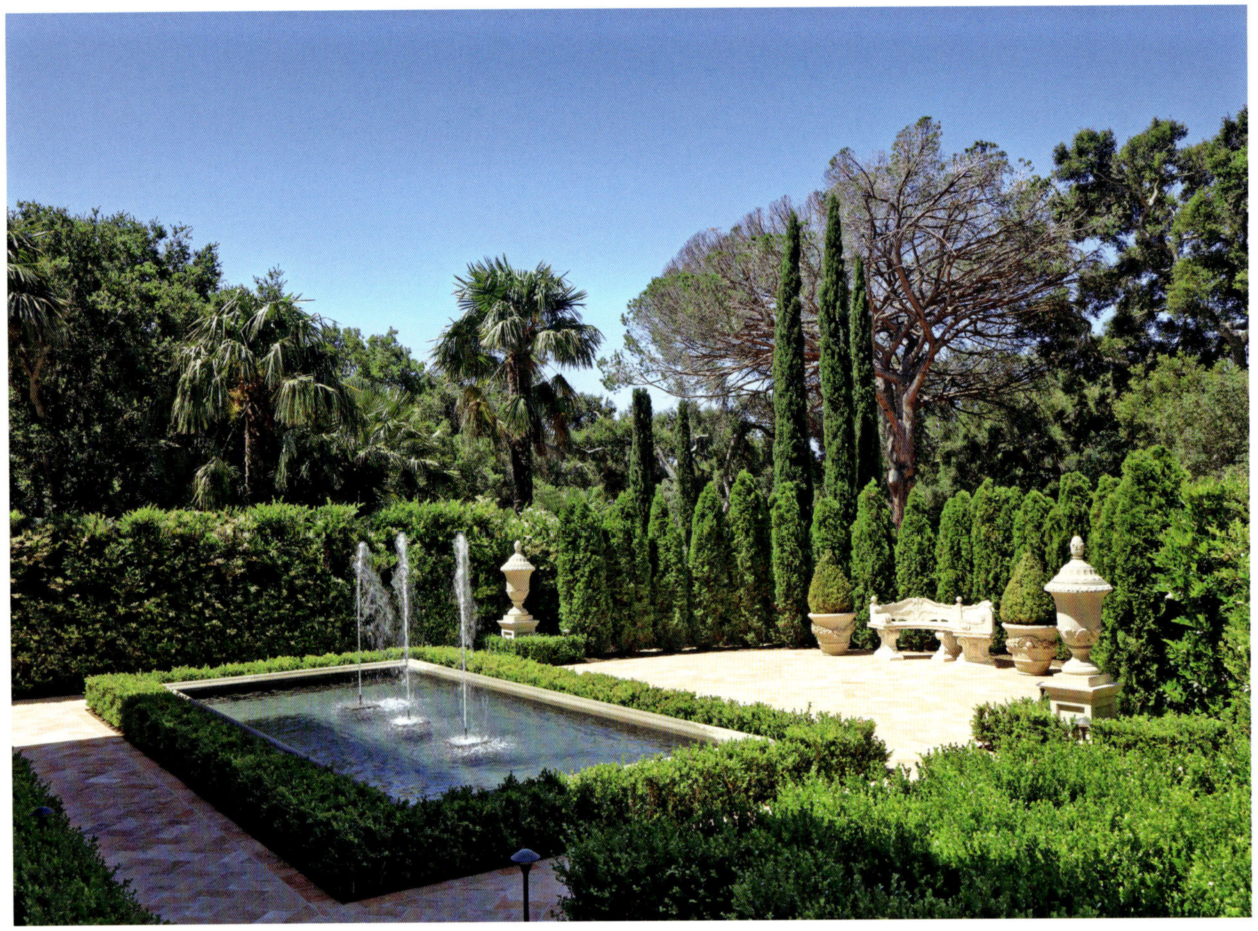

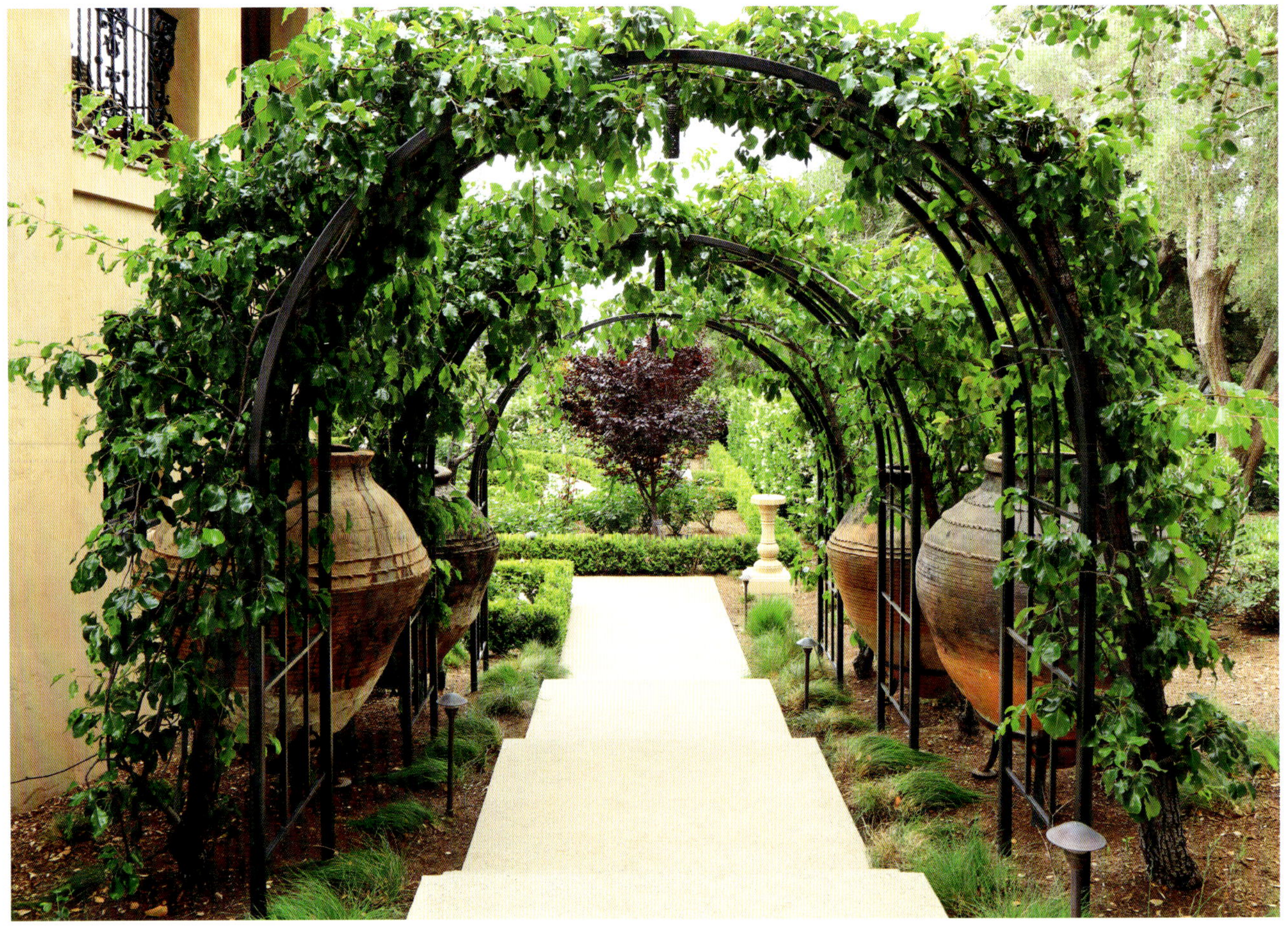

ABOVE LEFT: *The side garden off the library. When you start to meander down the hillside, you come across the other structures on the grounds, such as the lower guest houses and the pool house.*

ABOVE RIGHT: *An arbor with antique European urns.*

OPPOSITE LEFT: *An allée of mature olive trees leads to a bocce ball court. The gardens have axial walks and vistas and are an exploration of new garden traditions.*

OPPOSITE RIGHT: *A Thai spirit house.*

FOLLOWING PAGES, LEFT: *The pool's walls of local golden stone continue the motif of antiquity and tie the pool area to the house. A shell grotto with a spa is tucked into the end.* RIGHT: *The new pool house is a very open structure with gray plaster columns, metal arched doors, and reclaimed wood ceiling. It bridges the pool on one side and the lower tennis court on the other.*

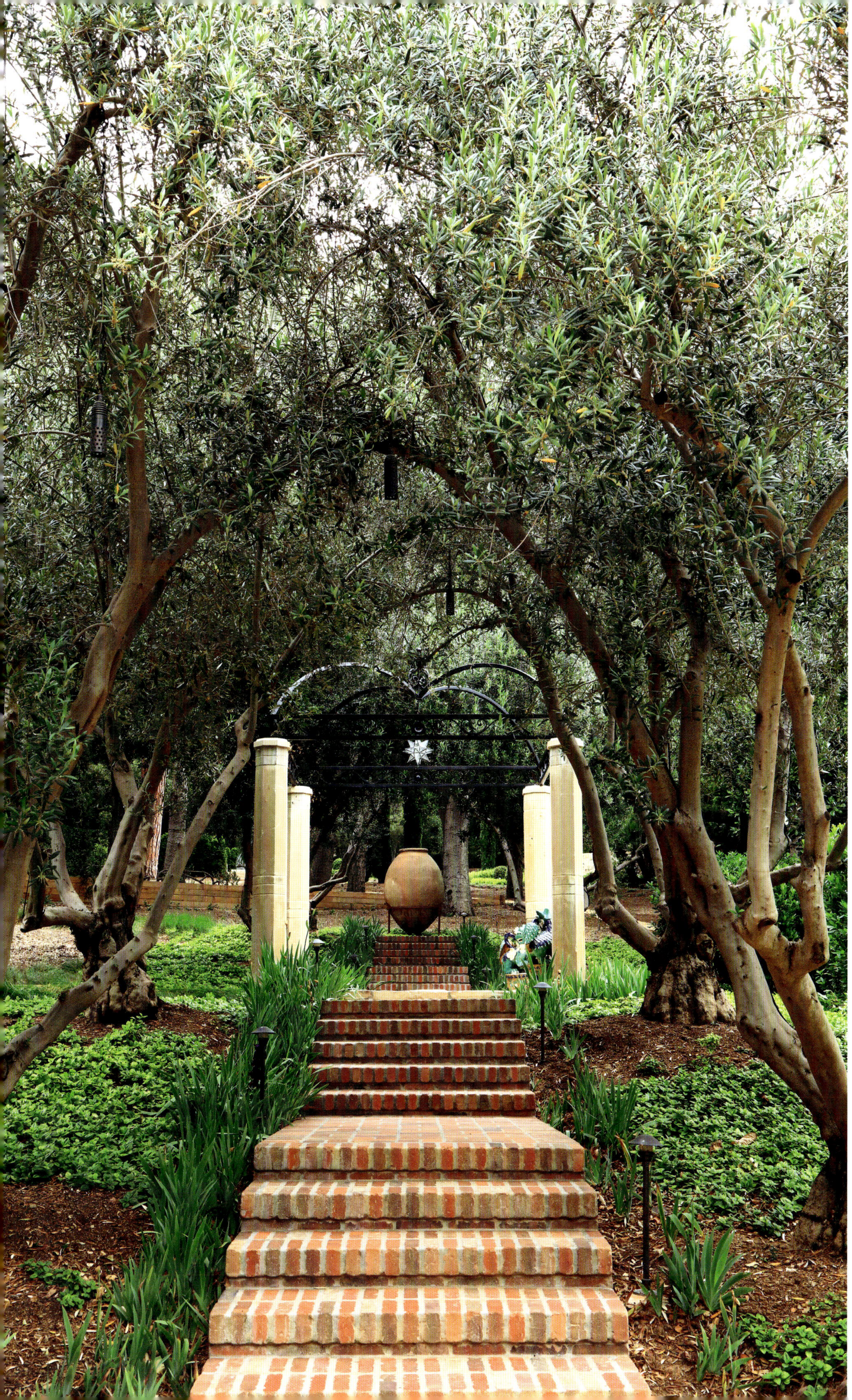

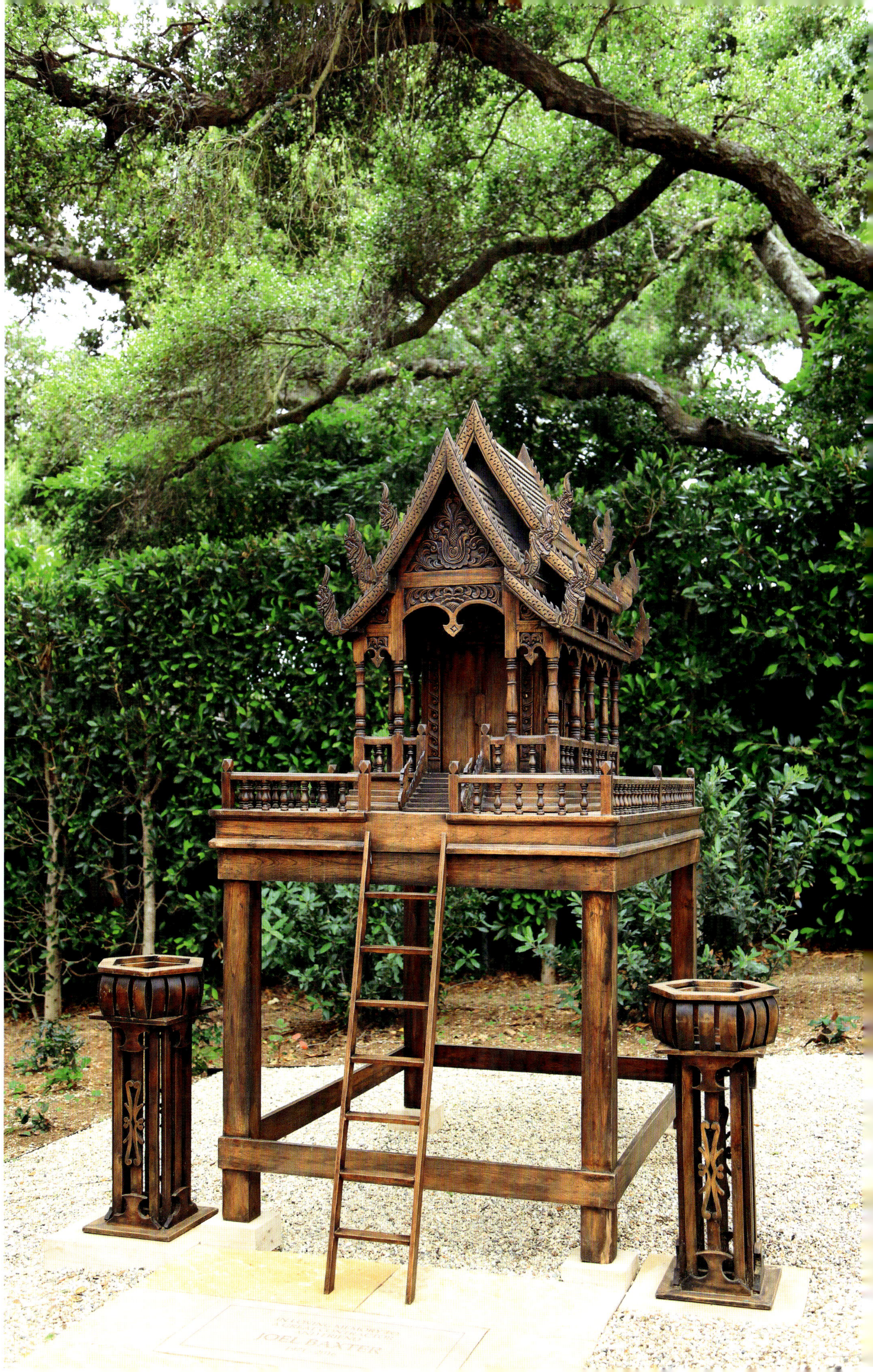
JOEL BAXTER

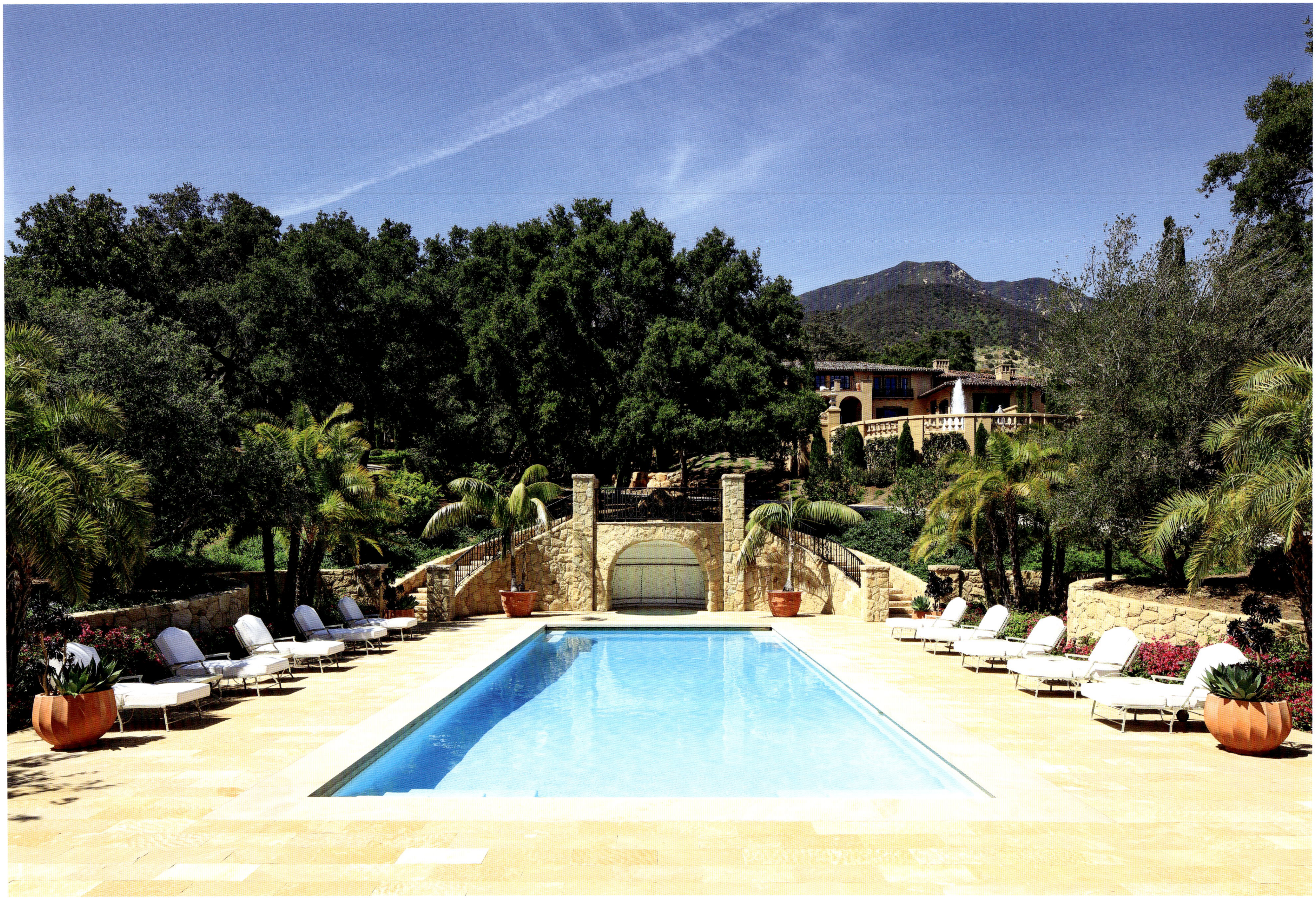

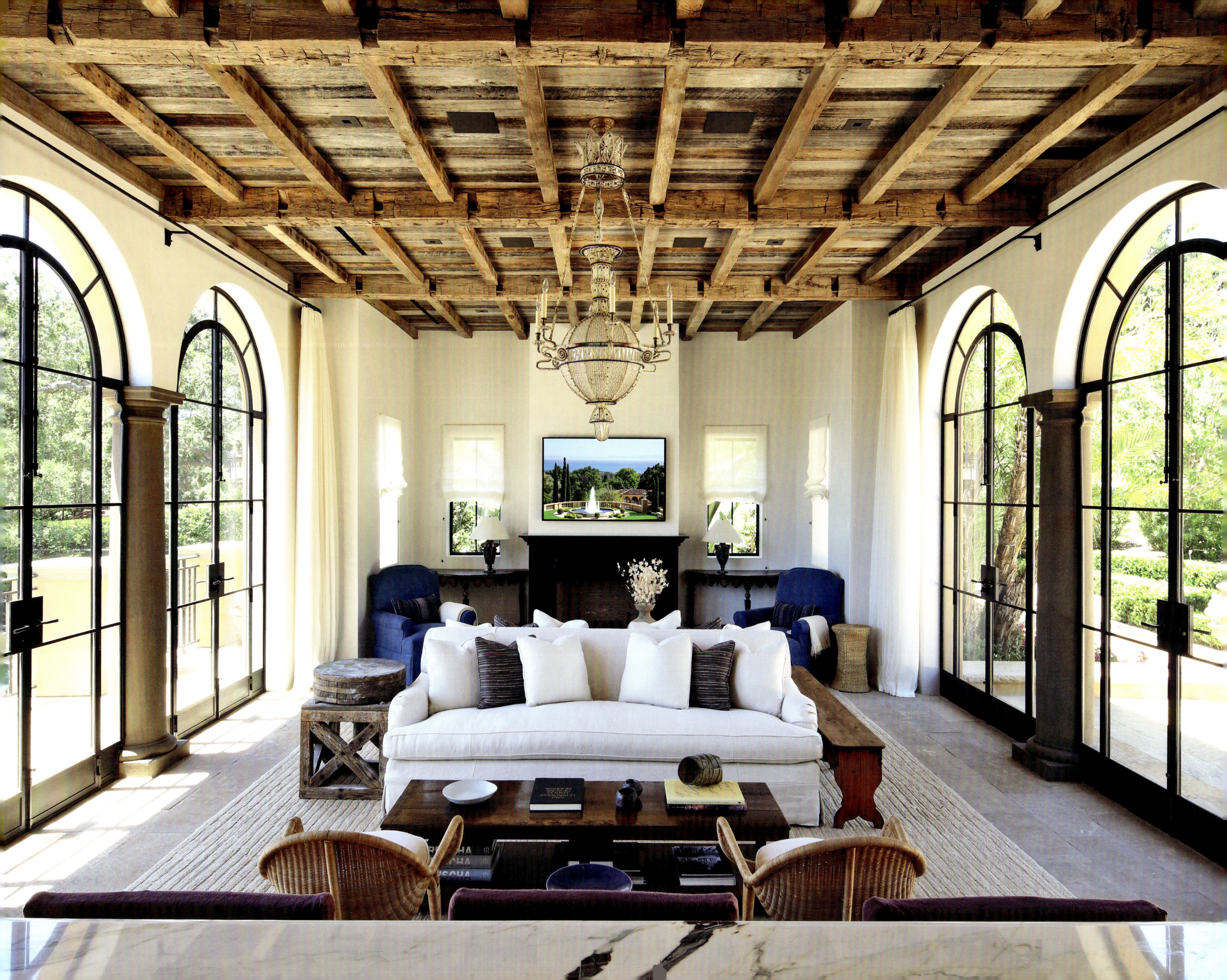

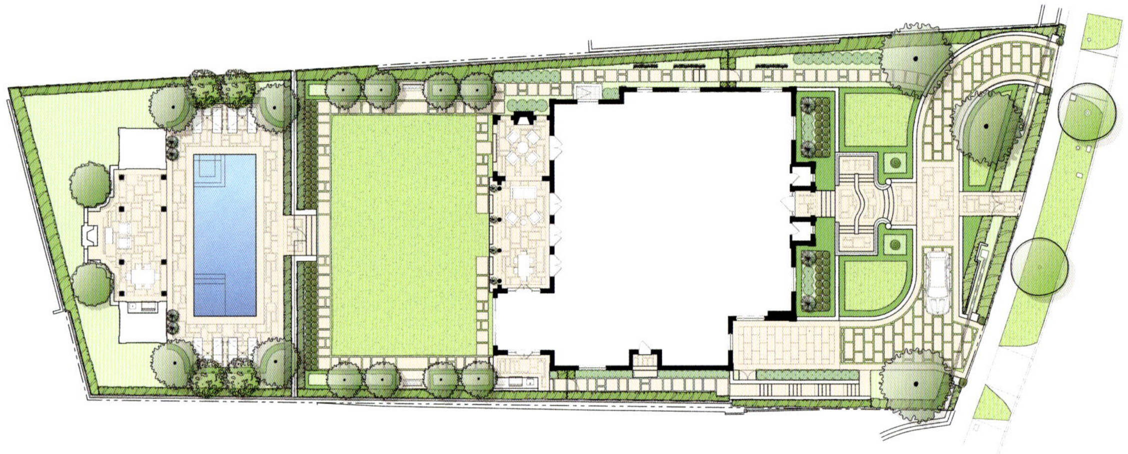

HOLMBY HOUSE

Holmby Hills

Located in an established neighborhood of historical homes, this house continues the great custom of uniting tradition with modernity that was the hallmark of Colonial Revival houses in the 1930s on the Westside of Los Angeles.

With the gently sloping topography, we elevated the main floor of the house to be level with the rear garden. That let us slip a garage and basement underneath the house and give the façade the sort of dramatic, raised entry that you typically see in London or the East Coast.

The classic white brick exterior with picture windows in thin steel and the stylized Doric entry surround over a recessed porch all look original to the period. But instead of painting all of the exposed metal white, as was common in the 1930s, we kept the steel black and the downspouts in gunmetal gray for a more contemporary look for our updated take on this style.

Since our clients are a young modern family and passionate art collectors, the interior architecture is a synthesis of a traditional Colonial framework of cornices, moldings, and casings that have been treated in a highly stylized way to be a bridge between the bold and the streamlined. When the element is traditional, we put a twist on it.

Interior architecture, developed with SFA Design, has a continuity of background. The color palette is black and white or charcoal and beige. Floors have a common color to tie them together, but with different tones and patterns to differentiate each space. To establish drama, there are large cased openings, coved ceilings, Moderne-inspired ironwork, and bold marble elements in geometric patterns.

The goal was to create a house of substance by layering luxurious architectural materials with the furnishings and finishes, all of which give the home its elevated, modern feel.

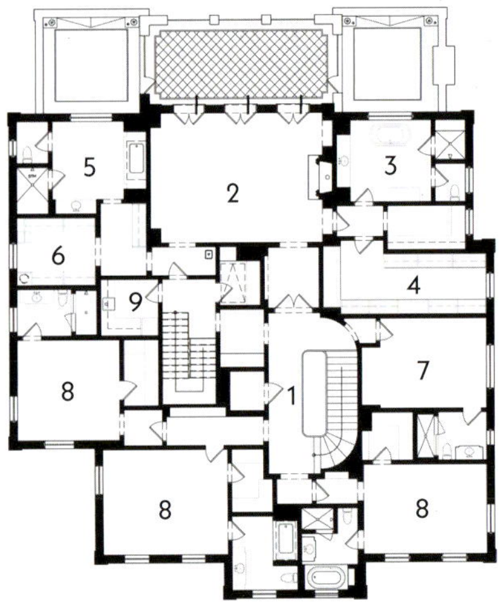

1 Upper stair hall
2 Master bedroom
3 Her bath
4 Her closet
5 His bath
6 Dressing room
7 Playroom
8 Bedroom
9 Linen closet

SECOND-FLOOR PLAN

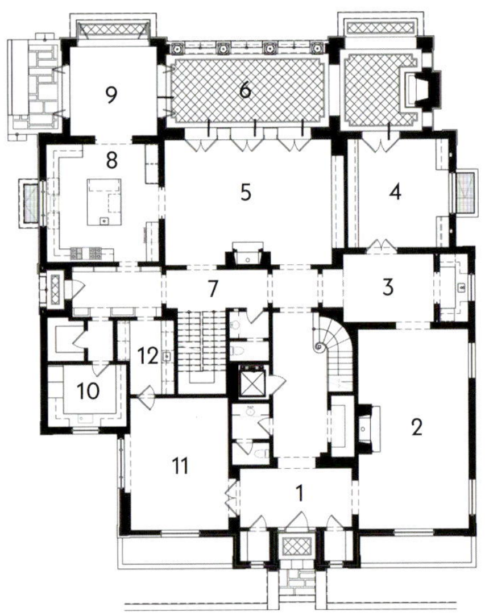

1 Entry hall
2 Living room
3 Lounge
4 Library
5 Family room
6 Loggia
7 Family hall
8 Kitchen
9 Breakfast room
10 Laundry
11 Dining room
12 Butler's pantry

FIRST-FLOOR PLAN

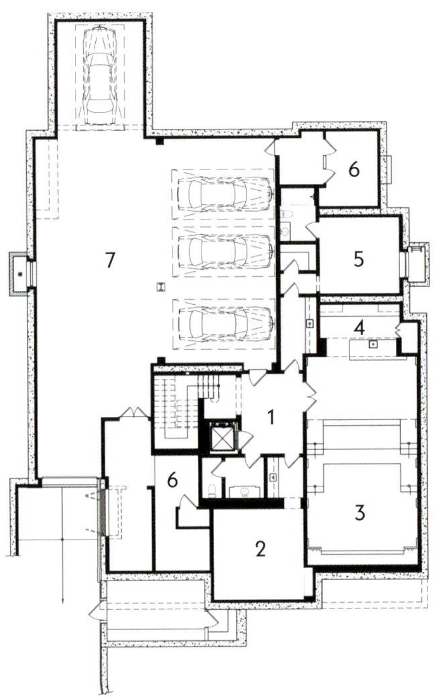

1 Basement foyer
2 Gym
3 Recreation room
4 Bar
5 Staff bedroom
6 Mechanical/storage room
7 Garage

BASEMENT FLOOR PLAN

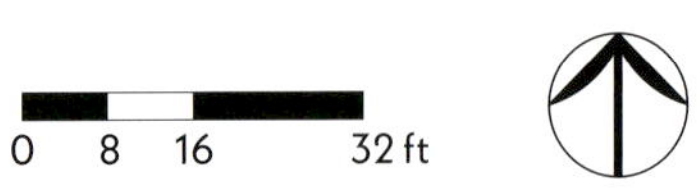

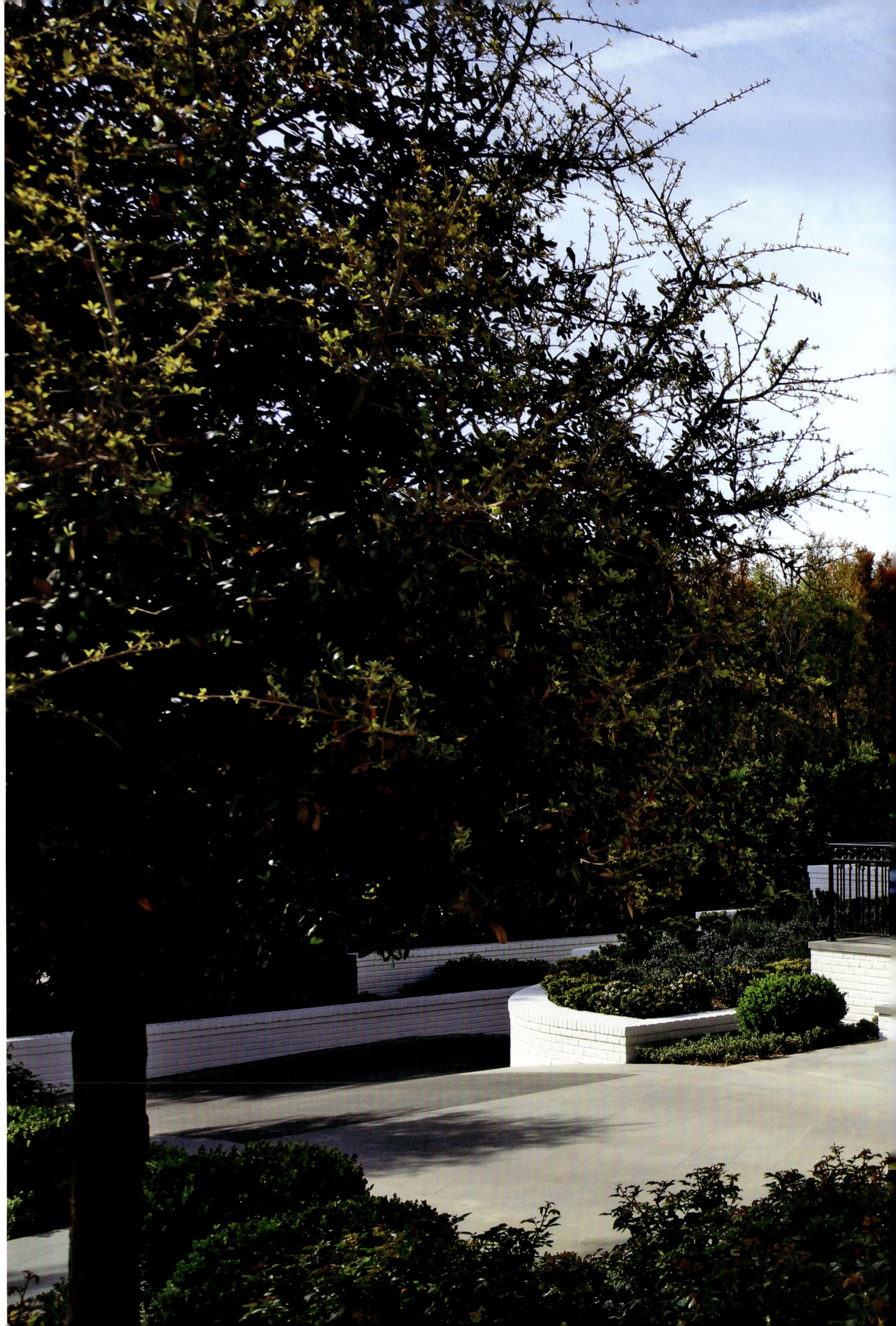

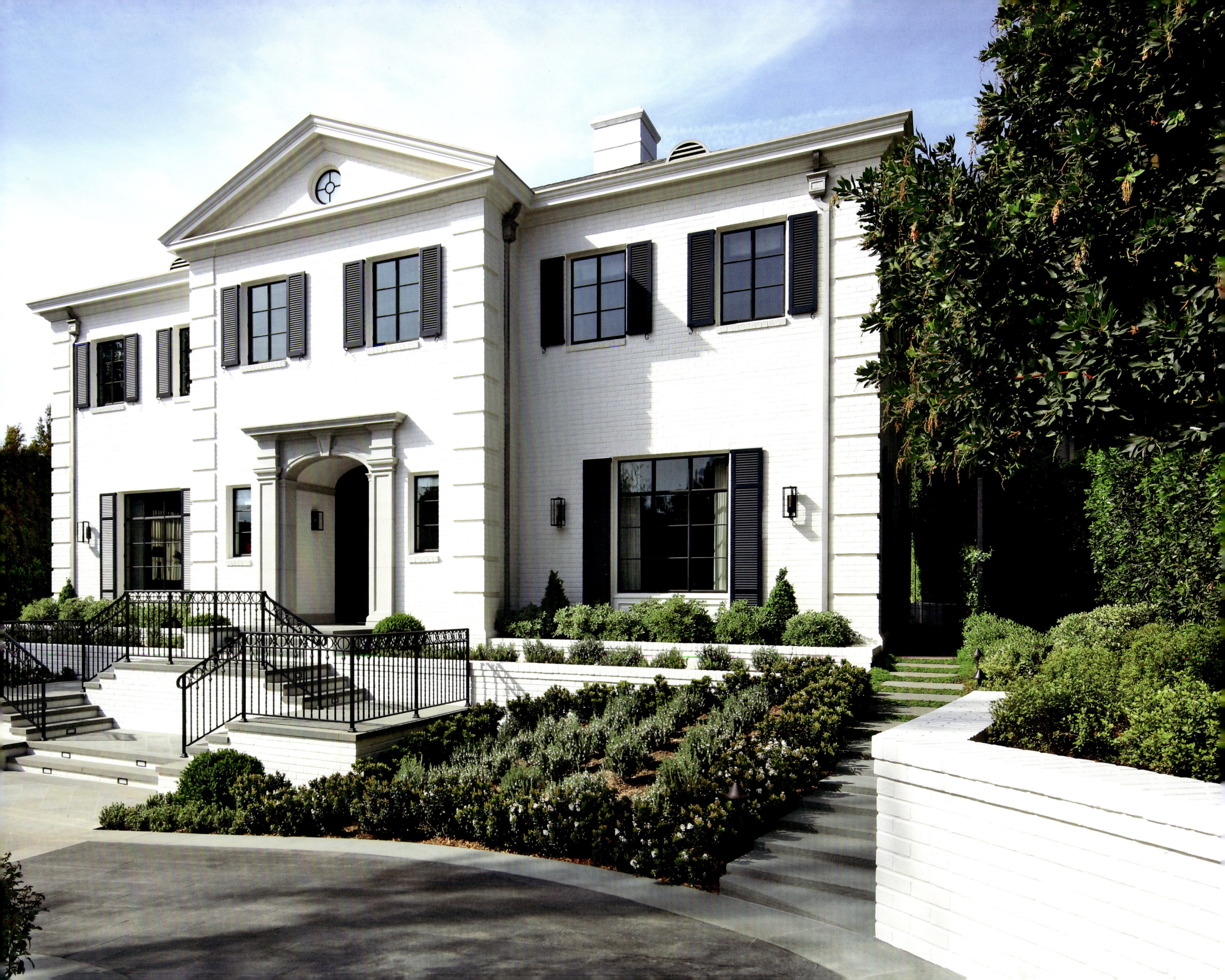

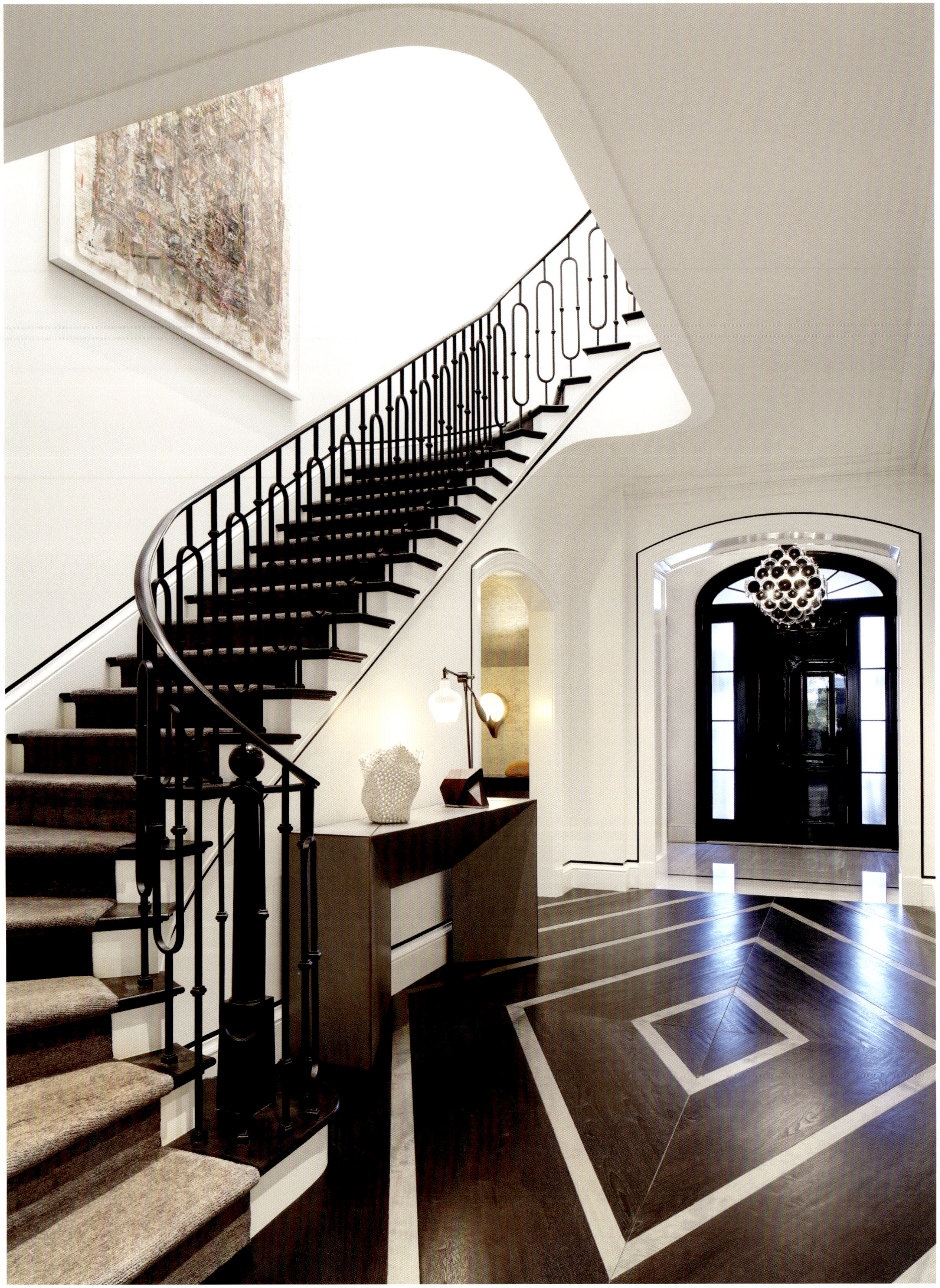

PREVIOUS PAGES: *A new Colonial Revival house in a neighborhood of historical homes has all the traditional exterior elements—white brick façade, picture windows in steel, Doric entry surround—that were streamlined for a more contemporary interpretation of the style.*

LEFT: *The interiors by SFA Design took the traditional framework of cornices and casings but stylized them to update this classic home for a family with young children. A mitered patterned marble floor defines the stair hall.*

OPPOSITE: *The entry hallway immediately establishes a sense of drama with grand cased openings, their classic entablatures painted glossy black for a more modern edge.*

FOLLOWING PAGES, LEFT: *The living room has a plaster ceiling and a black painted reveal around every molding and architectural feature. It was important to the clients to have a fireplace surround in a dramatic color to match the furniture and art.* RIGHT: *A softer dusty rose was used in the dining room, which is a more formal space used in the evenings.*

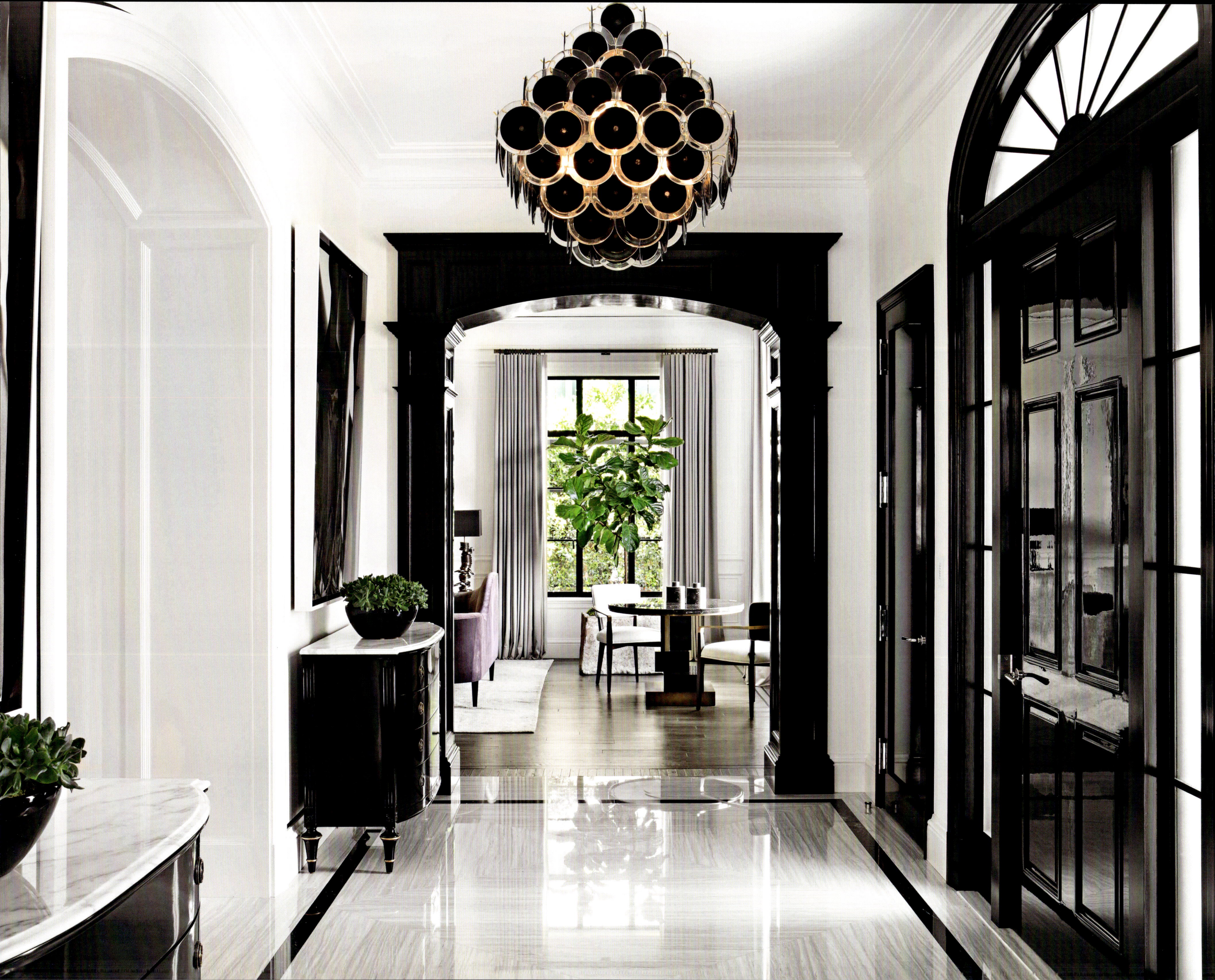

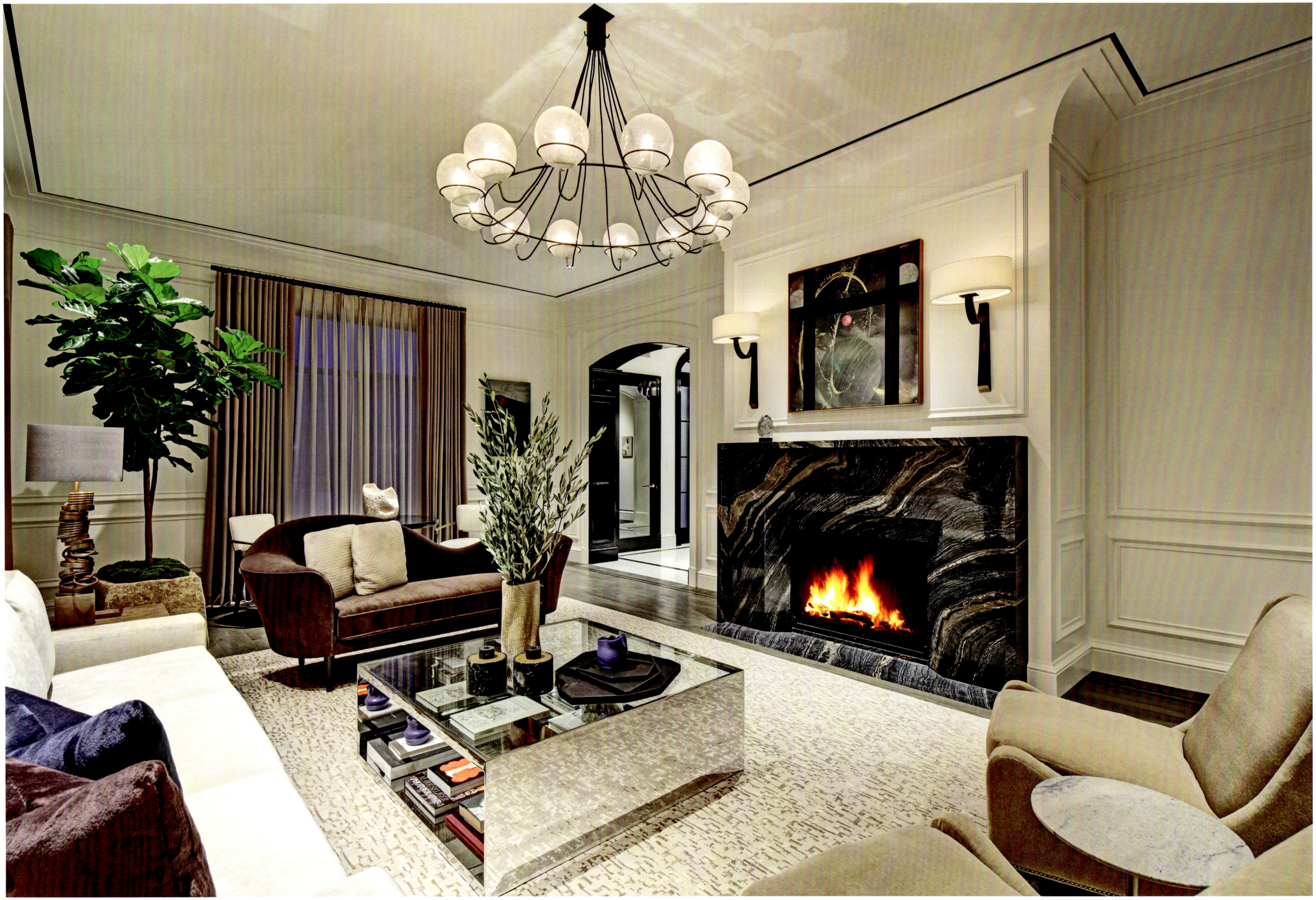

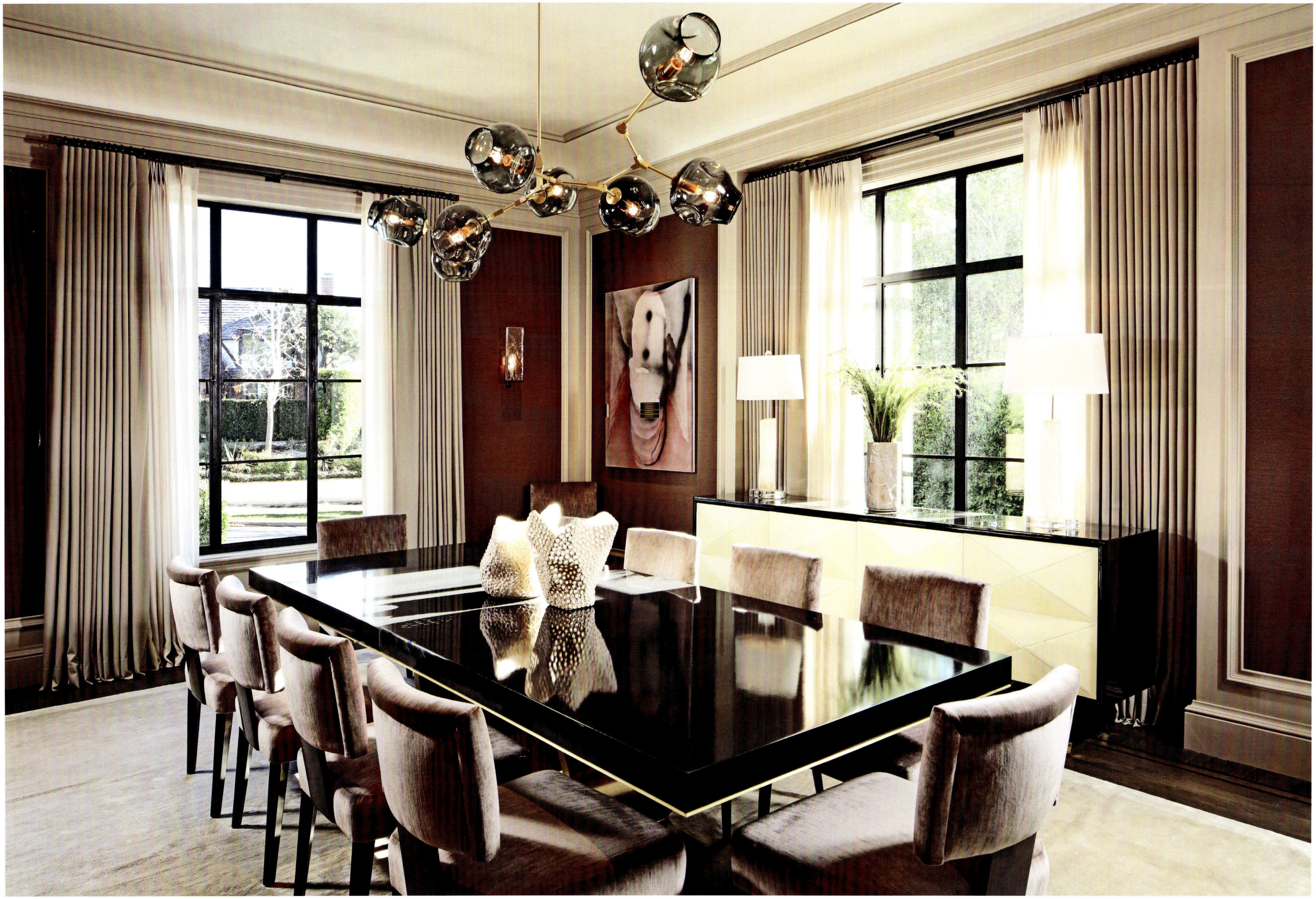

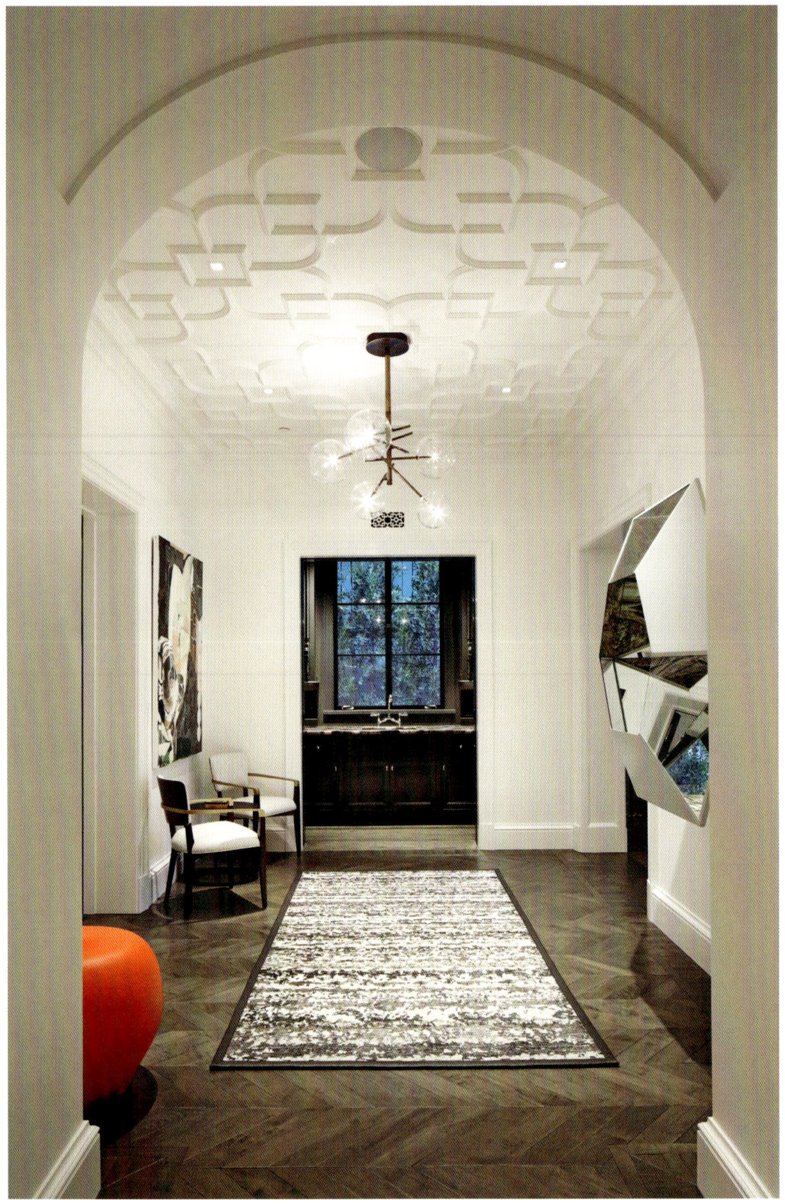

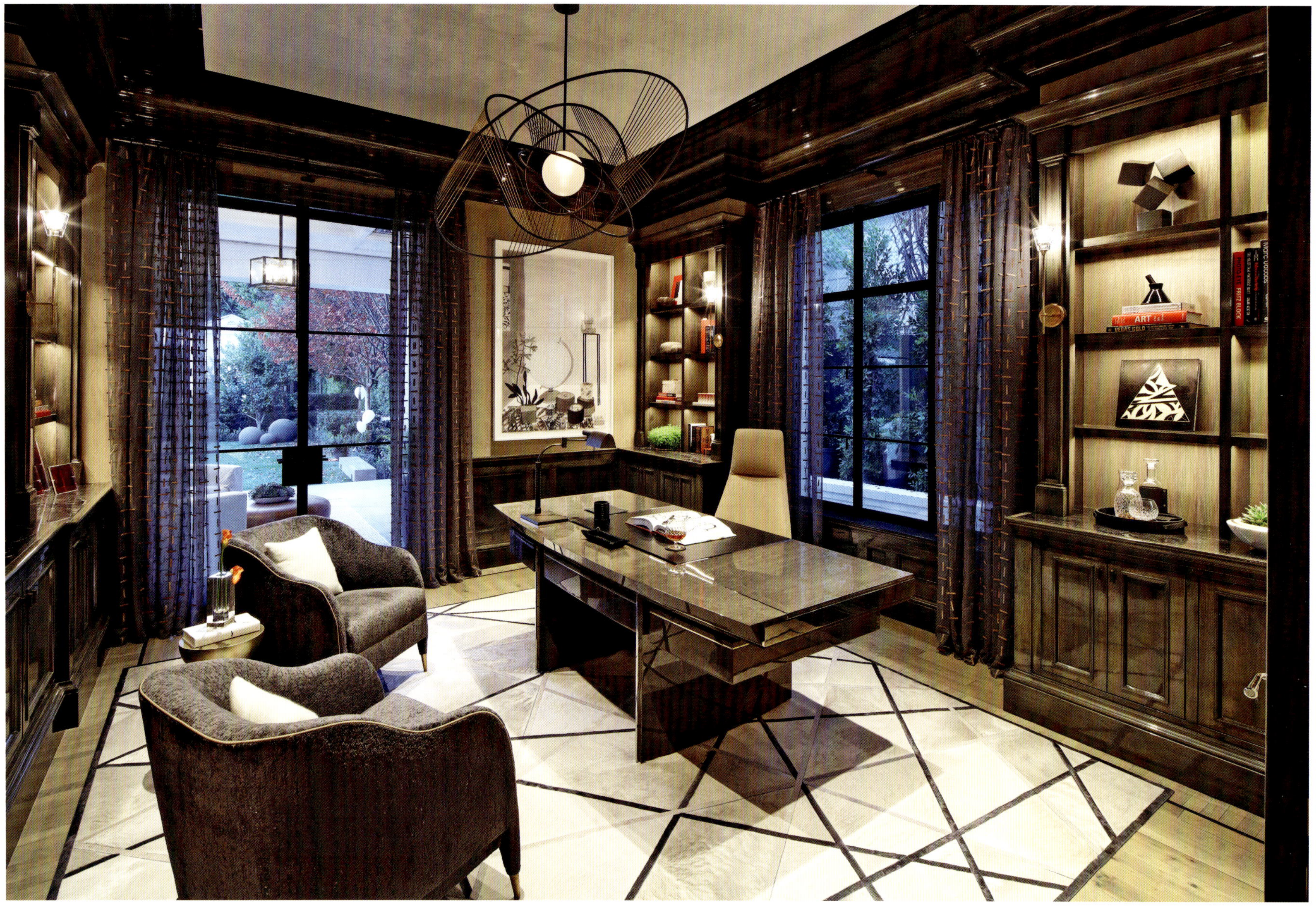

ABOVE LEFT: *A hallway that displays part of the clients' art collection has a strapwork ceiling that echoes the pattern in the steel and glass doors, which lead to the bar.*

ABOVE RIGHT: *A hip ceiling painted gray unites the brown and black in the husband's office. All the light fixtures are a combination of vintage and artisan.*

OPPOSITE: *The family room is a major focal point of the back of the house, with a very traditional coffered ceiling and wainscoting given a contemporary twist with cove lighting and a fireplace that relates to the cabinetry.*

FOLLOWING PAGES: *The kitchen opens through an elliptical entrance to the breakfast room, which was given a coffered ceiling and pocket doors. The same color floors are used throughout, but with different patterns to differentiate the spaces.*

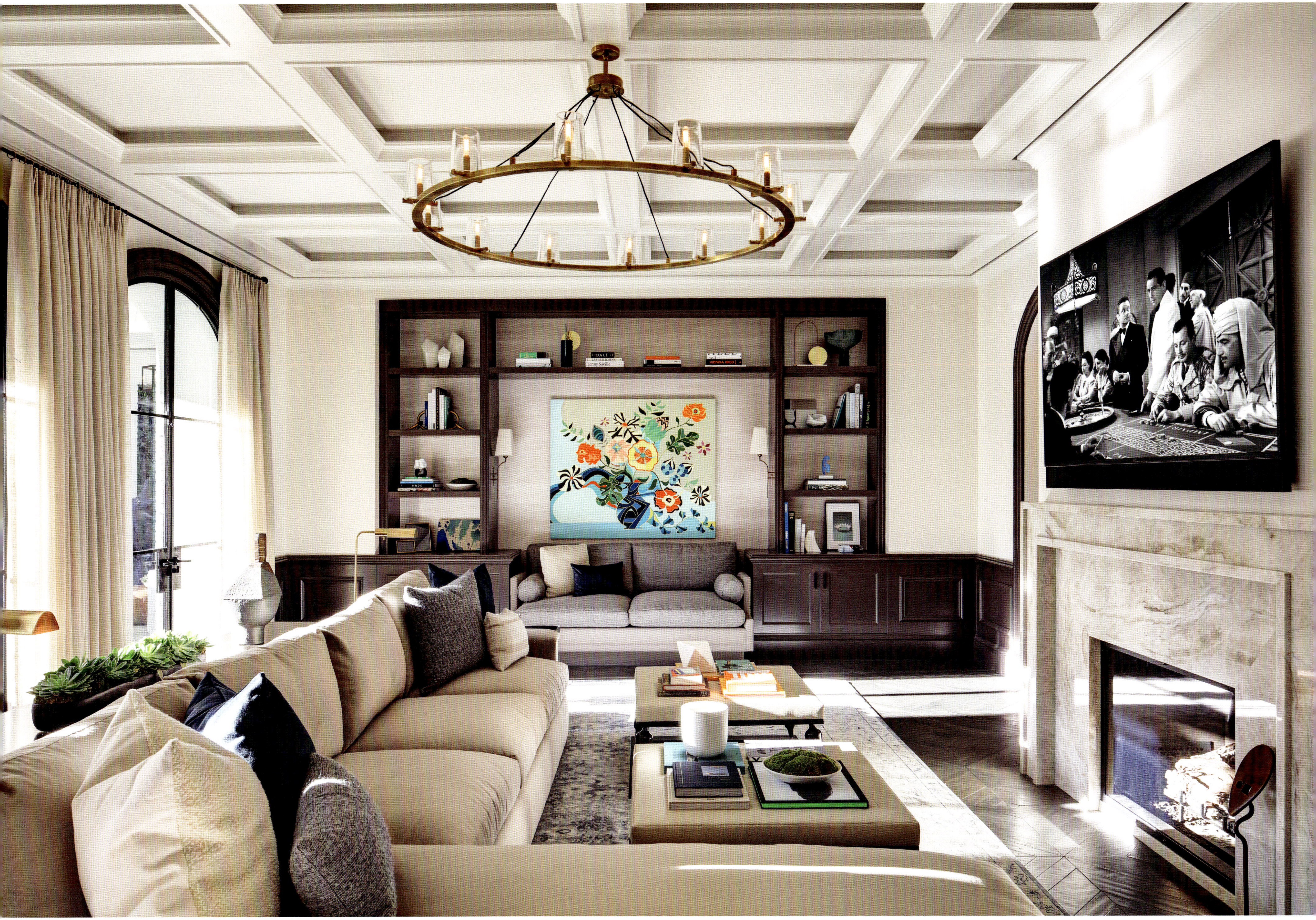

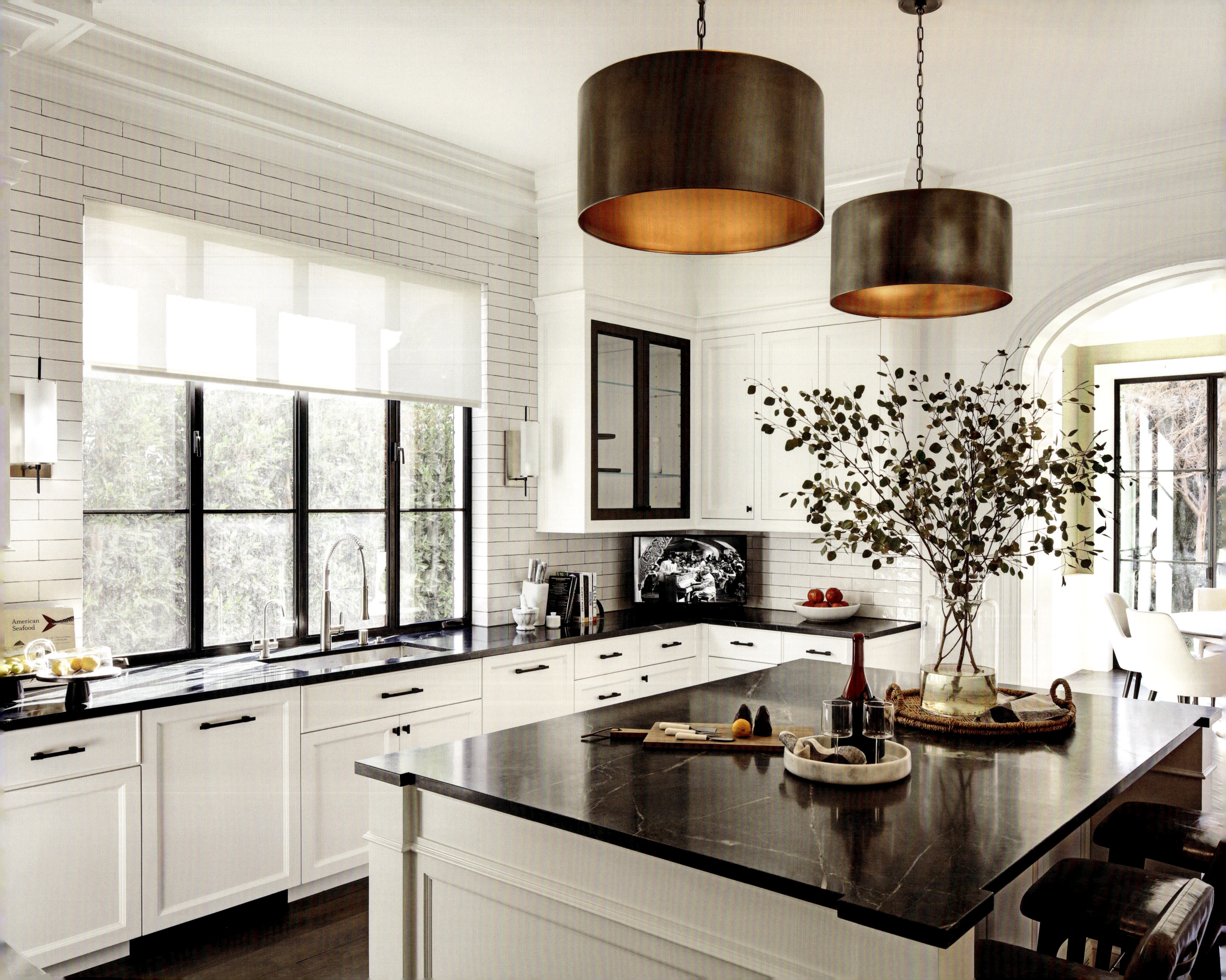
American
Seafood

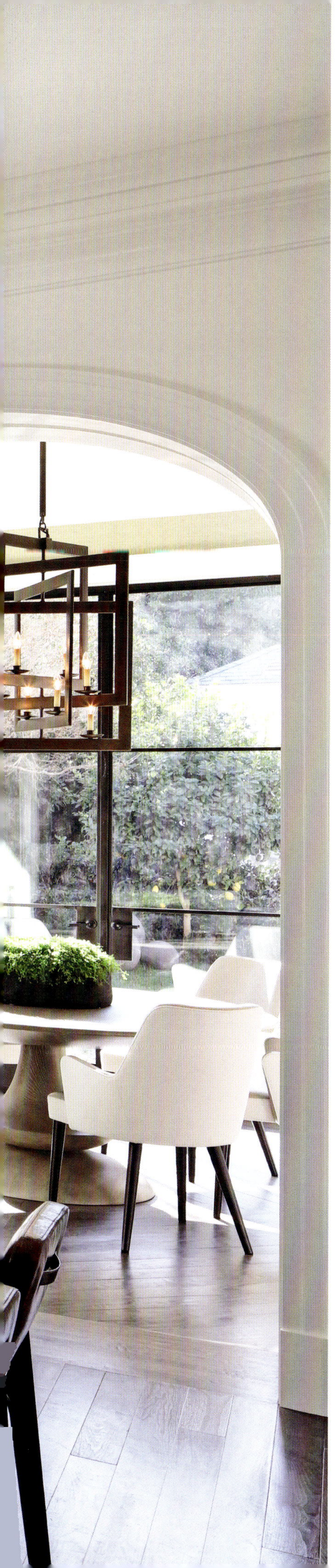

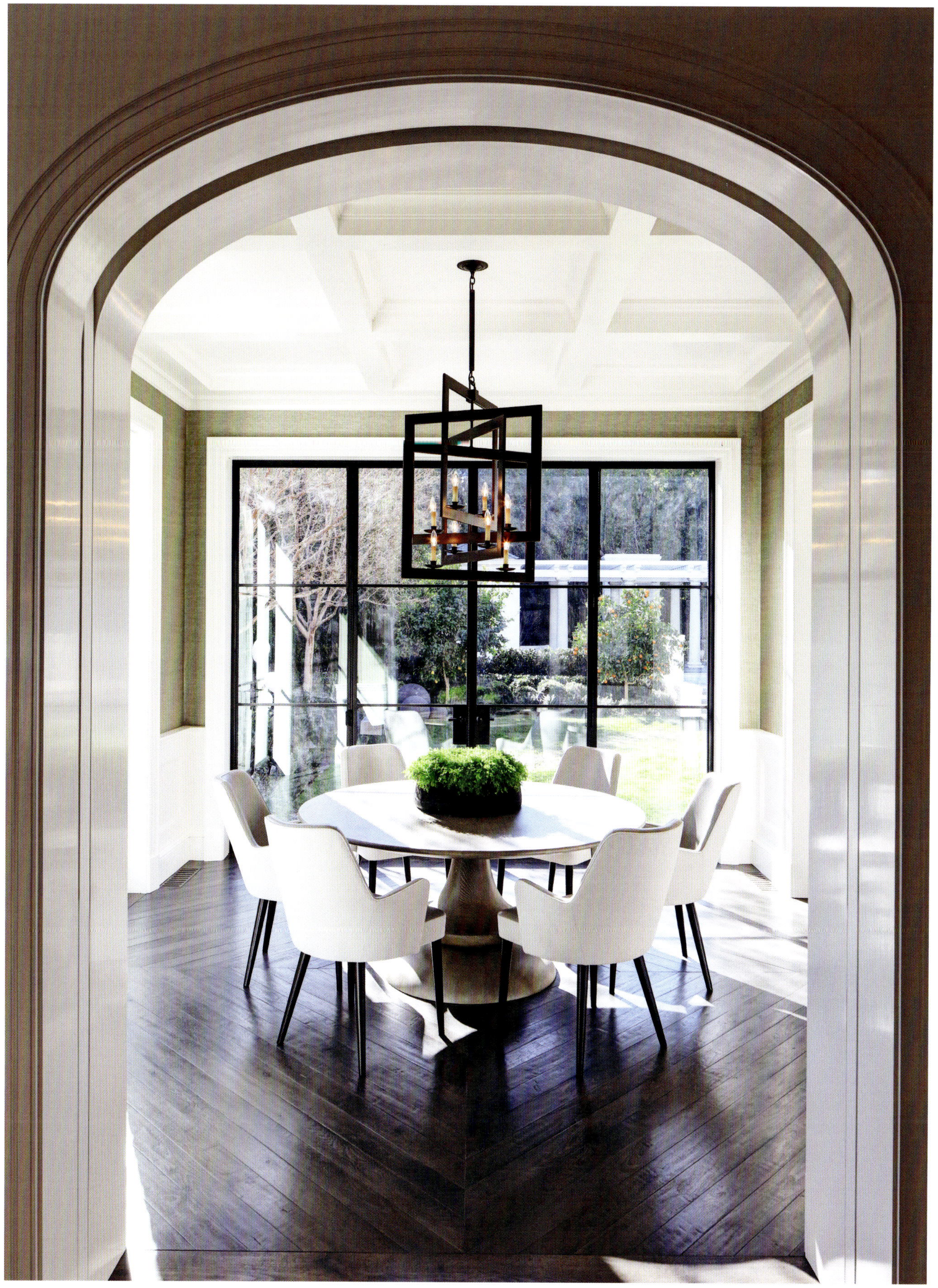

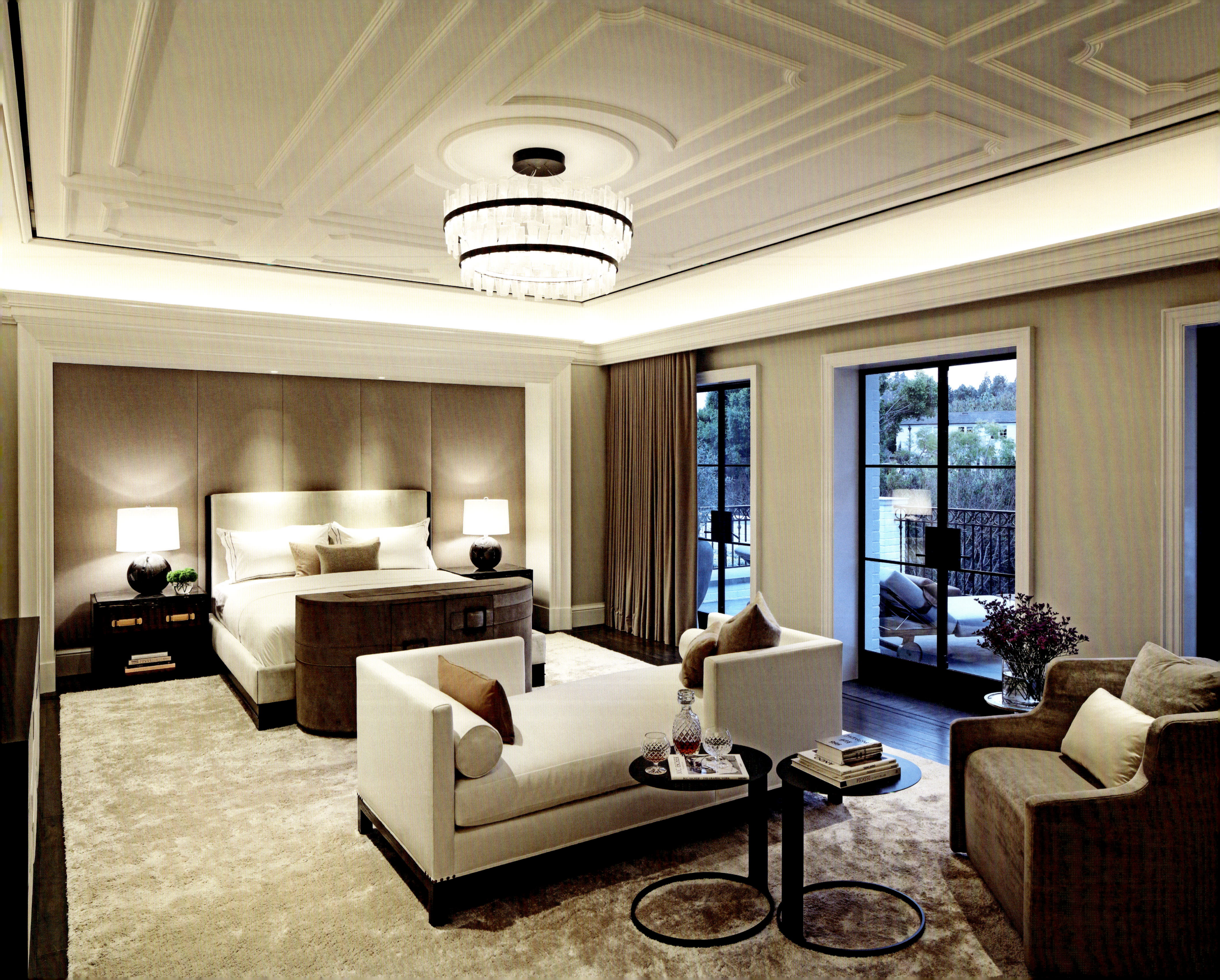

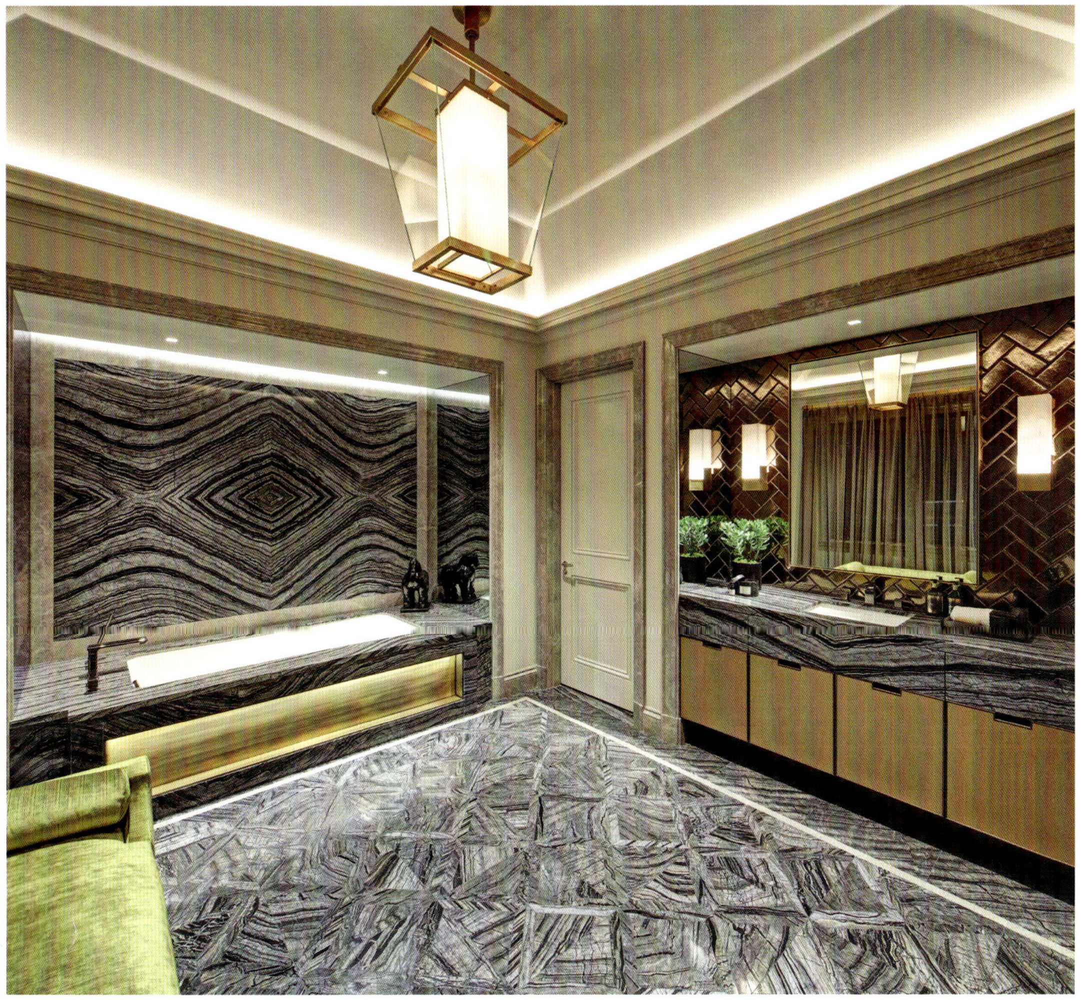

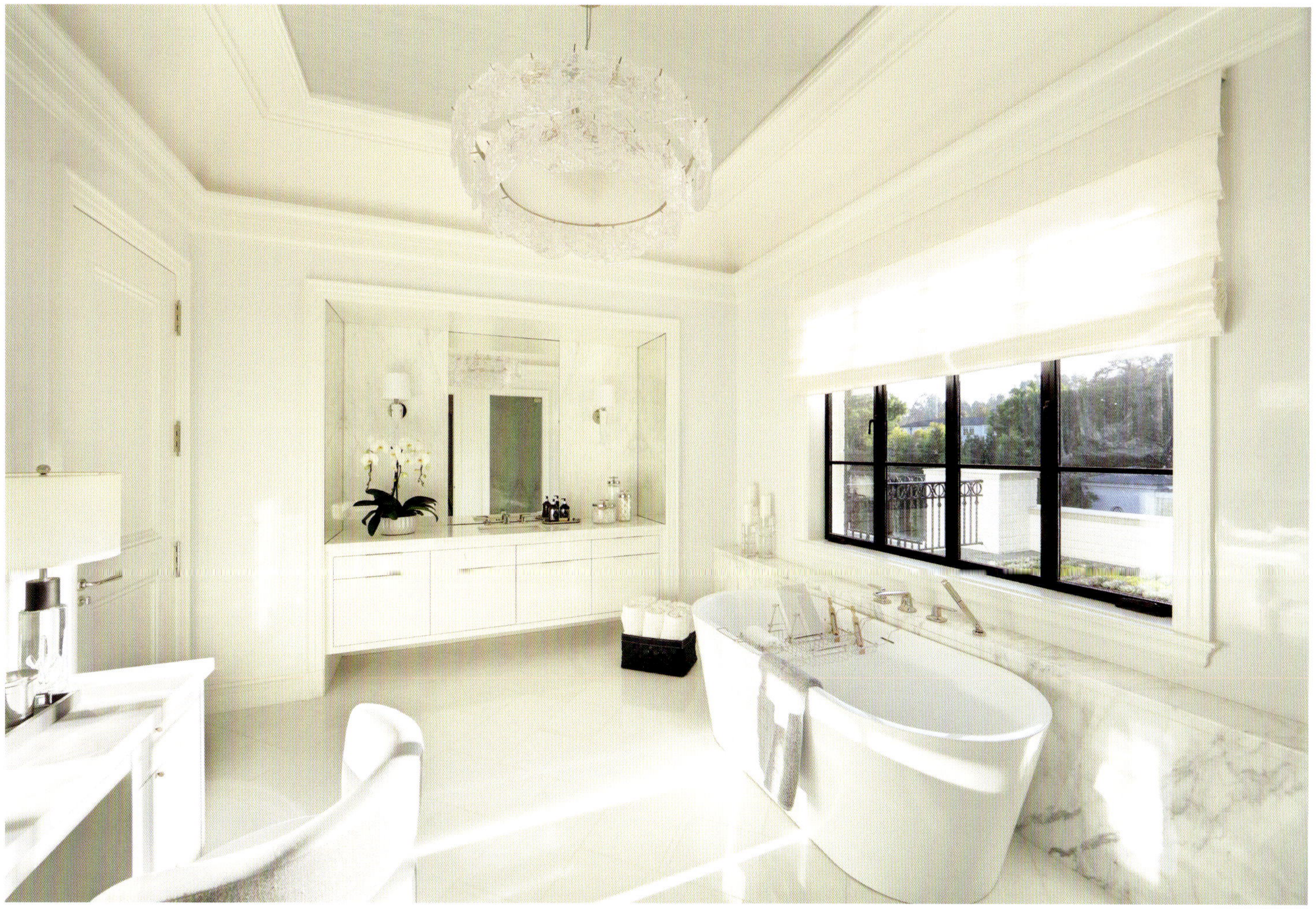

OPPOSITE: *Layering the architectural materials with those selected for the furnishings give the house an elevated feel. The master suite, with a terrace above the loggia, is a sophisticated room with a lighted cove and applied moldings to the ceiling.*

ABOVE LEFT: *The husband's bath is a play of bold patterns in the stonework on the floor, counter, and tub surround, book-matched marble panel, copper-bronze tile, and a metal panel on the tub.*

ABOVE RIGHT: *The wife's bath is a more serene, all-white space with restrained black accents.*

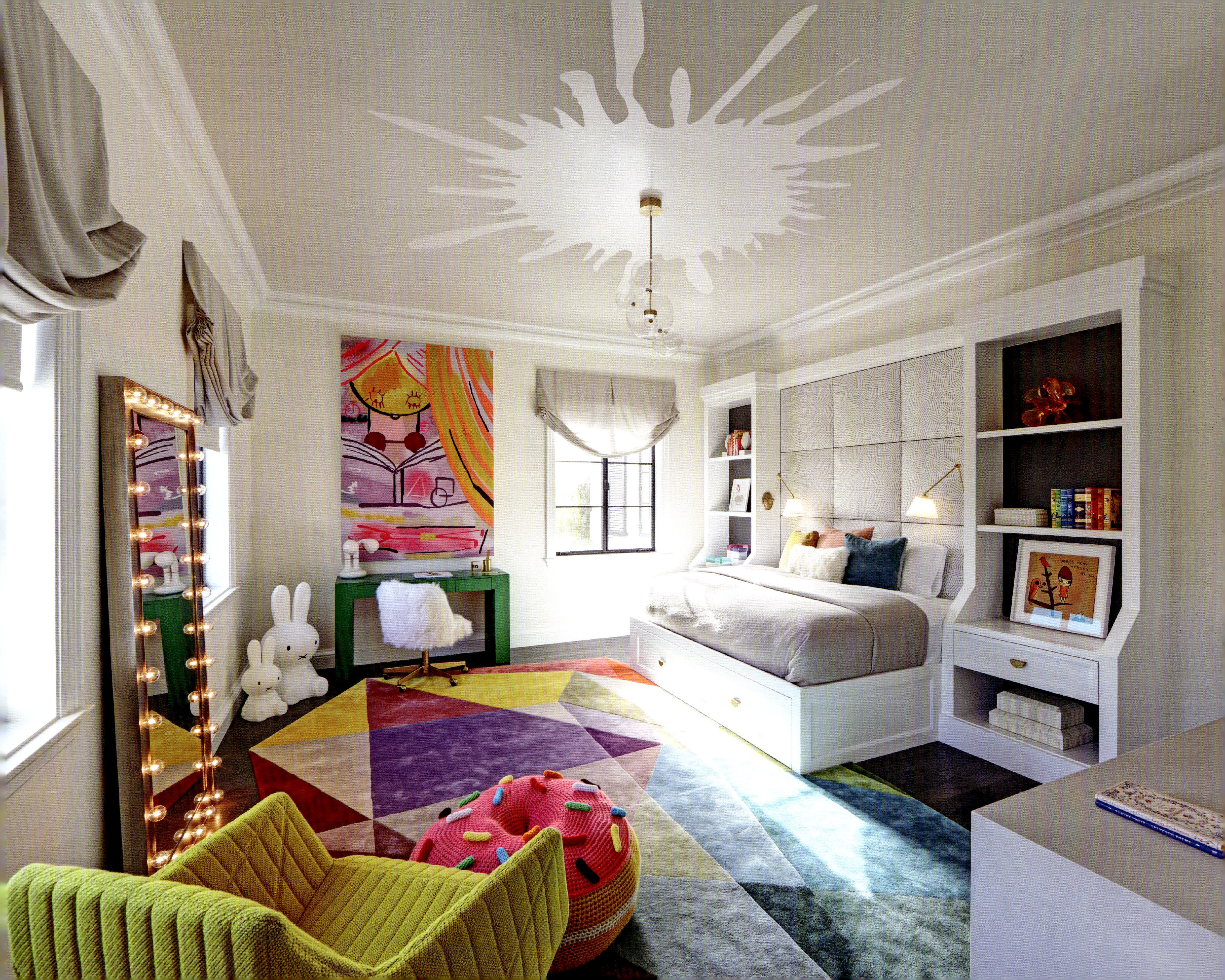

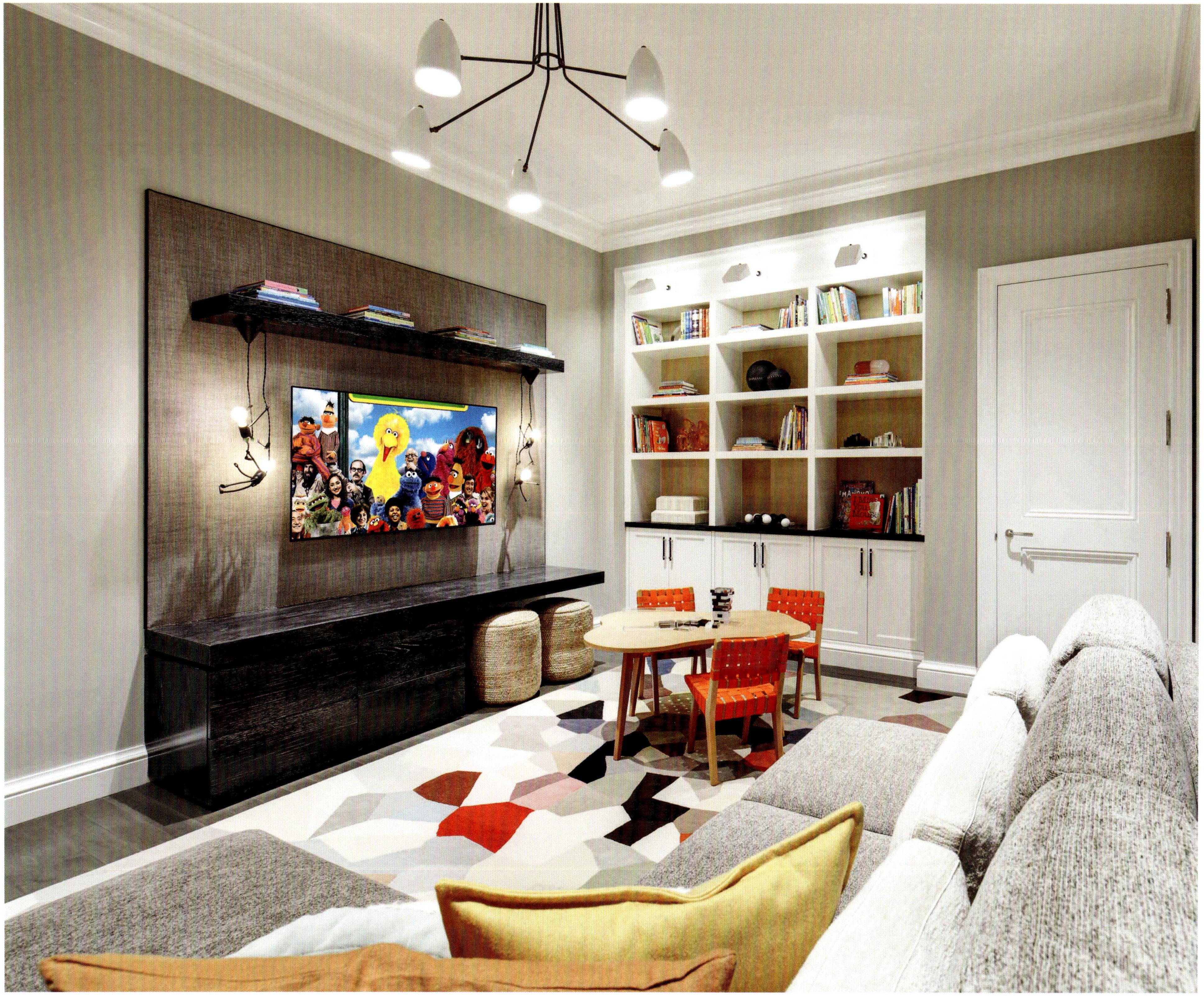

OPPOSITE: *The daughter's bedroom, with its colorful furnishings, which include a doughnut ottoman, is a fun, personal space that will evolve over time.*

ABOVE: *The playroom is also a flexible space that can be converted into a study later.*

FOLLOWING PAGES, LEFT: *The home theater is a light-hearted family space in Art Deco/Art Moderne motifs and features one of the first private home IMAX Palais theaters with a curved screen, installed by Future Home Theater.* RIGHT: *The powder room is a twist on the 1940s with bold marble and a modern console vanity with chrome fixtures.*

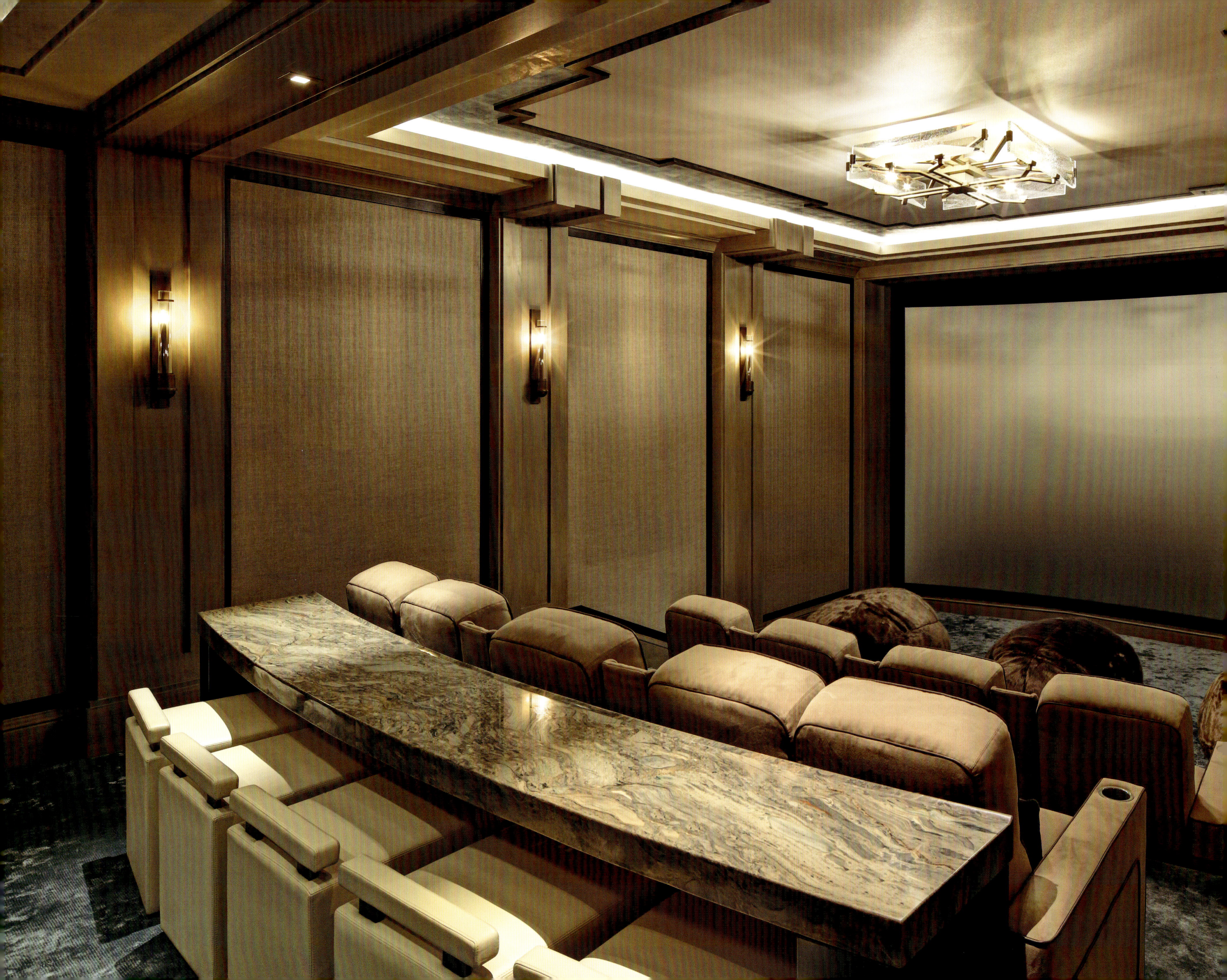

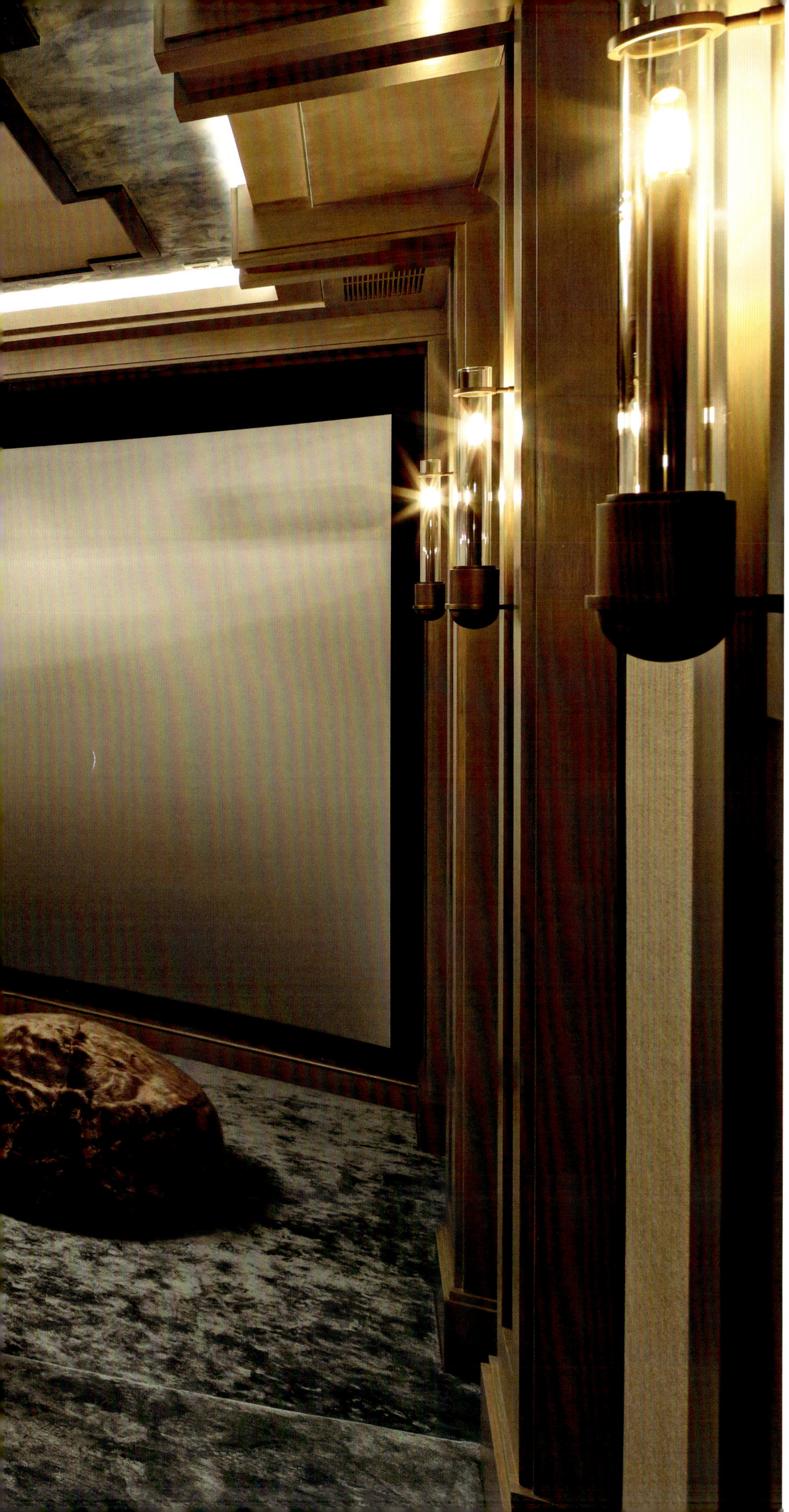

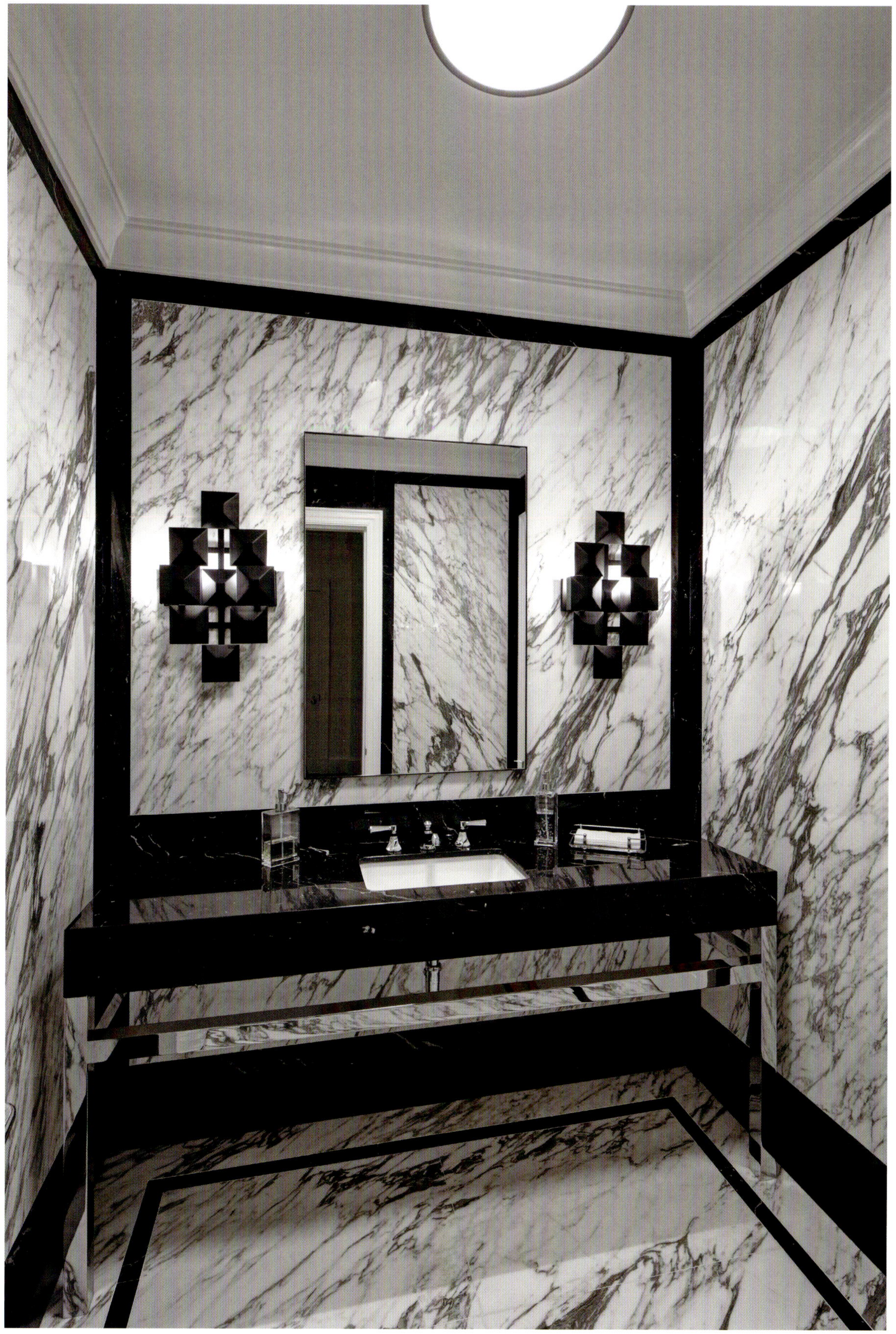

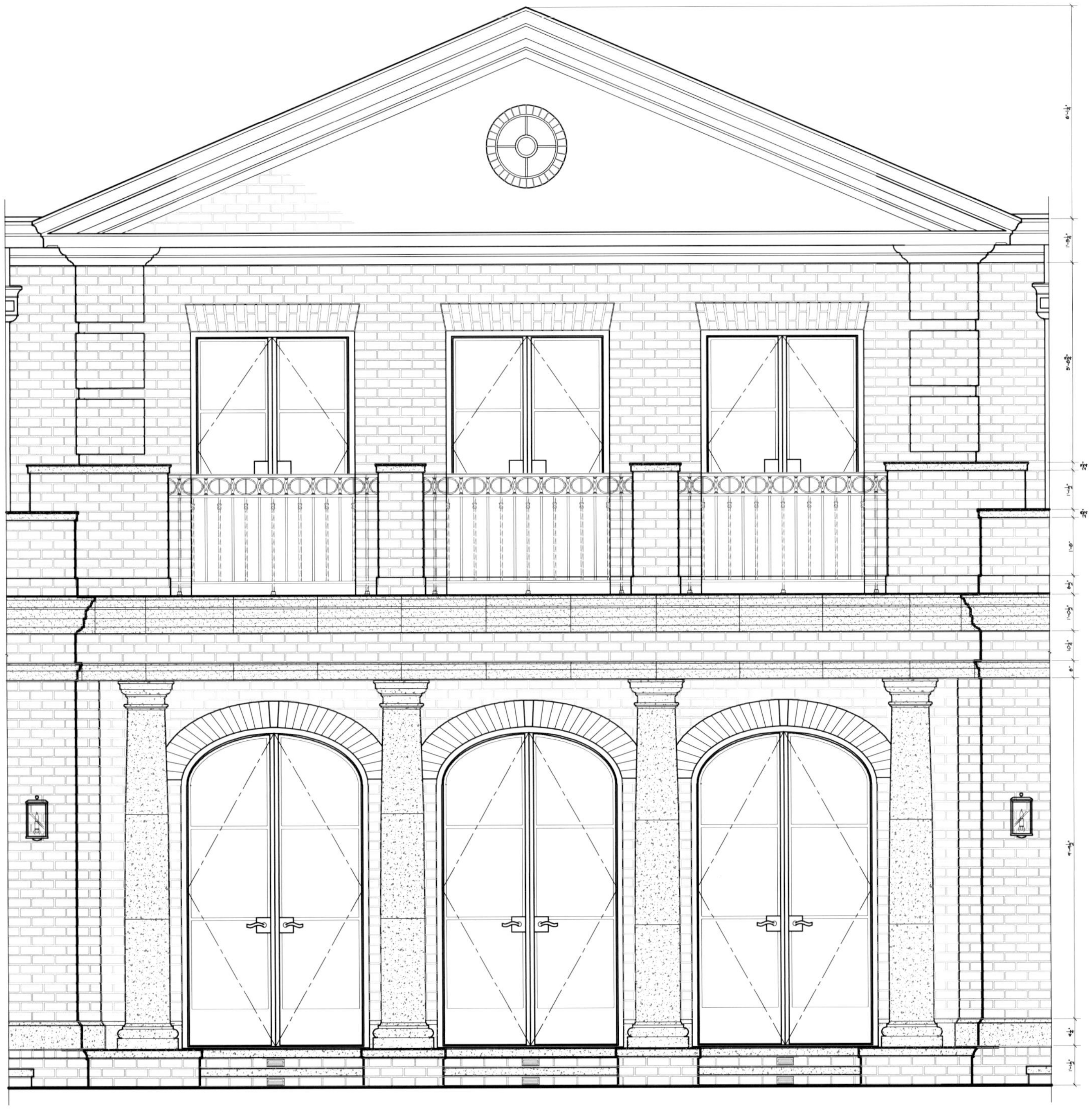

LEFT: *An elevation drawing of the rear colonnaded central loggia, and upper terrace.*

OPPOSITE: *The rear façade at twilight reveals the home's symmetry. The loggia ends at left in a seating area outside the library and flows into the dining room at right with bifold doors. The central loggia has bluestone paving and blue-gray limestone trim and features a long table with overhead heaters concealed in the ceiling beams. Above is a terrace roof garden of succulents bordered in stone, which breaks up the space and softens it.*

FOLLOWING PAGES, LEFT: *At the far end of the property is the pool and pool house, with changing rooms. The building codes dictated the idea of two pavilions united by a pergola and columns.*
RIGHT: *The pool house outdoor lounge area includes a fireplace and bar.*

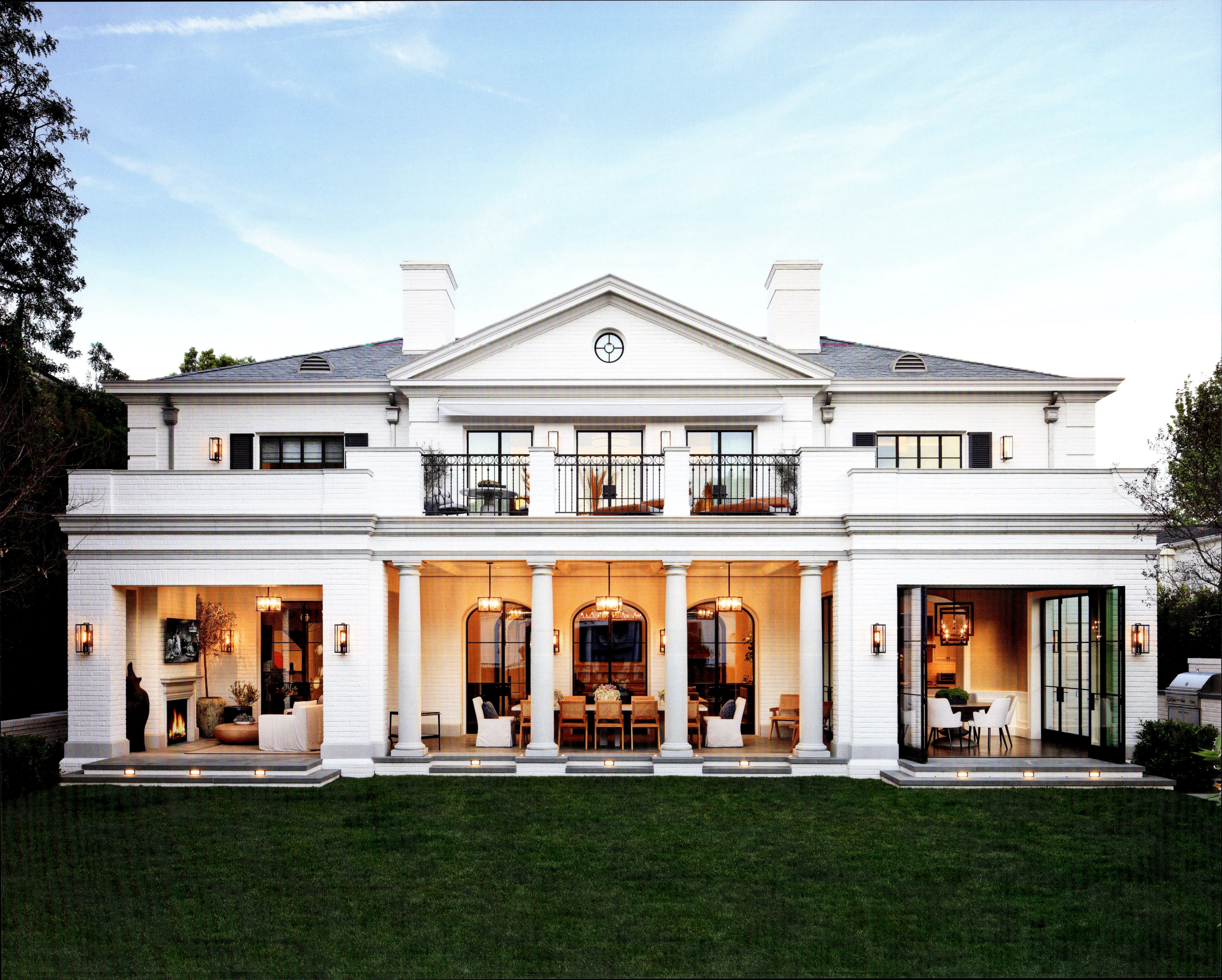

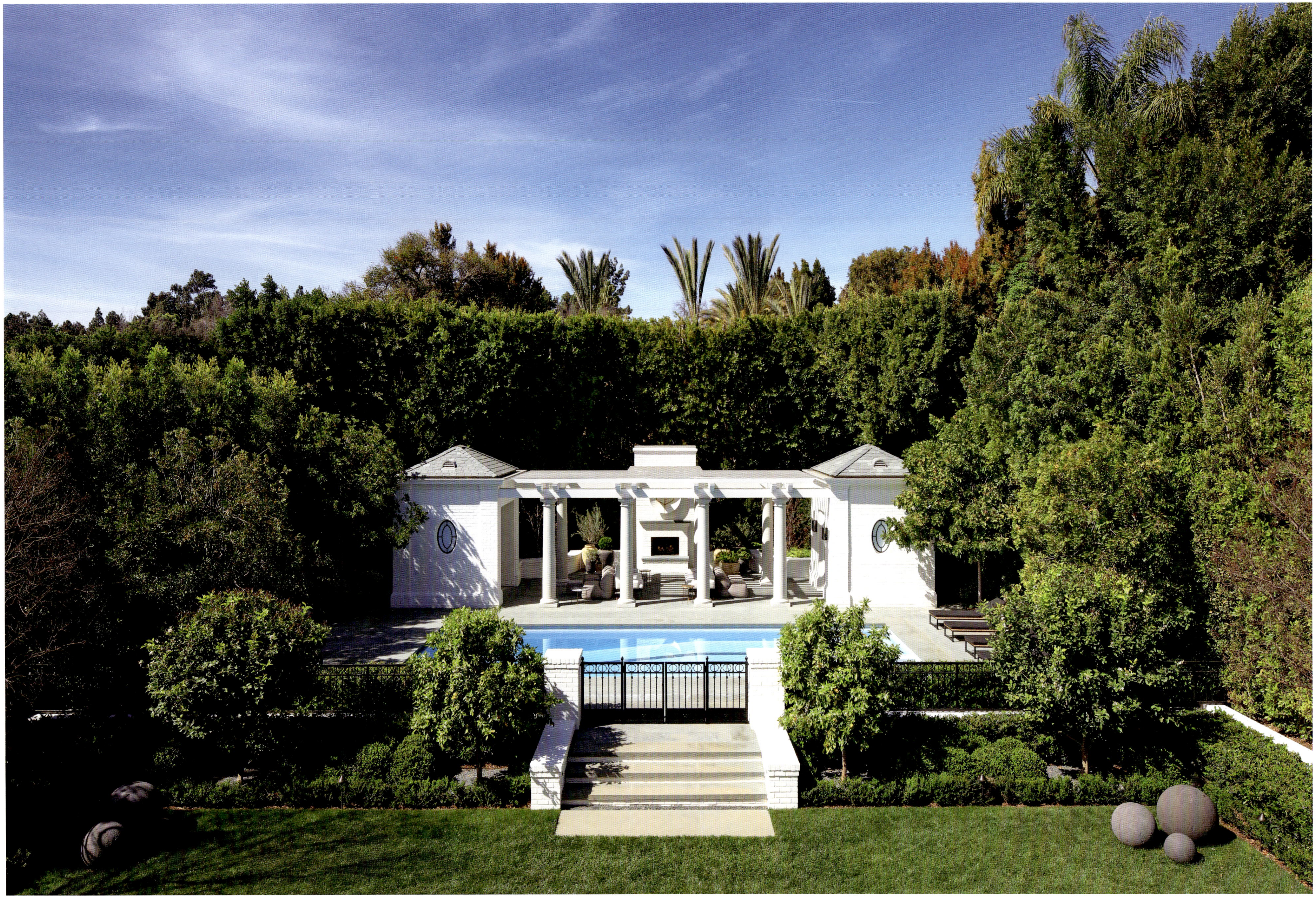

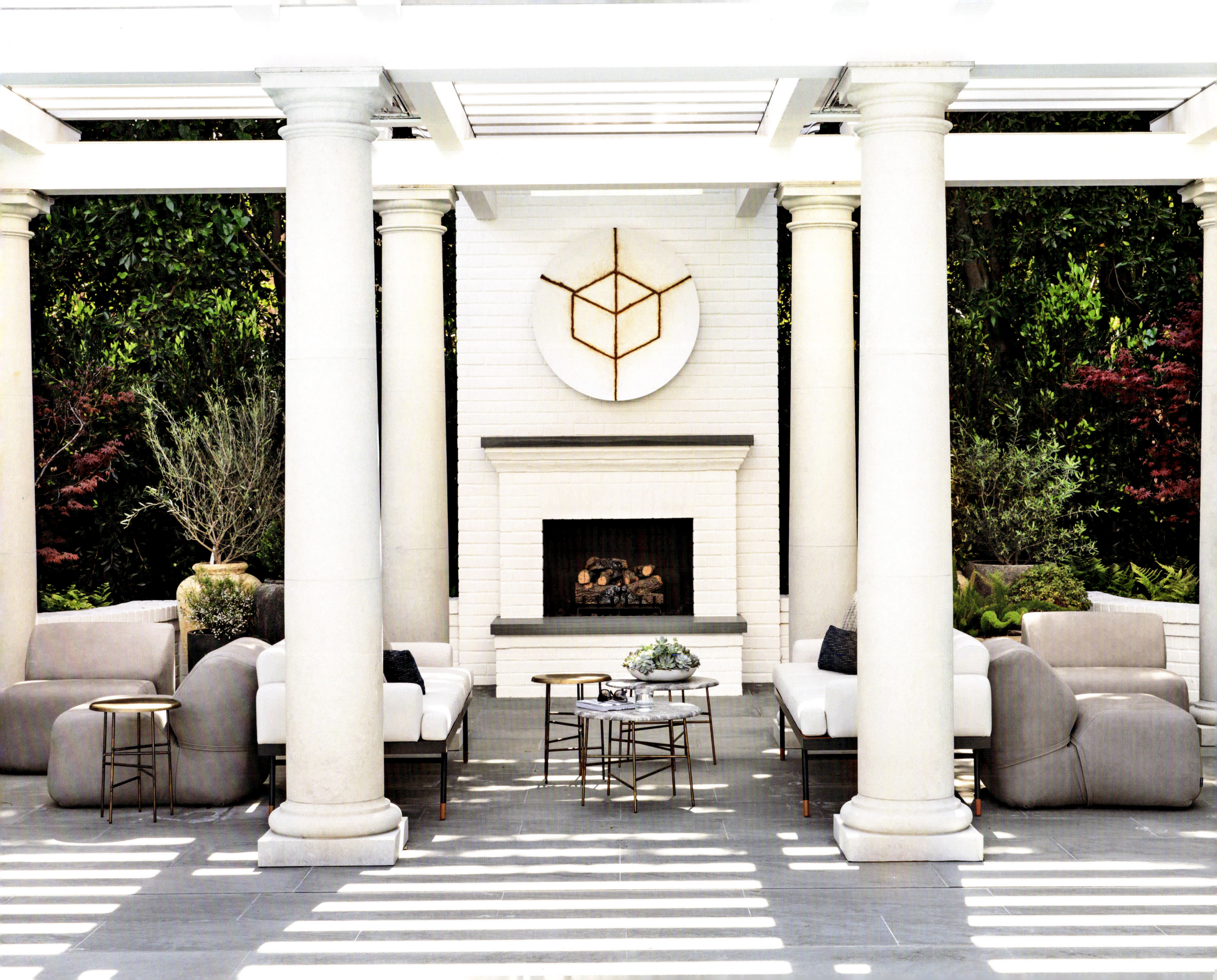

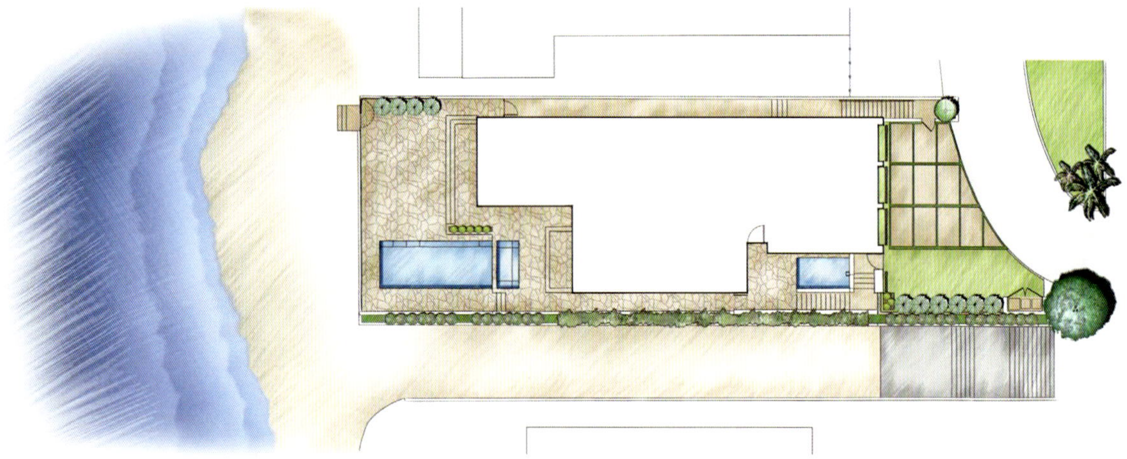

SEASIDE

Malibu

For a clients' weekend getaway in Malibu, we took a hodgepodge of an old home that had an unparalleled oceanfront location and existing pool, and turned it into a low-maintenance, minimalist retreat.

Our challenges included a steeply sloped narrow lot, height limitations that protected neighbors' beach views, a footprint dictated by the existing house, and a beach access pathway adjacent to one side of the property.

We all wanted to explore a contemporary vocabulary from the start that would be clean, warm and inviting. Our guiding principle was the idea of a pure, modern shape with all of the interest coming from geometric volumes, simple materials, and colors reflective of the sand and water.

From the street level, the house presents itself as a monumental, opaque, and solid mass that conceals the rewarding experiences to come. Once inside the gate, a set of stairs leads down to an entry courtyard past a reflecting pool and into a three-story skylit atrium with a dramatic floating brushed steel and rift-oak staircase.

The L-shaped house wraps around a pool and spa and reveals itself slowly as a progression of spaces that unfold as you walk through the rooms. At the core is an open-plan family room, living room, and dining room with limestone floors that flow out to the poolside terrace. Materials in muted and warm tones—beige plaster walls, floors in random-shaped limestone or wire-brushed oak, travertine counters and baths—maintain a unified and muted color scheme that is punctuated by colorful fabrics and the owners' collection of tribal art and twentieth-century furnishings.

The entire ocean-facing rear is the antithesis of the front, with banks of 10-foot-tall glass doors that slide open and disappear into stacks at the end of each of the façades, allowing the expansive waterfront views to dominate.

This striking beach house is a slow reveal, from a secretive façade to a knockout oceanfront panorama. It's a study in contrasts between complete privacy and total transparency.

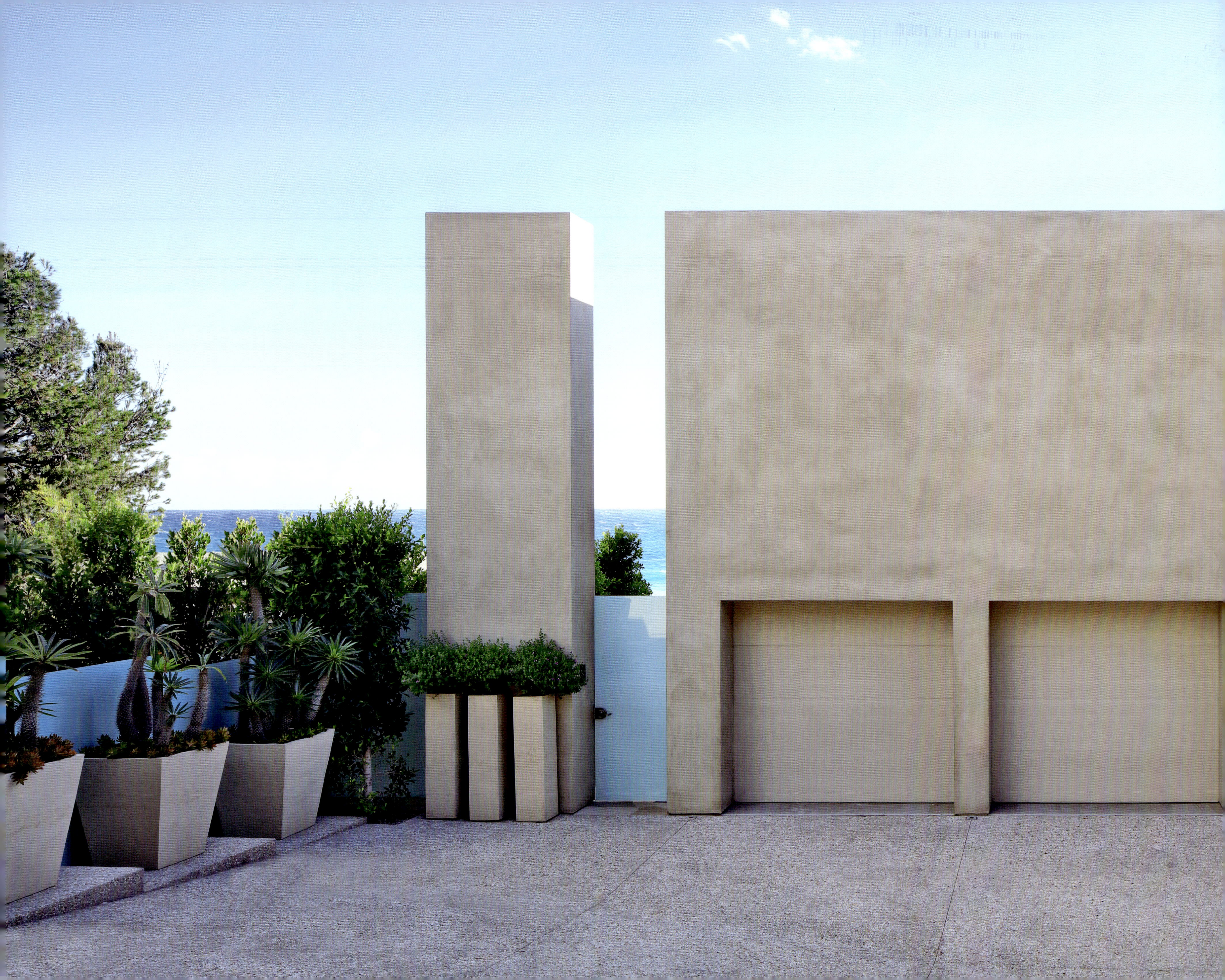

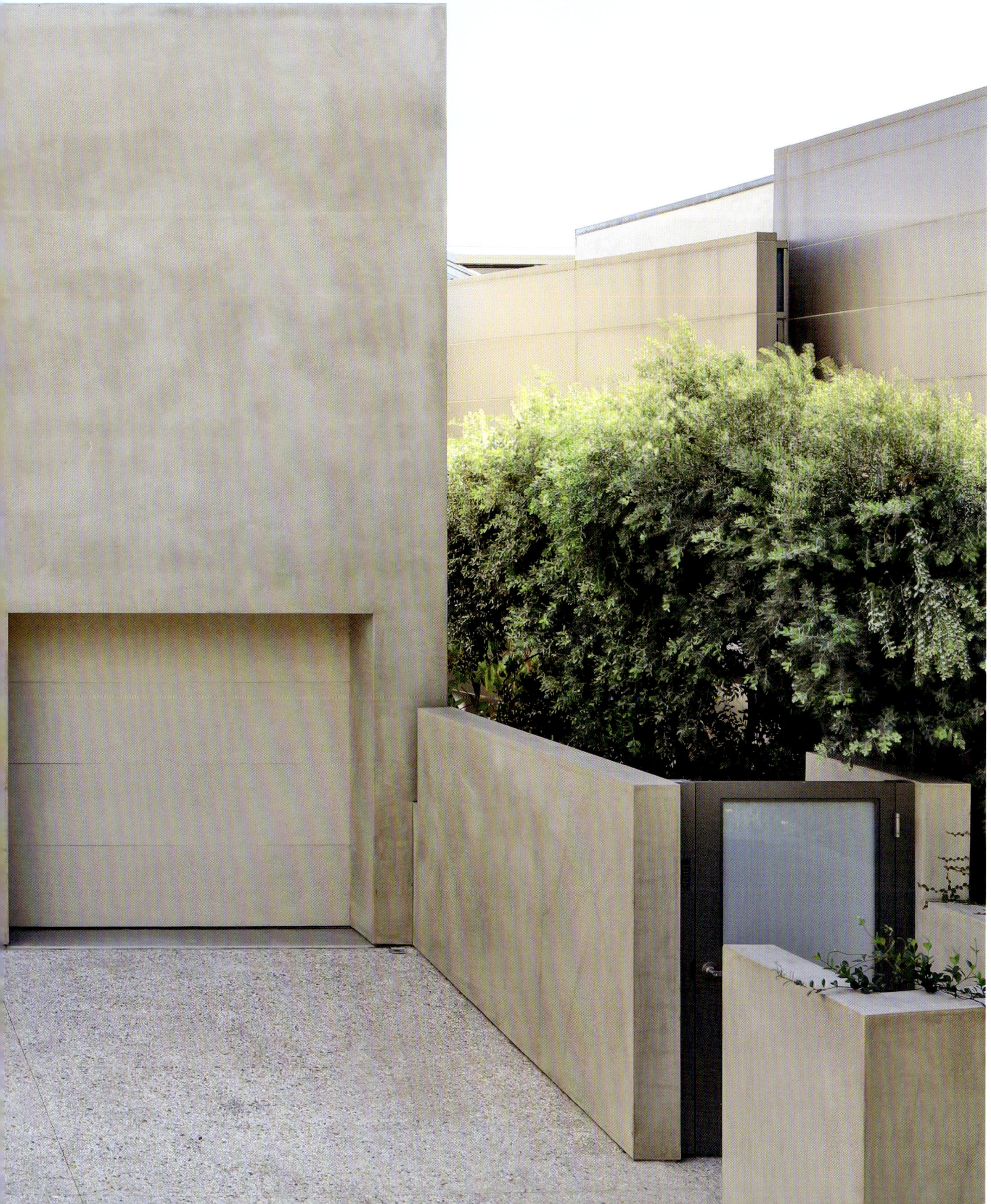

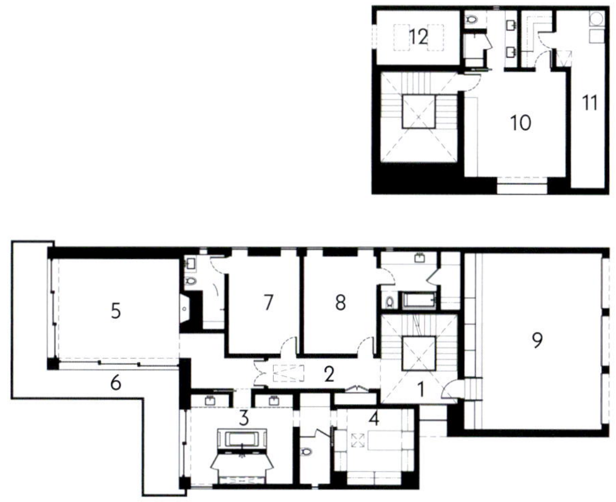

SECOND-FLOOR PLAN

1 Upper stair hall
2 Hall
3 Master bath
4 Master closet
5 Master bedroom
6 Deck
7 Guest bedroom
8 Bedroom
9 Garage
10 Loft bedroom
11 Mechanical room
12 Rooftop mechanical room

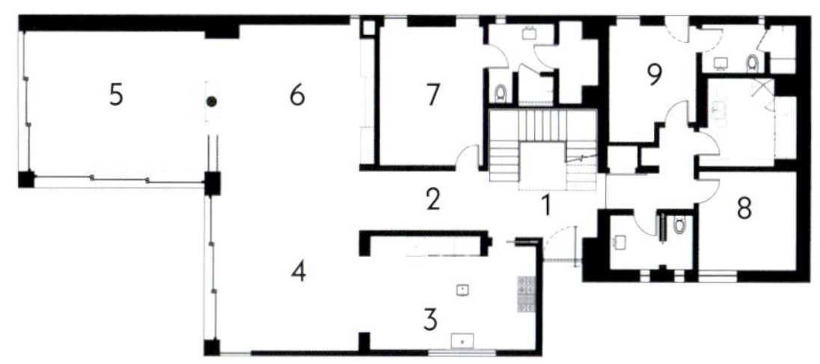

FIRST-FLOOR PLAN

1 Stair hall
2 Gallery
3 Kitchen
4 Dining room
5 Living room
6 Family room
7 Bedroom
8 Office
9 Gym

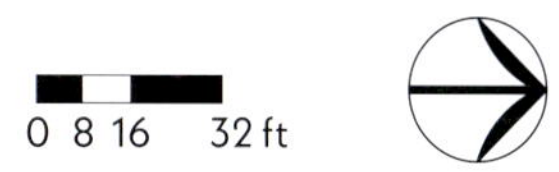

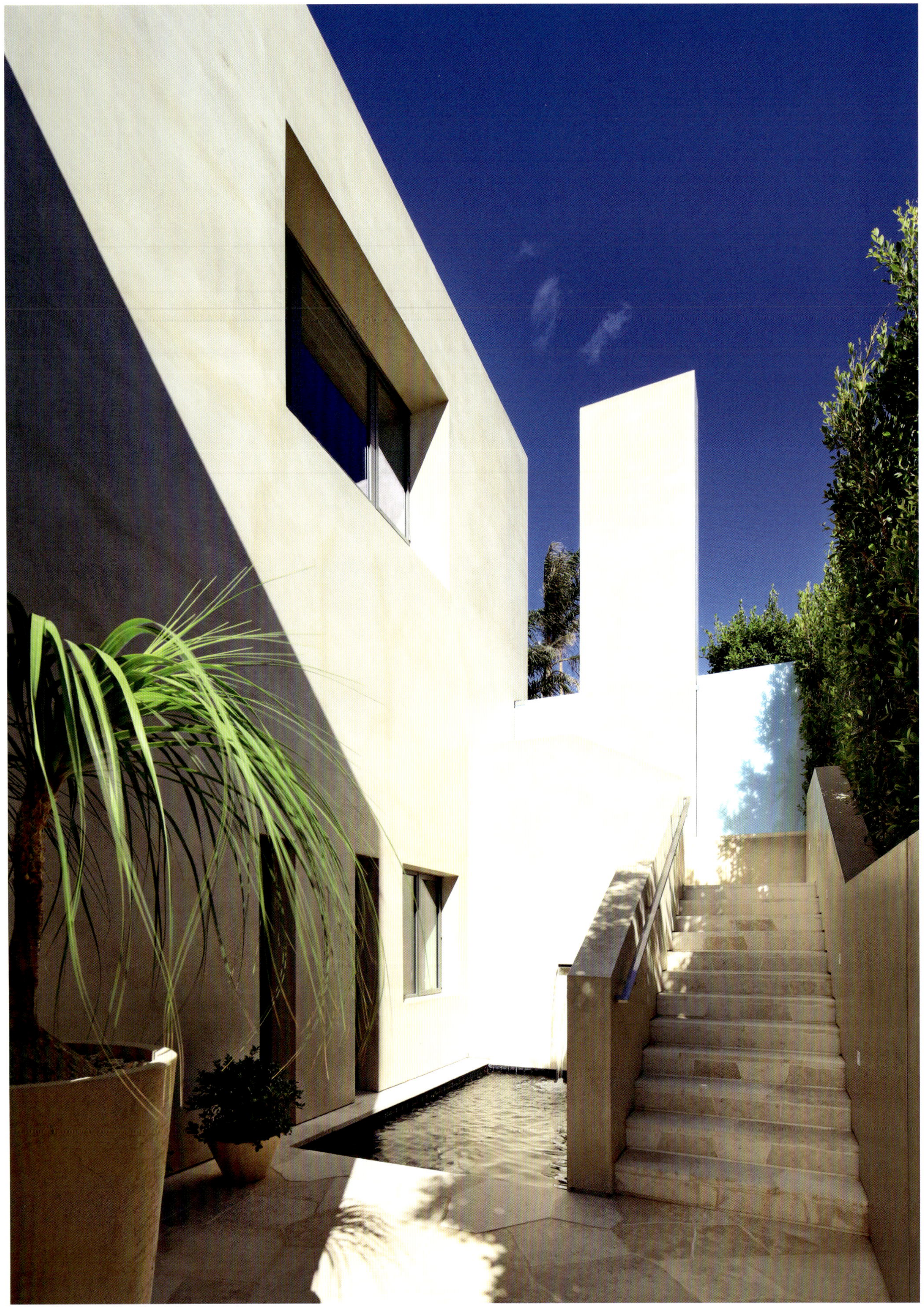

PREVIOUS PAGES: *Our intent was to create a contemporary beach house that combines the simplicity of geometrical volumes and spaces with warm materials. You enter from the upper street level through a translucent glass gate that is set between the home's geometrical volumes and monumental gate pier, giving the feeling of penetrating a solid volume of architecture to arrive at your destination.*

LEFT: *The stair leads down to the entry courtyard, defined by the bold architecture on three sides, dense landscape on the other, and a reflecting pool to contrast the manmade with the natural.*

OPPOSITE LEFT: *The powder room reveals the overall theme of warm modernism using materials in muted colors—1930s silver-framed mirror, beige plaster walls, travertine slab vanity, random ashlar limestone floors.*

OPPOSITE RIGHT: *The house is organized around a dramatic skylit central atrium with a monumental stair made of wood treads that seem to float on brushed stainless-steel supports.*

FOLLOWING PAGES, LEFT: *A plan elevation of the three-story staircase that is topped by a large skylight.* RIGHT: *The brushed stainless-steel, wood-and-glass staircase is both a piece of architecture and a sculptural work of art.*

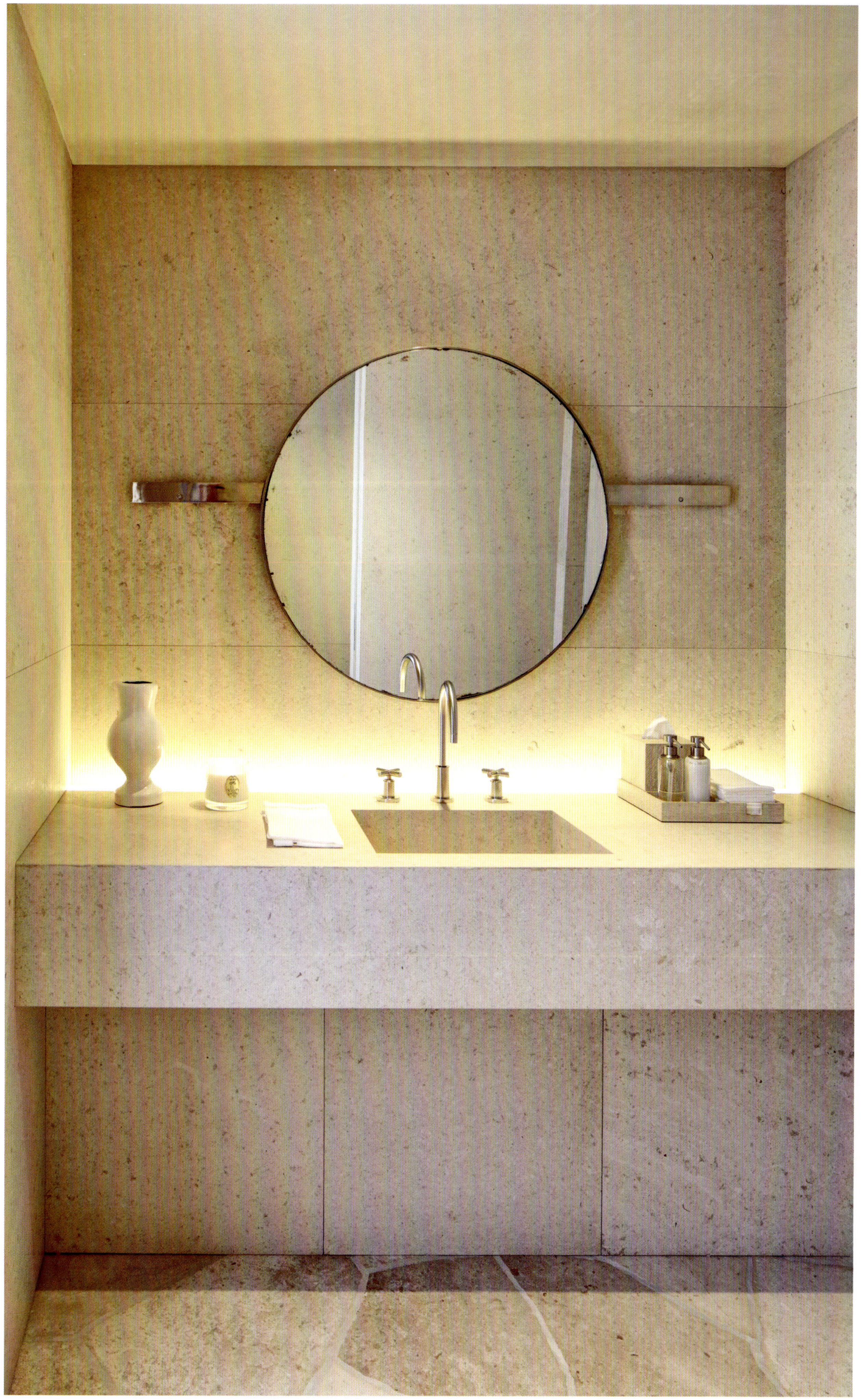

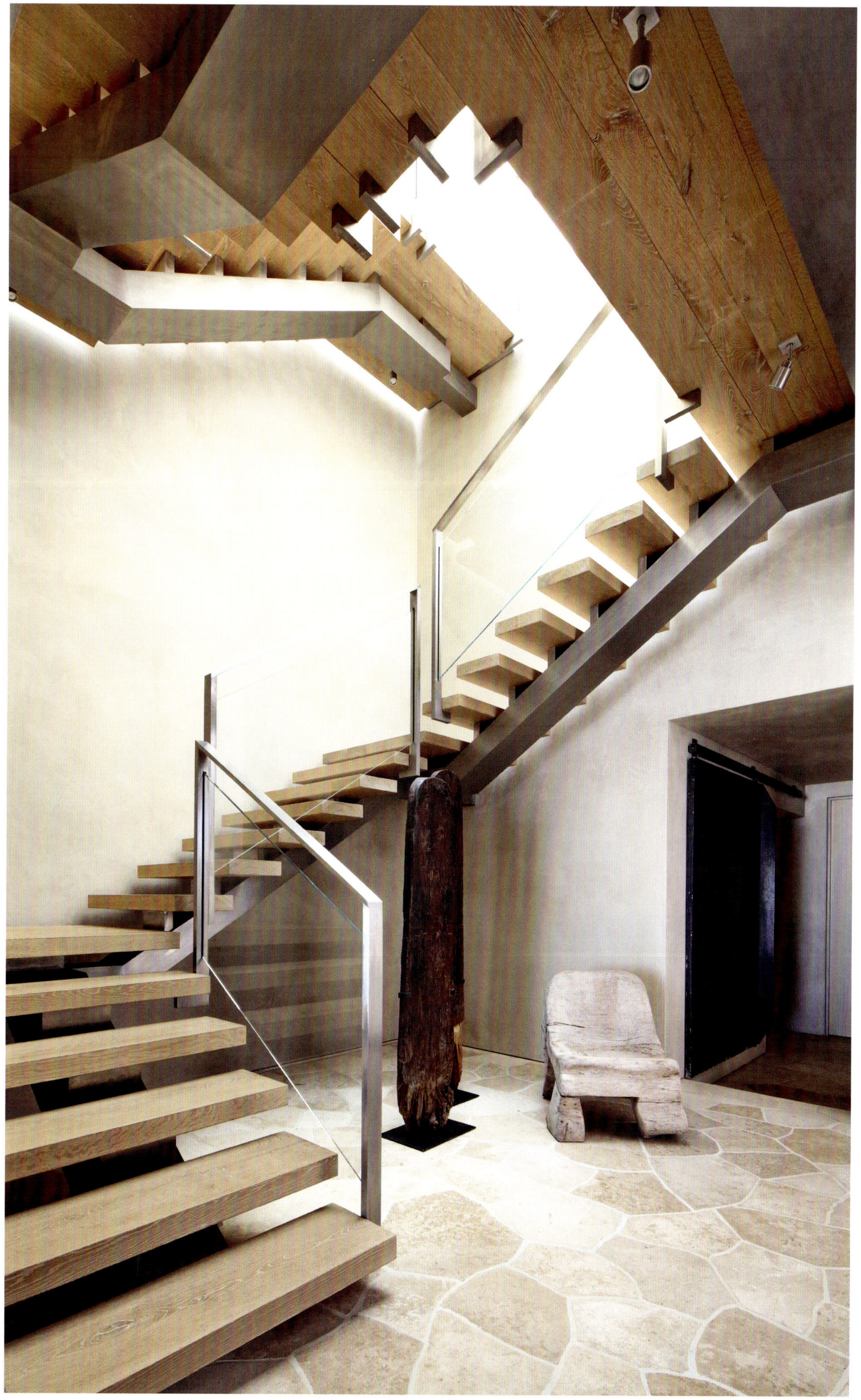

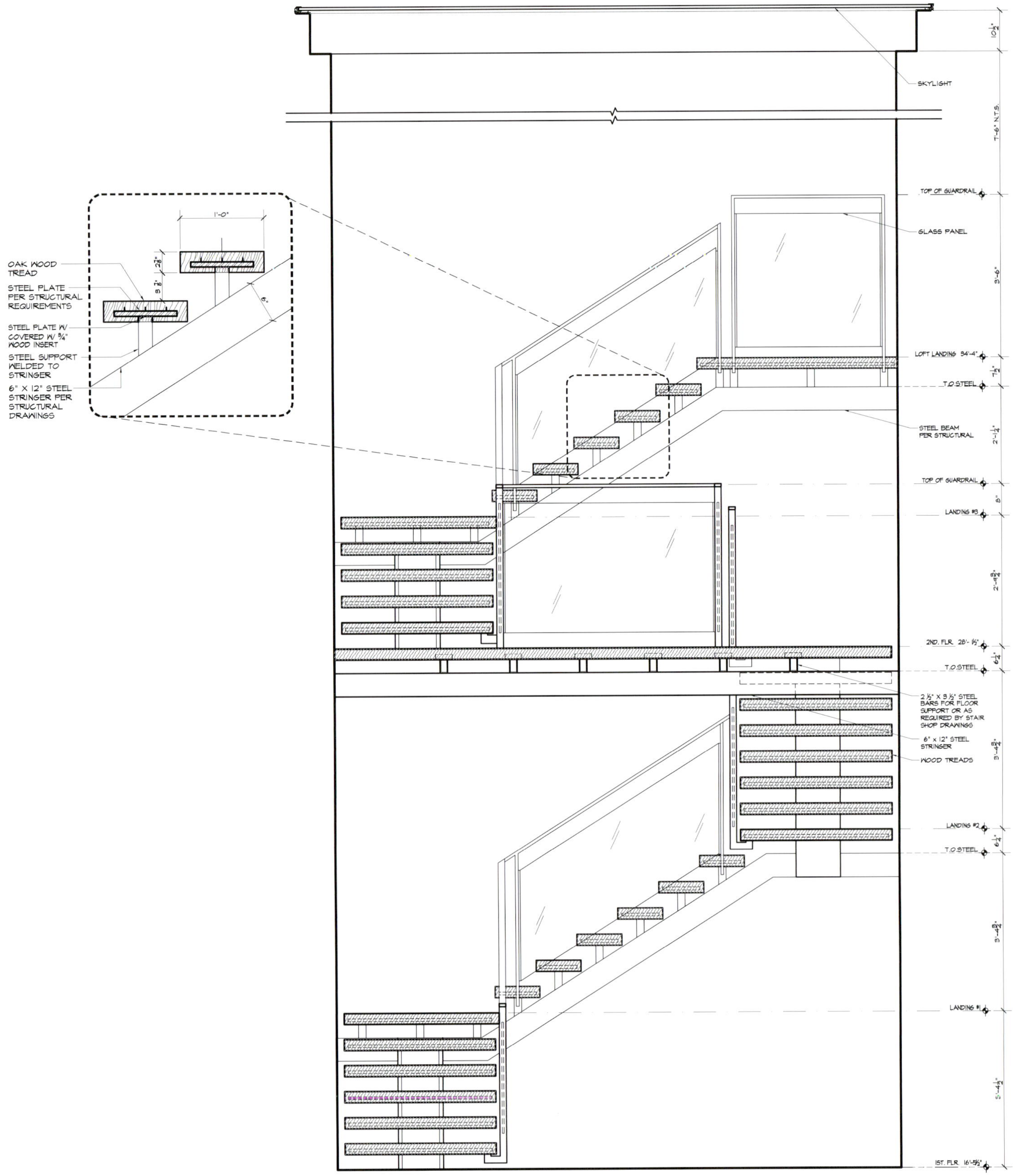
OAK WOOD TREAD
STEEL PLATE PER STRUCTURAL REQUIREMENTS
STEEL PLATE W/ COVERED W/ 3/4" WOOD INSERT
STEEL SUPPORT WELDED TO STRINGER
6" X 12" STEEL STRINGER PER STRUCTURAL DRAWINGS
1'-0"
6"
SKYLIGHT
10 1/2"
7'-6" N.T.S.
TOP OF GUARDRAIL
GLASS PANEL
3'-6"
LOFT LANDING 34'-4"
7 1/2"
T.O.STEEL
STEEL BEAM PER STRUCTURAL
2'-1 1/4"
TOP OF GUARDRAIL
8"
LANDING #3
2'-9 3/4"
2ND. FLR. 28'-1 1/2"
6 1/4"
T.O.STEEL
2 1/2" X 3 1/2" STEEL BARS FOR FLOOR SUPPORT OR AS REQUIRED BY STAIR SHOP DRAWINGS
6" x 12" STEEL STRINGER
WOOD TREADS
3'-4 3/4"
LANDING #2
6 1/4"
T.O.STEEL
3'-4 3/4"
LANDING #1
5'-4 1/2"
1ST. FLR. 16'-5 1/2"

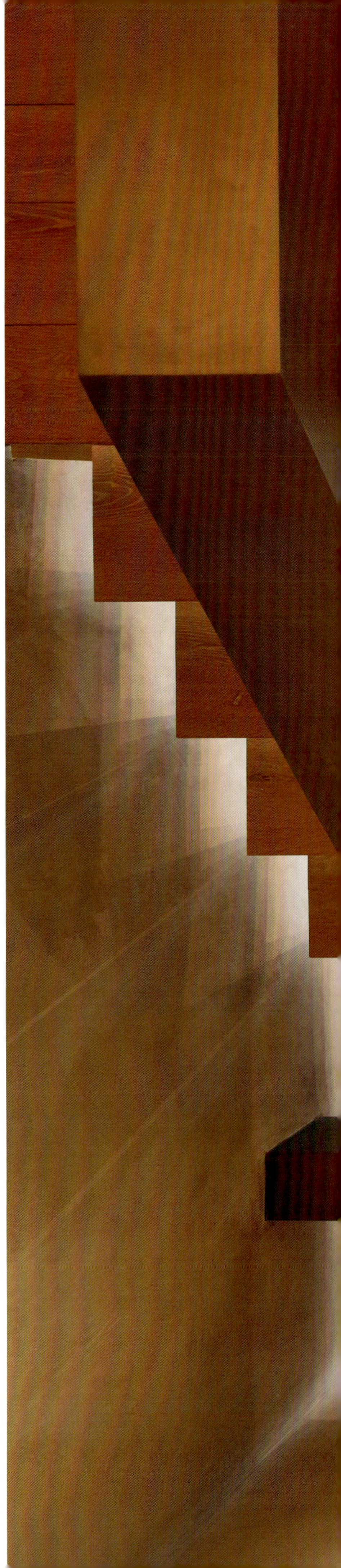

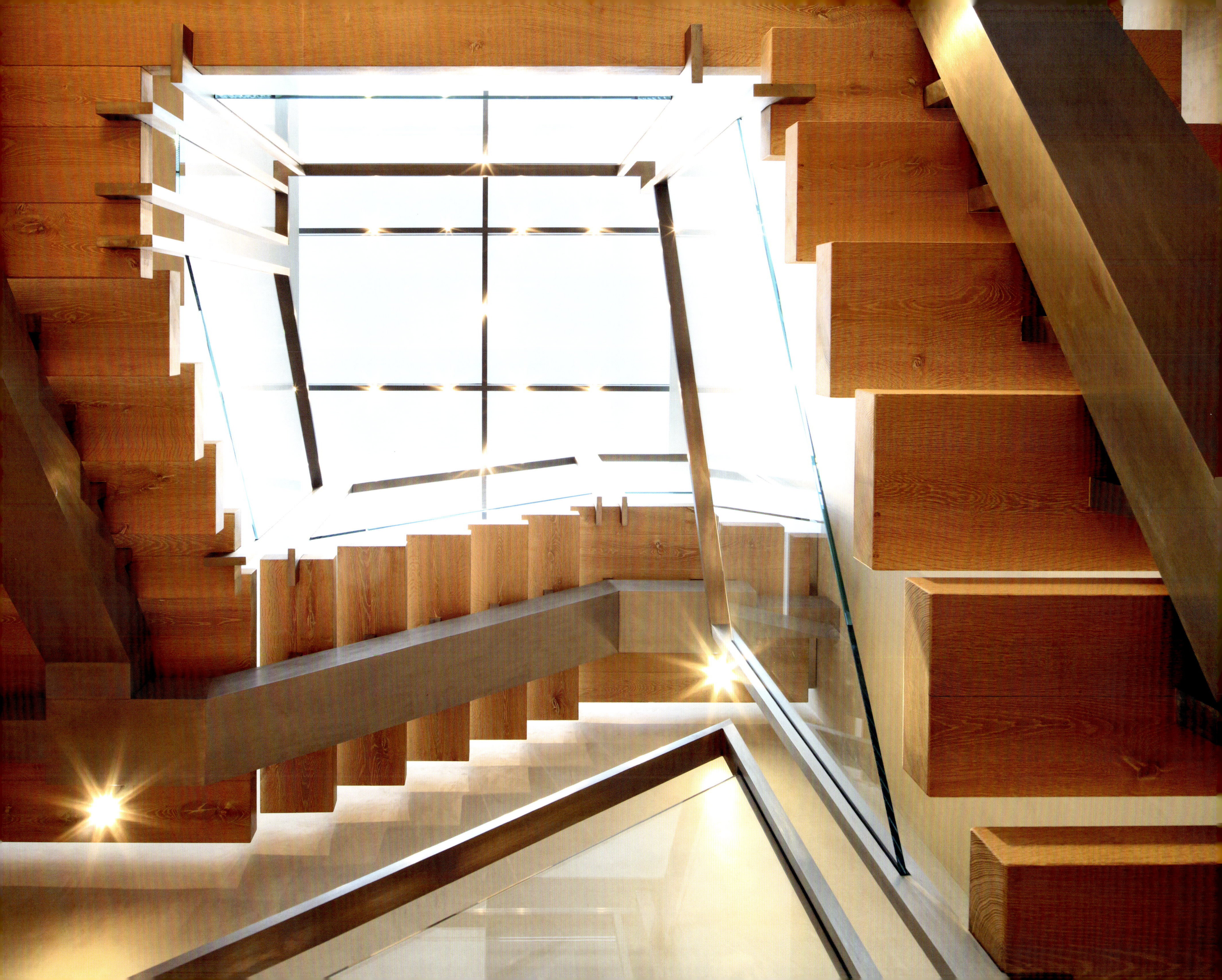

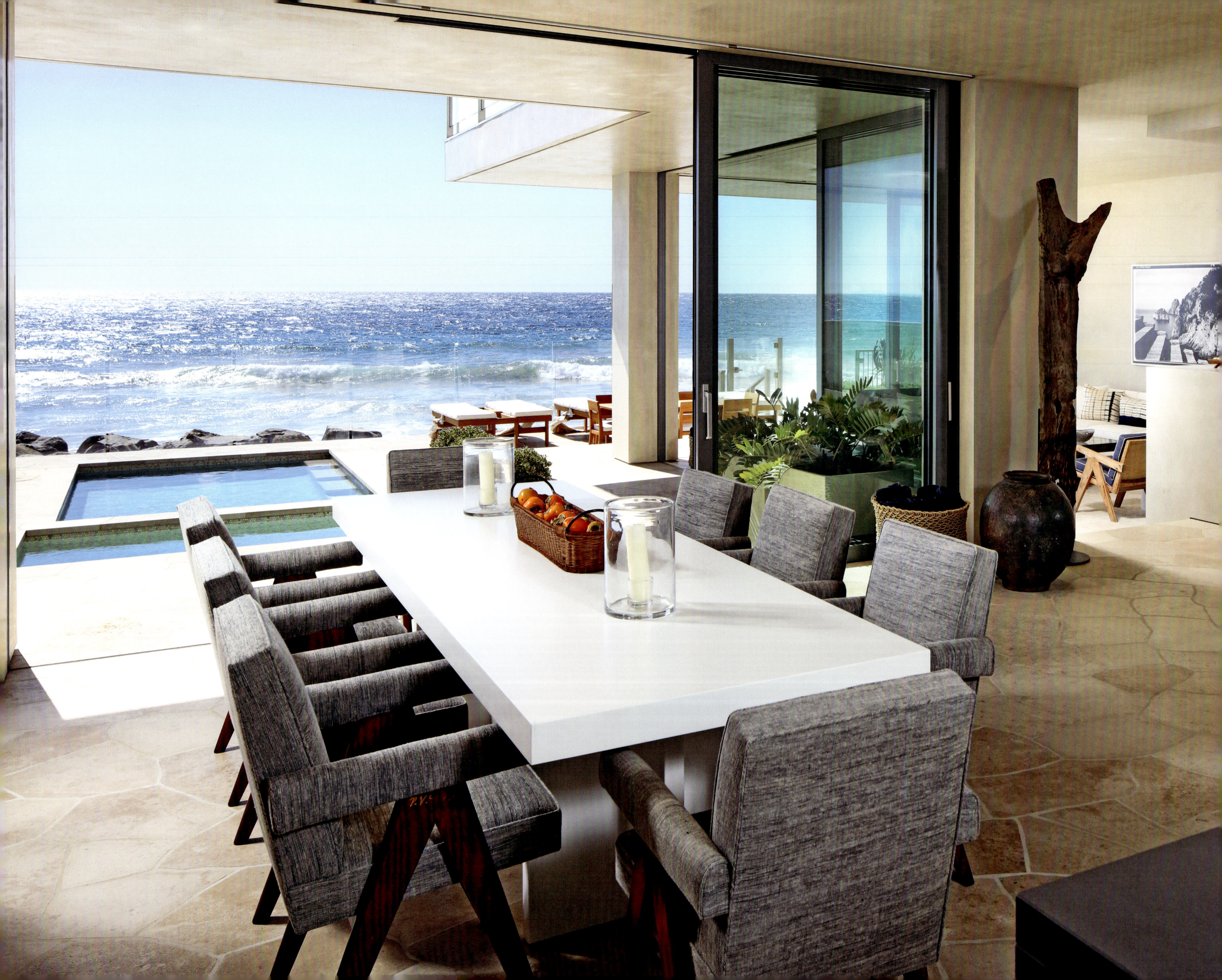

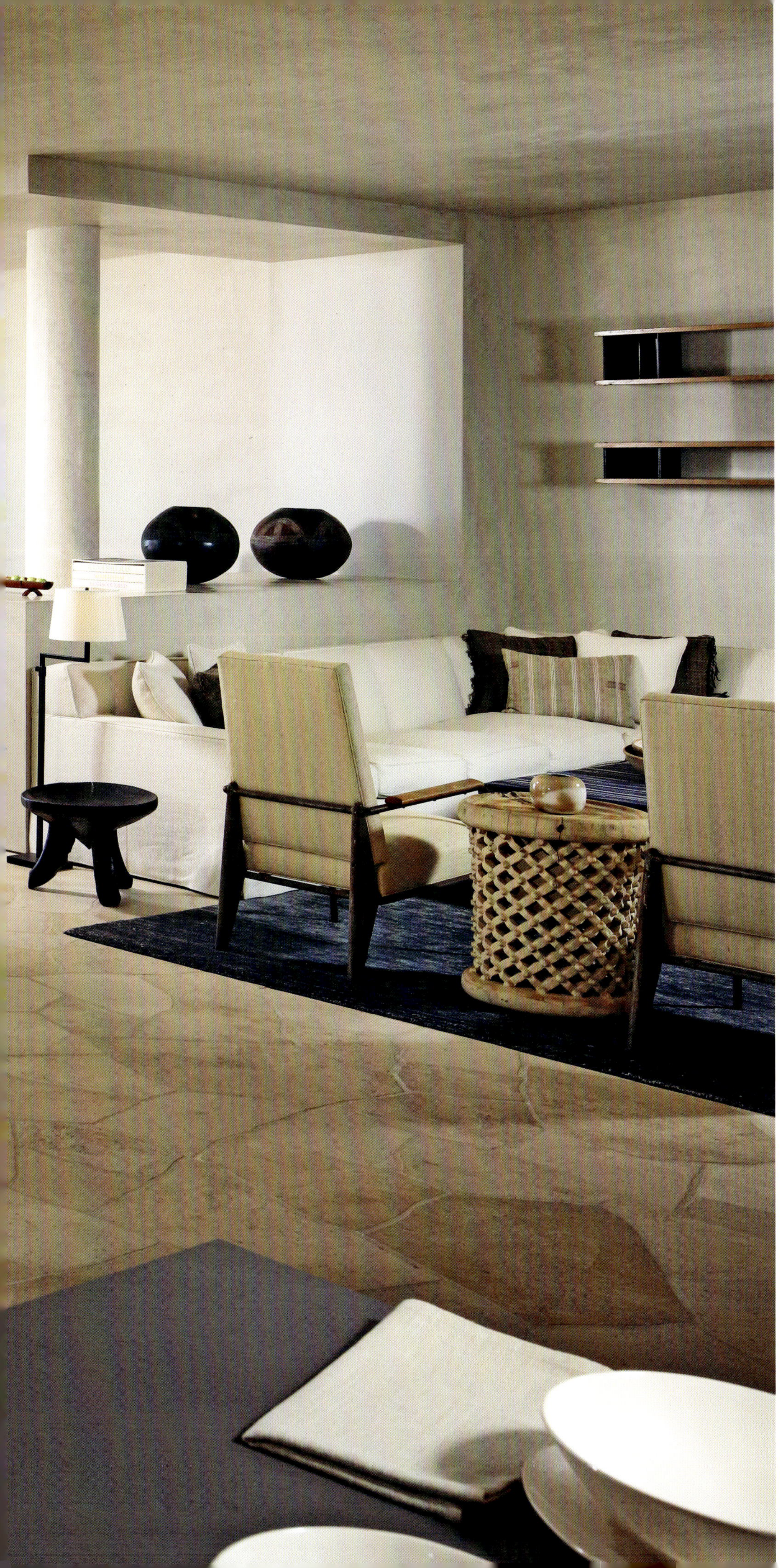

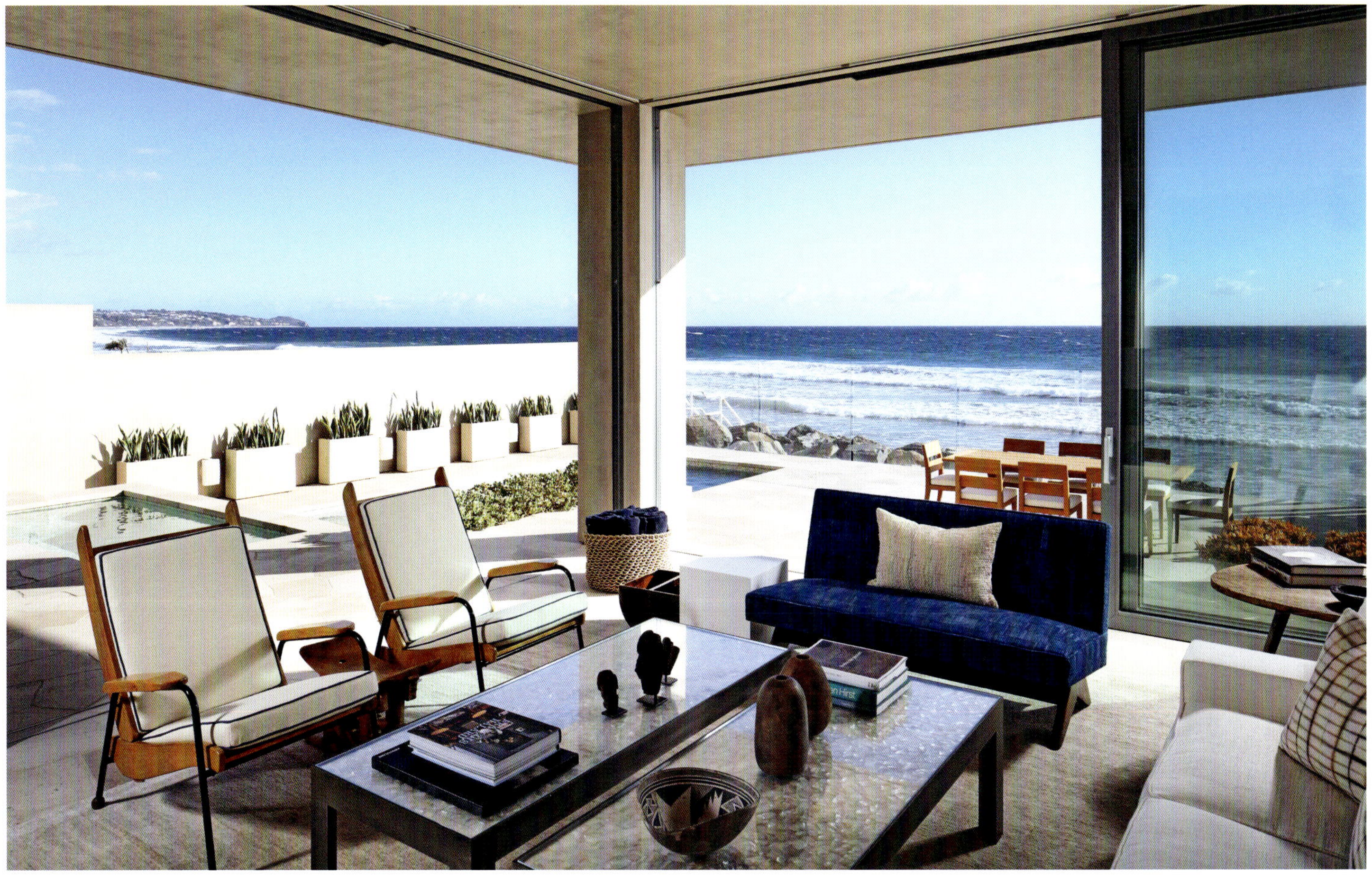

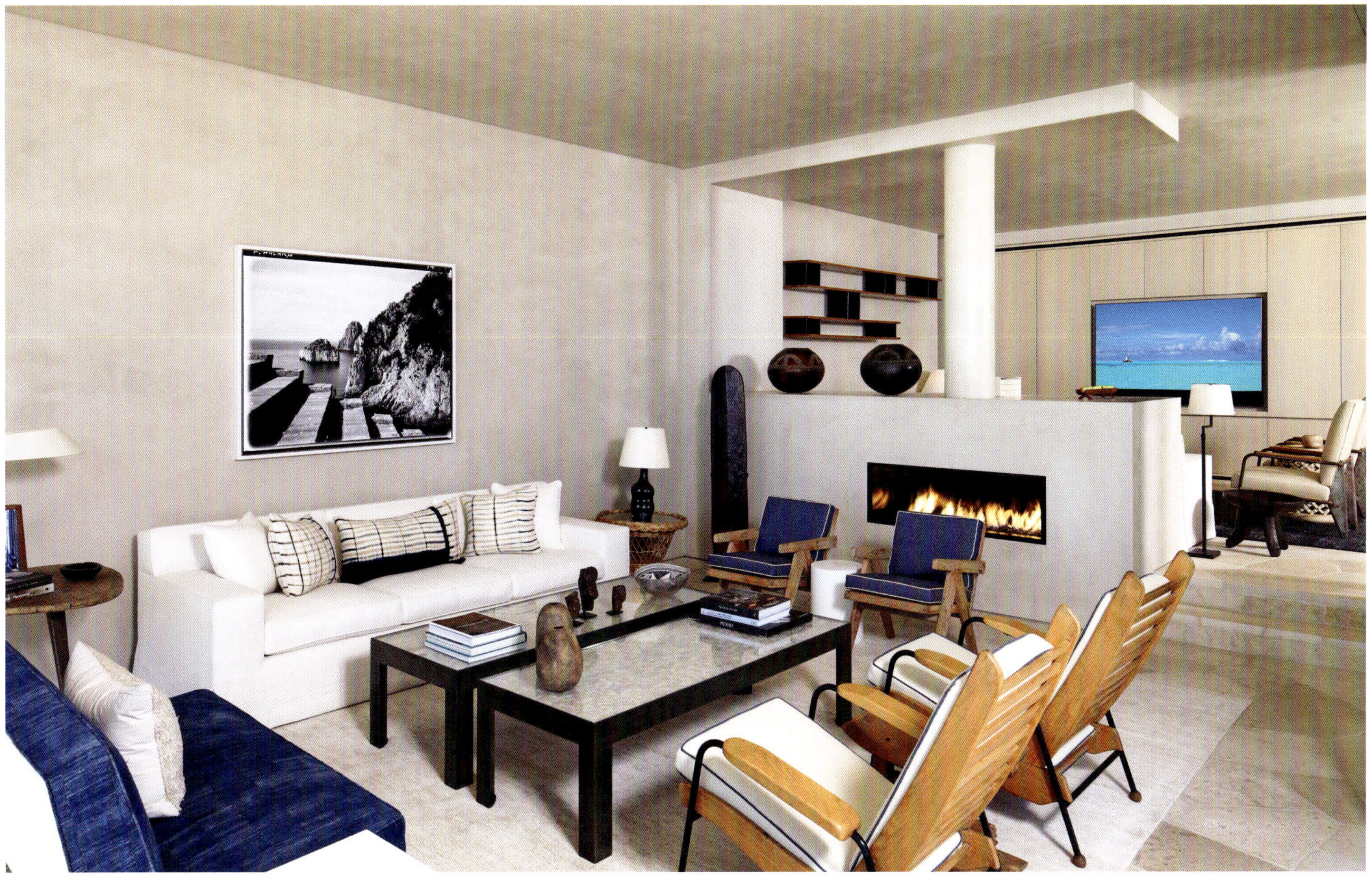

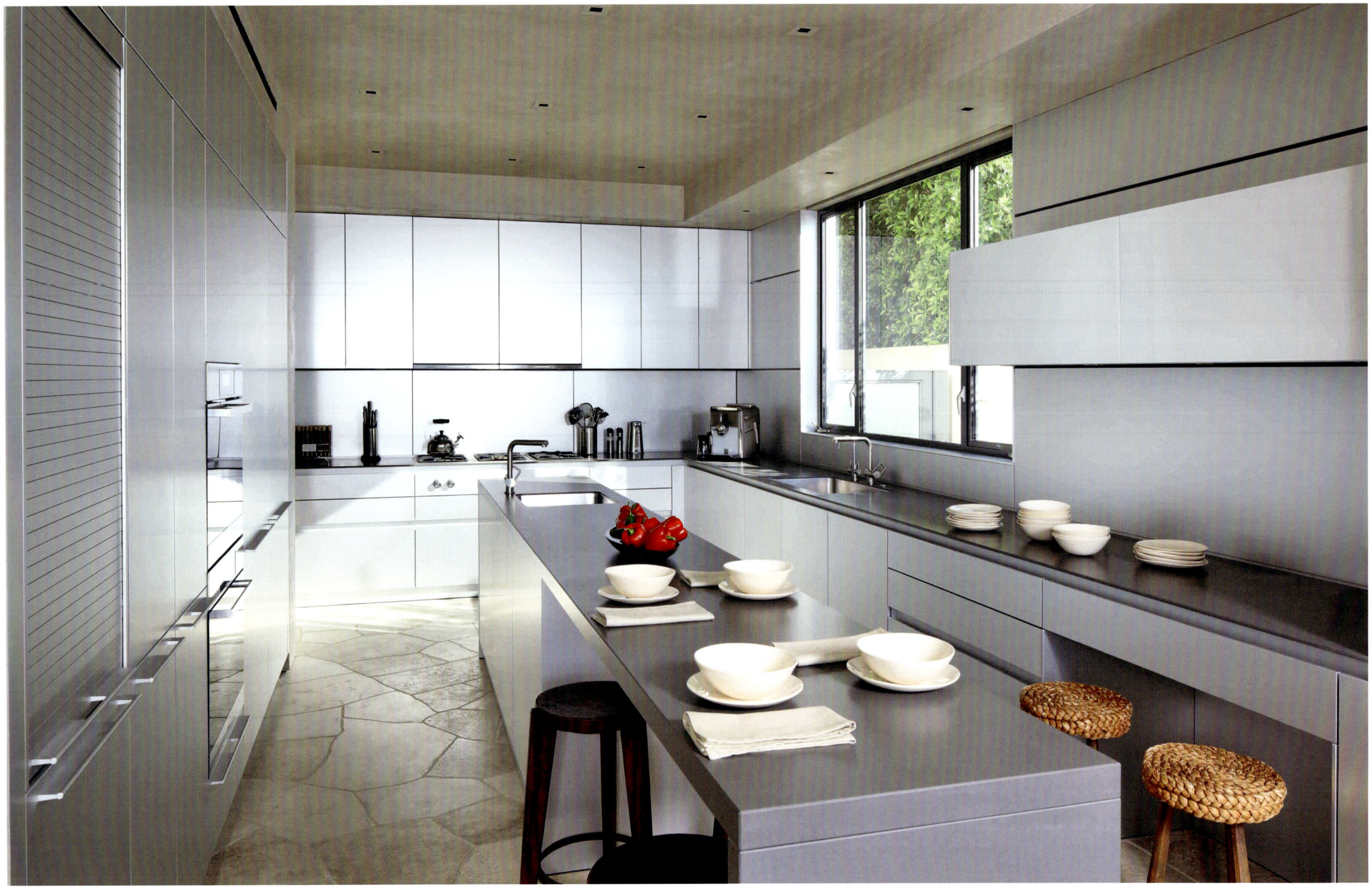

PREVIOUS PAGES, LEFT: *The open plan, split-level dining, family, and living rooms are united by limestone floors that continue out to the terrace. Most of our discussions revolved around how things unfold as you walk through the house. By the time you reach the back, the house becomes completely transparent.* TOP RIGHT: *The steel framing allowed us to create entire walls of glass that lift and stack along each end of the façade and offer access to the outdoors from every room.* BOTTOM RIGHT: *Atelier AM furnished the living areas with twentieth-century classic pieces by Jean Prouvé and Pierre Jeanneret. The television in the family room was placed on an interior wall away from the windows to reduce glare. Shelving by Charlotte Perriand.*

ABOVE: *The sleek, low-maintenance kitchen features Bulthaup cabinetry.*

OPPOSITE: *A wraparound second-floor terrace leading off the master bedroom overlooks the lower terrace.*

FOLLOWING PAGES: *A pair of 1950s Pierre Jeanneret chairs in a corner of the master bedroom.*

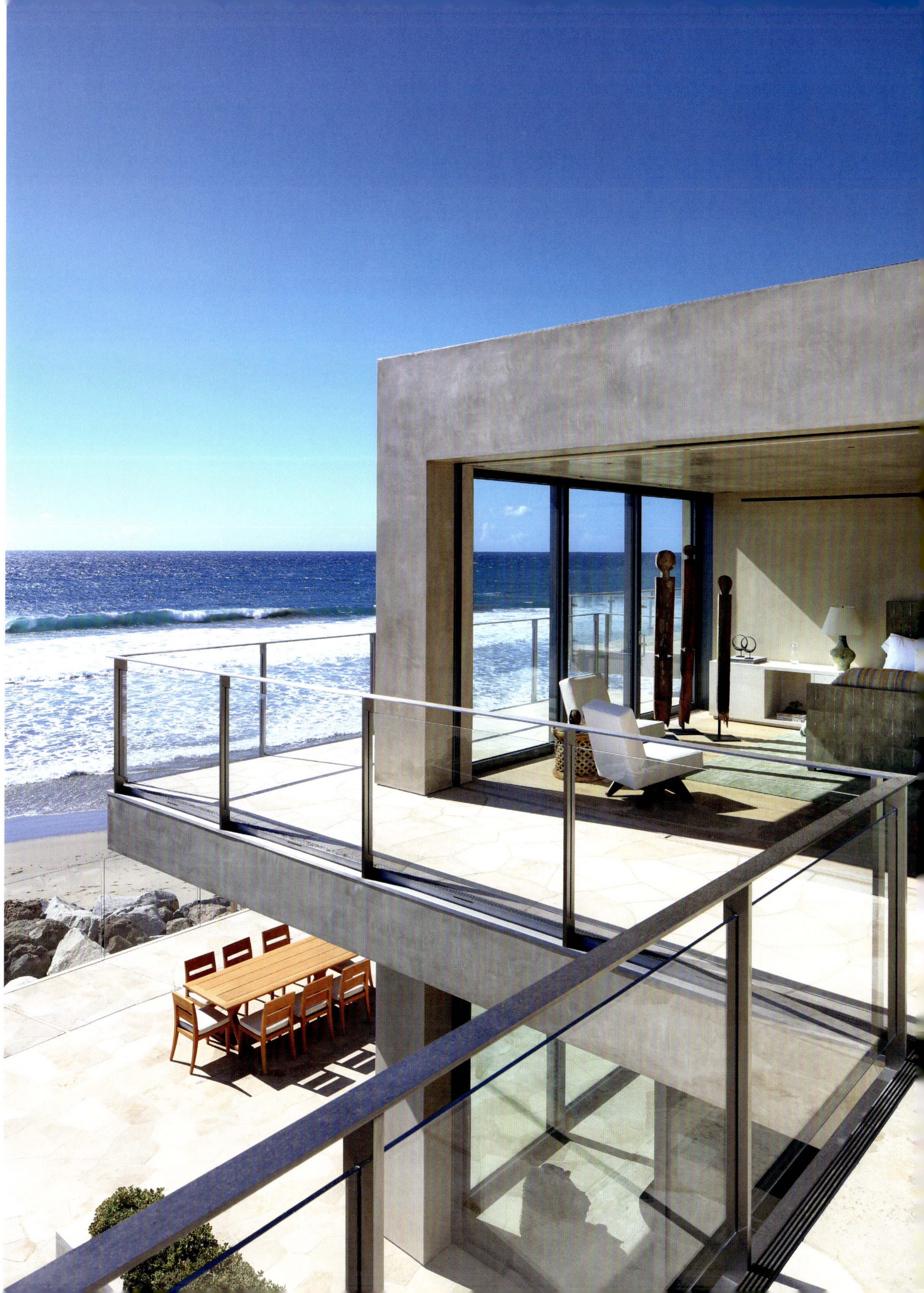

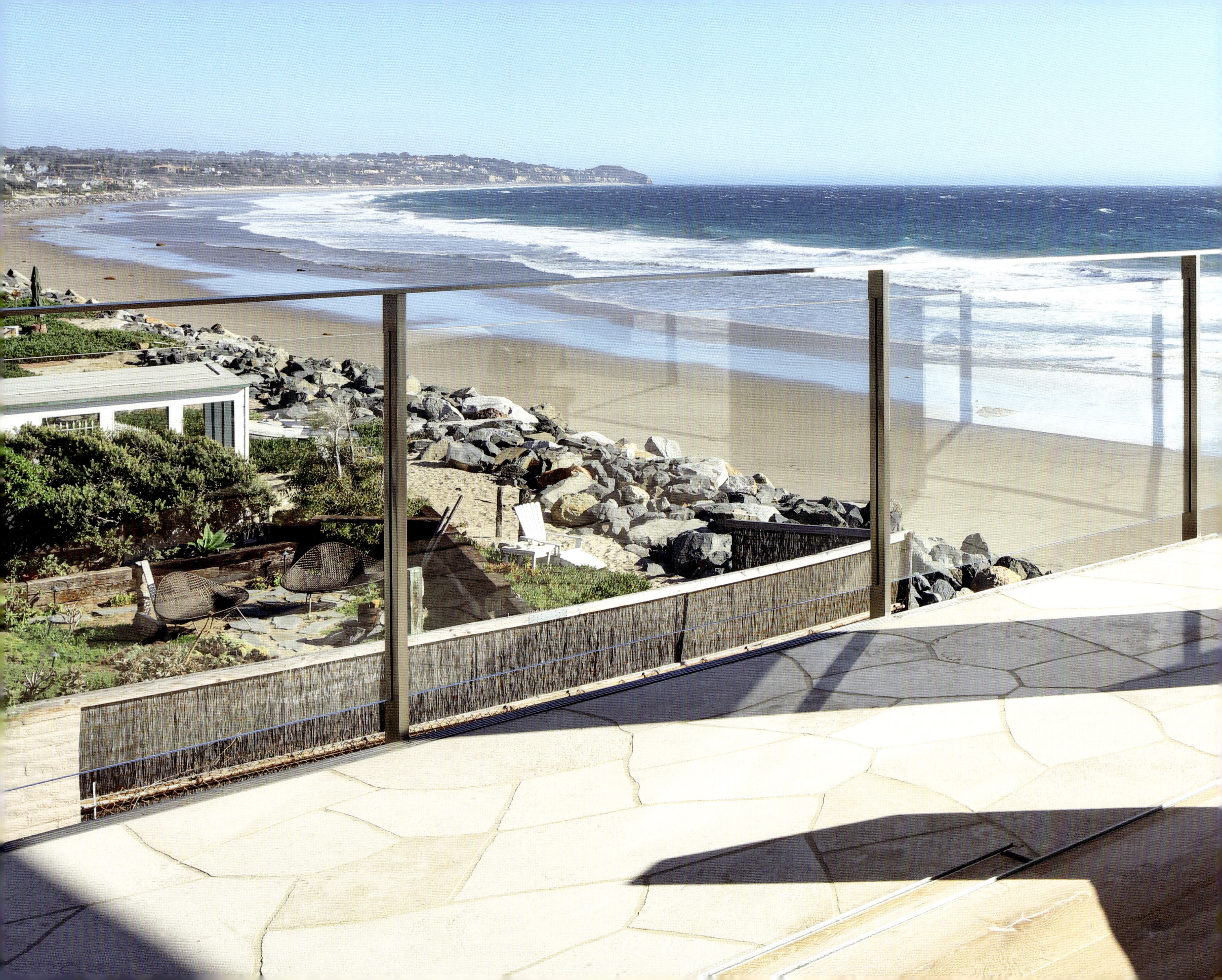

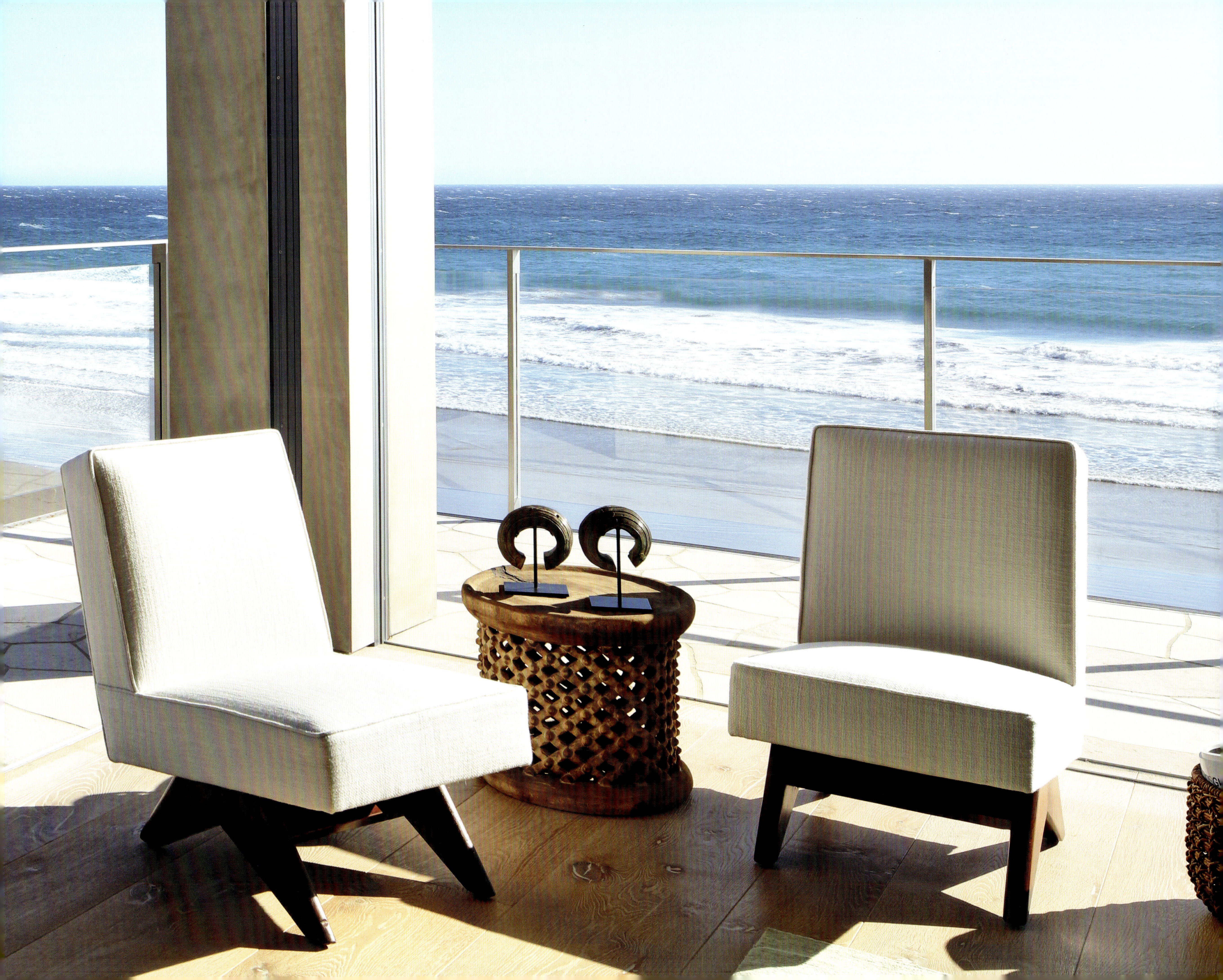

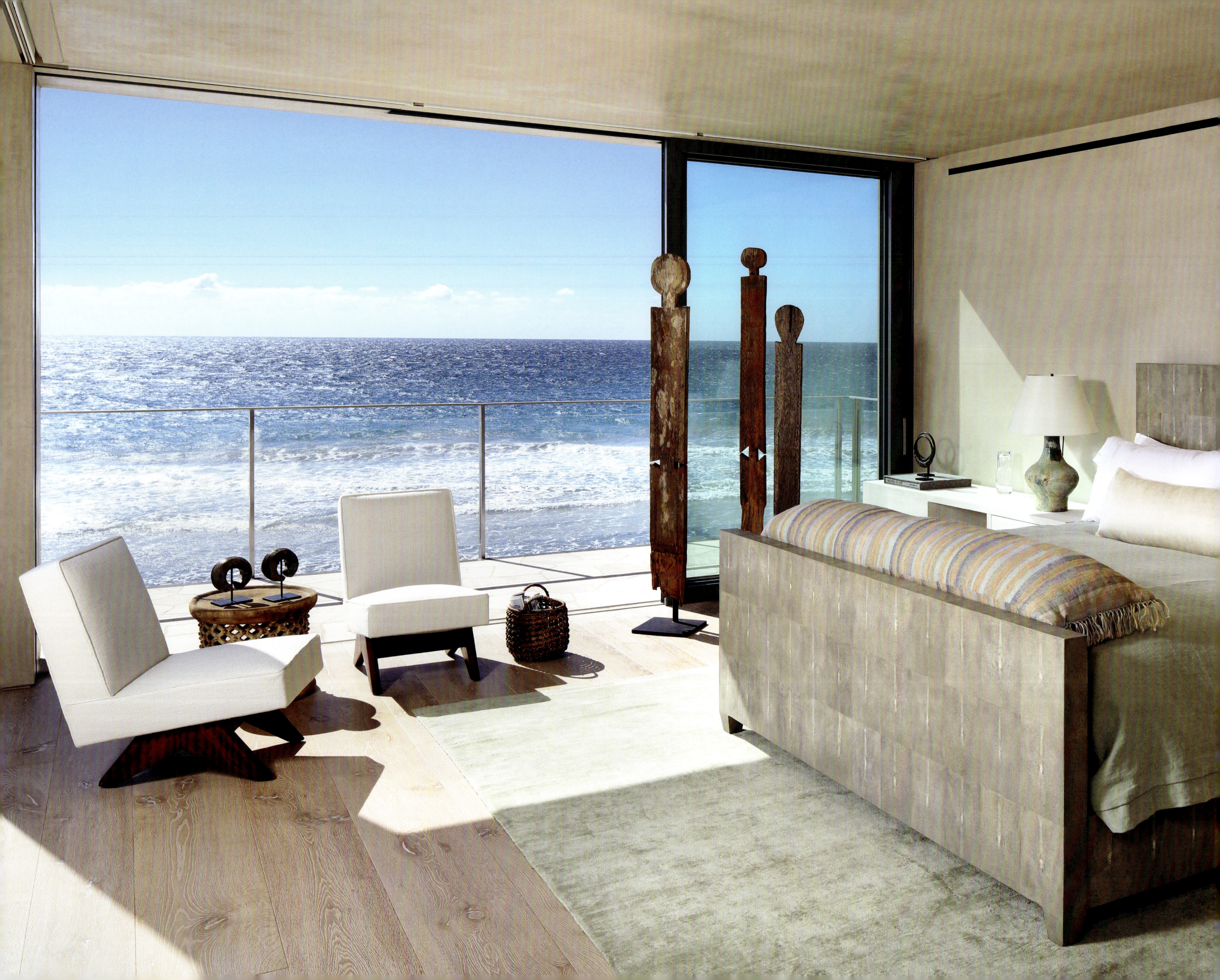

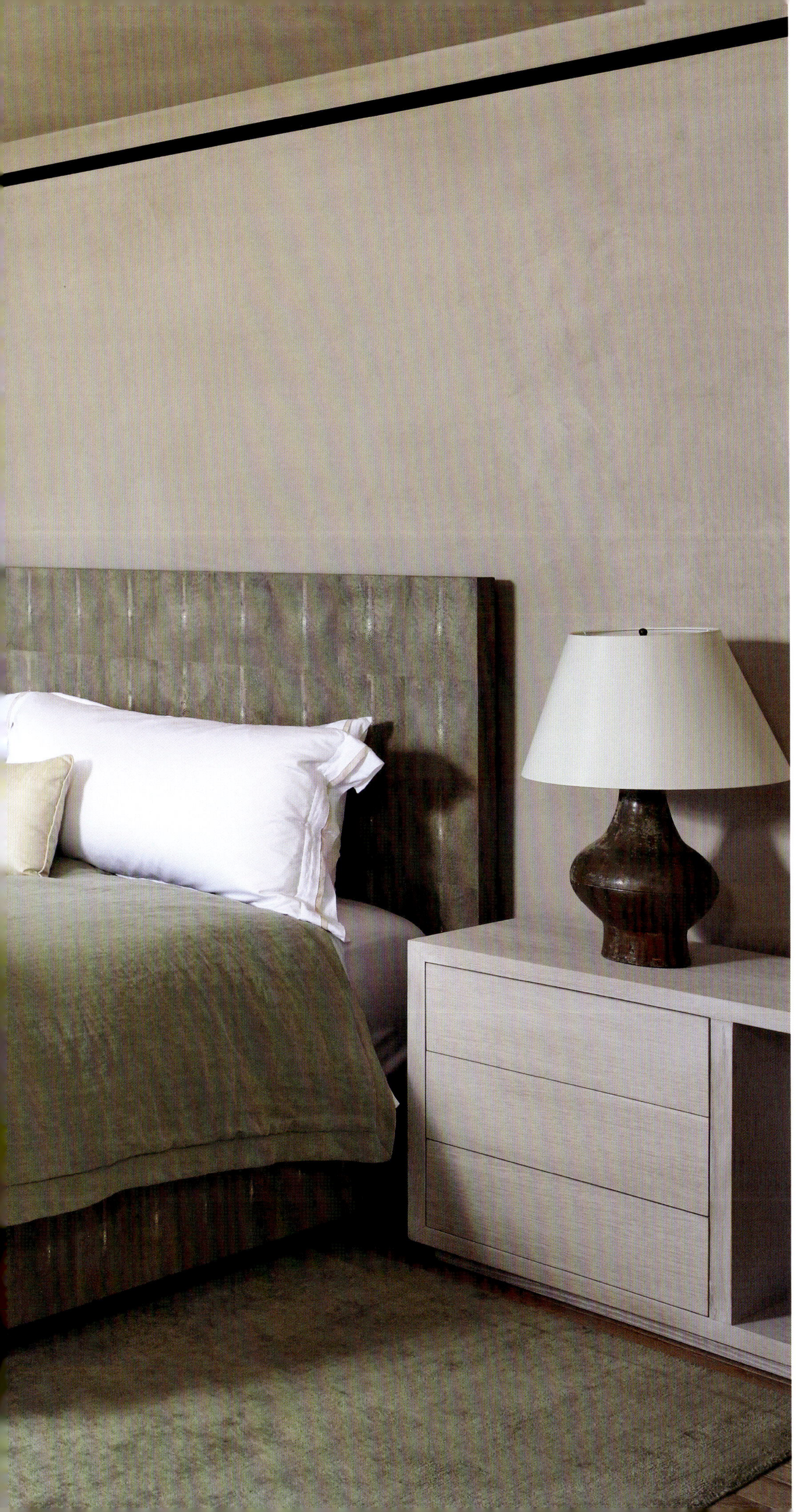

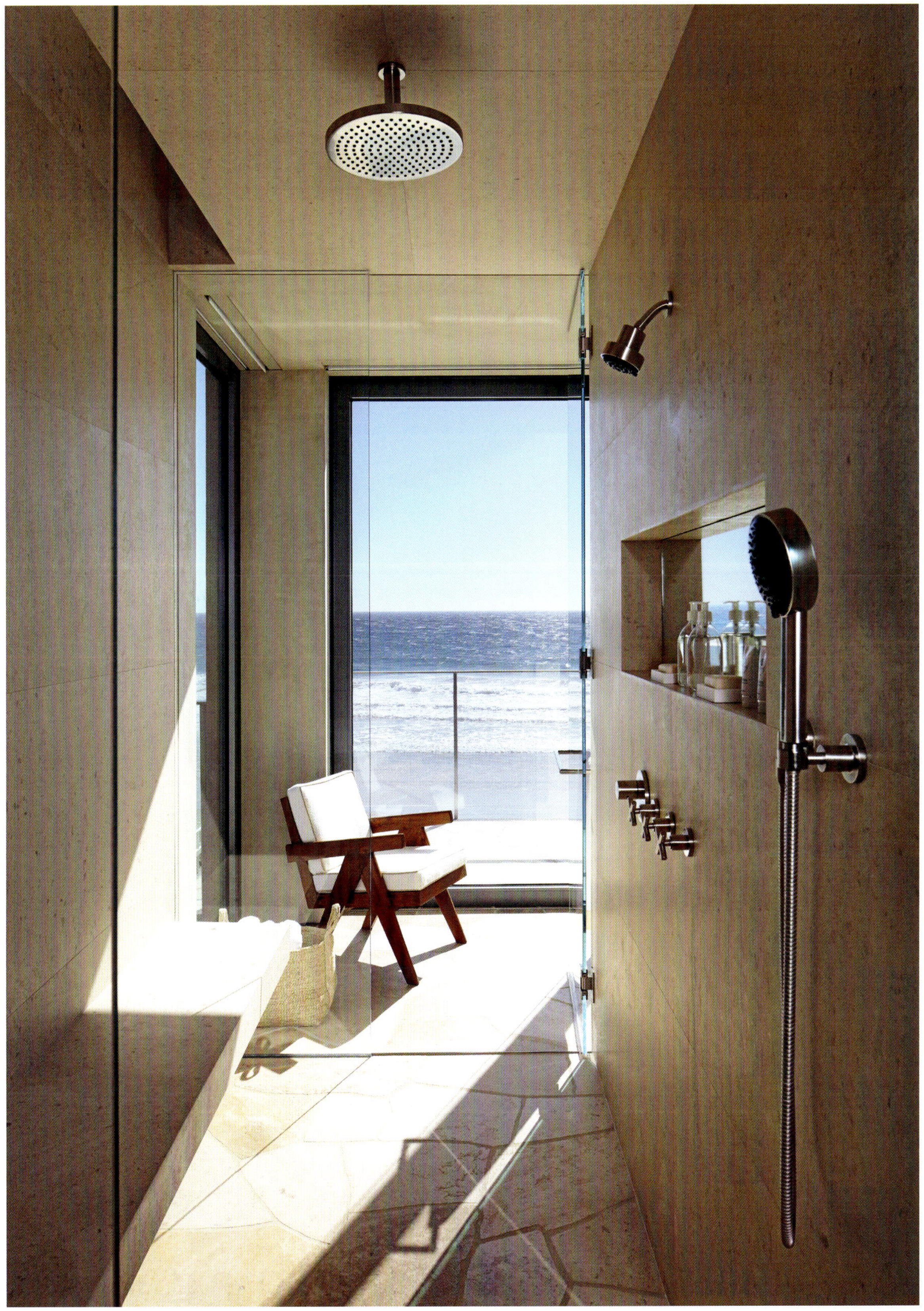

LEFT: *Nothing interrupts the ocean views from the upstairs master suite. The mix of flagstone and wire-brushed oak floors maintains a united color scheme that is punctuated by the owner's collection of tribal art and modern French furnishings.*

ABOVE: *One side of the master bathroom has a large walk-in limestone shower and a Pierre Jeanneret chair.*

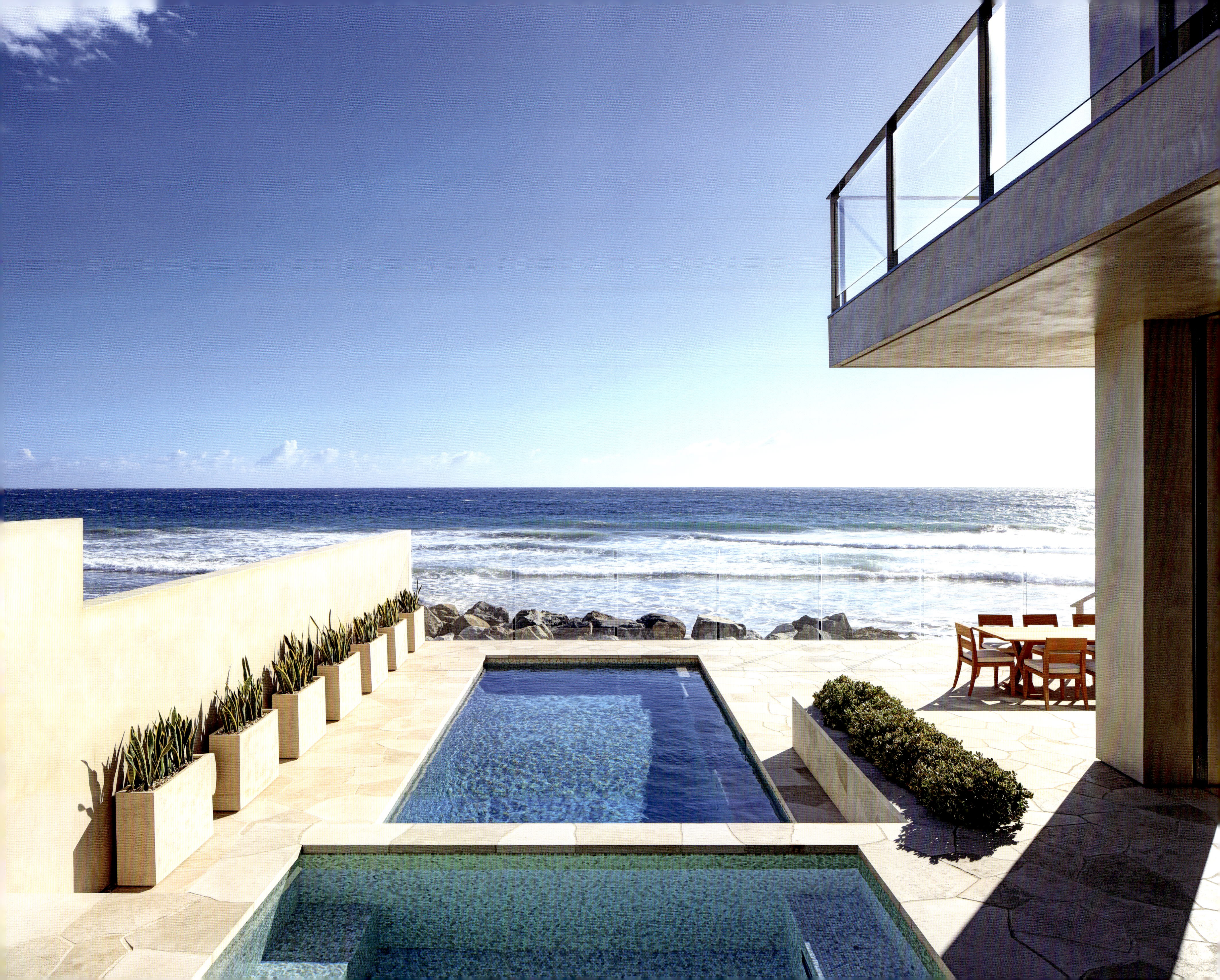

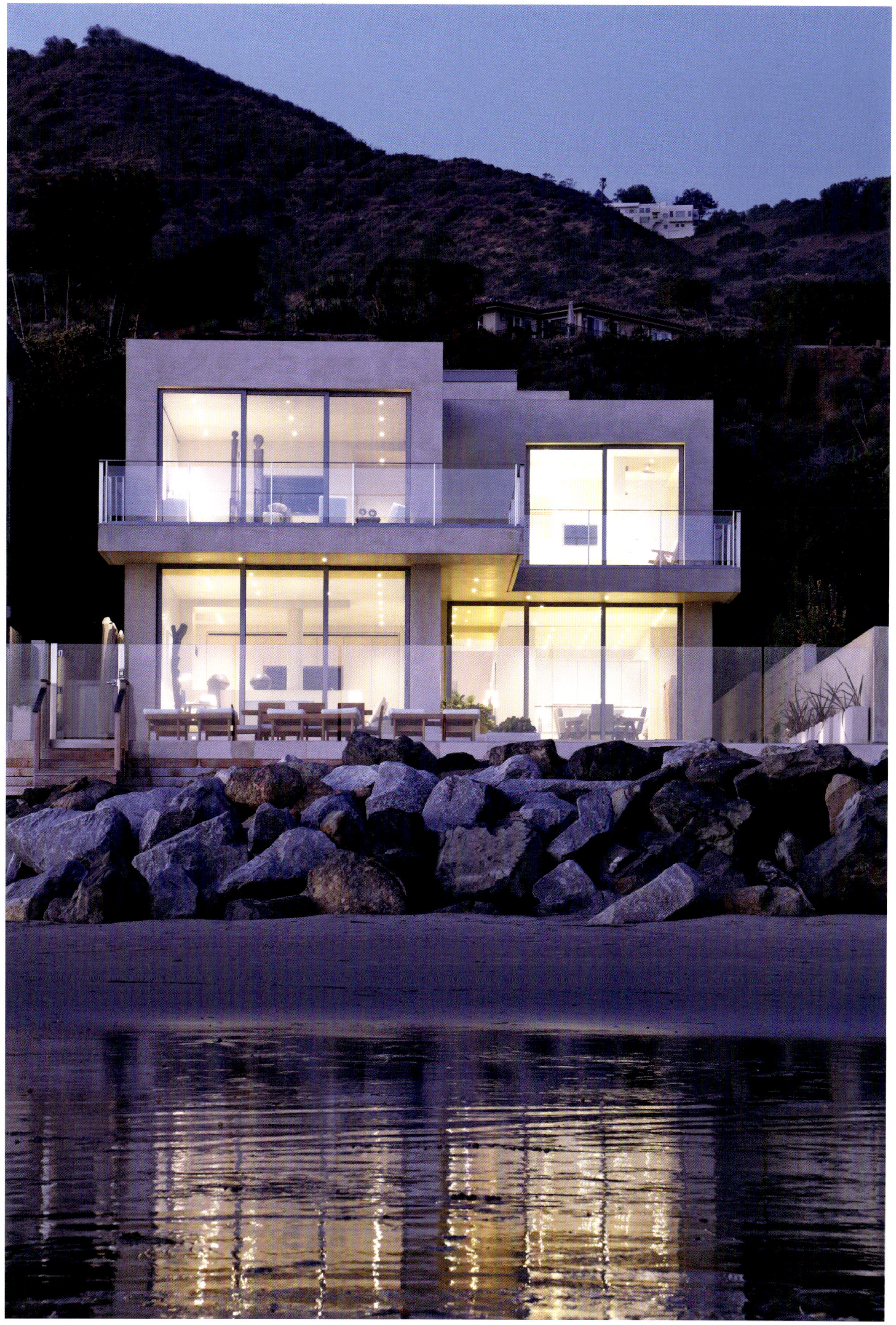

OPPOSITE: *While the front façade provides both privacy and security, this slowly dissolves as you progress through the house and reach the serenity and drama of the beach. The L-shaped floor plan wraps around the pool and spa.*

RIGHT: *The home's palette takes its cues from the sky, ocean, and landscape. At dusk, the house, as seen from the rear, glows with a minimalist simplicity that is warm and soft.*

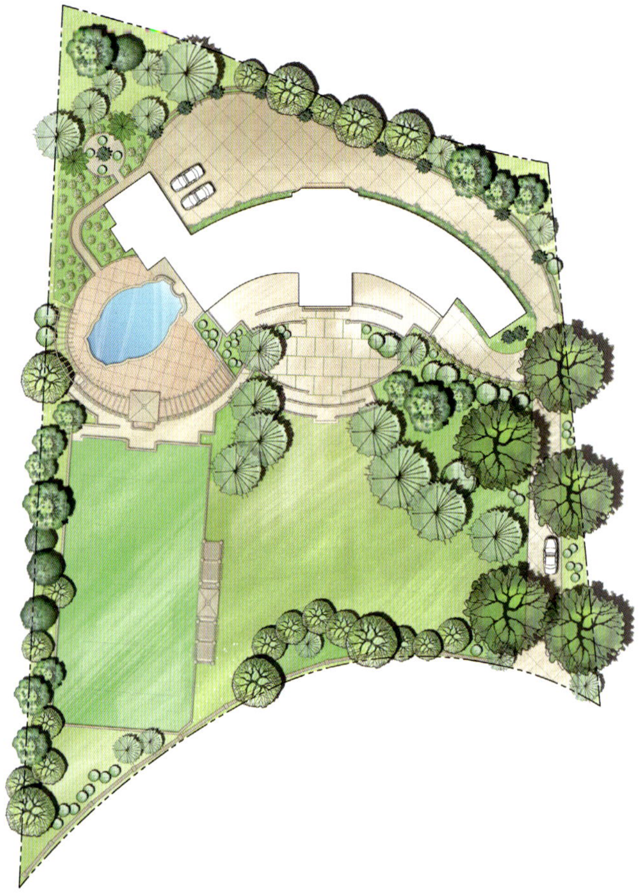

VILLA MEZZALUNA

Bel-Air

The bones of this Italianate villa in Bel-Air remain exactly as Wallace Neff—one of the masters of Mediterranean Revival architecture in Southern California in the first half of the twentieth century—created them in 1931. Neff had taken Giacomo Barozzi da Vignola's Villa Giulia in Rome as his inspiration for the steep, bowl-shaped site, and used its natural contours to design a semicircular structure whose outermost concave façade faced out over the gardens and views of the Bel-Air Country Club.

The villa's original owner was Sol Wurtzel, a movie executive and producer, whose vision for a grand European villa was brought to life during the Depression. It was then owned from the early 1960s to 1990 by Dolly Green (a daughter of one of the founders of Beverly Hills), who added a layer of ornamental detailing. The next owners undertook a massive renovation, which included excavating a full basement for an exercise room and spa and putting in a tennis court, and they gave the main rooms more of an Art Deco/Art Moderne feel.

The scope of our work included adding new windows to lighten the rotunda entrance hall, enlarging the south loggia, enclosing the west loggia to function more like a conservatory, creating a direct garage entry and elevator, redesigning the entire master suite, restoring the exterior and gardens, installing new art lighting, and updating the systems.

Our clients appreciate the layering of history that the villa now encompasses. There is the original Italianate work by Neff, changed by the previous owners and modified by the current ones. In a sense it feels like an old country house that has been adapted through the ages by owners who each put their own stamp but kept the original gist of the house in place.

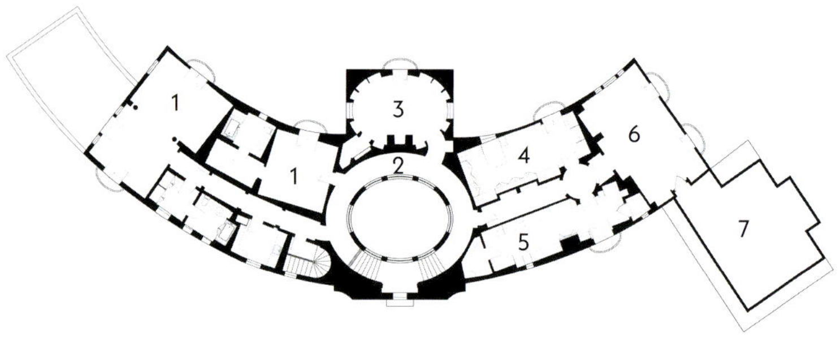

SECOND-FLOOR PLAN

1 Bedroom suite
2 Balcony
3 Study
4 Her dressing room
5 His dressing room
6 Master bedroom
7 Master bath

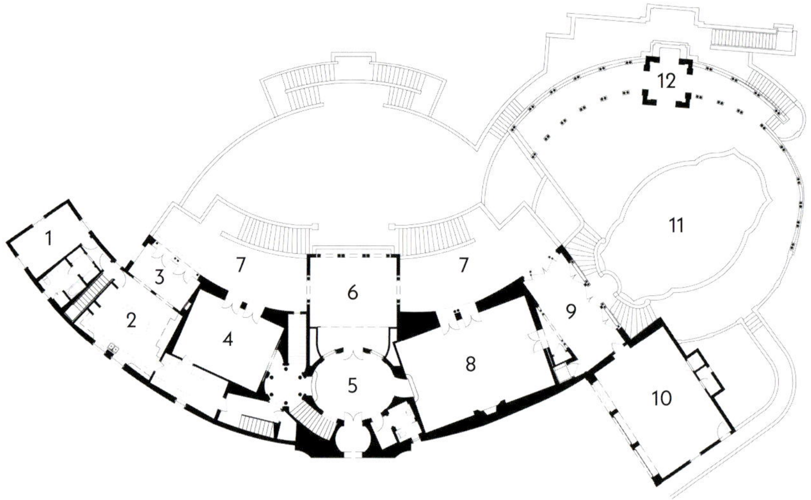

FIRST-FLOOR PLAN

1 Staff quarters
2 Kitchen
3 Breakfast room
4 Dining room
5 Entrance hall
6 Loggia
7 Upper terrace
8 Living room
9 Conservatory
10 Garage
11 Pool
12 Pergola

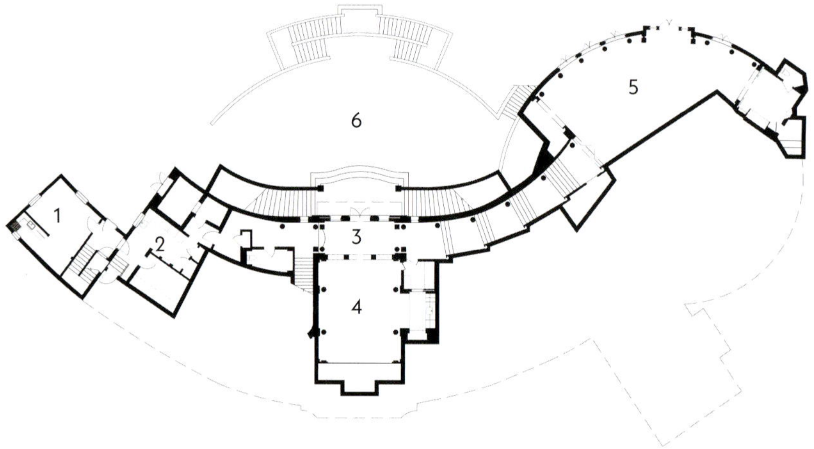

LOWER-LEVEL PLAN

0 8 16 32 ft

1 Staff quarters
2 Service area
3 Gallery
4 Theater
5 Exercise room
6 Lower terrace

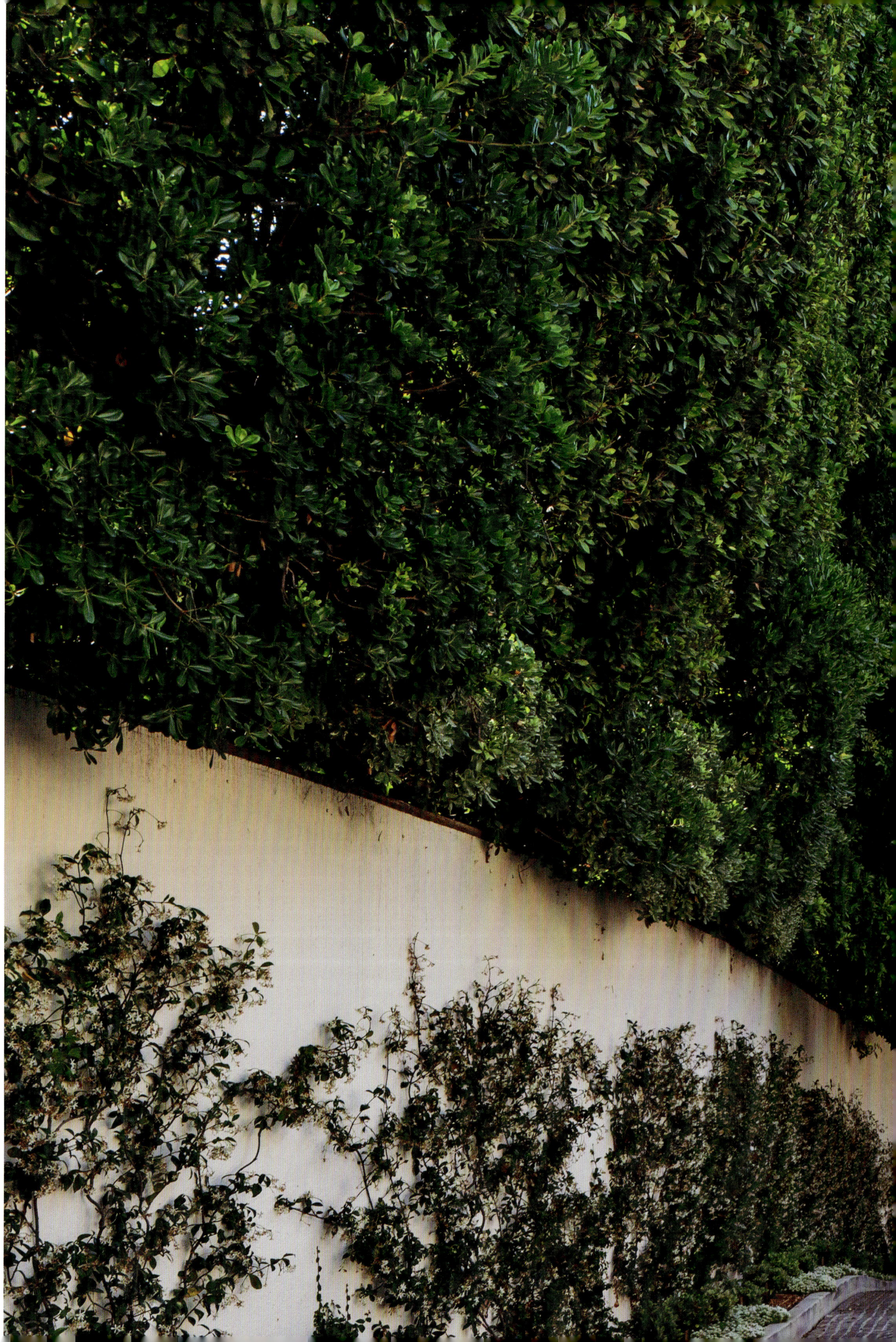

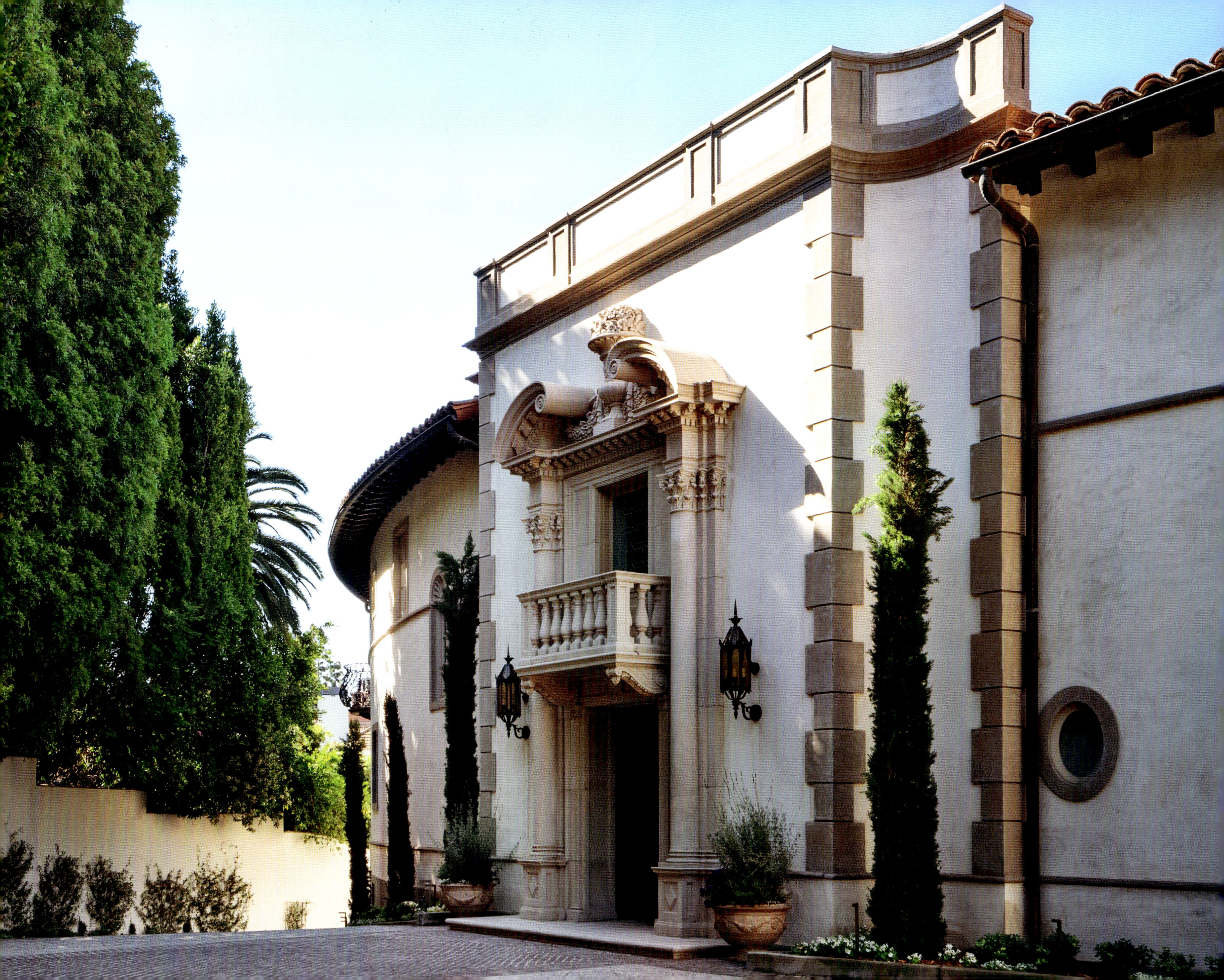

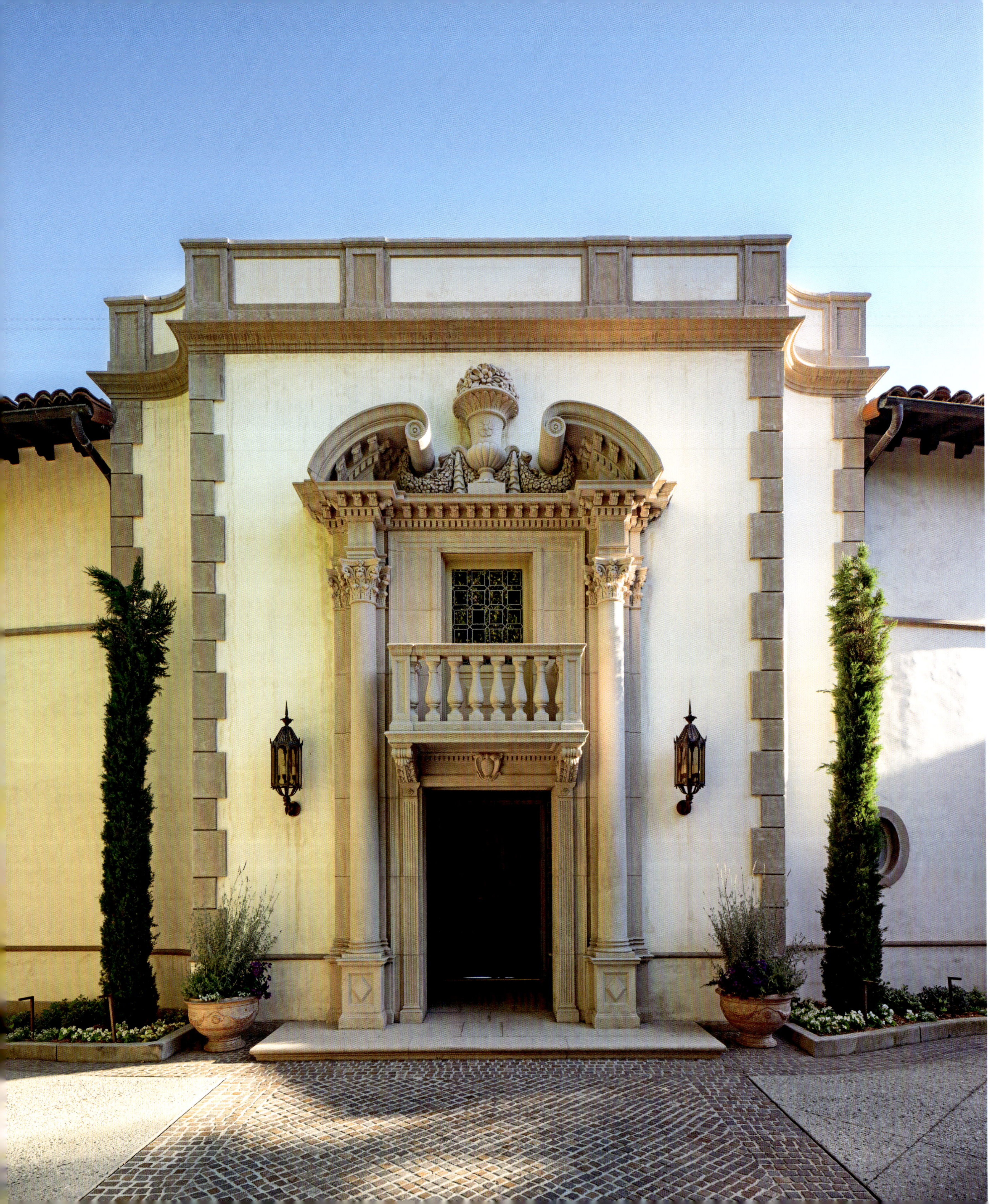

PREVIOUS PAGES: *Completed in 1931 by architect Wallace Neff on a sloping lot in Bel-Air, Villa Mezzaluna was designed to fit the natural contours of the land. The entry courtyard, hidden from the street, leads up to the crescent-shaped villa that stretches 176 feet long and 50 feet deep.*

LEFT: *Neff's skills with proportion, scale, craftsmanship, and attention to detail are apparent in the ornate Italianate cast stone front façade, which, with columns, a broken pediment, and a balustraded balcony that protects an amber-leaded window, is Neff at his most exuberant.*

OPPOSITE: *The faux-painted walls in the entry vestibule were inspired by a pattern that the clients saw in Florence.*

FOLLOWING PAGES, LEFT: *The core of the house revolves around the double-height oval rotunda entrance hall, where new windows were added to lighten the space.* RIGHT: *Elevation drawing of the entrance hall.*

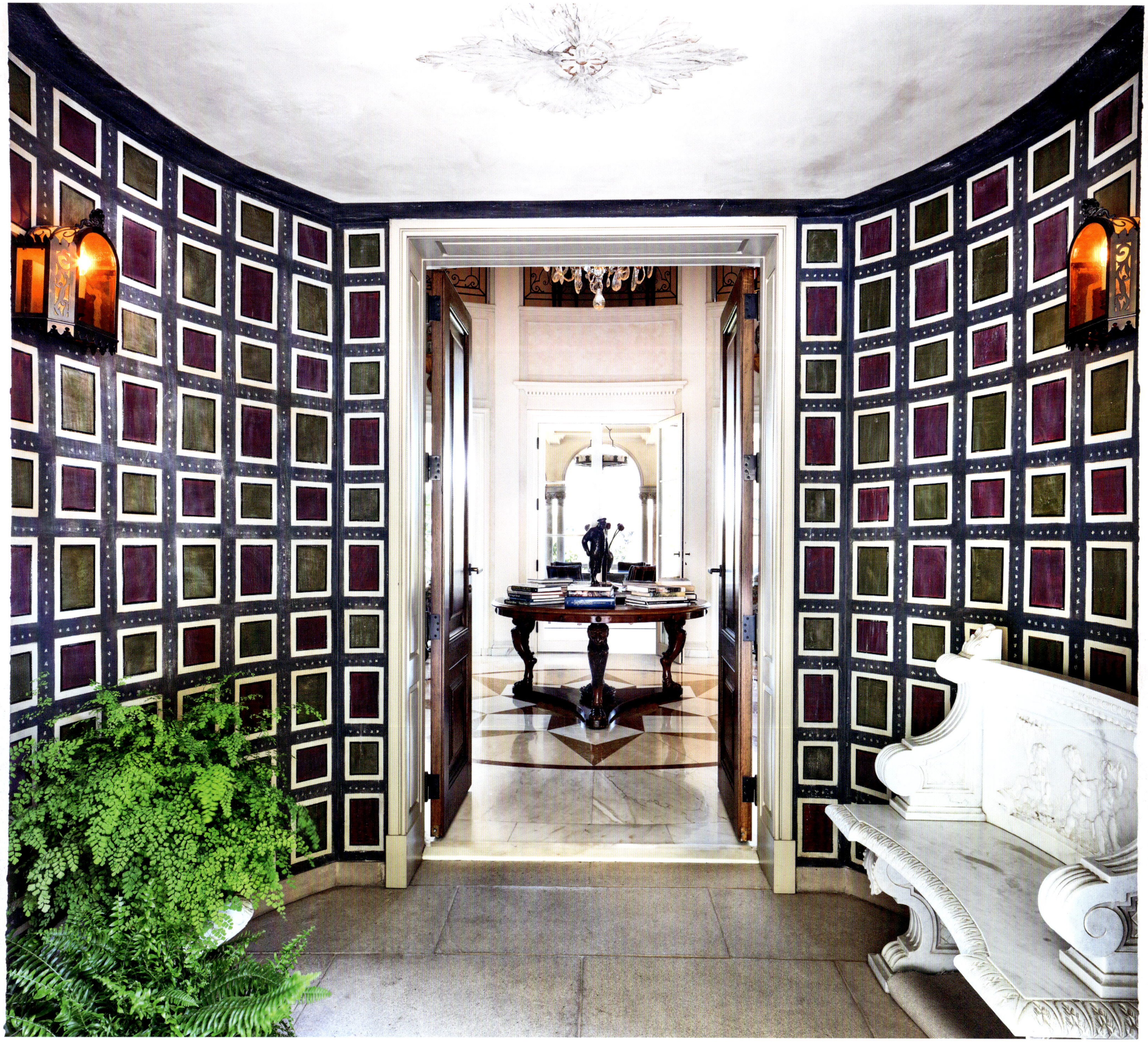

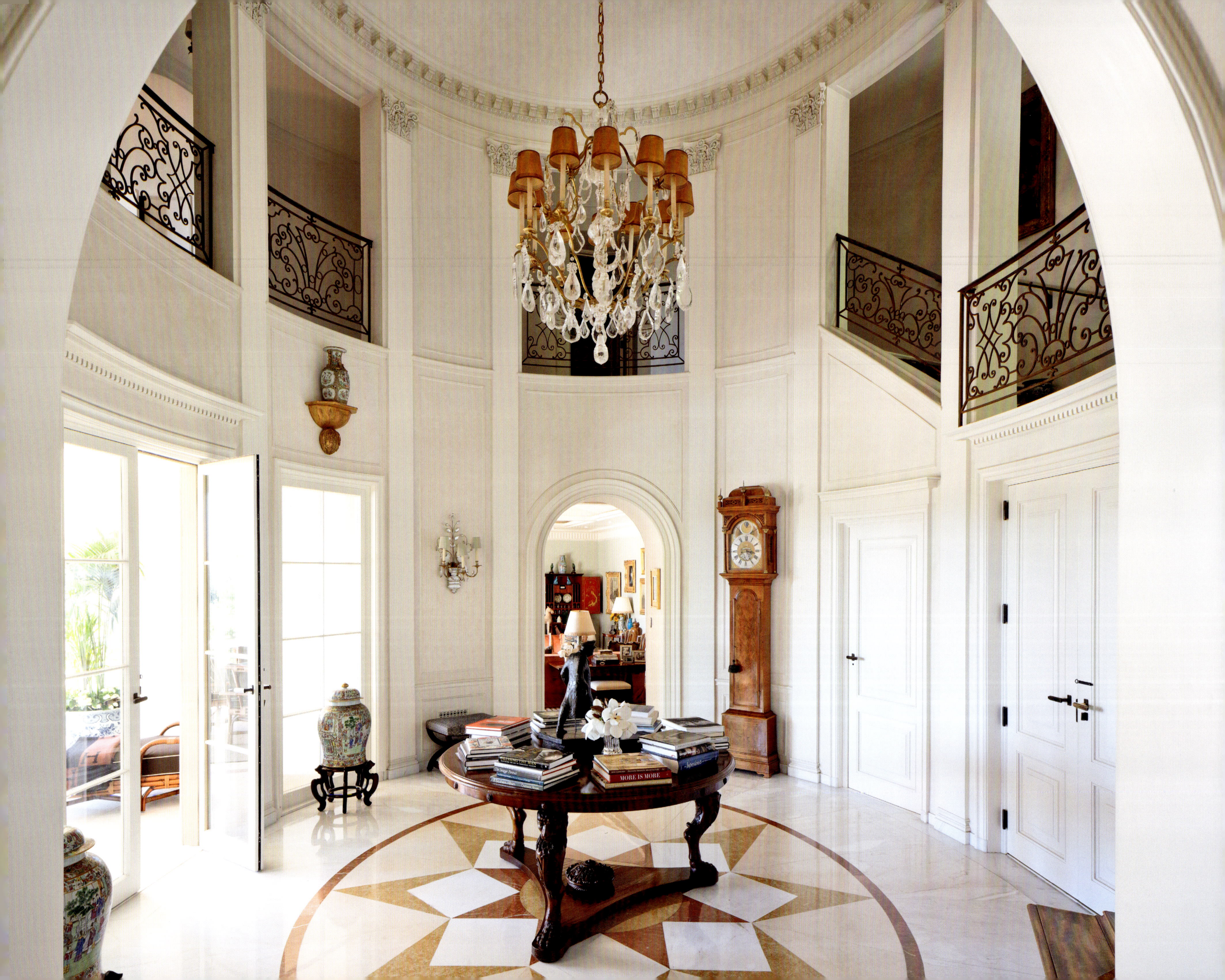
MORE IS MORE

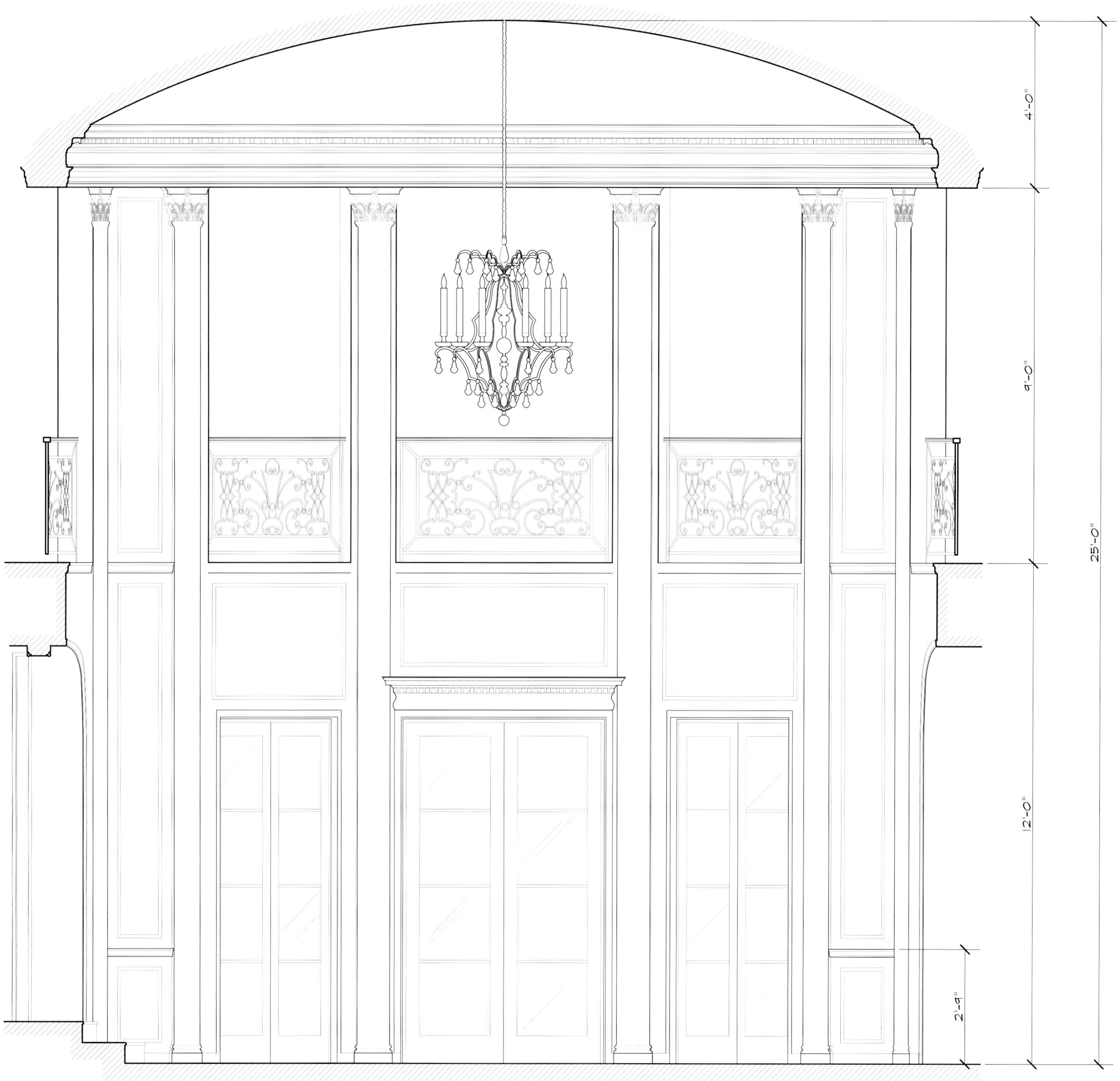
4'-0"
9'-0"
12'-0"
2'-9"
25'-0"

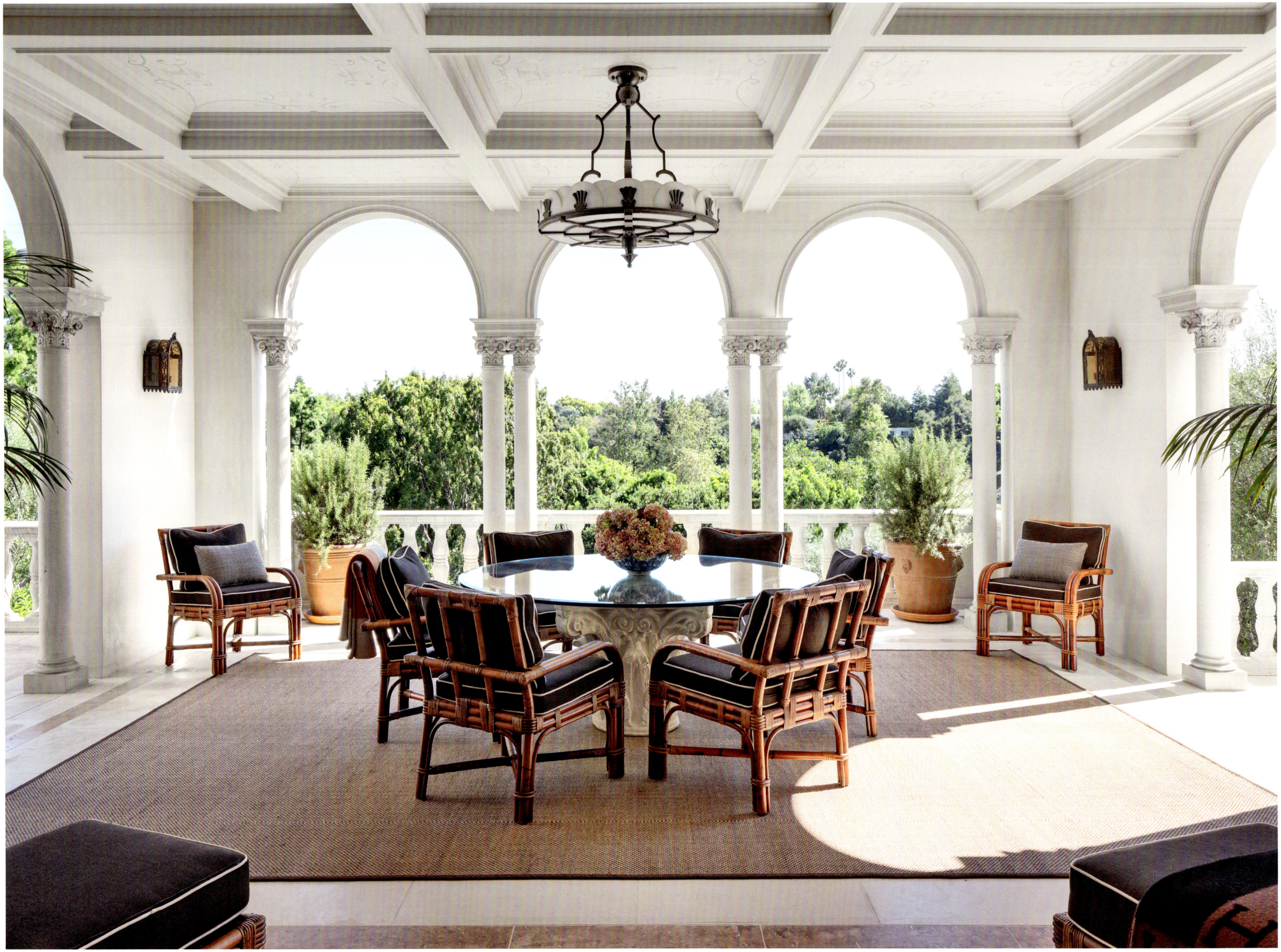

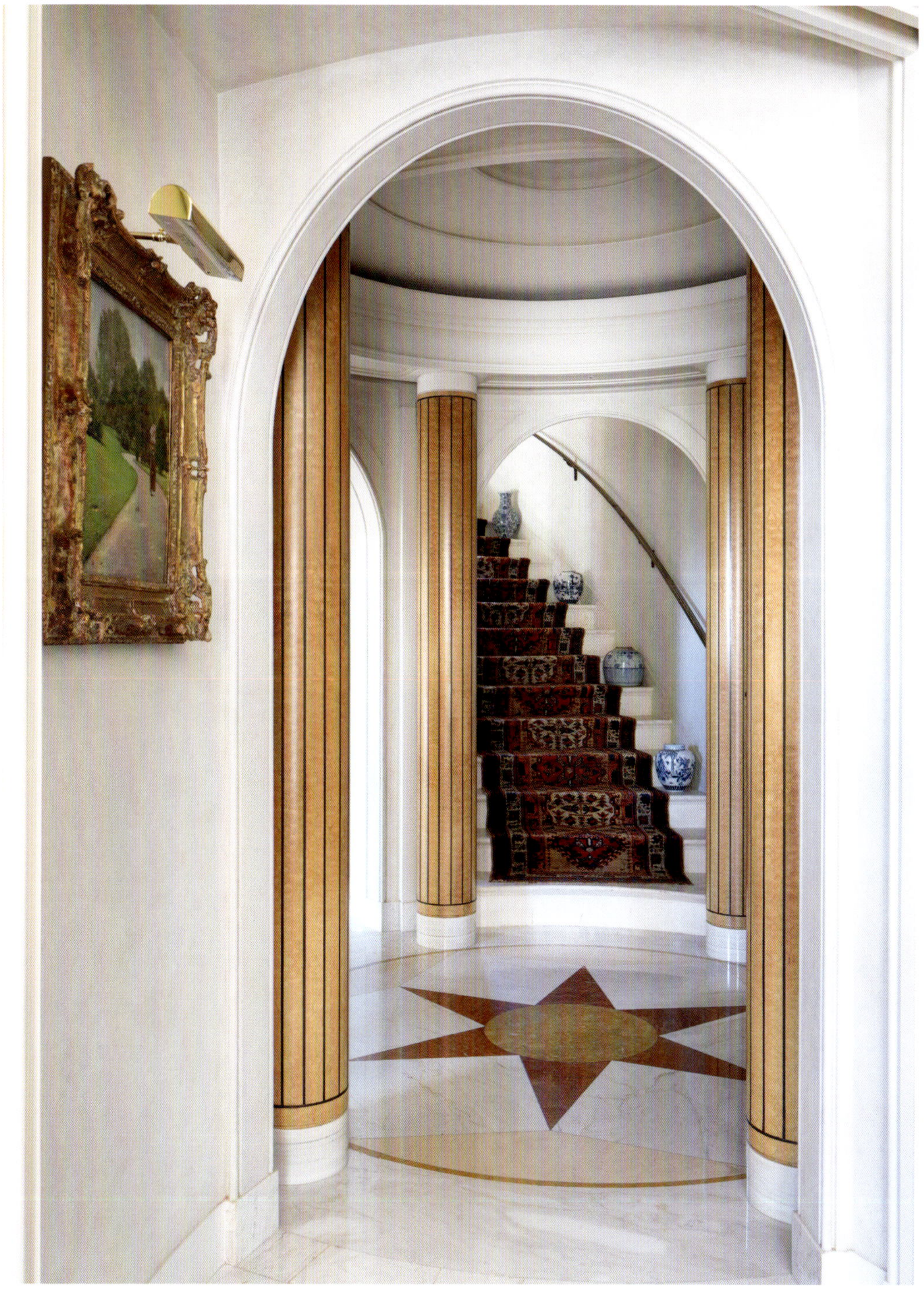

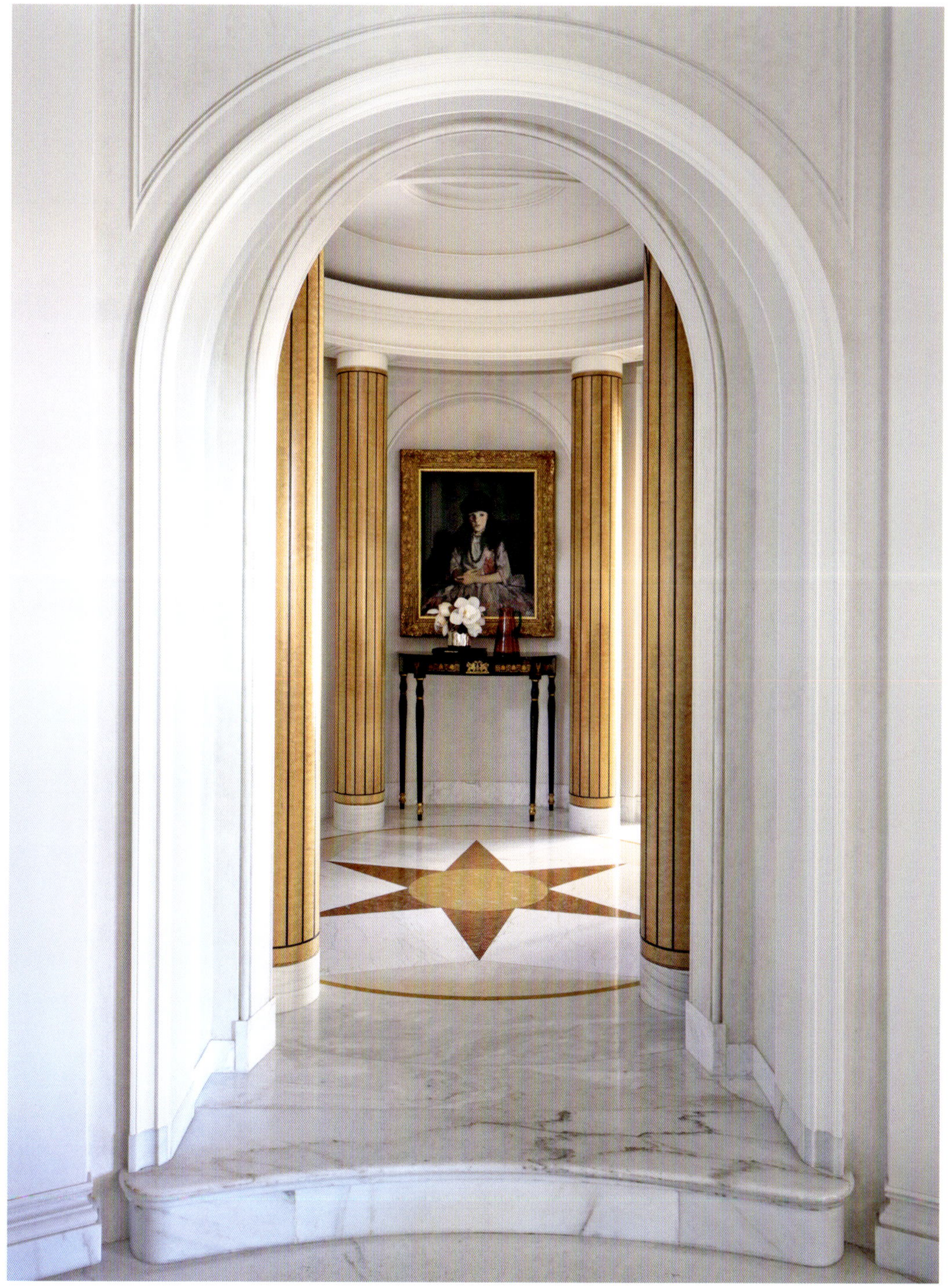

OPPOSITE: *The open south loggia was enlarged and furnished with rattan chairs to capture the feel of old Hollywood glamour.*

ABOVE: *A small rotunda was added in the 1990s by the previous owners as a central accessway to the upstairs and family wings.*

FOLLOWING PAGES, LEFT: *Interior designer Trevor Howells gave the living room a jewel-toned Florentine look with moss green walls, velvet upholstery, Moorish patterned drapes, woven flooring, and a Baroque mirror. The wall sconces in cut stone are original.* RIGHT: *The west loggia was originally open, but the owners wanted an enclosed casual space on this level, so 10-foot-tall arched doorways and hand-troweled plaster were added to match the existing casing.*

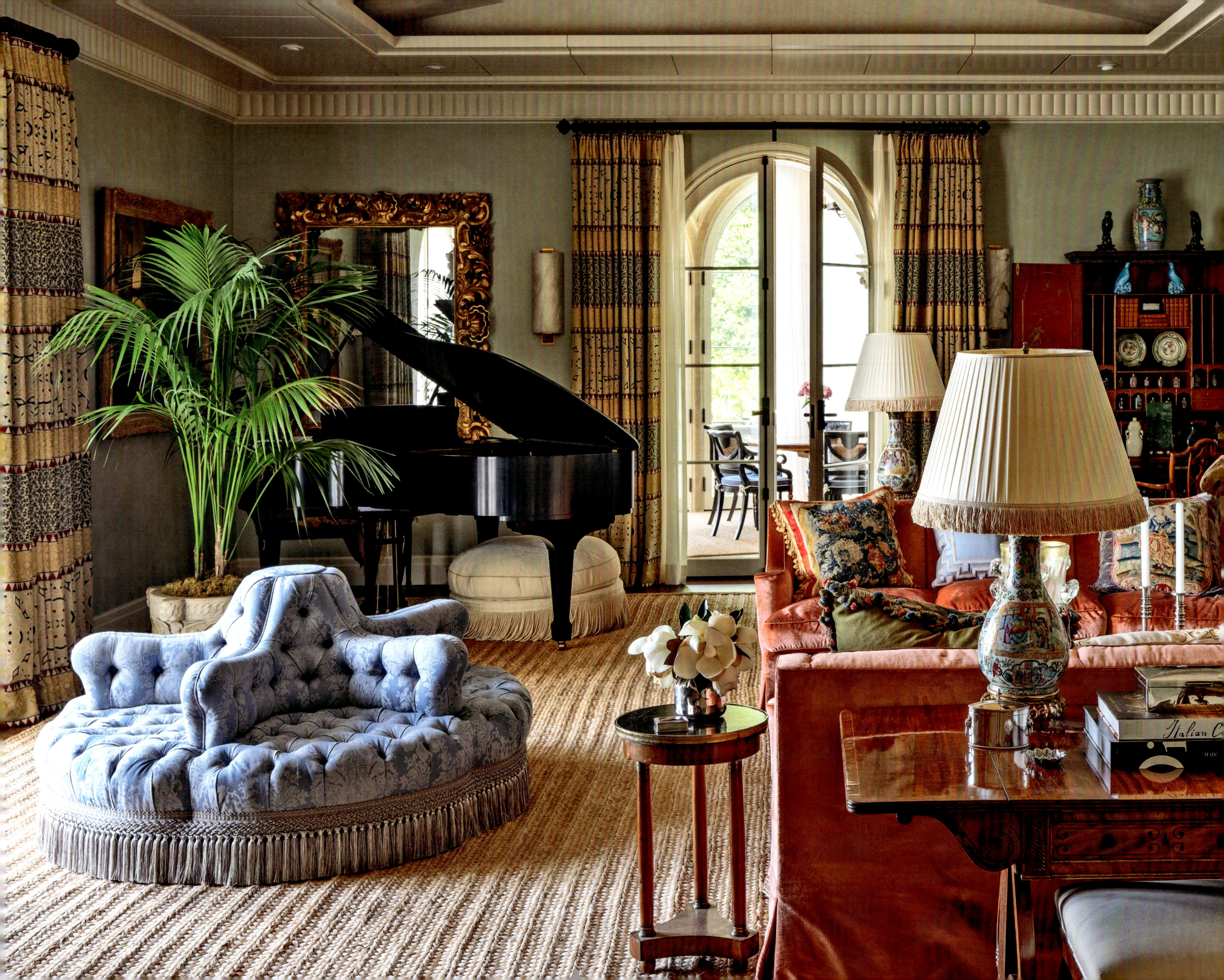

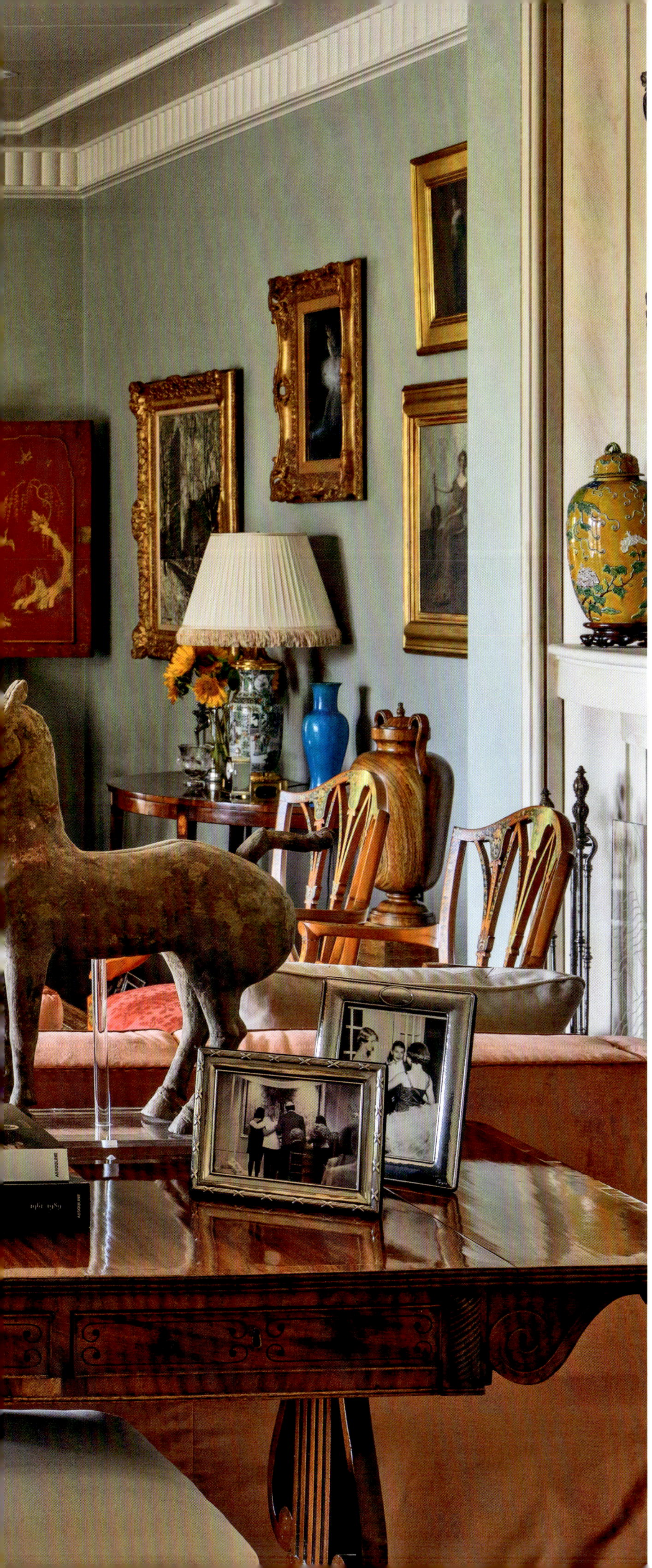

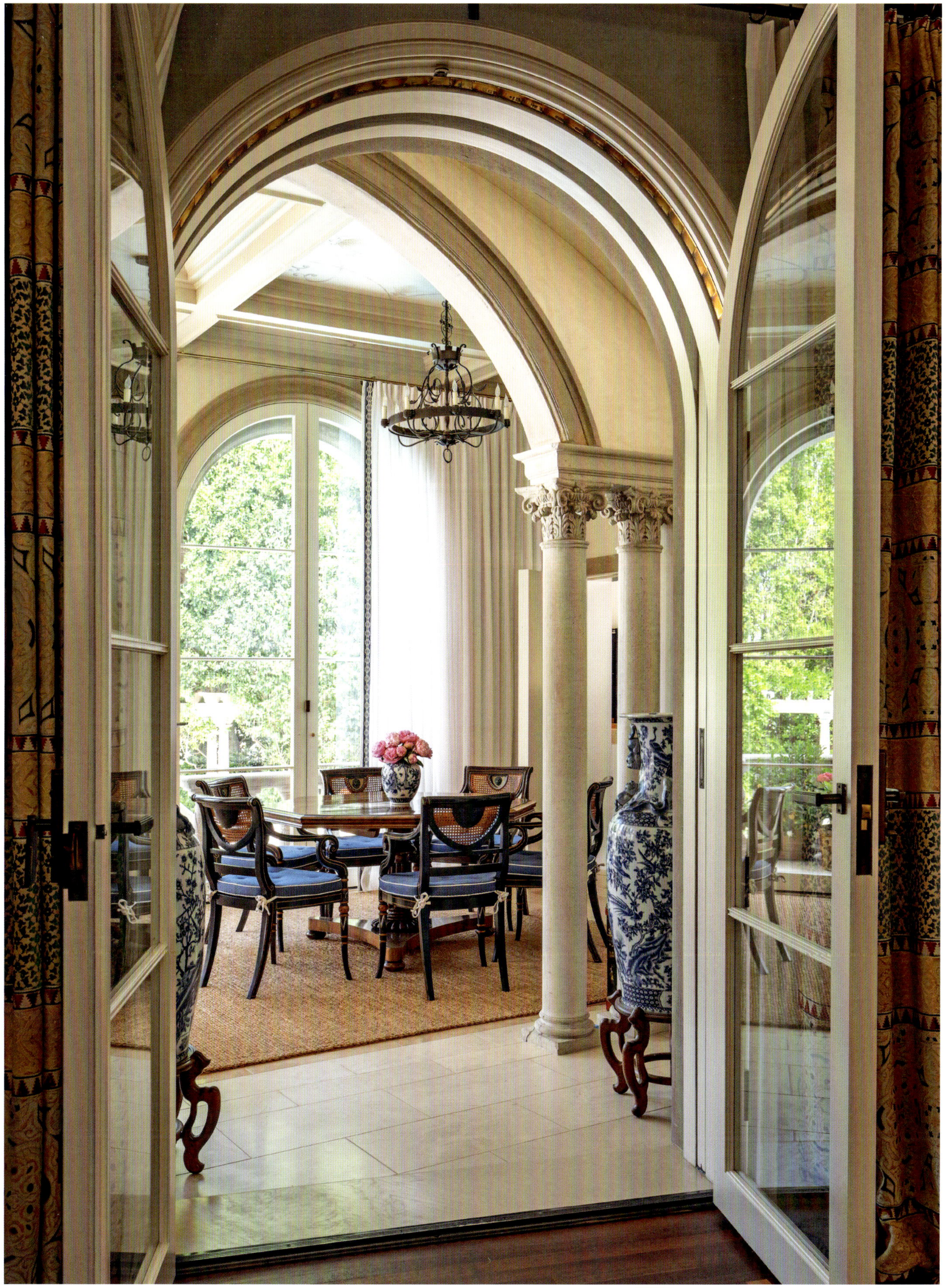

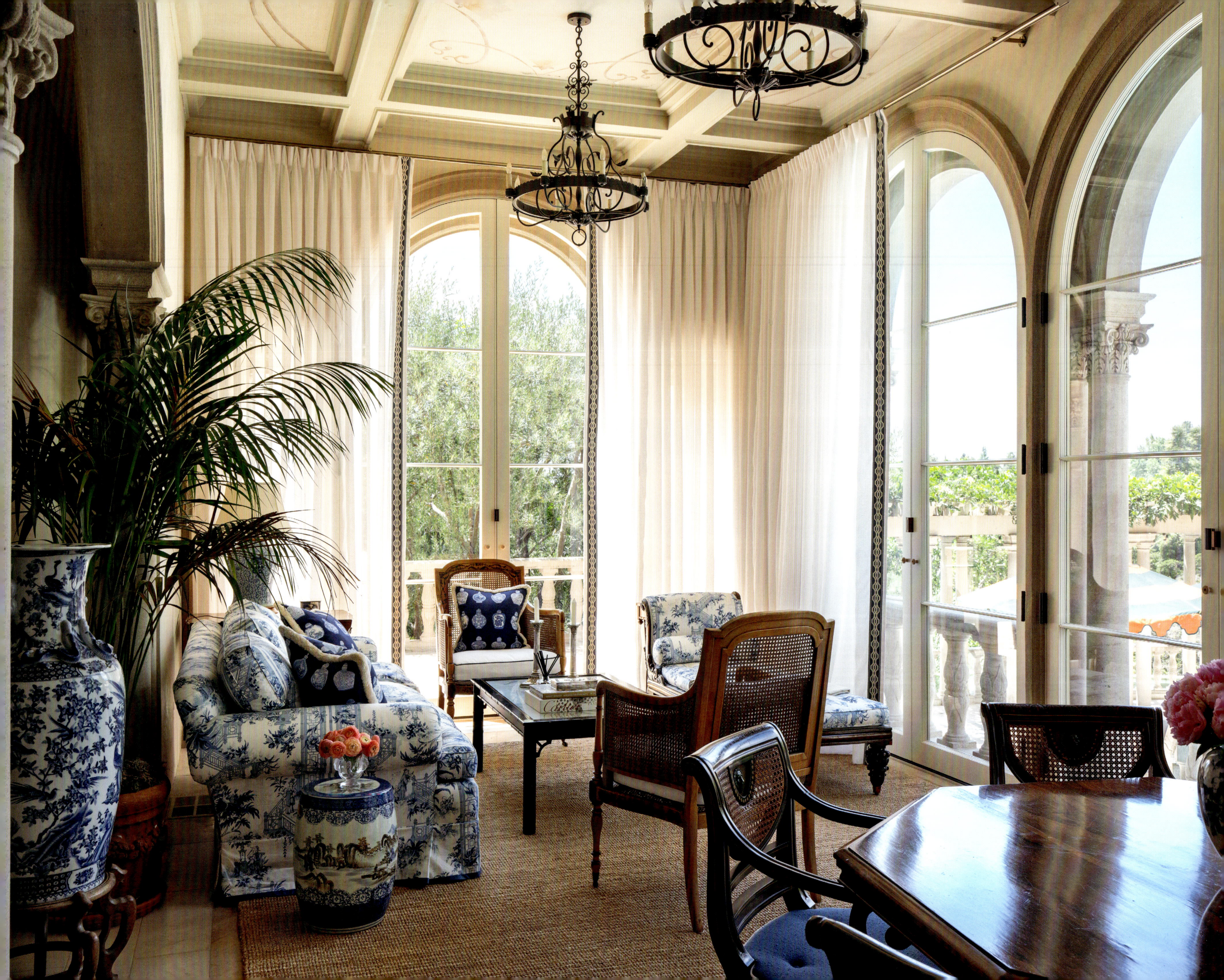

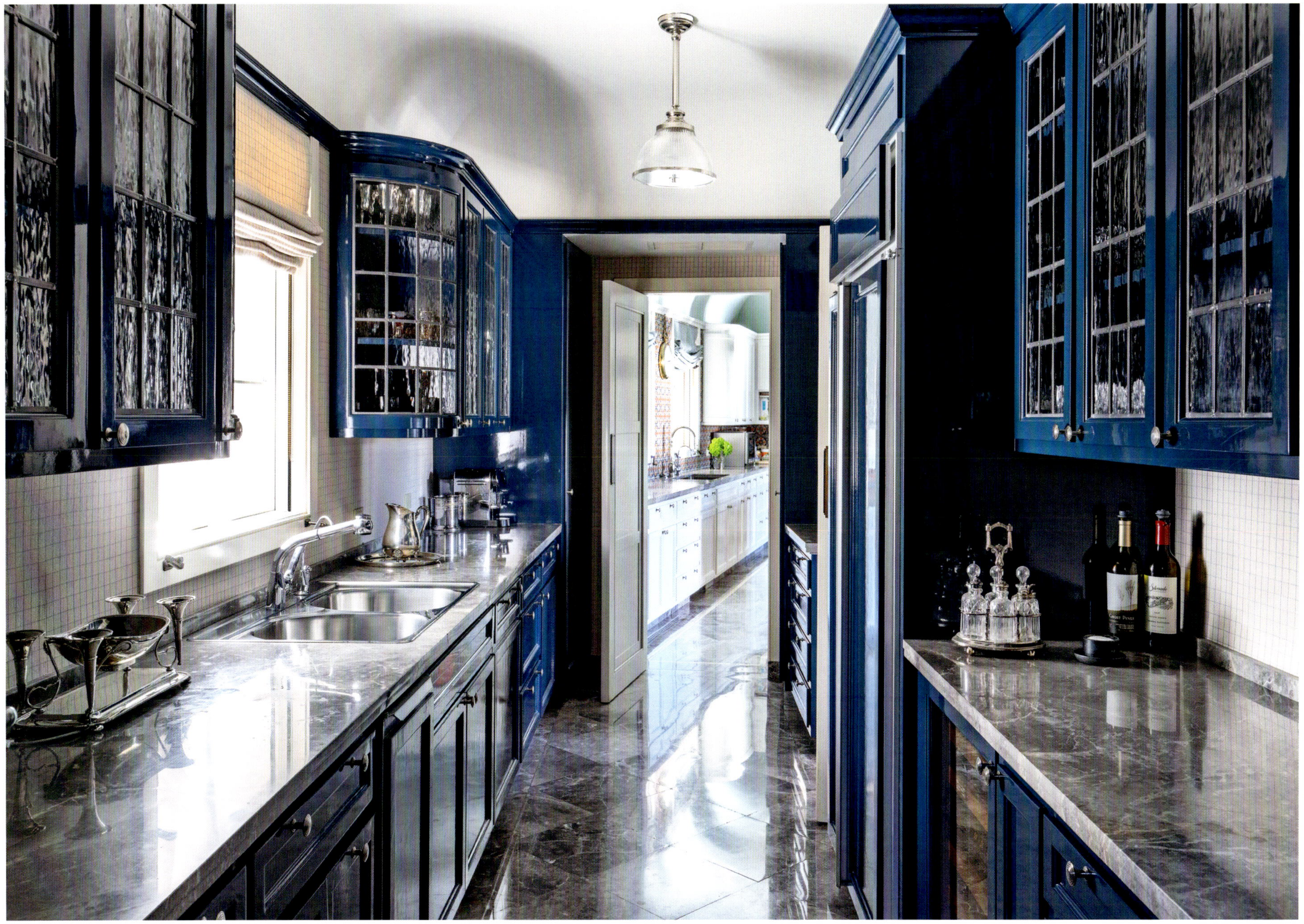

OPPOSITE: *Another view of the enclosed west loggia with its pared-down coffered ceiling.*

ABOVE: *The kitchen and pantry were given a decorative facelift by adding blue lacquered cabinetry and tile and by wallpapering the breakfast room to give it more personality.*

FOLLOWING PAGES, LEFT: *De Gournay wallpaper lines the formal dining room, which was furnished with the clients' collection of American art and European antiques.* RIGHT: *Wallace Neff's original wood-paneled oval library. All the rooms were given more lighting for warmth accenting artwork, and more layers to make them more inviting.*

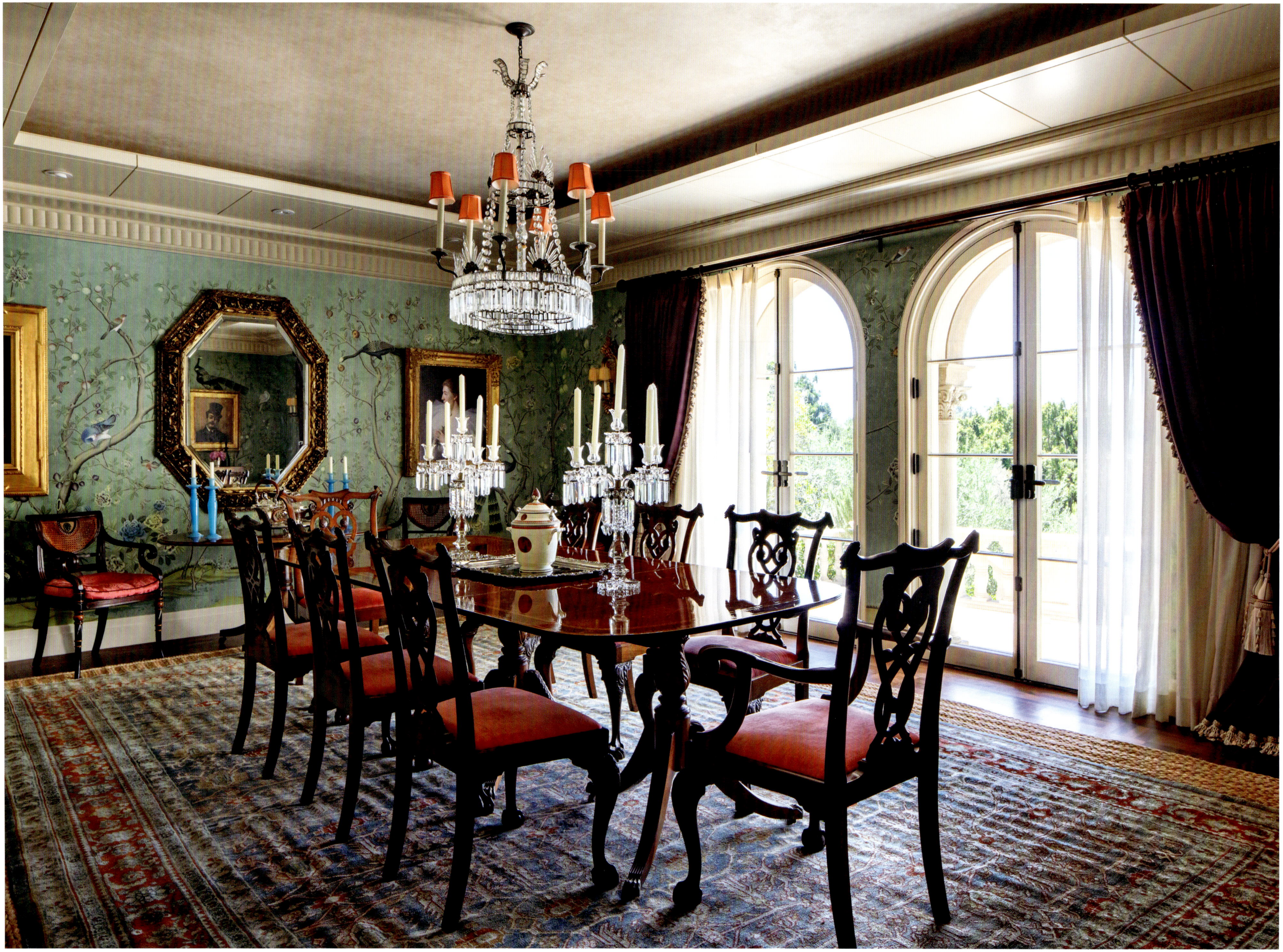

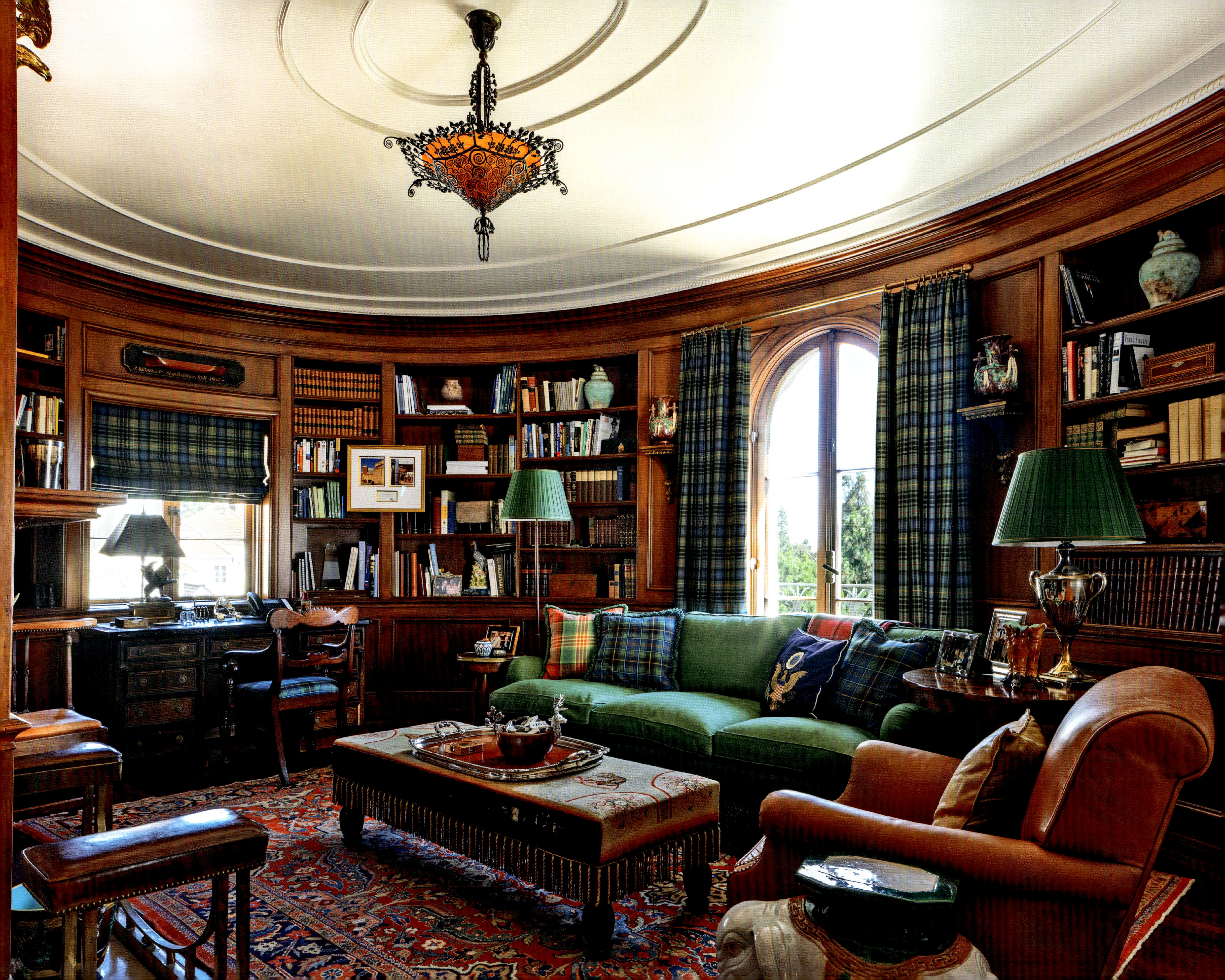

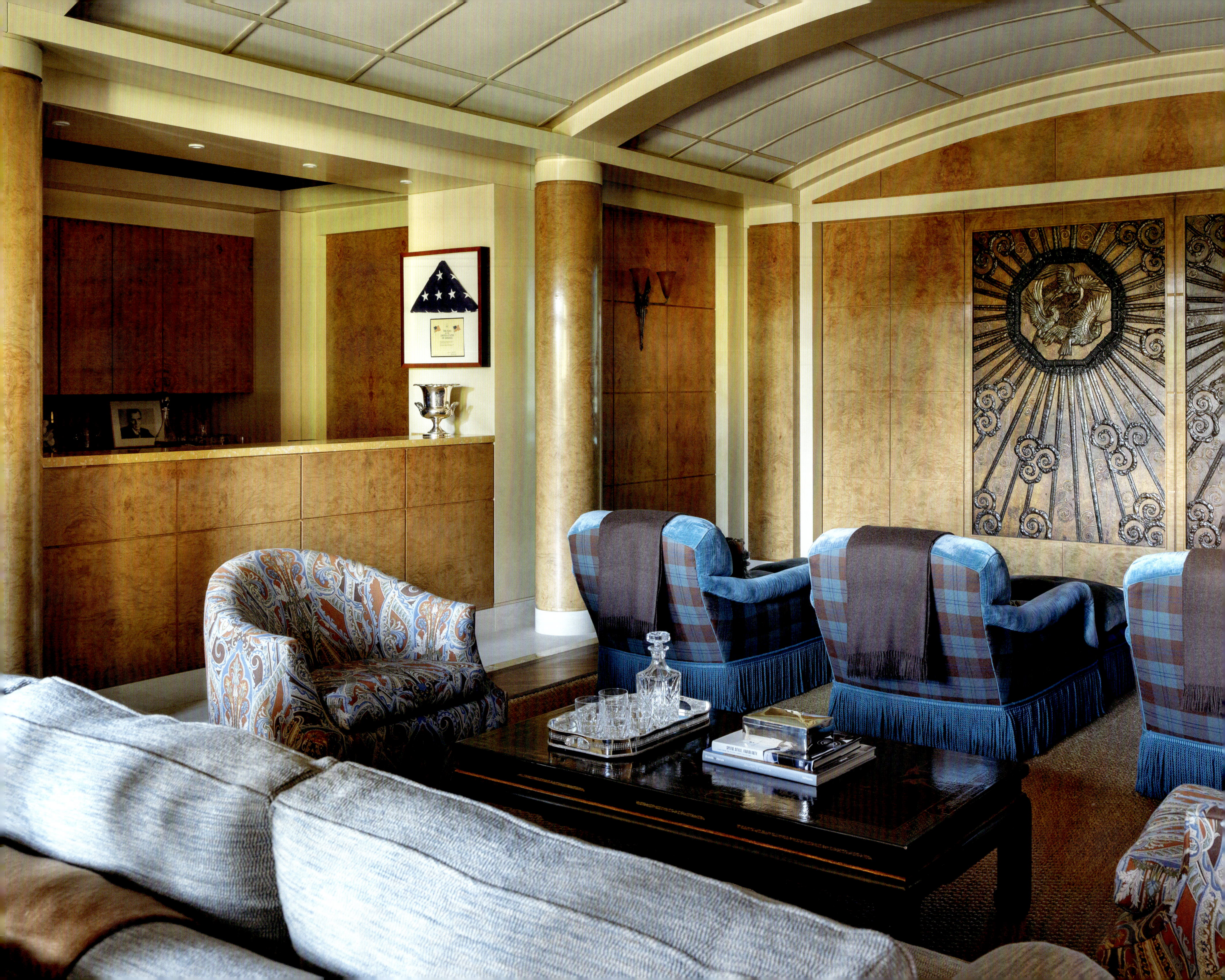

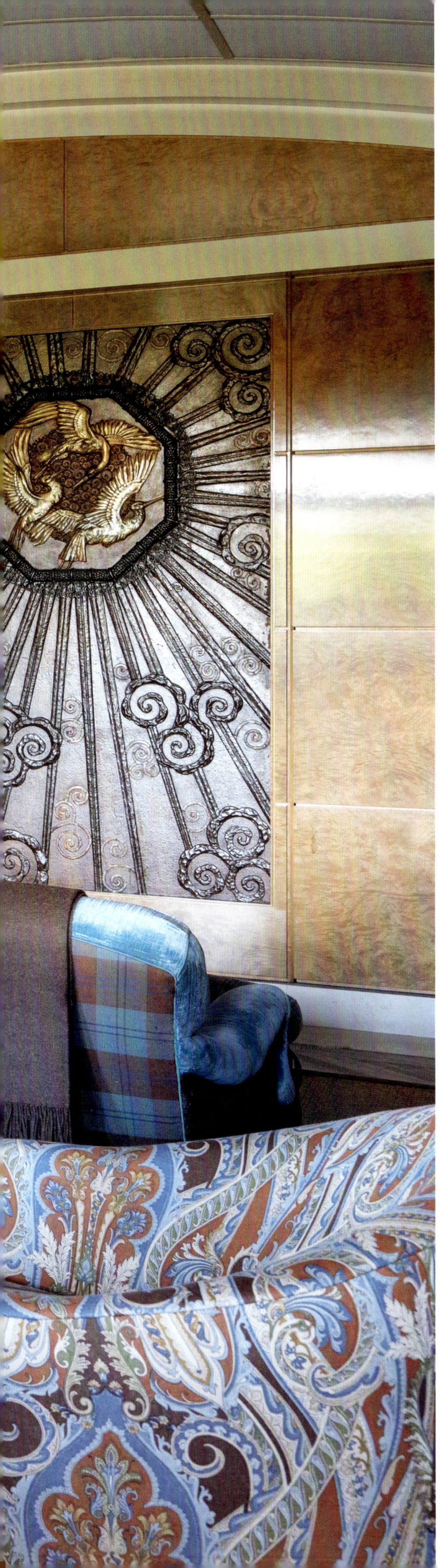

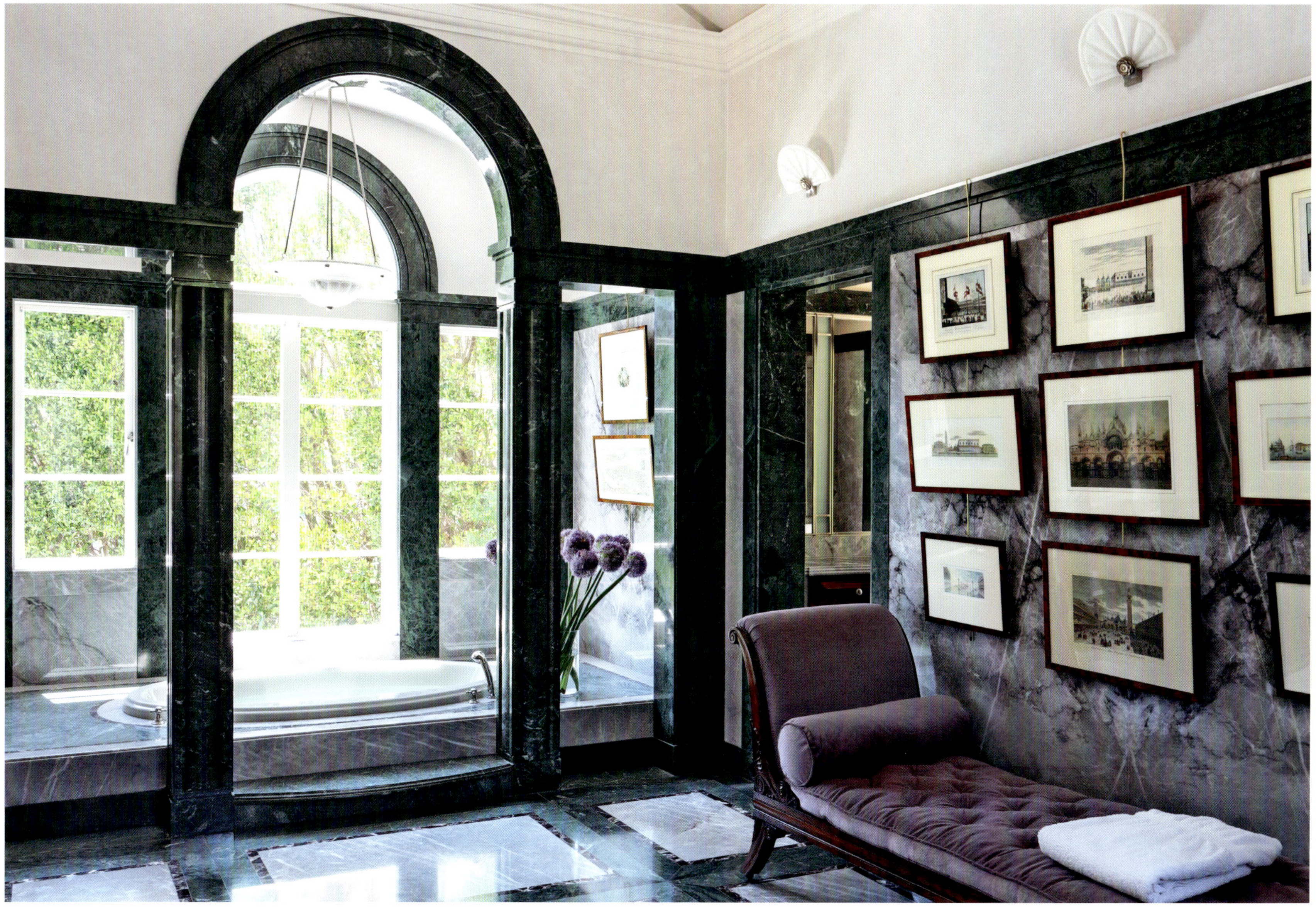

LEFT: *The lower-level home theater was originally a projection room for the first owner, film producer Sol Wurtzel. It was renovated in the 1990s with olive ash walls and sliding panels that were designed in the 1920s by Edgar Brandt for the elevator doors of Selfridges in London.*

ABOVE: *The house has had four owners and has been documented at each stage of ownership. The marble master bath was redone in the 1990s as a version of a 1931 bathroom.*

RIGHT: *Among the exterior details created by Neff are terra cotta finials and ornamental ironwork balconies. Steps lead down from the enclosed west loggia to the pool.*

FOLLOWING PAGES: *Neff pushed the property to the northernmost edge so that the entire house faces south and its siting gives a sense of a much larger space. The upper set of stairs is original. The lower set was added in the 1990s when an extension was excavated under the pool and a tennis court installed.*

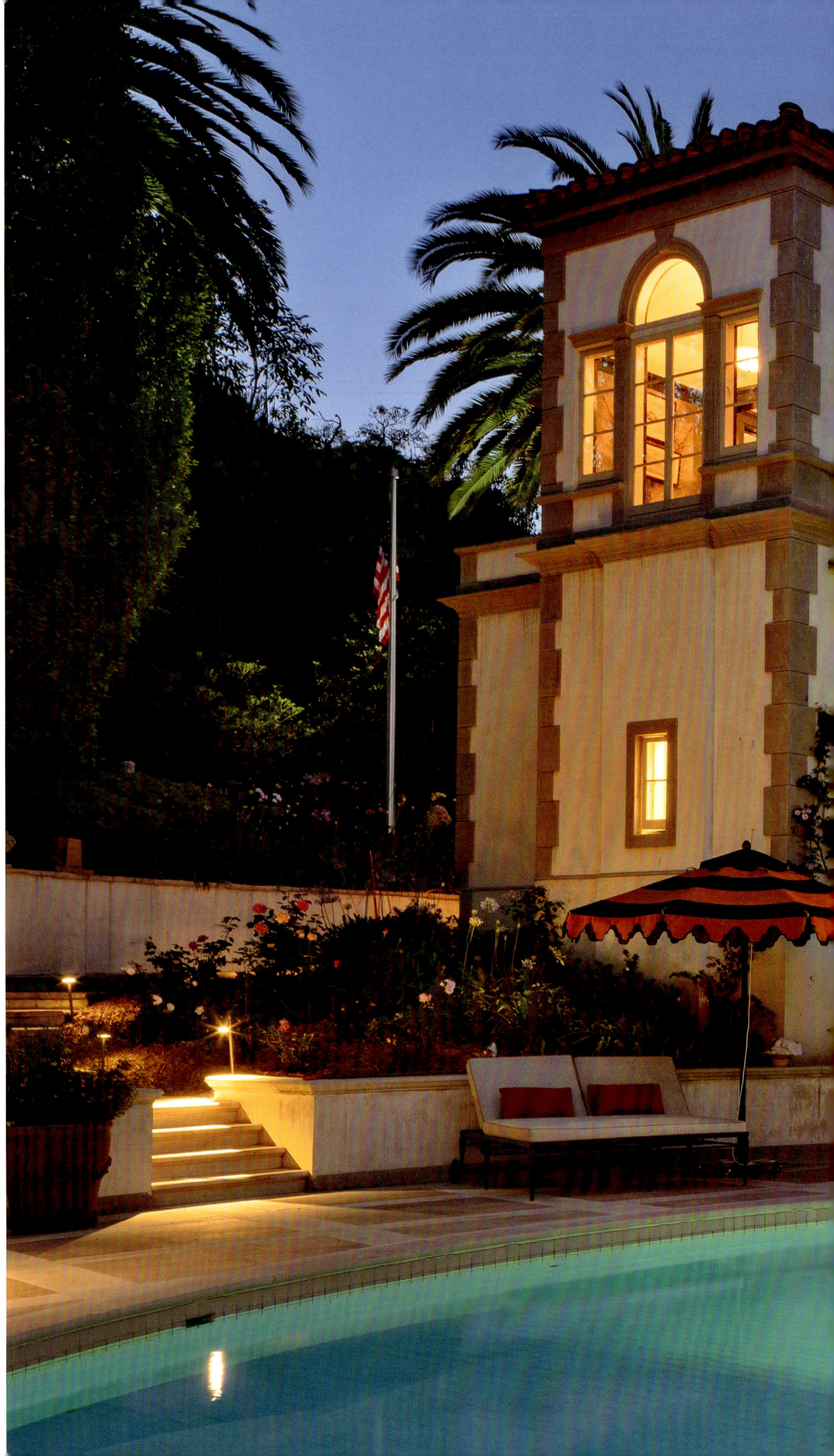

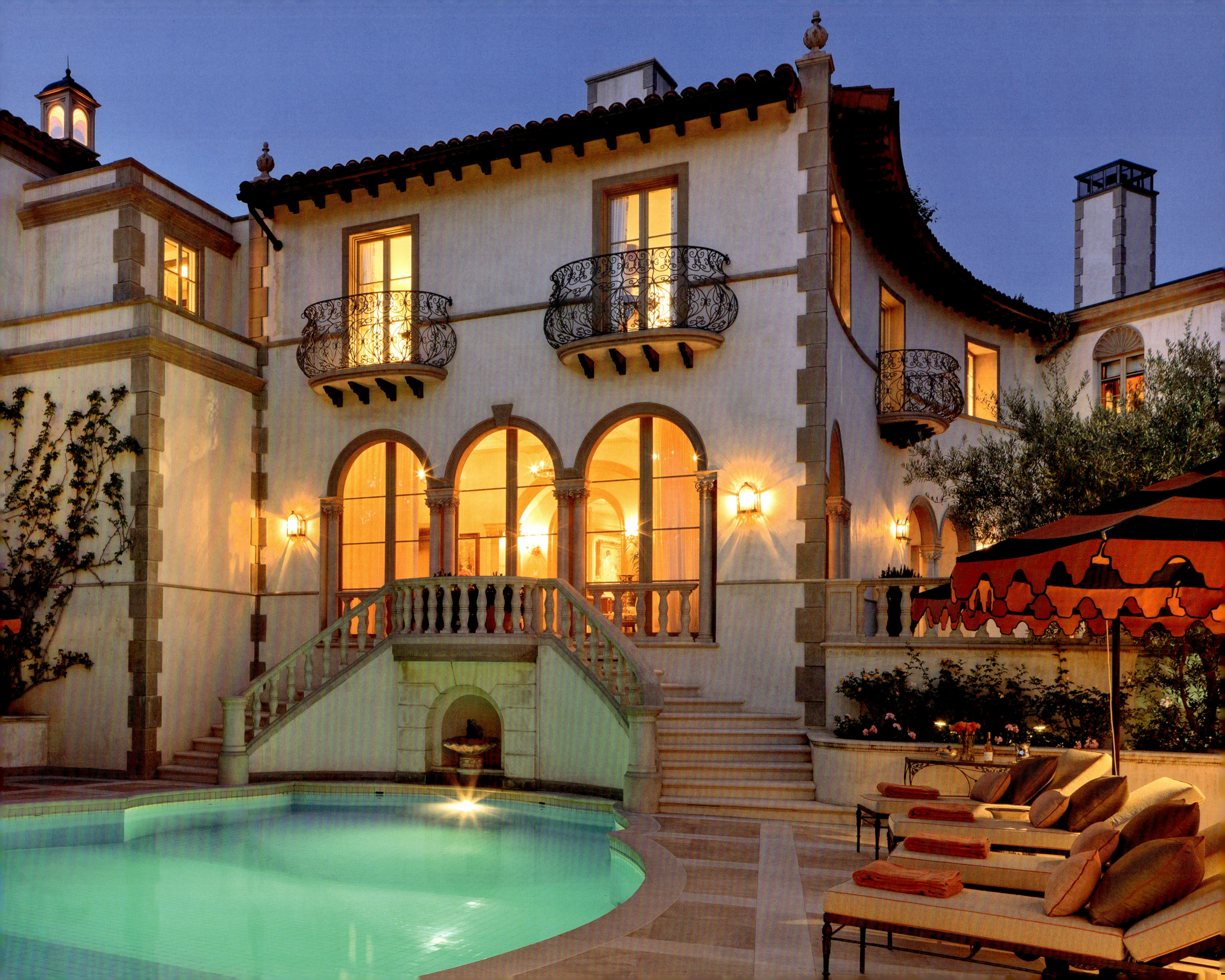

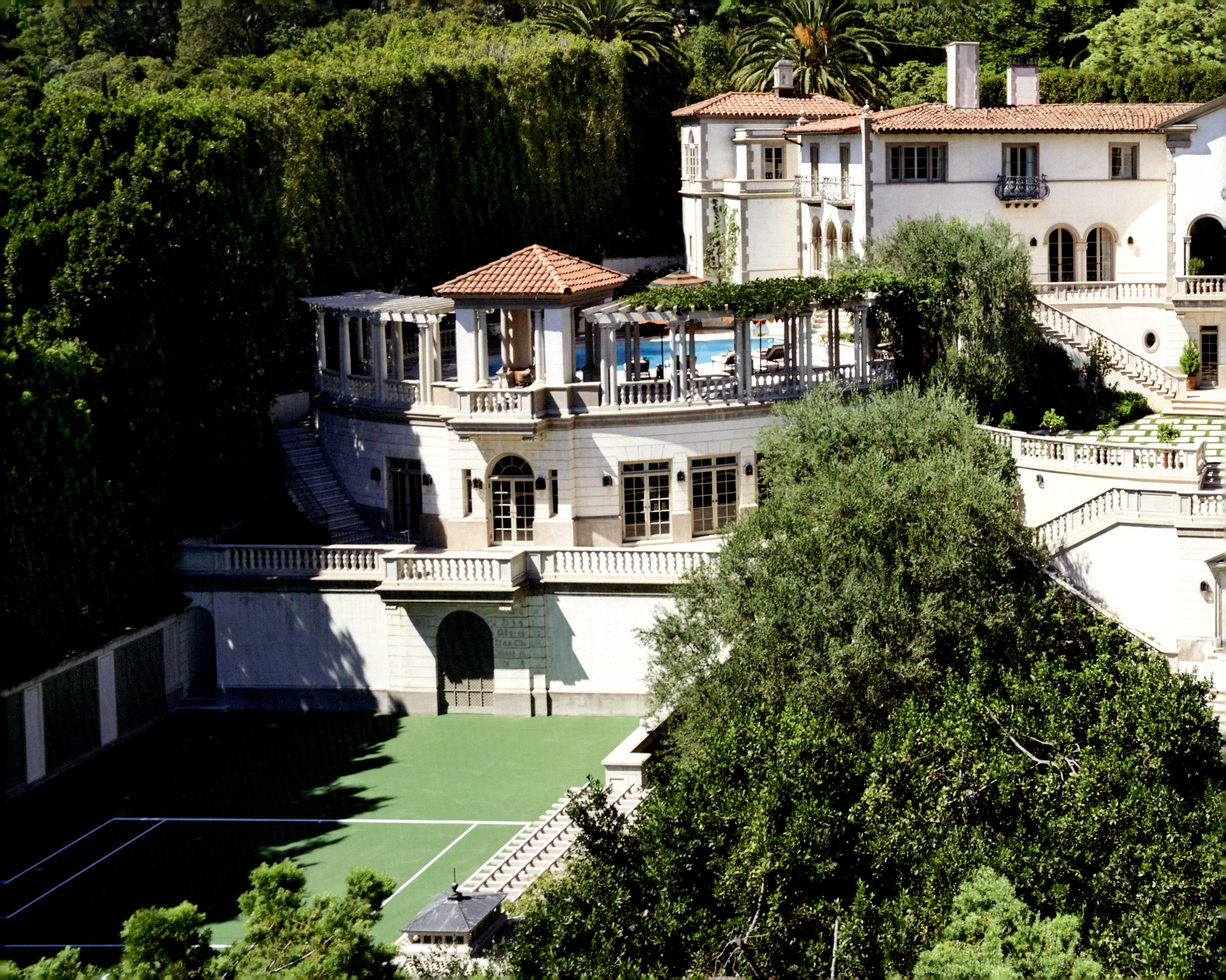

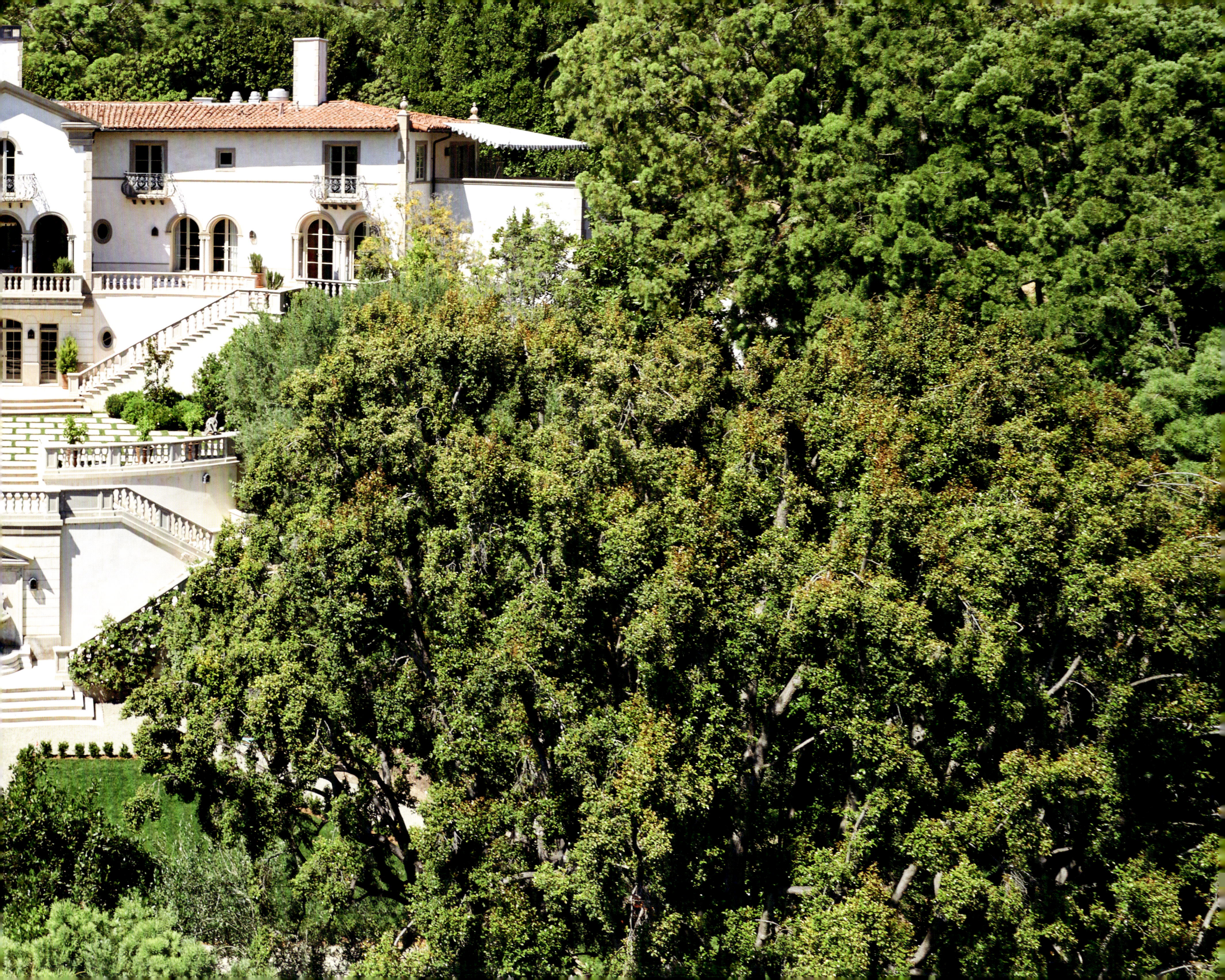

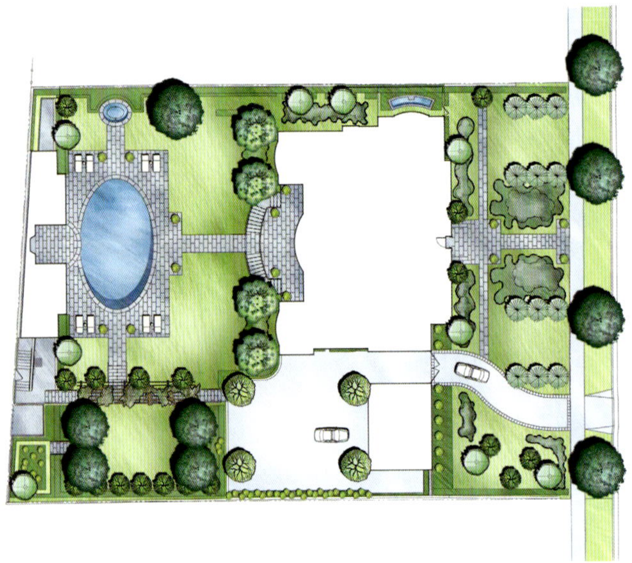

RUTHERFORD HOUSE

Beverly Hills

This elegant residence was built in 1938 for Beverly Hills property developer Edward Paul Dentzel by architect Herbert Reisenberg. Designed in a stately French Provincial style and inspired by the Art Deco screen period popular in Los Angeles during the 1930s, it became the longtime home of actress Ann Rutherford.

Since the architect was a prestigious practitioner of his day and the client became mayor of Beverly Hills and a noted developer of this period, the house was designated by the city of Beverly Hills as having historical value. We could not alter the façade, except for the removal of a metal porch that was not original, but we were able to remove the back half of the house that had been insensitively added in a 1970s remodel and shape the direction of the interiors.

The front façade has been restored to its original splendor. The painted handmade brick exterior is capped by a steeply pitched hipped roof accented by tall brick chimneys and bow windows. The primary entrance is recessed, with a paneled wood embrasure with fluted pilasters flanking the doorway, topped by an elegant scrolled pediment.

The rear and sides of the house had been altered so substantively that it was incoherent with the original design. We kept the classic oval stair hall, living room and family room in front, then literally sawed the house in half, enlarged and redesigned all the rear rooms, and added a new kitchen, dining room, master suite upstairs, basement staff quarters, an elevator, a new guest wing over the garage, and a pool house replete with gym and hammam.

The interiors by David Desmond maintain the elegant scale of the original rooms and blend Art Deco pieces with contemporary furnishings and the client's antiques and art. Along with the home's balanced proportions and tasteful appointments, the finishes and color palette are consistent throughout and create a sense of unity in all the major spaces.

The entire site—landscape design, driveways, terracing, pool—was completely reworked and reimagined, using the oval as the unifying theme. We took a very utilitarian pool house and made it into a beautiful focal point, like the famous one Paul R. Williams designed for Jay Paley. So while the house appears to be traditional, many of the treatments are decidedly "moderne" *and* modern. It is a case study in taking a historical home and updating it for the twenty-first century while honoring its past.

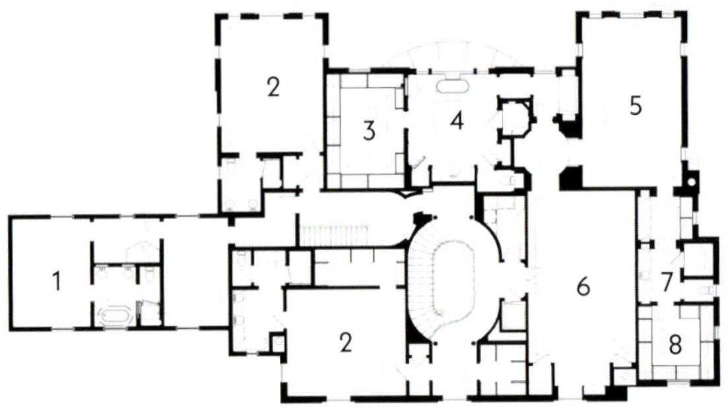

1 Guest suite
2 Bedroom
3 Her dressing room
4 Her bath
5 Master bedroom
6 Master sitting room
7 His bath
8 His dressing room

SECOND-FLOOR PLAN

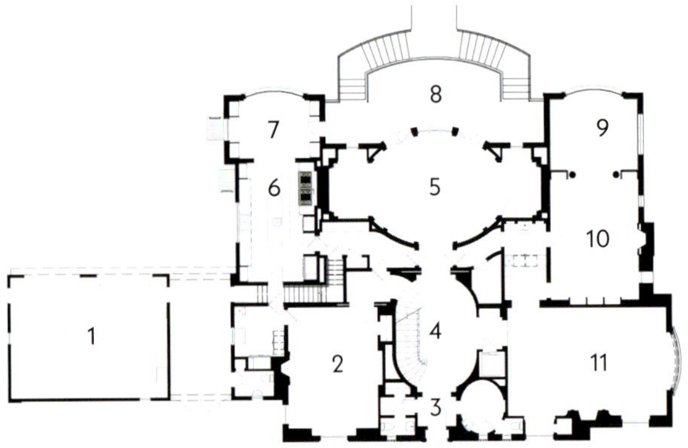

1 Garage
2 Den
3 Foyer
4 Stair hall
5 Dining room
6 Kitchen
7 Breakfast room
8 Terrace
9 Study
10 Library
11 Living room

FIRST-FLOOR PLAN

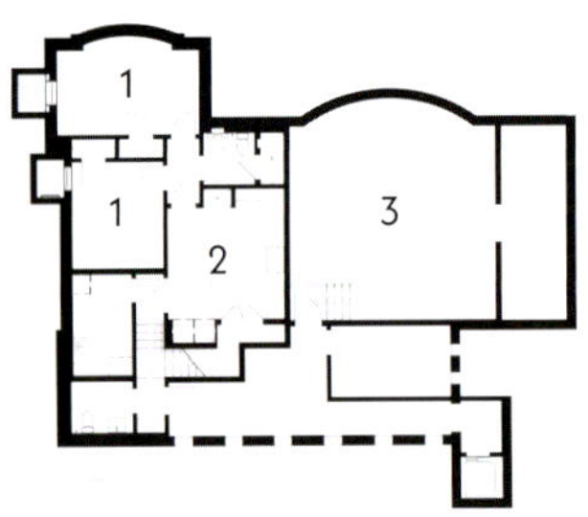

1 Staff quarters
2 Service area
3 Equipment

BASEMENT FLOOR PLAN

0 8 16 32 ft

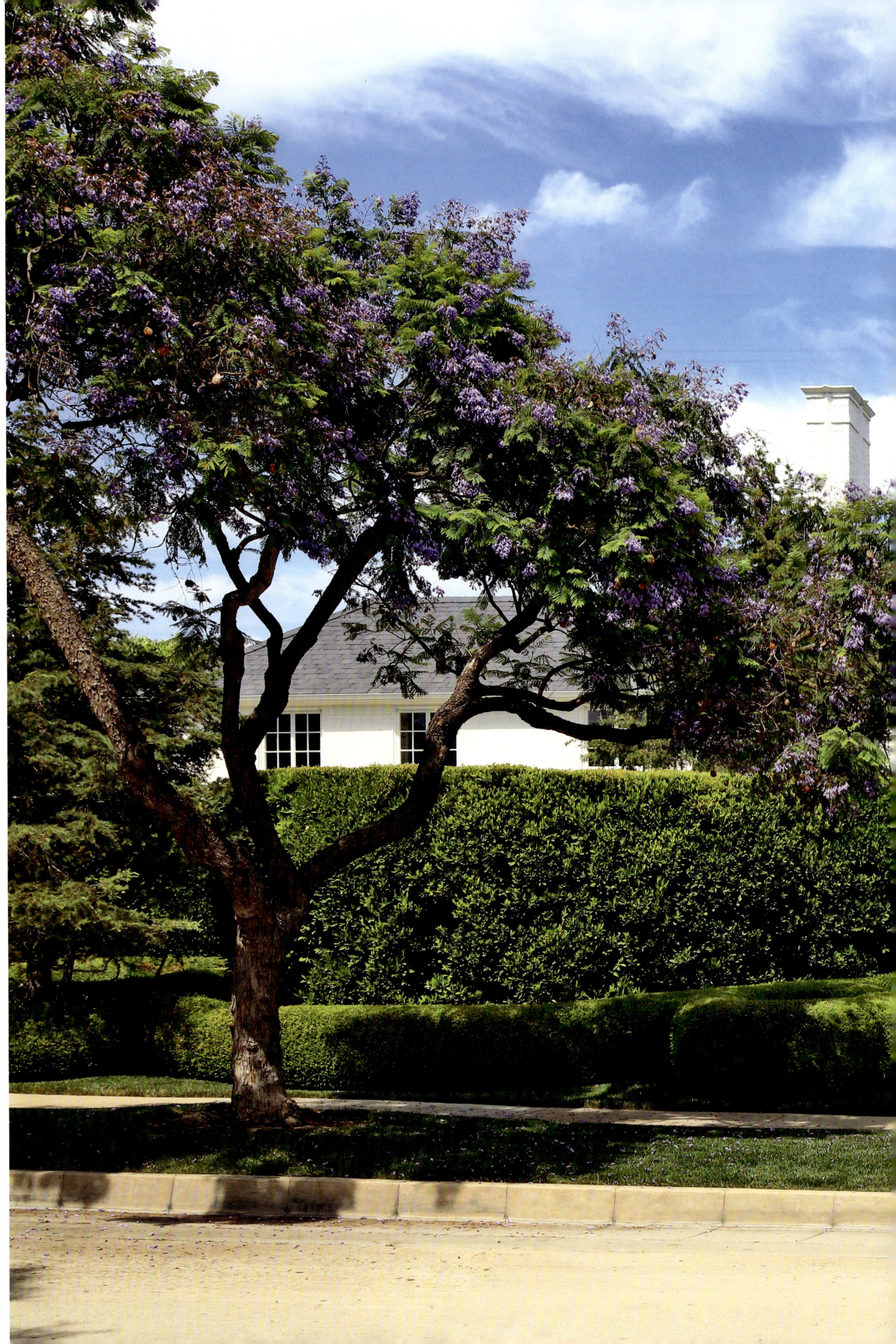

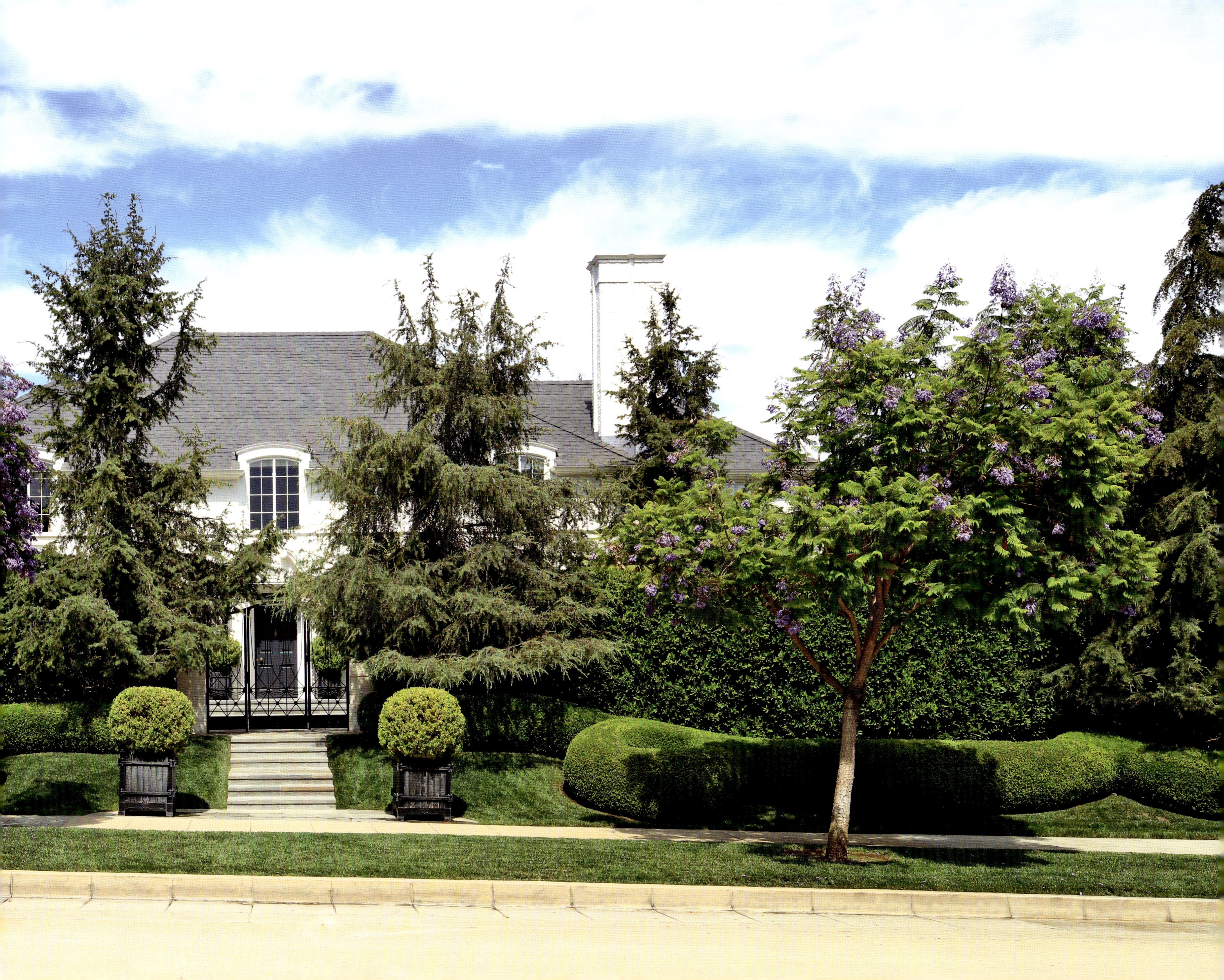

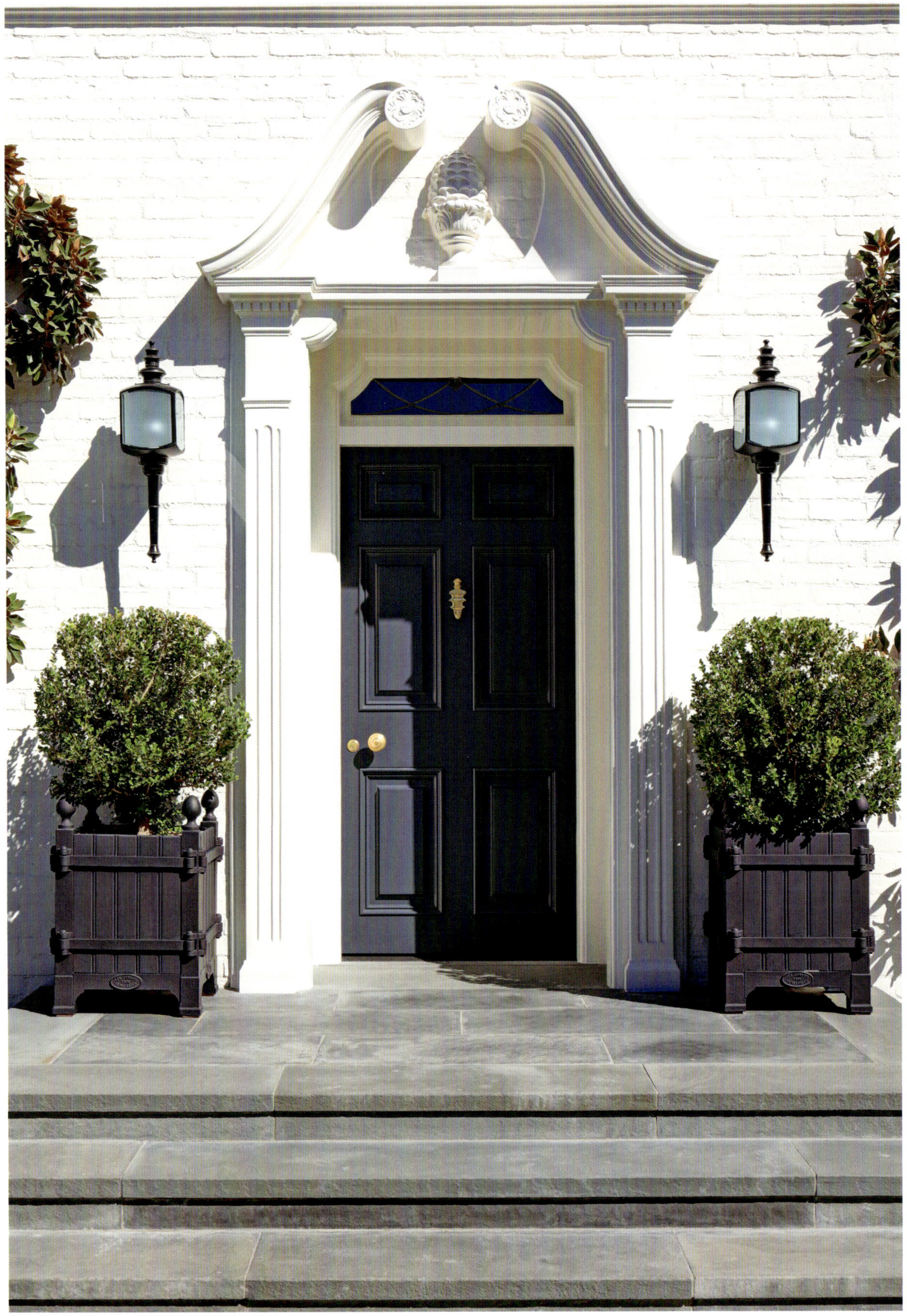

PREVIOUS PAGES: *A steeply pitched roof, tall chimneys, handmade white brick façade, and shallow boxed eaves distinguish this newly renovated 1938 residence that is restrained French Provincial on the outside and glamorous Art Deco/Art Moderne inside. Among the new additions was a guest wing above the garage at left.*

LEFT: *An elegant plaster scroll bracket curls over the recessed front door.*

OPPOSITE LEFT: *The circular ladies powder room, designed by Craig Wright with fluted walls and black marble and onyx floor, was based on Paul R. Williams's design for Saks Fifth Avenue in Beverly Hills. The oval bronze table was made in Paris, and the stool was based on one in a Jean Harlow movie.*

OPPOSITE RIGHT: *This classic oval stair hall with original stair railing and a dramatic rock crystal sunburst skylight and chandelier set the overall oval theme that was repeated in the home's bow windows, terrace, knot garden hedges, and pool.*

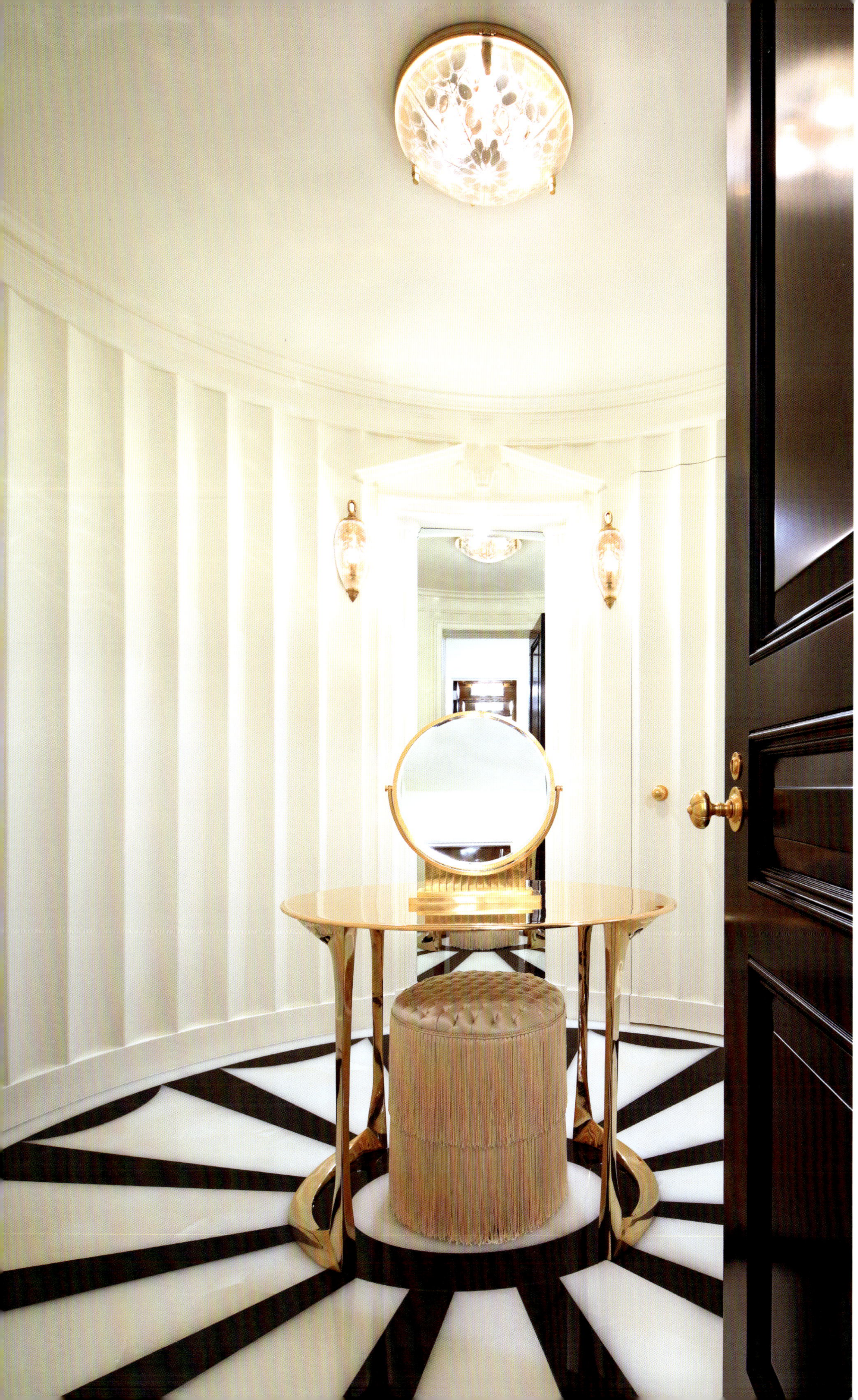
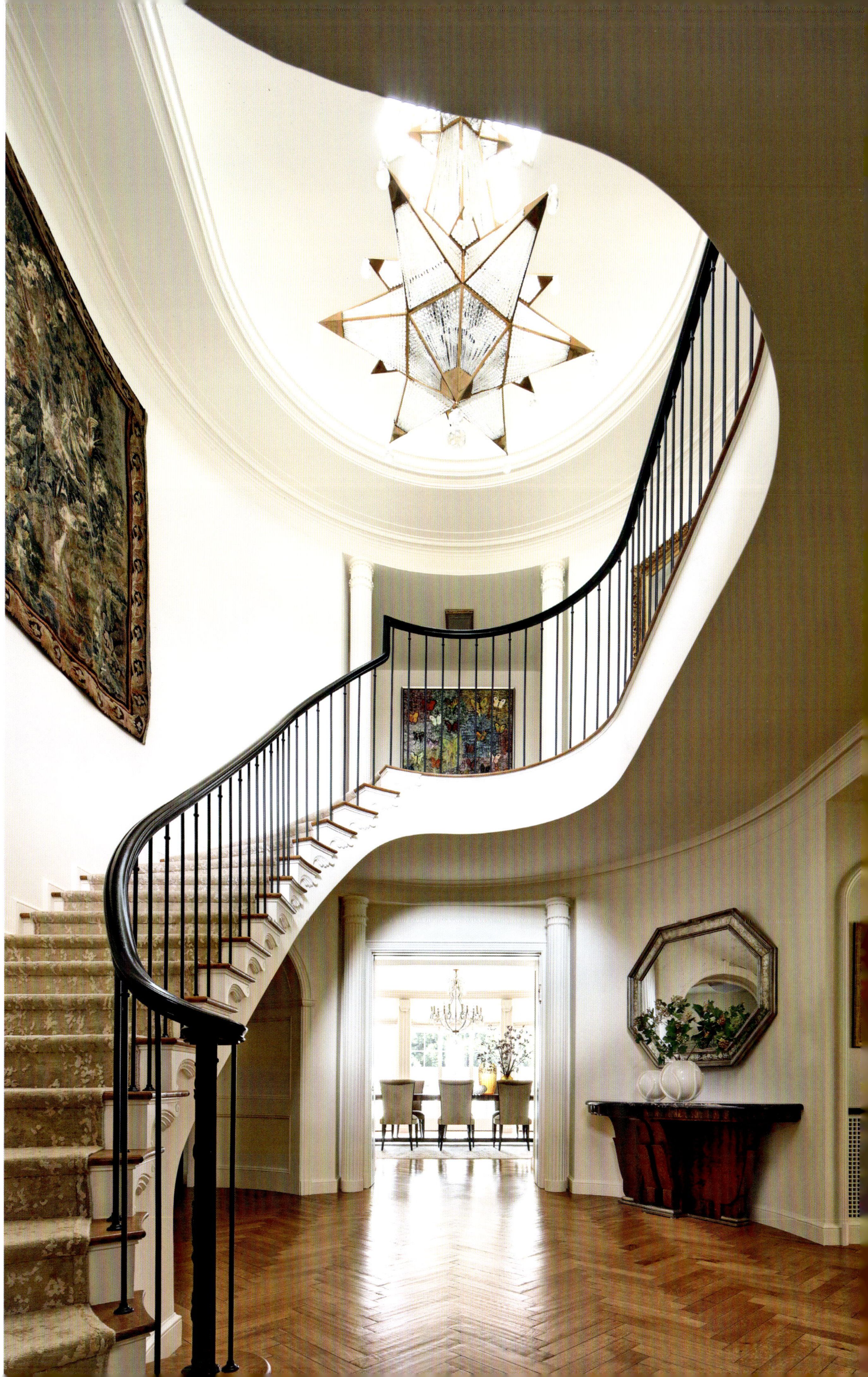

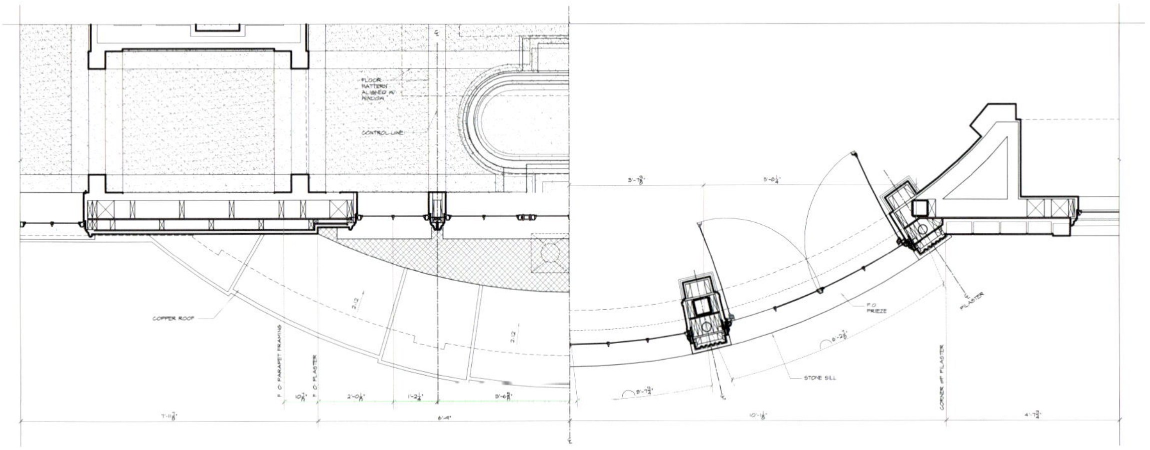

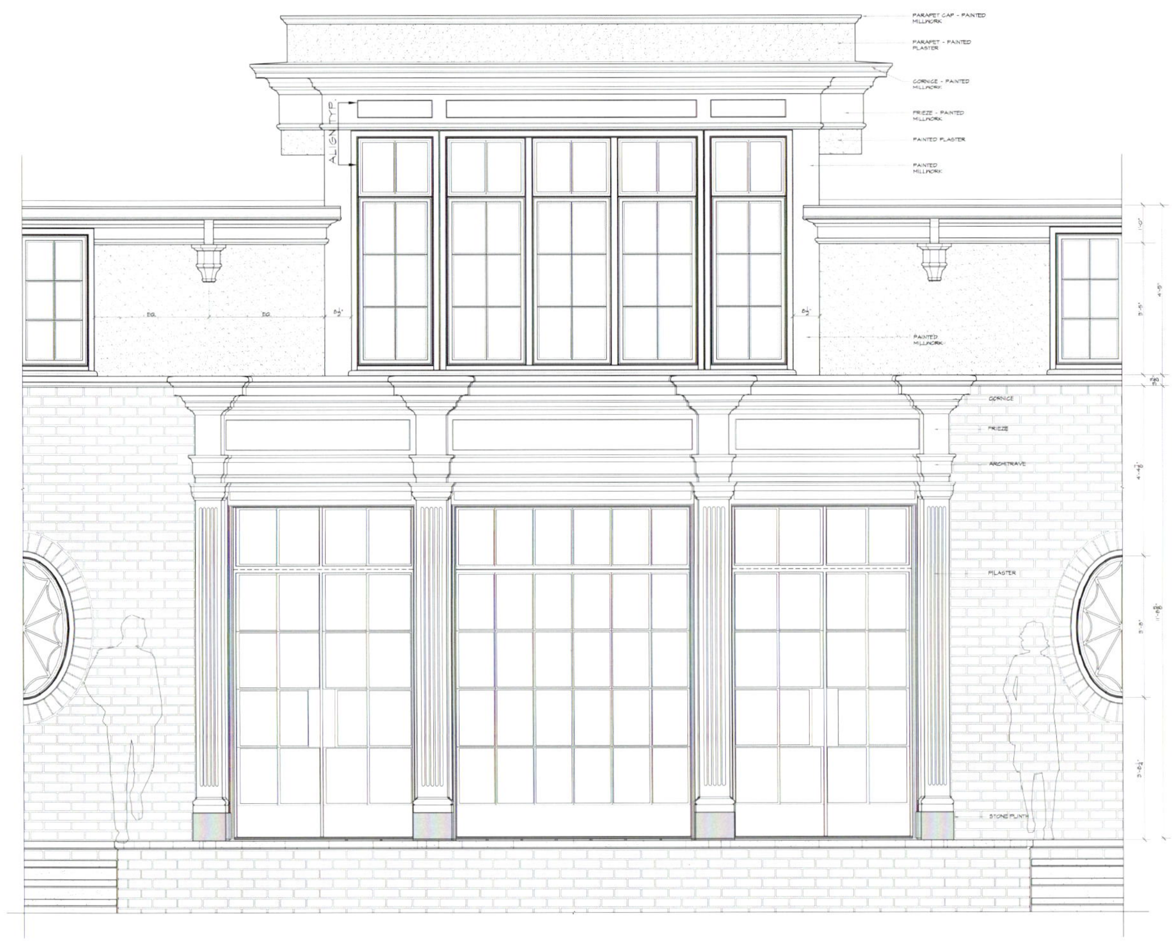

ABOVE: *Drawings of the new bay window in the dining room.*

RIGHT: *The entire back half of the house, which had been altered in the 1970s, was rebuilt to make the residence one cohesive whole. For the Art Moderne elliptical dining room (with the bay window that overlooks the pool pavilion and matching end alcoves with illuminated hammered-iron screens after designs by Edgar Brandt), interior designer David Desmond brought in a 17-foot-long macassar ebony dining table that can seat twenty.*

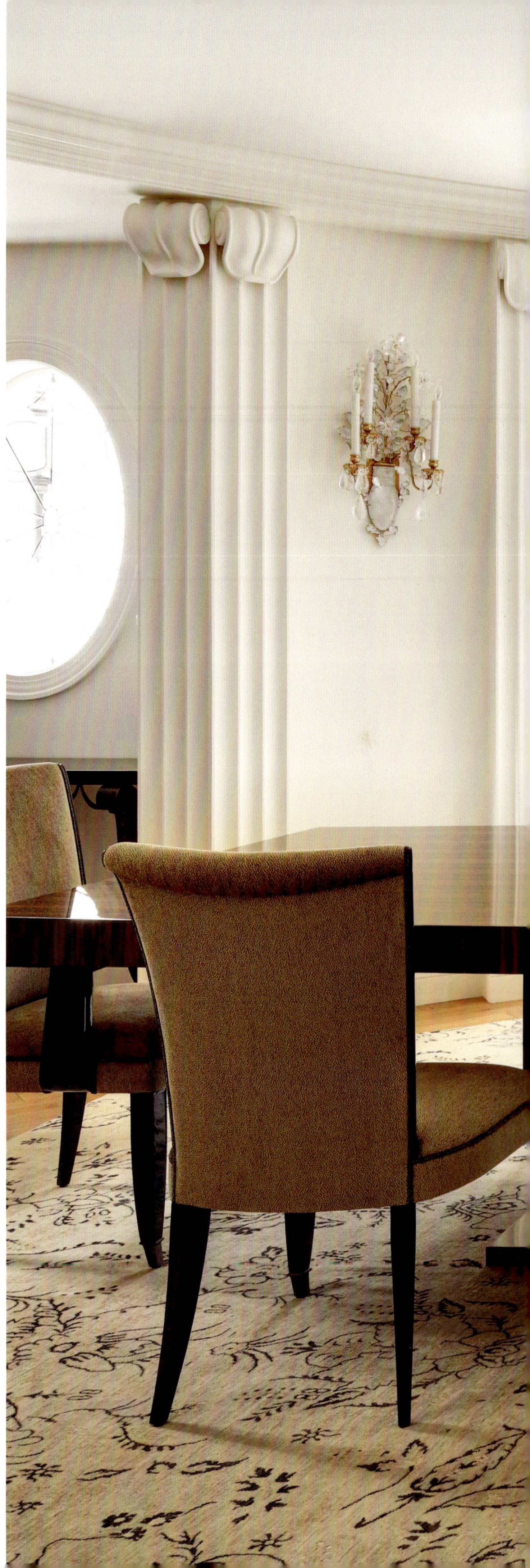

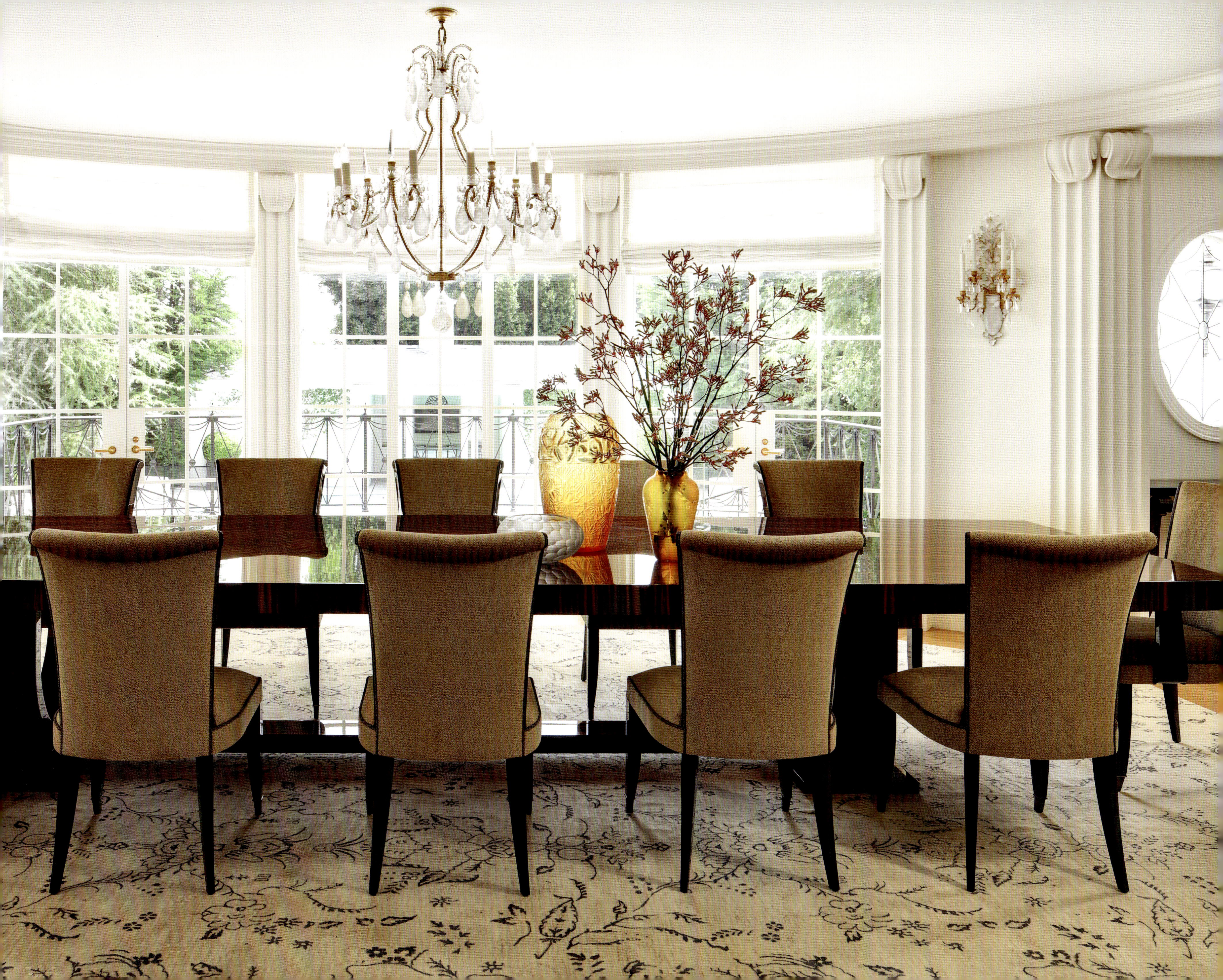

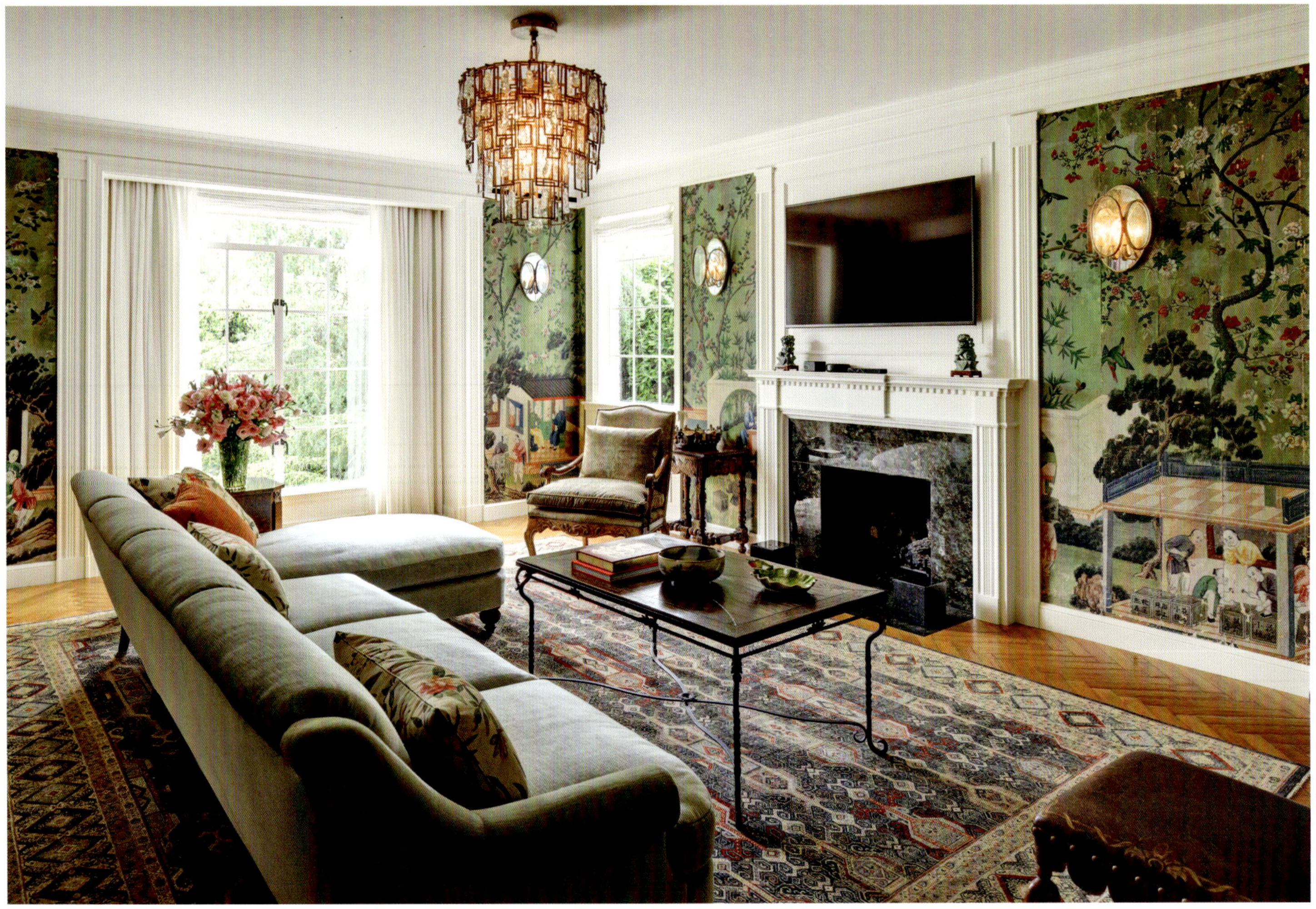

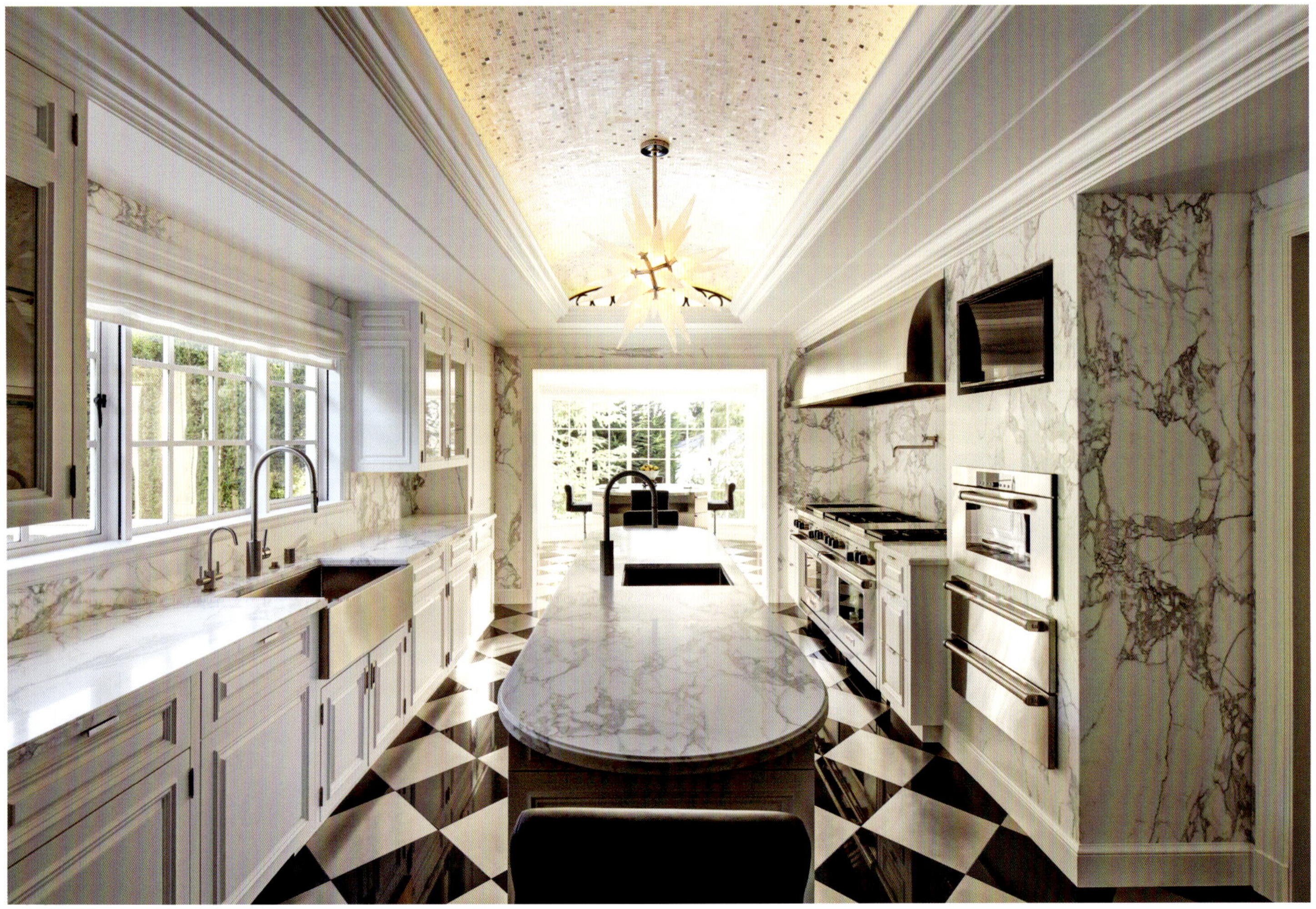

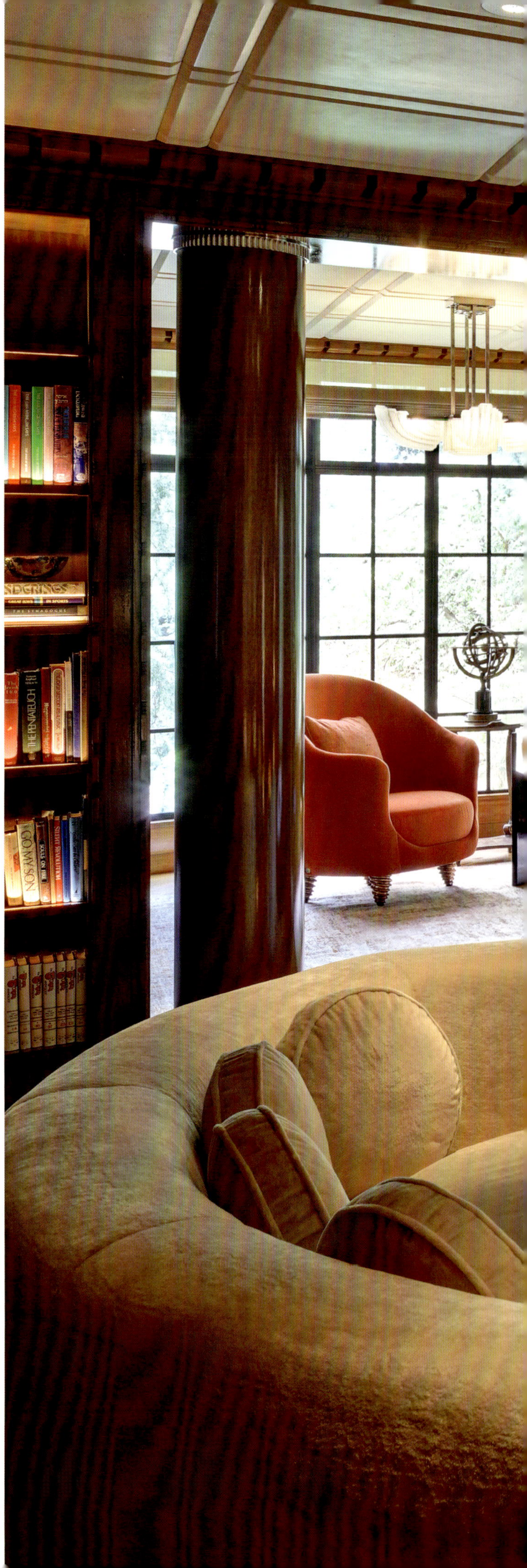

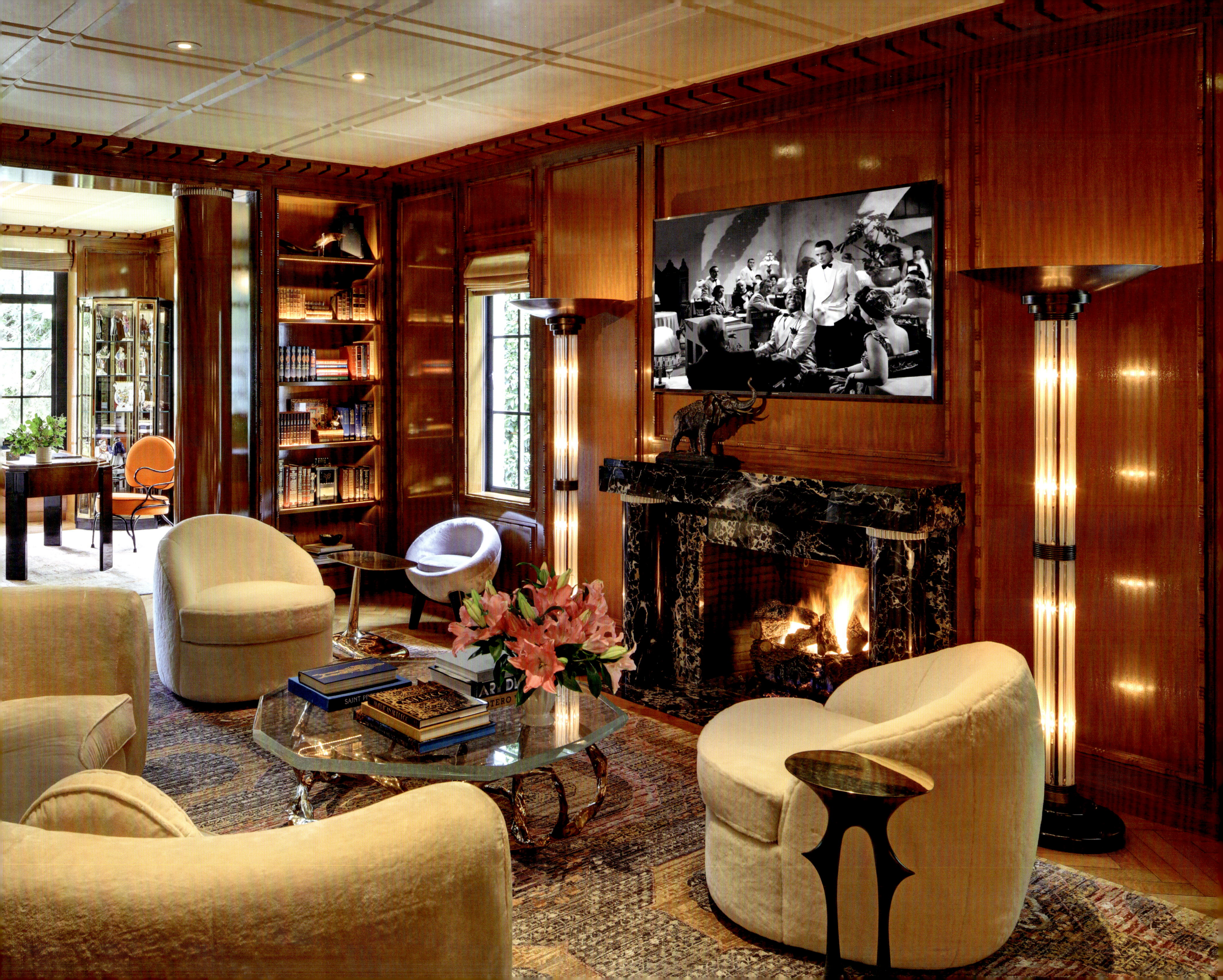

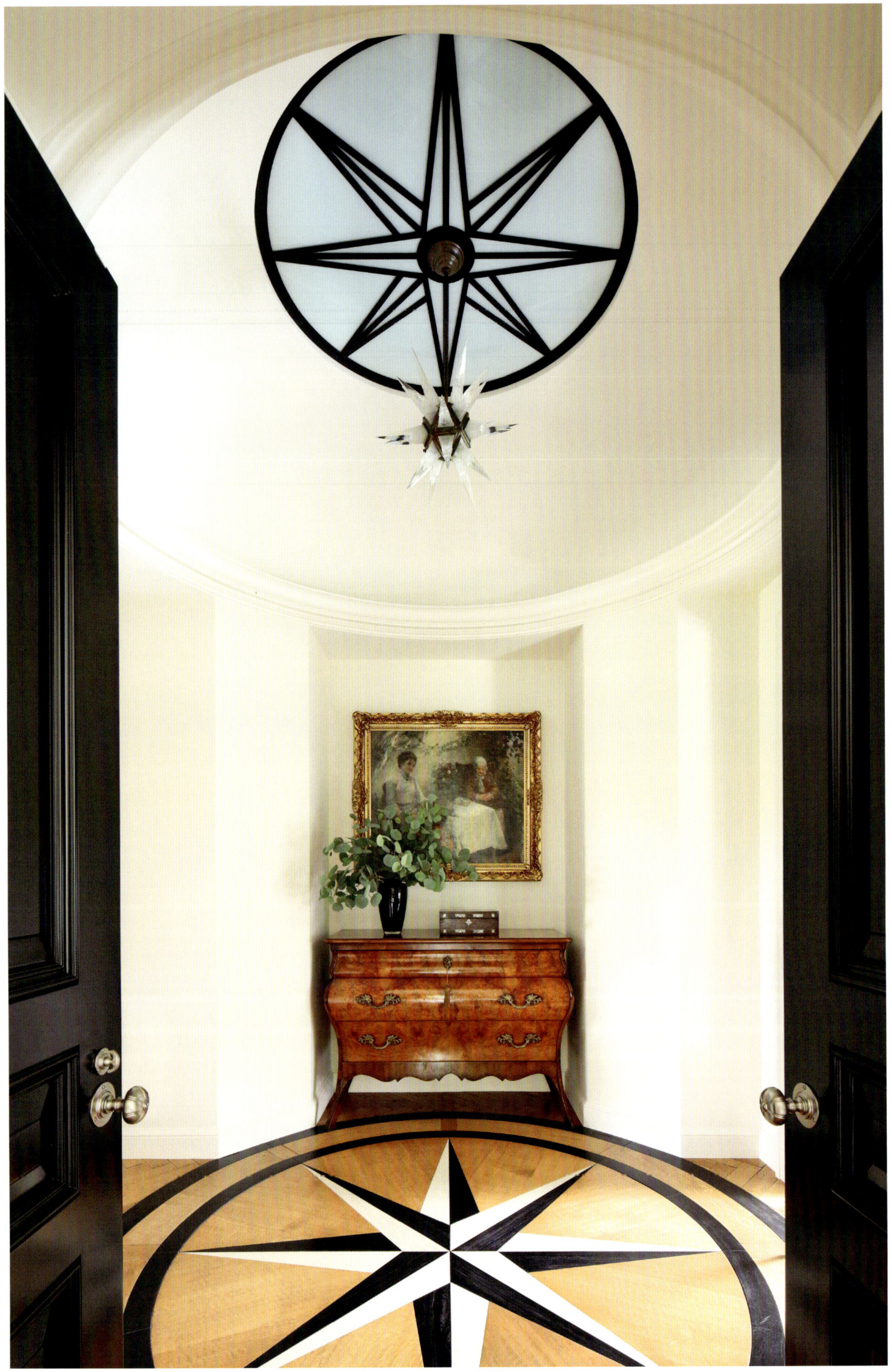

PREVIOUS PAGES, TOP LEFT: *Rare eighteenth-century Chinese Export wallpaper used by the Doheny family in their various Beverly Hills homes lines the family room.* BOTTOM LEFT: *The black granite, white marble, and stainless-steel floors, walls, and ceiling in the kitchen and breakfast area give the illusion of height in a long, narrow space.* RIGHT: *In the Art Deco wood-paneled library and office is a collection of contemporary furnishings by India Mahdavi, Paul Mathieu, Herve Van der Straeten, Patrick Naggar, and Elizabeth Garouste.*

LEFT: *An inlaid wood floor and a skylight that was inspired by the central stair hall fixture, highlight the circular domed vestibule, which is the entrance to the master suite.*

OPPOSITE: *One of the home's most dazzling features, and one of its most complex installations, is the rock crystal sunburst skylight and crystal chandelier hanging over the stair hall.*

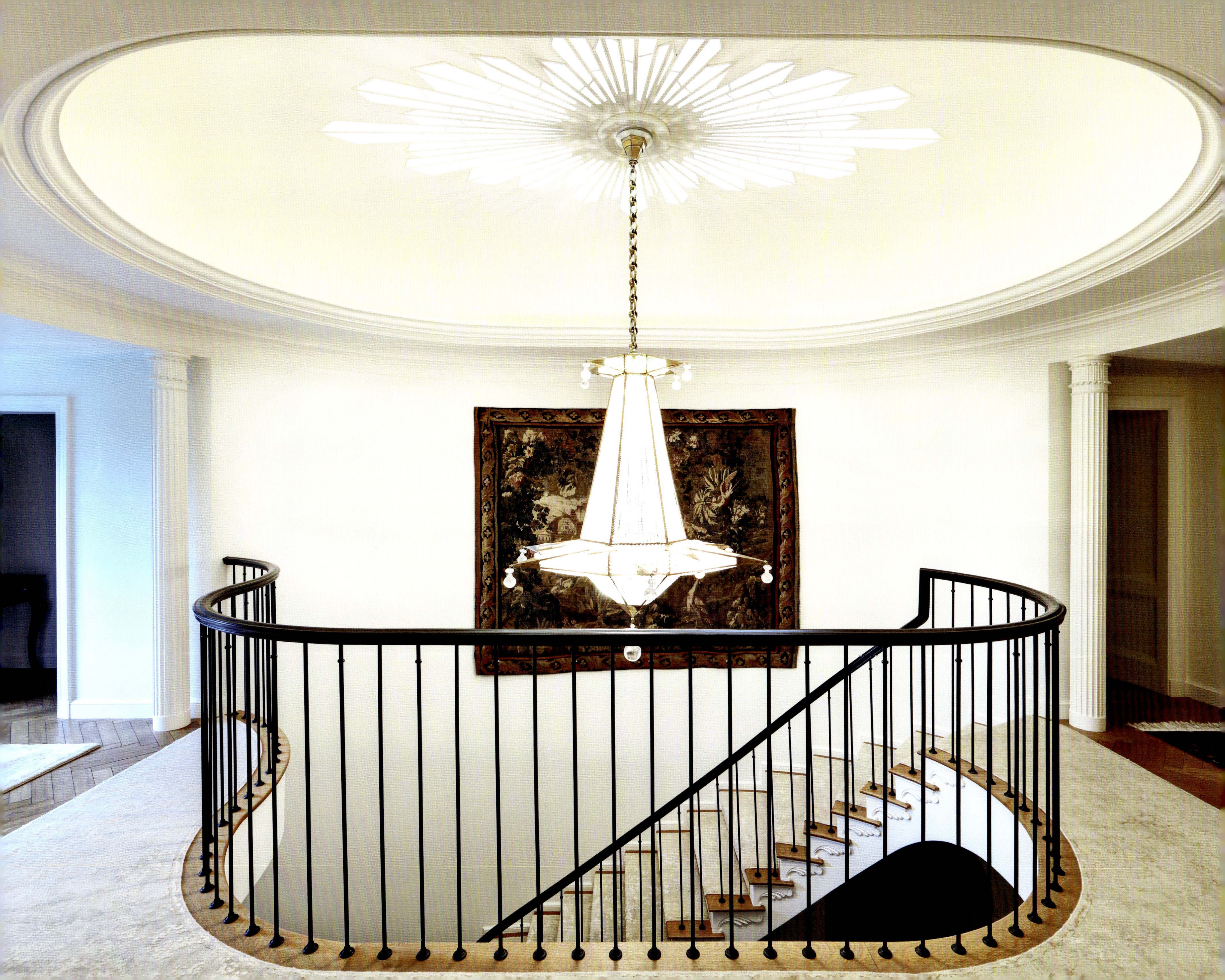

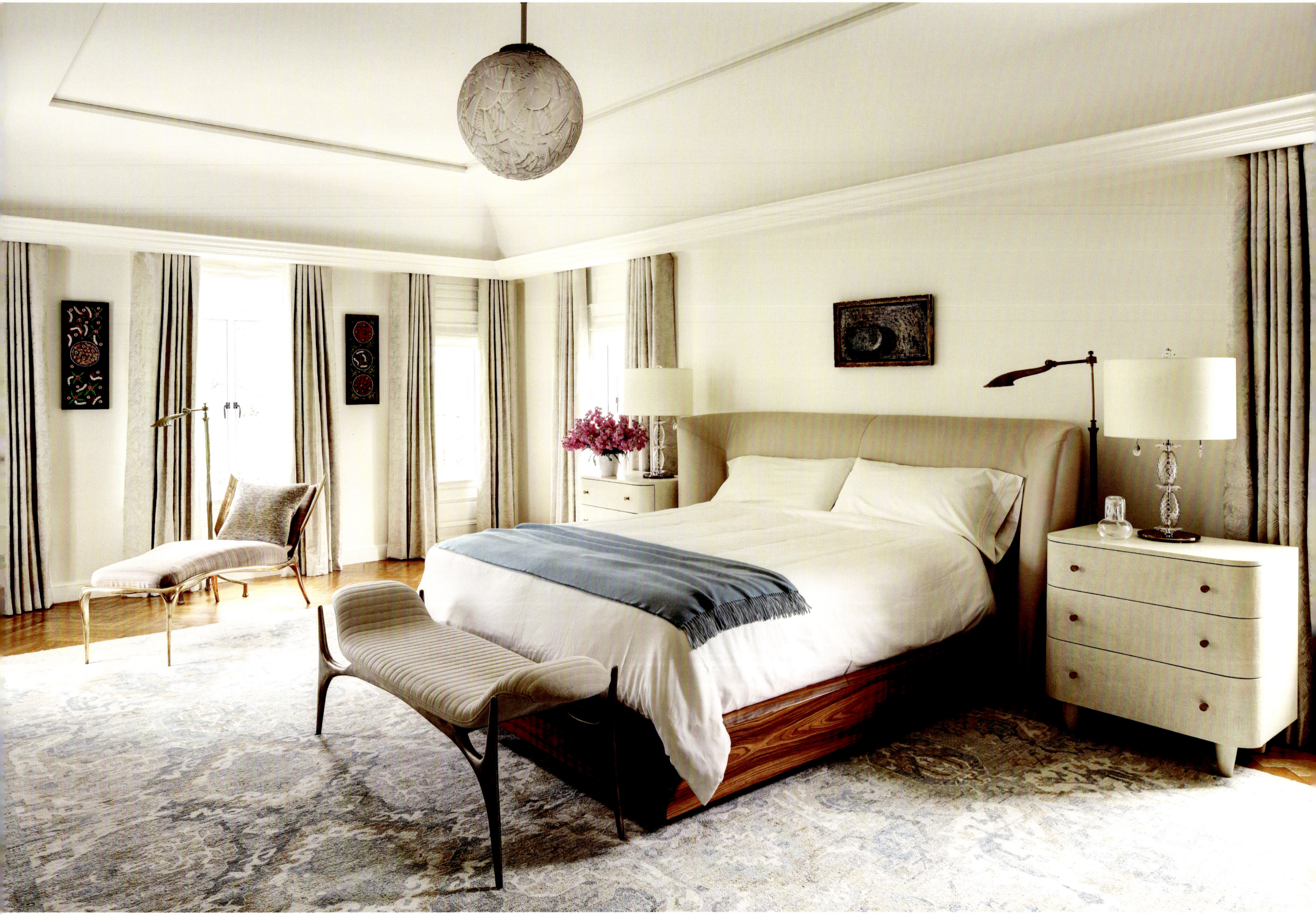

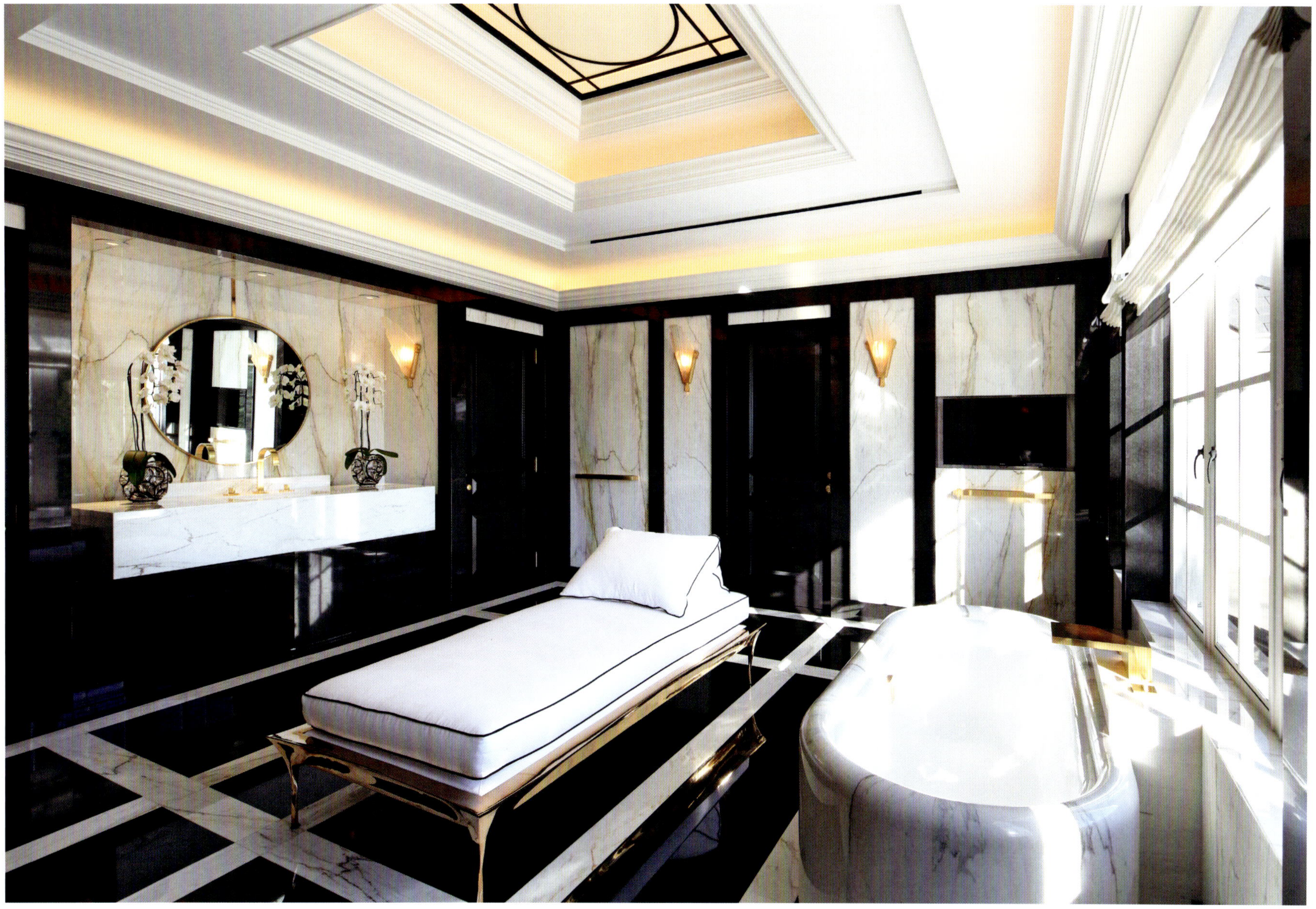

OPPOSITE: *A quietly sumptuous master bedroom blends a polished bronze bench by Vladimir Kagan and a white-gold chaise longue by Paul Mathieu with a custom rosewood and embossed leather bed and the client's art collection.*

ABOVE: *Clad in black and white marble with gold accents and with a white milk glass lay light that looks like a skylight, the master bath is an Art Deco riff on French architect Joseph Dirand's Mahal bath in Paris.*

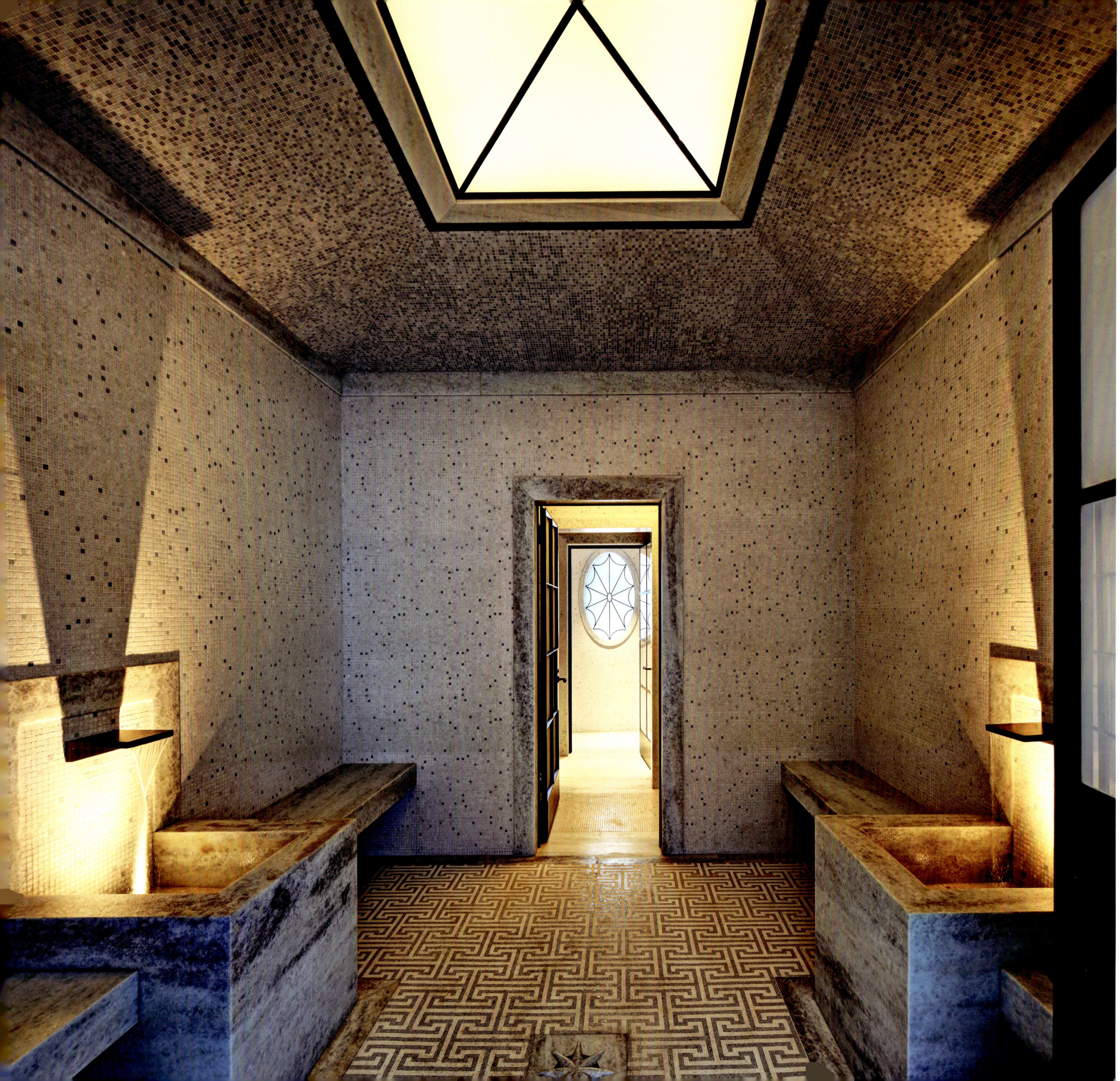

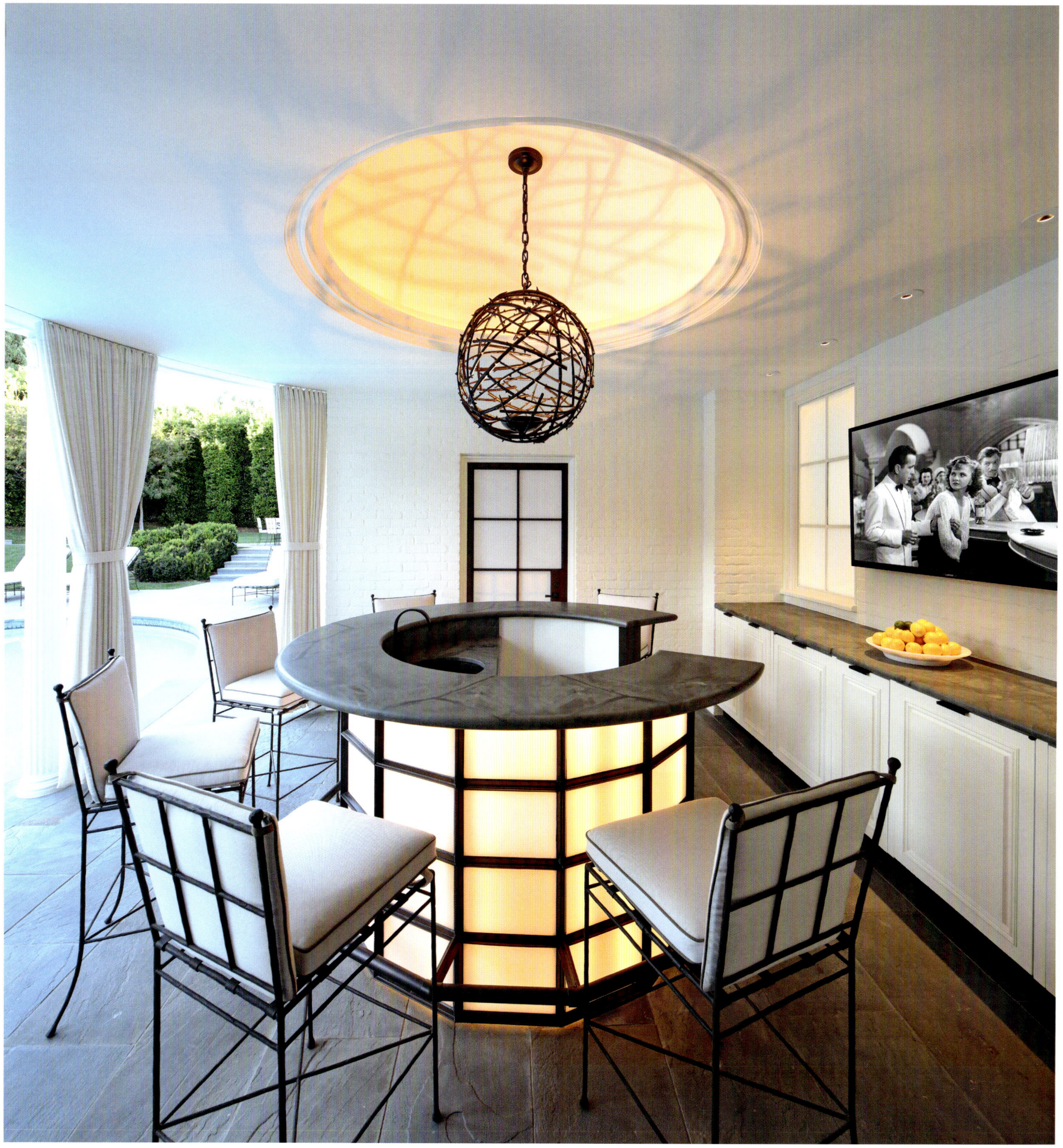

OPPOSITE: *Inside the pool pavilion on one side is the hammam, a Middle Eastern-inspired spa with marble mosaics, two fountains, a steam room, shower, and dressing room.*

RIGHT: *In the center of the pool house is the loggia that projects into the pool.*

FOLLOWING PAGES, LEFT: *The pool house with decorative oval windows is topped by a lit cupola and contains a lounge, bar, gym, and hammam. Both the oval pool house and pool, which acts as a reflecting pool by day, were based on Paul R. Williams's renowned design for Jay Paley's house in Beverly Hills.* RIGHT: *The new rear façade of the house, with the addition of the central bay window in the dining room, is now consistent with the front.*

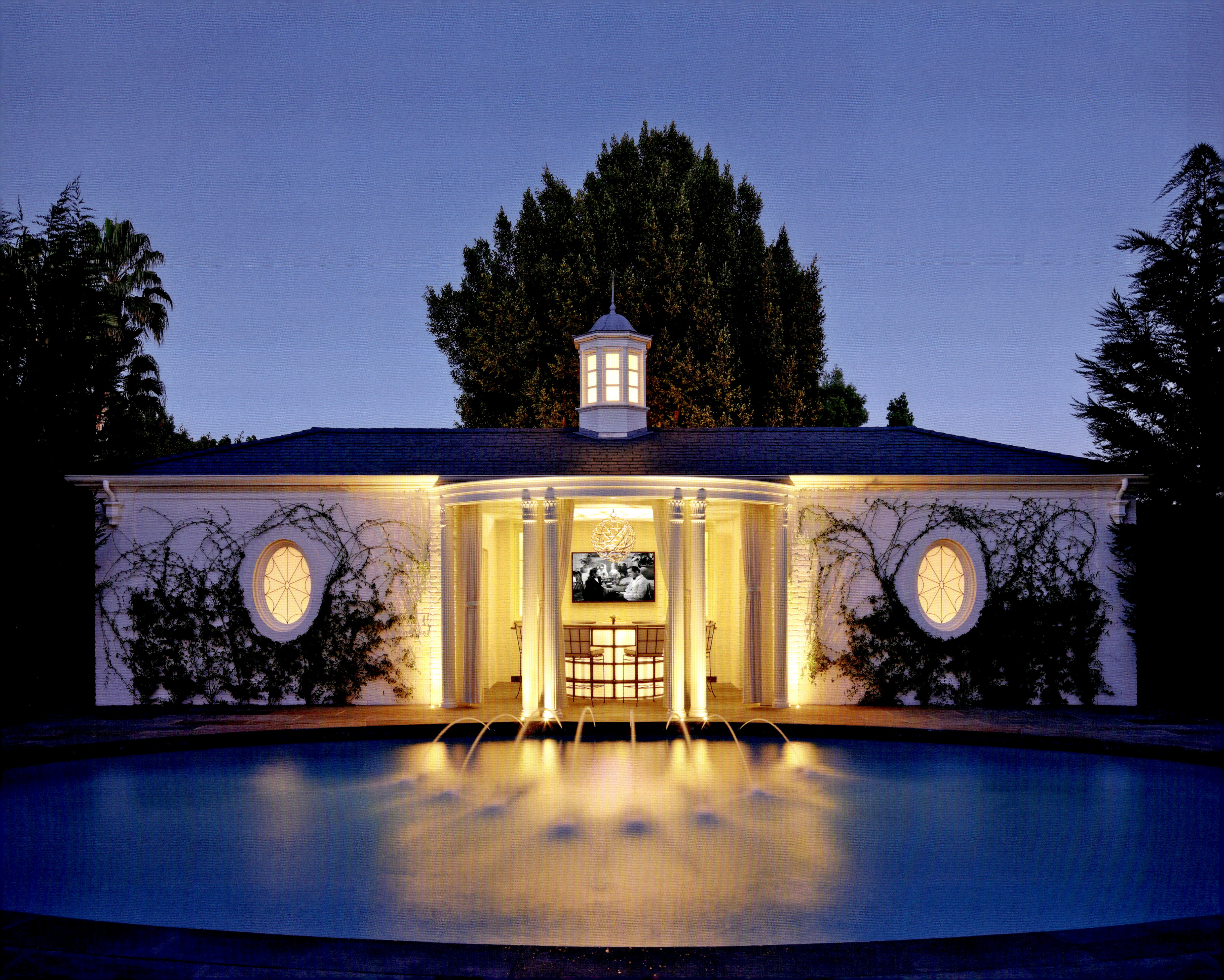

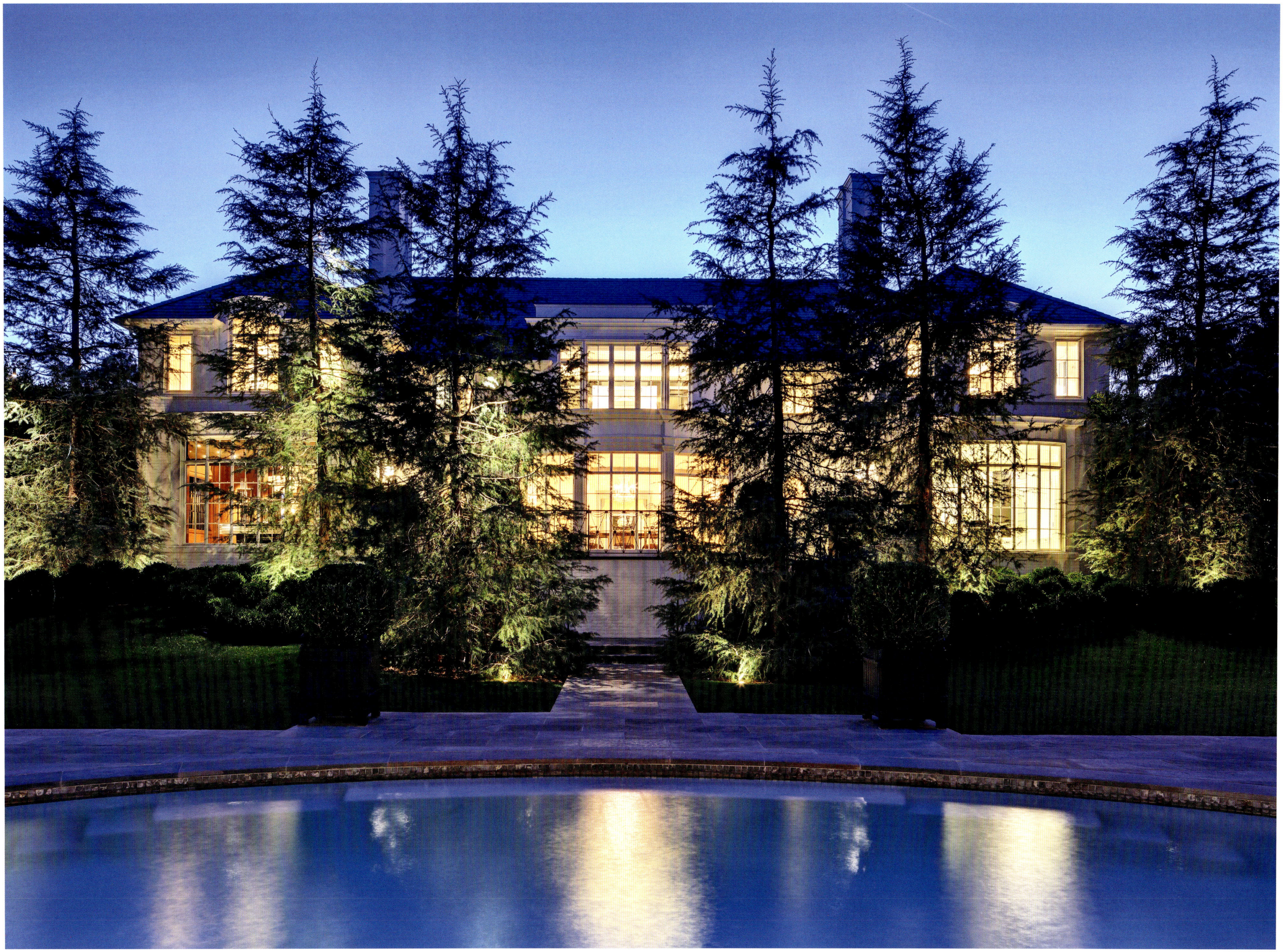

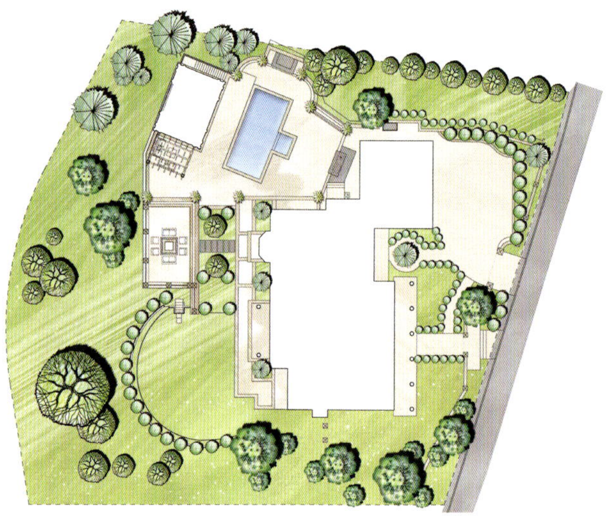

COLONIAL REVIVAL POOL HOUSE

Bel-Air

The challenge was to design a new pool house for an existing estate that wouldn't detract from the original Colonial Revival residence. Our solution was to echo the strong Doric-inspired columns of the main house with pilasters.

Sited on an existing pool deck with panoramic city views, the new pool house ties in with the character of the main house while becoming its own destination space with lounge seating around a fireplace, television, bar, fire pit, and outdoor dining.

We redesigned the pool terrace, continued the brick paving, added brick piers with low railings, and created a pergola off the view side of the pavilion that provides the necessary shaded seating for outdoor dining and avoids the need for umbrellas. Heaters were mounted discreetly on the inside of the beams.

Grand columns at the main house entrance helped us envision the pool house as a temple-like open pavilion with one solid wall at the north side accommodating a fireplace and cabinetry. Three other sides facing the pool and view have pilasters with French doors and door pockets so that the pavilion can be opened up completely or made to look like a loggia. We felt that the architectural details should be complementary to the main house, such that the pilaster details are similarly classically inspired but employ features and materials that are obviously a product of the modern era with a metal roof and steel windows and doors.

Inside, the idea was to create an updated traditional space using a simple but classic tray ceiling, limestone fireplace, built-in cabinetry, and a streamlined décor. Furnishings are by Nancy Corzine.

The pool house has a solid presence, anchored by the Doric pilasters and entablature, but it is also very light due to its transparency. At night there is a soft, romantic glow from the lighting, which makes the interiors stand out in greater detail.

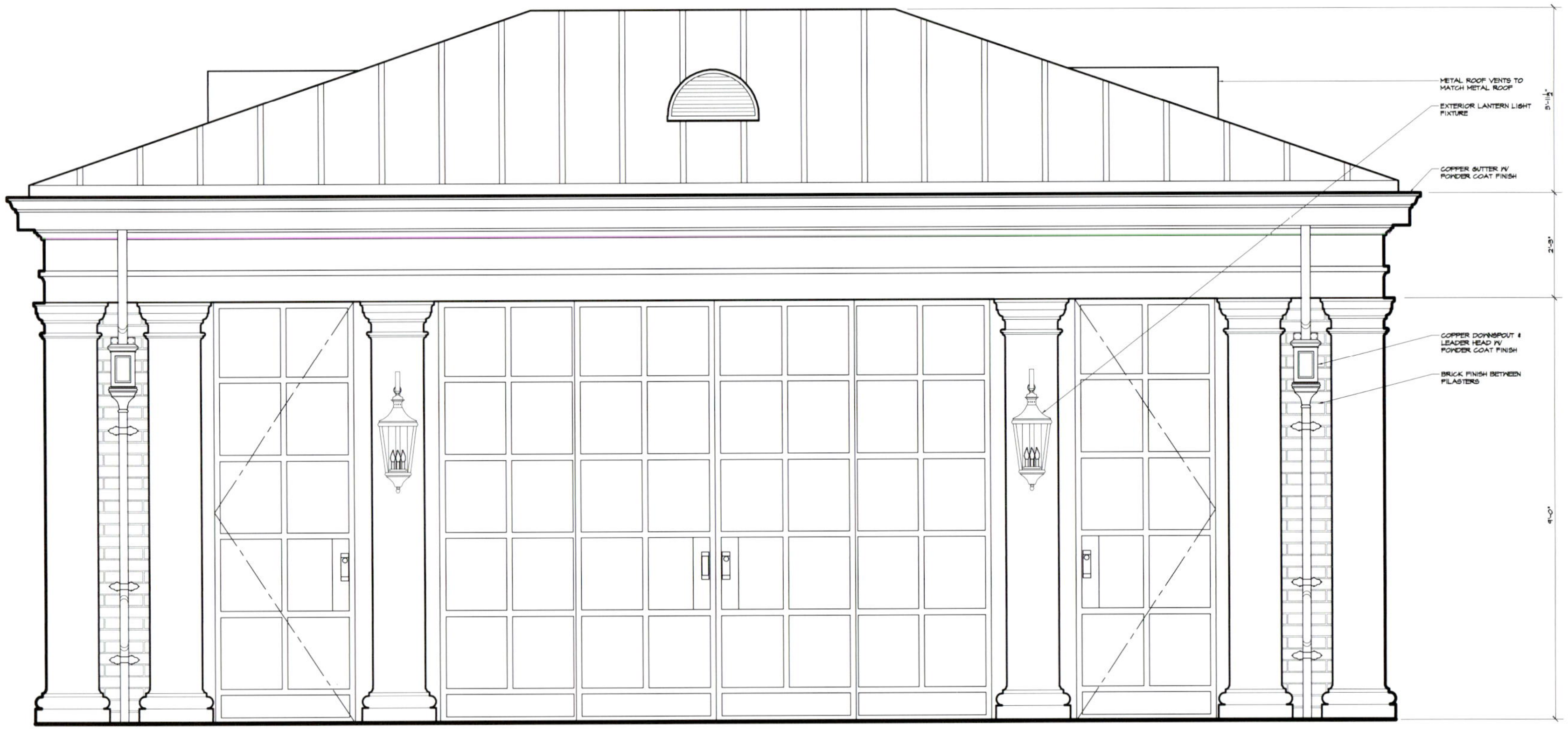

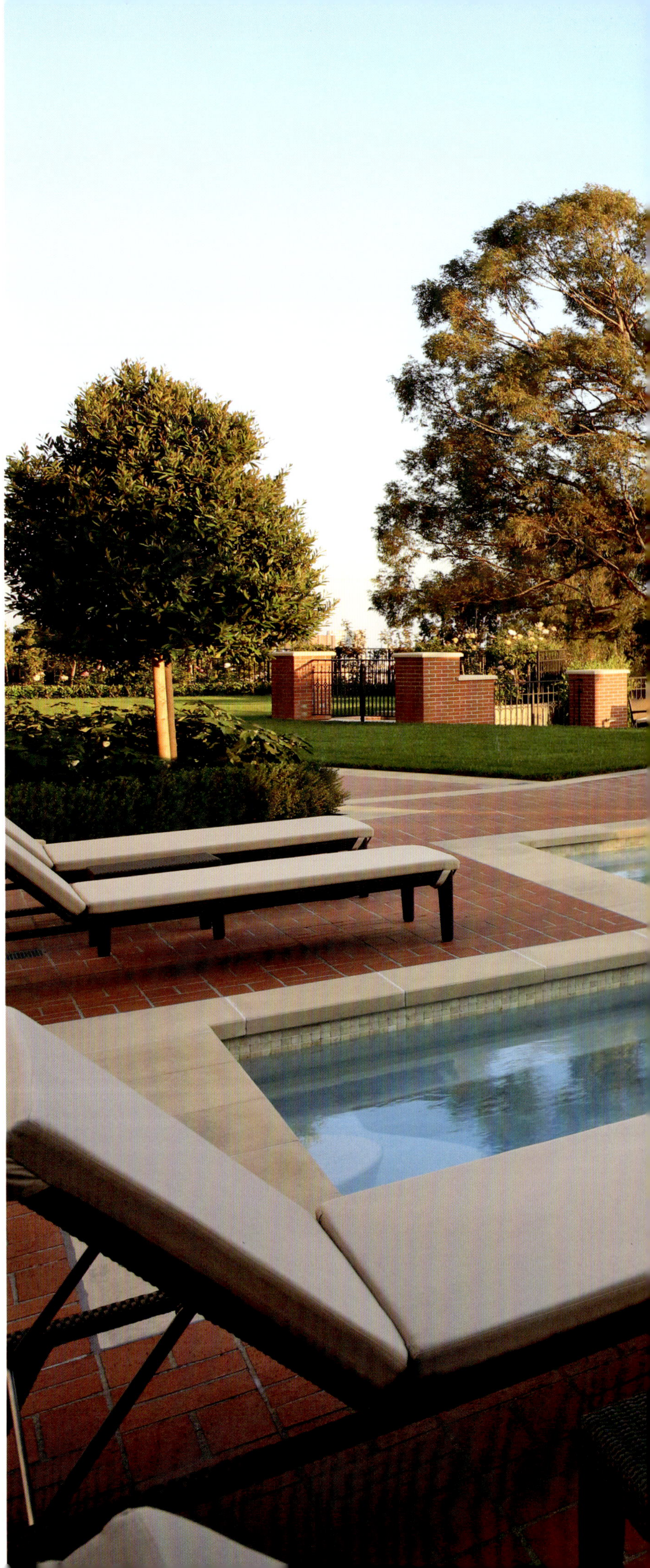

ABOVE: *A drawing of the pool house's exterior pilasters.*

RIGHT: *To maintain continuity with the Colonial Revival main residence, the new pool house was envisaged as a temple-like open pavilion in the Doric order that retains the same overall feel. Three sides of the pavilion have pilasters with French doors and door pockets so that the pavilion can be opened completely or made to look like a loggia.*

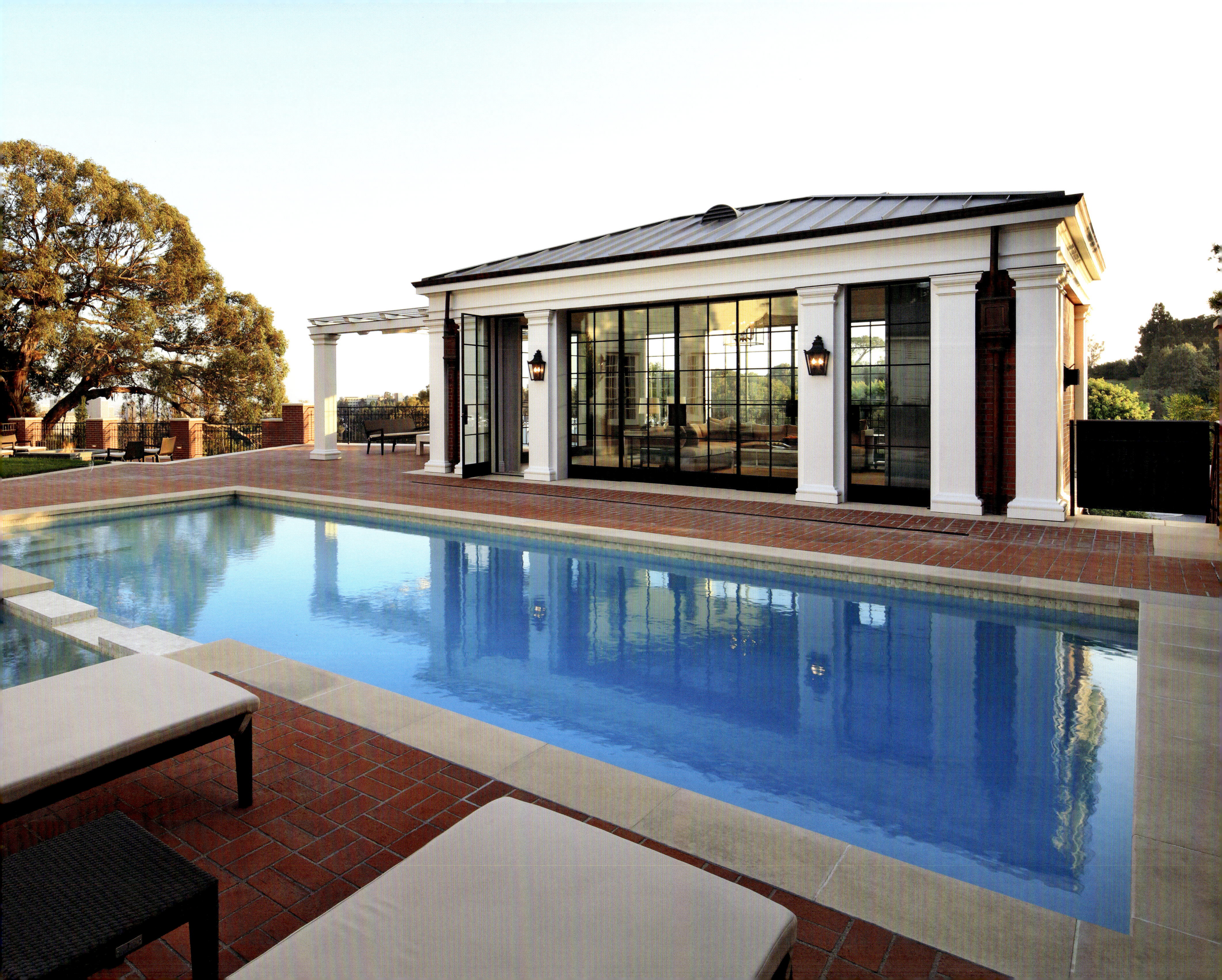

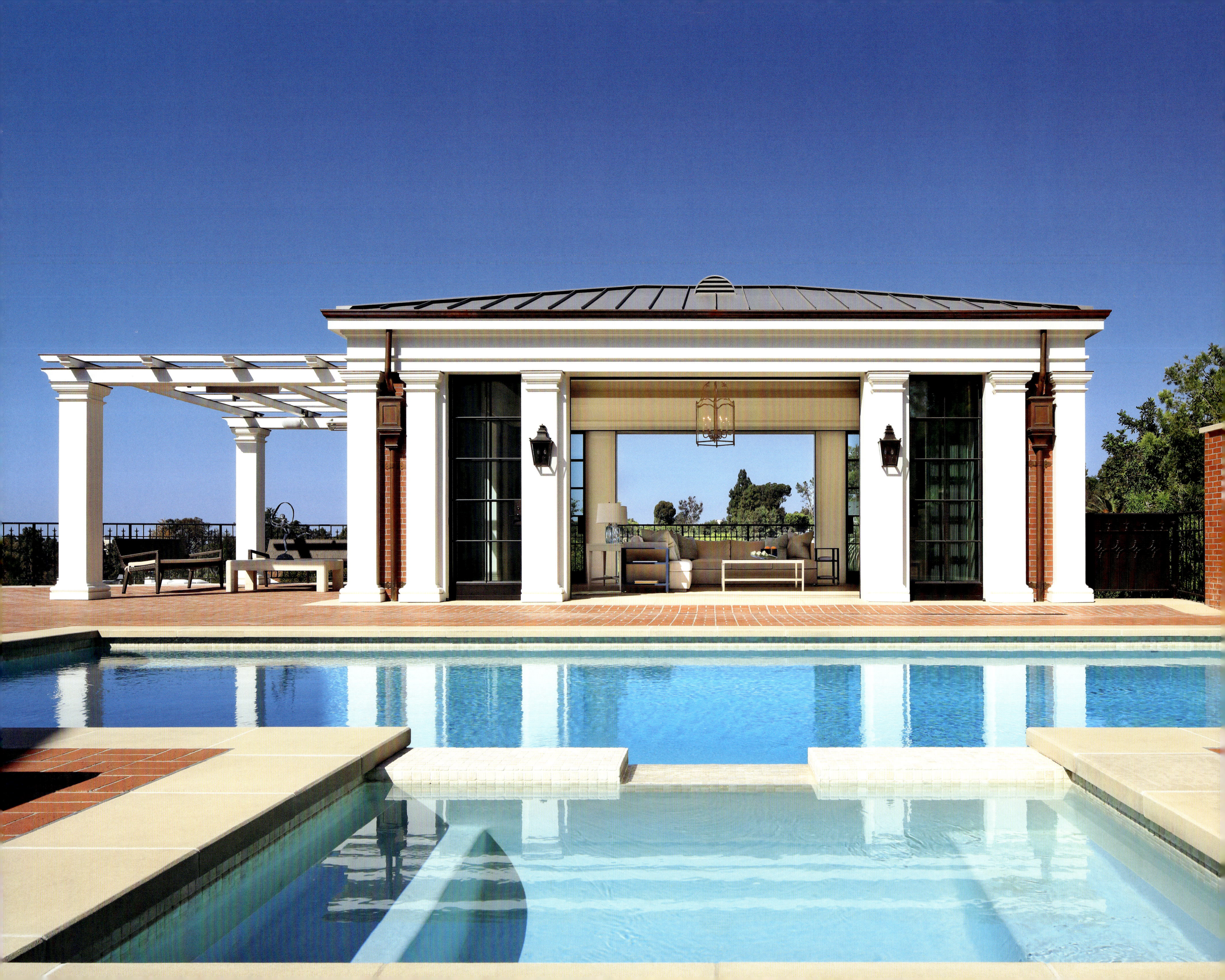

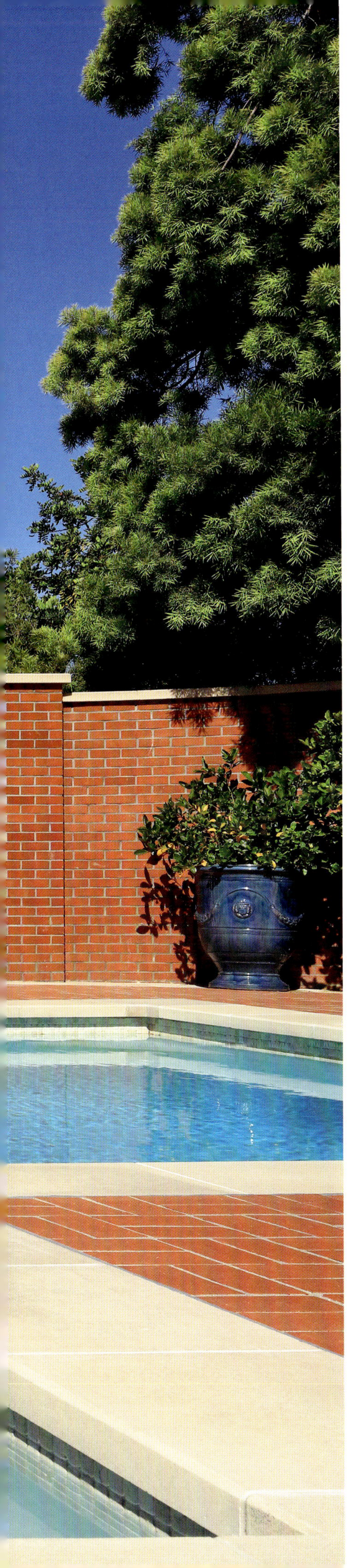

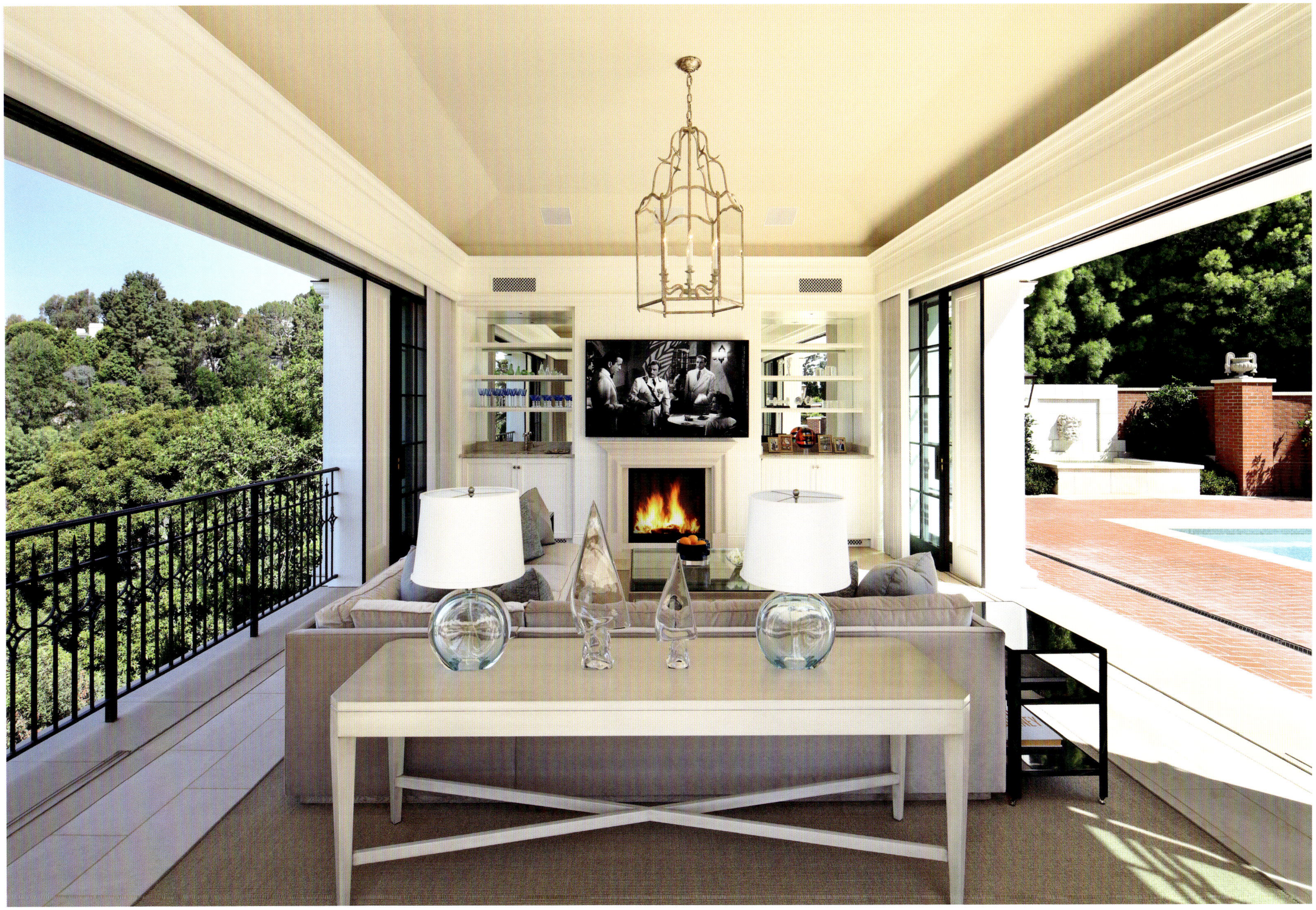

LEFT: *We used the footprint of the existing pool deck, continued the brick paving, and added a pergola off the city-view end of the pavilion for dining.*

ABOVE: *The pavilion's interior is an updated traditional space with a classic tray ceiling, limestone fireplace, and built-in cabinetry on the solid wall, and streamlined furnishings by Nancy Corzine.*

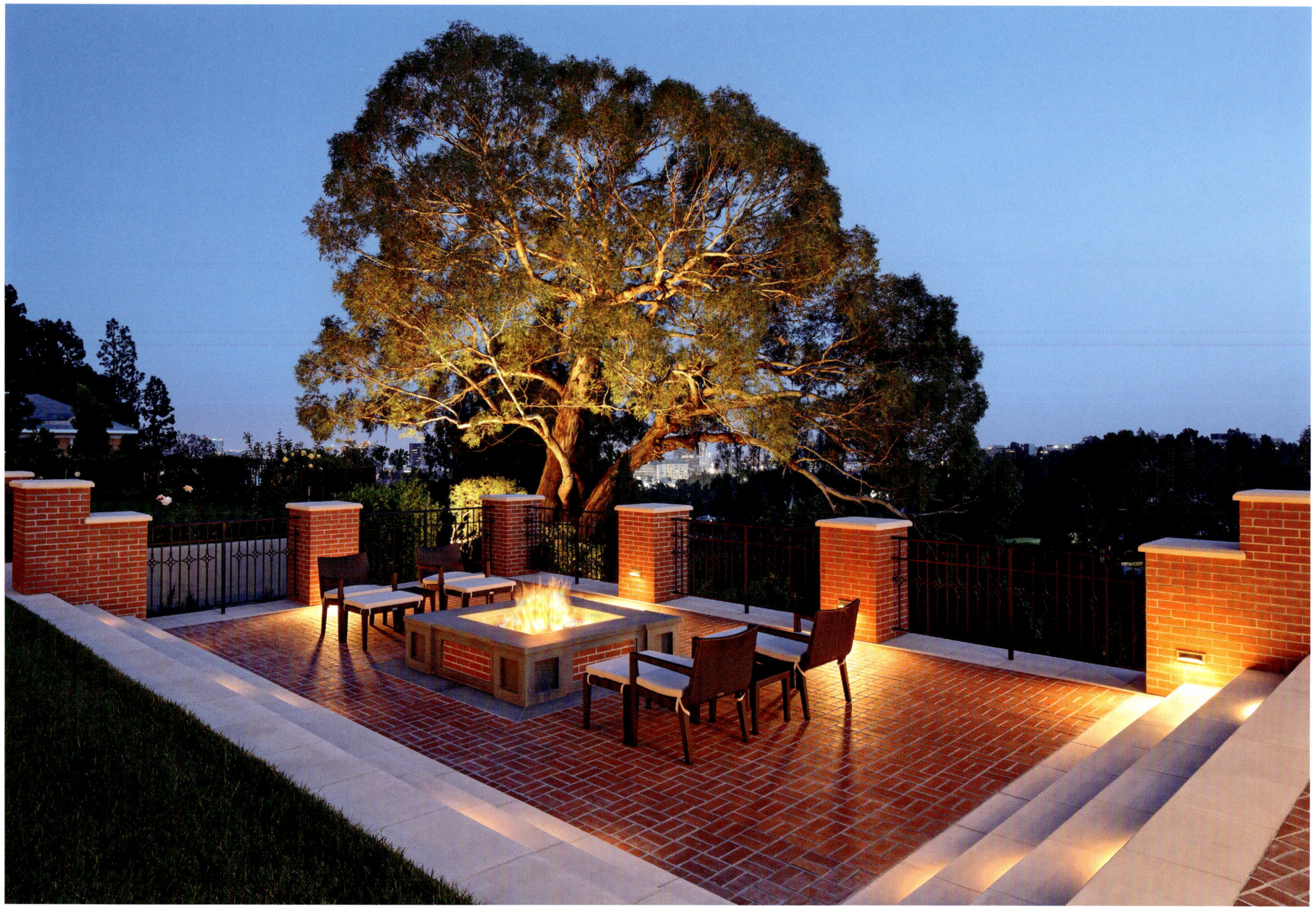

ABOVE: *Steps lead down to the fire pit area, framed with brick piers and iron railings.*

OPPOSITE: *The heaters for the pergola are mounted on the inside of the beams, so they are hidden very discreetly. The pergola also has space for tiny spotlights, which accent it at night.*

FOLLOWING PAGES: *The goal with the bench-height fire pit was to unite the brick with the bluestone trimwork so that people could sit and put their feet up. In the evenings, the pool house becomes its own destination, with areas for watching television, dining, and gathering around the fire pit.*

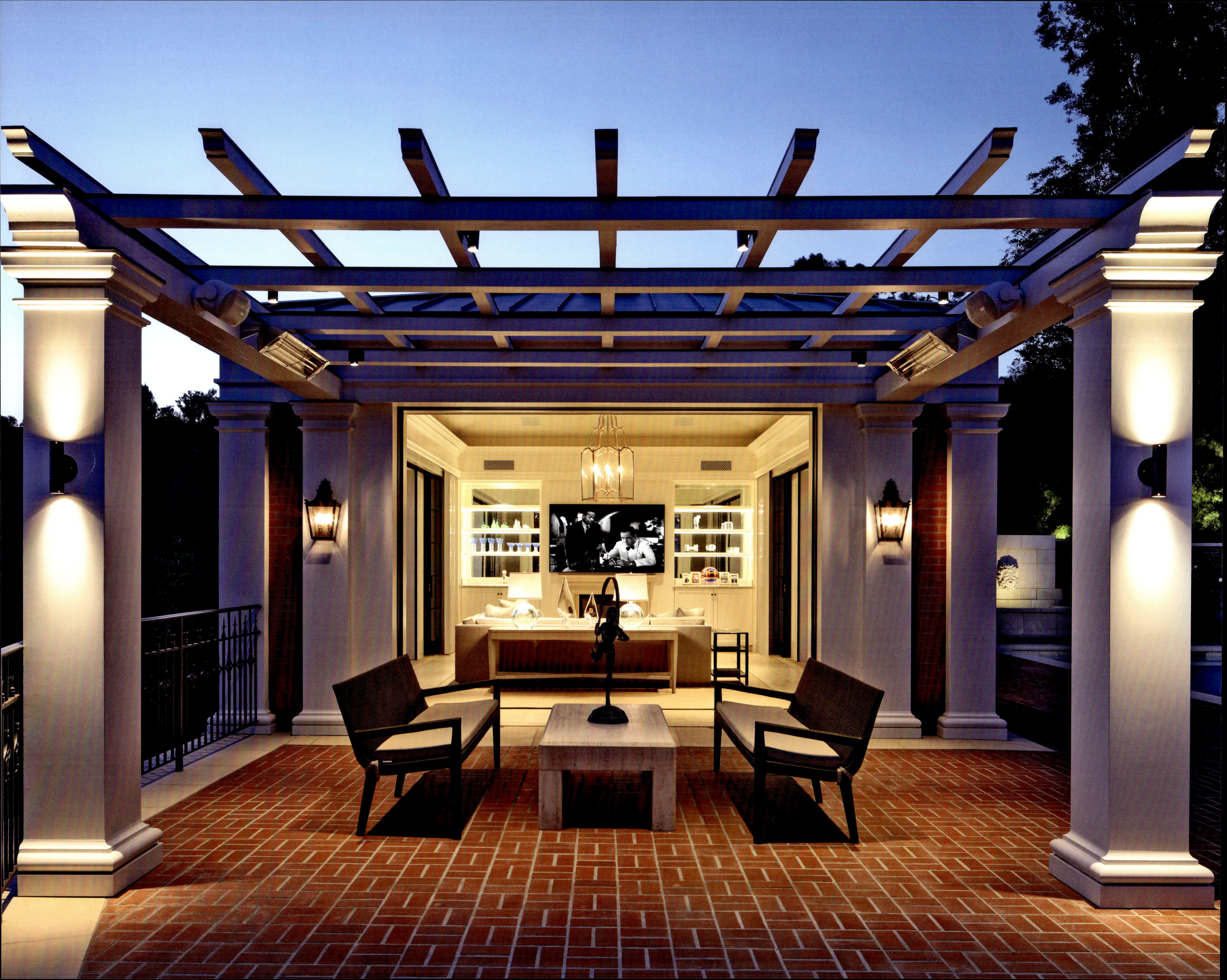

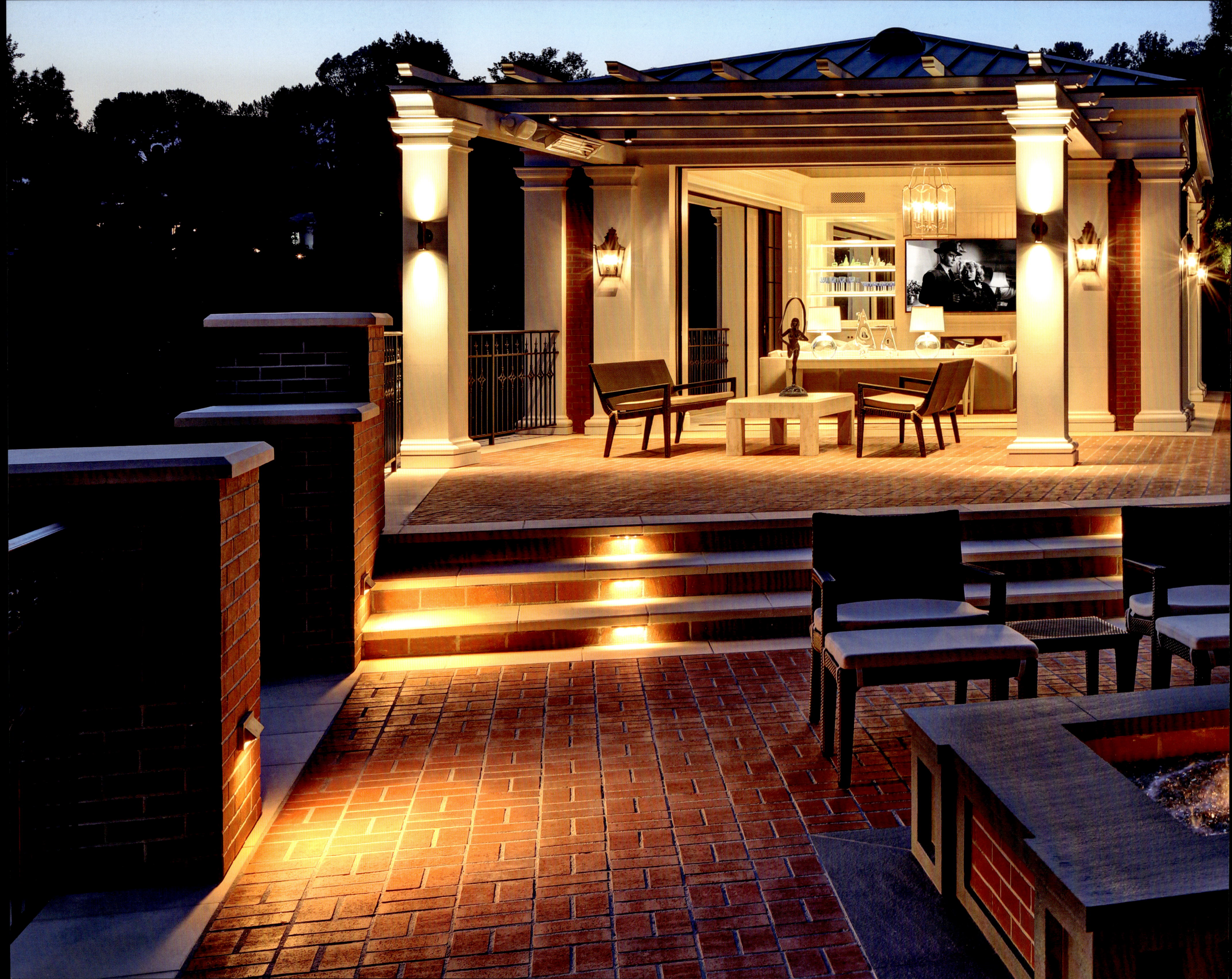

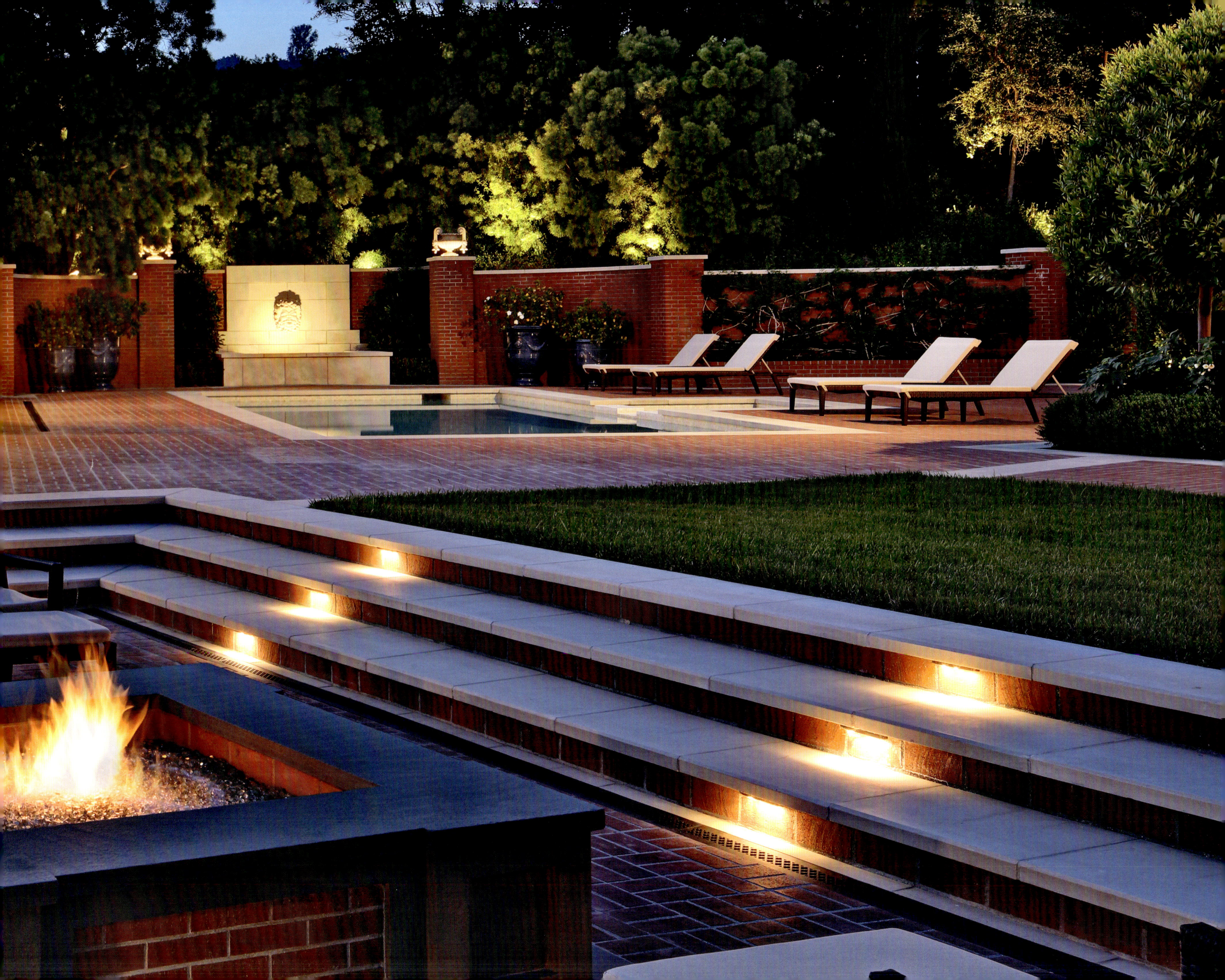

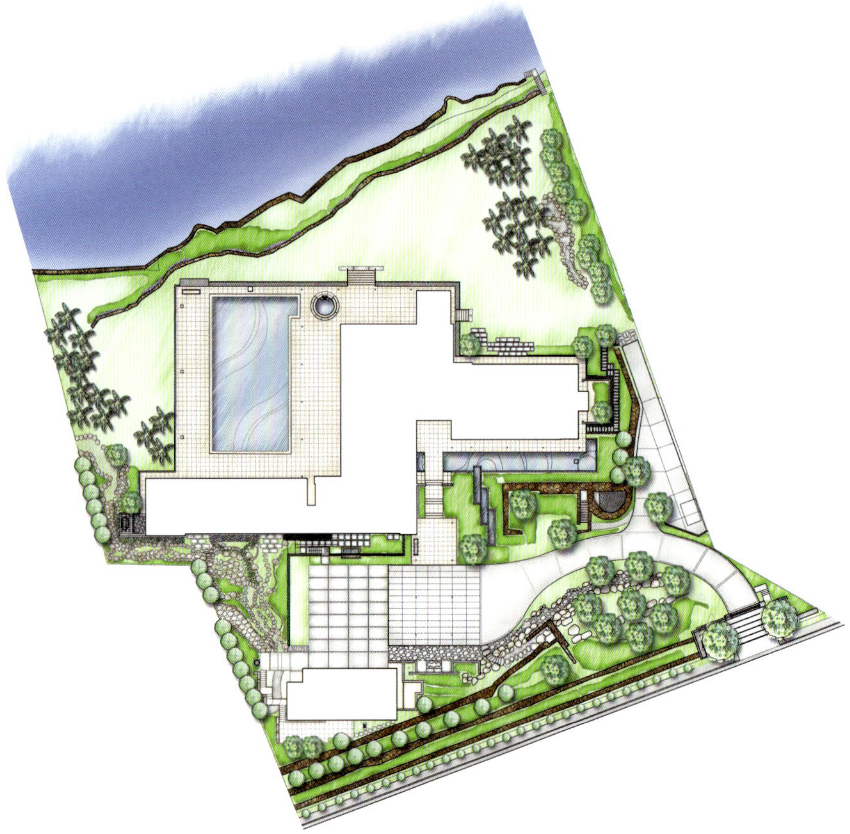

KAISER ESTATE

Hawai'i

One of the most significant modernist residences in Hawai'i, the Kaiser Estate was designed in 1959 for industrialist Henry Kaiser and his wife Alyce. After building the Hoover Dam, Liberty ships during World War II, Kaiser Aluminum, Kaiser Steel, and Kaiser Permanente, Henry Kaiser retired in 1954 to Honolulu, where he extended the length of Waikiki Beach, developed what is now known as the Hilton Hawaiian Village and the 521-acre housing tract Hawaii Kai, and built a house for himself.

The International Style residence was inspired by the work of Mies van der Rohe and is attributed to local architects Edwin Bauer and George Wright, but years of abandonment, neglect, and water damage had taken a toll.

Our extensive six-year remodel started with the remains of the original 1950s framework, with fragments of an iconic 1970s remodel by Palm Springs interior designer Steve Chase, and became the background for a new concept that incorporates the best elements of these two distinct design eras into a unified theme of what a modern Hawaiian house can be today.

Set on a prime oceanfront site on O'ahu with views across Maunalua Bay to Diamond Head, the single-story house follows Mies's architectural vocabulary with an off-center cross-shaped plan, broad flat roof, book-matched travertine marble walls, and huge expanses of sliding glass doors reminiscent of his Barcelona Pavilion. Kaiser tackled the construction of his house with the same verve of his large-scale engineering feats. Slender steel columns support the sheltering roof along the ocean-facing perimeter and 10-foot-by-10-foot sliding glass doors provide views of the ocean from virtually every room.

Many original features remain and were restored: the living room's marble fireplace, the dining room's semicircular segmented marble walls, and the media room's stained-glass skylight depicting the history of Hawai'i. Many new materials were introduced: walls clad in teak, onyx, marble, limestone, hand-troweled plaster, glass mosaic tile and bronze mirror, and floors laid in limestone, marble, and walnut.

The formality of the architecture forms the ordered backdrop for a collection of vintage and custom traditional furnishings and site-specific art that emphasize the softer shapes and patterns of nature. Interior designer David Desmond took color cues from the environment, from the sky and ocean to local volcanic earth tones and dramatic hues from flowering plants, and even the pink of Honolulu's famed Royal Hawaiian Hotel.

The Kaiser Estate has presence, pedigree, and provenance. This restoration has reinforced its original intent—a house inspired by Mies van der Rohe that bridges past and present, the International Style and modern Hawai'i.

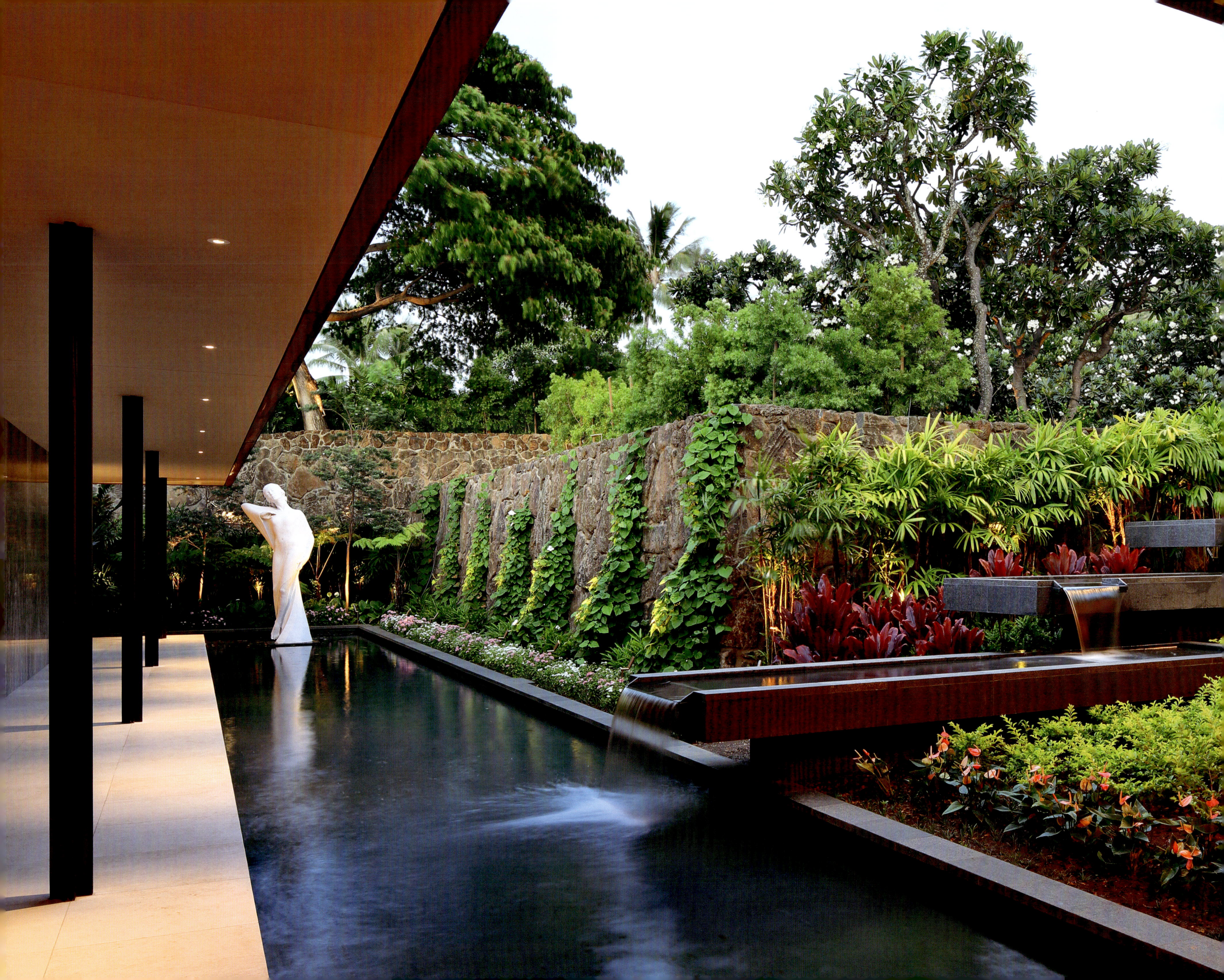

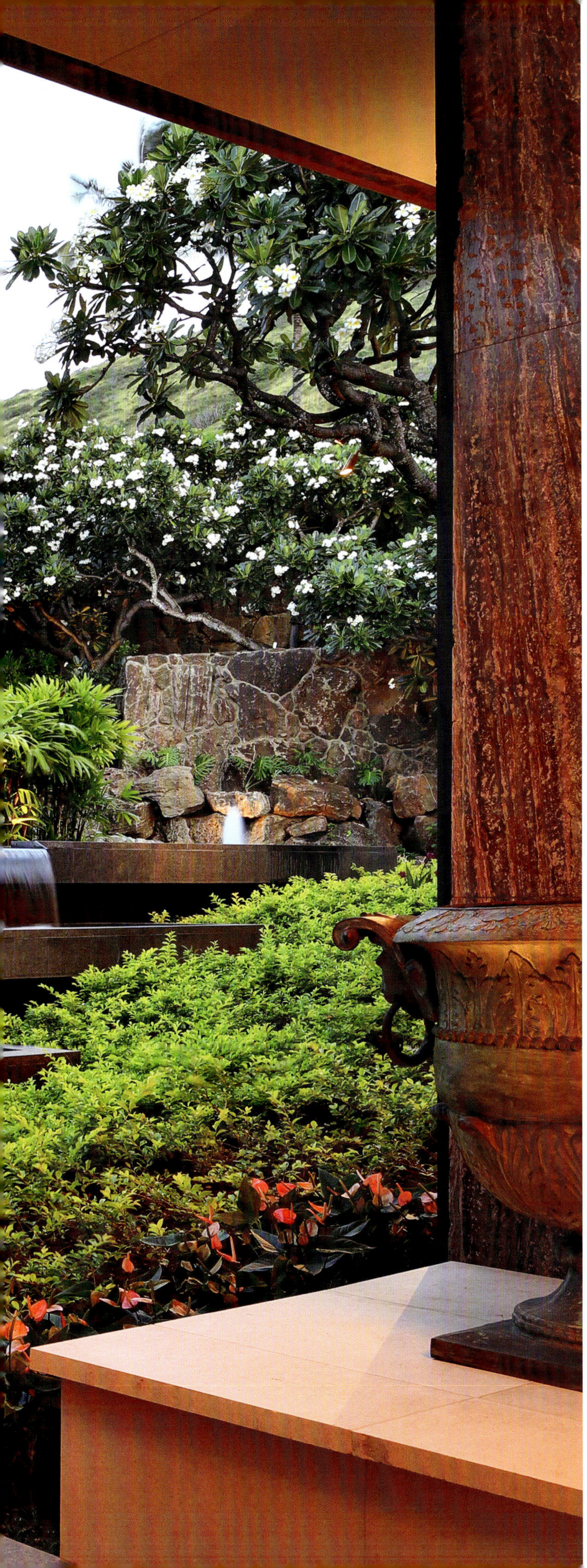

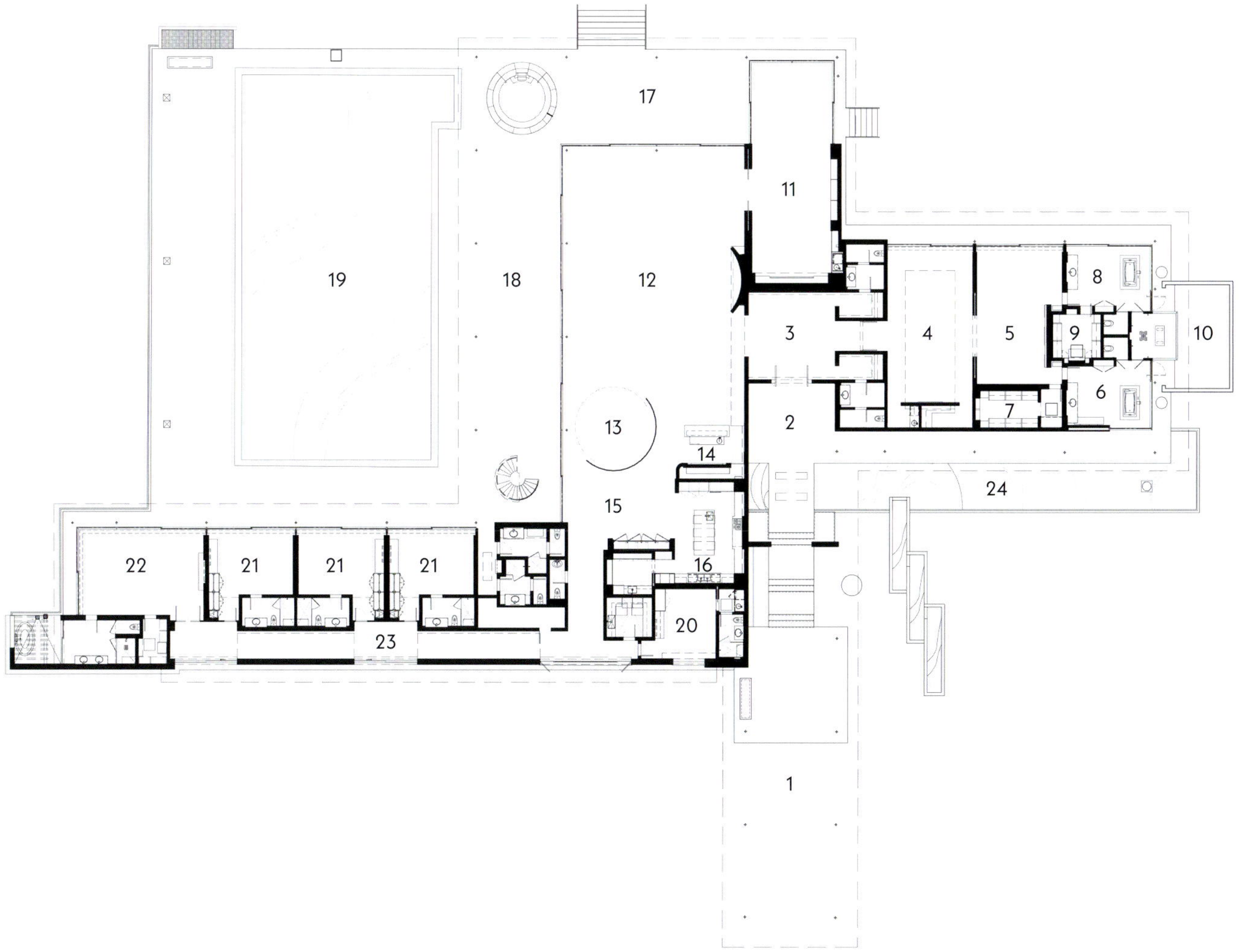

1 Porte-cochère
2 Entry court
3 Foyer
4 Master sitting room
5 Master bedroom
6 Her bath
7 Her closet
8 His bath
9 His closet
10 Garden
11 Media room
12 Living room
13 Dining room
14 Bar
15 Breakfast area
16 Kitchen
17 Lanai
18 Pool lanai
19 Swimming pool
20 Staff quarters
21 Bedroom
22 Junior master bedroom
23 Gallery
24 Reflecting pond

MAIN HOUSE FLOOR PLAN

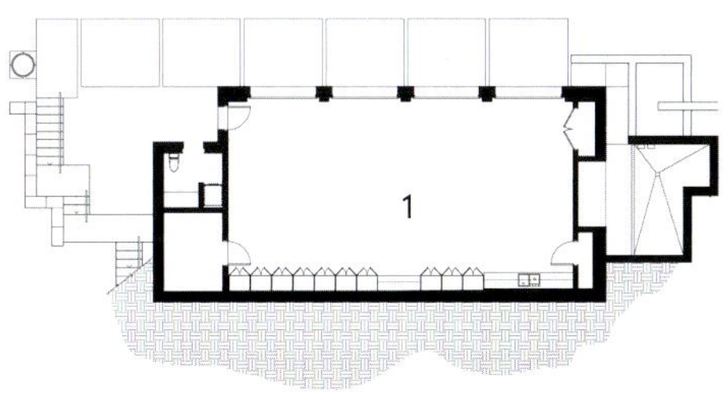

1 Garage

GUEST HOUSE LOWER-LEVEL PLAN

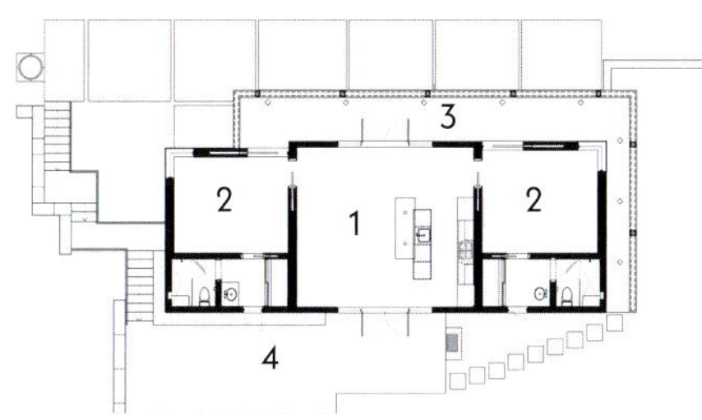

1 Lounge
2 Bedroom
3 Lanai
4 Terrace

GUEST HOUSE UPPER-LEVEL PLAN

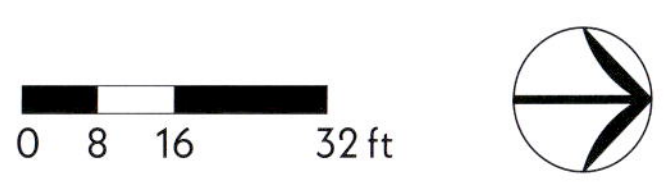

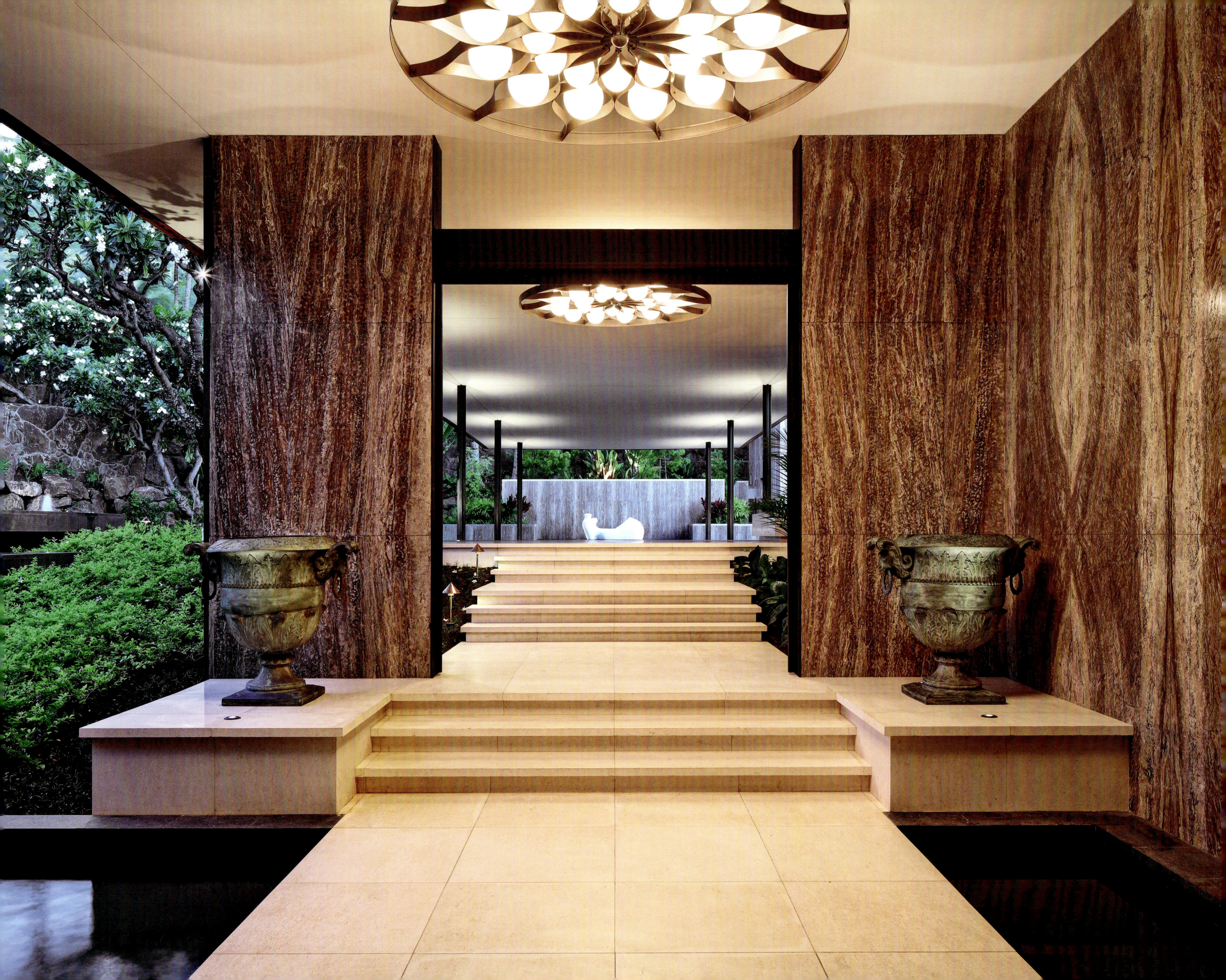

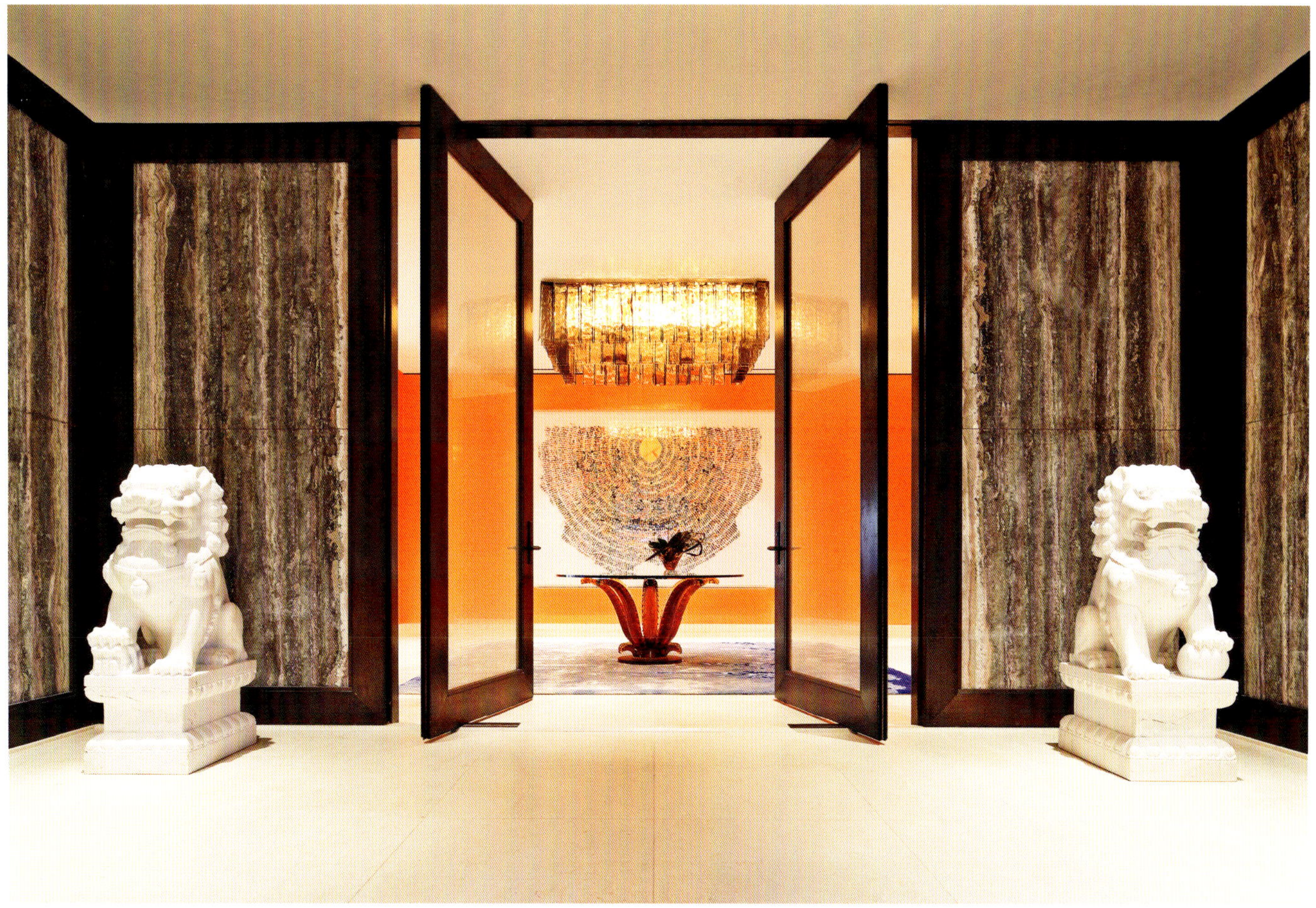

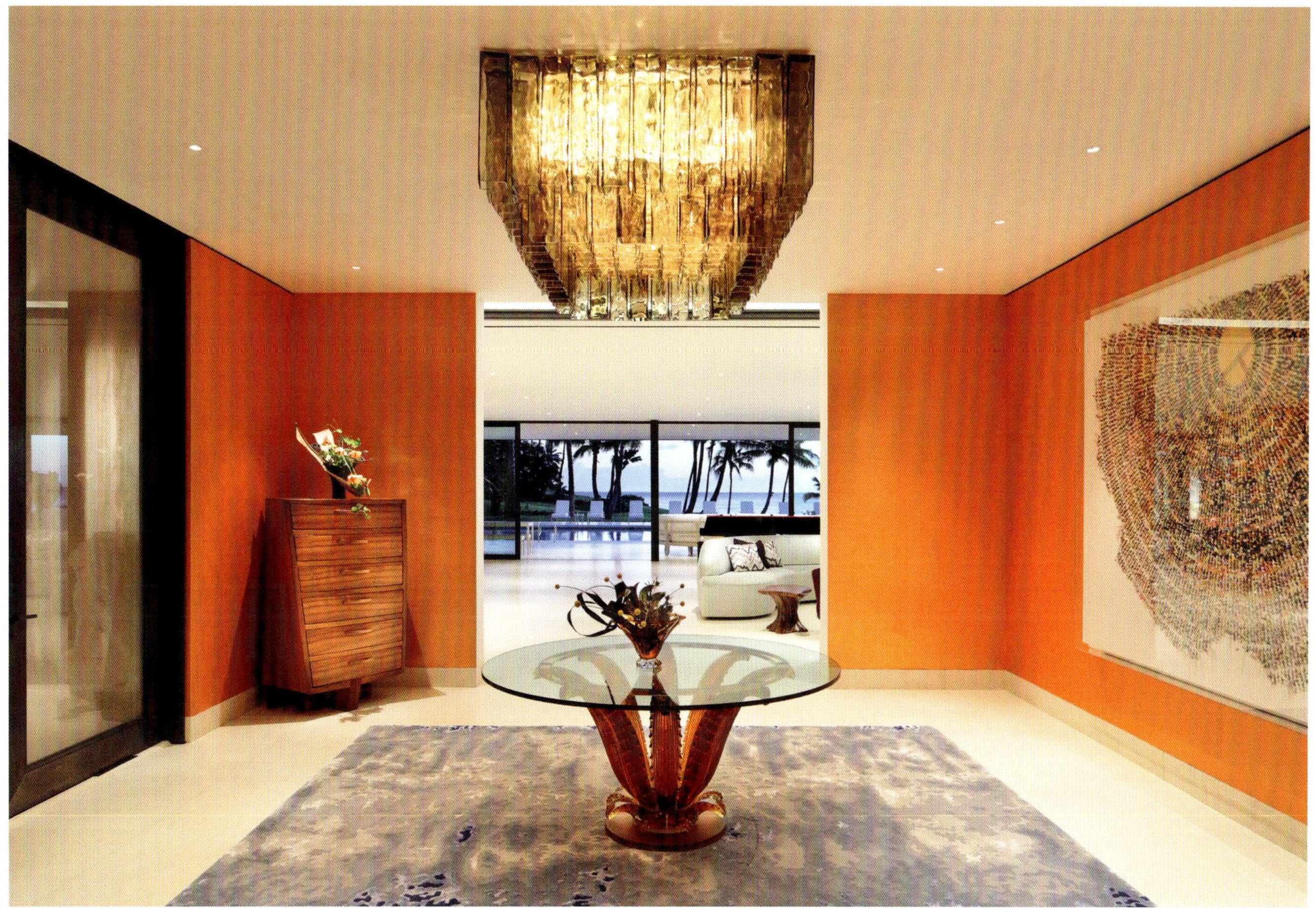

PREVIOUS PAGES: *Our intensive six-year restoration of Kaiser Estate, designed for industrialist Henry Kaiser in 1959, preserved all the International Style architectural elements made popular by Mies van de Rohe: flat roof, steel frame, huge expanses of glass sliding walls, and an open floor plan. The entrance sequence starts with a series of waterfall pools and lush tropical landscaping.*

OPPOSITE: *Framed by the porte-cochère, the main entry reveals rough landscape walls of local lava rock, exterior façade walls in polished book-matched travertine, original Gio Ponti chandeliers, and a pair of antique Danish classical urns.*

TOP RIGHT: *A pair of white marble Foo dogs guard the front entrance. Pivoting glass entry doors with bronze frames open to the entrance hall.*

BOTTOM RIGHT: *Metallic orange wallcovering wraps the entrance hall, with a view to the living room and ocean beyond. The interiors by David Desmond spotlight such vintage pieces as the 1951 Lalique Cactus table and a 1970s Venini Murano glass chandelier.*

RIGHT: *Cream limestone paving flows from the outdoors through the interiors. The restored Italian silver travertine fireplace is surmounted by a skylight that brings light to the center of the living room. A new onyx bar with teak paneling anchors one end, and the 26-foot-long custom serpentine sofa divides the living room into two main seating areas. The tree-trunk side tables are among numerous pieces handmade for the house by local master craftsman Vedad Kulalic.*

FOLLOWING PAGES, LEFT: *The ocean-facing end of the living room has a view across Maunalua Bay to Diamond Head. New Italian furniture and vintage modern pieces (including side tables and lamps by interior designer Steve Chase) and custom hand-tufted rugs add texture. The majority of the finishes—walls clad in teak, onyx, marble, limestone, hand-troweled plaster, glass mosaic tile, and bronze mirror; floors laid in limestone, marble, and walnut—are new.* RIGHT: *The formal dining room is carved out of the living room with a semicircular wall of freestanding book-matched slabs of travertine. Gold mesh floor-to-ceiling curtains on a track form the other half of the circle and provide an intimate dining experience when closed. The custom table has a bronze base and rose quartz top. A vintage midcentury Venini textured glass tube chandelier hangs from the ceiling.*

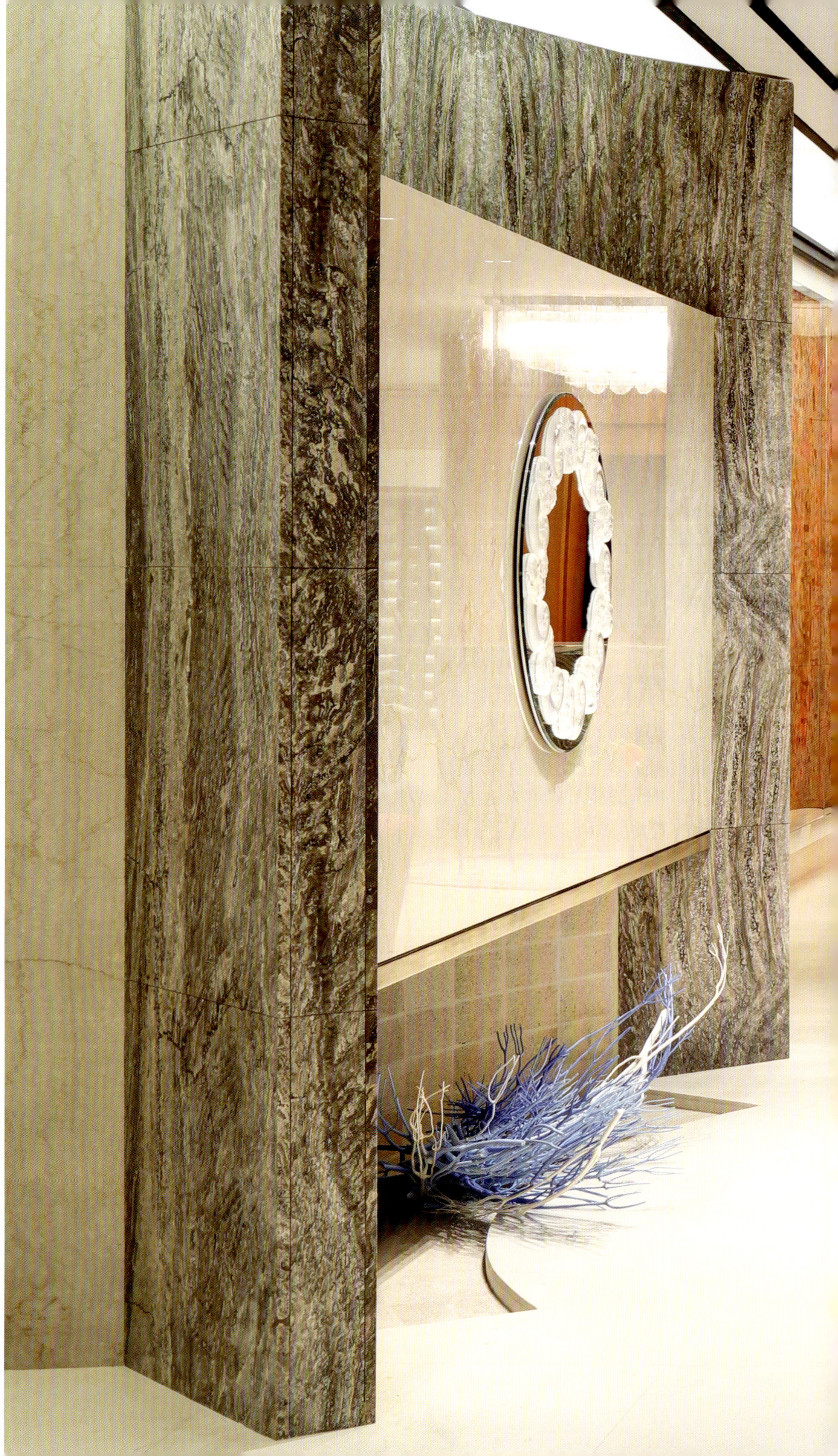

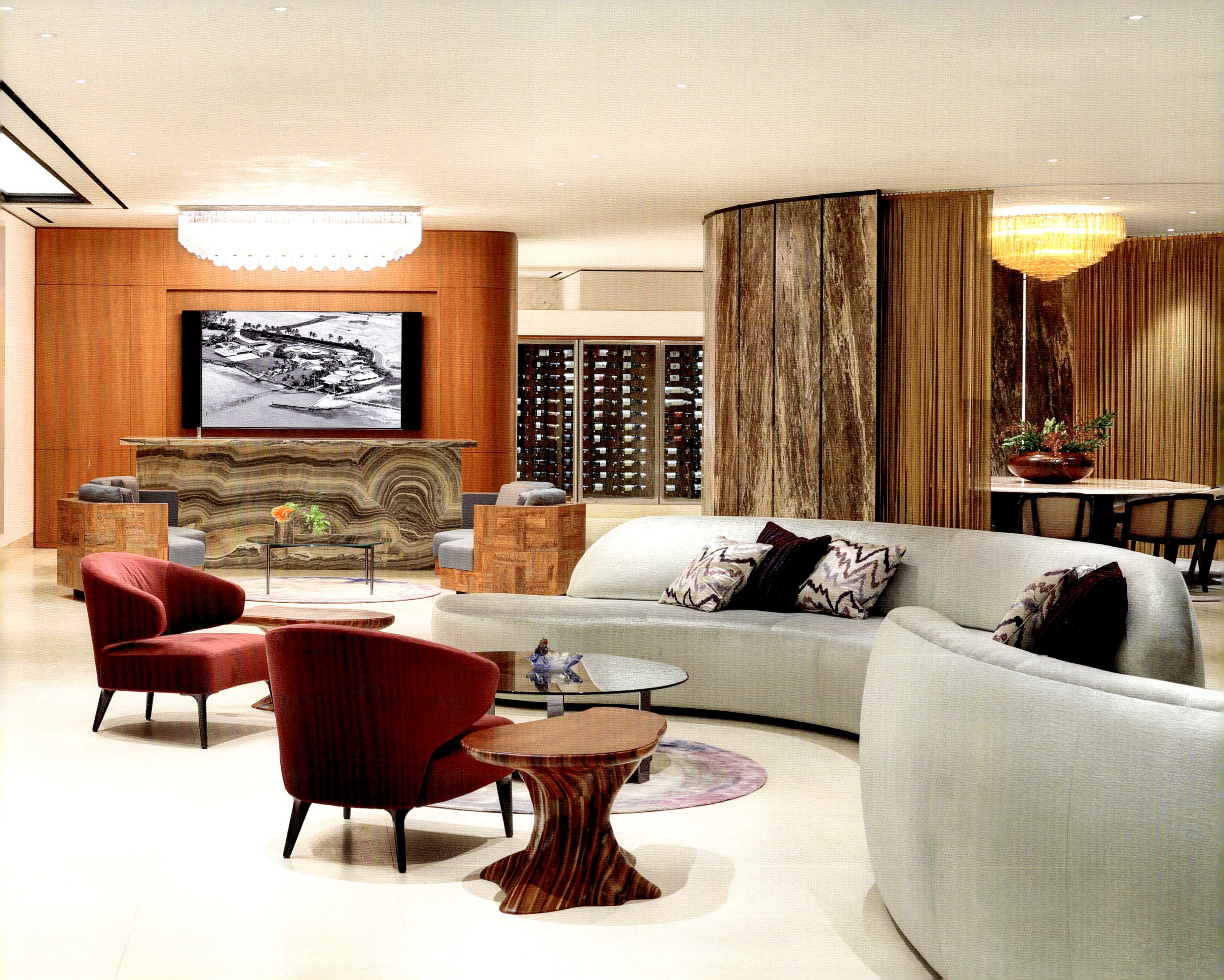

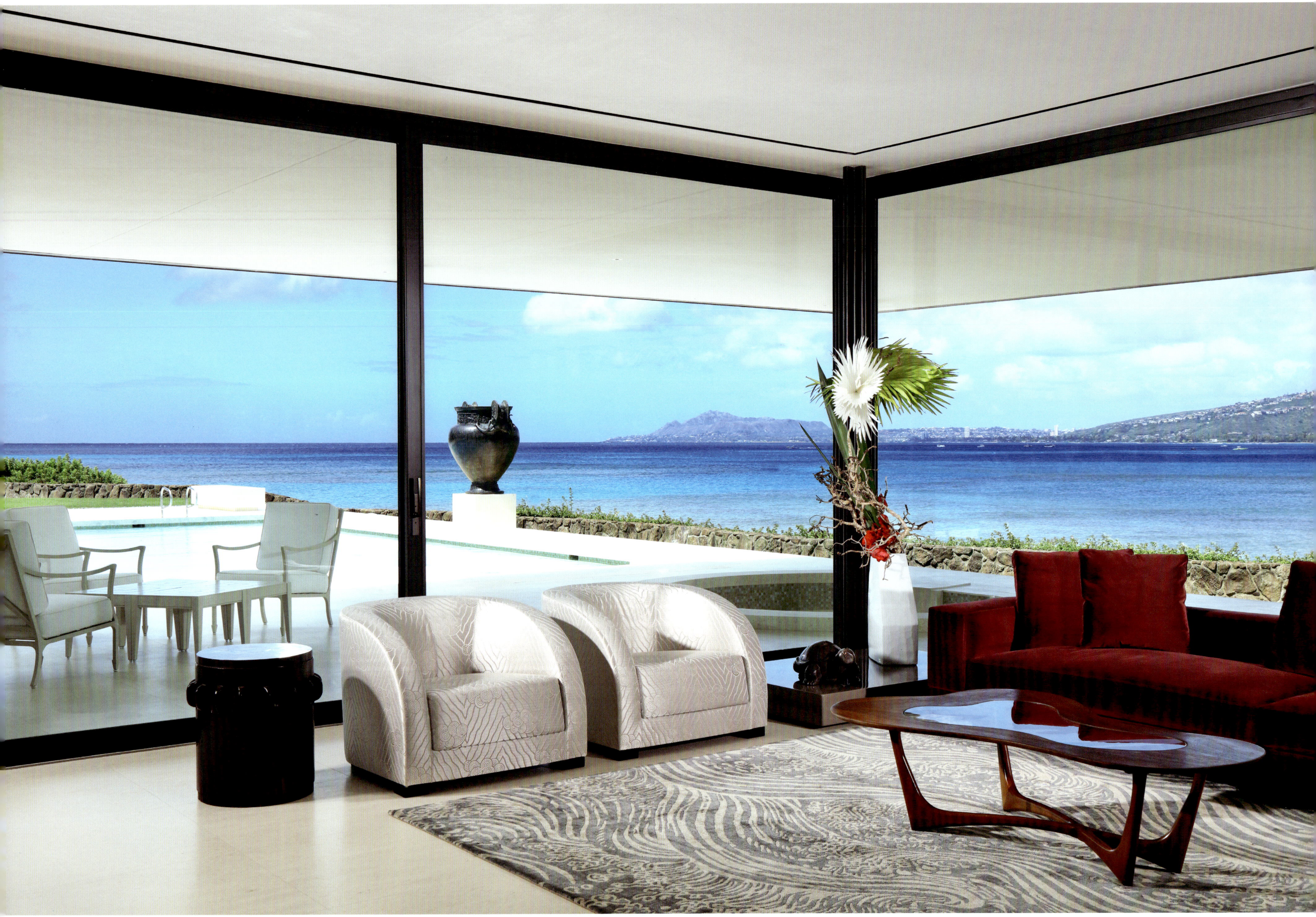

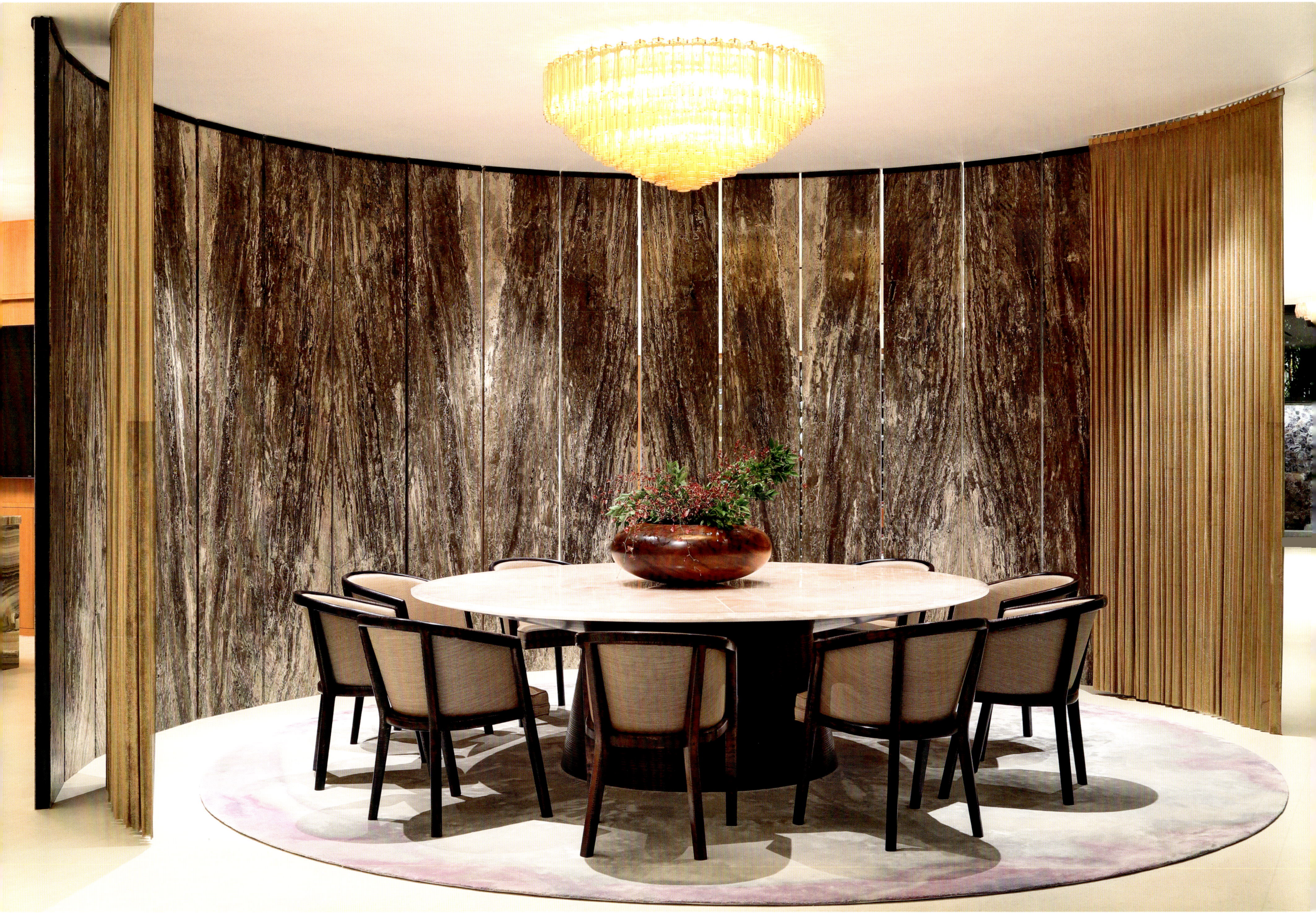

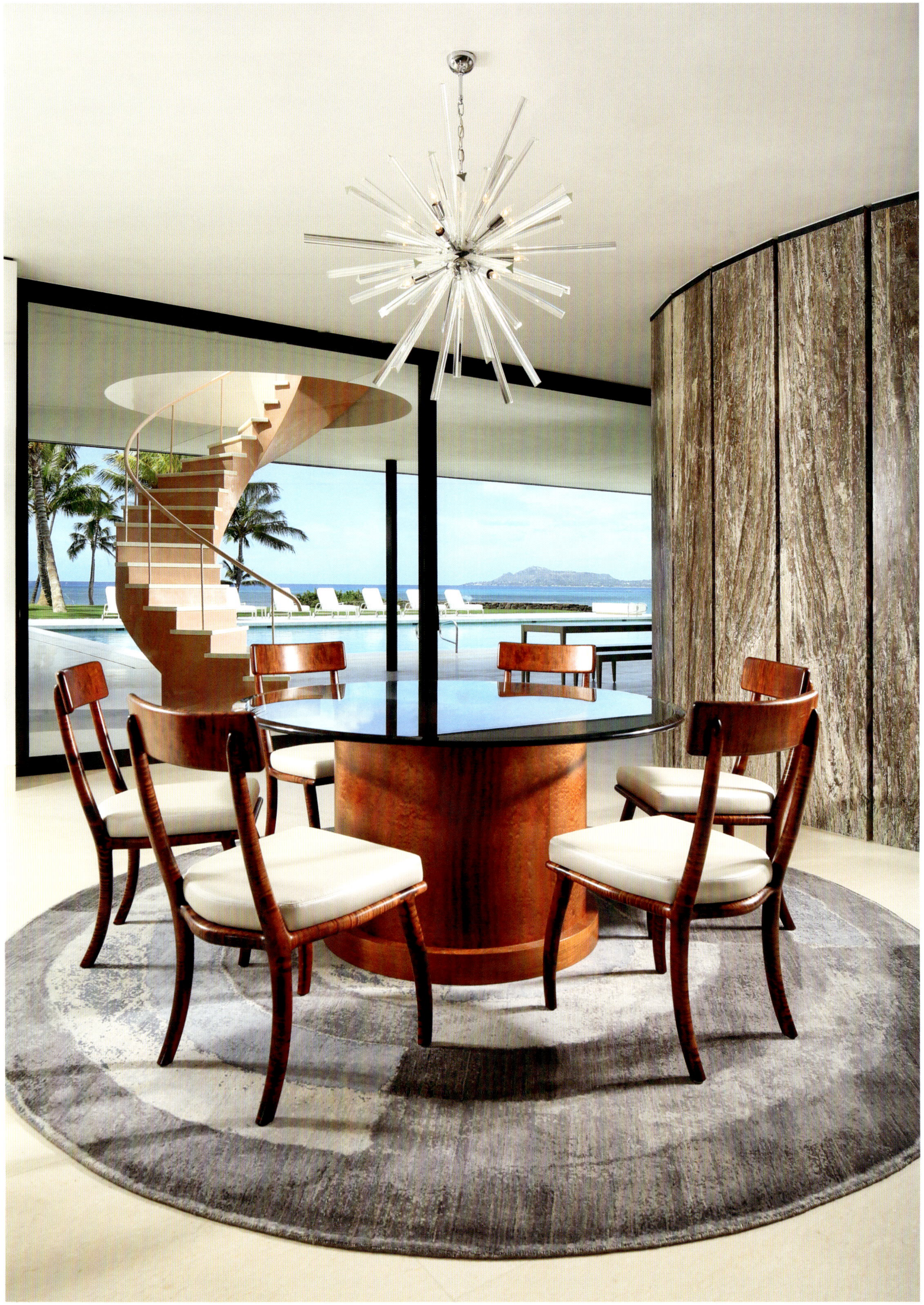

LEFT: *The family dining area adjacent to the kitchen has a view out to the spiral staircase, painted pink in homage to the Royal Hawaiian Hotel, which used to lead up to Henry Kaiser's heliport.*

OPPOSITE: *The all-new kitchen is in Calacatta marble with oak Studio Becker cabinets and custom range hood with pewter finish. A pair of vintage Venini crystal bar chandeliers hangs above the island. Temperature-controlled wine storage is at right.*

FOLLOWING PAGES, LEFT: *The color scheme for the teak-paneled media room comes from the stained-glass dome, designed in the 1970s by Steve Chase of Arthur Elrod Associates. The dome documents the accomplishments of King Kamehameha and was restored to its original splendor. Open shelves in cobalt blue optical-grade resin display a collection of Lalique vases.* RIGHT: *At the far end of the media room is a pool table by Porsche Design.*

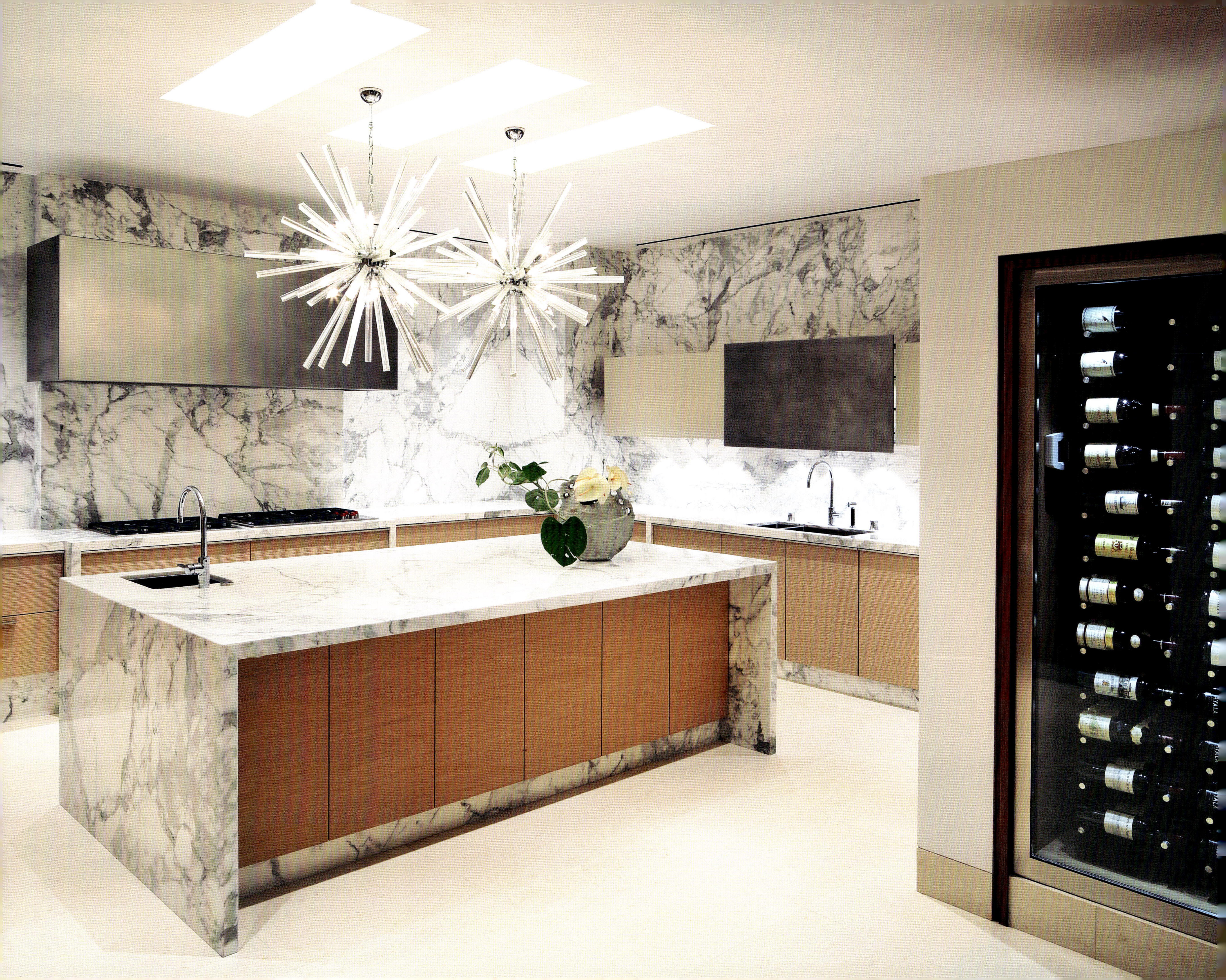

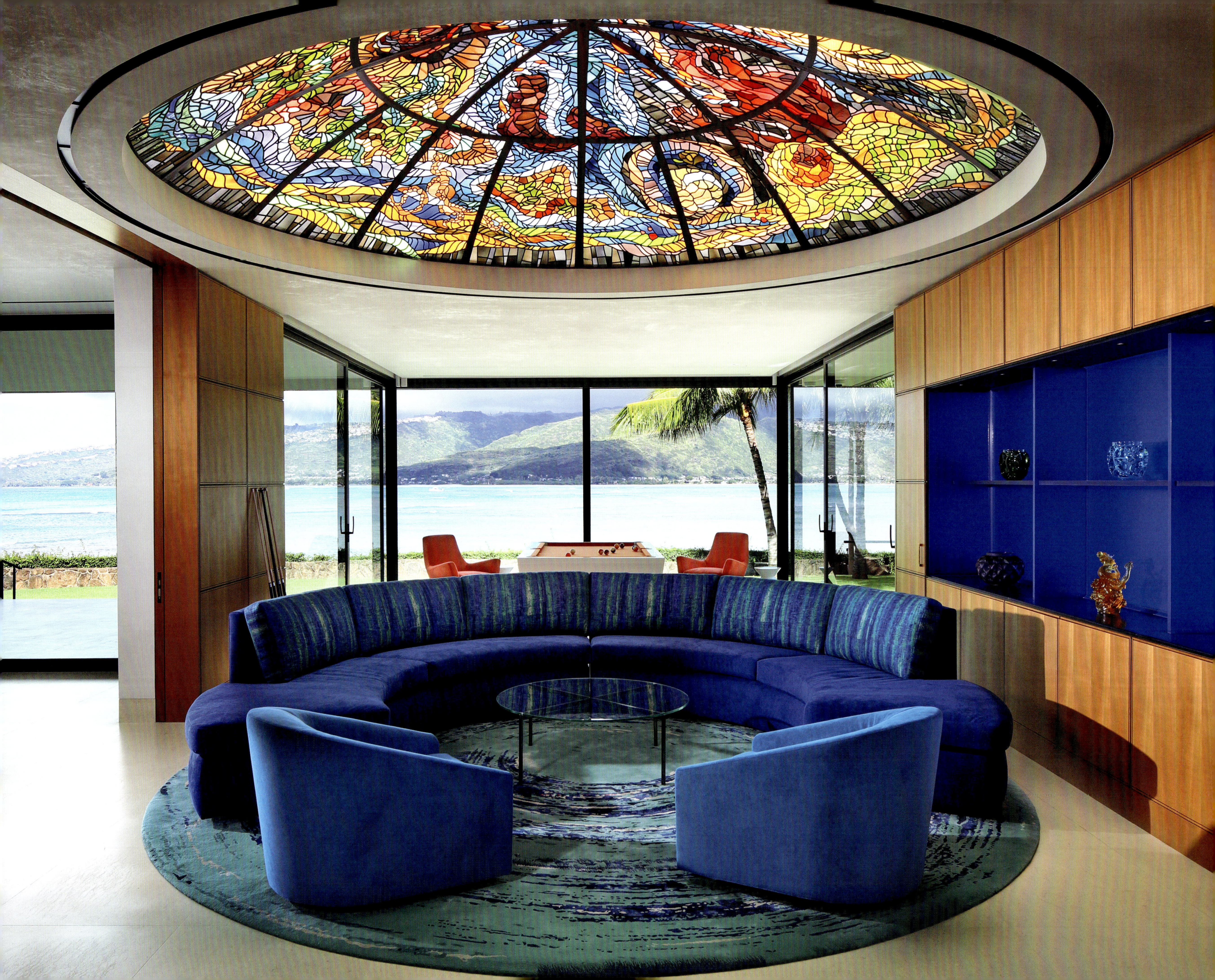

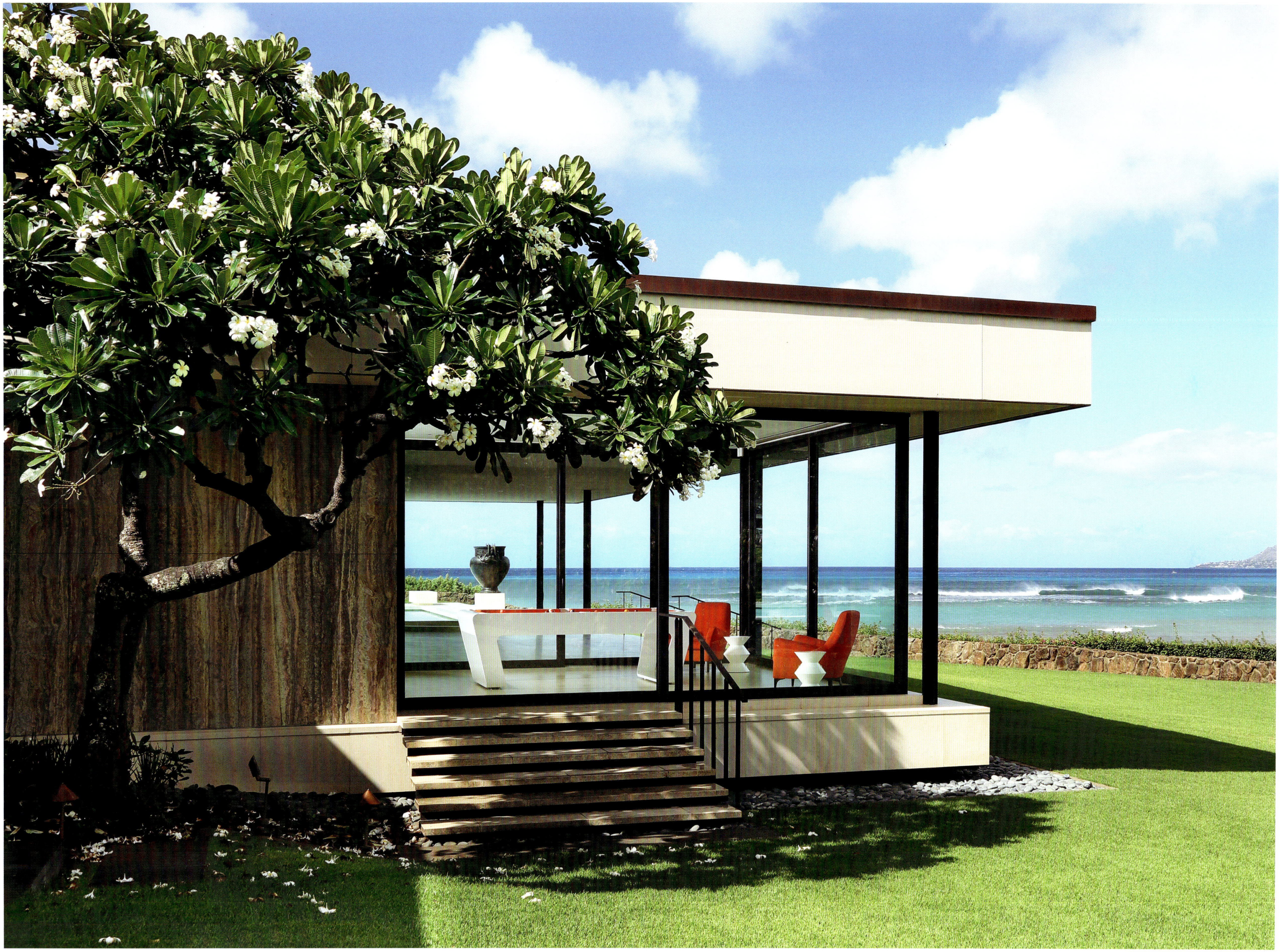

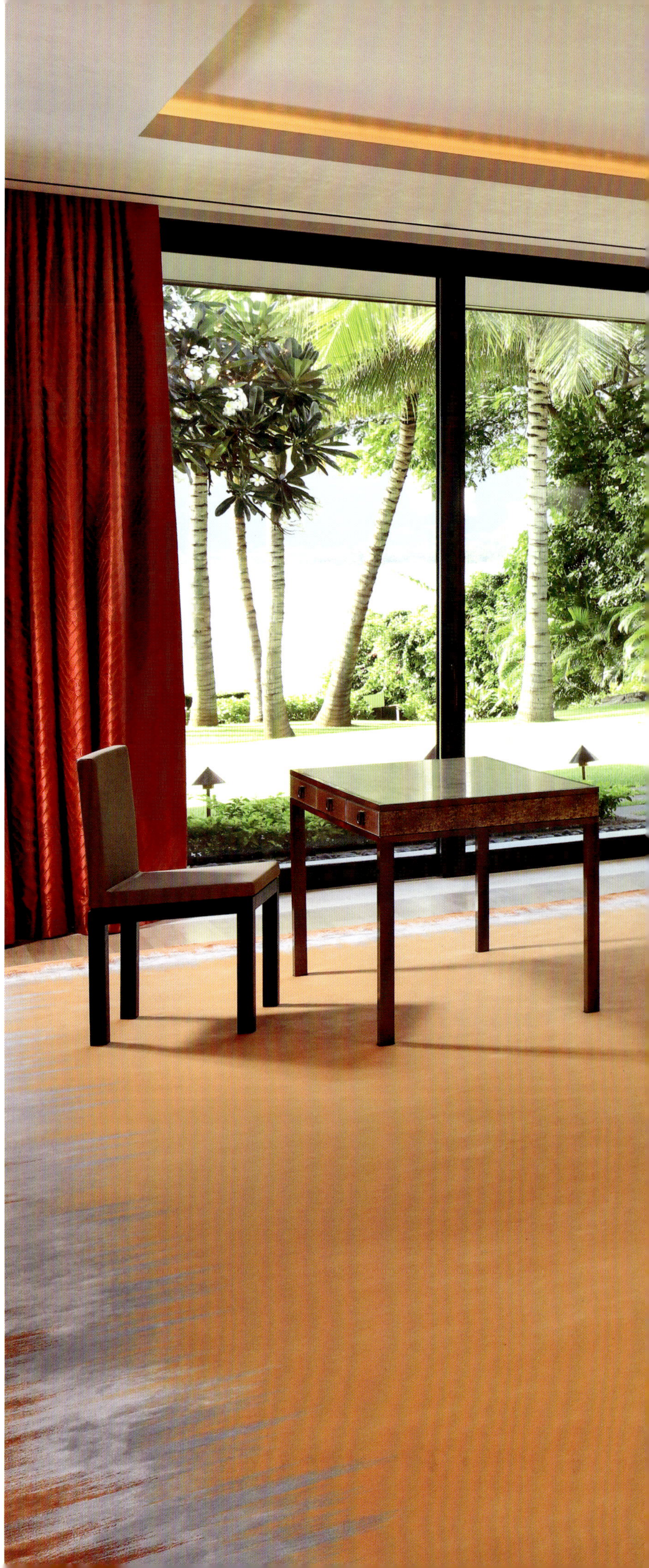

RIGHT: *The teak-paneled master sitting room leads into the bedroom. One master craftsman made more than sixty chairs, tables, chests, and beds in solid Koa, mango, quilted mahogany, and other exotic woods. Each piece was conceived for its purpose and exact place, and adds to the feeling that this house could only be in Hawai'i. Sliding glass doors open to a broad lawn overlooking Maunalua Bay.*

FOLLOWING PAGES, LEFT: *One of two master baths overlooks a lawn ringed by plumeria trees. The walls and floating vanity, with a white onyx countertop, are clad in teak. Drawer pulls are by Lalique, as is the Orgue chandelier designed by Studio Andrée Putman.* RIGHT: *Drawings of the master bath cabinetry.*

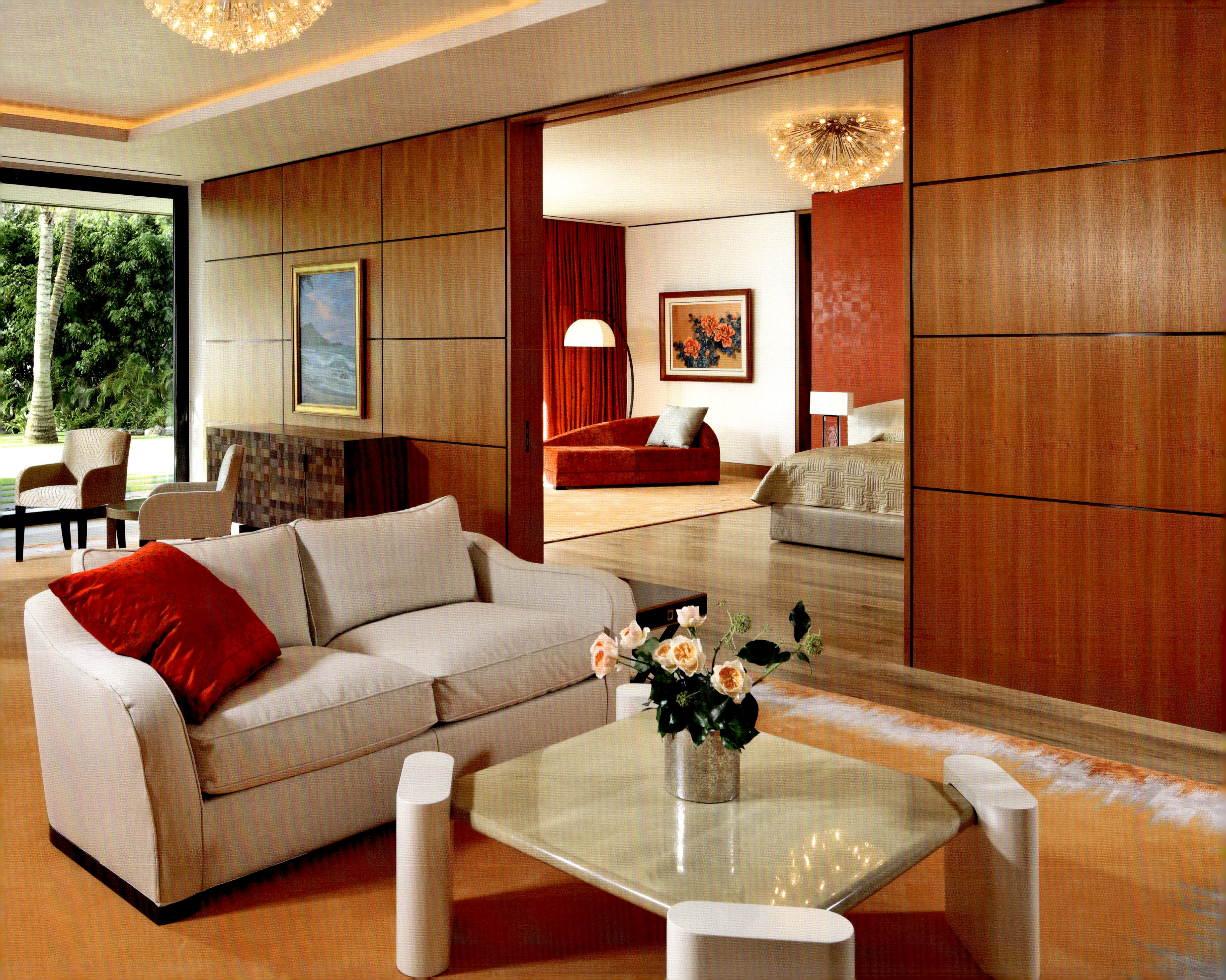

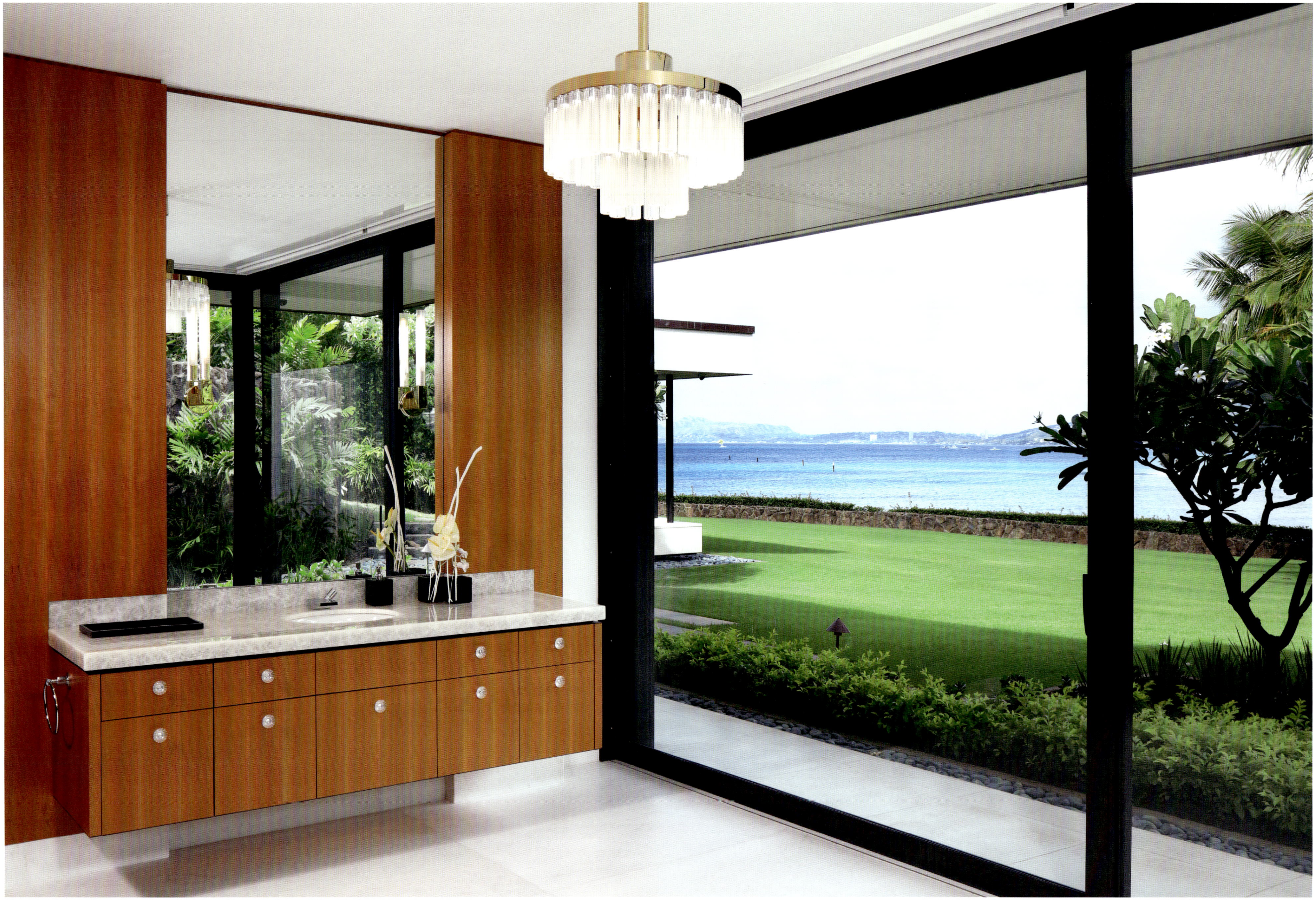

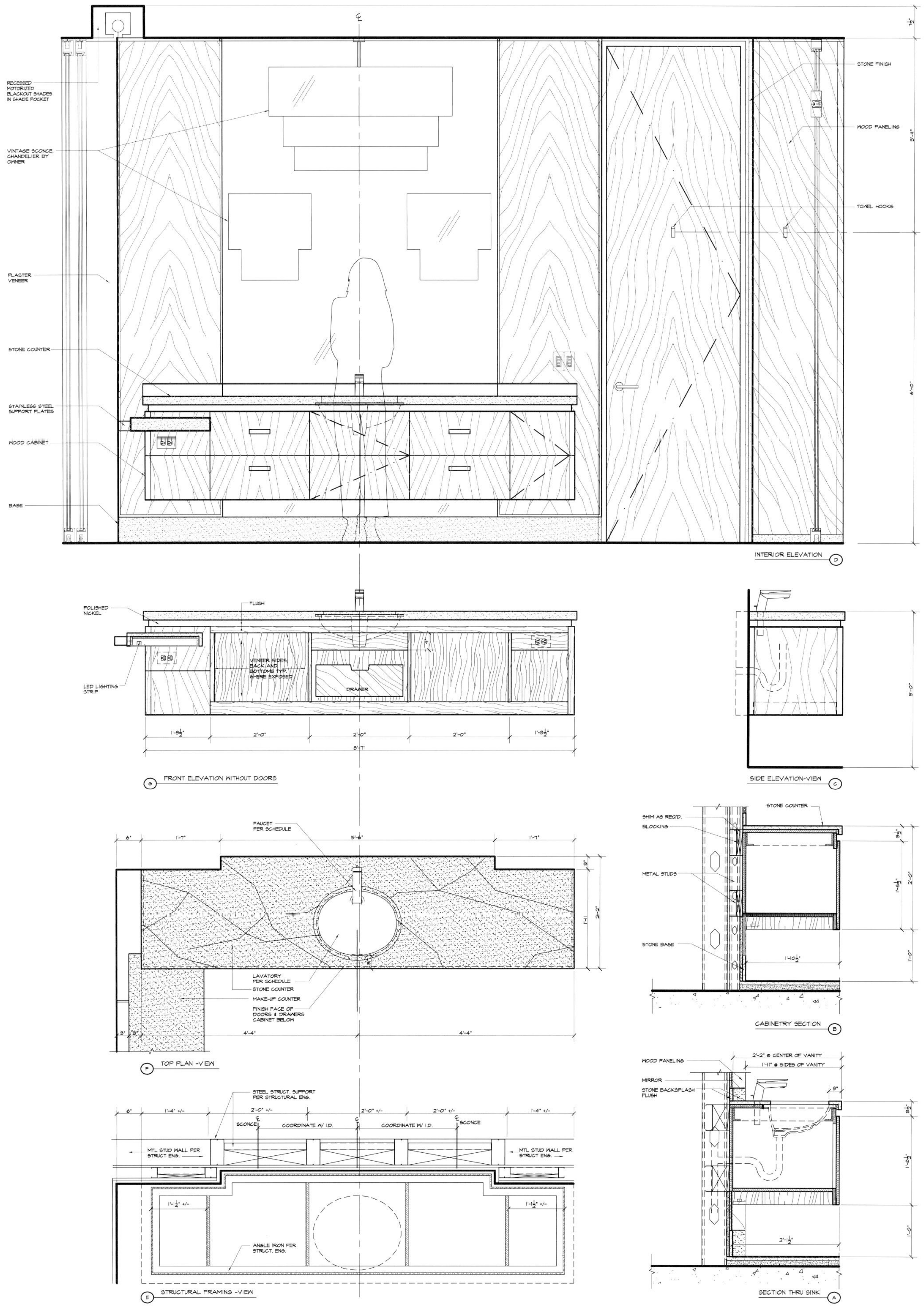

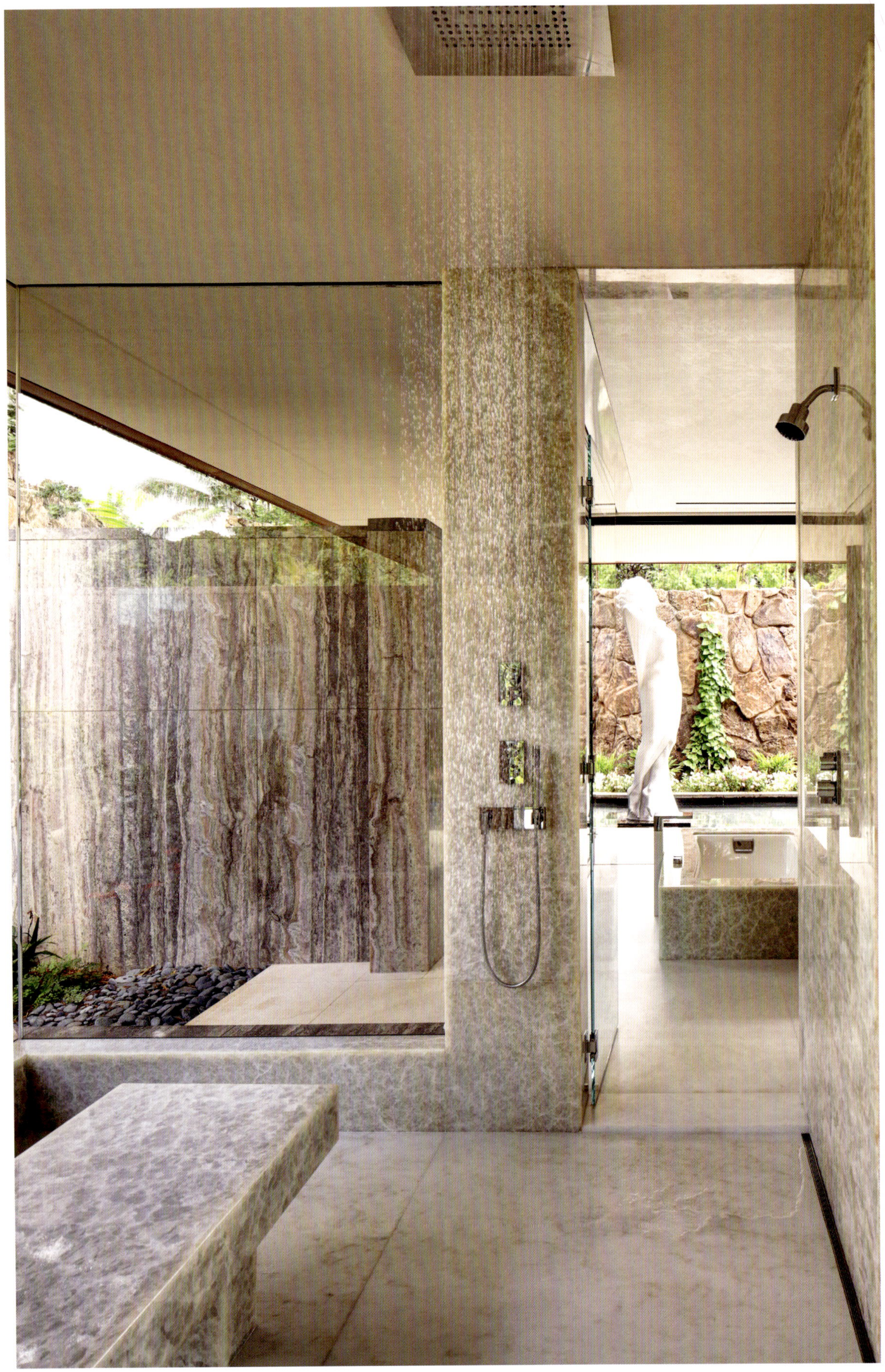

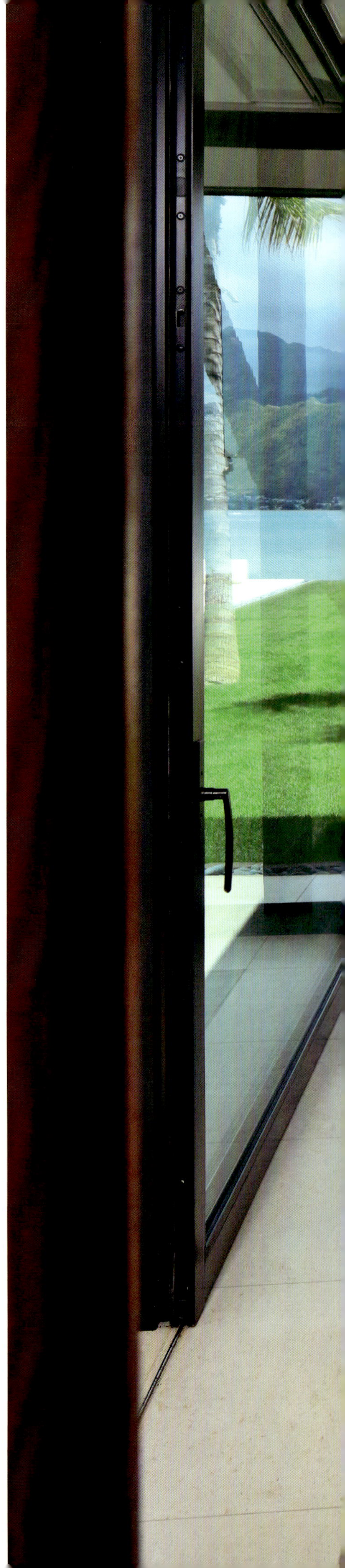

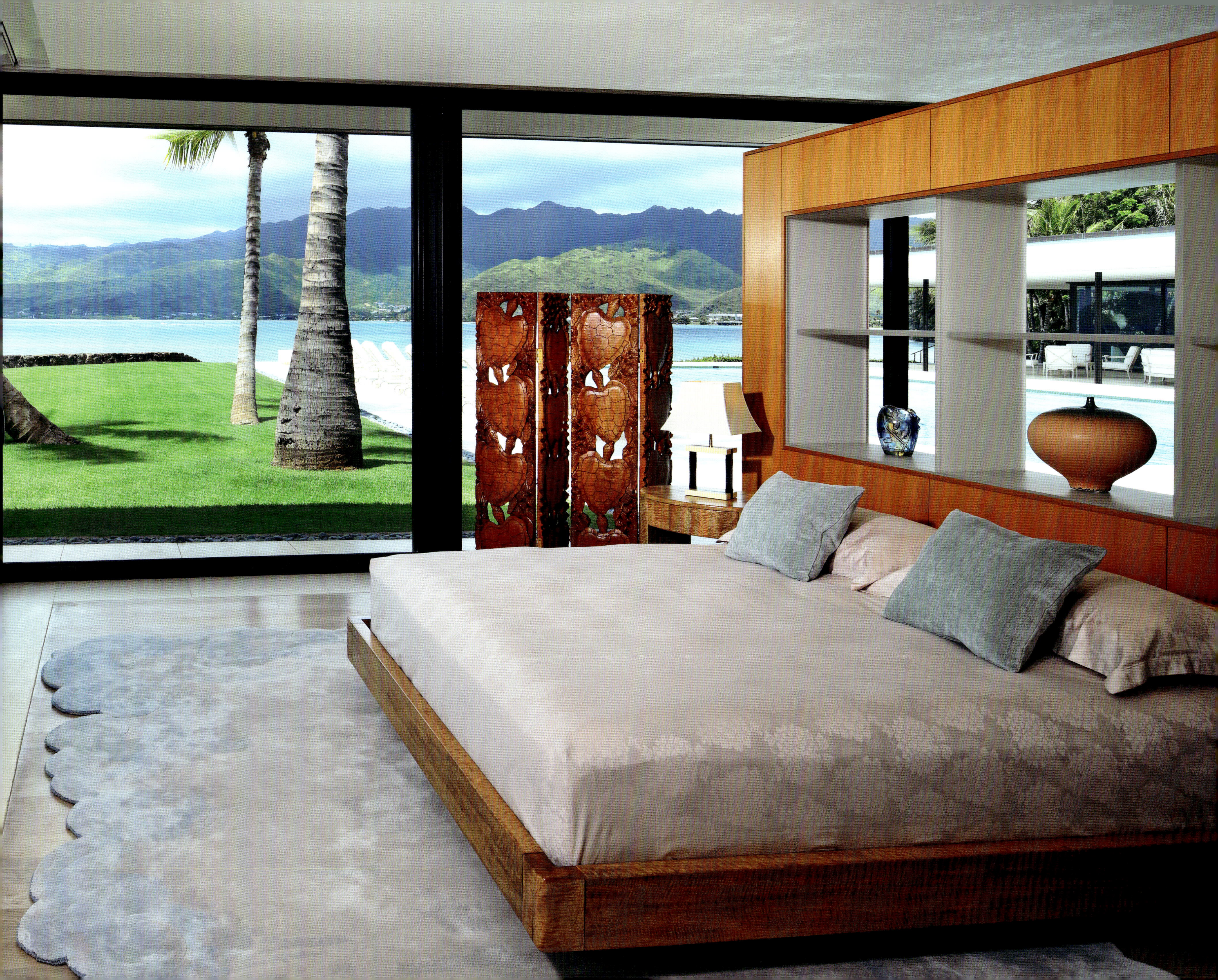

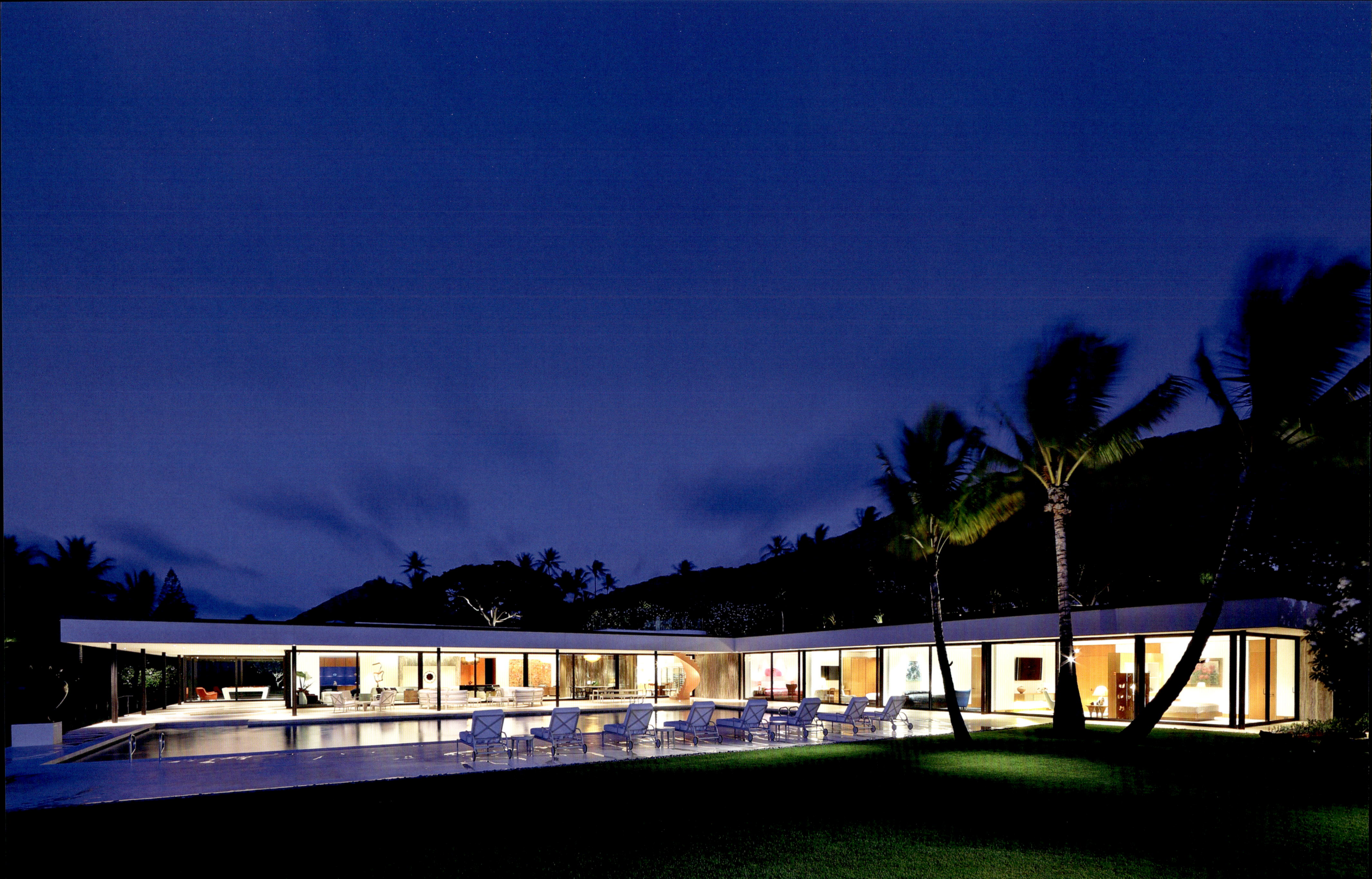

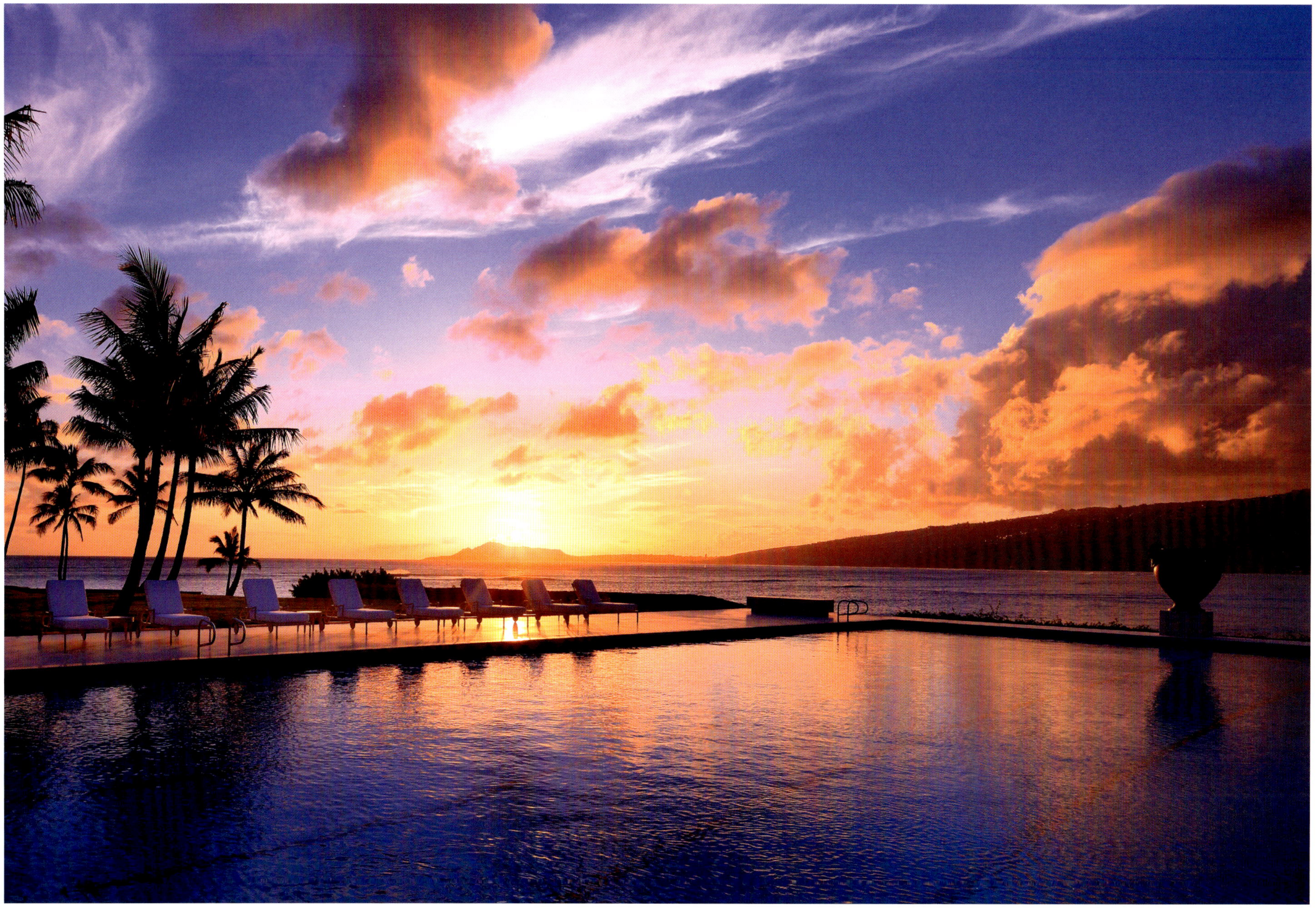

PREVIOUS PAGES, LEFT: *The master shower, with walls, floor, and bench clad in white onyx, connects the two master bathrooms. Three glass walls look out to a Japanese-inspired garden defined by exterior walls in travertine. The view is to a reflecting pool with a monumental white marble sculpture by Emmanuel Fillion.* RIGHT: *The junior master bedroom is sited at a far corner of the house where sliding glass doors open to a lawn overlooking the pool and Maunalua Bay.*

OPPOSITE: *A view from the guest rooms toward the living areas reveals the 20-foot-deep covered lanai that creates a substantial outdoor lounge.*

ABOVE: *The 82-foot-long swimming pool has its shallow end closest to the ocean. The original pool walls and bottom are of white Carrara marble with inlaid dark green marble to form the pool lanes. At sunset, a focal point is the Fonderia Artistica Ferdinando Marinelli's* Vix Krater *in bronze on a limestone pedestal.*

FOLLOWING PAGES: *With its floating horizontal planes, extensive glass walls, and delicate cruciform-shaped columns, the house incorporates its previous 1950s and '70s incarnations to present a modern Hawaiian house for today.*

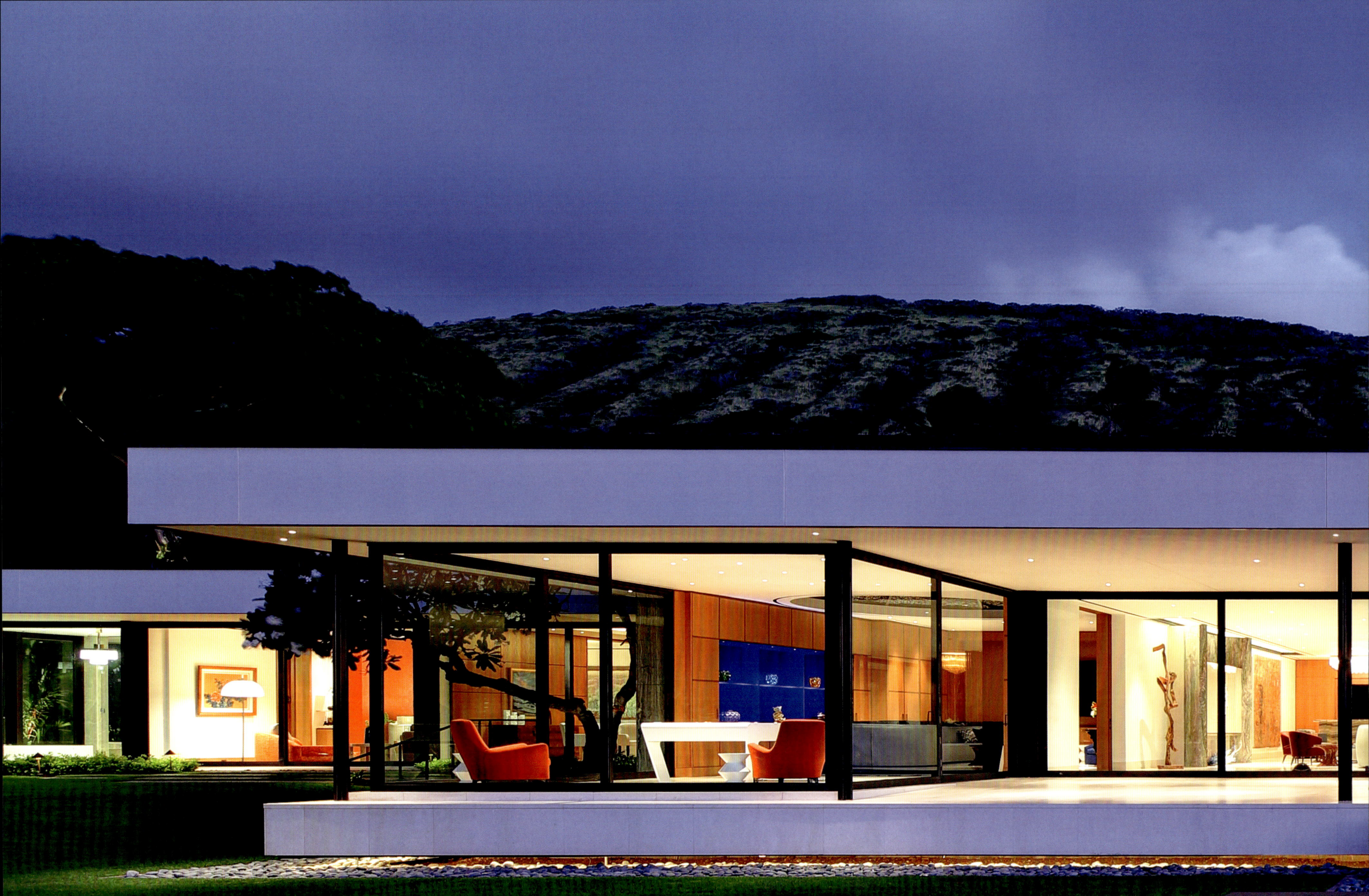

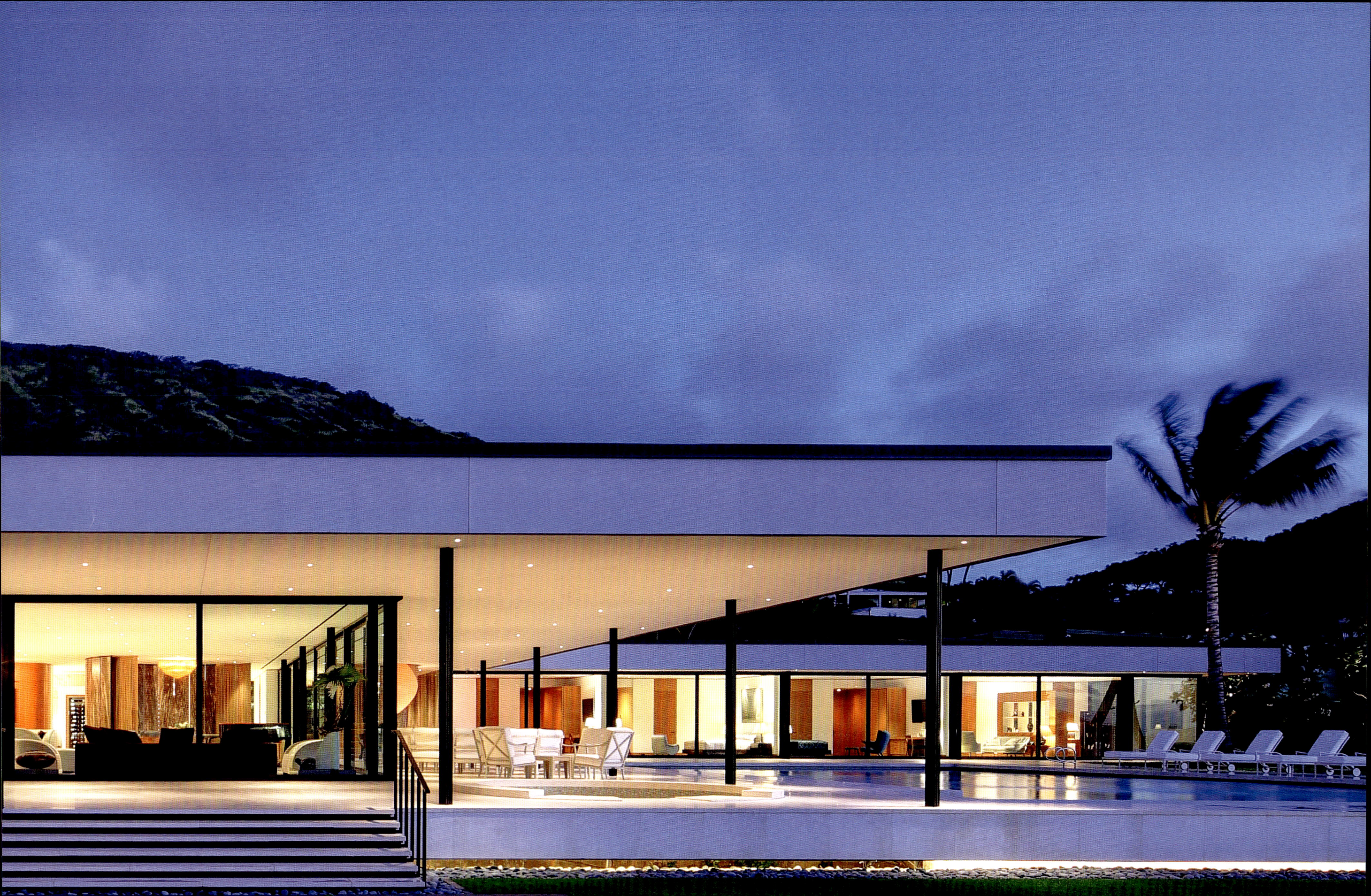

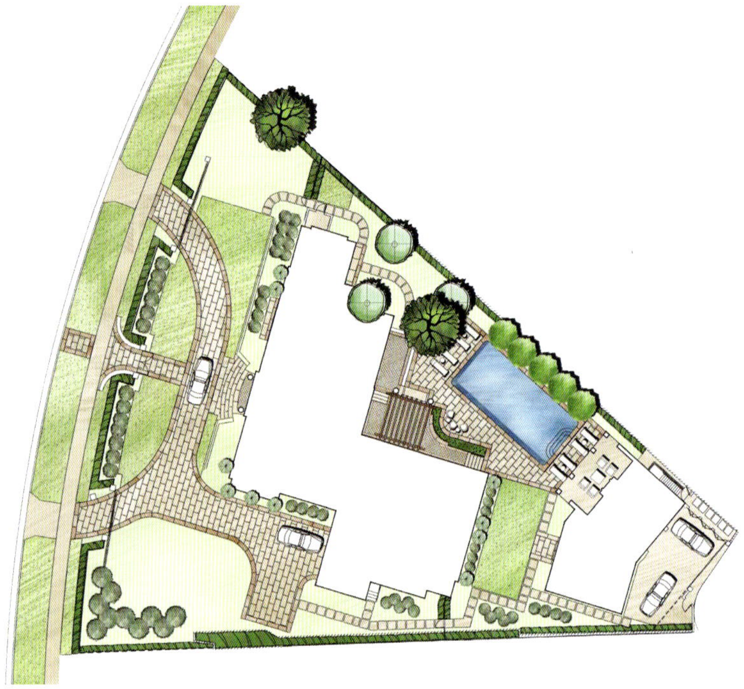

CASA CALIFORNIA

Beverly Hills

With a dramatic presence on a gracefully curving street and long double driveway, Casa California offers a tantalizing reveal of its distinctive California Mediterranean Revival features. Built in 1926 by the architectural firm Camduff and Camduff as one of the partners' own homes, Casa California embodies the eclectic amalgamation of Spanish and Italian influences that prevailed in Los Angeles at the time.

Our intent was to keep that same vision, remove unattractive alterations that had been made over decades, and add more family rooms and bedrooms, a basement with entertainment spaces, and a new garage and guest house, all pulled together with a redesigned landscape.

The façade retains its original elegant features, including various loggias and multiple sets of arched French doors, which were used to form wider panoramic openings in traditional structures. We selected stained wood windows and doors, and matching stained eaves and beamed rafter tails, which are prevalent in central Italy. New additions followed the same grouping of arched windows and openings, flooding their interiors with natural light.

The interior was gutted and added onto substantively using motifs from Spanish and Italian architecture in California from that era. Because our client has an extensive collection of antiques and art, we kept the wood flooring in a dark walnut parquet for all the formal rooms and stone integrated with walnut banding in the family areas, features that you see frequently in central Italy.

The back of the property has a discreetly located service entry from an alley that was a perfect location for the new guest house, which hides the garage and provides a focal point for the termination of the pool with a loggia and outdoor fireplace. The guest house provides additional quarters for our client's family and friends in a private setting.

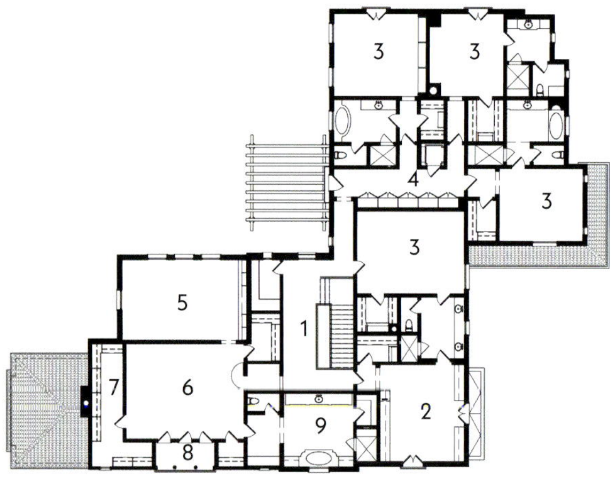

SECOND-FLOOR PLAN

1 Stair hall
2 Study
3 Bedroom
4 Hall
5 Master sitting area
6 Master bedroom
7 Closet
8 Loggia
9 Master bath

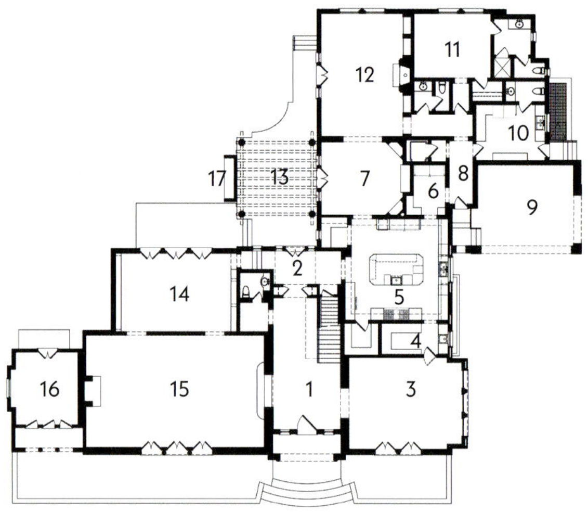

FIRST-FLOOR PLAN

1 Entrance hall
2 Hall
3 Dining room
4 Butler's pantry
5 Kitchen
6 Pantry
7 Breakfast room
8 Hall
9 Porte-cochère
10 Laundry
11 Guest room
12 Family room
13 Terrace
14 Library
15 Living room
16 Gym
17 Barbecue

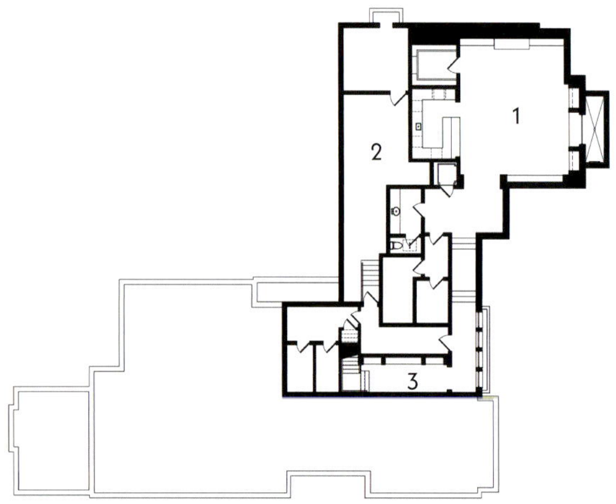

LOWER-LEVEL FLOOR PLAN

1 Media room
2 Equipment
3 Hall

0 16 32 ft

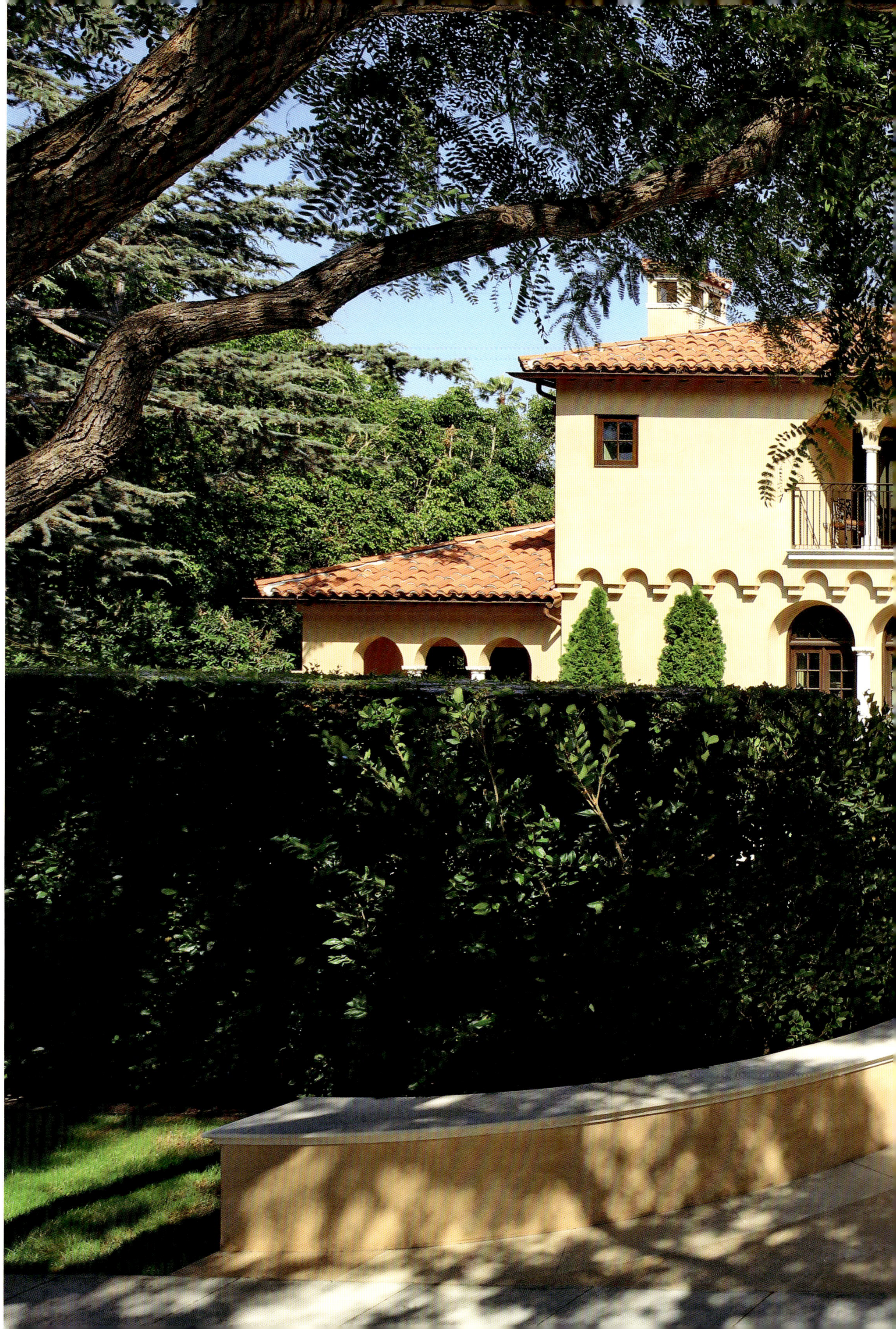

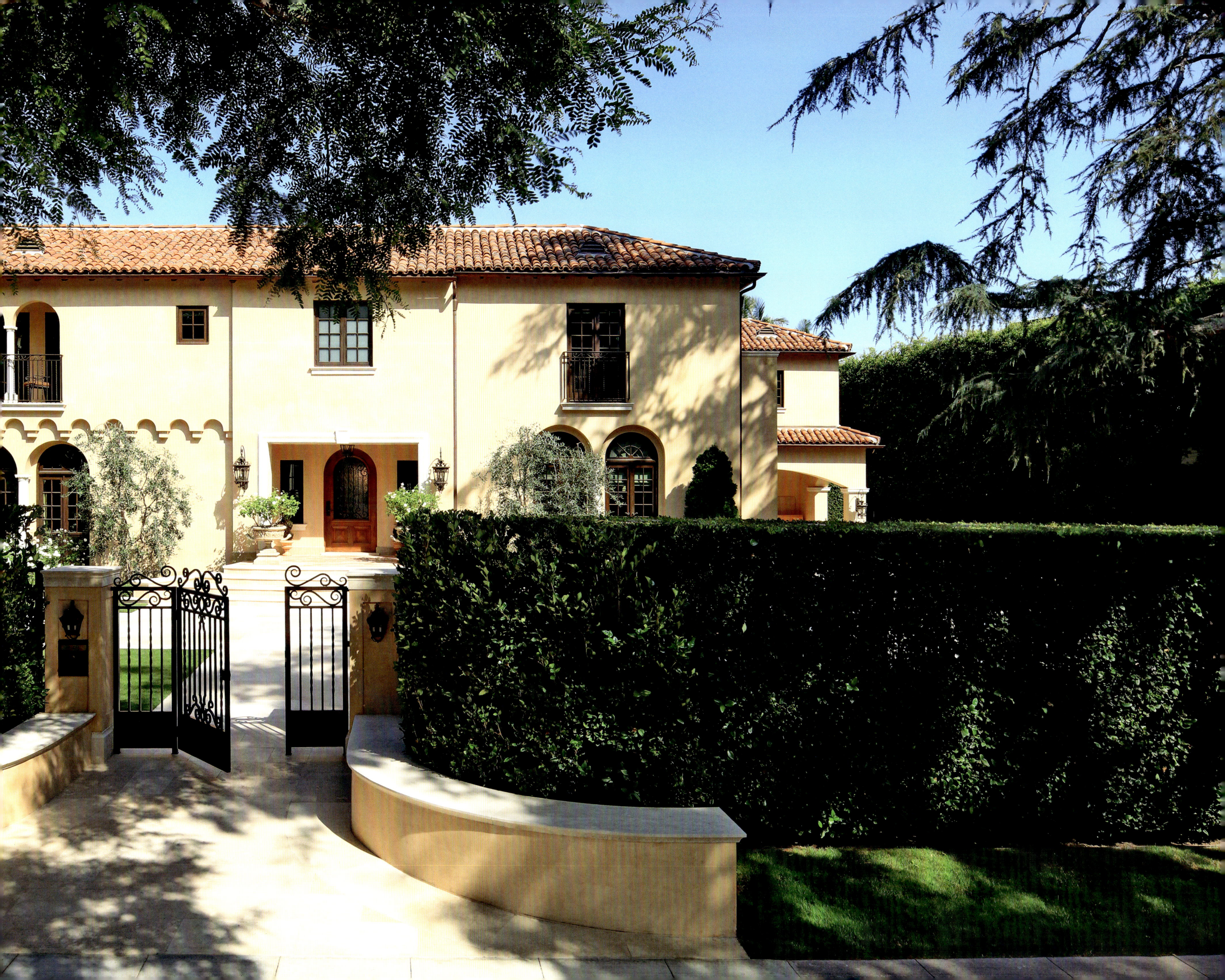

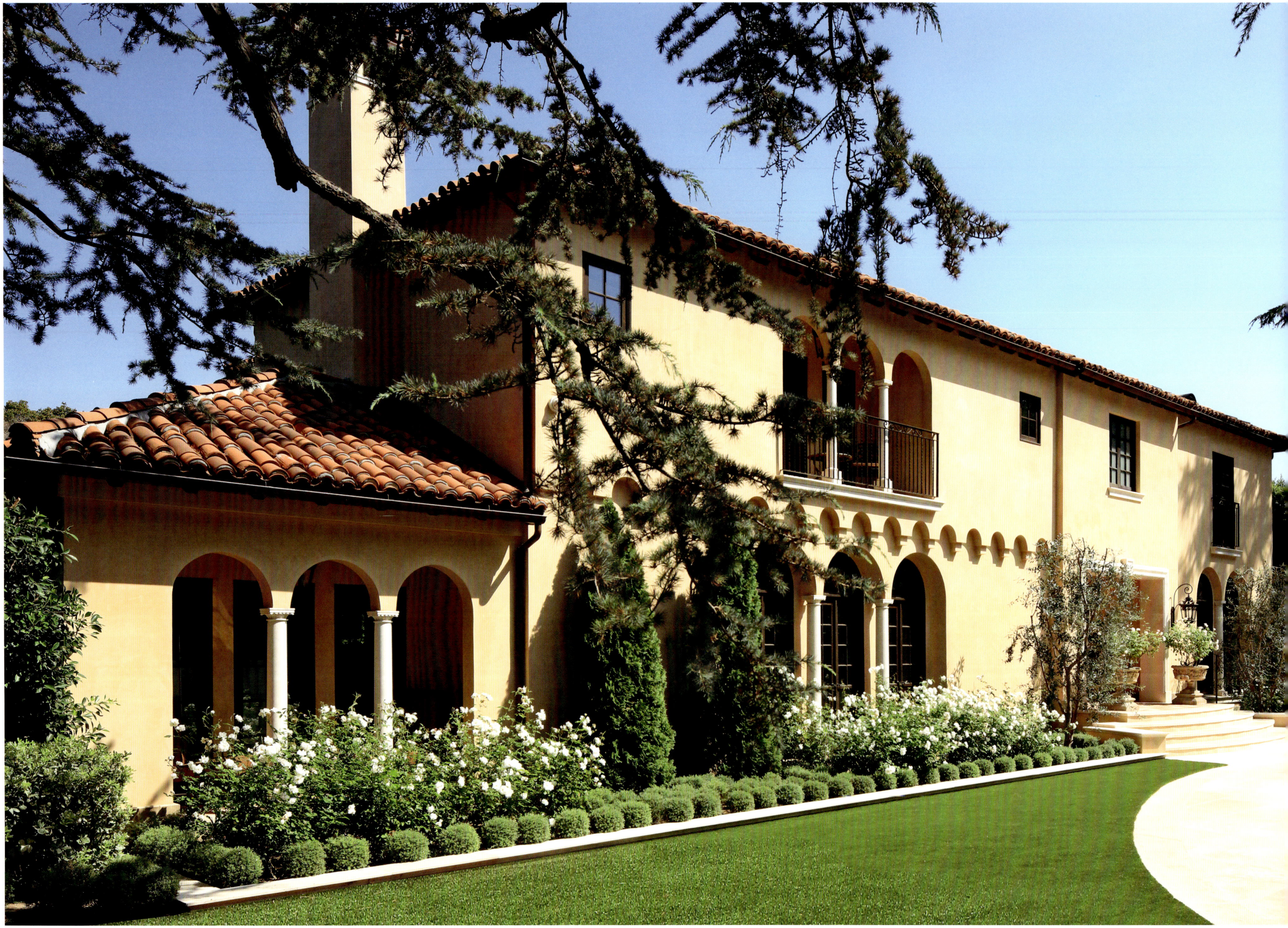

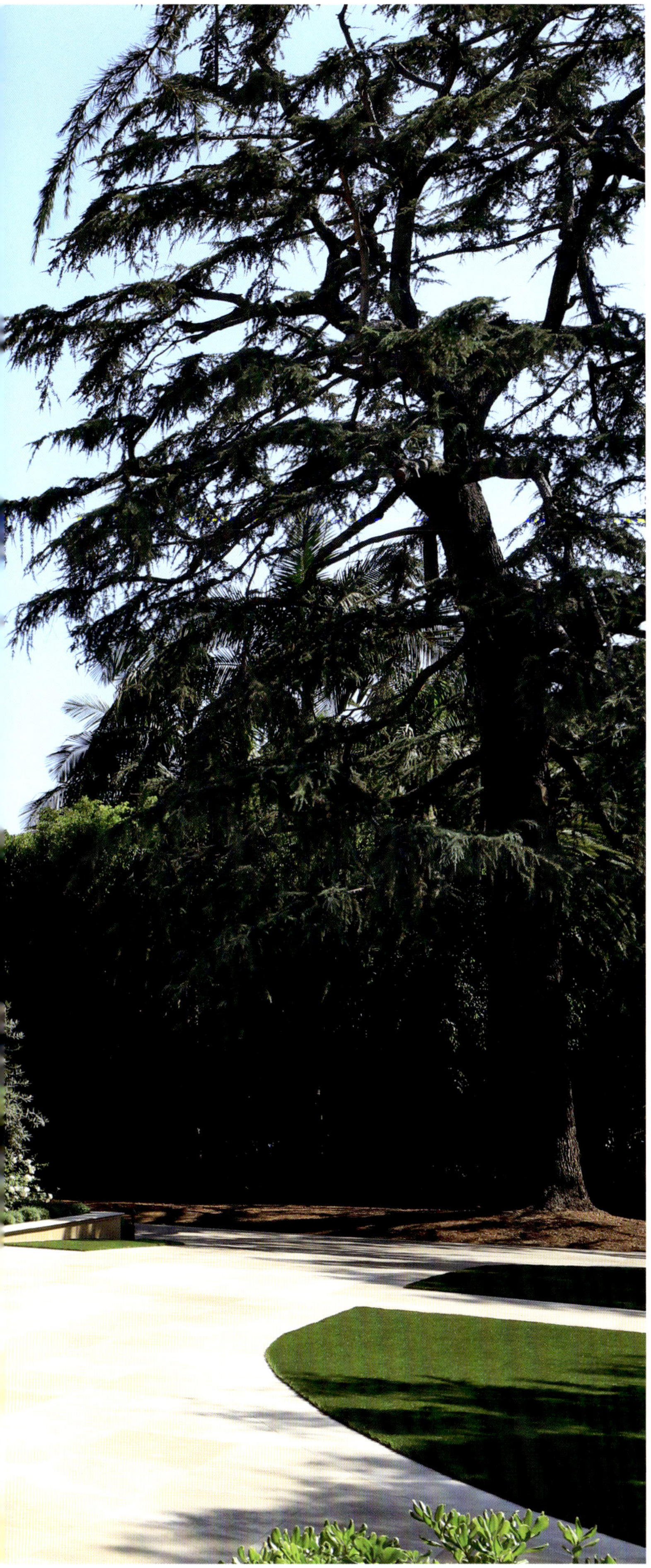

PREVIOUS PAGES AND LEFT: *Framed by massive Atlas cedars and cypress trees, Casa California's front façade displays many of its signature California Mediterranean Revival features—red-tile roof and long loggias framed by arched openings. Sited on a pie-shaped lot, the driveway approach is a long curve up to the dramatic entrance.*

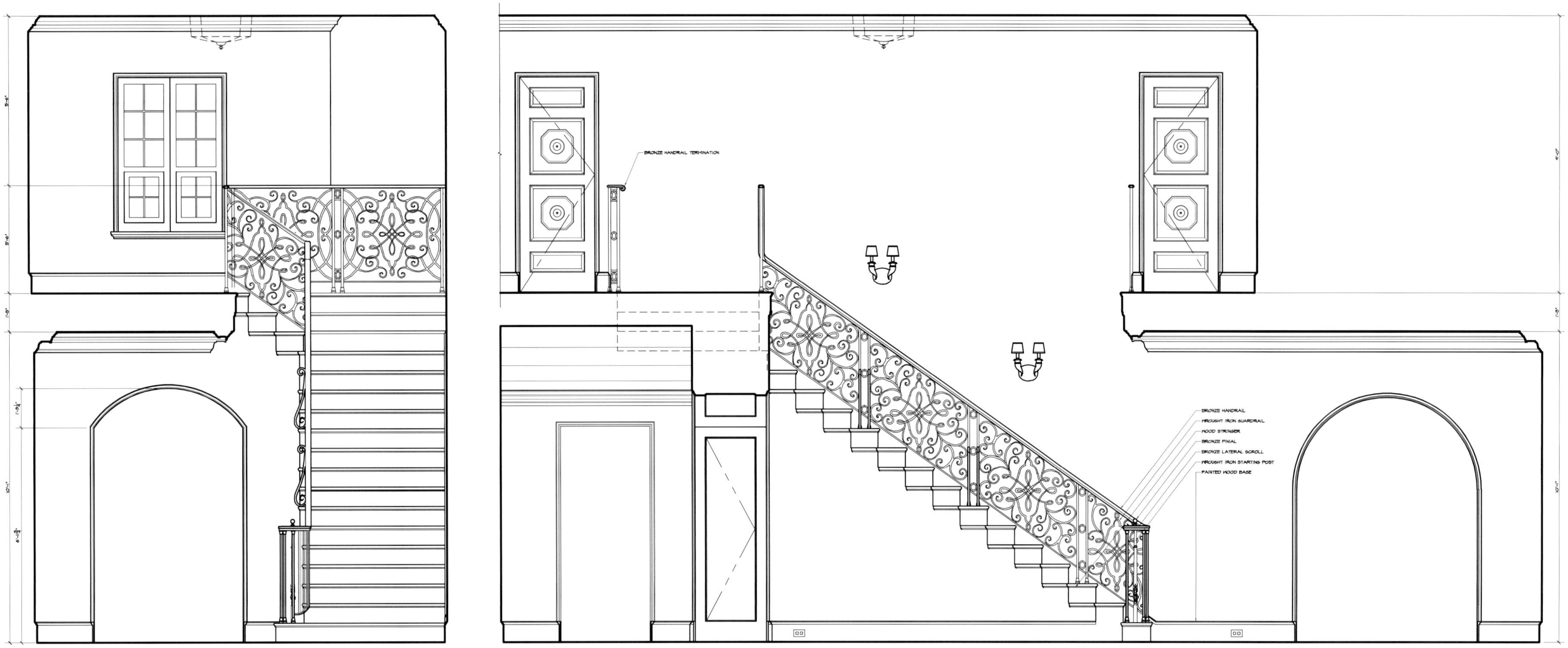

ABOVE: *Detail of the main stair and railing.*

OPPOSITE: *Our client wanted to maintain the elegant Mediterranean style while updating all the systems and finishes throughout. The entire interior was gutted and added onto substantively. The two-story stair hall sets the tone with dark walnut floors and ornate railing that is a nod to the more Baroque style of Spanish Renaissance architecture.*

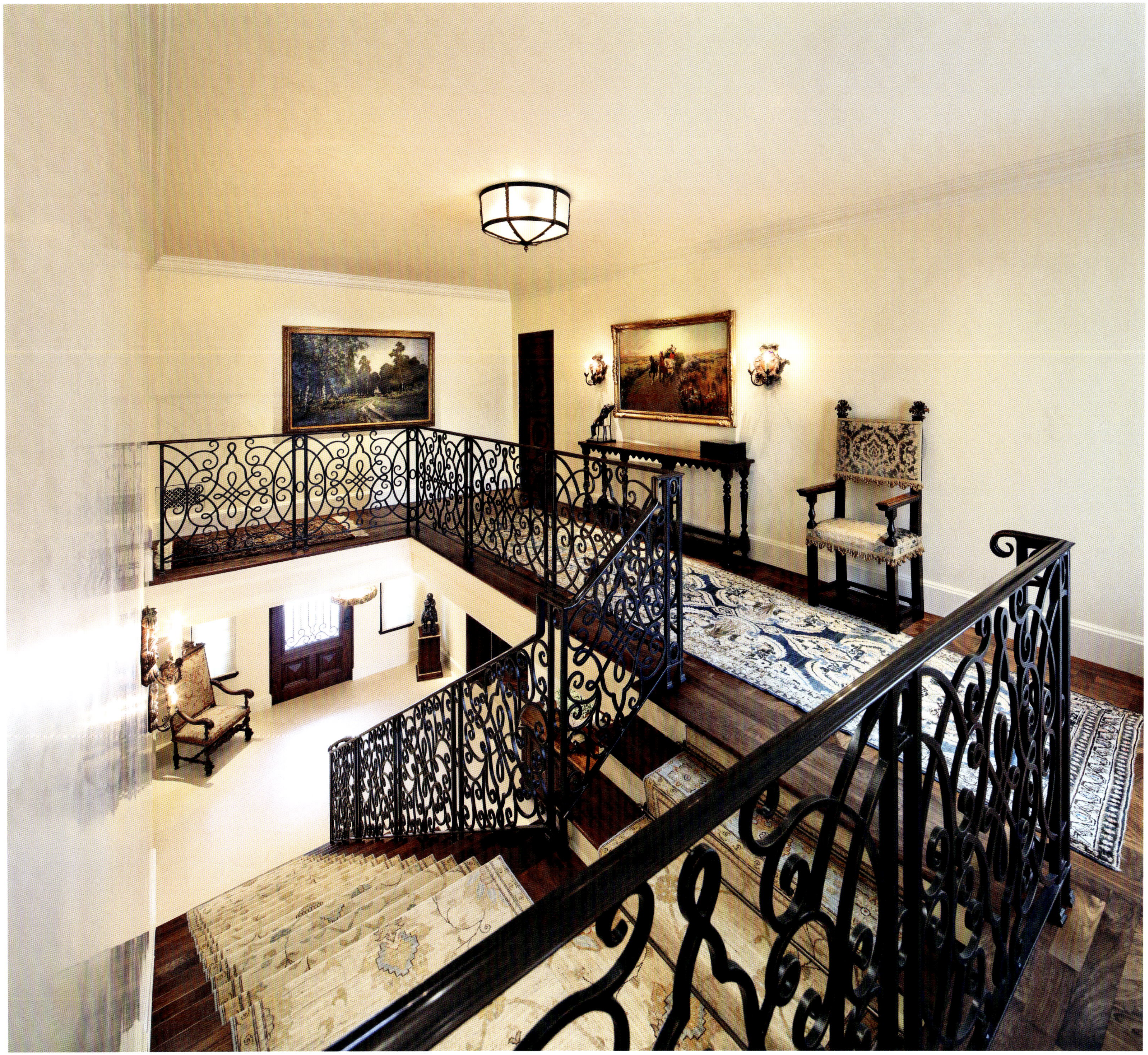

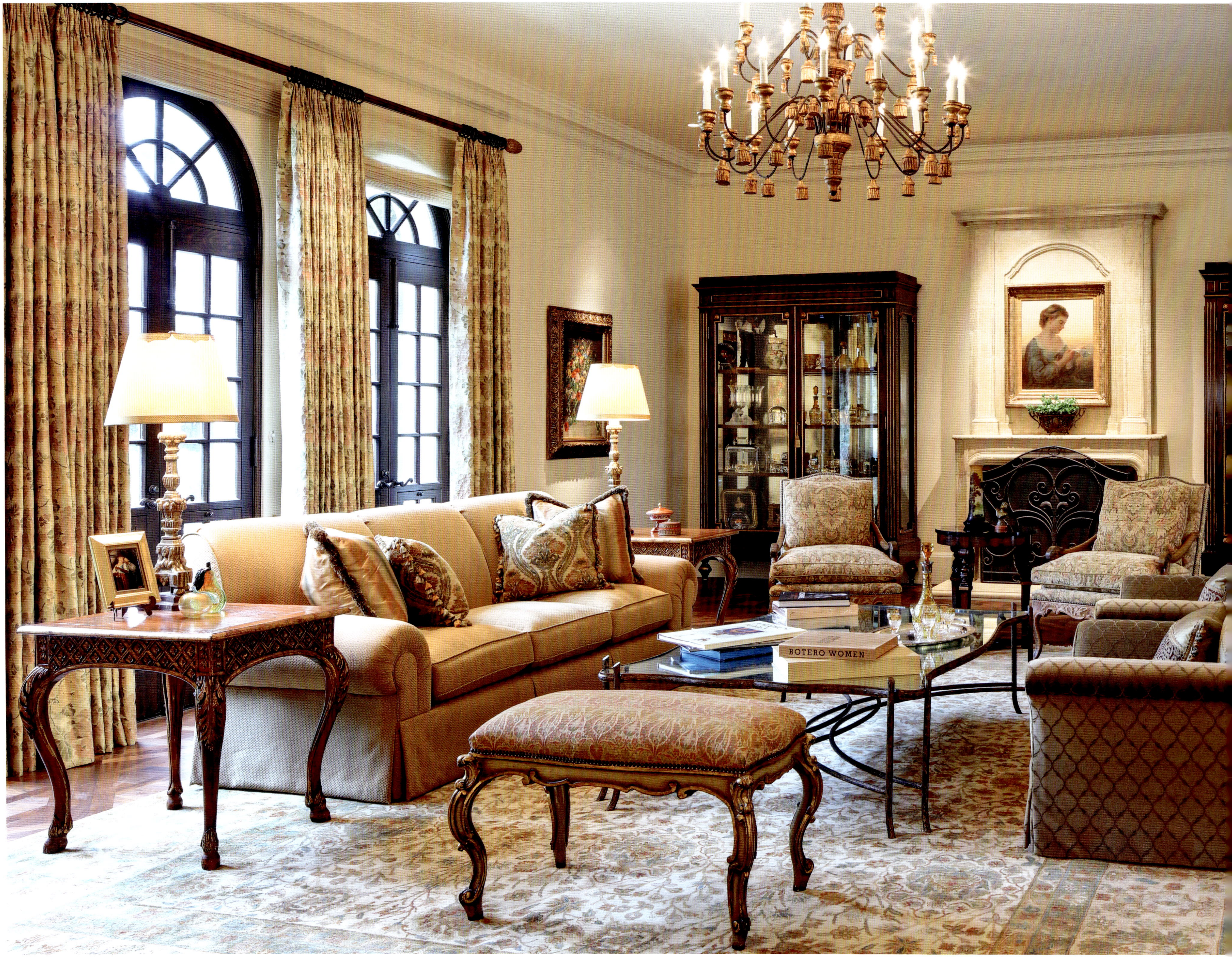
BOTERO WOMEN

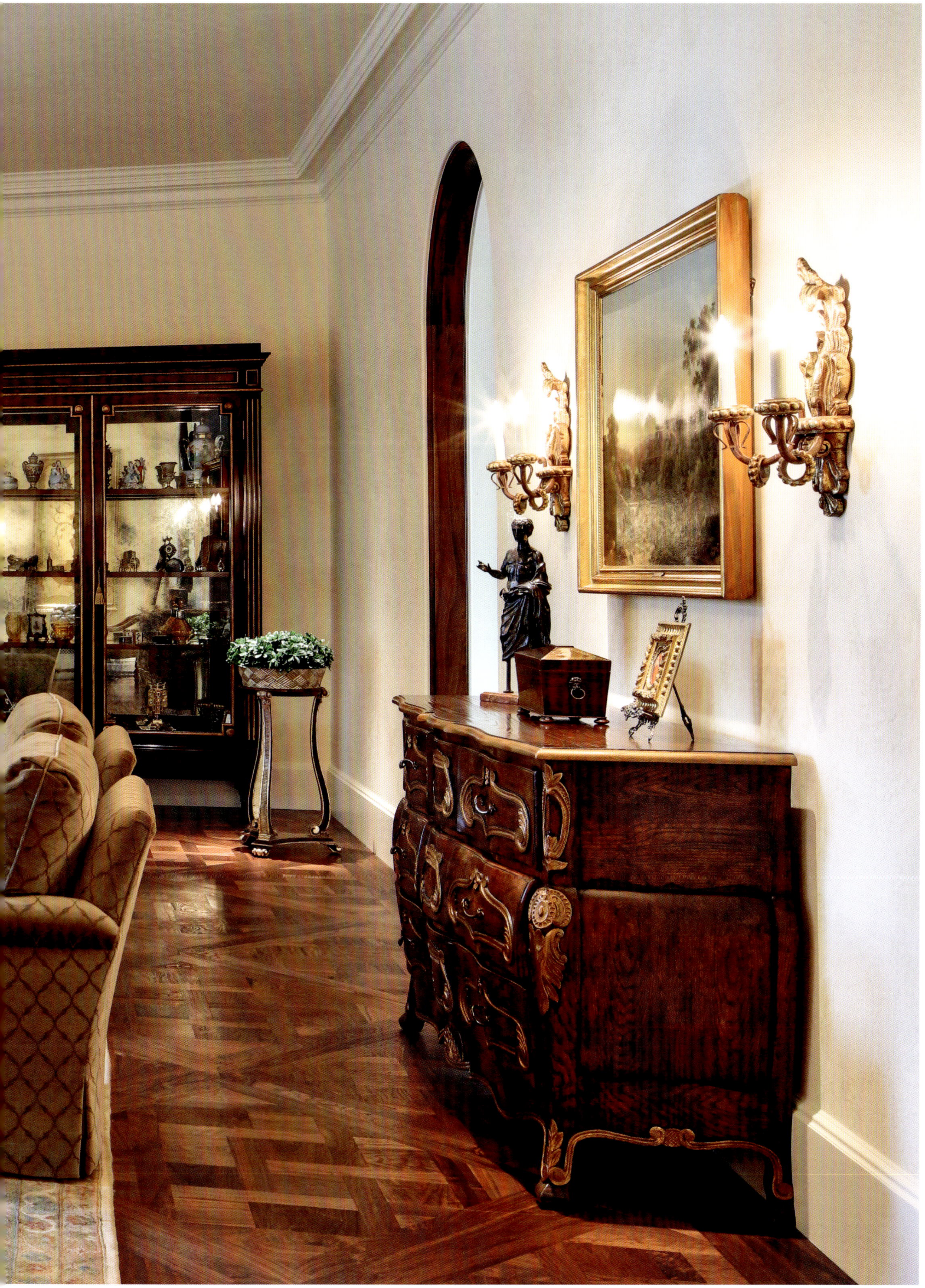

LEFT: *The vision of a classic villa was brought to life by interior designer Melissa Partridge, who used the client's antiques and paintings mixed with custom furnishings.*

FOLLOWING PAGES, LEFT: *The view into the dining room shows how wood was used in every door opening. Instead of casing the archways, we used inset walnut panels to accent the transition between rooms. It ties the millwork together from the mahogany windows and doors to the floors, cabinetry, and the furnishings.* RIGHT: *The library's stone fireplace with scroll brackets was inspired by Italian architecture and the coffered ceiling with beams has painted panels to lighten up the space.*

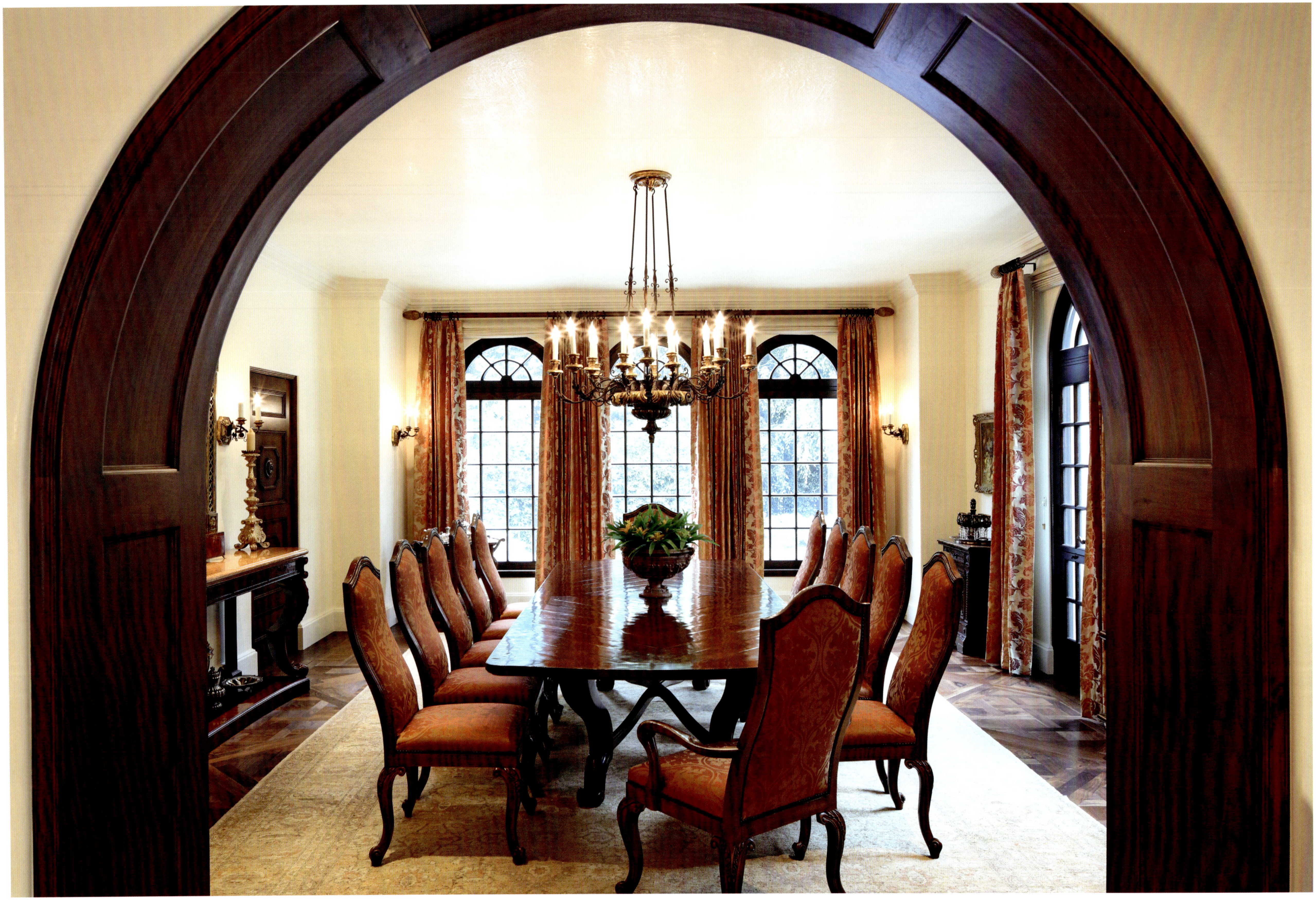

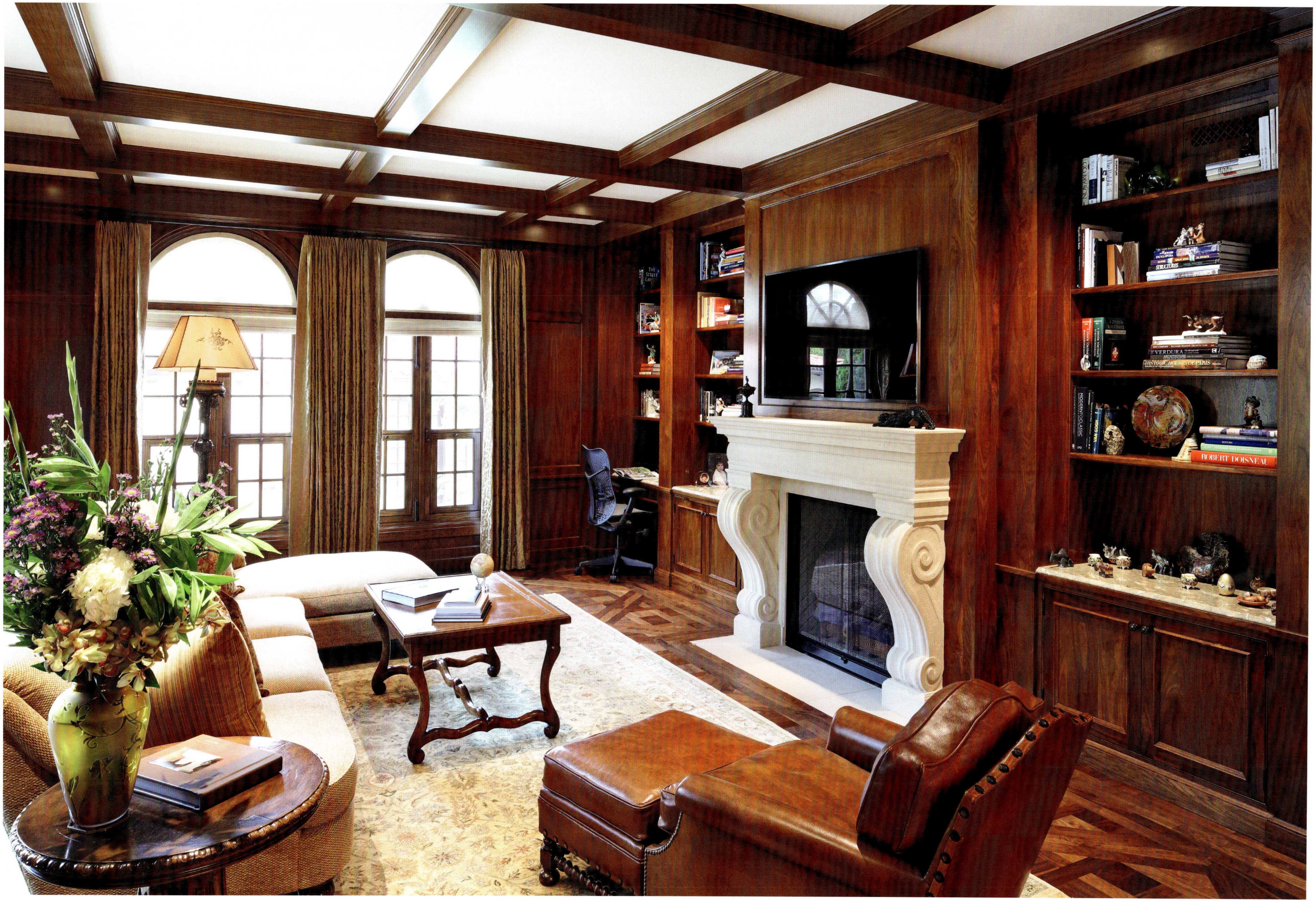
ROBERT DOISNEAU

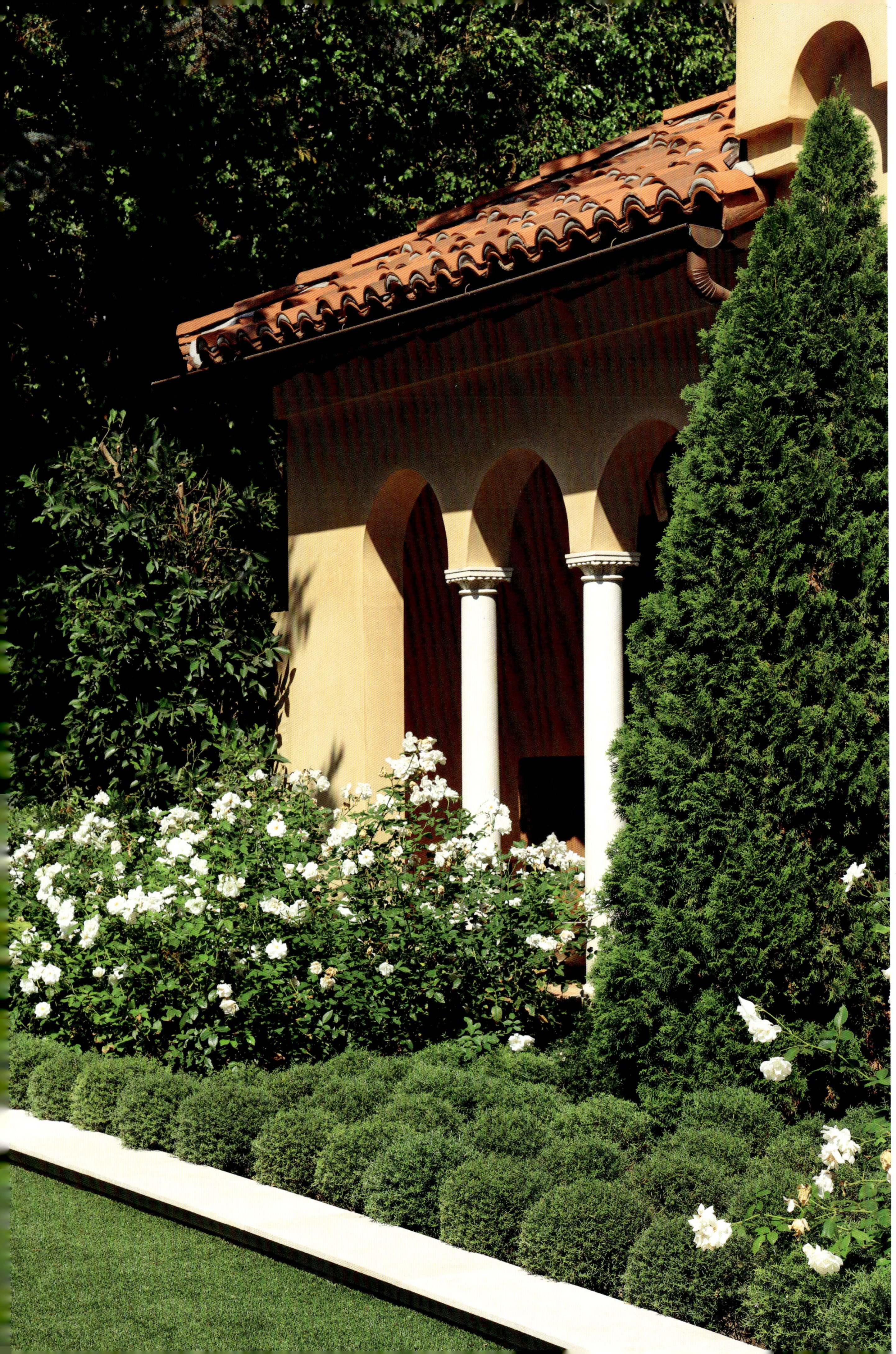

LEFT: *A detail of the front arched loggia.*

OPPOSITE: *The pool house was designed to look like a loggia for outdoor entertainment, with a fireplace and a guest house that conceals the garages. It is a focal point for the termination of the pool and provides covered outdoor seating. Landscaping is by Leyva & Wilde.*

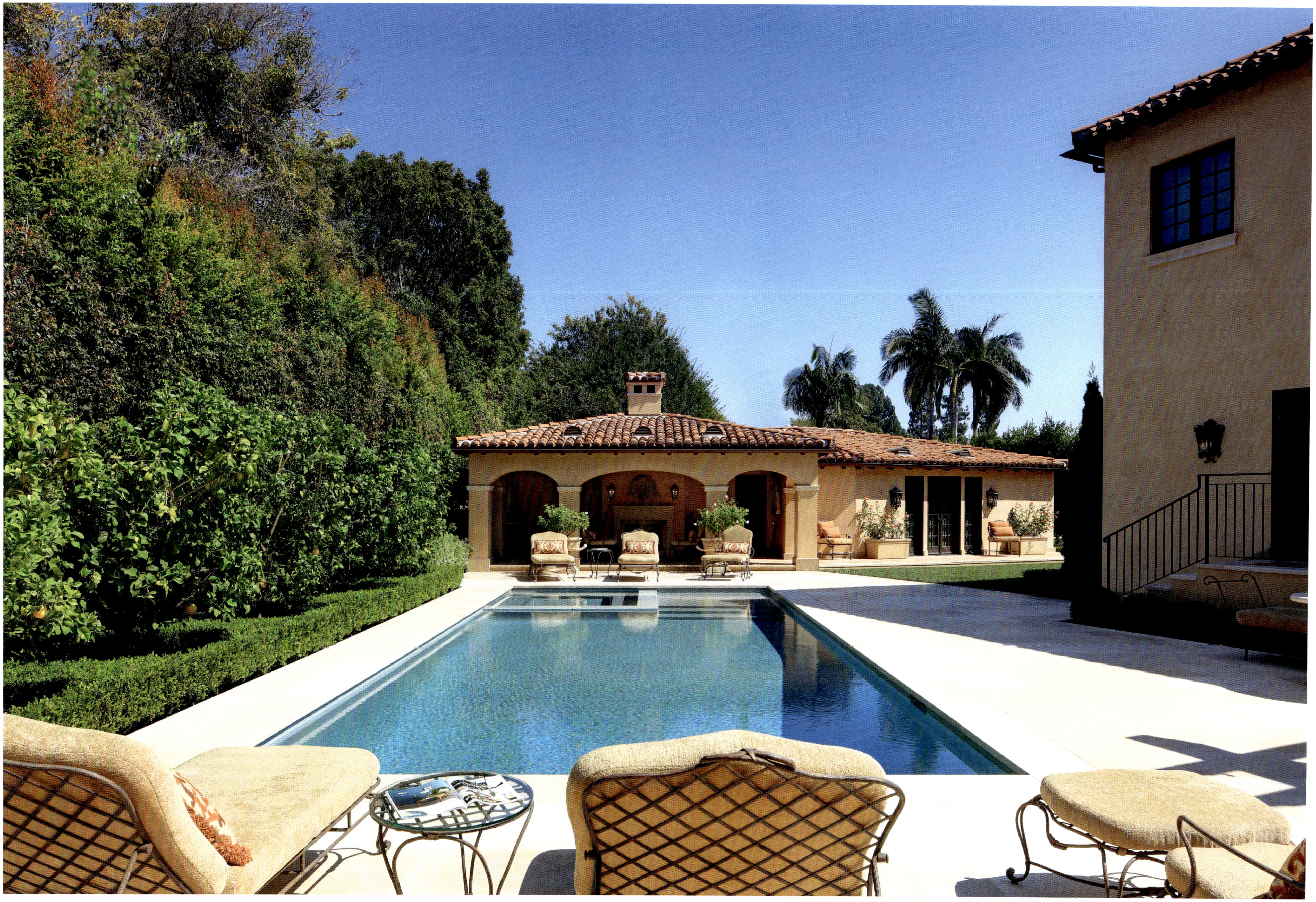

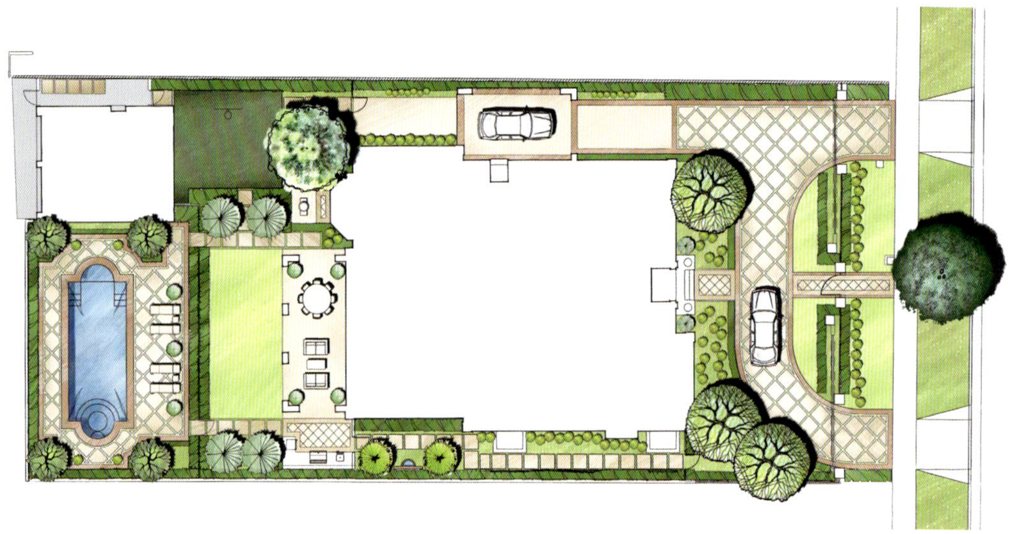

MAISON DUNAND

Beverly Hills

Built from the ground up for a couple with young children, this Beverly Hills residence is a contemporary interpretation of a French Provincial country house.

Our narrative for the project was envisioning a house that was built decades ago and our clients undertook an extensive remodel and reinvention of the interiors. This fit nicely within the Beverly Hills' design requirement that the exterior of every new traditional home must be designed in one of a number of historical styles and emulate the features of that style.

The exterior has a tailored rusticity with handmade tan brick, limestone, and brick-shaped moldings, a steep roofline evocative of French manor houses, and an overscaled entry surround of limestone. Steel doors and windows bridge the transition between exterior and interior, and the more contemporary sconces and lanterns are a subtle hint that, once inside, it becomes a different type of house.

The interior organization is classical, with a central two-story skylit stair hall that becomes the focal space around which all rooms flow. Our goal was to maximize room sizes and minimize unneeded circulation space.

The room shapes and organization might seem traditional, but the finishes, colors, and patterns are bolder, stronger and largely tone-on-tone to modernize the design. Open-plan interiors mix traditional architectural elements with a contemporary sensibility inspired by the work of French designer Jean-Louis Deniot, who blends modern interiors with traditional architecture.

Rooms with beautiful paneling and woodwork mixed with edgy, modern, and bold pieces was our clients' goal. They wanted a home that was elegant, welcoming, and comfortable, a place where they could entertain guests and a family home to enjoy and watch their children grow.

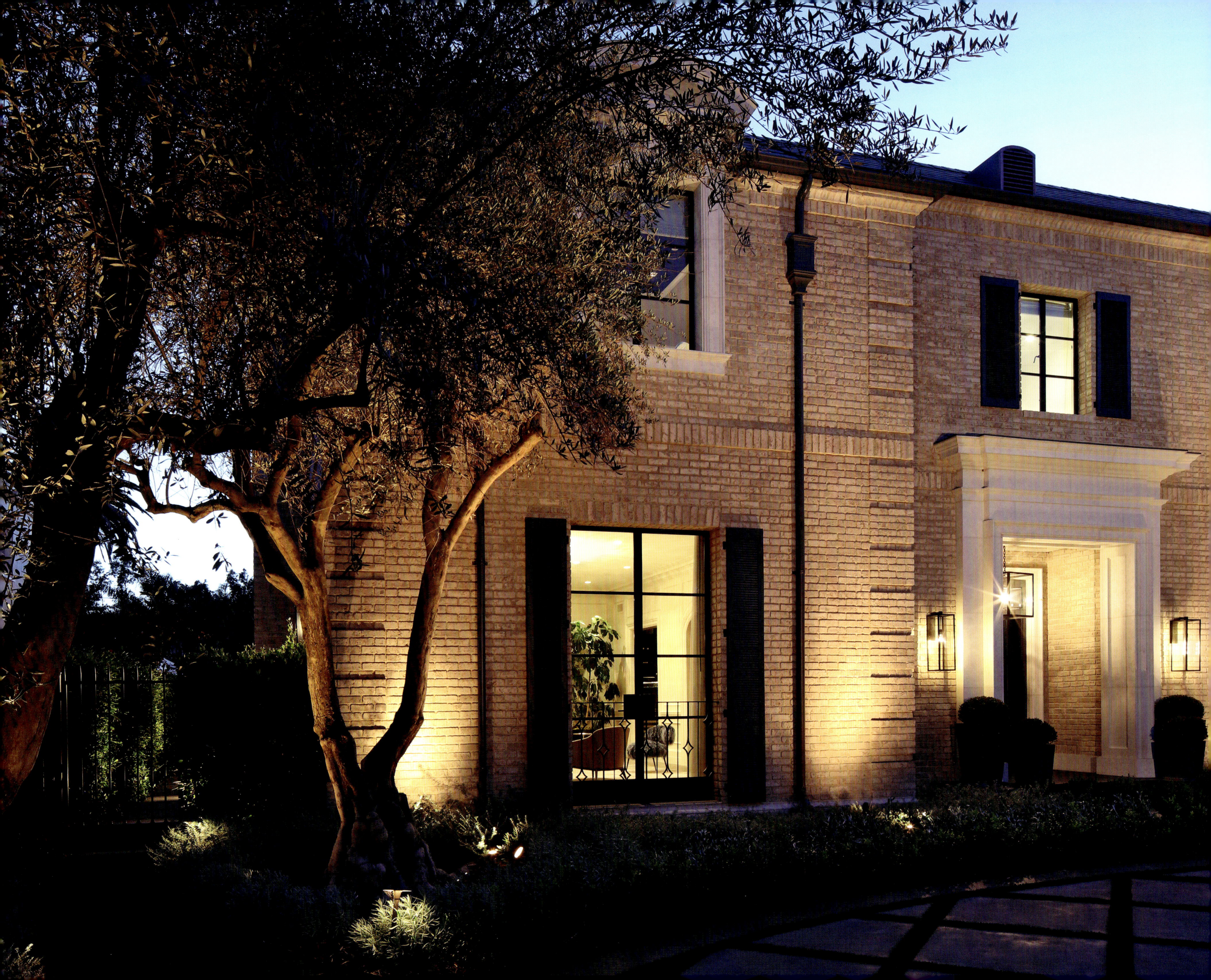

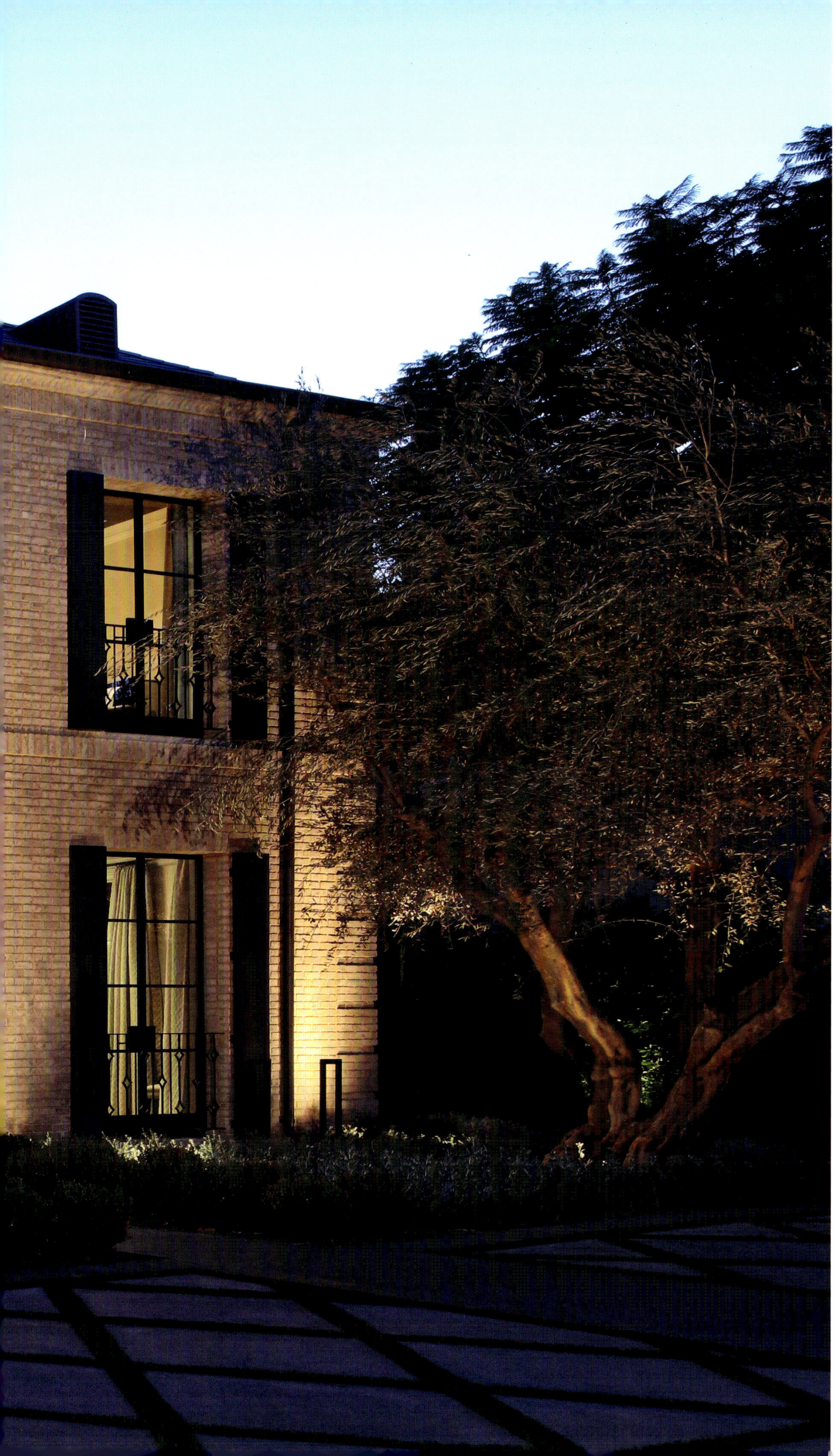

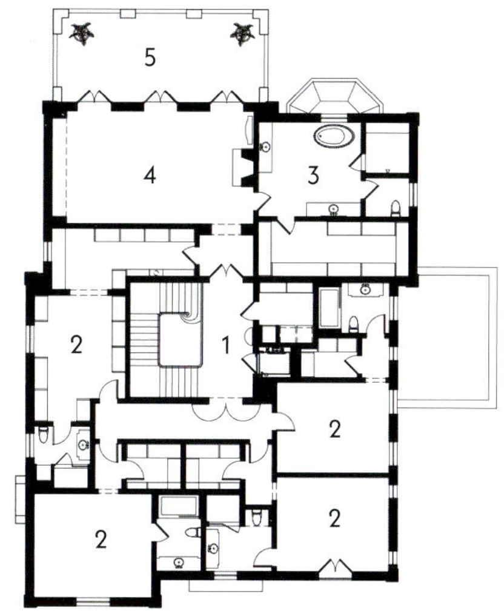

SECOND-FLOOR PLAN

1 Upper stair hall
2 Bedroom
3 Master bath
4 Master bedroom
5 Master terrace

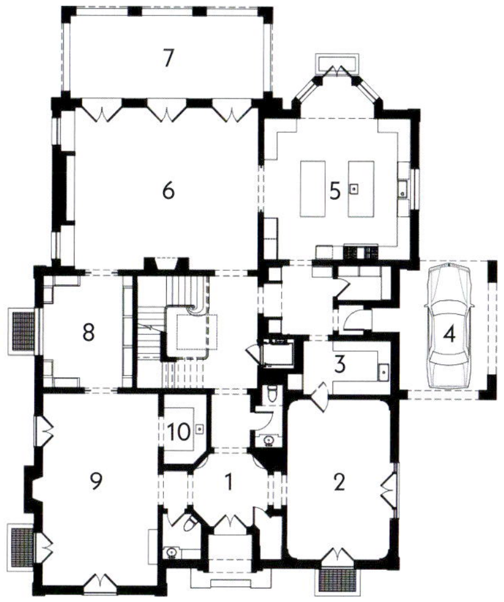

FIRST-FLOOR PLAN

1 Foyer
2 Dining room
3 Butler's pantry
4 Porte-cochère
5 Kitchen
6 Family room
7 Veranda
8 Library
9 Living room
10 Bar

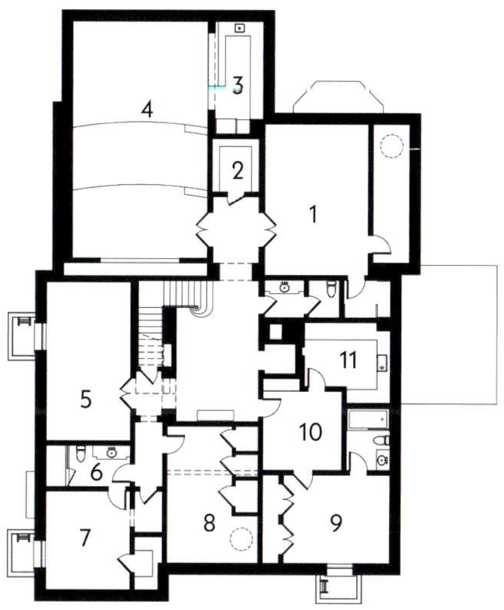

BASEMENT FLOOR PLAN

1 Playroom
2 Wine room
3 Bar
4 Games/screening room
5 Exercise room
6 Guest bath
7 Guest room
8 Mechanical/storage area
9 Staff quarters
10 Staff sitting room
11 Laundry

0 8 16 32 ft

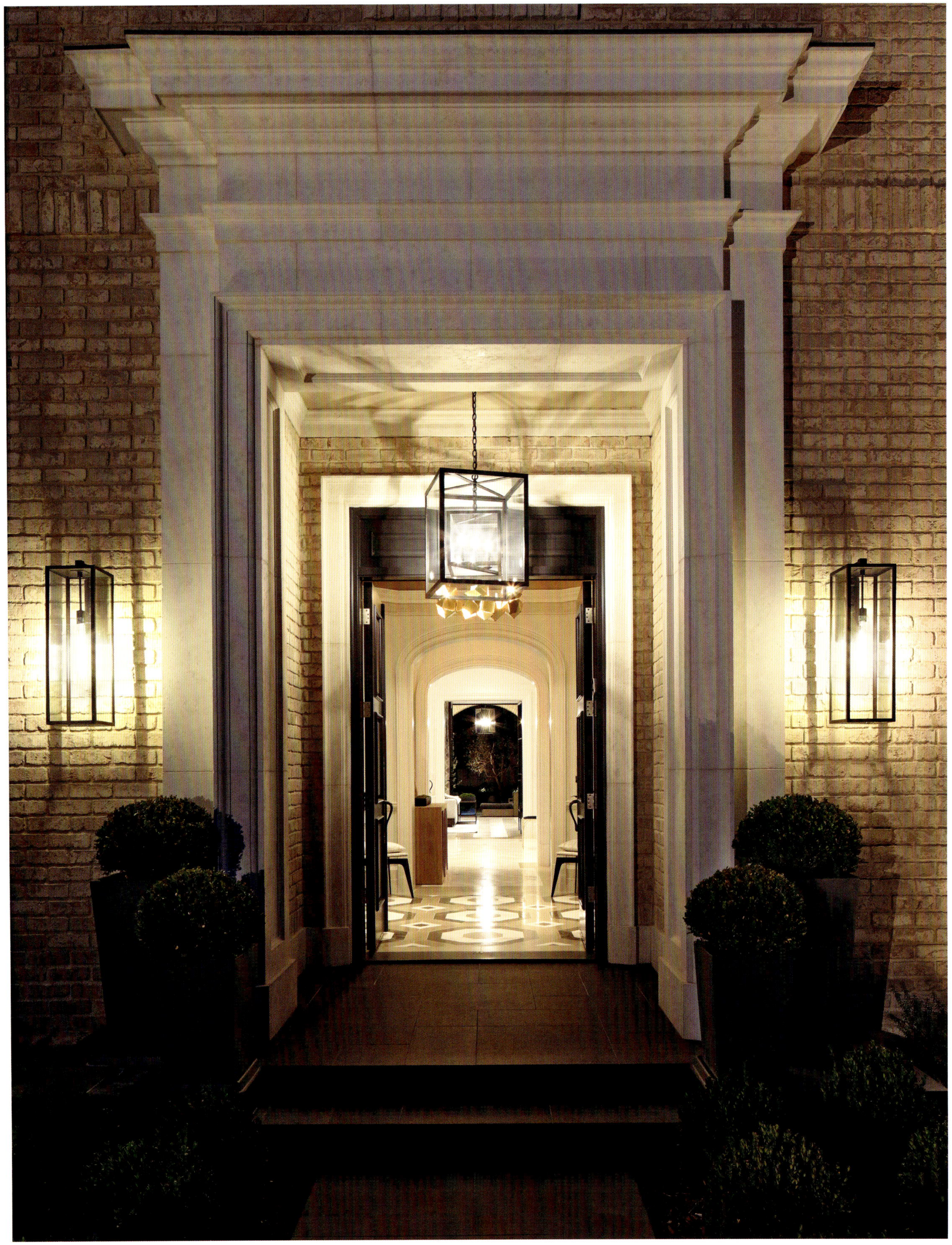

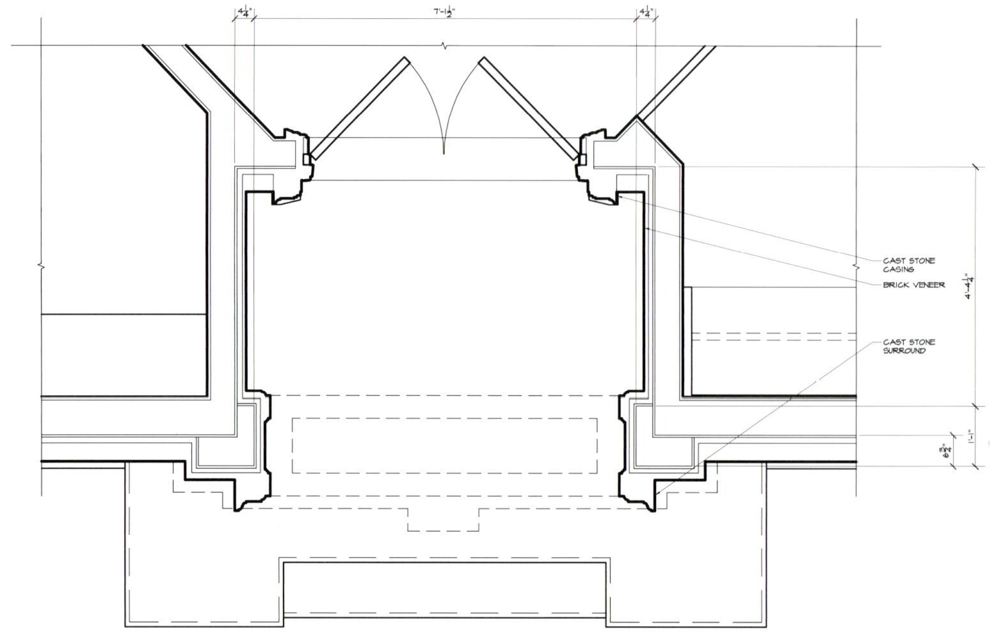
CAST STONE CASING
BRICK VENEER
CAST STONE SURROUND

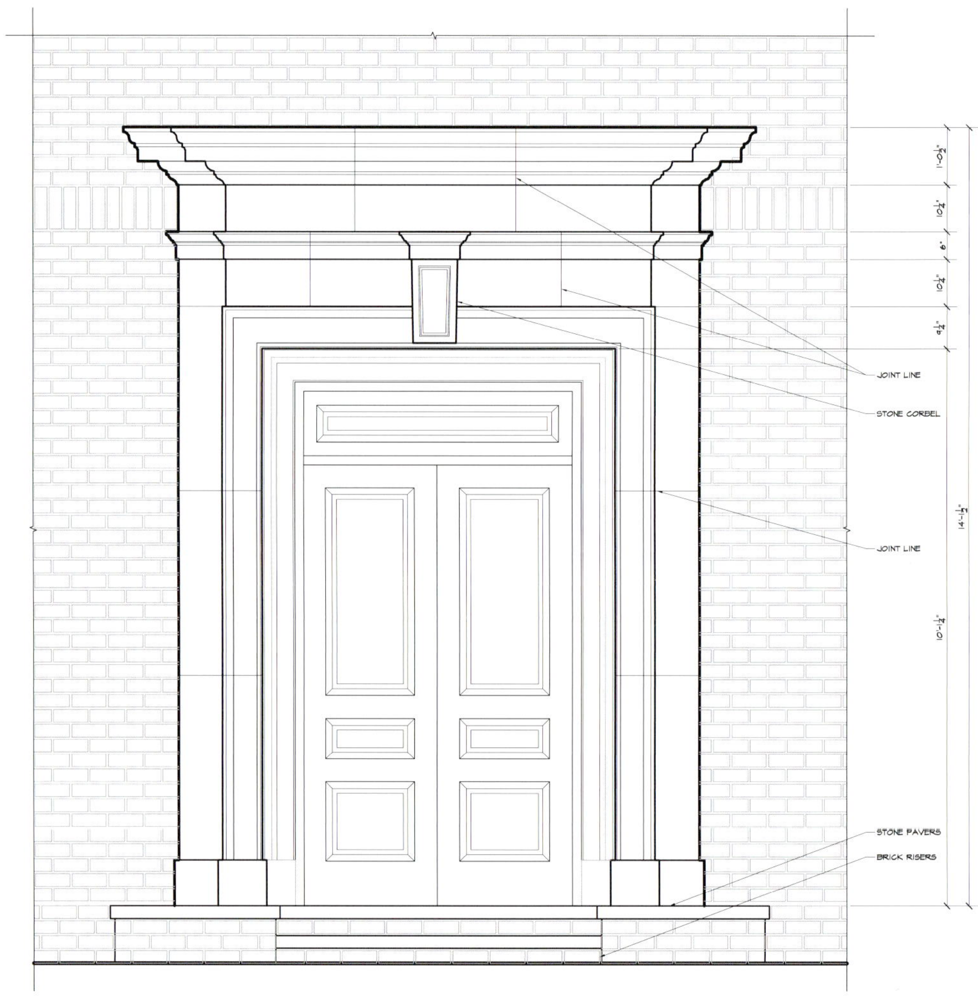
JOINT LINE
STONE CORBEL
JOINT LINE
STONE PAVERS
BRICK RISERS

PREVIOUS PAGES: *Our contemporary interpretation of a French Provincial country house starts with a rustic façade of handmade tan brick made modern with steel doors and windows.*

OPPOSITE LEFT: *The overscaled limestone entry surround.*

OPPOSITE RIGHT: *Drawing detail of the surround.*

RIGHT: *The clients' goal was a traditional French home with contemporary interiors. The classic stair hall has a Neoclassical flooring of cabochons and a streamlined railing. Contrasting light fixtures from the 1960s and '70s are by Fontana Arte.*

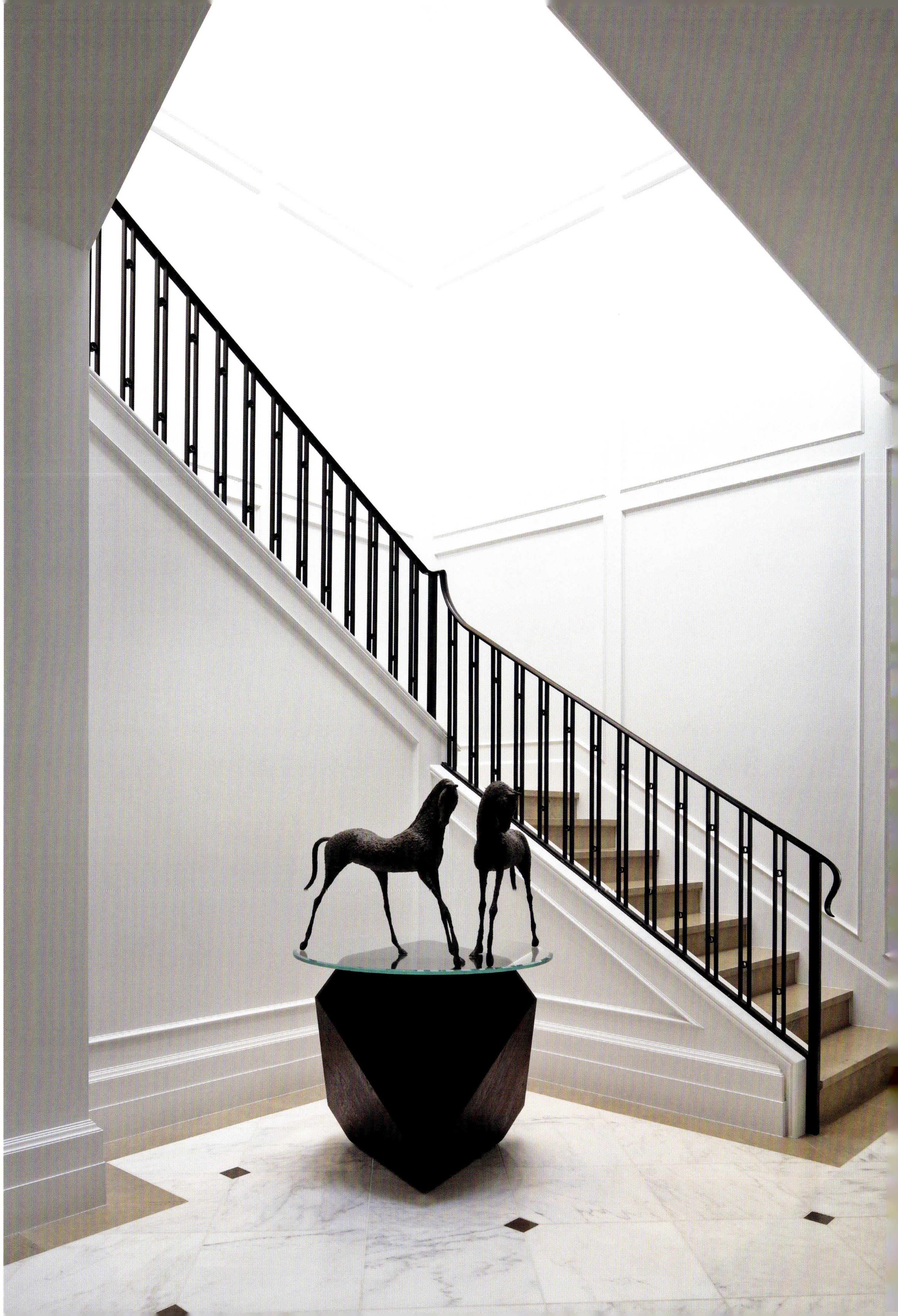

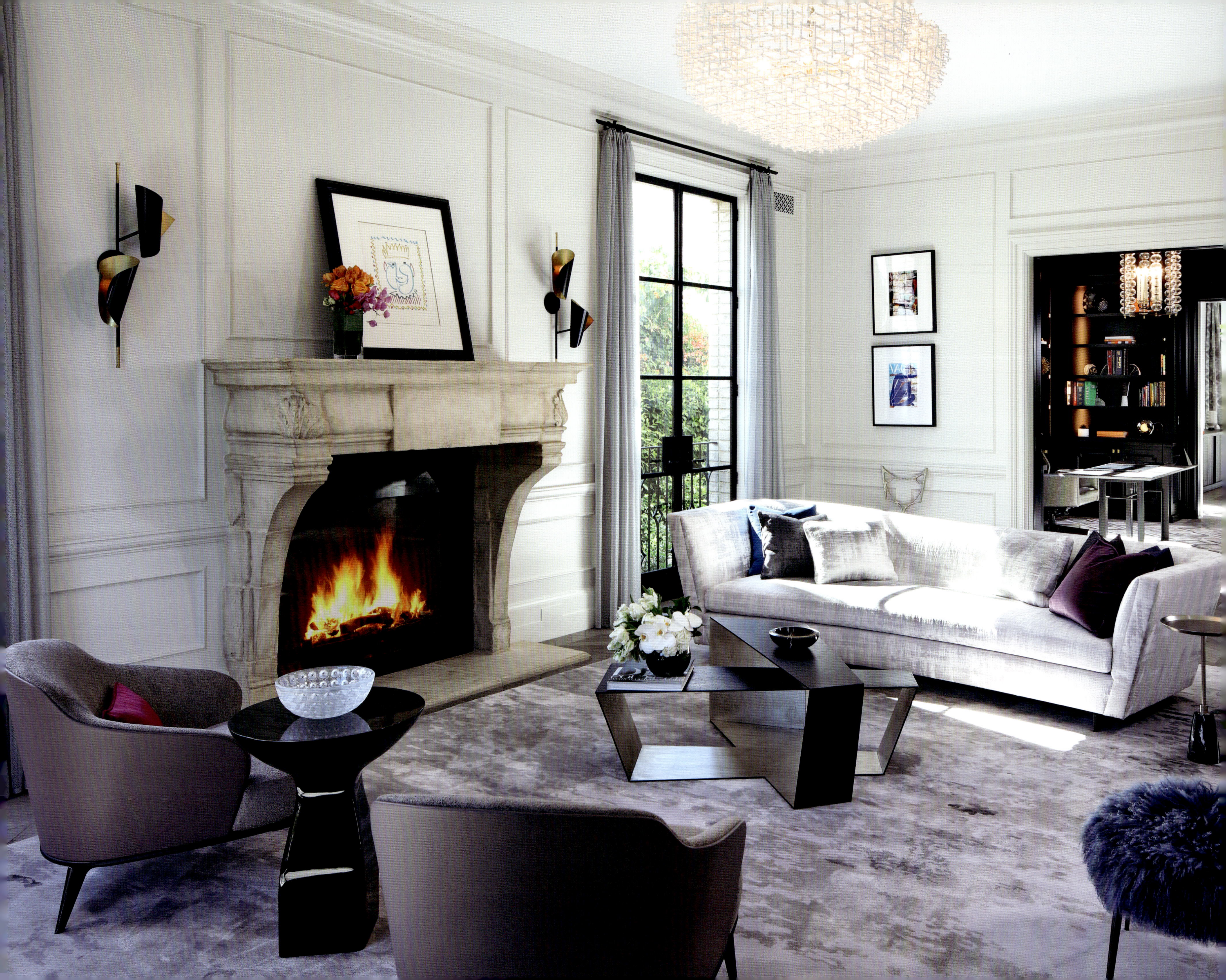

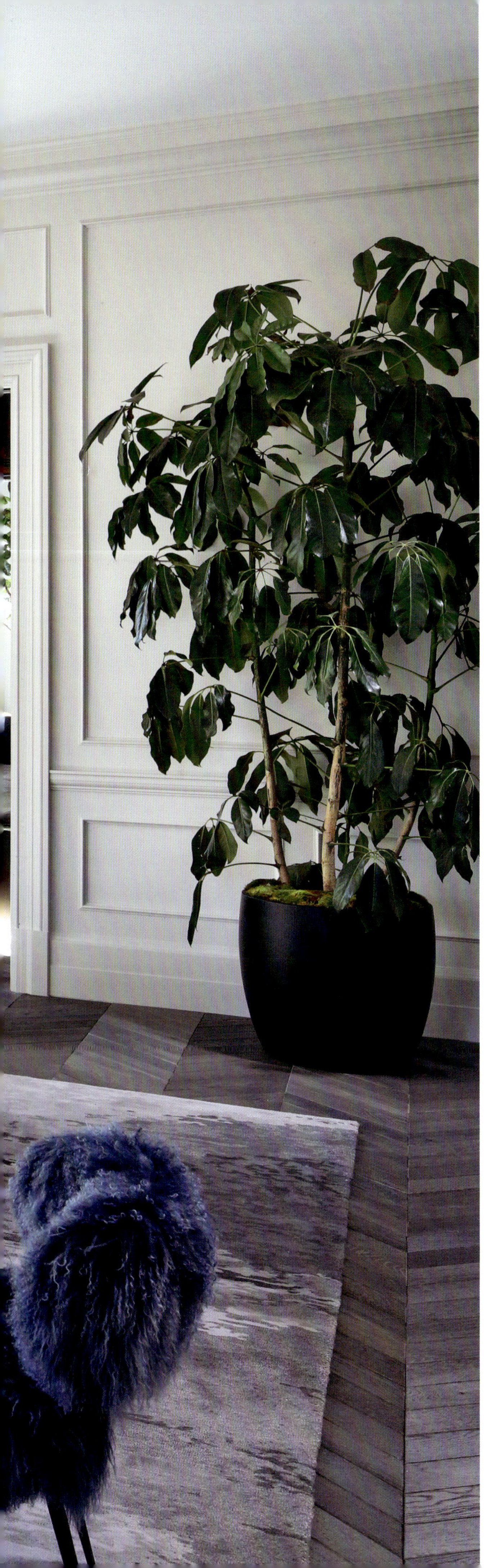

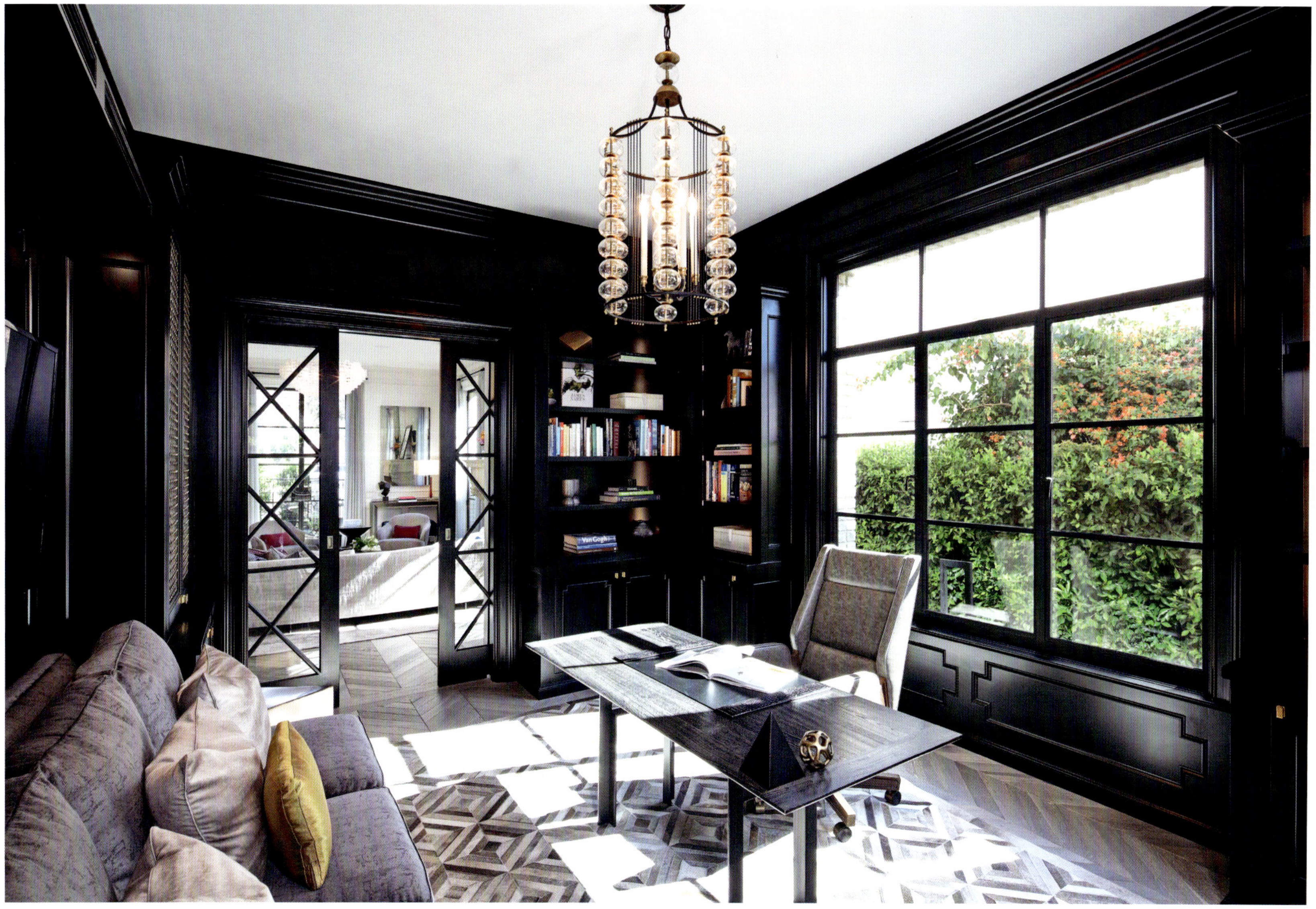

LEFT: *The antique fireplace in the living room combines elements from the past with chic modern furniture and lighting for a more curated look. French chevron oak floors were stained in gray as opposed to the typical honey color.*

ABOVE: *The study, which connects the living and family rooms through pocket doors, is a twist on a darker, traditional library but done in black lacquer. Thanks to numerous windows, the room is very bright, which makes the contrast intense. Interior designer Dory Novian used a vintage modernist steel desk with a cerused wood surface.*

FOLLOWING PAGES, LEFT: *The dining room's strapwork ceiling is a Tudor/Jacobean design done in a flat, streamlined way to unite tradition and modernity. The modern furnishings, drapery, and lighting work within the traditional framework of the chevron floor and cornices.* RIGHT: *The elegant, informal family room, which bridges the more structured living and dining rooms, is a symmetrical space with a subdued coffered ceiling and multiple doors and windows. Pocket doors open to our version of a modern French kitchen. The kitchen opens to the family room, but can be closed off during formal events.*

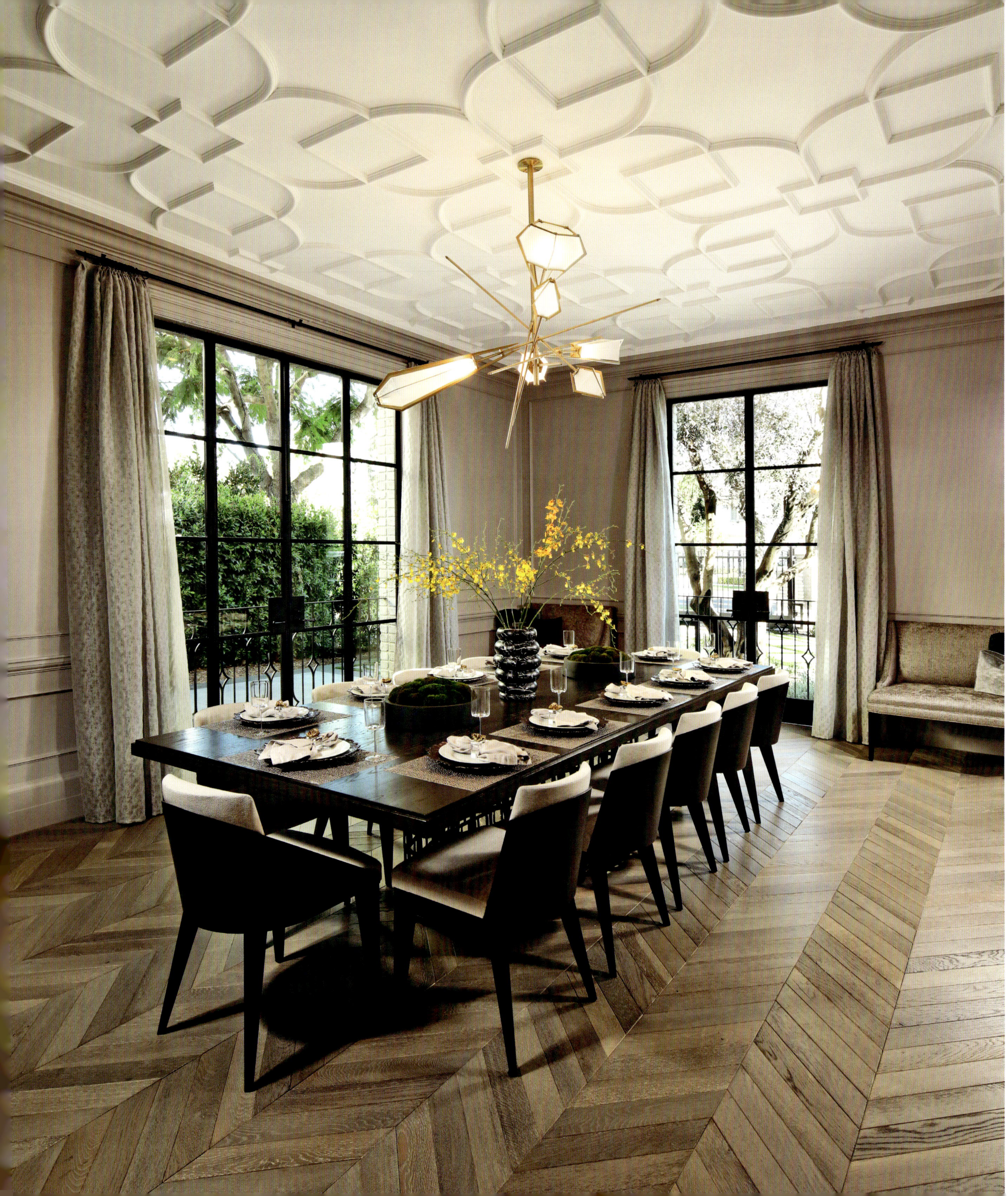

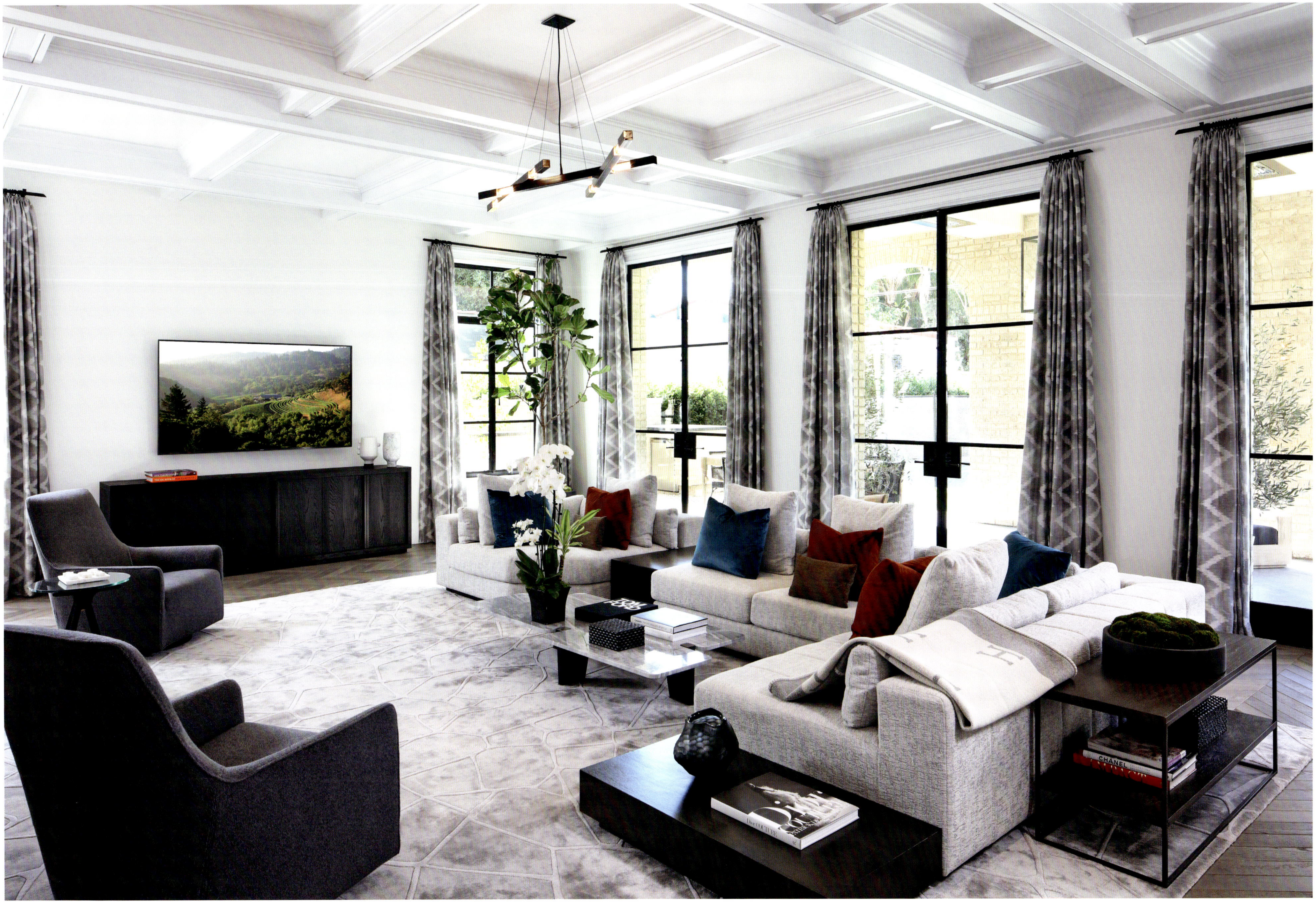

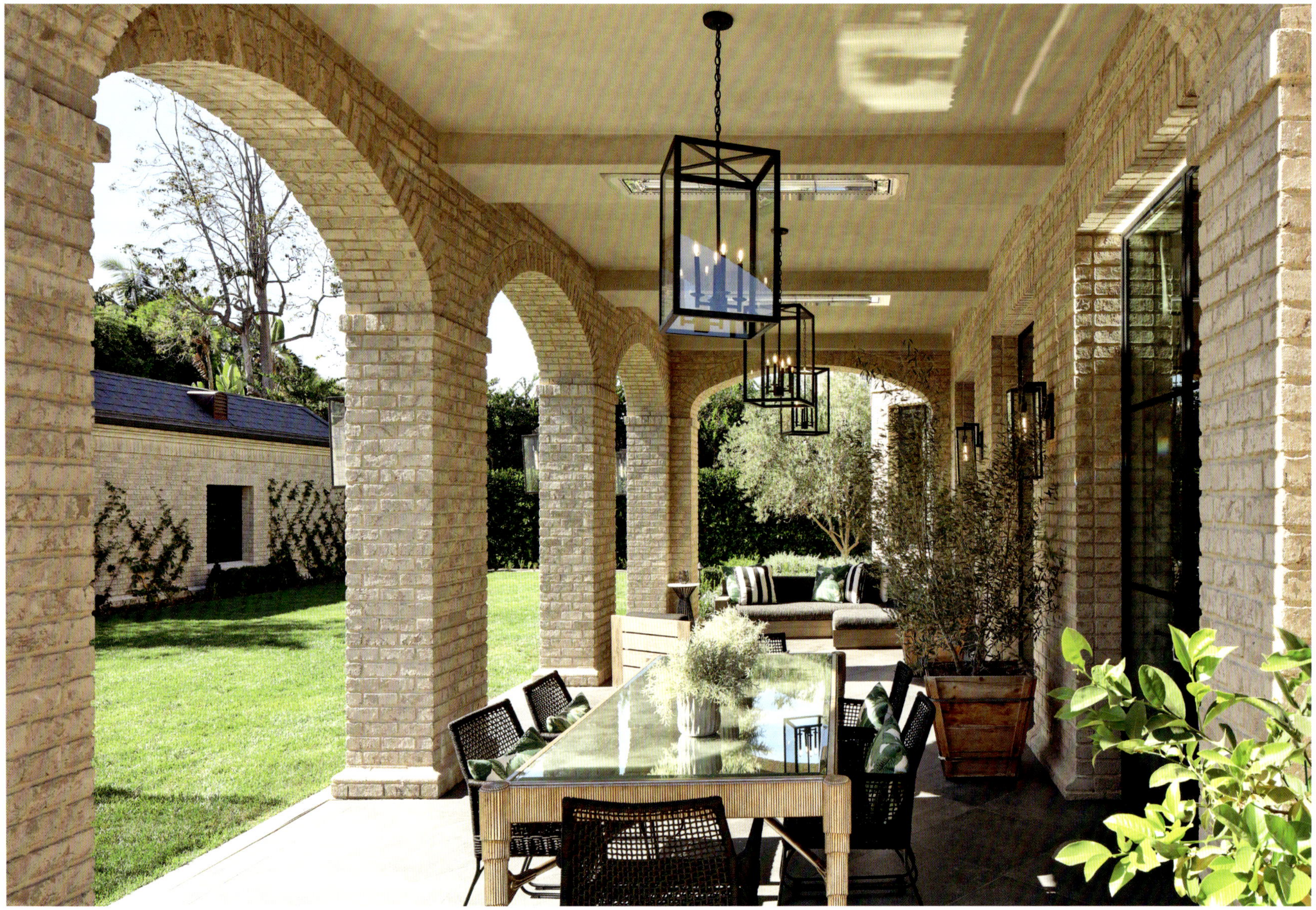

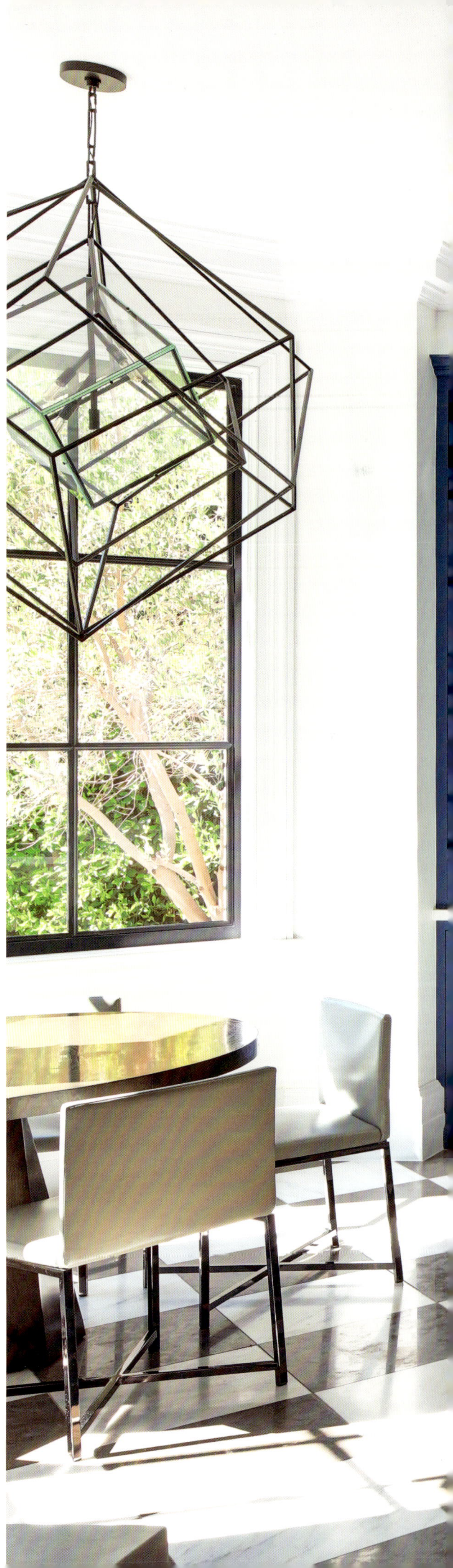

ABOVE: *As in many of our homes, the loggia becomes an outdoor living room. Directly off the family room, it is meant as a bright and welcoming space that combines dining and lounging and overlooks the back yard and pool. With oversize hanging lanterns and heaters integrated into the flat beams, it's a space the clients can use year-round.*

RIGHT: *The kitchen, with a breakfast area in a half-octagonal bay, is the heart of the house. A gray-and-white floor in a bold checkerboard pattern offers a contrast to the rich indigo blue kitchen cabinetry. Lacanche stove and hood are a nod to antiques. The oak-stained, marble-topped island is more like a piece of furniture. The geometric chandelier is by Kelly Wearstler.*

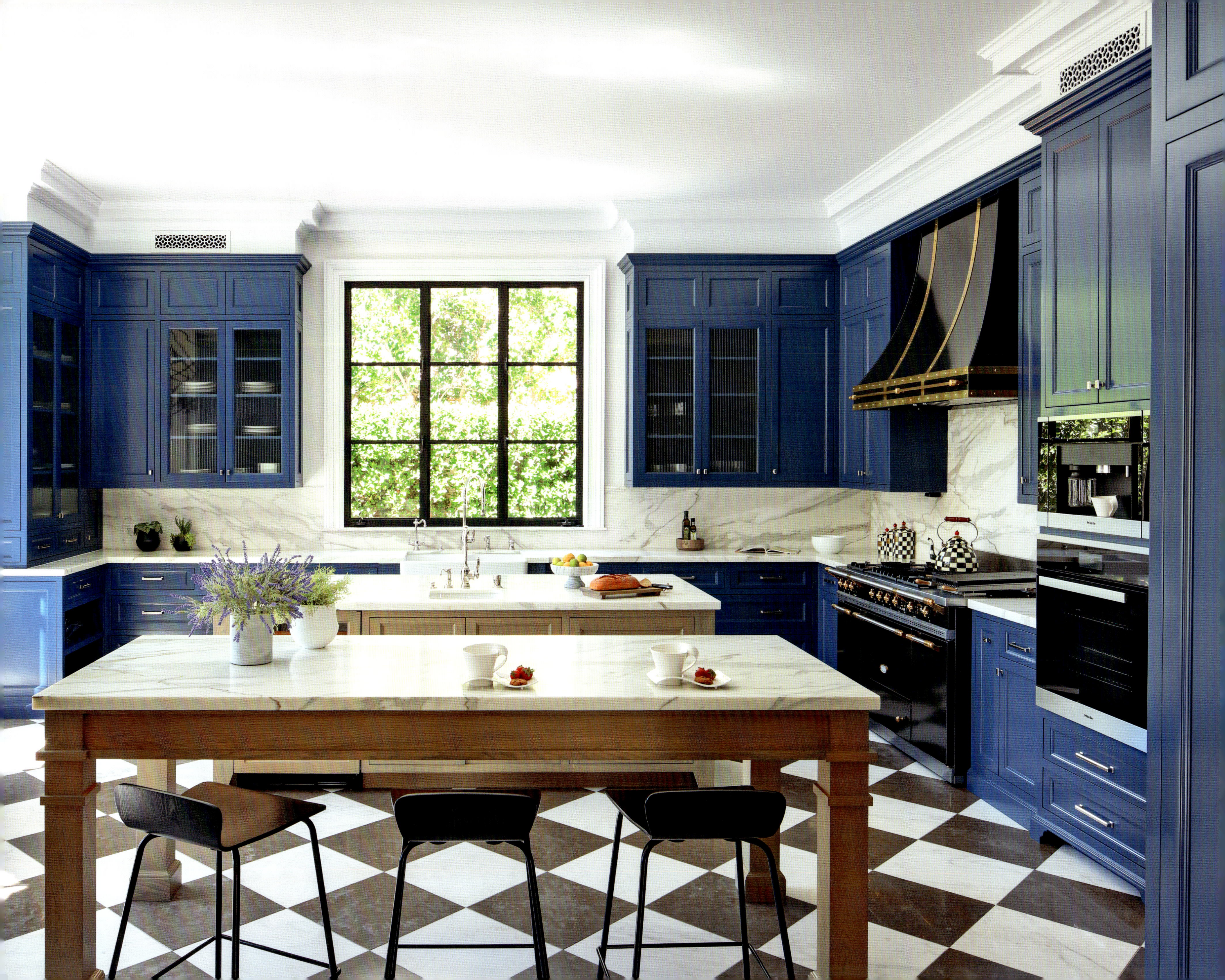

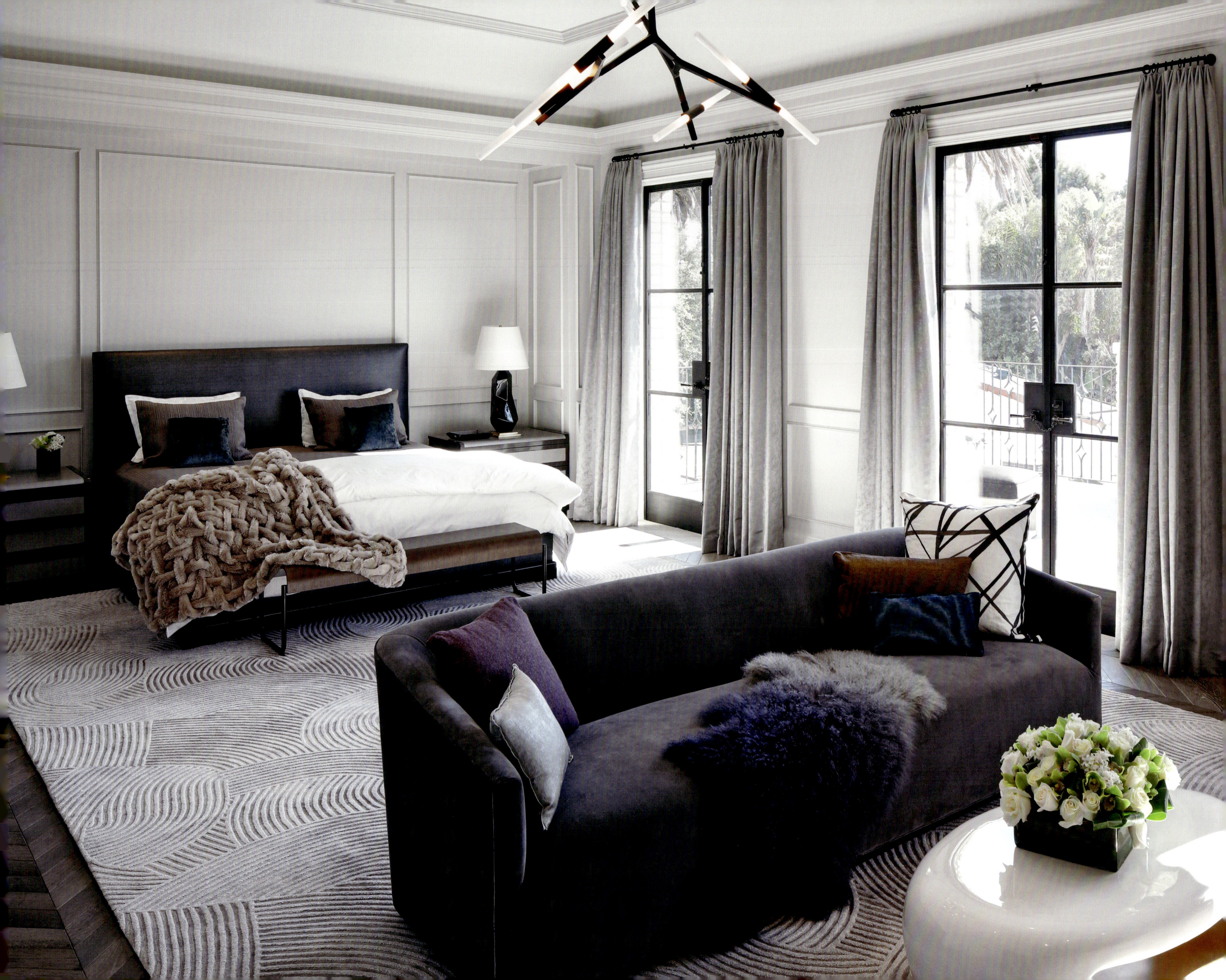

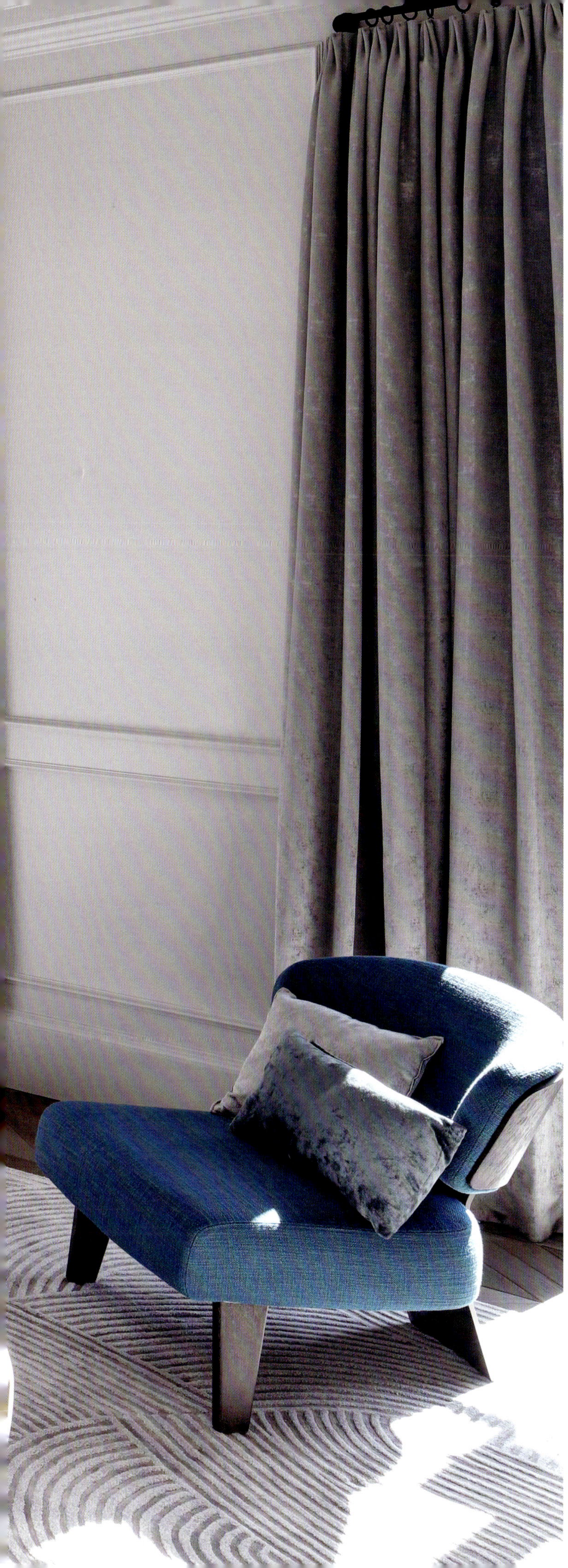
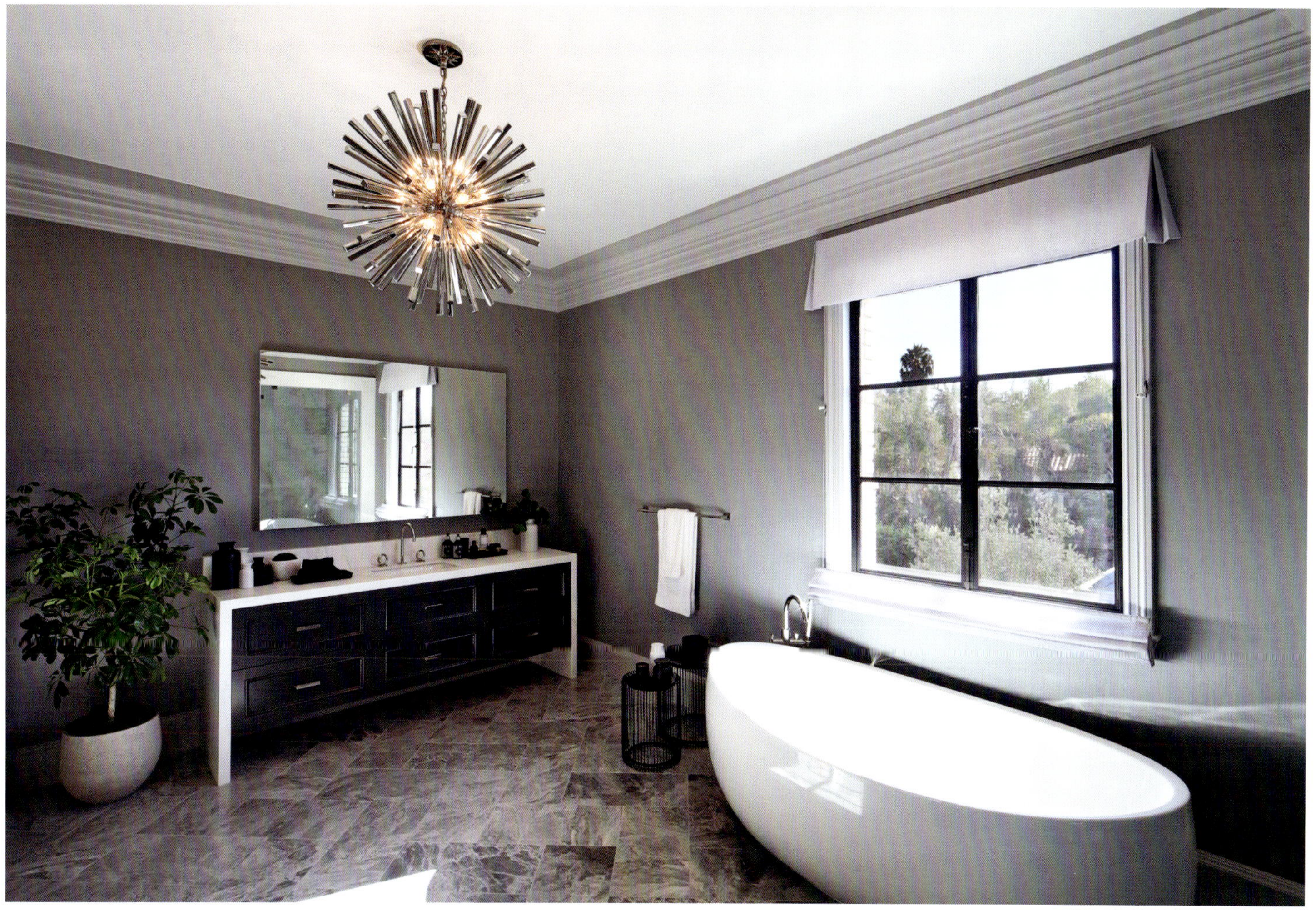
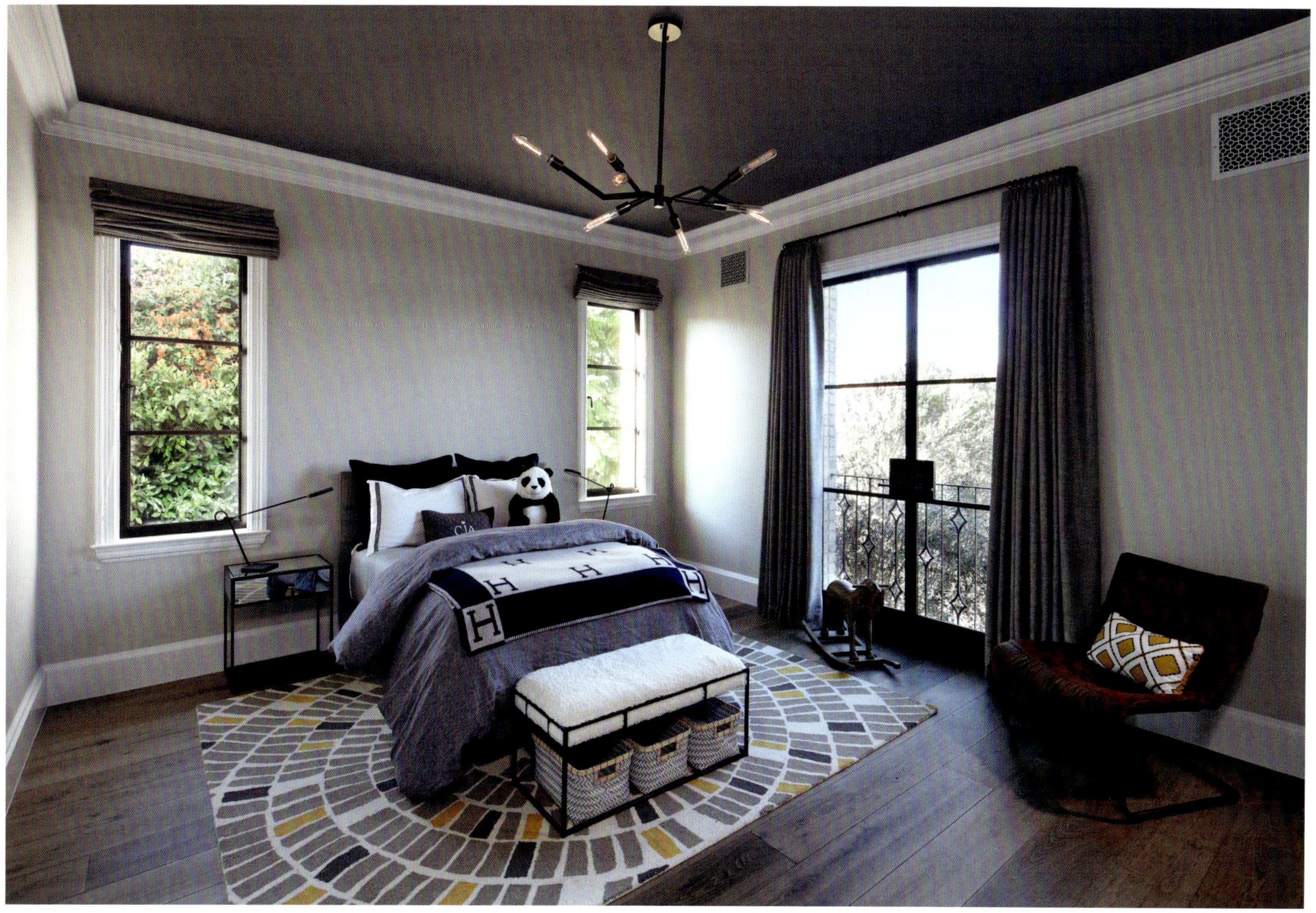

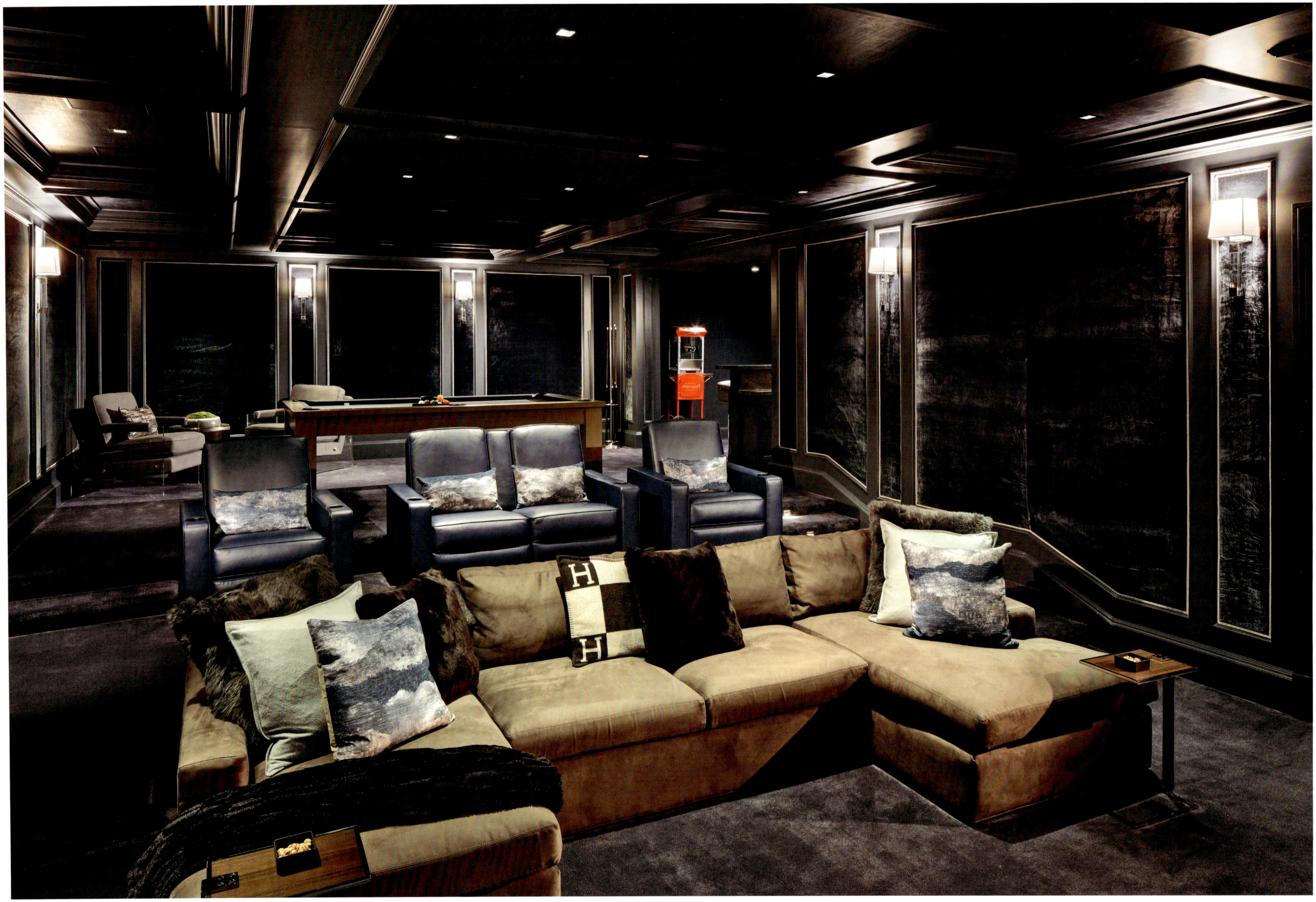

PREVIOUS PAGES, LEFT: *The master bedroom echoes the more formal elements of the living/dining rooms with a tray ceiling to add height, paneled walls, classic cornices, and the same gray chevron oak flooring, all balanced with contemporary lighting and neutral gray furnishings.* TOP RIGHT: *The master bath is a streamlined interpretation with a traditional bathtub, but the fixtures are a more sculptural twist on tradition. The vanity is done with a waterfall marble motif and traditional drawers, and a supernova light fixture steals the show.* BOTTOM RIGHT: *Each of the children's rooms has its own color scheme. The son's room is done in a French gray-blue and made more casual with plank flooring and contemporary lighting.*

OPPOSITE: *The theater is a combination of family room and cinema, with casual seating and bean bags at the front for the kids and theater-like chairs for adults in the middle. With a billiard table and popcorn machine, it's a multipurpose space where the family can watch movies and shows or play video games.*

RIGHT: *Instead of a traditional cellar, the wine-tasting room is a relaxed spot to open a bottle and enjoy it in a setting where the play of light from the chandelier together with the racking system create a mesmerizing pattern.*

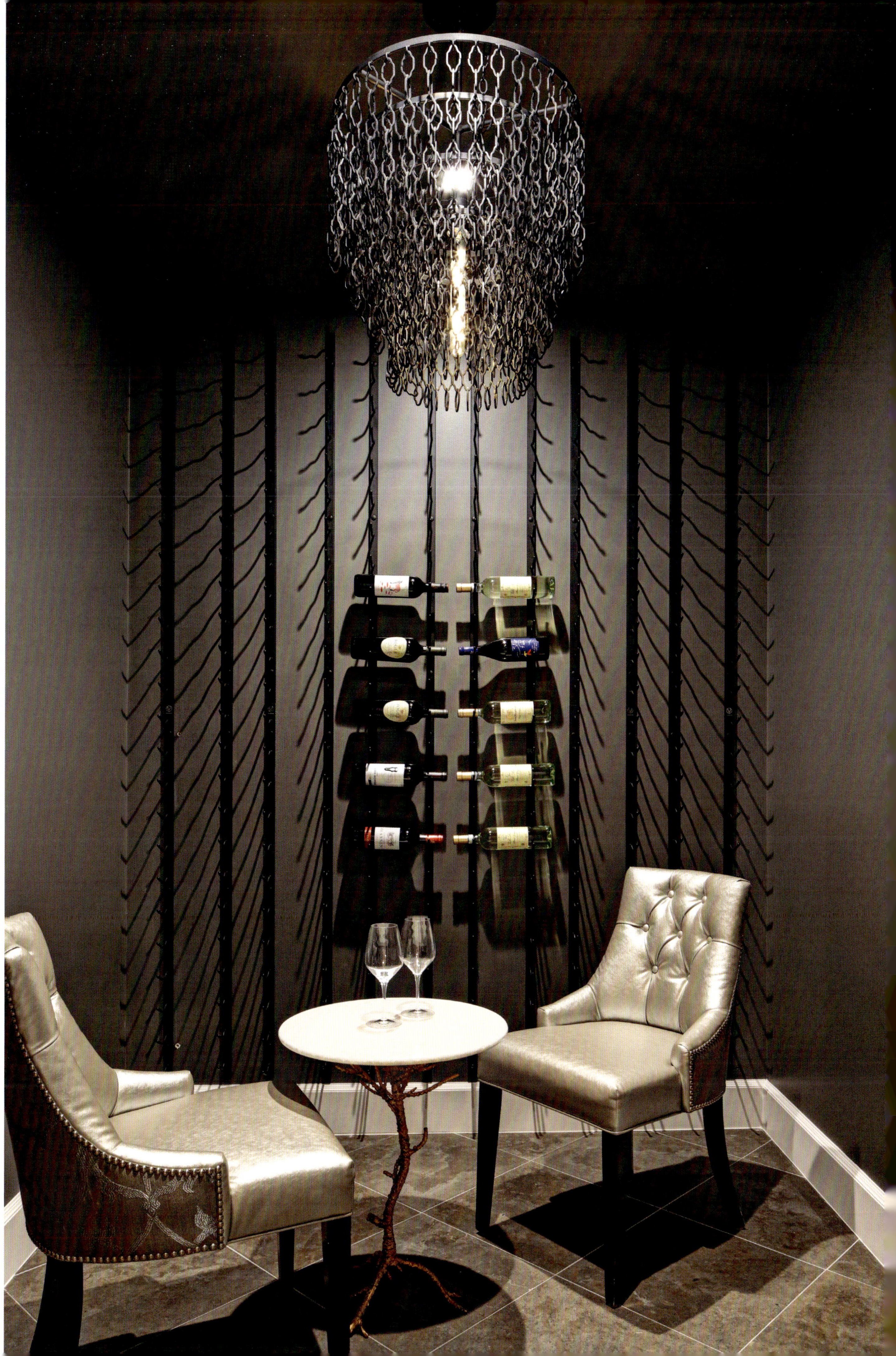

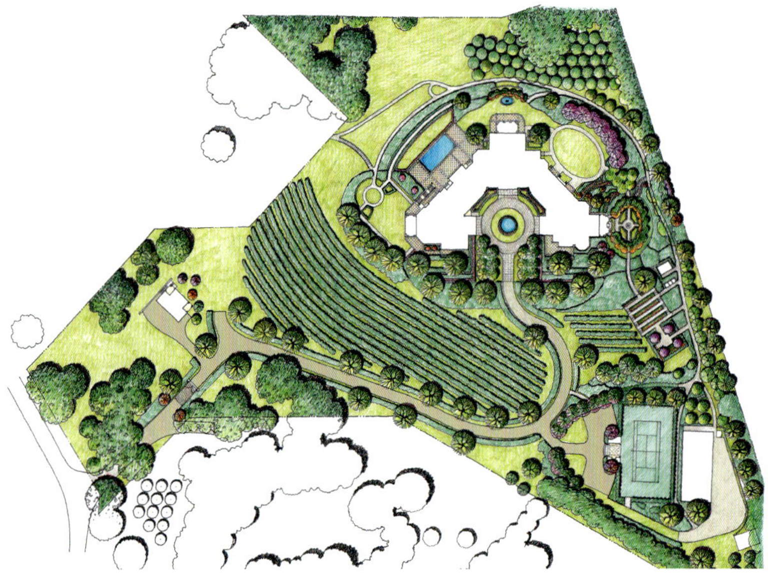

COLLINE D'OR

Bay Area

Set on 18 acres with panoramic views of San Francisco Bay, this formal French limestone mansion was built to showcase our clients' interests in architecture and the decorative arts. The directive was for a Neoclassical estate that would emulate the style and proportions of eighteenth-century French design and continue the heritage of classical architecture in the Bay Area, from Willis Polk and A. Page Brown to today's practitioners. The patrons had tremendous interest in Europe, particularly Paris, and so there was an attraction to the French aesthetic with the idea of taking inspiration from châteaux and Parisian houses but streamlining them for modern California living.

The property was a blank slate, and one of the challenges was the height limit imposed by the local jurisdiction due to the prominent hilltop setting. We worked within the code restrictions to make the house appear taller by introducing numerous vertical elements on the façades: Ionic pilasters, Doric columns, and quoins. Where we could place balconies, we would have a pair of French doors with iron railings that accentuated verticality and accomplished our clients' goal of bringing light deep into the house, which is found often in French architecture of this period.

As you approach the house from below along a winding drive, it unfolds in façade vignettes, which helps reinforce the idea that the house is tall, even though it is not. To enhance the views of the Bay, major rooms are located on the second floor with first-floor spaces devoted to secondary requirements—guest suites, an indoor pool and spa, billiards, and garages.

Part of the design evolution was devising various themes that would tie the house thematically together but create unique spaces throughout. The large U-shaped plan has far wings at each end but is narrow in depth to allow light into all of the rooms. The heart of the house is a two-story entry façade and stair hall on the main axis, which becomes the space that orients family and guests alike, forming the focus of daily circulation to the major rooms and galleries. Anchoring the far ends of the main floor are the formal living room and loggia with Bay vistas and the master suite with private gardens.

During the course of the project there were many trips to Europe to find original materials for the architecture and interiors: limestone from France, marble from Italy, muralists from Florence, and light fixtures and hardware from Paris. Artisans and artists were given the opportunity to create unique works of art, from stone pediment carvings and murals to Venetian plaster and garden statuary. Throughout the process, our clients were involved with every decision. It was a very personal and very collaborative project for them, a way for them to continue the great heritage of Bay Area patronage of the arts.

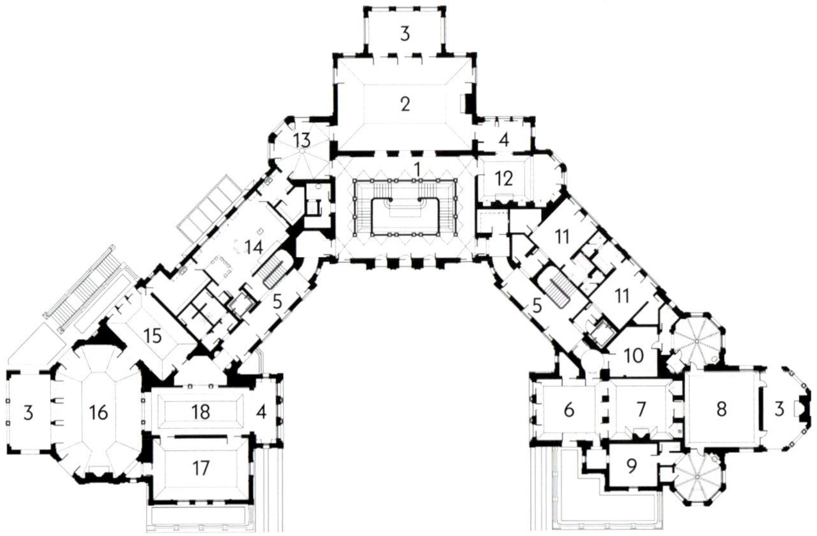

SECOND-FLOOR PLAN

1 Upper stair hall
2 Family room
3 Loggia
4 Bar
5 Hall
6 Foyer
7 Sitting room
8 Master bedroom
9 His bath
10 Her bath
11 Bedroom
12 Library
13 Family dining room
14 Kitchen
15 Formal dining room
16 Formal living room
17 Media room
18 Lounge

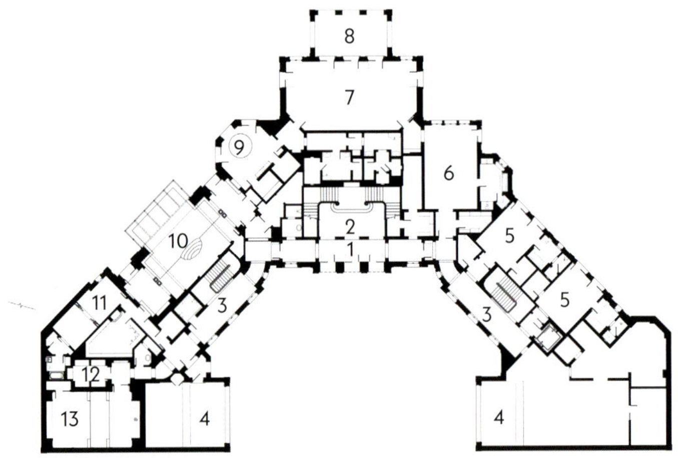

FIRST-FLOOR PLAN

1 Foyer
2 Stair hall
3 Hall
4 Garage
5 Bedroom
6 Game room
7 Dance salon
8 Loggia
9 Spa
10 Pool
11 Staff quarters
12 Wine cellar
13 Theater

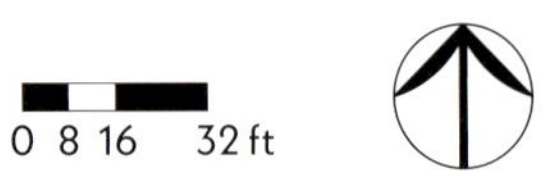

RIGHT: Organized around a central entry court enclosed on three sides, the formal limestone façade of this eighteenth-century-style château has a central pediment carved in France that incorporates symbols important to the client—two reclining cherubs that connote children and family through the imagery of art and music.

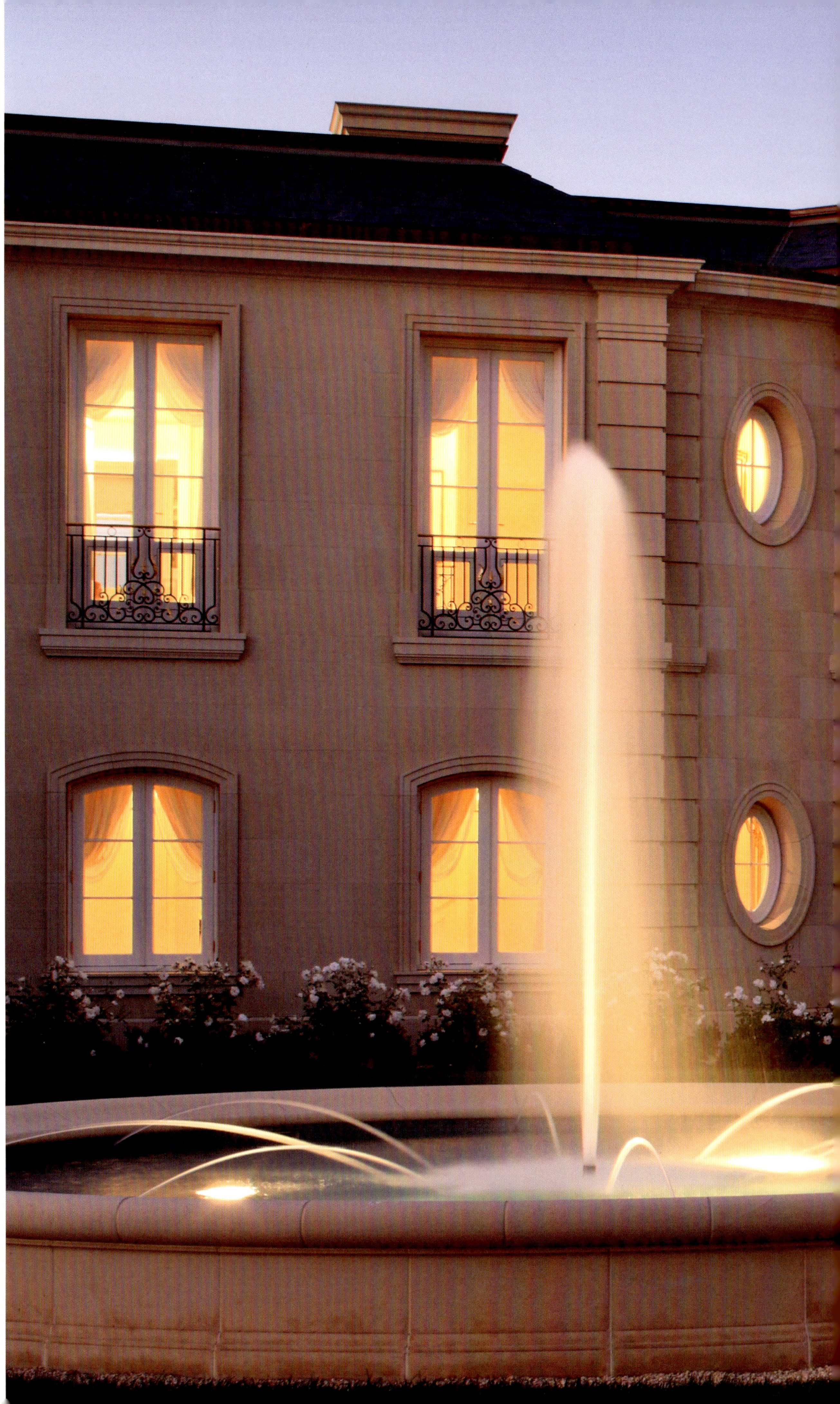

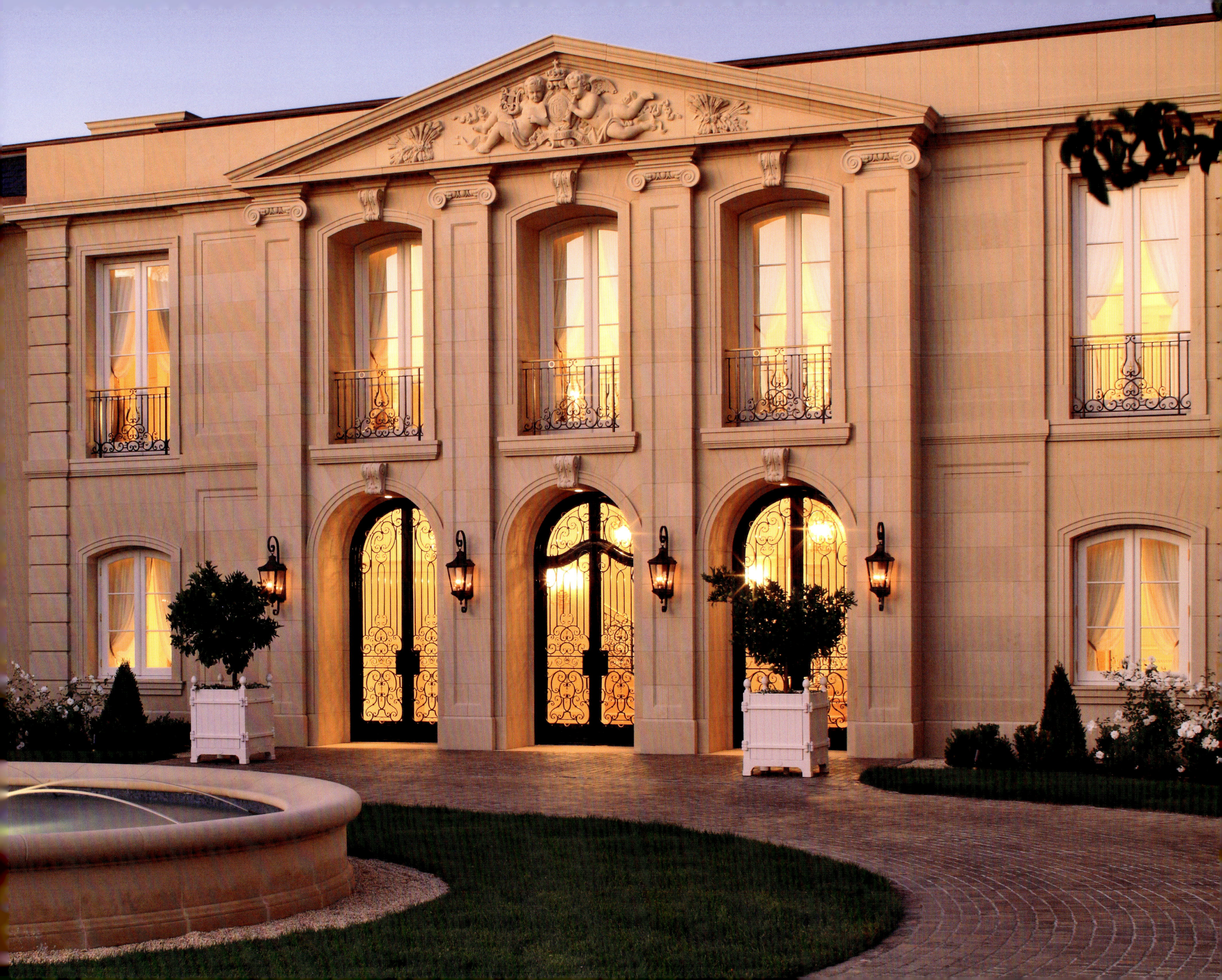

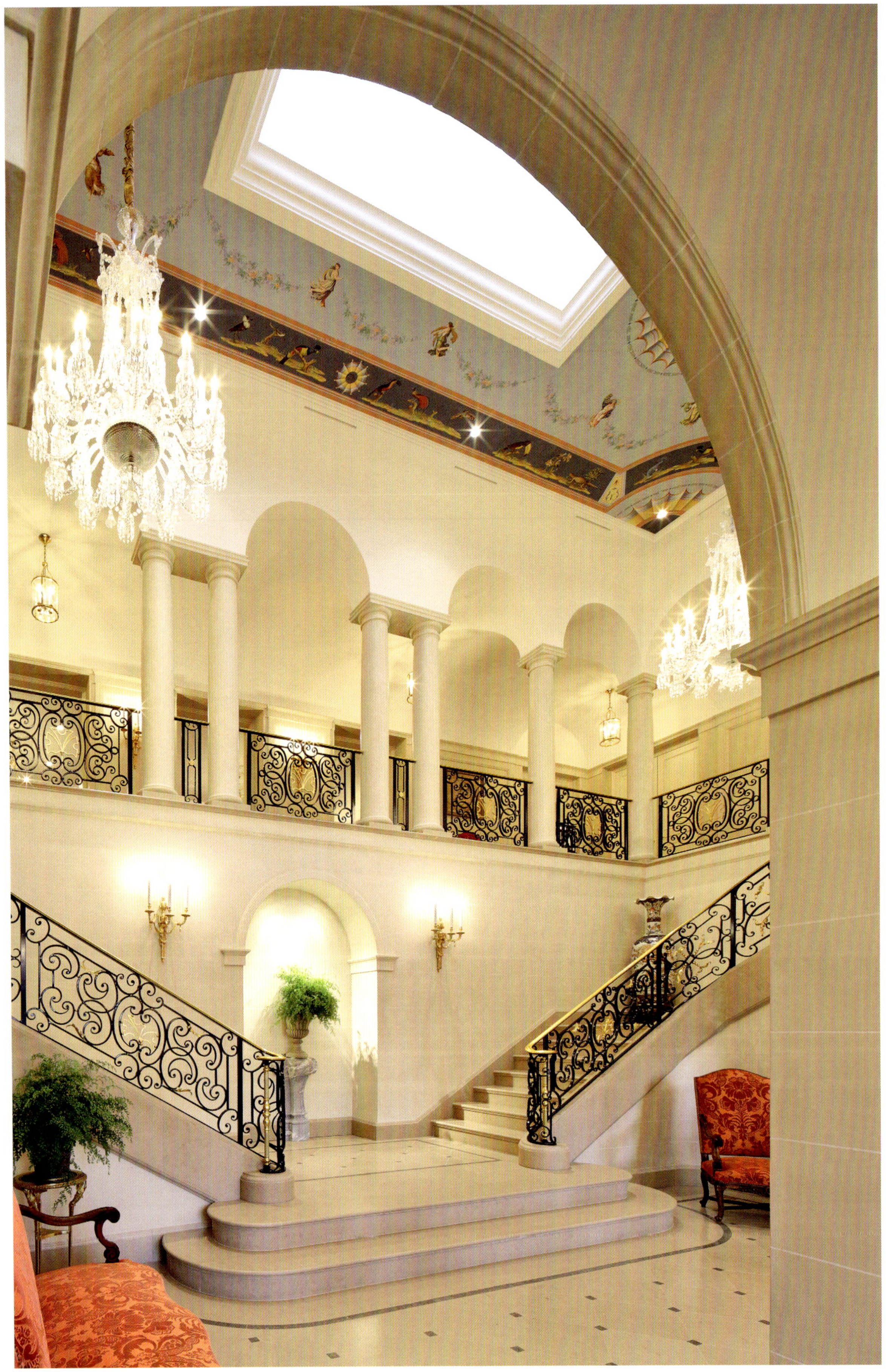

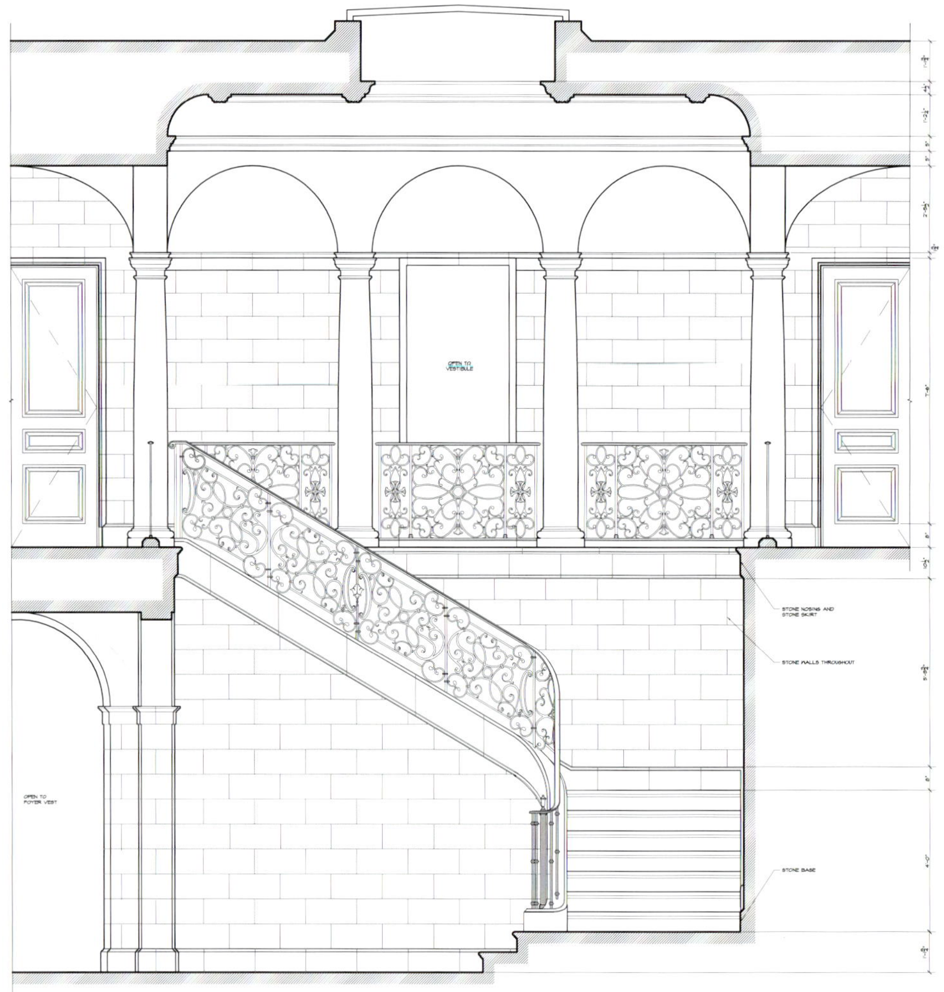

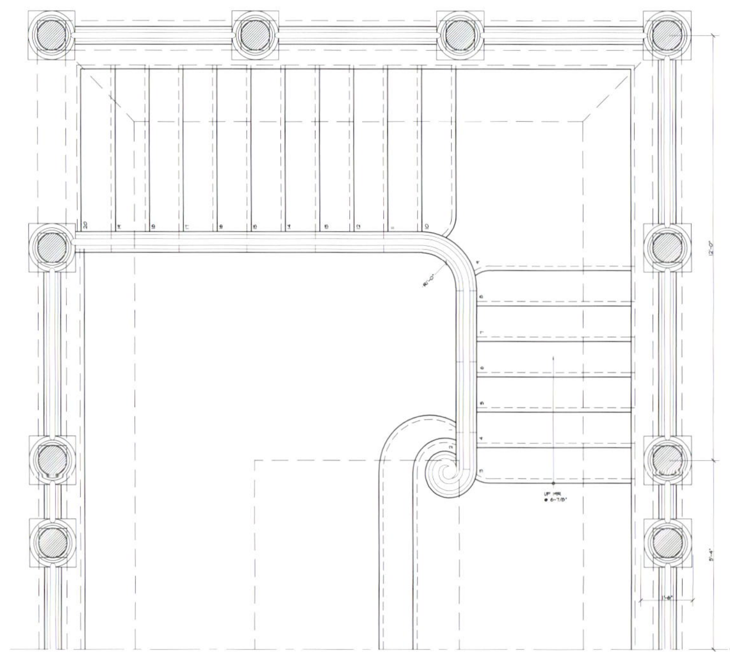

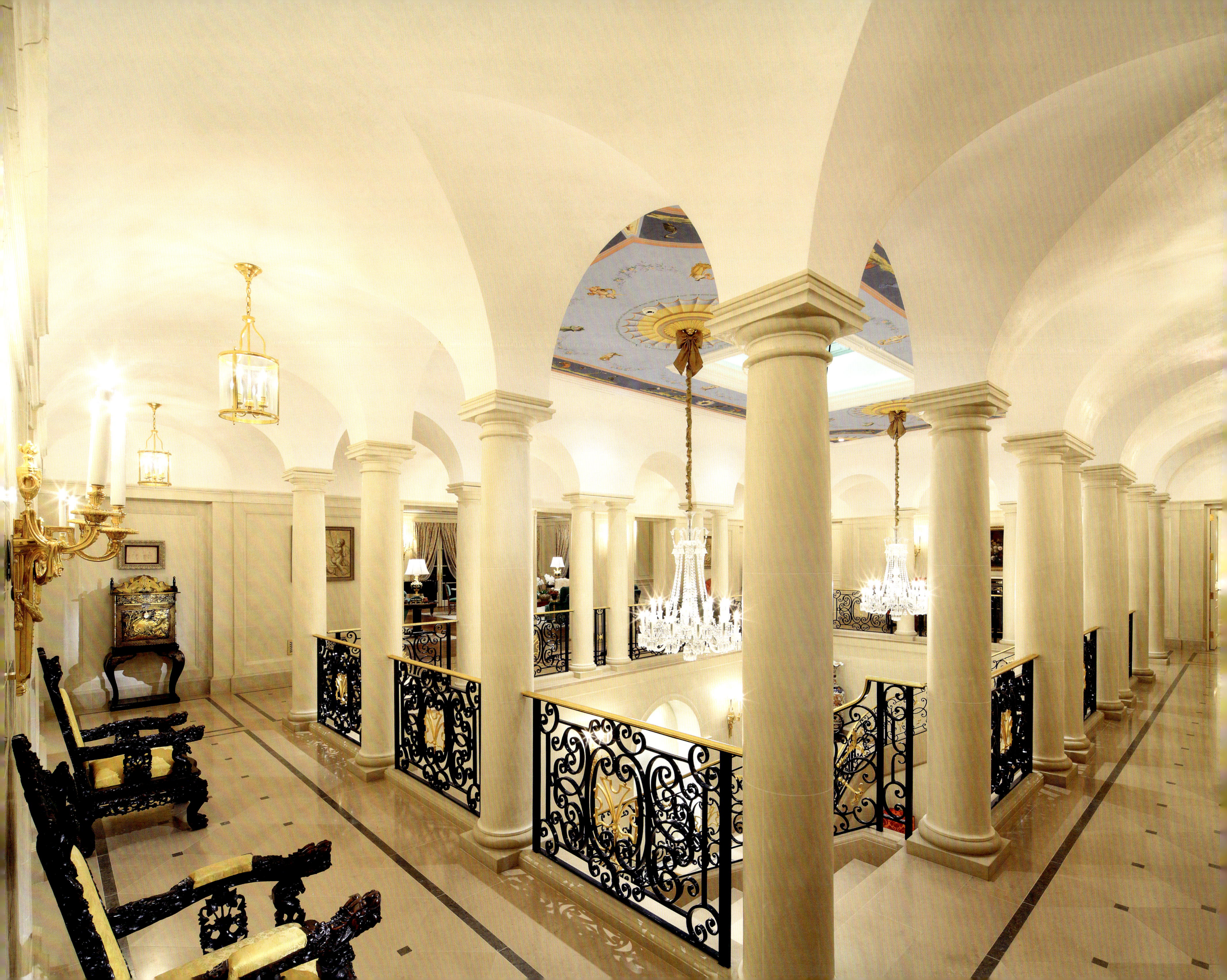

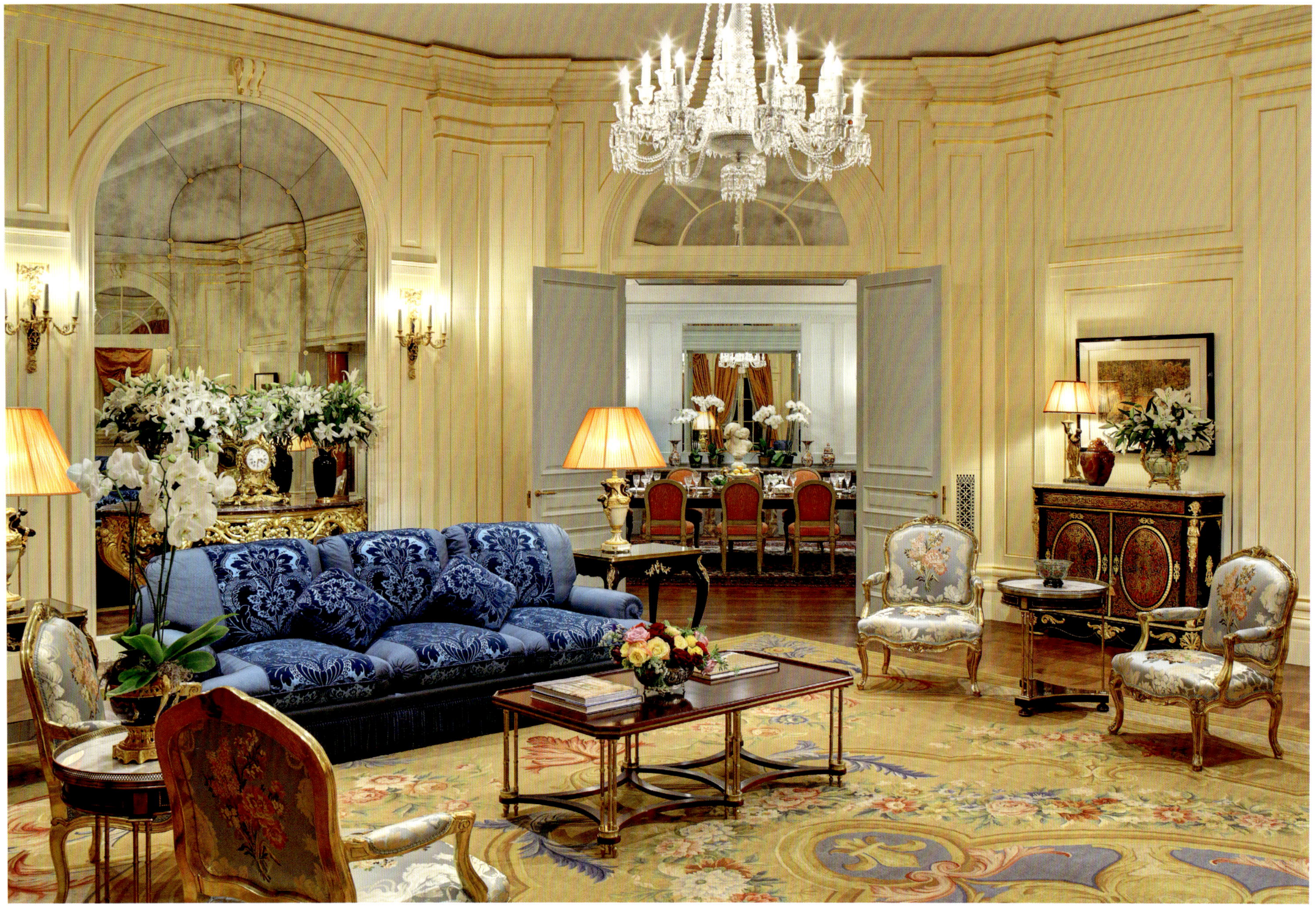

PREVIOUS PAGES, LEFT: *The two-story entrance hall and grand stair is reminiscent of Renaissance courtyards and is the main circulation space. Custom stair railings, Baccarat crystal chandeliers, and Régence-style seating in crimson silk velvet.* MIDDLE: *Drawings of the main stair.* RIGHT: *The upper stair hall is a geometric tour de force of vaulted ceilings and columns. The ceiling was hand-painted by Florentine artists with motifs from Herculaneum—a reminder of the classical past and a link to the architectural traditions that inspired this new French château.*

ABOVE: *The octagonal formal living room is designed for entertaining on a grand scale. All the formal rooms are paneled in the French tradition and have Doric pilasters and wood floors for displaying custom rugs. The Louis XV-style rug's predominant tones of gold, rose, and blue unite the room with the formal dining room, visible through the double doors.*

OPPOSITE: *The formal living room's painted and gilded wall paneling has recessed panes of antiqued mirror. Sets of French doors open to a limestone columned loggia overlooking San Francisco Bay.*

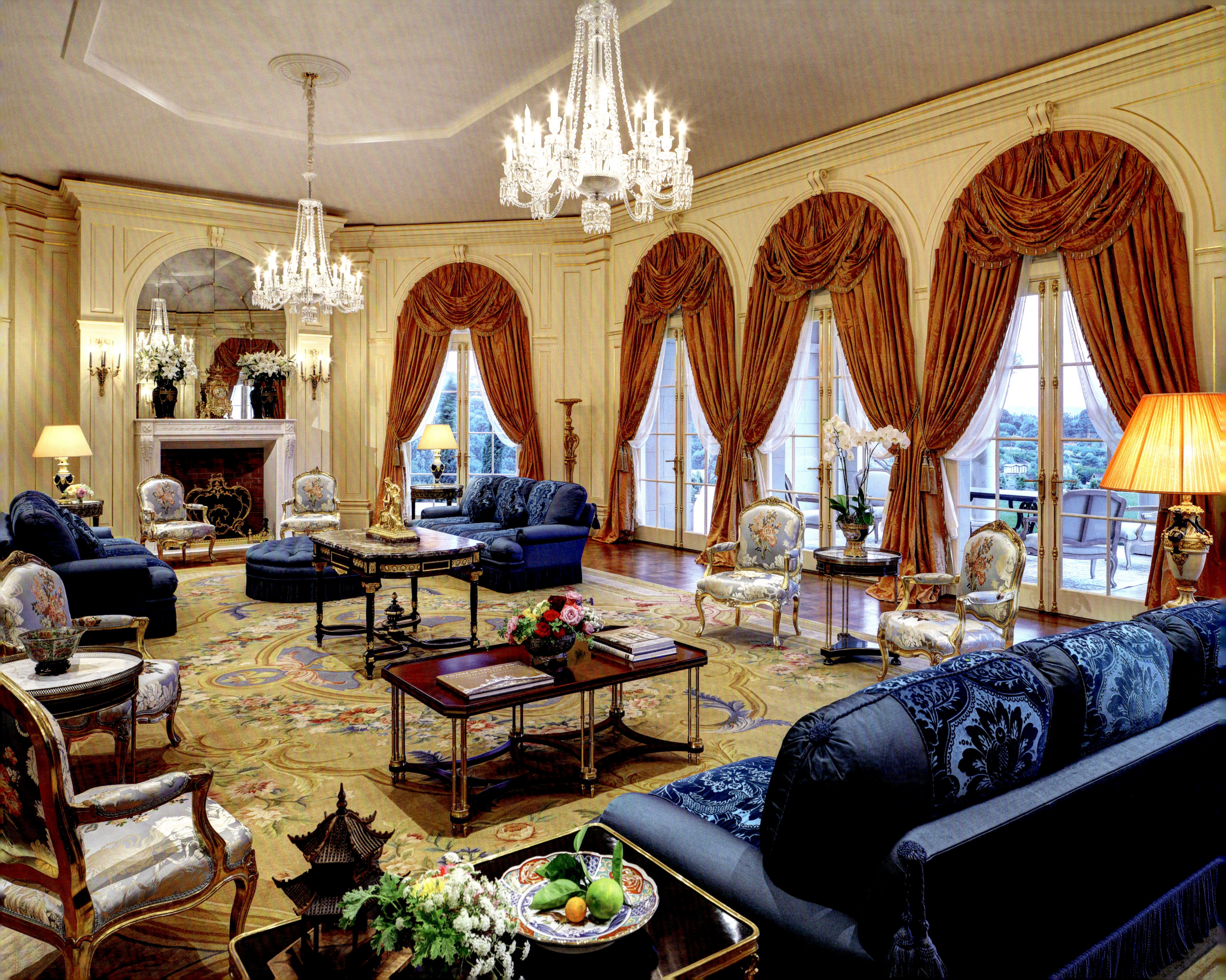

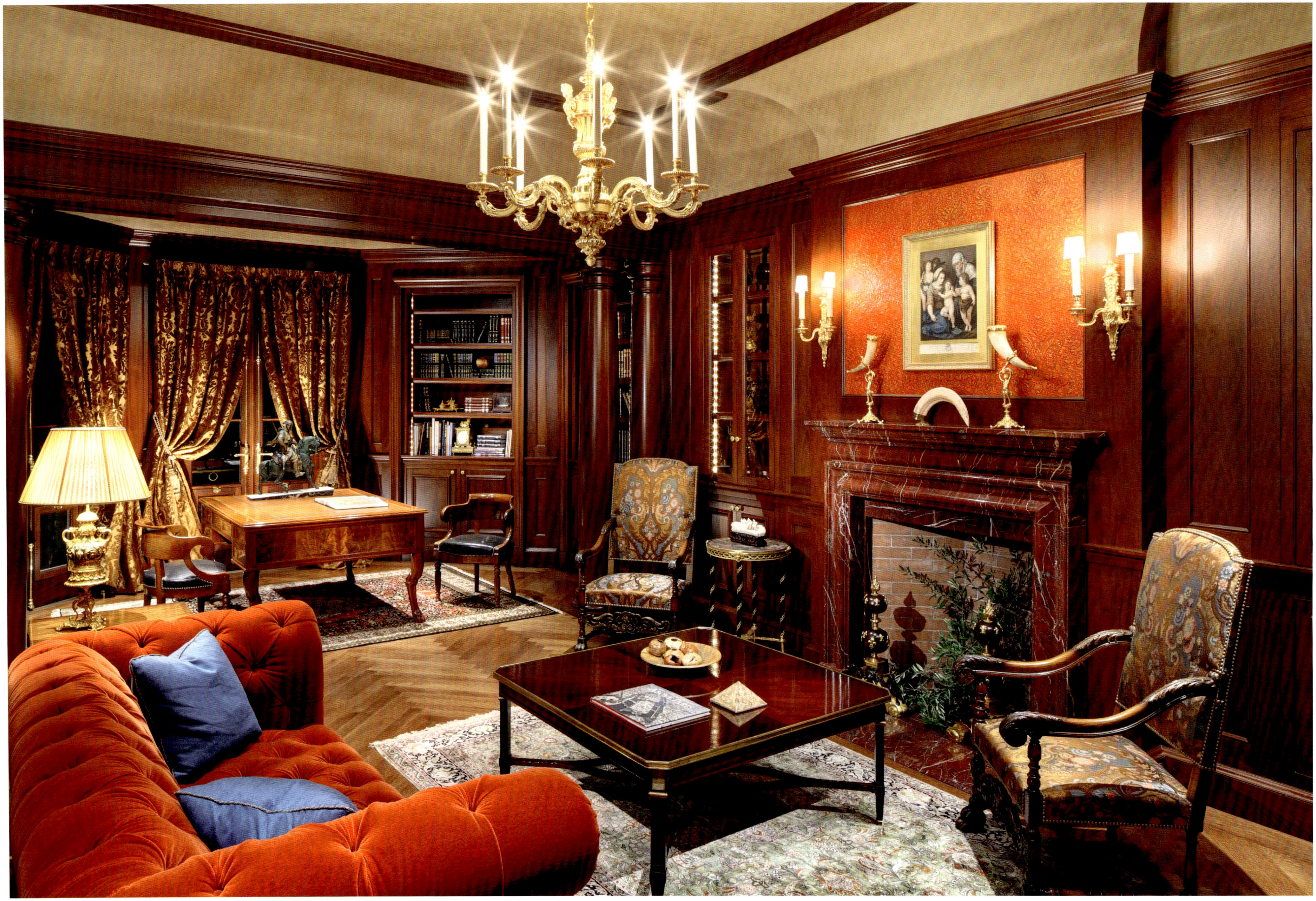

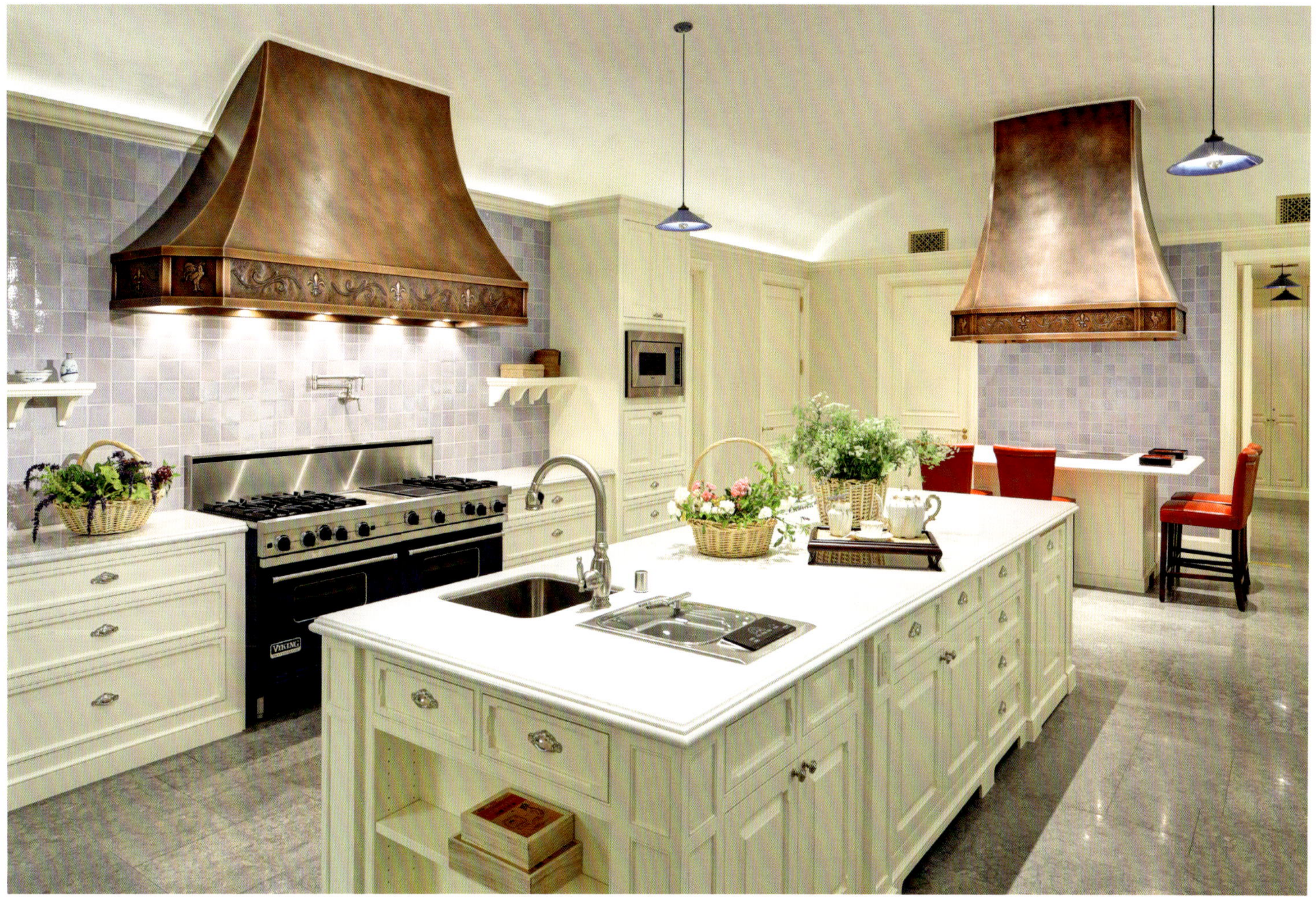

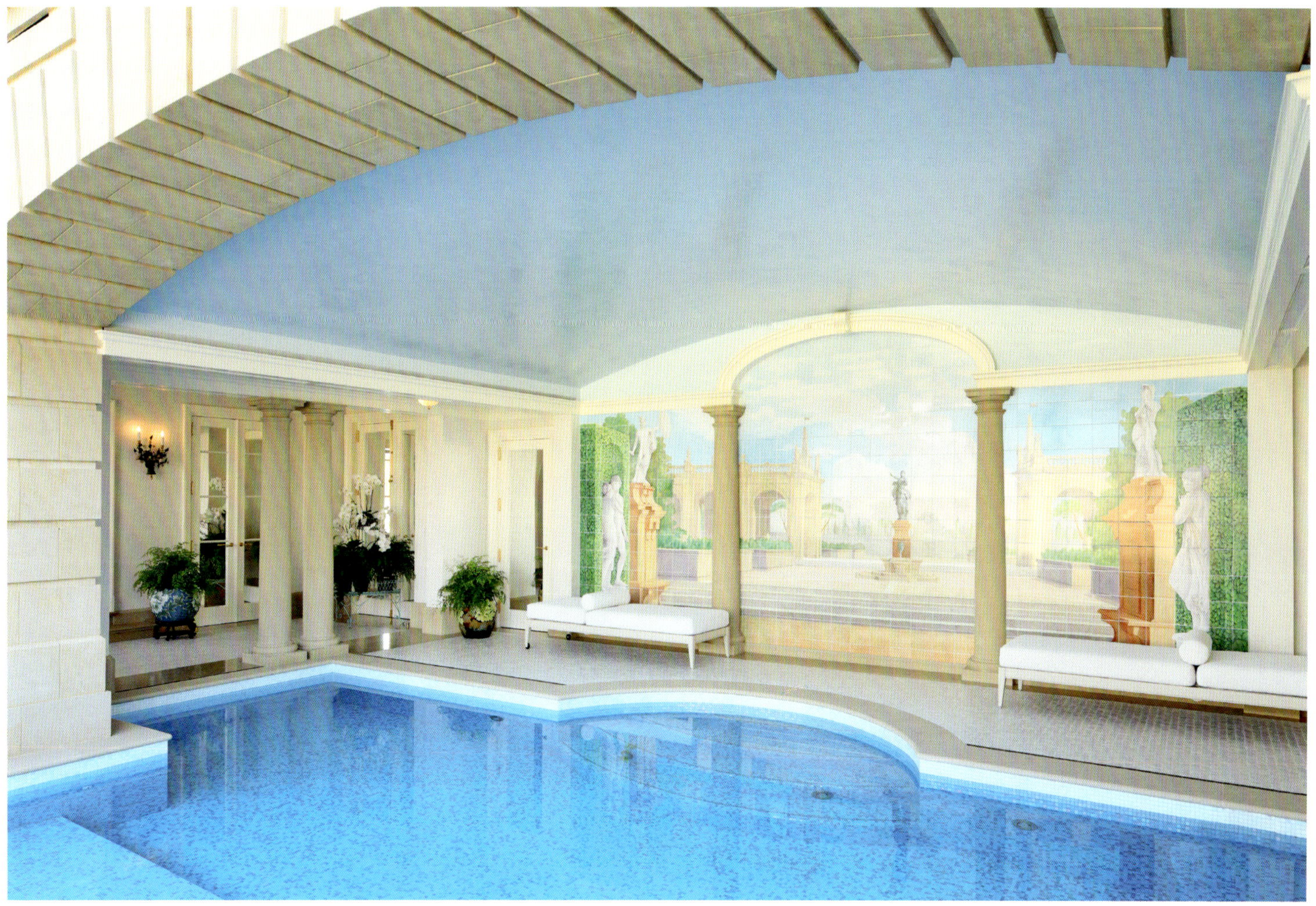

OPPOSITE: *Mahogany paneling and oak chevron floors dictated the library's warm tones. The ceiling was done in tobacco-colored plaster, which made it lighter, and with a large cove that brought the paneling down in height. The solid mahogany informed the reds and oranges in the furnishings introduced by interior designer David Desmond.*

TOP RIGHT: *The family enjoys cooking, so the kitchen is an interpretation of a classic French country kitchen with off-white/ivory cabinetry, a simple vaulted ceiling to accent the rectangular space, pale blue/gray Provençal tile, and hammered copper hoods. A teppanyaki grill, a favorite hobby of our client, was placed behind a separate stone counter that required its own ventilation hood.*

BOTTOM RIGHT: *On a lower level, the indoor pool and spa has a garden view, which inspired the mural with images of a classical garden with architectural fragments, hedges, and antique statuary.*

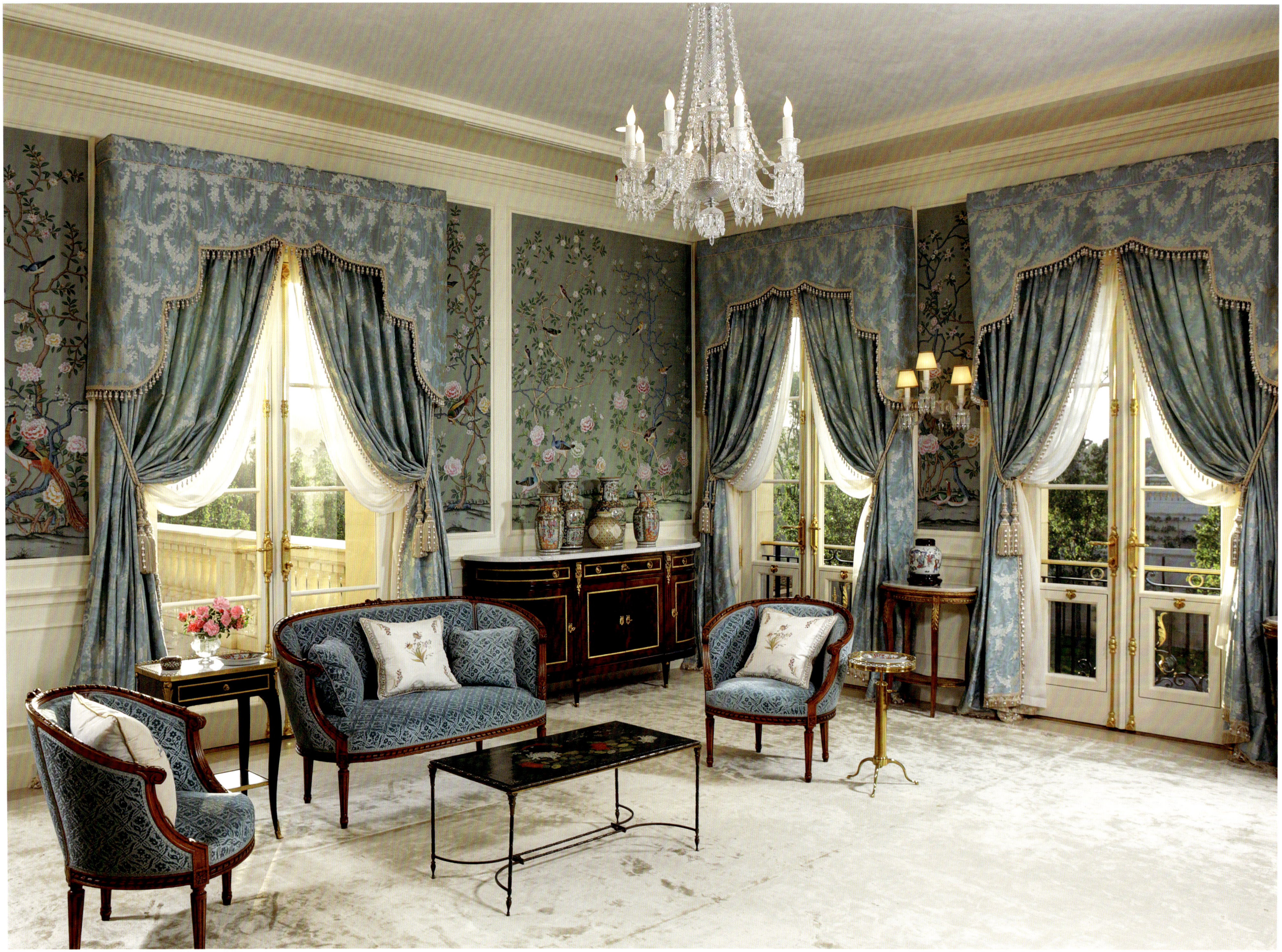

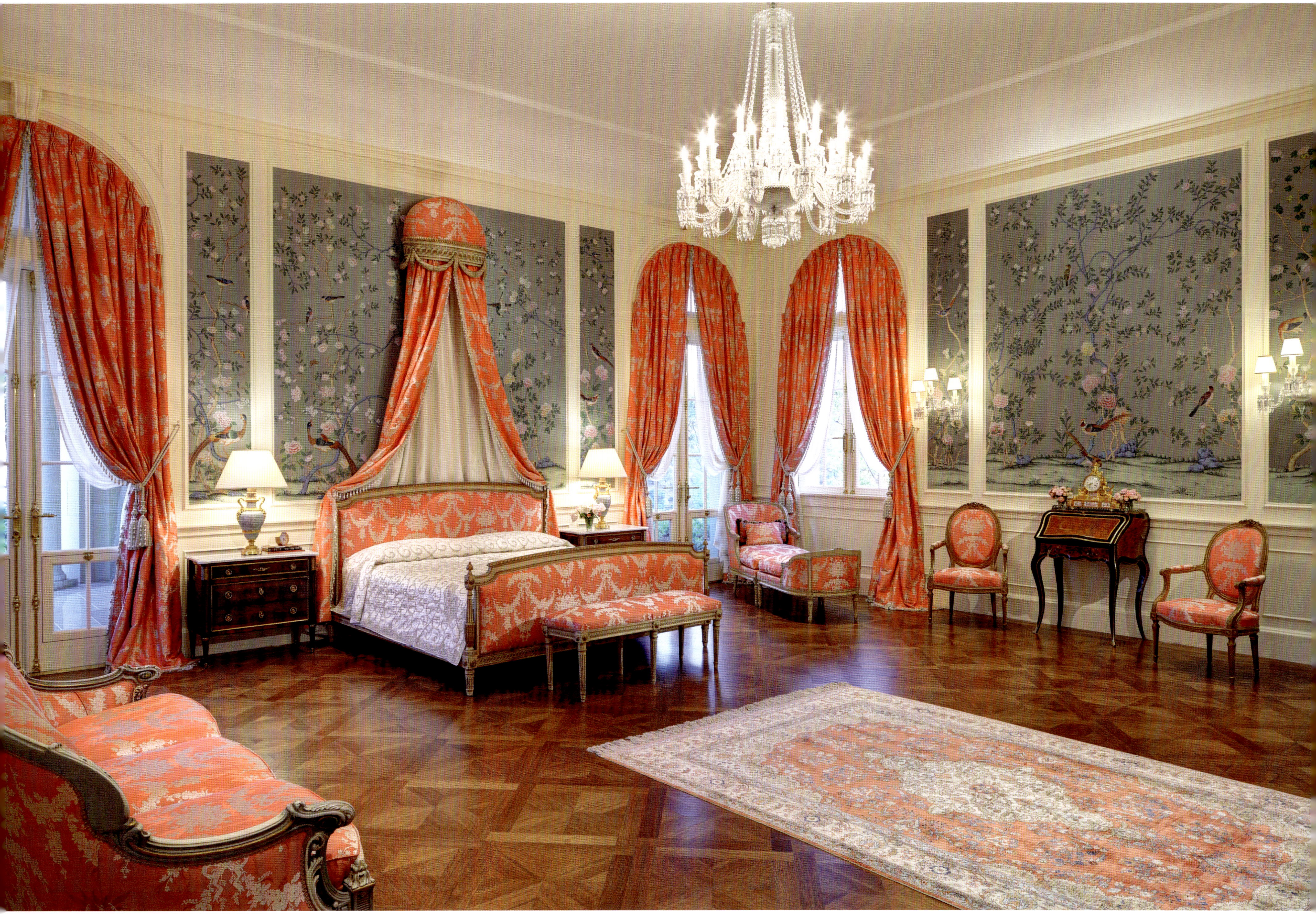

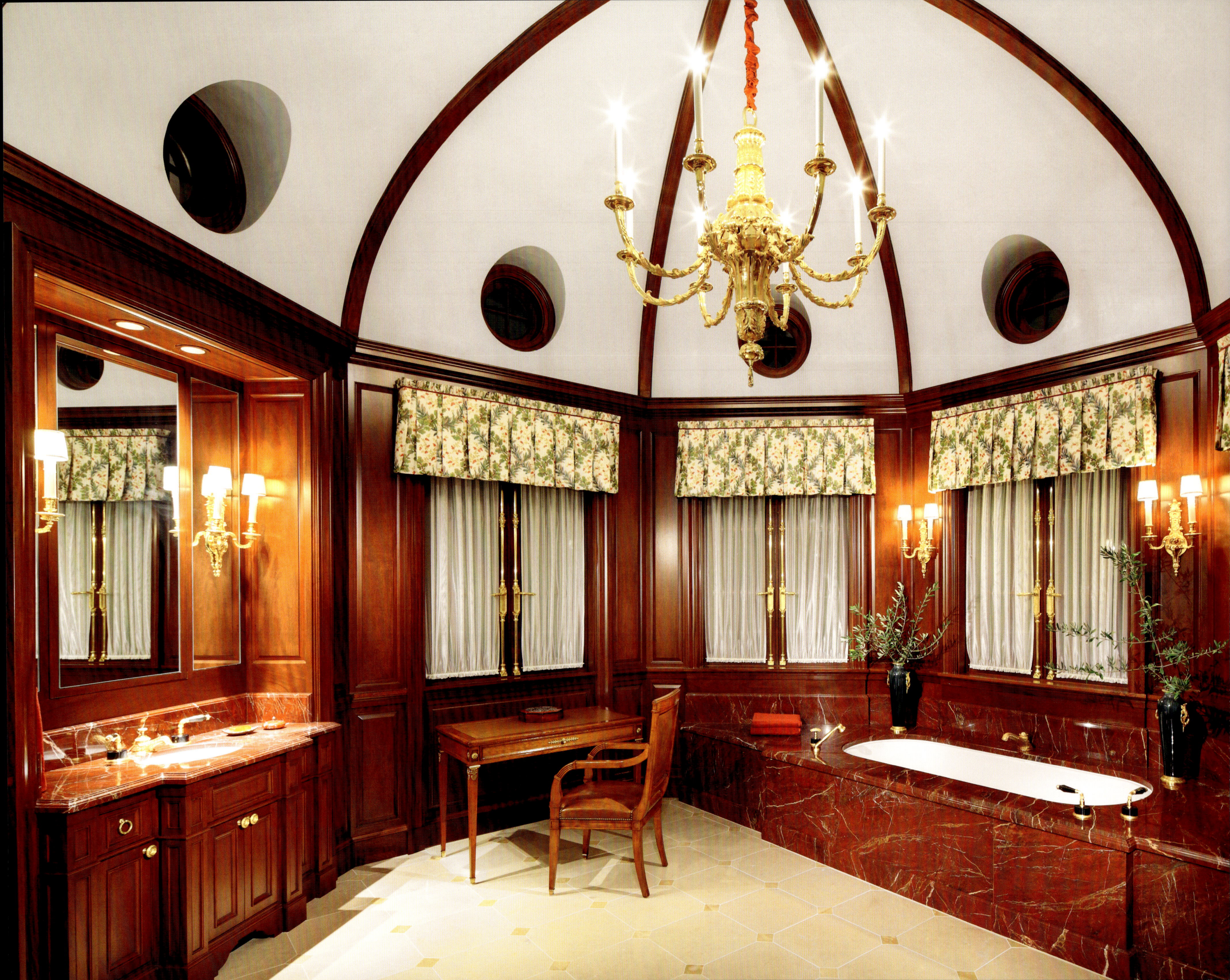

PREVIOUS PAGES, LEFT: *The private master wing has its own spacious sitting room with high ceilings, architectural moldings as the framework, and panels that are wallpapered instead of being painted. Hand-painted silk wallpaper in celadon and robin's-egg blue is enhanced by the hand-woven silk carpet, Louis XVI-style furniture and a collection of famille-rose porcelain.* RIGHT: *The impressive volume of the master bedroom is amplified by the oak parquet de Versailles floor and Baccarat crystal chandelier and sconces. The furnishings balance the patterns of a celadon green hand-painted silk wallpaper with a pink Chinoiserie silk lampas fabric on the drapes, bed, and seating.*

OPPOSITE: *Flanking either side of the master suite are identical octagonal bathrooms. His bath continues the theme of the library with mahogany paneling and King's Red (Rouge du Roi) marble crowned by a segmented dome in sky blue Venetian plaster. The floor is patterned in two colors of French limestone. Mahogany dressing table and chair are in the Empire style.*

RIGHT: *Her octagonal bath took on a more delicate tone with dominant colors of white and peach. The octagonal dome ceiling is in shell-colored Venetian plaster; the Statuario marble floor features a pietra dura central medallion, and the countertops are violet onyx. The fabric at the windows and on the furniture was designed for the Queen's Bedchamber at Versailles.*

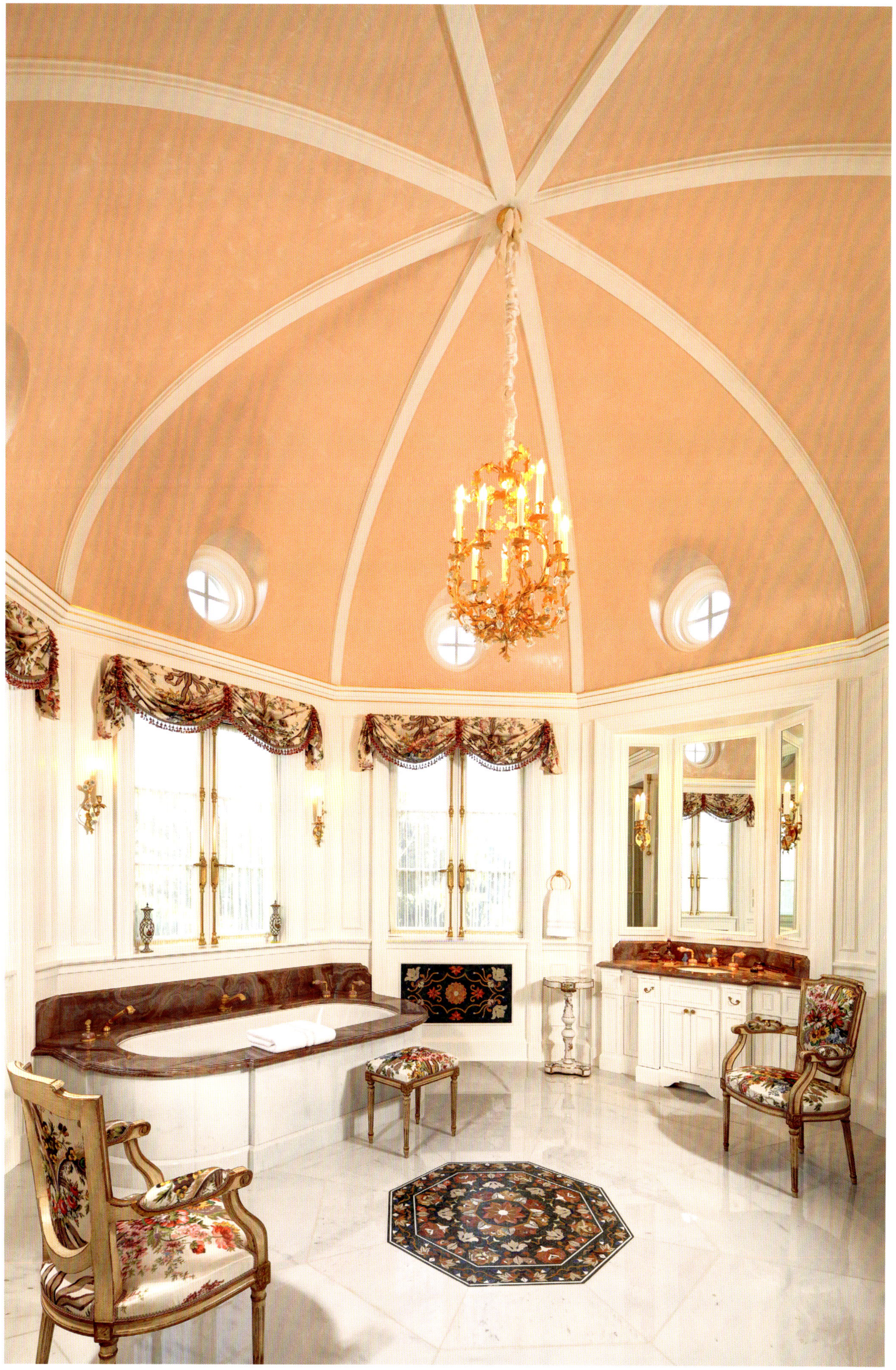

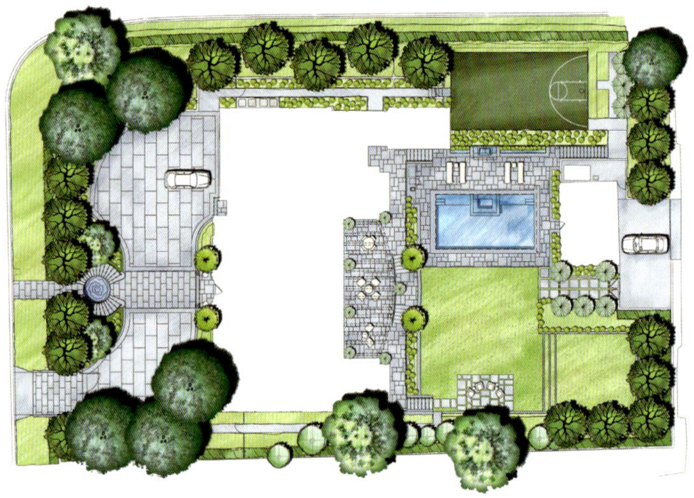

BUCKHEAD

Brentwood

The spark for the design of this home was a Colonial Revival house we had built in Bel-Air, which our clients had admired, and in turn had been inspired by the wonderful Colonial Revival estates built around Atlanta in the 1920s and '30s.

But this property was more challenging because it abutted a busy street and intersection. By using an L-shaped plan, we placed the garages and service wing along the main road and fronted the family wing on the quieter side of the street. By grading the lot down 12 feet, we were able to maximize the building height and minimize the sound and view of traffic.

While the home's framework is Colonial Revival, with white-painted brick, paneling and moldings organized around a classic center hall floor plan, the interiors evolved in a different direction, harking to Hollywood's Golden Age of movie glamour. The inspiration for the interiors came from architect Paul R. Williams and from William Haines, the former silent screen star who became one of Hollywood's top decorators, for elements such as the black lacquered interior doors and black-and-white marble floors.

The home swivels in two directions. To the right of the entry hall is the entertaining area, with a grand living room that spills into a bar, a wine tasting room, and the husband's office/library. To the left is the family wing, with the media room, dining room, kitchen, and breakfast alcove.

We added several distinctive features. The entry has a 10-foot-tall ceiling that leads into a double-height center hall. Instead of lowering the height on the second floor, we kept the ceiling height on both floors the same, as our clients enjoyed tall ceilings throughout the house. And in a pattern we are seeing increasingly with our younger clients, the couple wanted a self-contained master suite with a sitting room and bedroom, but preferred to share one large master bath.

This new house now fits within Los Angeles's architectural tradition and an evolving vision of Hollywood glamour.

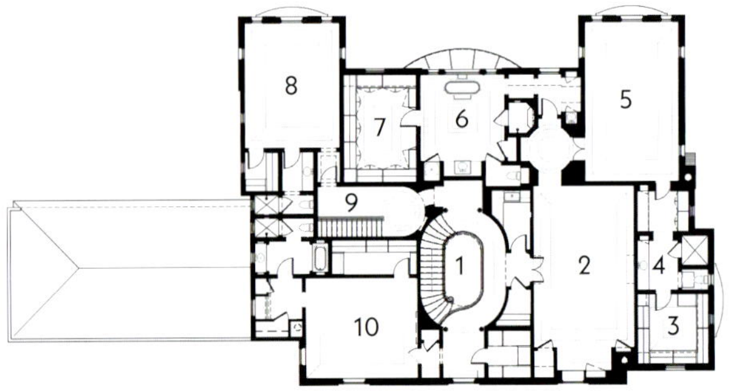

SECOND-FLOOR PLAN

1 Upper stair hall
2 Master sitting room
3 His closet
4 His bath
5 Master bedroom
6 Her bath
7 Her closet
8 Guest bedroom
9 Hall
10 Bedroom

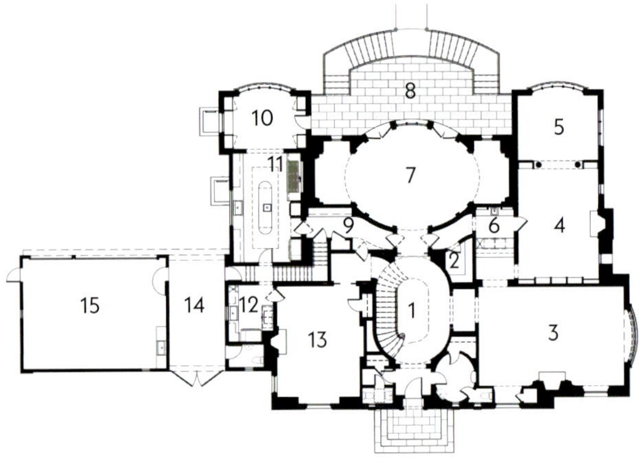

FIRST-FLOOR PLAN

1 Stair hall
2 Wine room
3 Drawing room
4 Club room
5 Pool room
6 Bar
7 Formal dining room
8 Terrace
9 China storage
10 Office
11 Kitchen
12 Pantry
13 Morning room
14 Breezeway
15 Garage

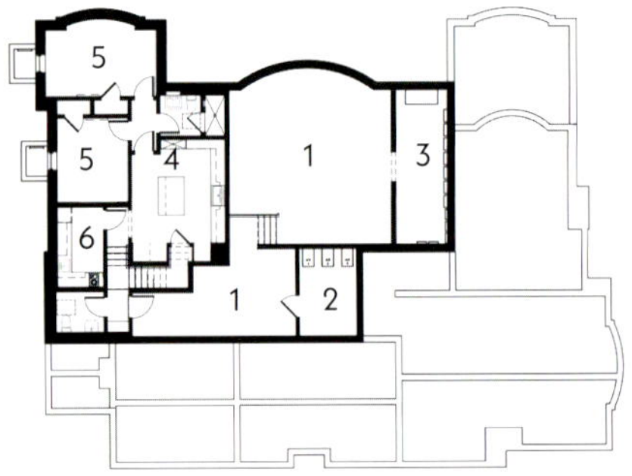

BASEMENT FLOOR PLAN

1 Mechanical room
2 Audio-visual system
3 Electrical room
4 Laundry
5 Staff quarters
6 Pantry

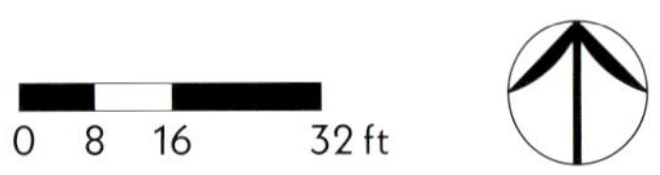

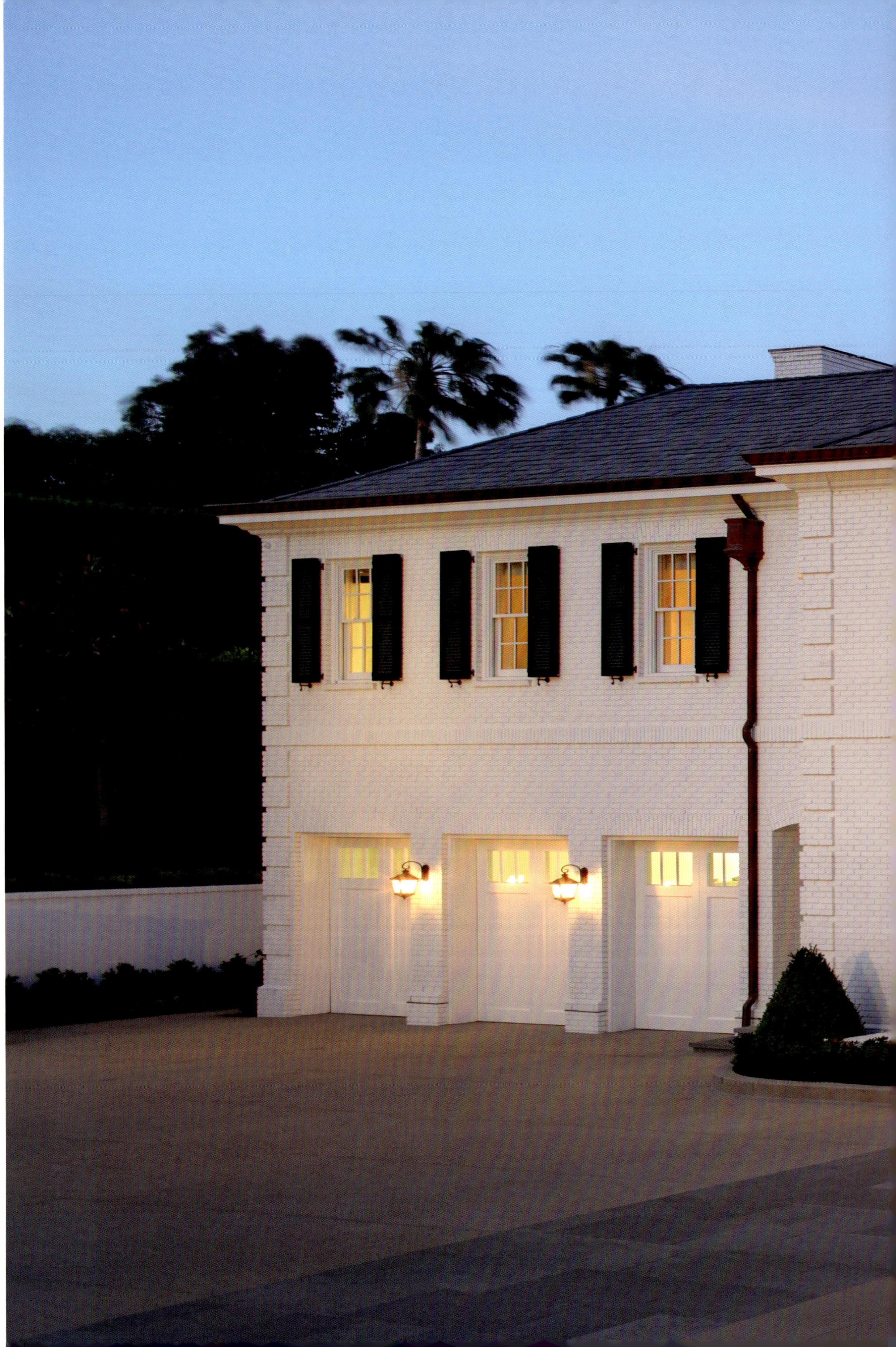

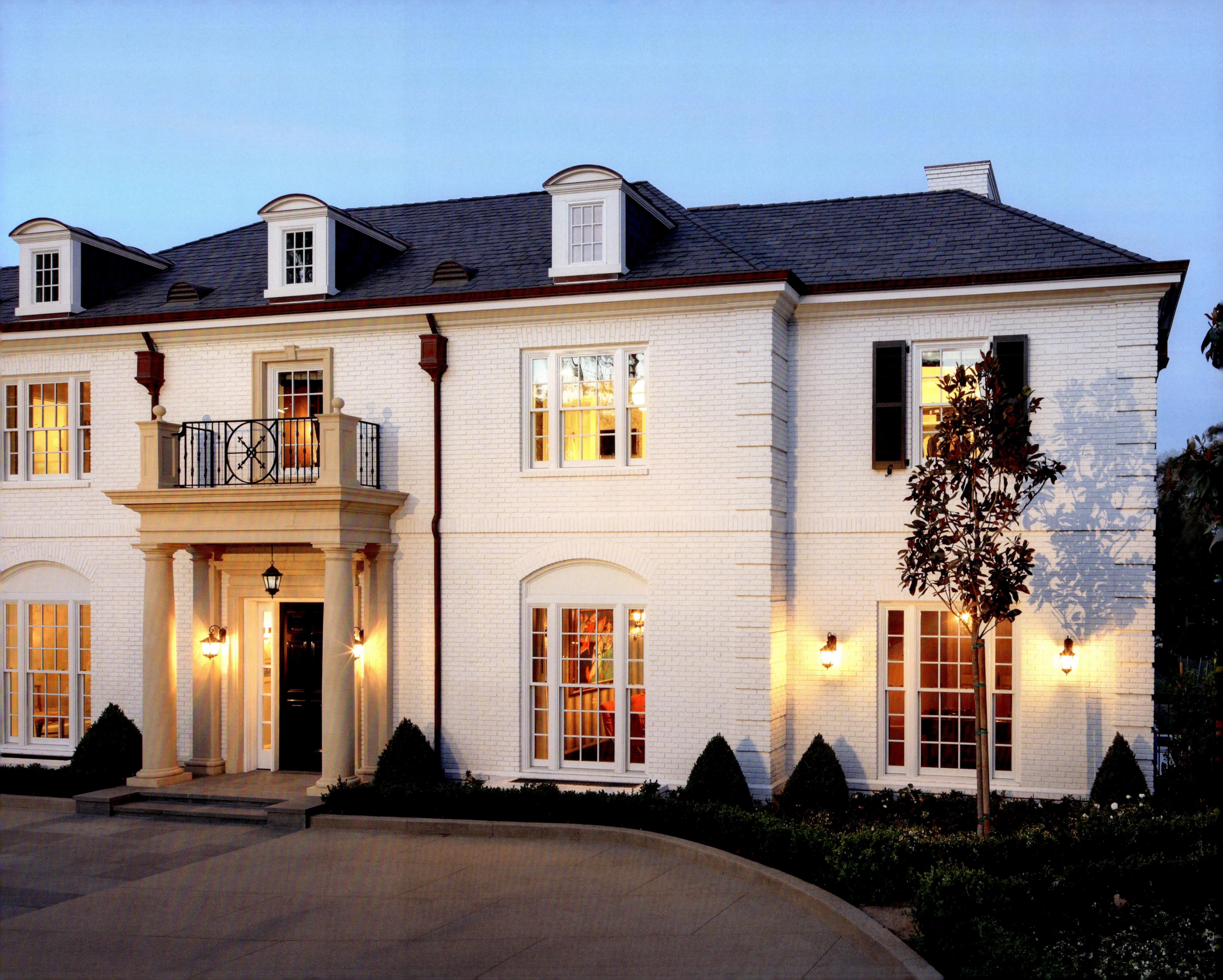

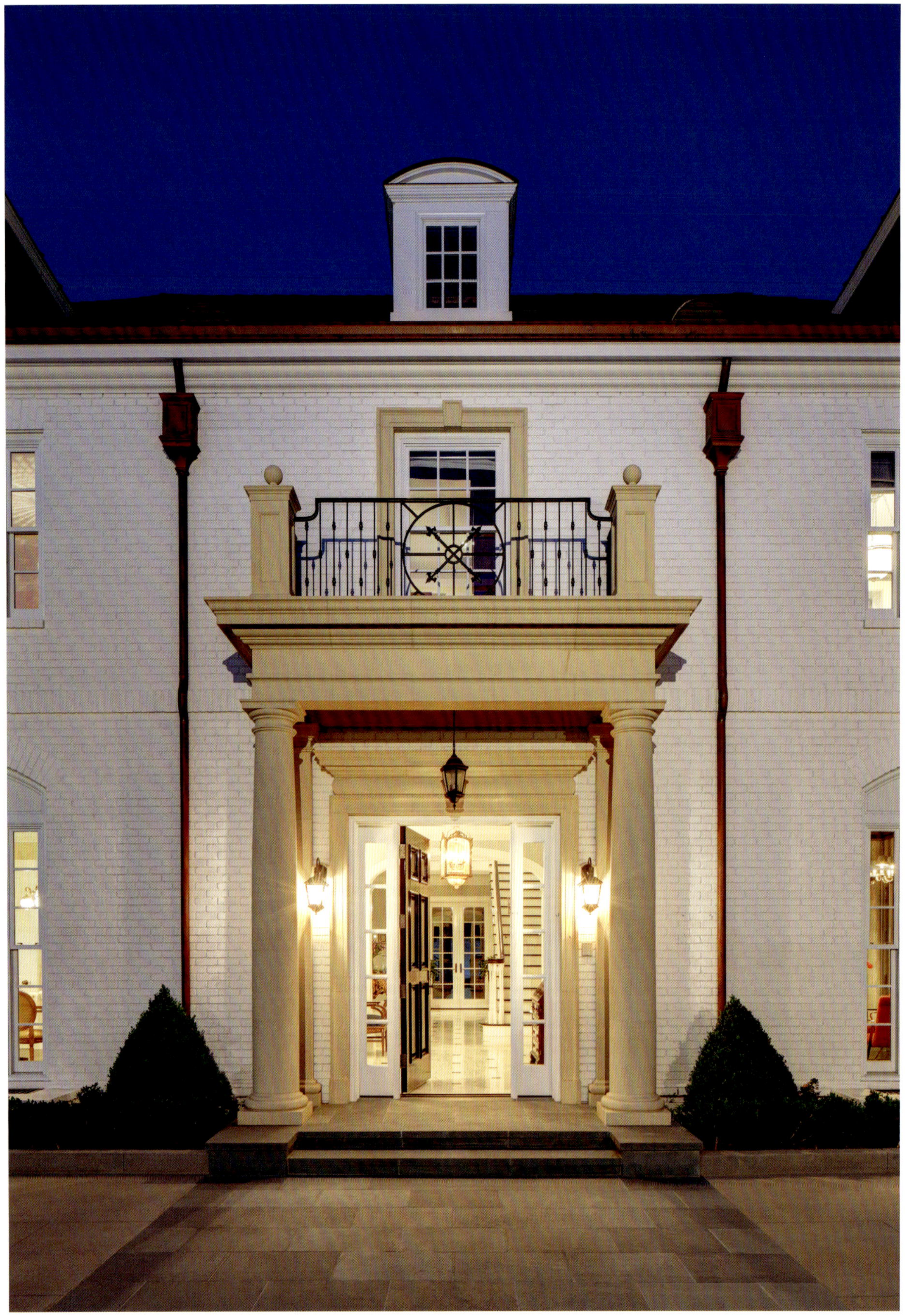

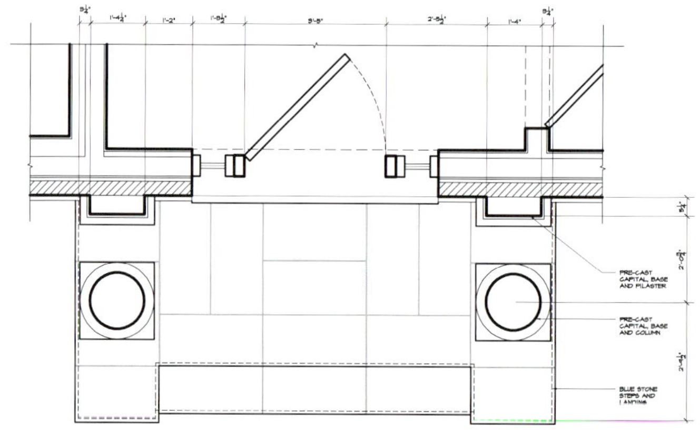

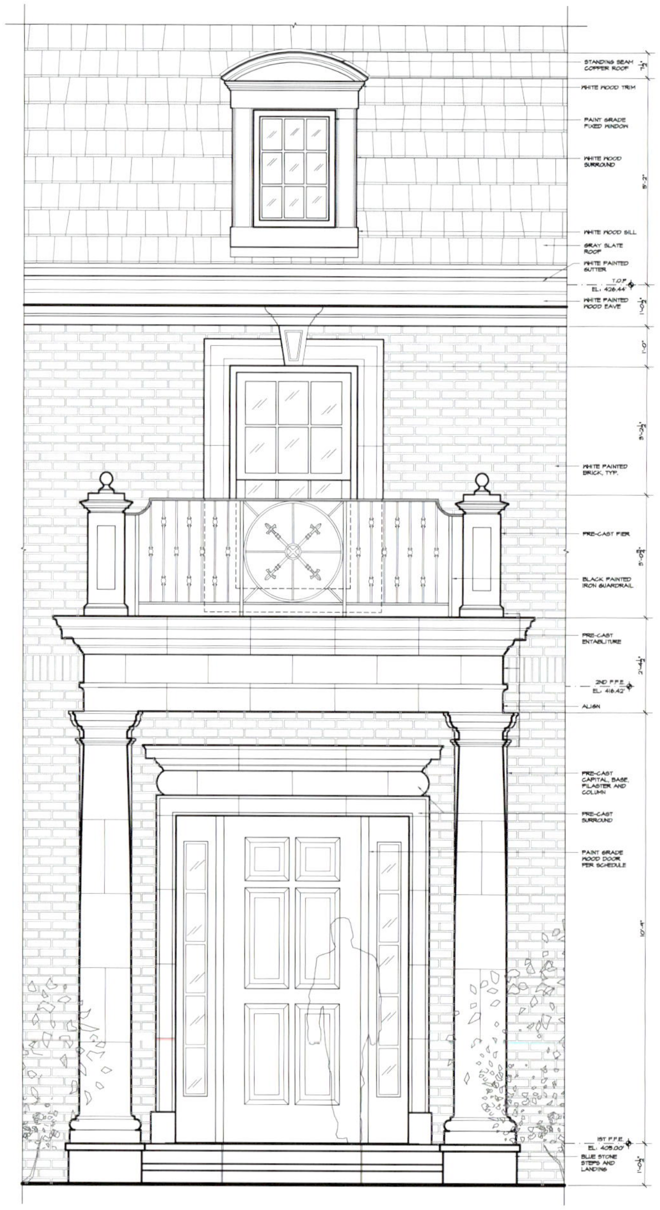

PREVIOUS PAGES: *This new Colonial Revival house fits within the architectural tradition of Hollywood's golden age, when movie stars commissioned classical homes, which had in turn been inspired by the Colonial Revival estates, such as those built around Atlanta in the 1920s and '30s.*

OPPOSITE LEFT: *The front façade consists of white brick, slate roof, strong dormers, groupings of different-size windows, a cast stone porch, and copper downspouts.*

OPPOSITE RIGHT: *Drawing of the entry porch.*

RIGHT: *The symmetrical floor plan is organized around a classic center hall, with its color scheme of black, white, silver, and gray that creates a polished, modern look within a traditional framework.*

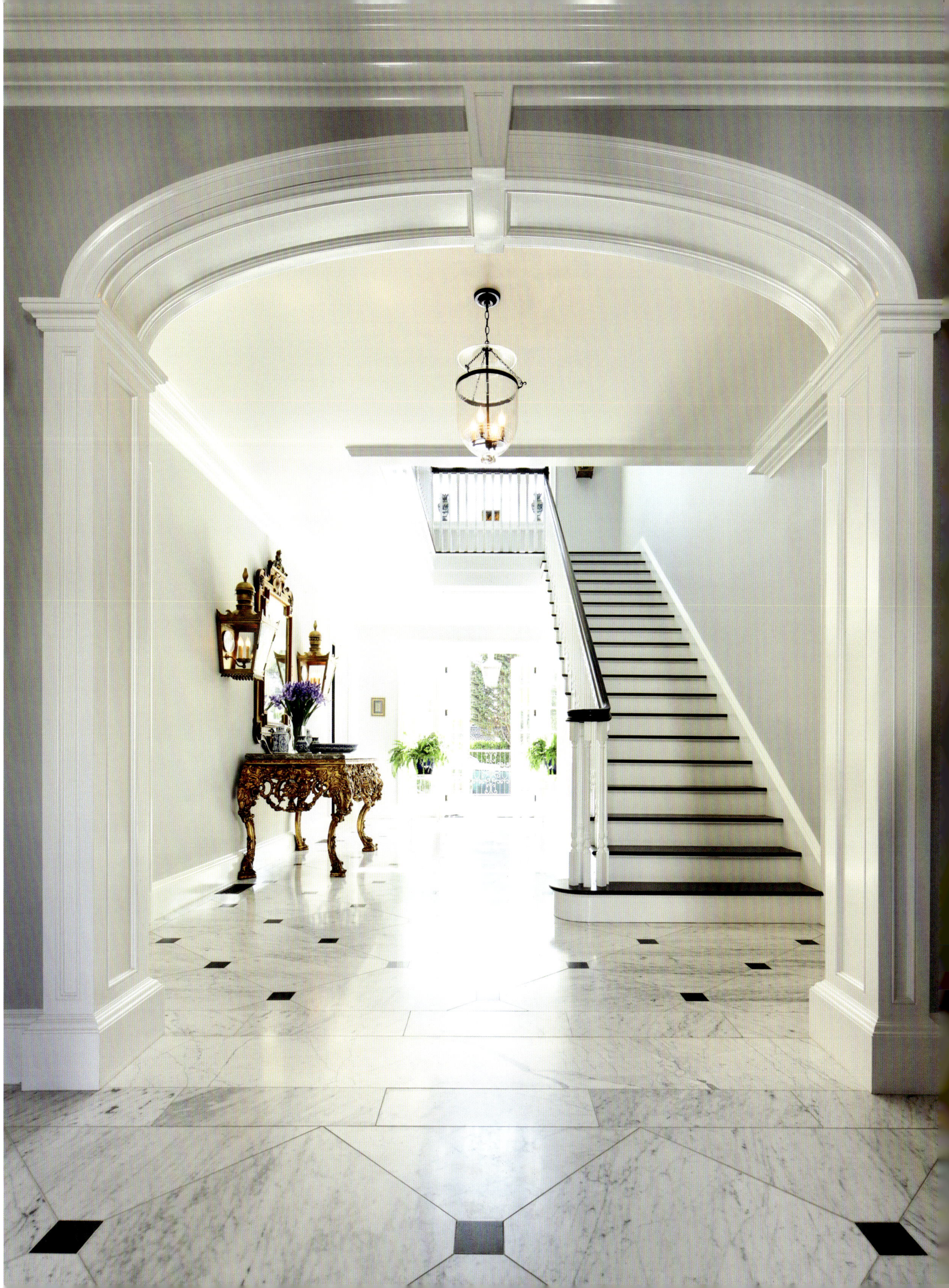

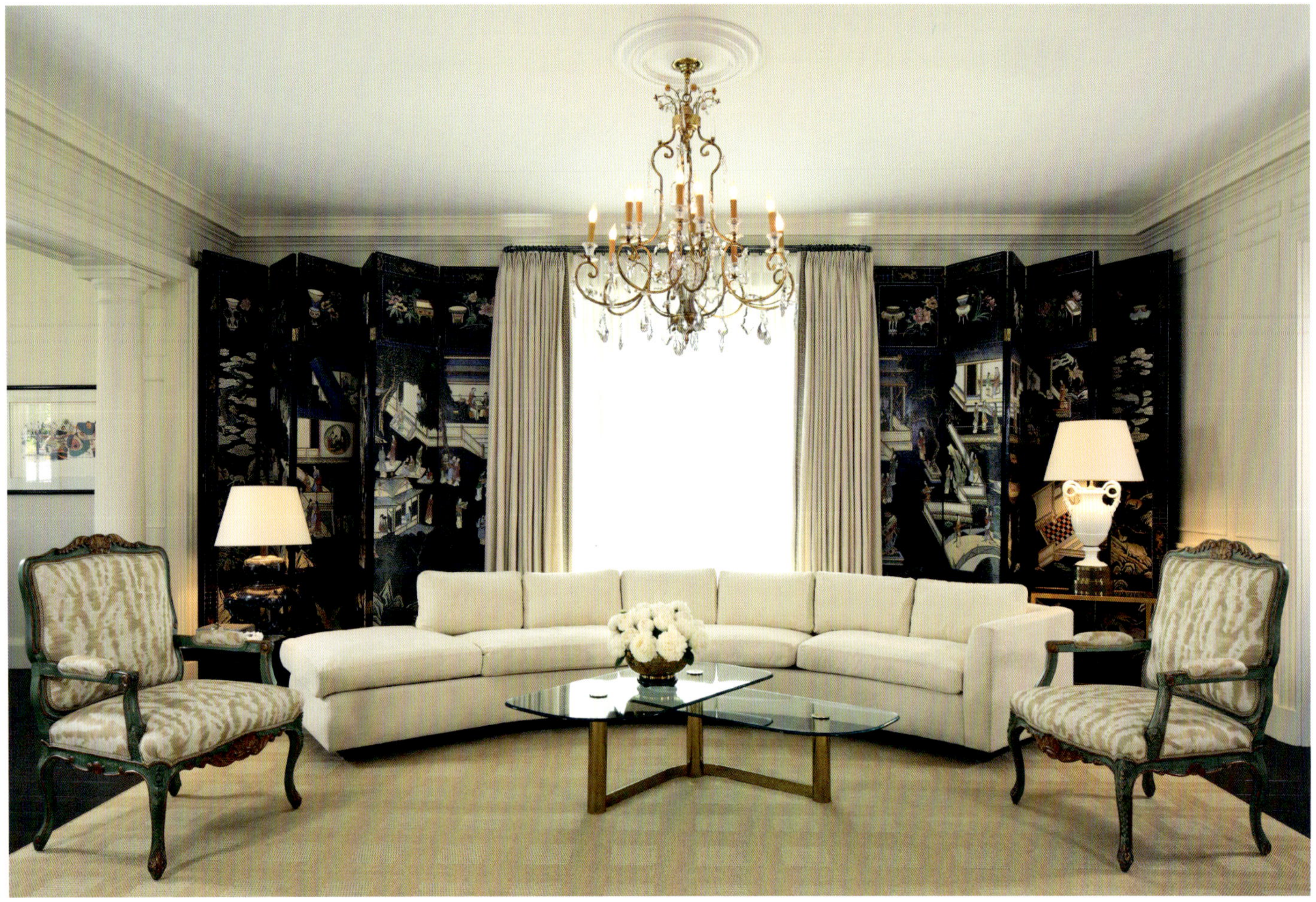

ABOVE: *The interiors by David Desmond explore the influences of Hollywood designer William Haines and the French design firm Maison Jansen. The living room's 1920s Coromandel screen and crystal chandeliers are a nod to Coco Chanel's Paris apartment.*

RIGHT: *At the other end of the living room, the dark wood floors, light rug and eighteenth-century European antiques are integrated with such 1970s pieces as Milo Baughman curving sofas and Pace Collection cocktail tables.*

FOLLOWING PAGES, LEFT: *The formal dining room was placed at the front for evening use, and is softened by the hand-painted Chinese wallpaper and chairs upholstered in gold leather and linen batik.* RIGHT: *Tall doors with cremone bolts help maintain the wine room's temperature. Python-textured wallpaper is in three shades of silver.*

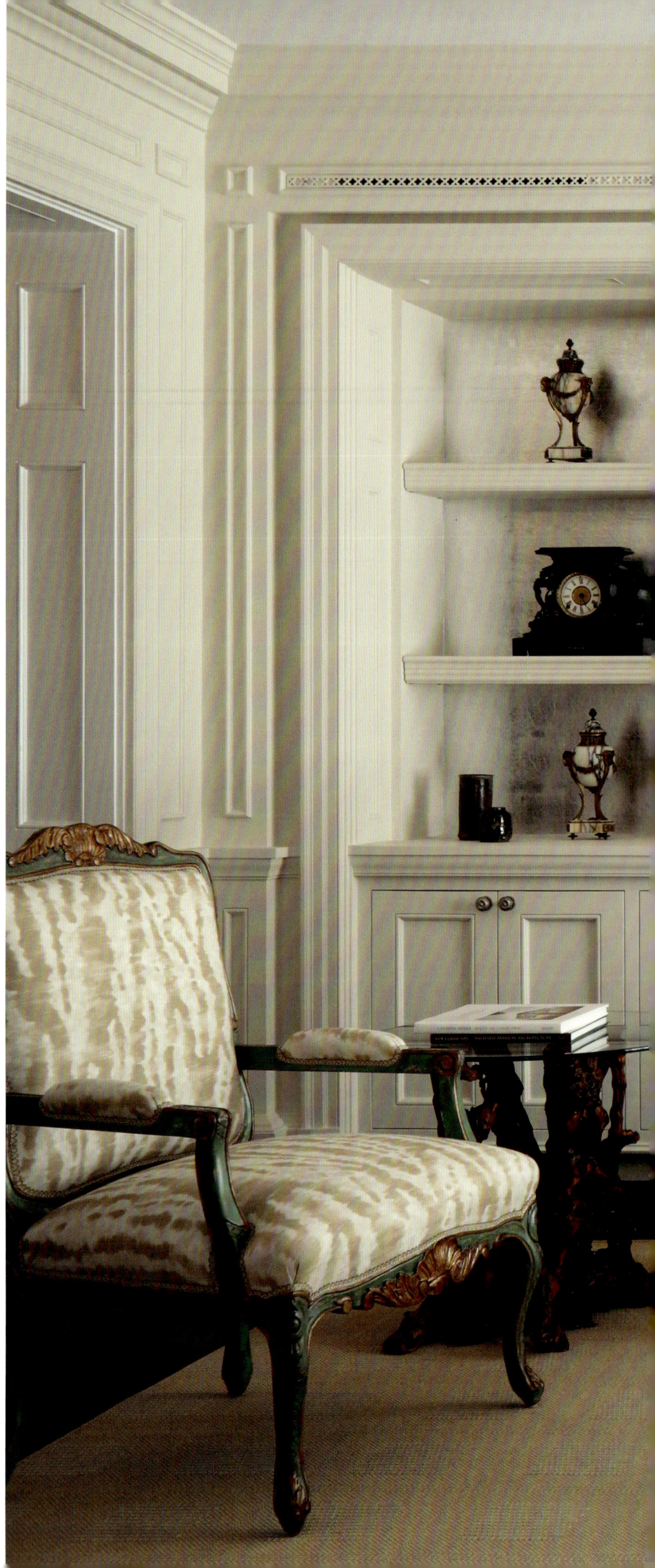

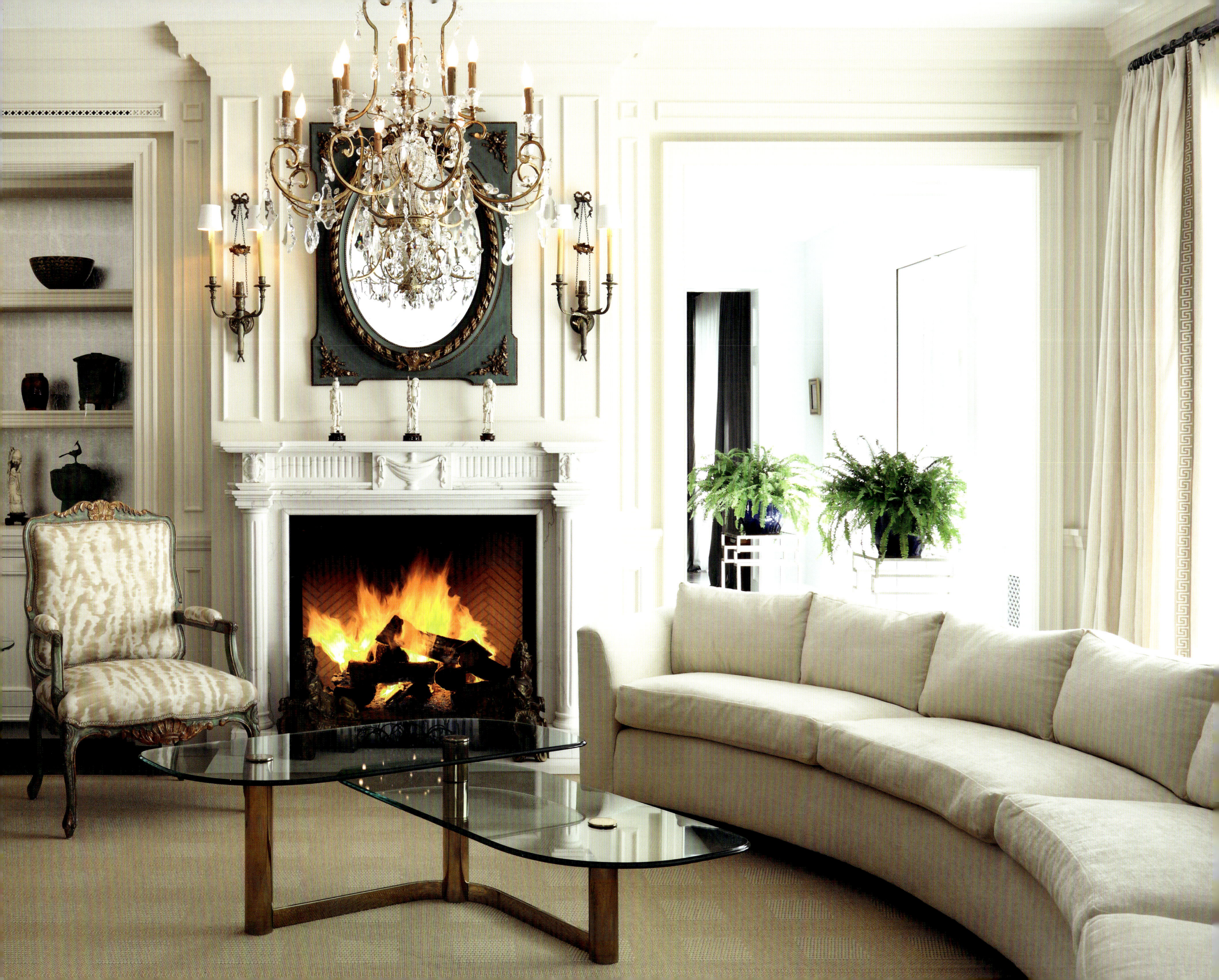

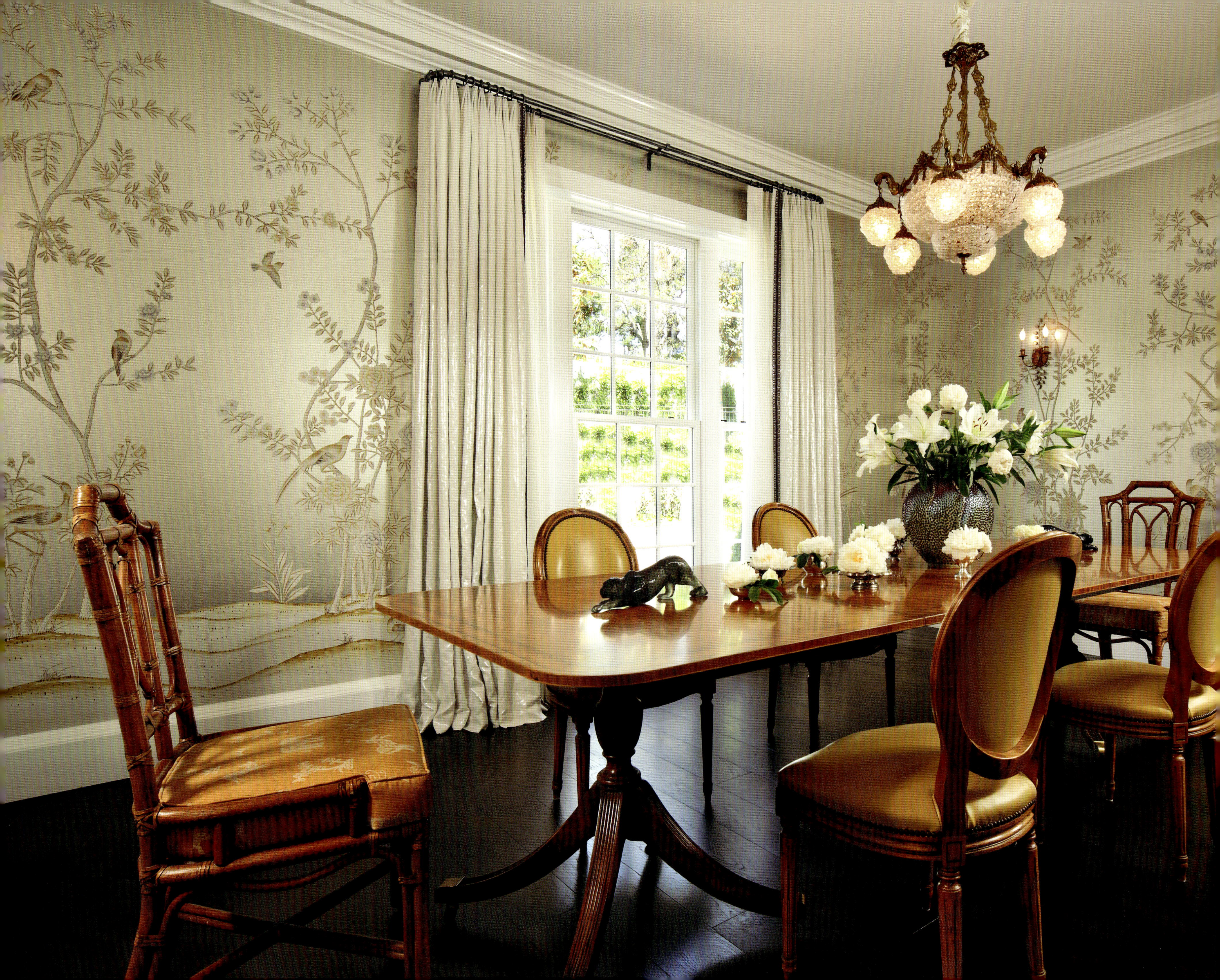

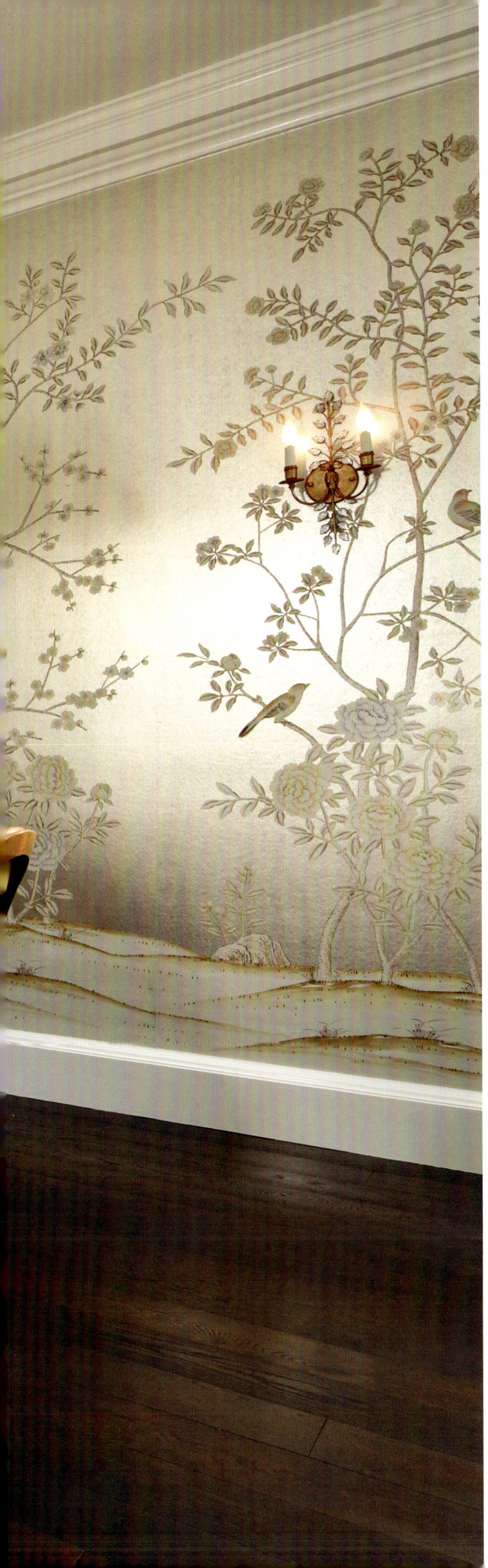

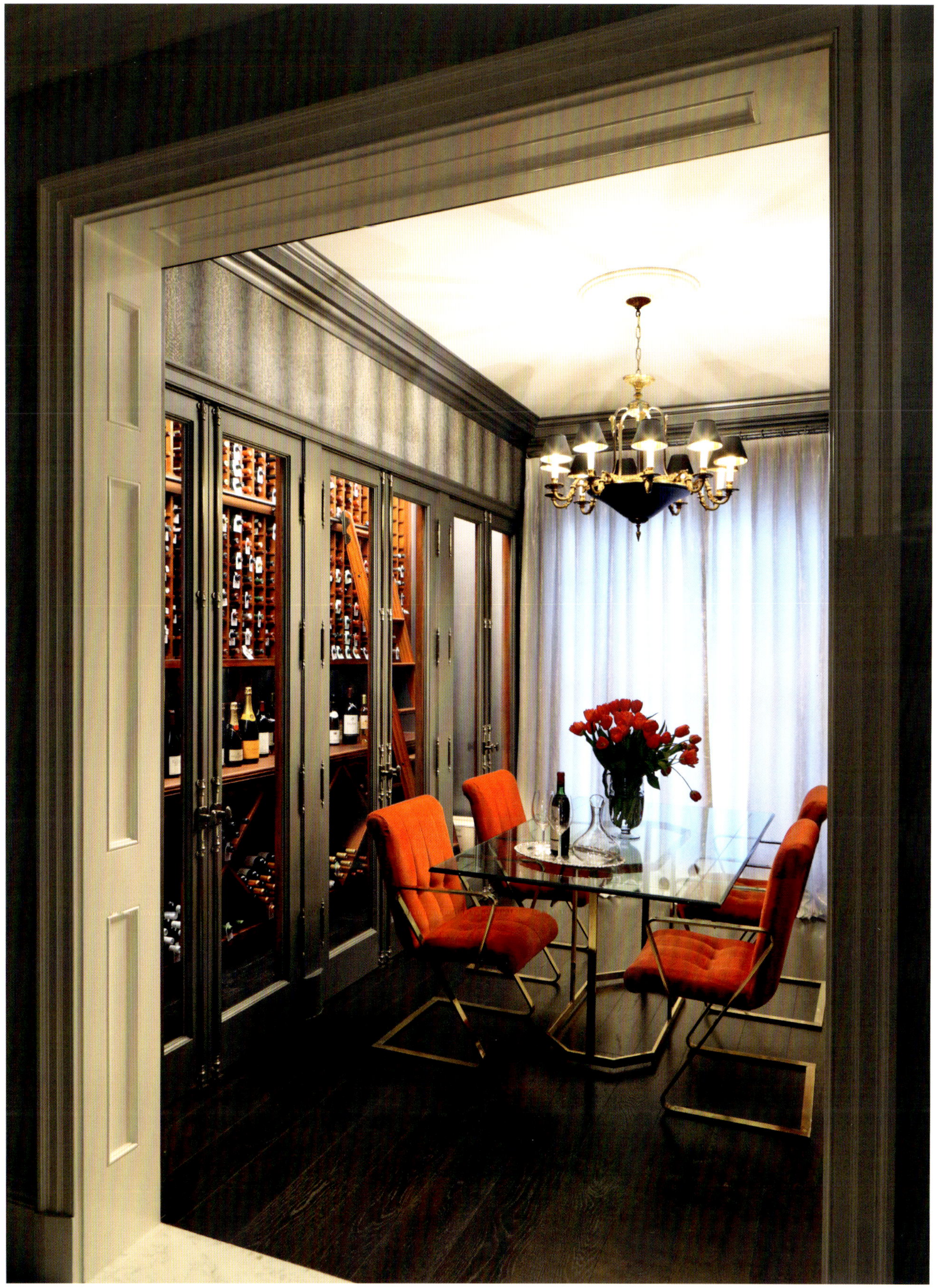

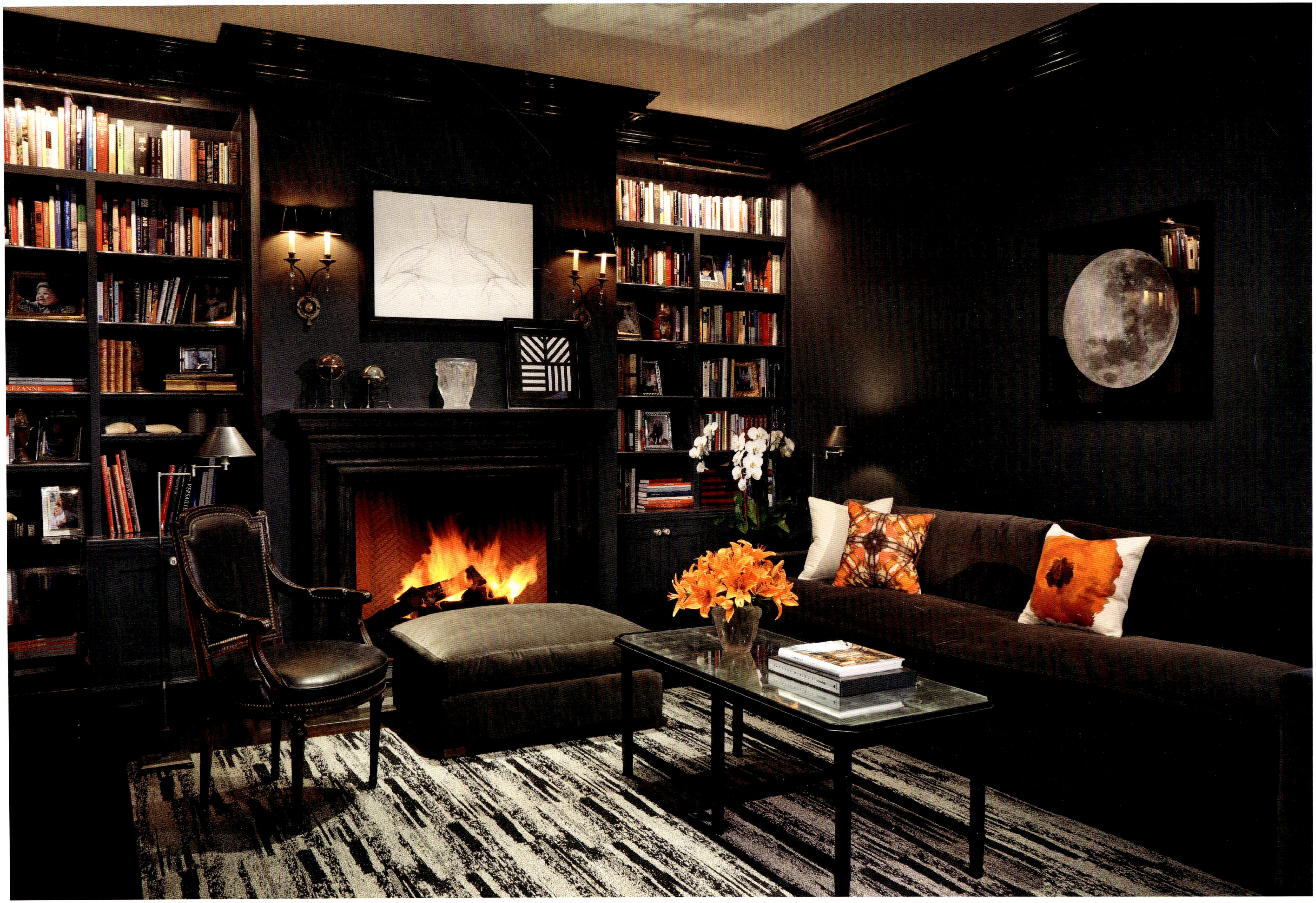

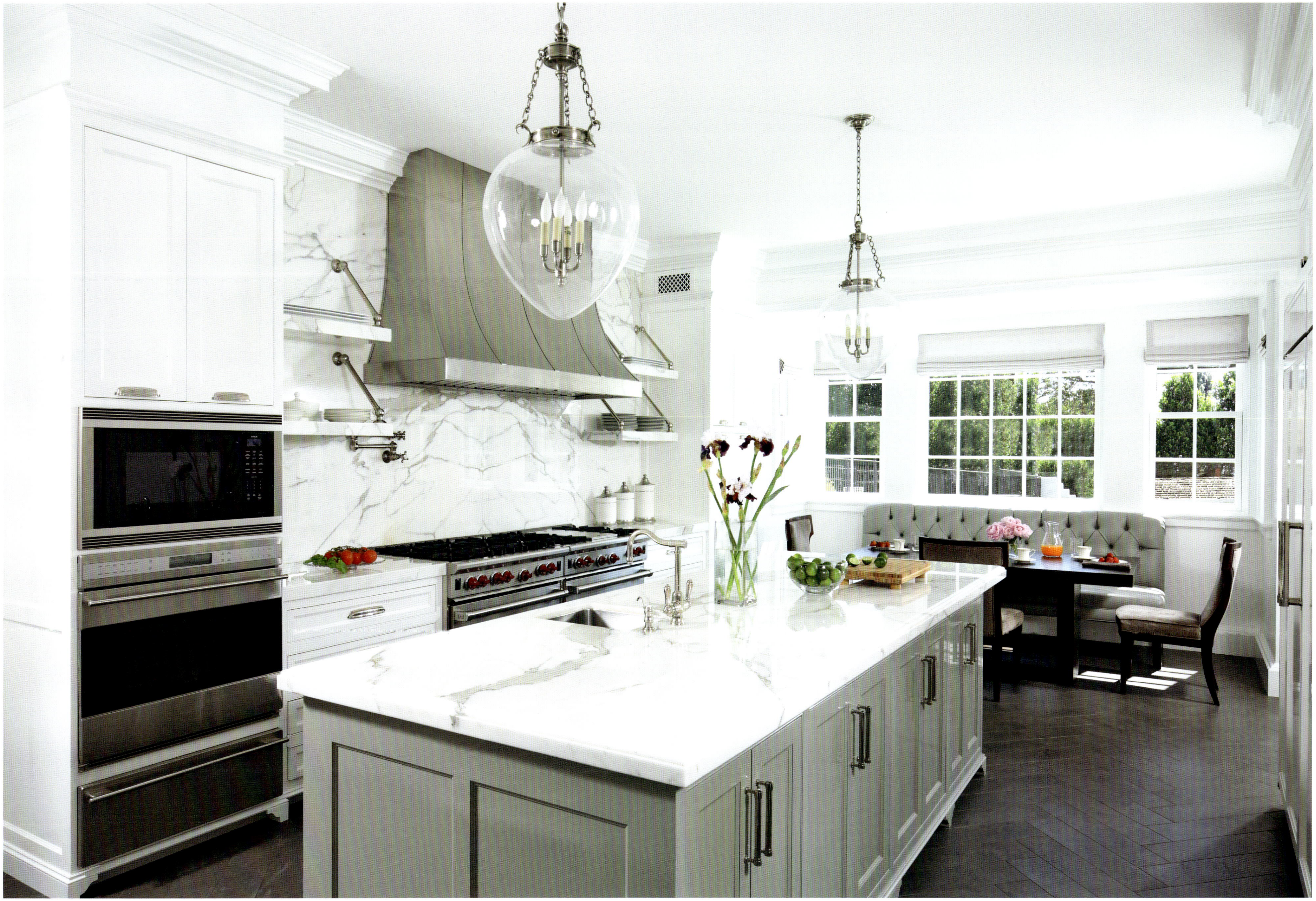

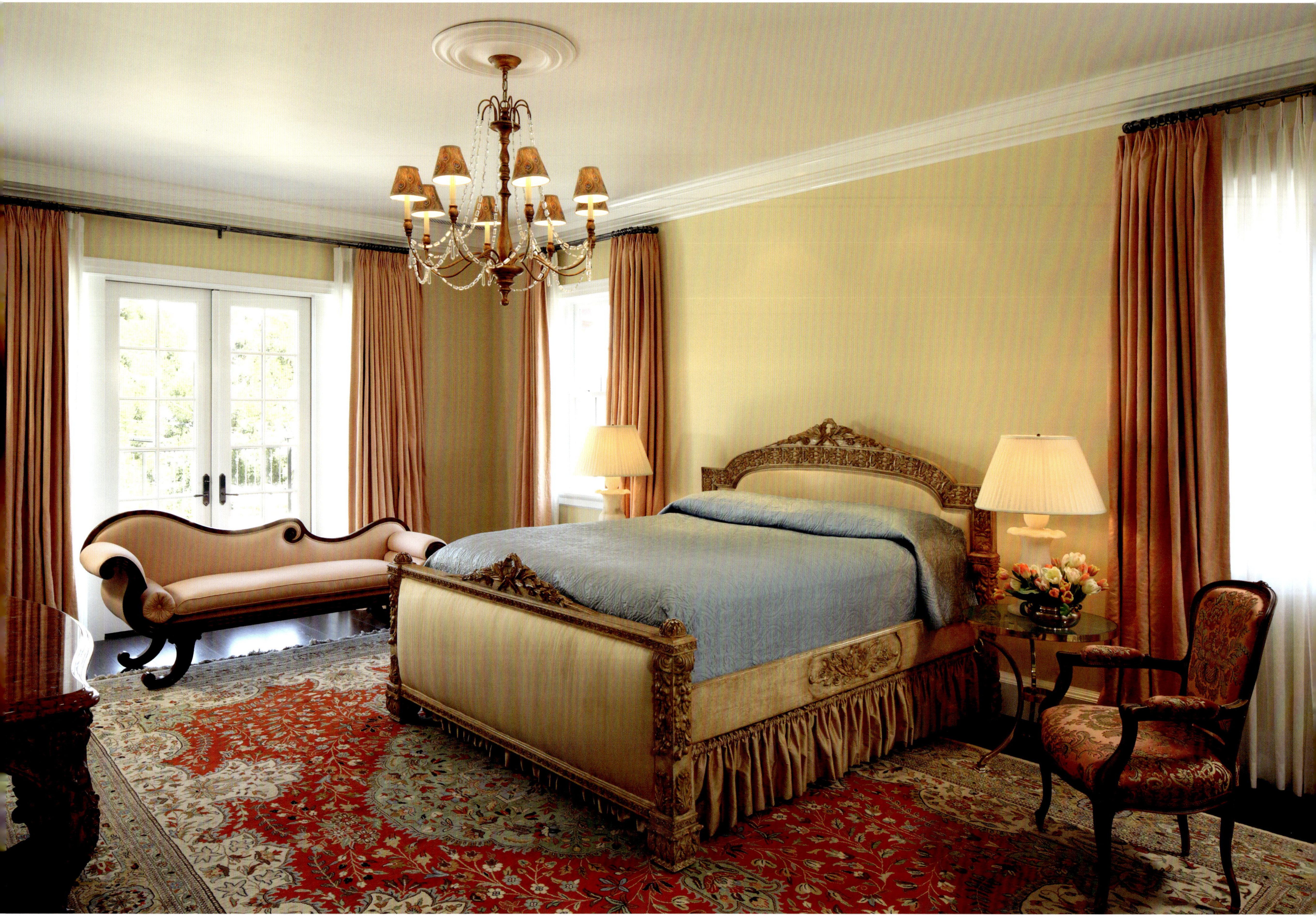

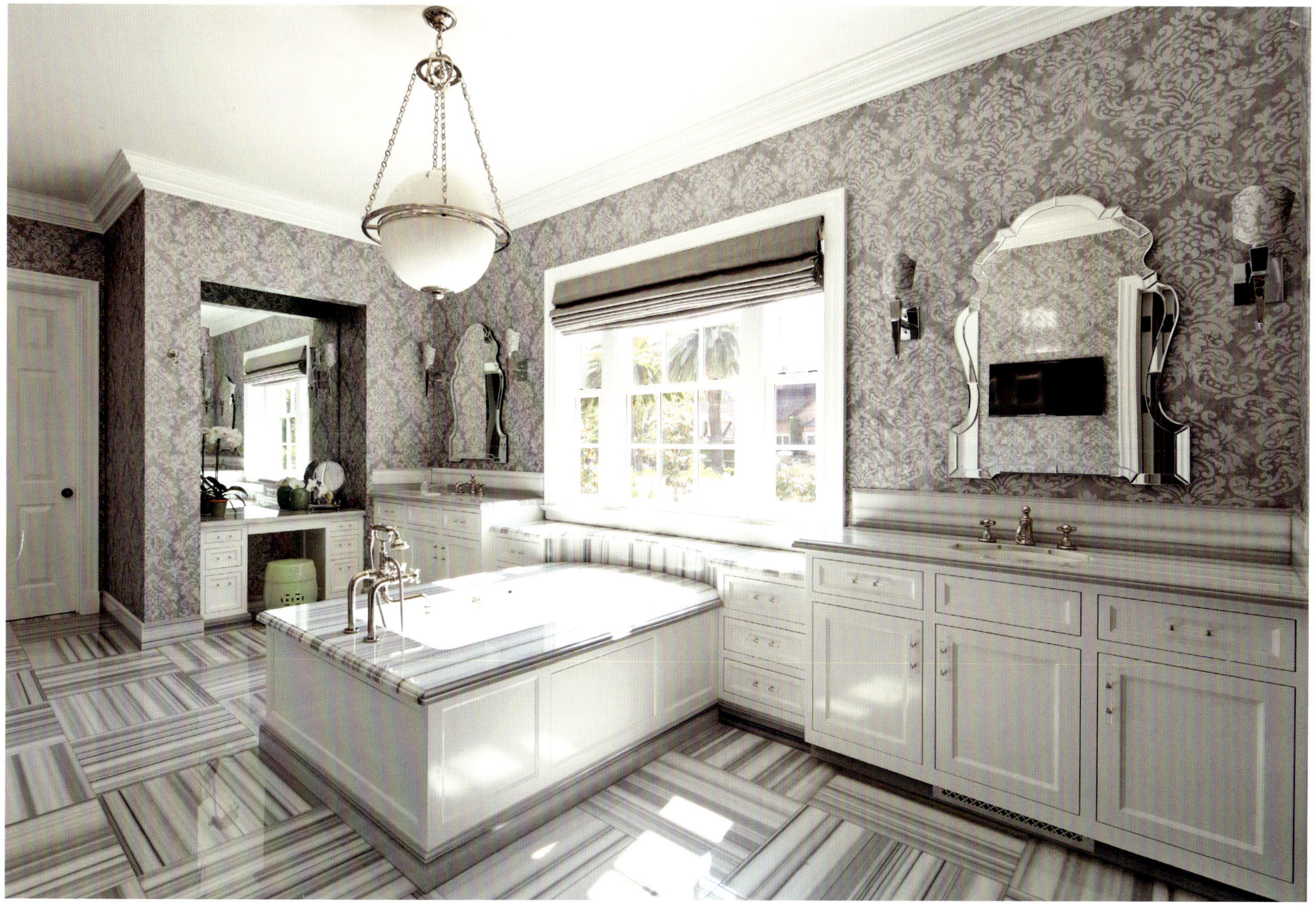

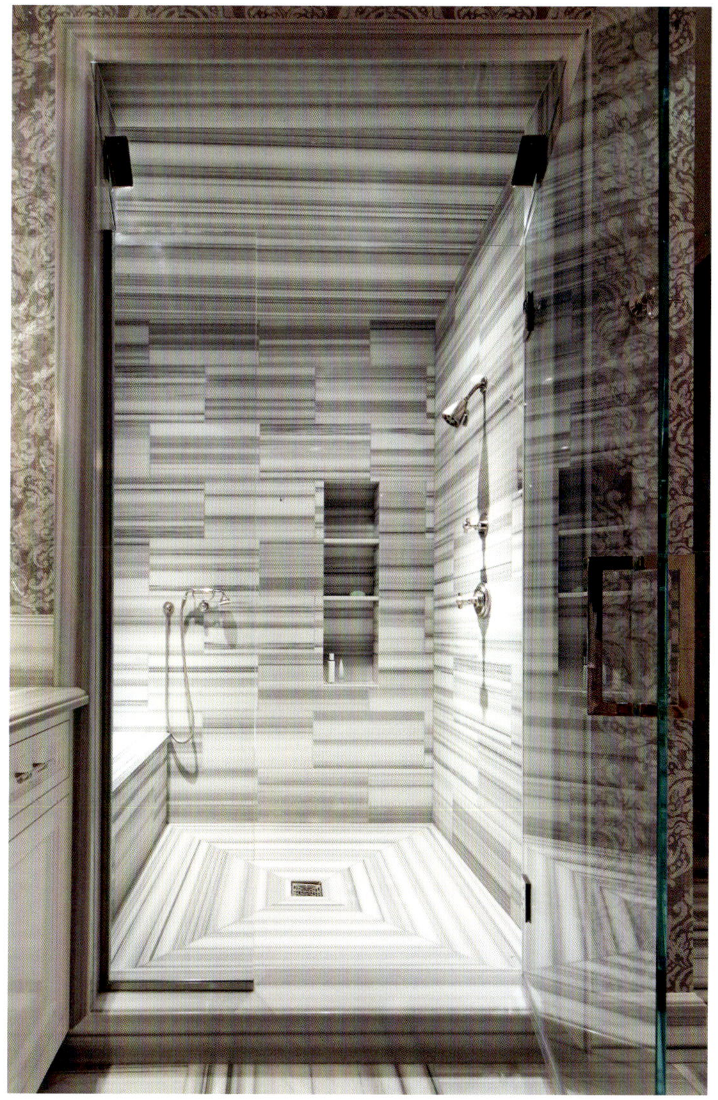

PREVIOUS PAGES, LEFT: *The family wing on the left side of the house includes the media room, which is clad in charcoal and gray and is an ideal cocoon for watching television at night.* RIGHT: *The wife, who loves to cook, wanted a restaurant-style eat-in kitchen with no upper cabinets, so we made open marble shelves. The island is very functional, not too wide or long, with enough room to move around.*

OPPOSITE: *For the master bedroom, the clients, who are a young, cosmopolitan couple with children, chose to adapt a classical style to the way they want to live today.*

ABOVE LEFT: *Most of our younger clients choose to share the master bath. This bathroom is a study in gray and white with the sharp, geometric lines of Marmara Equator zebra marble from Turkey cut into 18-inch squares, and silver damask wallpaper.* RIGHT: *The shower with the same precision-cut marble.*

FOLLOWING PAGES: *The symmetrical rear façade with a colonnaded central loggia and double stairs that lead down to the lawn.*

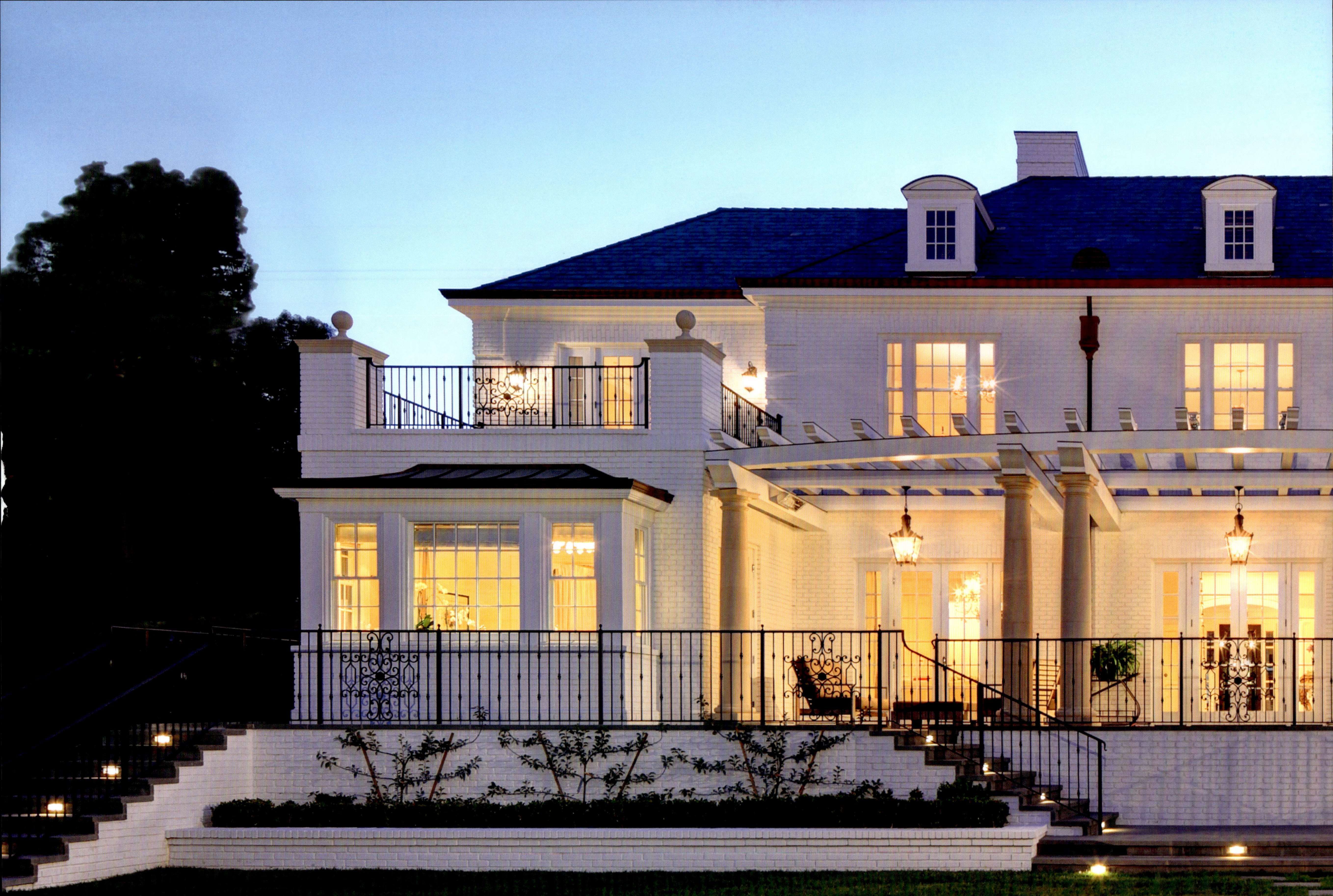

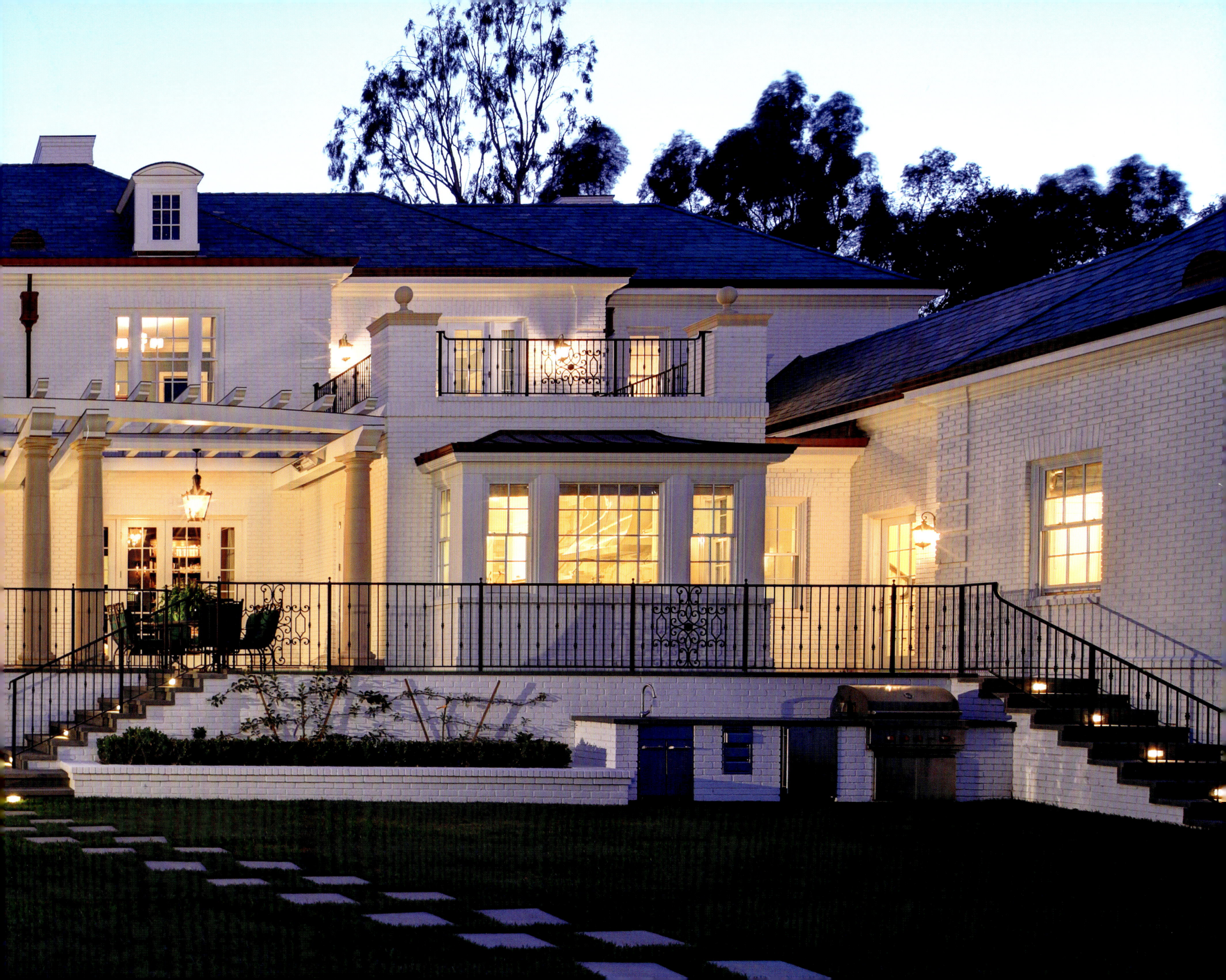

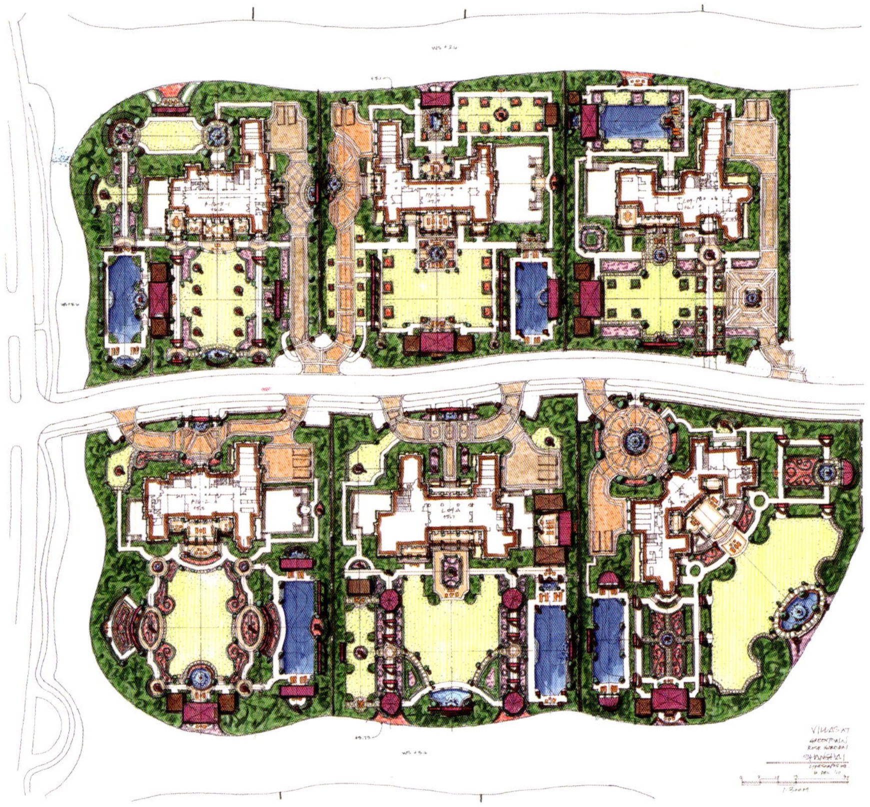

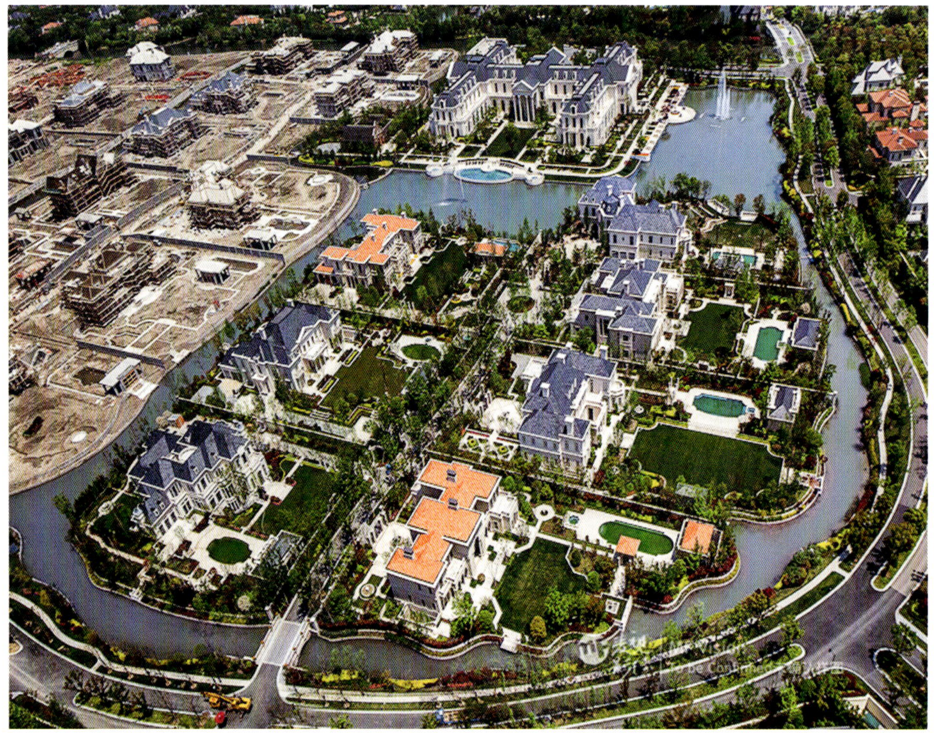

ROSE GARDEN VILLAS

Shanghai

Located west of Shanghai, Rose Garden is a gated residential community developed by Greentown China Holdings. Since this was the first luxury development of its kind in China, the developer was very conscious of wanting to make a major statement, so the community and its estates were based on such esteemed communities as Tuxedo Park, Beverly Hills, and Palm Beach.

At the center of the development, on an island surrounded by water, are the seven most exclusive estates—the Rose Garden Villas. The architectural inspirations were the classical houses of Europe and their American counterparts: eighteenth-century French châteaux, Italian Renaissance villas, and English Georgian manors. We designed four of the villas in formal French and Italianate styles.

One of the most notable features of the site plan is that, regardless of the entry orientation of the house from the street, the back of the house had to face south—the developer felt it was essential to have primary family rooms face the south sun. Thus, houses located on the northern side of streets were entered from the far northern end or the side of the property so that the major rooms would face south. It was sometimes a challenge—on those lots, vehicular circulation often required a fair amount of space because the entrance court and front façade had to be grand and impressive.

Most of the clientele are prominent businessmen and there was a degree of social prestige and cachet in having houses created by Western designers—hiring an international design team was a significant status symbol. Trish Wilson designed the grand French eighteenth-century clubhouse, and the landscaping and gardens were by Mario Nievera. The quality of the streetscapes, parkways, and gardens is world-class and stands alongside the great precedents that inspired Rose Garden.

French Villa

For this eighteenth-century-inspired French villa, which sits on two acres at the end of the island with views on three sides and facing the clubhouse, we based the design on a favorite Houston house of ours by John Staub. The front façade wraps around the entry court in facets and fans out in the rear garden. A conventional plan wouldn't work—it needed to be a shape that was more Baroque and dramatic to take advantage of the many views.

Greentown insisted on authentic materials; each villa is clad in full limestone with slate or tile roofing. We were given carte blanche with the architectural detailing and worked intimately to develop the floor plans and interior architecture in concert with local preferences and programmatic requirements that included adherence to feng shui rules of organization; first-floor guest suites; family and chef kitchens; and separation of the entry court from the garages in the tradition of grand estates of the past.

Each estate featured a rich history of architectural detailing: ornate exterior and interior spaces, ceilings with beams or coffers or vaulting, elaborate paneling and trimwork in the formal rooms and master suites, stained wood in family rooms and libraries, and painted millwork elsewhere.

One of the more unusual features was a two-story living room, which the developer identified as very desirable for their clientele, who live a very formal lifestyle. They didn't care as much about the entrance hall being large, but they wanted one entertainment room that was truly grand in scale.

Each villa also features a full basement with an indoor pool, spa, gym, dramatic Art Deco theater, bar, wine cellar, and staff accommodations. As part of the basement, the client also requested sunken gardens to provide daylight. Since the lots are flat, this was an interesting feature we had to accommodate.

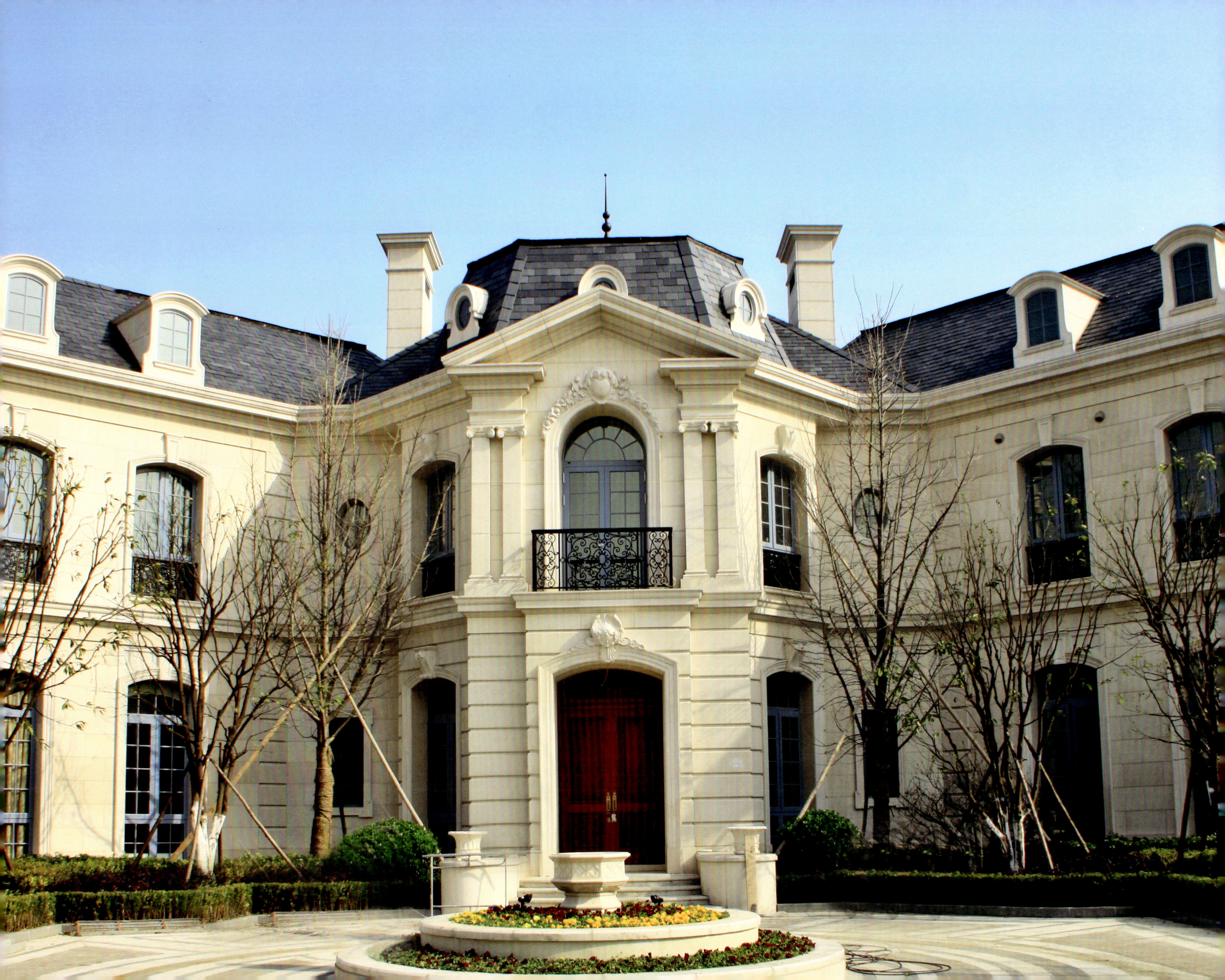

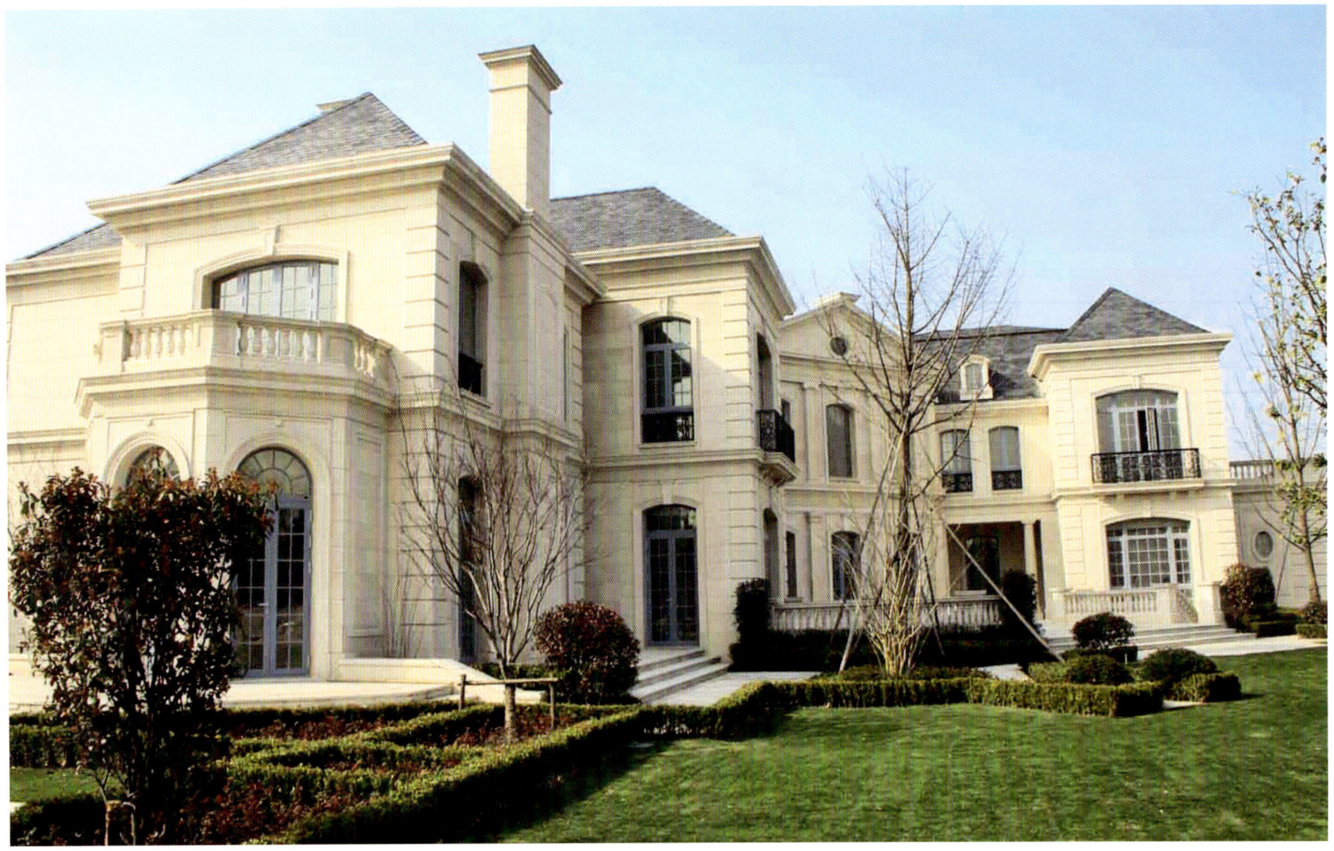

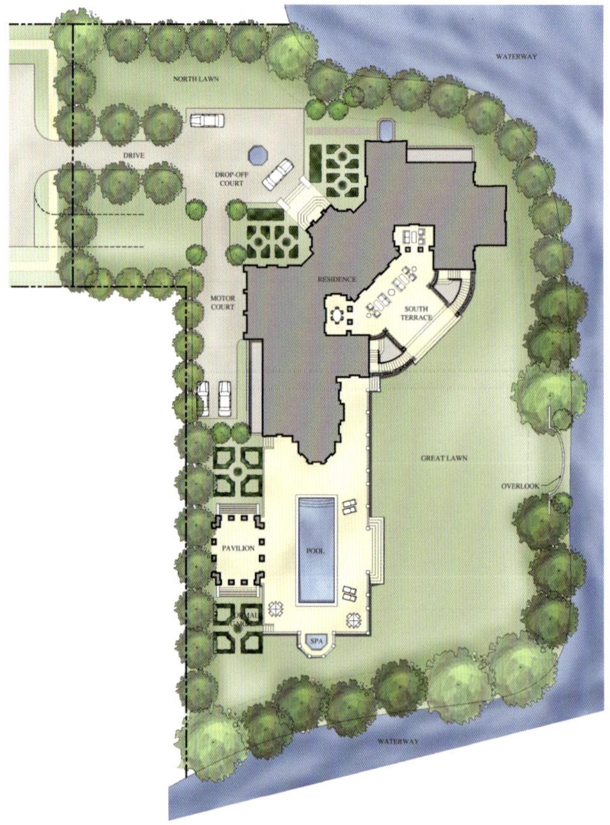

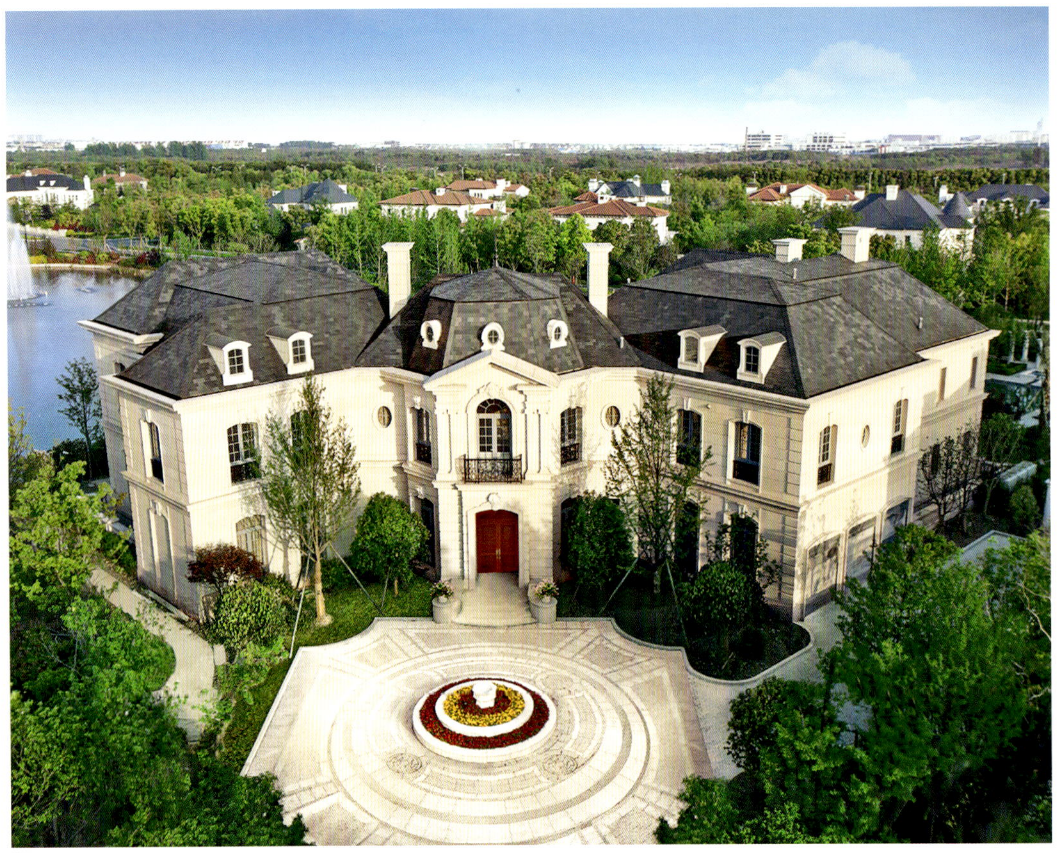

PAGE 210, LEFT: *Site plan of the Rose Garden Villas outside Shanghai.* RIGHT: *An aerial view of the seven Rose Garden Villas at the center of the Rose Garden development on an island facing the grand French-inspired eighteenth-century clubhouse.*

PREVIOUS PAGE: *The design of the French villas was based on the formal architecture of eighteenth-century French châteaux. The front façade is clad in limestone with a slate roof.*

ABOVE LEFT: *Rear façade of the French villa.*

ABOVE RIGHT: *Site plan of the French villa that sits on two acres facing the clubhouse.*

LEFT: *Inspired by the work of John Staub in Houston, the French villa is a dramatic Baroque design that wraps around the entry court to take advantage of the multiple views.*

OPPOSITE: *A drawing of the front elevation of the French villa.*

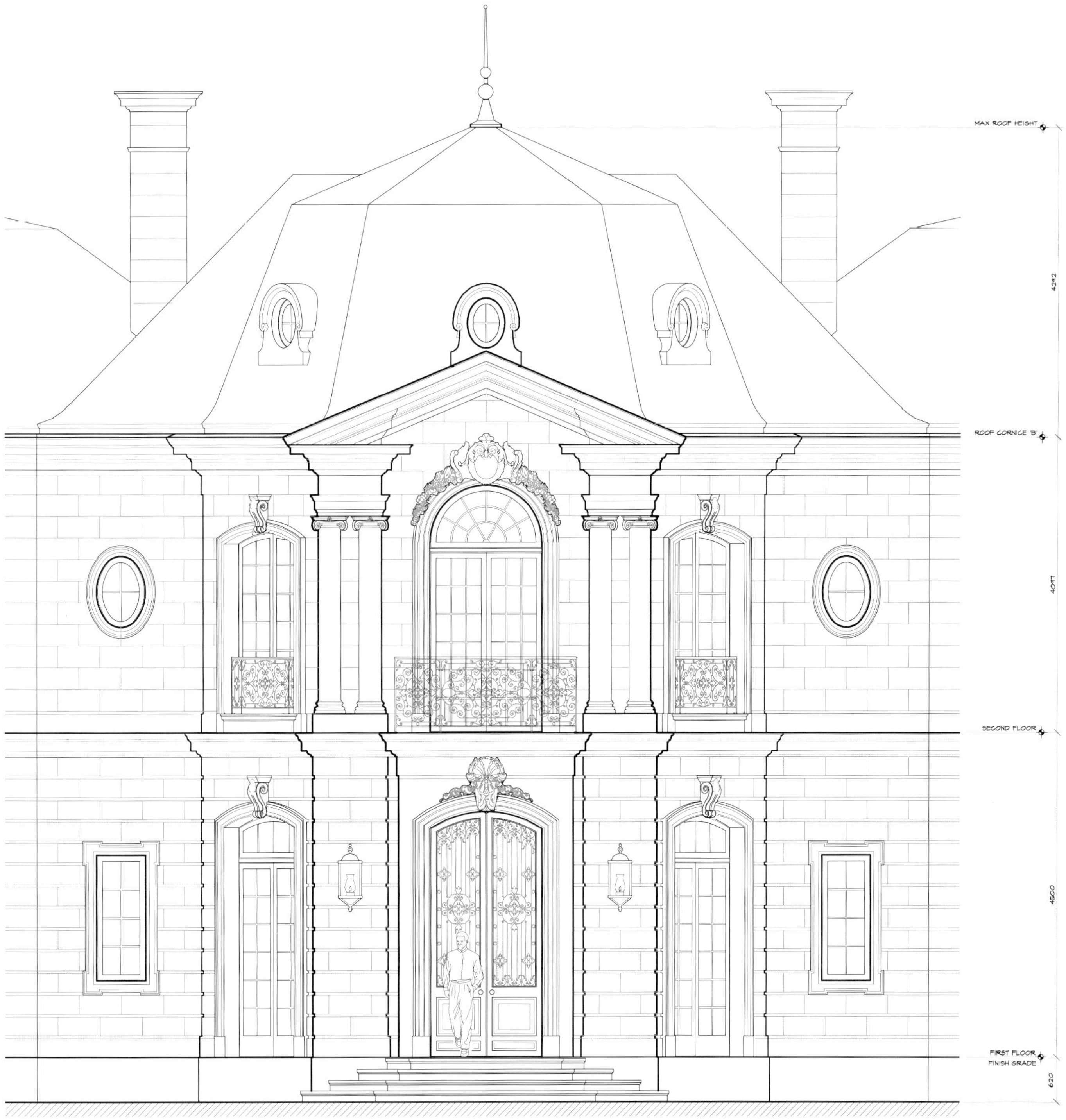

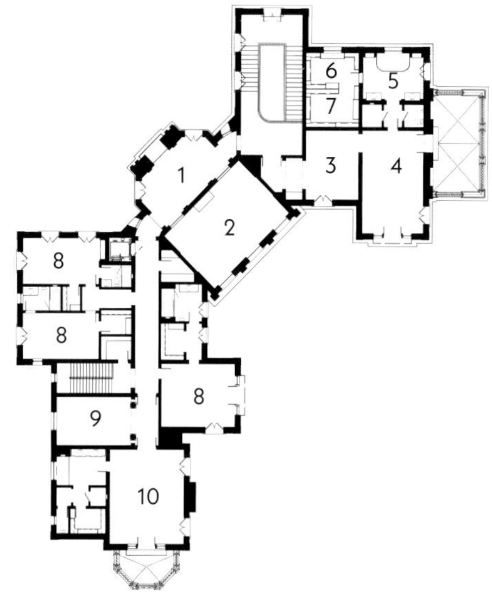

SECOND-FLOOR PLAN

1 Sitting room
2 Open to below
3 Sitting room
4 Master bedroom
5 Master bath
6 His closet
7 Her closet
8 Bedroom suite
9 Sitting room
10 Junior master bedroom

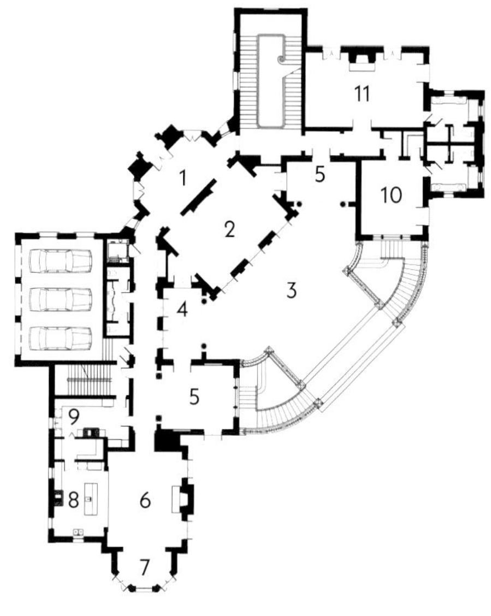

FIRST-FLOOR PLAN

1 Entrance hall
2 Formal living room
3 Formal terrace
4 Loggia
5 Formal dining room
6 Family room
7 Family dining room
8 Western kitchen
9 Chinese kitchen
10 Guest bedroom
11 Library/office

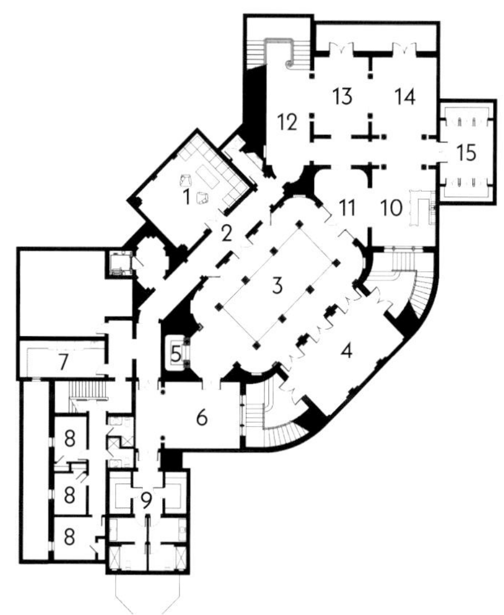

LOWER-LEVEL PLAN

1 Theater
2 Gallery
3 Swimming pool
4 Sunken garden
5 Spa
6 Exercise room
7 Laundry
8 Staff quarters
9 Spa
10 Bar
11 Card room
12 Foyer
13 Game room
14 Billiard room
15 Wine cellar

0 8 16 32 ft

Italian Villa

The Italianate villas were created in the style of the eclectic mansions of Palm Beach. From the exterior you can see the desire to incorporate an elaborate canon of classical detailing, from paired Corinthian columns and elaborate balustrades to roof eaves with limestone brackets, carved limestone panels below the windows, finials, and ornamentation.

In this Italianate villa, we had to place a double-height entry on the side of the property as well as a two-story living room. The foyer forms the cross-axis with a gallery continuing into the living room and terminating at the far end with furnishings for feng shui compliance. The formal staircase is located off the side of the entry so that it wouldn't be immediately visible since it is just for family use, but it provides a glimpse of its elegance as it leads to a balcony that wraps around the entry and continues to overlook the living room.

Primary rooms feature elaborate ceilings and moldings, marble columns with gilded details, ironwork, and carved stone, all fabricated with local craftsmen and artists. Most of the formal rooms were paneled and have intricate, geometric, Escher-like parquet floors inlaid with three or more different woods.

The size of the two-acre estates along with the absence of tennis courts afforded grand lawns and gardens that were formally laid out by landscape architect Mario Nievera. The Italian villa won the Best of the Best Villa award in 2010 from Robb Report China.

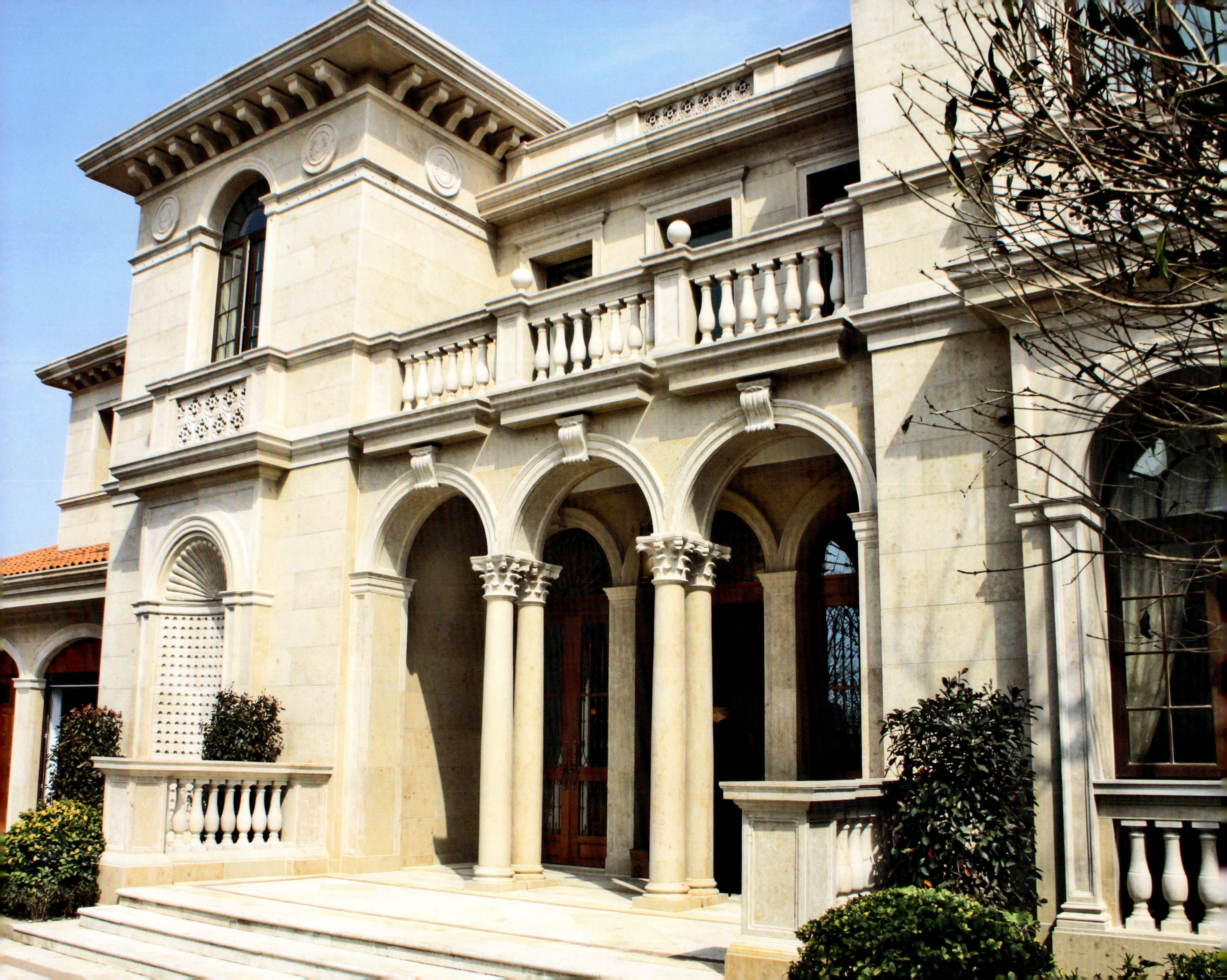

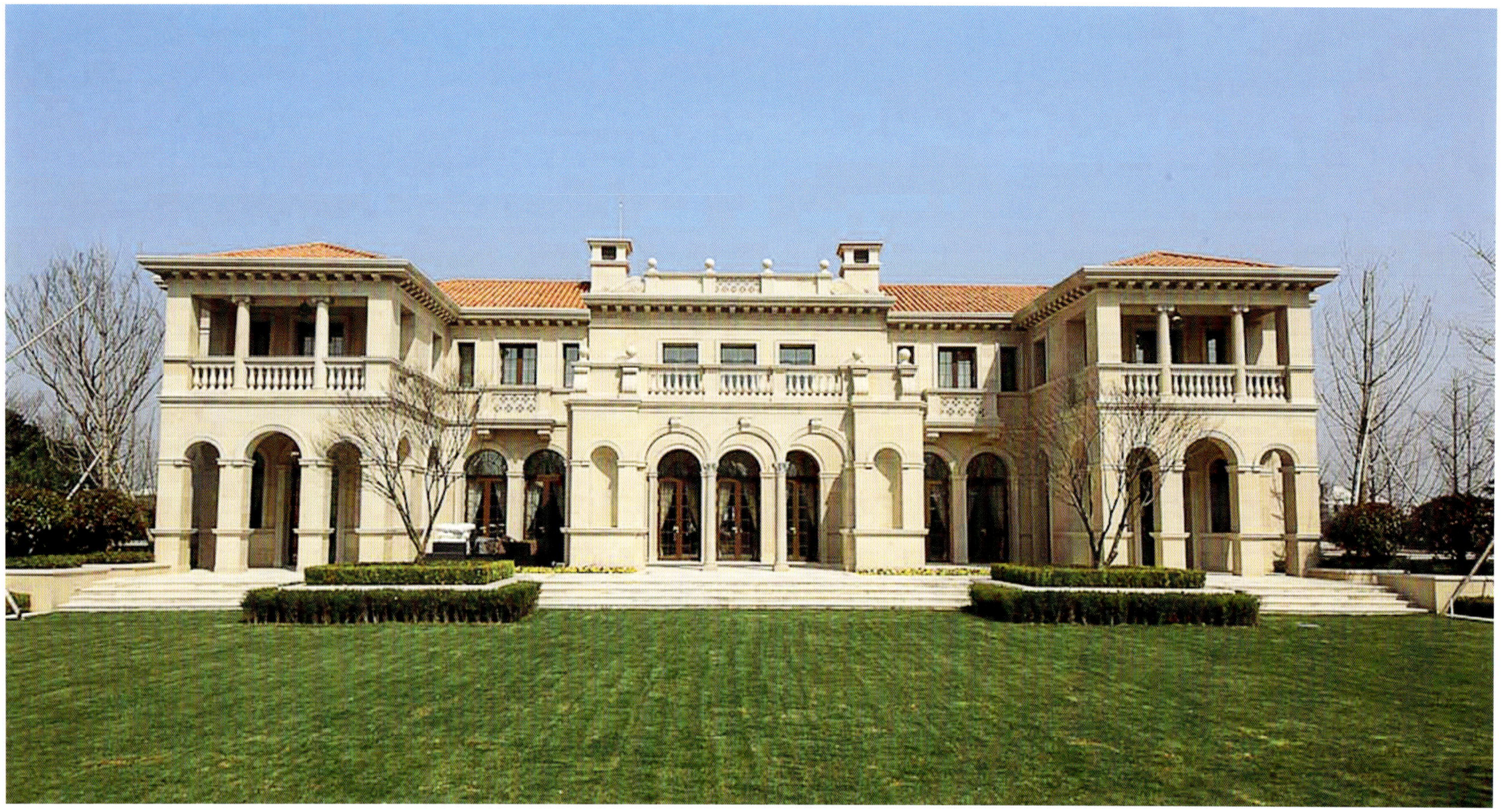

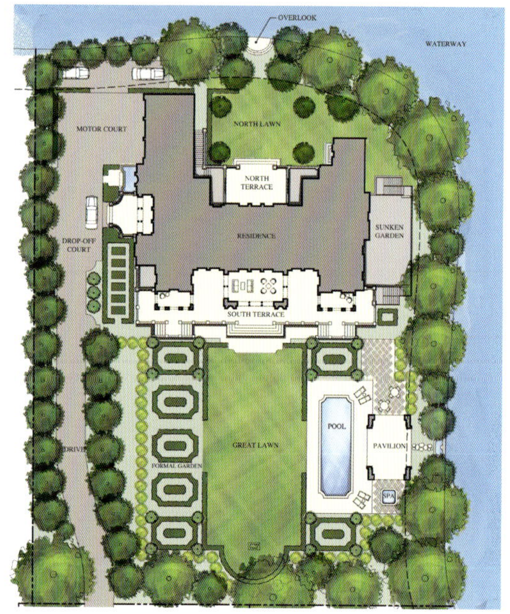

PREVIOUS PAGE: *The Italianate villa is a modern interpretation of the great early twentieth-century Mediterranean Revival mansions in Palm Beach, with a golden limestone façade, three-arched entrance veranda, carved stone balustrade, and a terra cotta tile roof.*

ABOVE LEFT: *The rear garden façade is a dramatic U-shape with an elaborate display of classical detailing, including Corinthian columns and balustrades, roof eaves with limestone brackets, finials, and ornamentation.*

ABOVE RIGHT: *The site plan shows how all the rear garden façades of the villas had to face south, and how accommodations were made to create a driveway and entry regardless of the home's orientation on the street.*

OPPOSITE: *A drawing of the pergola for the Italianate villa.*

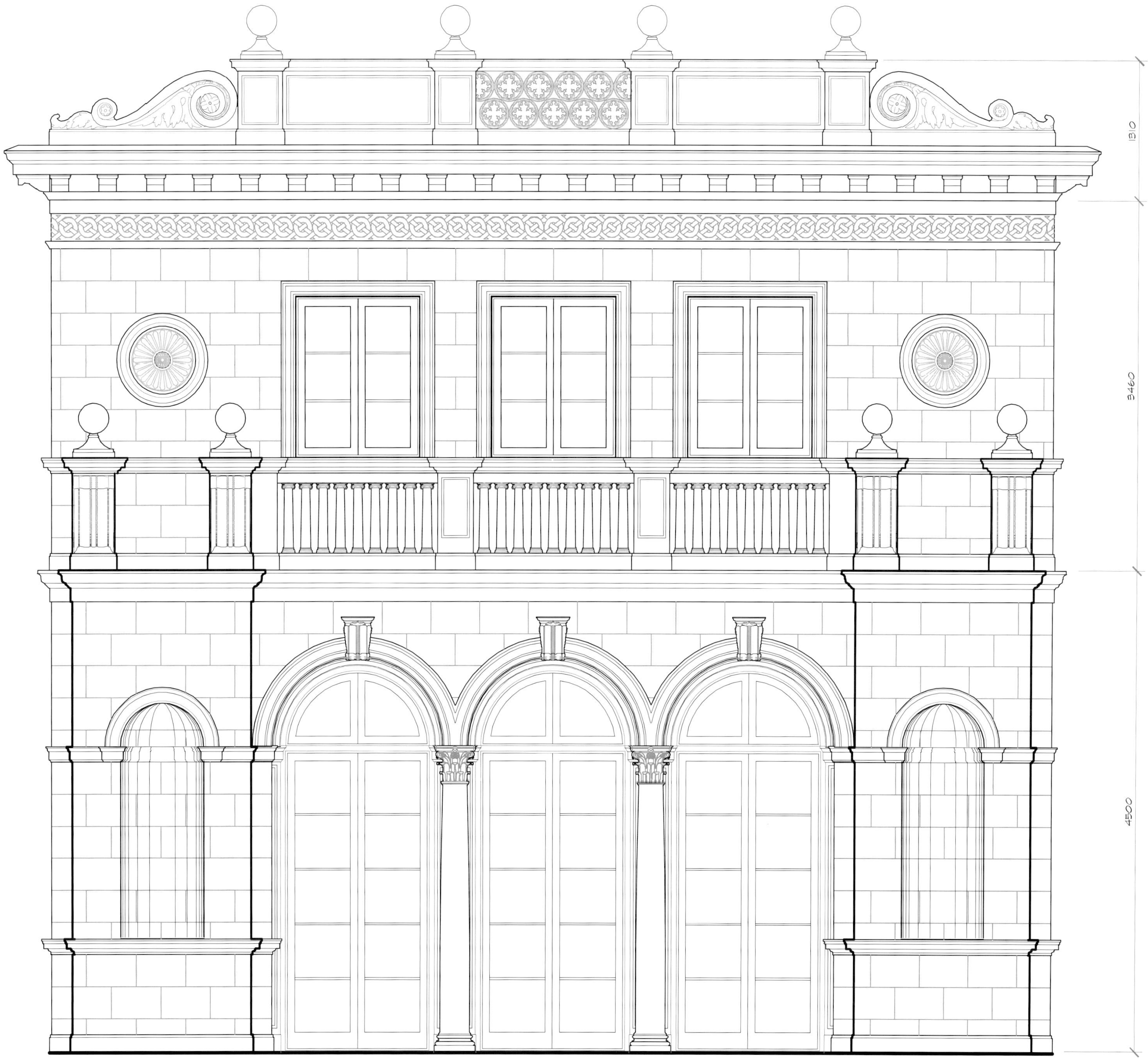
1310
3460
4500

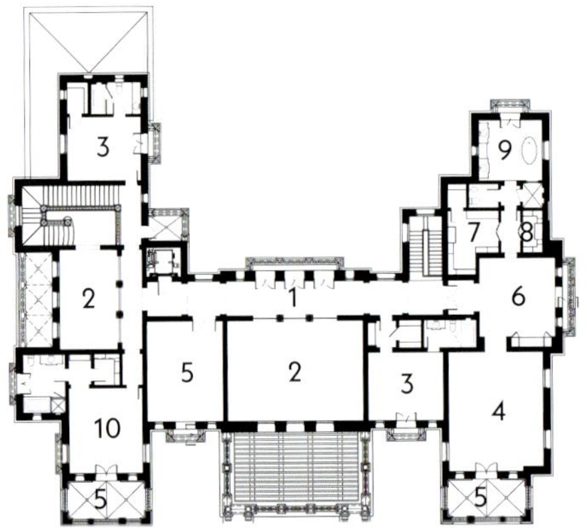

SECOND-FLOOR PLAN

1 Gallery
2 Open to below
3 Bedroom suite
4 Master bedroom
5 Terrace
6 Sitting room
7 Her closet
8 His closet
9 Master bath
10 Junior master bedroom

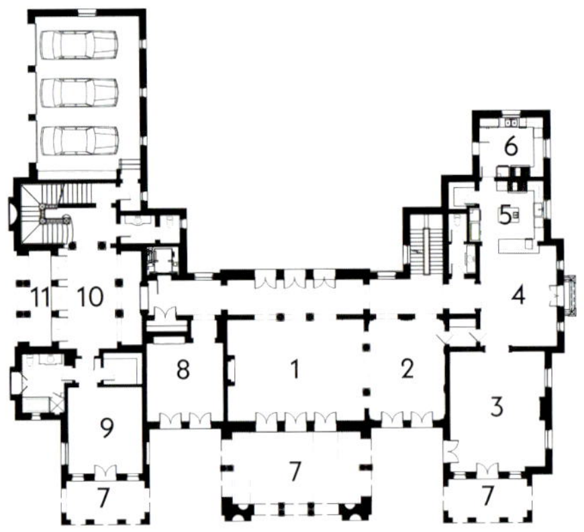

FIRST-FLOOR PLAN

1 Formal living room
2 Formal dining room
3 Family room
4 Family dining room
5 Western kitchen
6 Chinese kitchen
7 Pergola
8 Library
9 Guest bedroom
10 Entrance hall
11 Entry porch

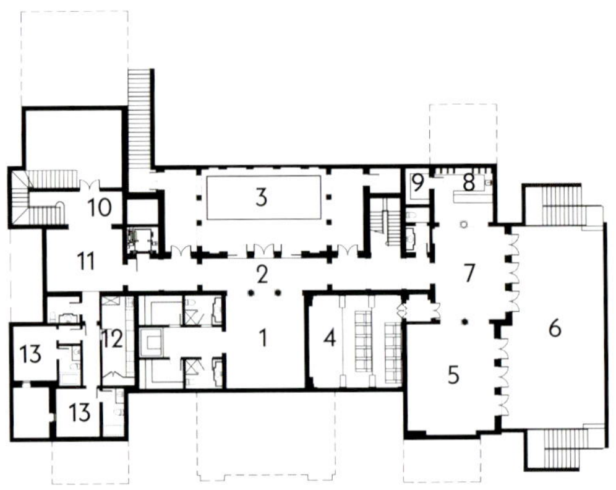

LOWER-LEVEL PLAN

1 Exercise room
2 Gallery
3 Swimming pool
4 Theater
5 Game room
6 East sunken garden
7 Card room
8 Bar
9 Wine cellar
10 Foyer
11 Stair lounge
12 Laundry
13 Staff quarters

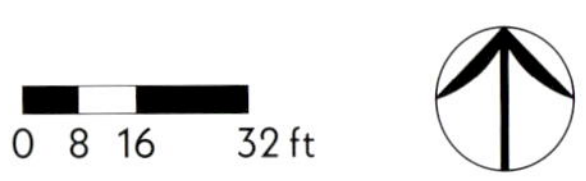

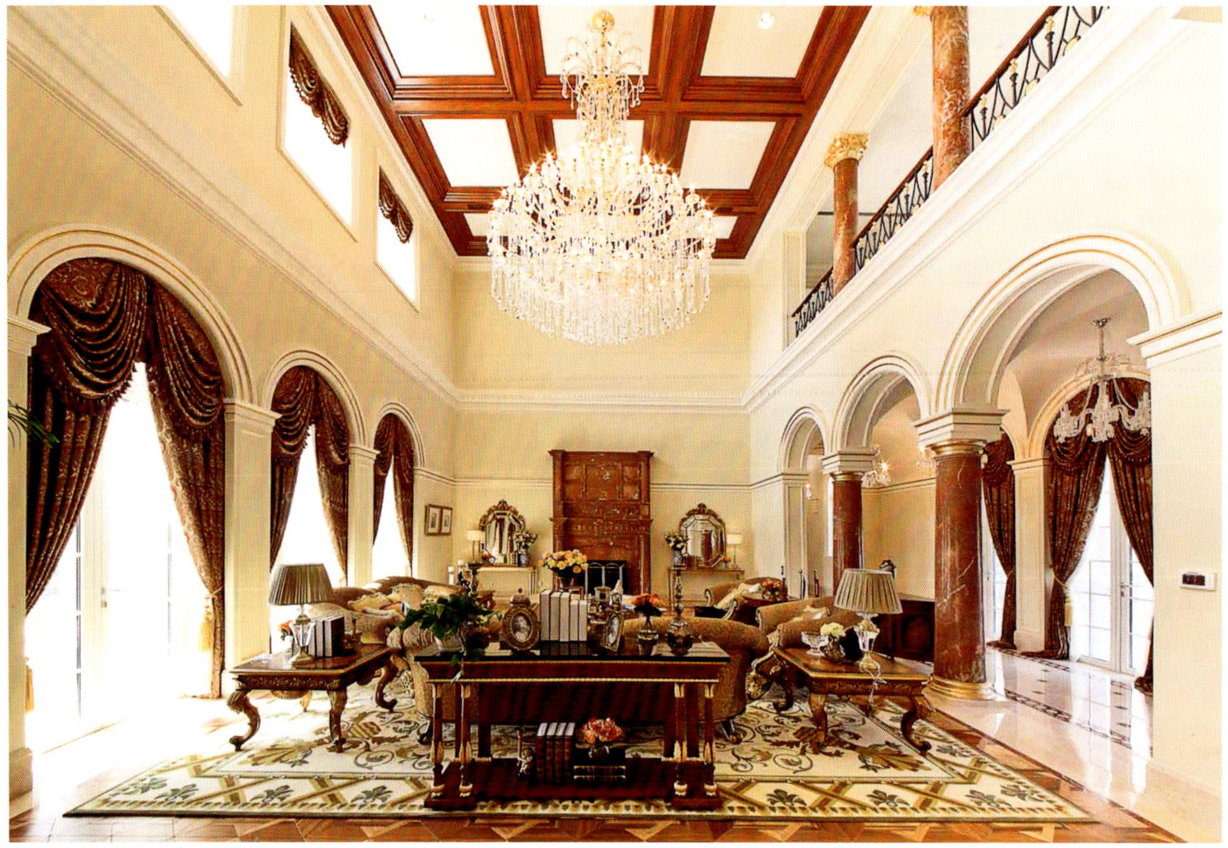

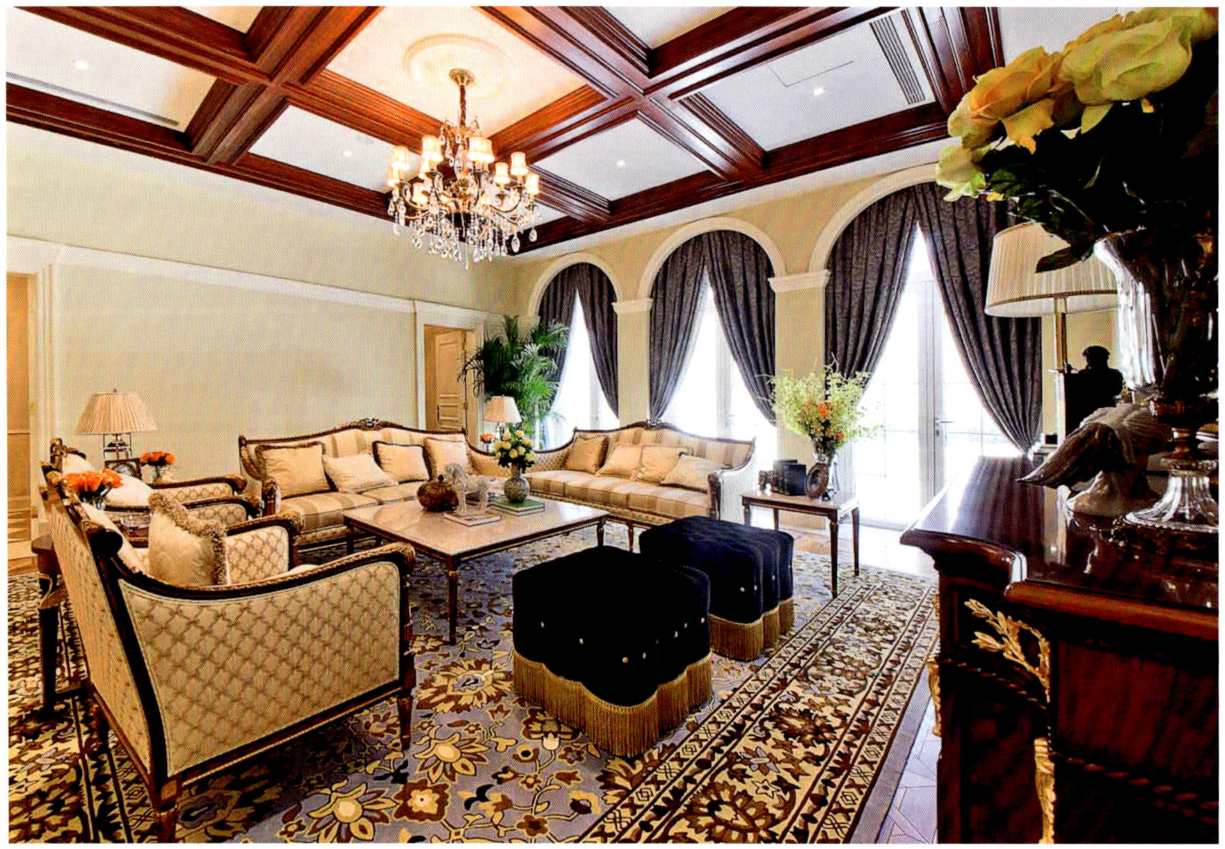

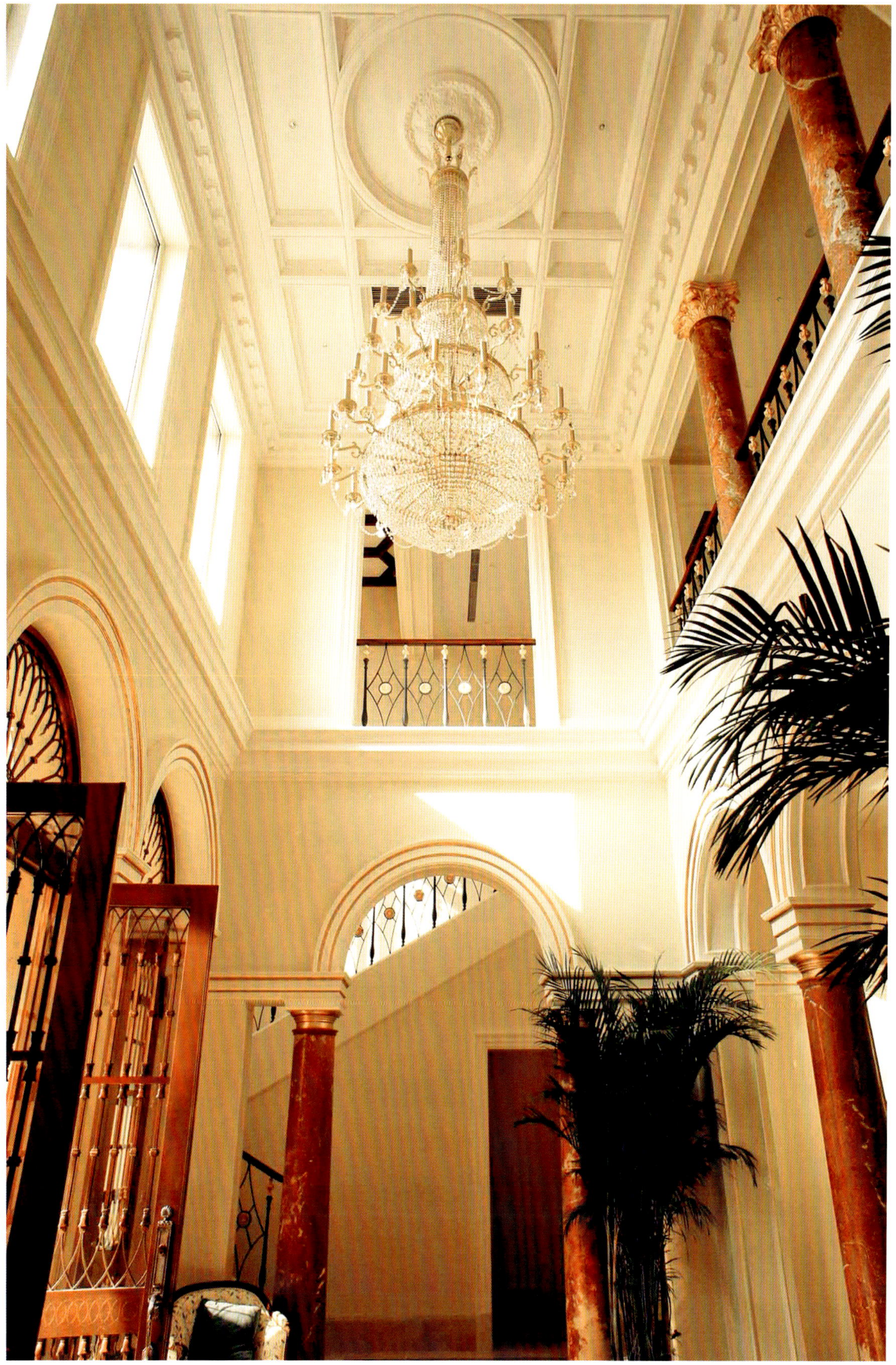

OPPOSITE TOP: *The double-height living room of the Italianate villa has a mahogany coffered ceiling and an open second-floor arcaded gallery. Natural light floods in from Palladian arched windows on each side and the second-floor windows. The oak parquet floor is bordered in polished beige limestone.*

OPPOSITE BOTTOM: *In the family lounge is the same mahogany coffered ceiling and a row of Palladian arched windows that lead to the rose garden.*

RIGHT: *A view of the upper entry hall highlights the Rosa Verona marble columns with gilded capitals and a three-tier crystal chandelier.*

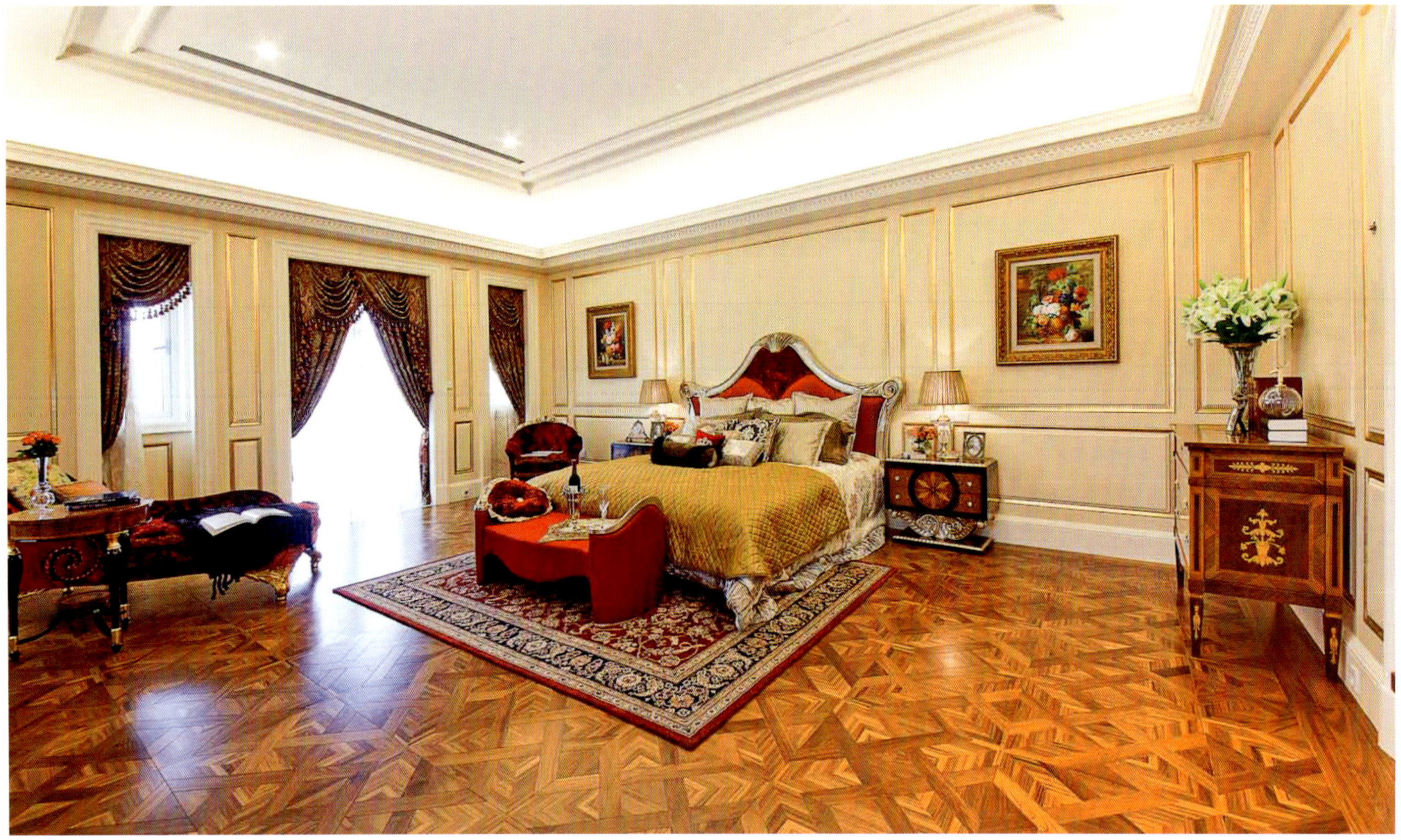

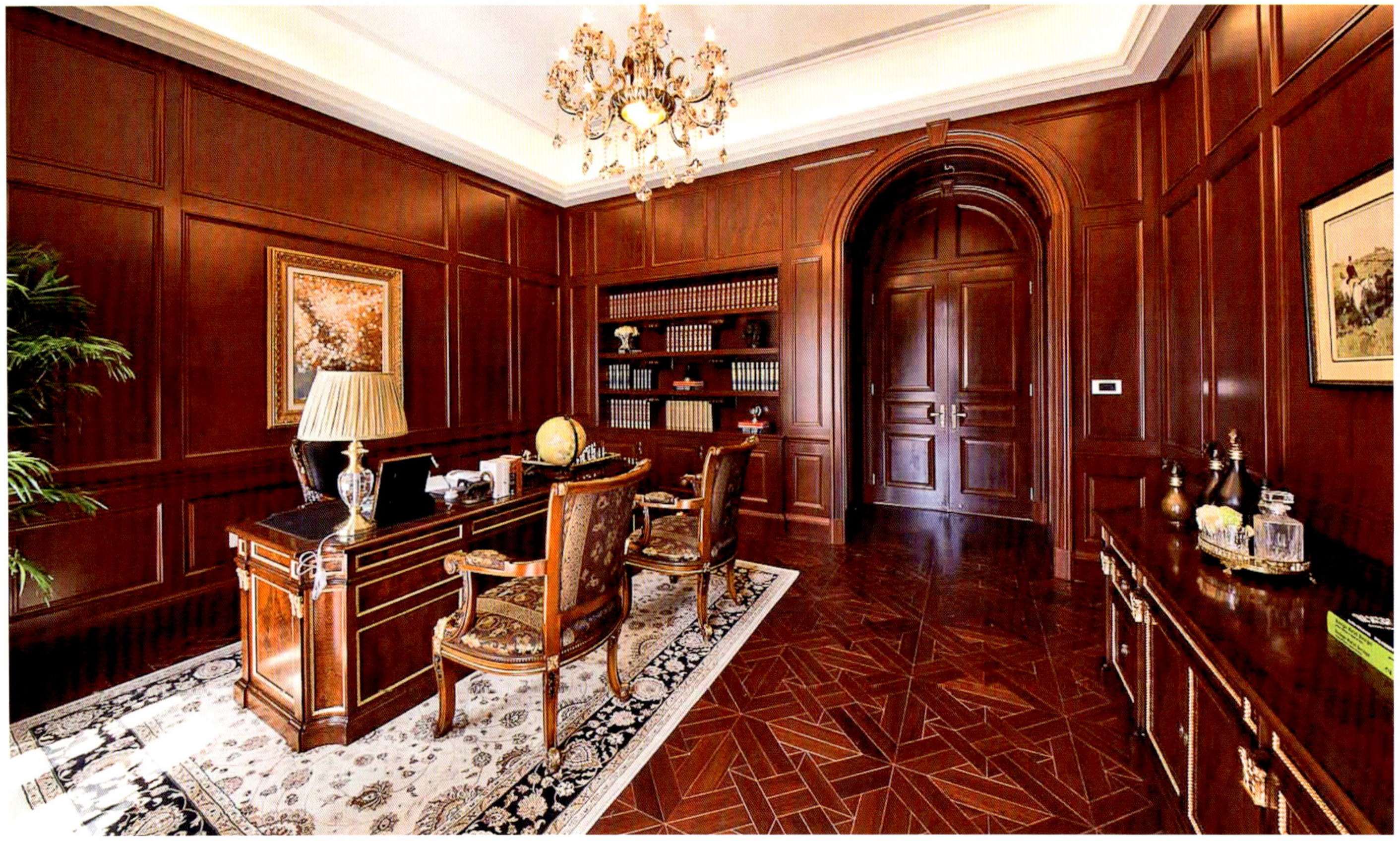

ABOVE LEFT: *Interior designer David Desmond gave the master bedroom ivory painted paneling with gold trim, oak parquet de Versailles floor, and a tray ceiling with cove lighting that create a backdrop for the elaborate marquetry inlaid furniture.*

LEFT: *The library is enveloped in mahogany, with paneled walls and doors, and parquet de Versailles floor. Natural light from one side balances the richness of the polished wood.*

OPPOSITE: *Pale yellow walls, white coffered ceiling, beige limestone fireplace, and Louis XV-style sofa and chairs in blue and yellow create a master sitting room that is light and bright, with windows overlooking the rose garden.*

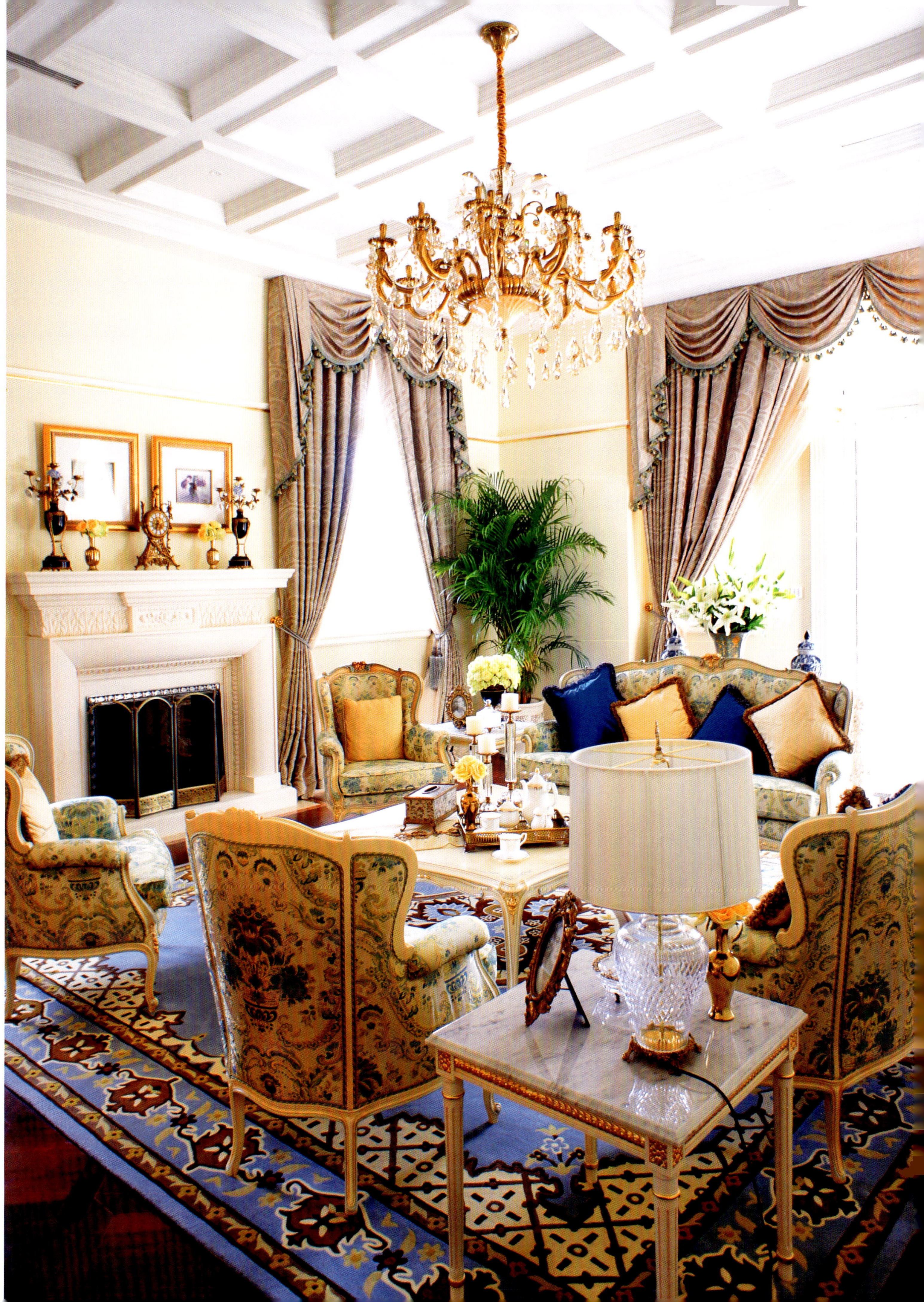

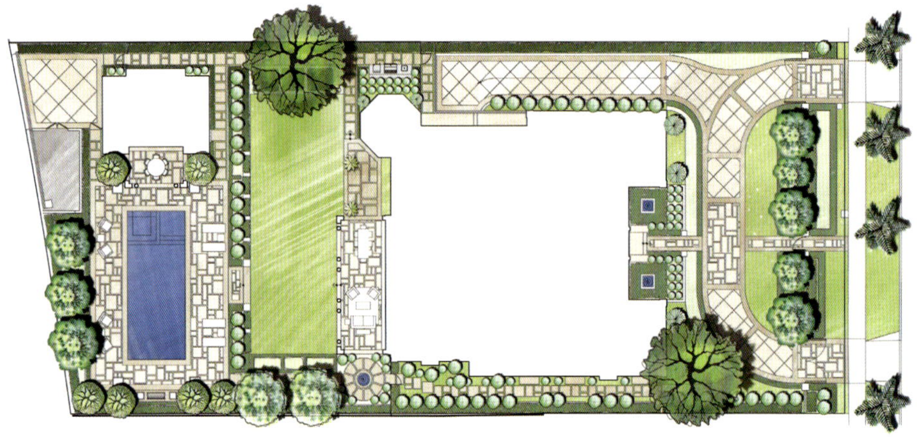

MAGNOLIA

Beverly Hills

The white brick Colonial Revival homes popular in Los Angeles in the 1930s have never gone out of style. People have always responded to their stylized and theatrical elegance, while their East Coast roots conveyed a sense of heritage and history. This streamlined style unites tradition and modernity, and was a favorite of Los Angeles architects Paul R. Williams and Roland Coate and other practitioners further east, from David Adler to John Staub. Our contemporary interpretation was designed for clients who are interested in homes with classical foundations that are built for twenty-first-century living.

The exterior colors are bold with white brick walls accented with black window frames and shutters, and gunmetal zinc downspouts. The brickwork adds a subtle texture to the planar white façades with moldings inspired by the Doric order. A bold segmental pediment articulates the main entrance. Inside, surfaces are brighter, more modern and cleaner to fit with a contemporary L.A. lifestyle. The classic two-story center stair hall makes a large house feel more compact and simpler in layout—you're always coming back to the center space. The major rooms are organized enfilade: foyer leading to living room to library and bar, and continuing to the family room and kitchen, creating a fun flow for parties as well as daily living. All the formal rooms have chevron walnut floors and classical fireplaces so that bold, modern patterns and colors can exist within a classical framework.

The rear façade is dominated by a spacious loggia with columns, the capitals of which were inspired by the Tower of the Winds in Athens, a favorite with this architectural style, and overlooks the rear gardens and pool. A pedimented pavilion anchors the north end of the pool terrace and serves as a sheltering respite from the California sun.

With urban land values soaring, basements are becoming increasingly common to optimize the accommodation of garages and needed secondary spaces. This provided the perfect location for extensive subterranean parking along with a movie theater, bar and wine cellar, and home gym. Everything one would need at home.

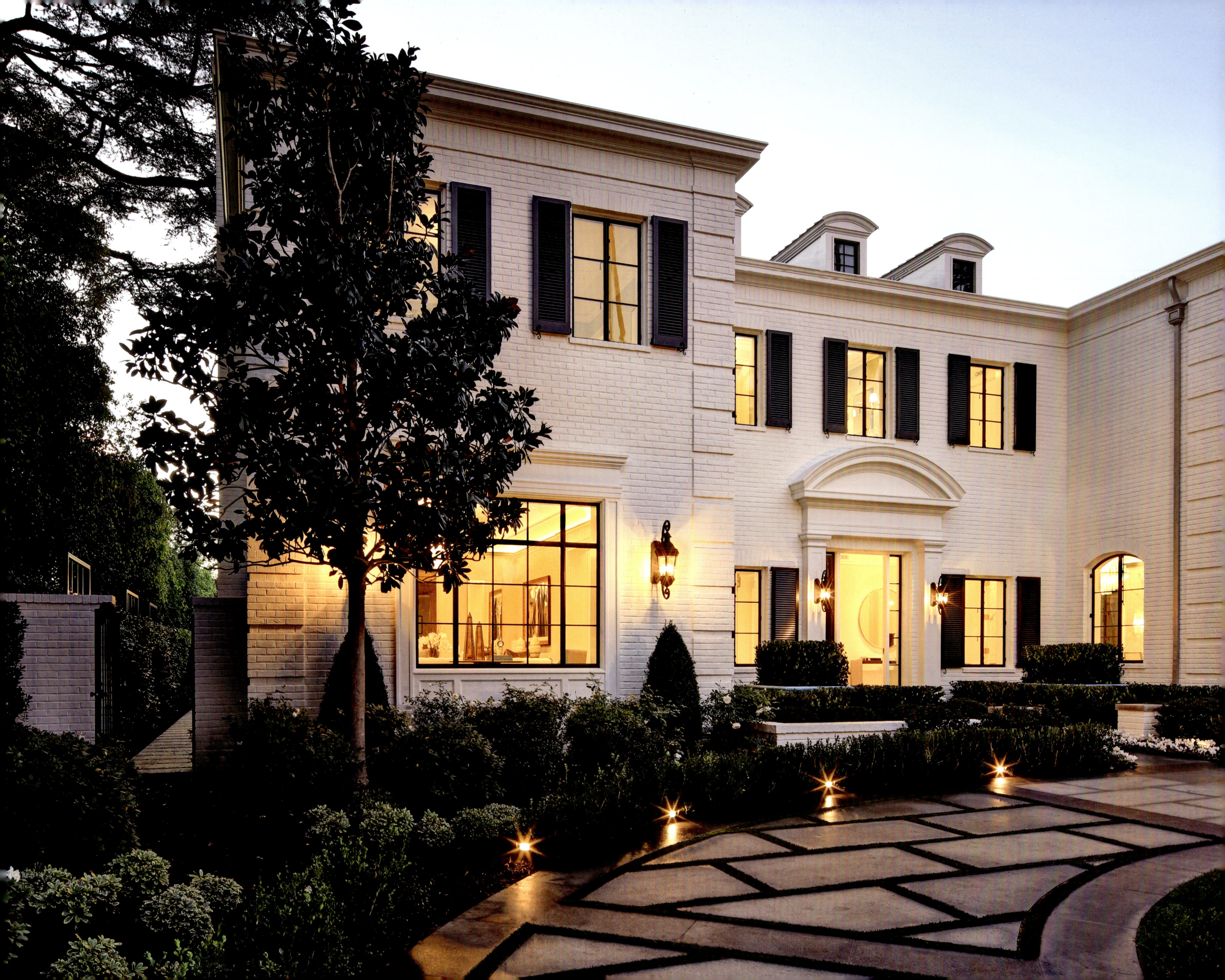

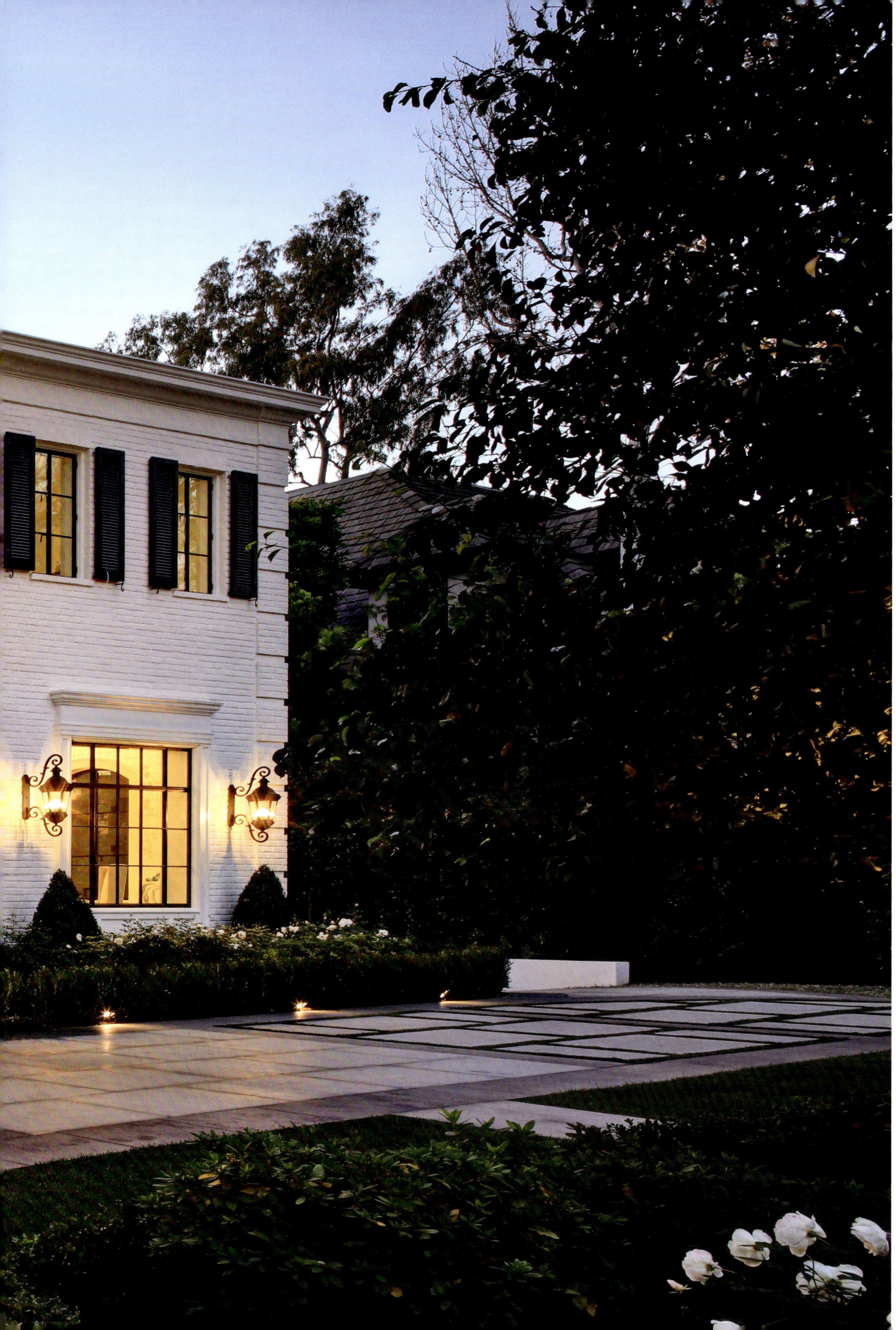

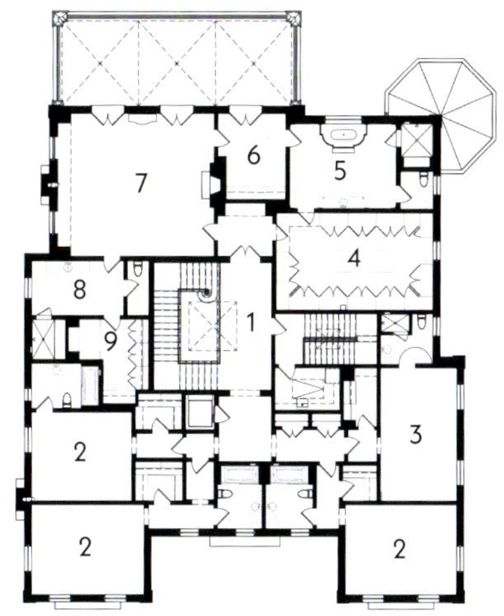

SECOND-FLOOR PLAN

1 Upper stair hall
2 Bedroom
3 Playroom
4 Her closet
5 Her bath
6 Her office
7 Master bedroom
8 His bath
9 His closet

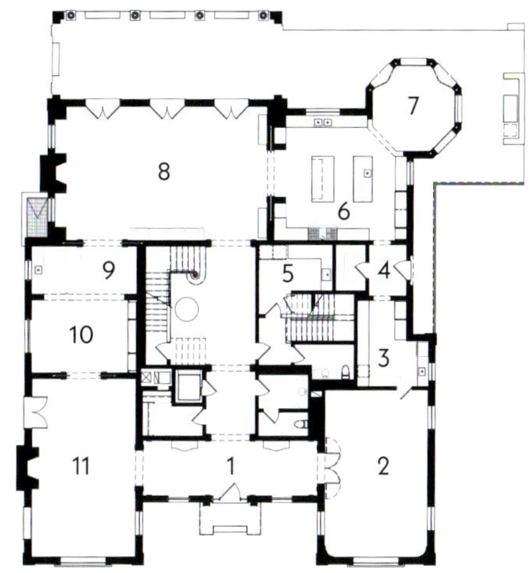

FIRST-FLOOR PLAN

1 Entry hall
2 Dining room
3 Butler's pantry
4 Staff quarters
5 Laundry
6 Kitchen
7 Breakfast room
8 Family room
9 Bar
10 Library
11 Living room

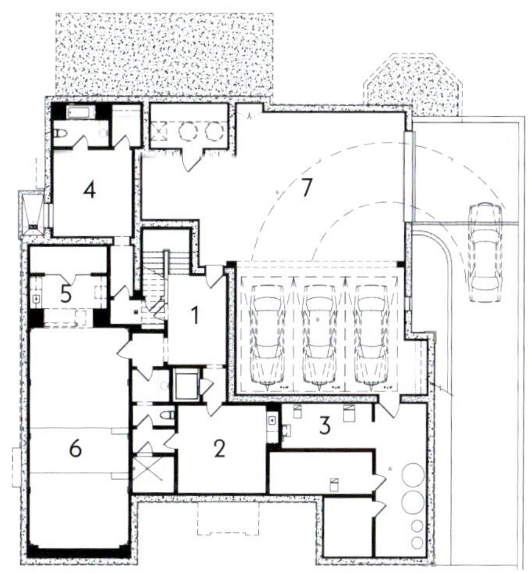

BASEMENT FLOOR PLAN

1 Basement foyer
2 Exercise room
3 Mechanical/storage room
4 Staff quarters
5 Bar
6 Recreation room
7 Garage

0 8 16 32 ft

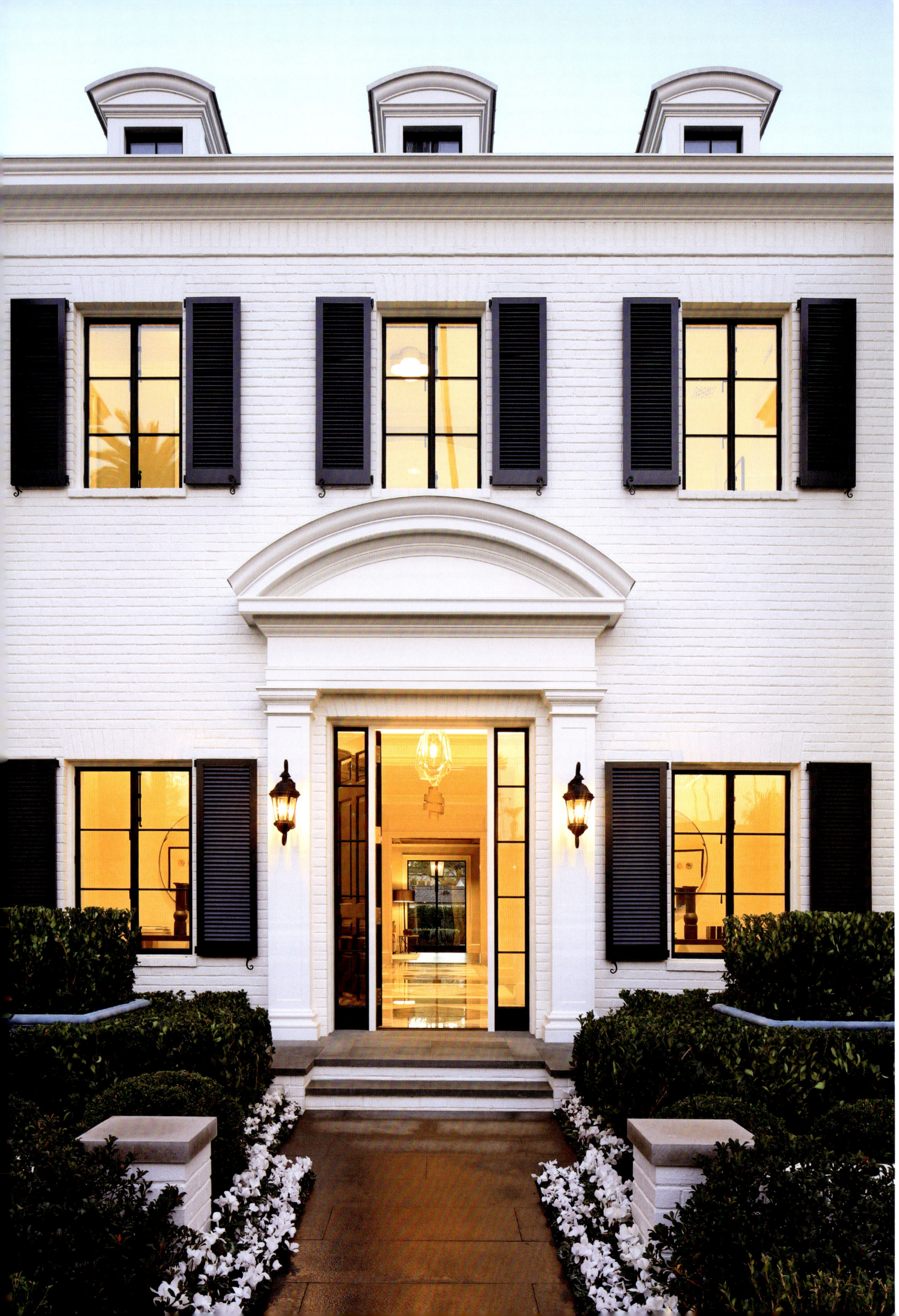

PREVIOUS PAGES: *Our contemporary interpretation of a classic Colonial Revival design remains true to its heritage—white brick, moldings, dormers—but is updated with black window frames and shutters, and gunmetal zinc downspouts.*

LEFT: *A Doric overdoor door-surround makes for a bold entry.*

OPPOSITE LEFT: *A plaster cornice with cove lighting adds drama to the entrance gallery, which is balanced by pilasters, fluted and reeded moldings, and floors patterned in four varieties of marble.*

OPPOSITE RIGHT: *The patterned marble continues into the skylit main stair hall where it forms a large-scale checkerboard pattern. The Louis XVI-style iron stair rail has gilded accents and a brass cap.*

FOLLOWING PAGES, LEFT: *A Lutyens-inspired fireplace highlights the living room. All the formal rooms are laid out en suite and have classical fireplaces, Ionic columns, and chevron walnut floors.*
RIGHT: *With a silver leaf ceiling, hand-printed Chinoiserie wallpaper on a silver leaf background, Murano glass chandelier and sconces, the dining room has a glamorous Art Deco feel.*

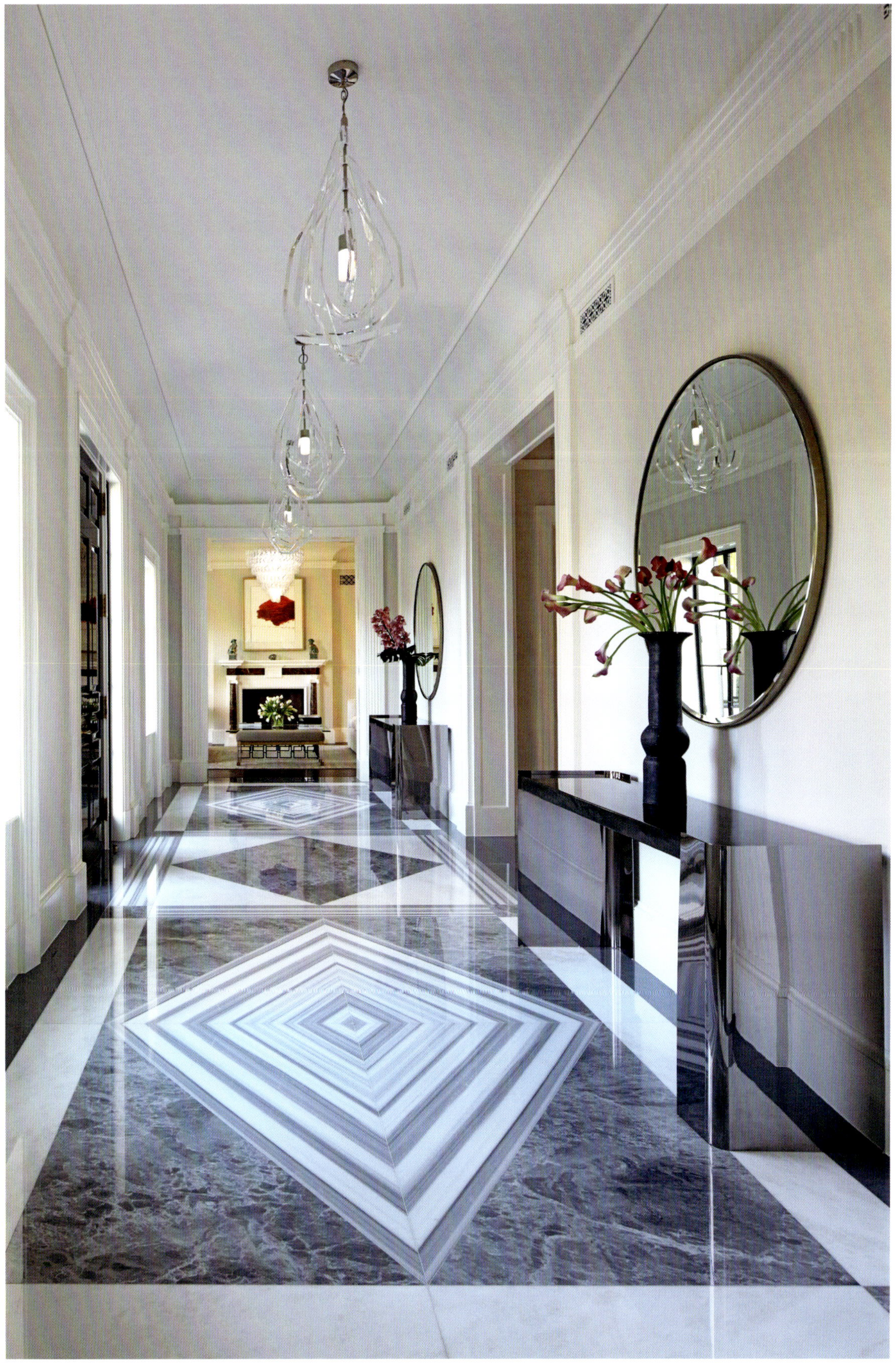

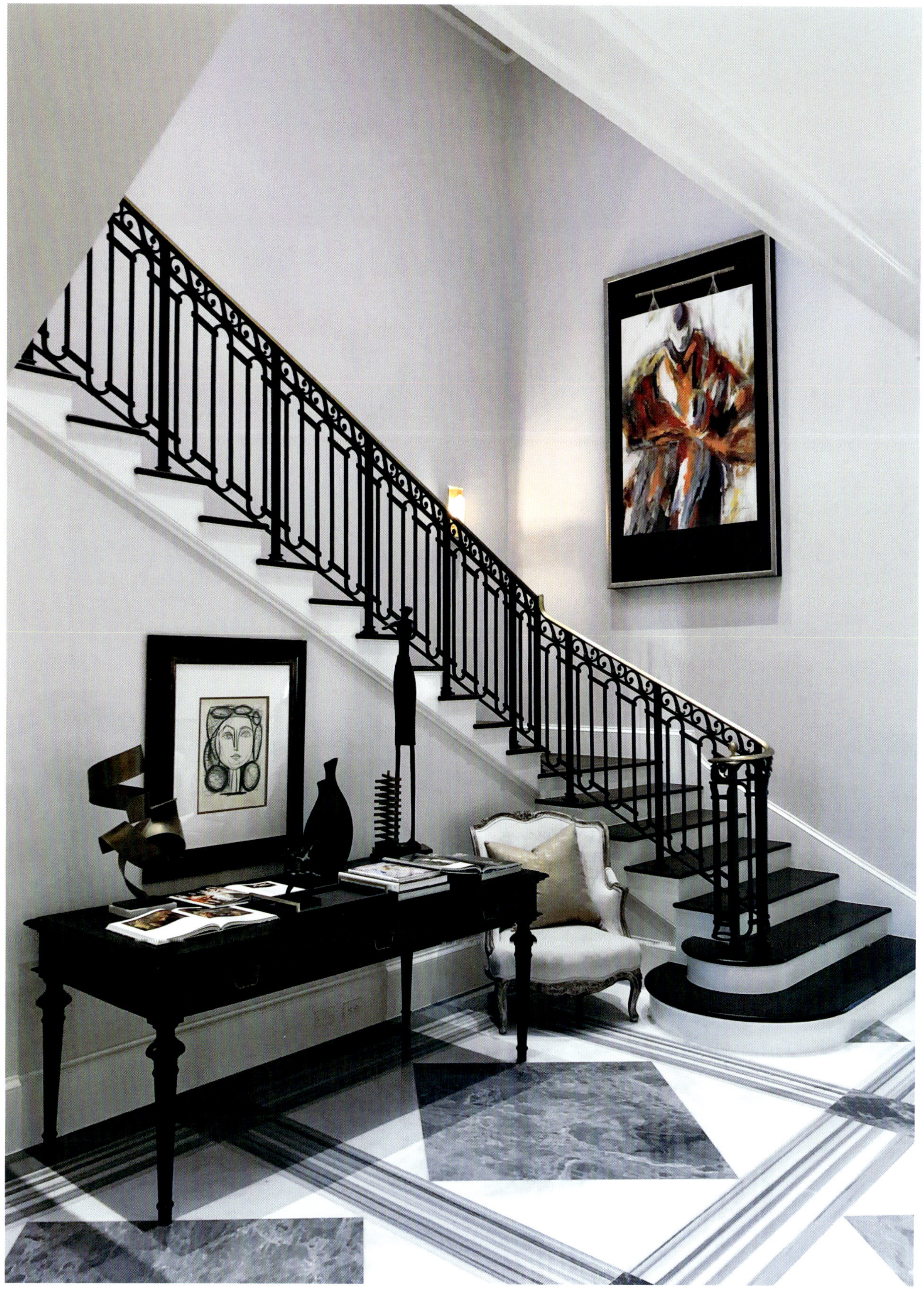

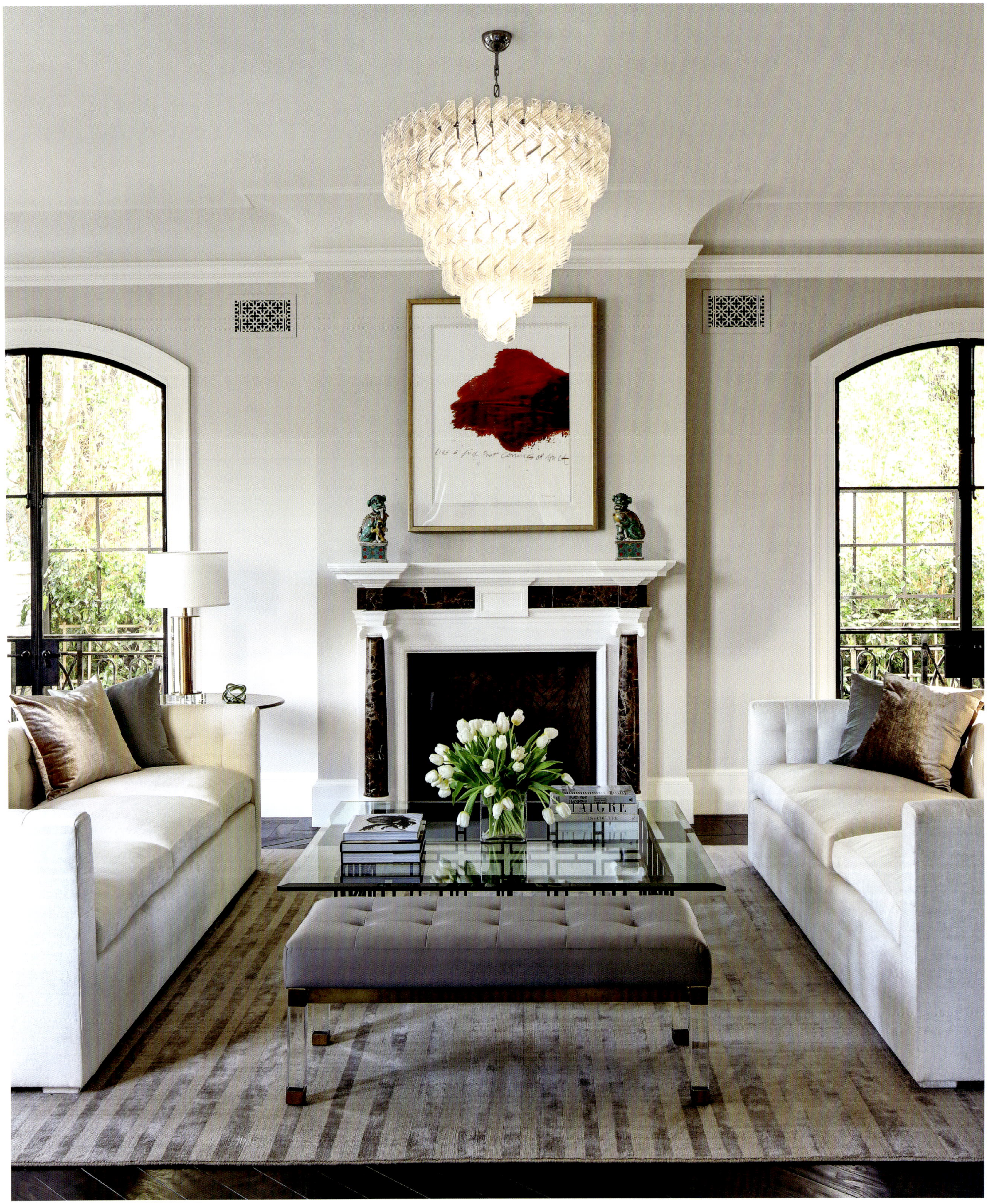

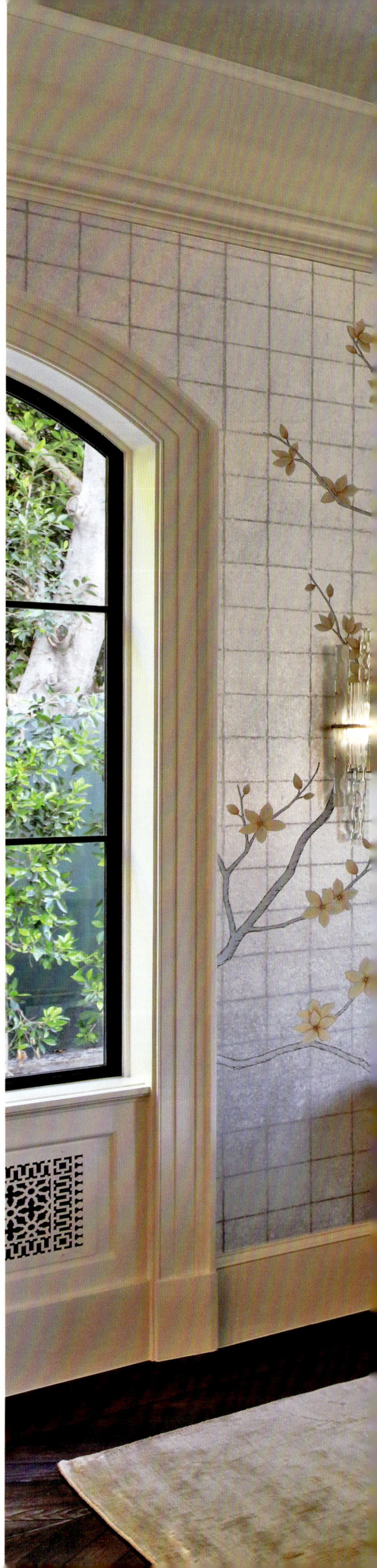

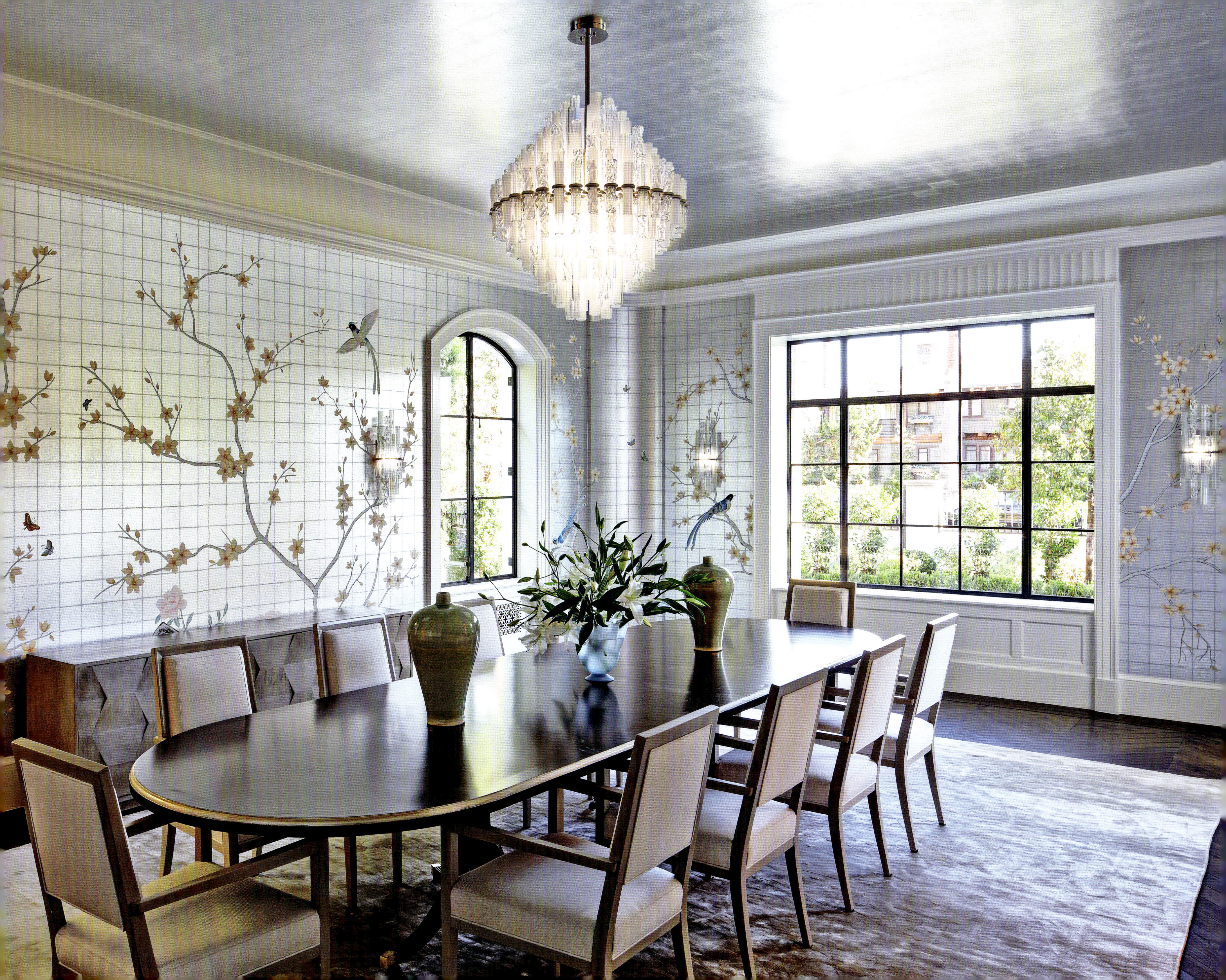

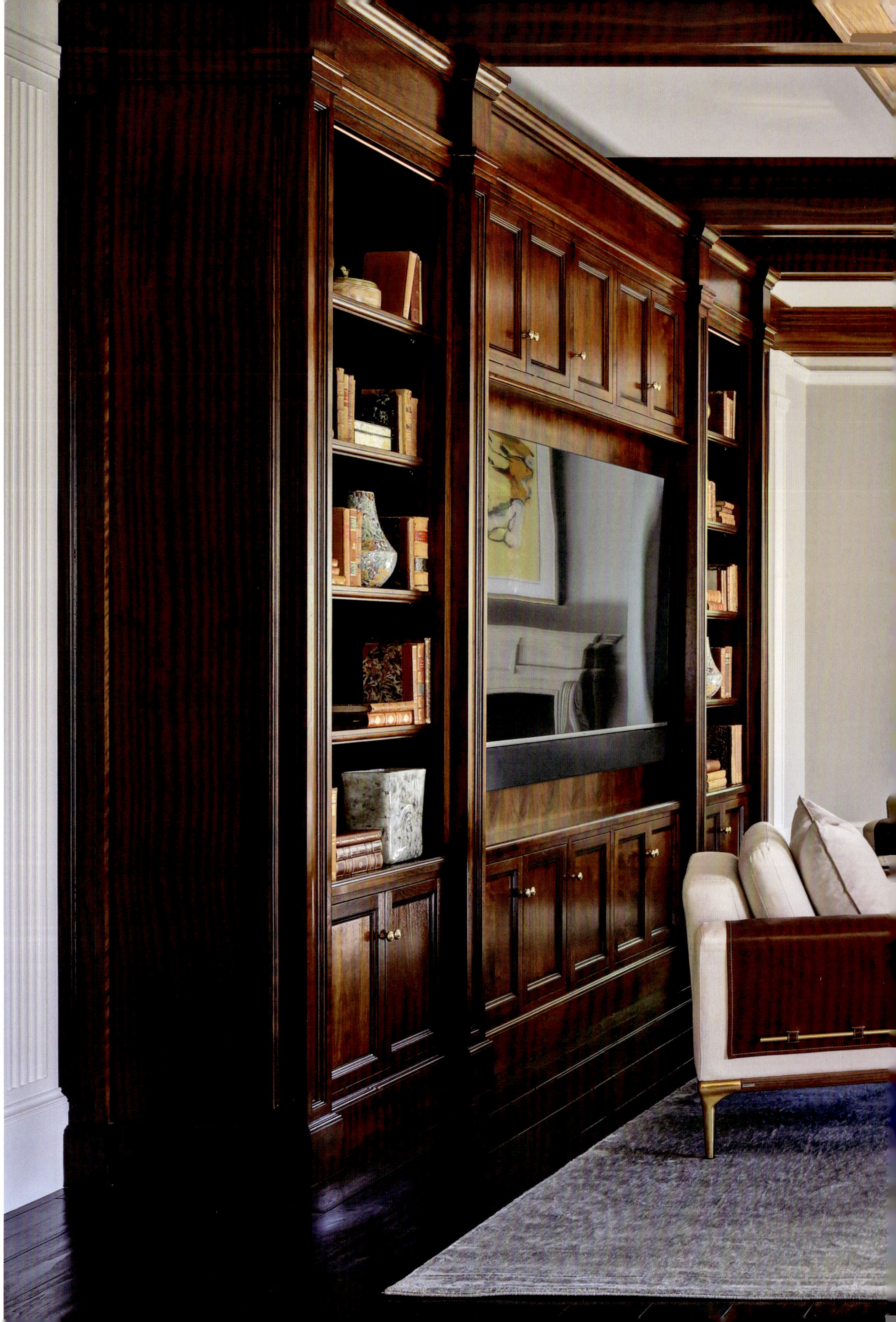

RIGHT: *The comfortable family room has hand-distressed solid walnut floors, coffered ceiling, built-in cabinetry, and a Neoclassical fireplace in beige limestone. Three sets of steel-framed French doors open to the loggia. Interior designer David Desmond chose furnishings upholstered in wool bouclé and saddle leather to add warmth.*

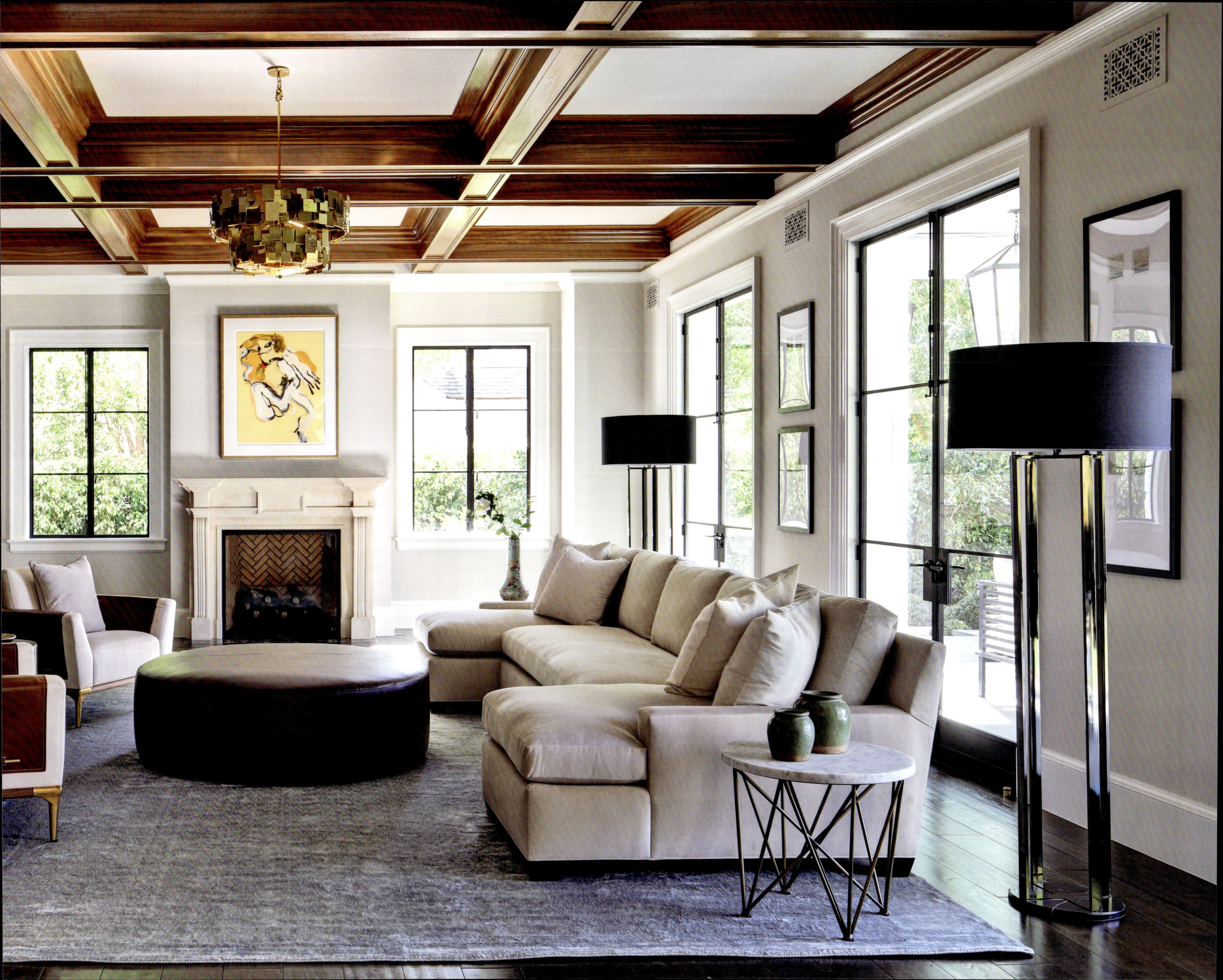

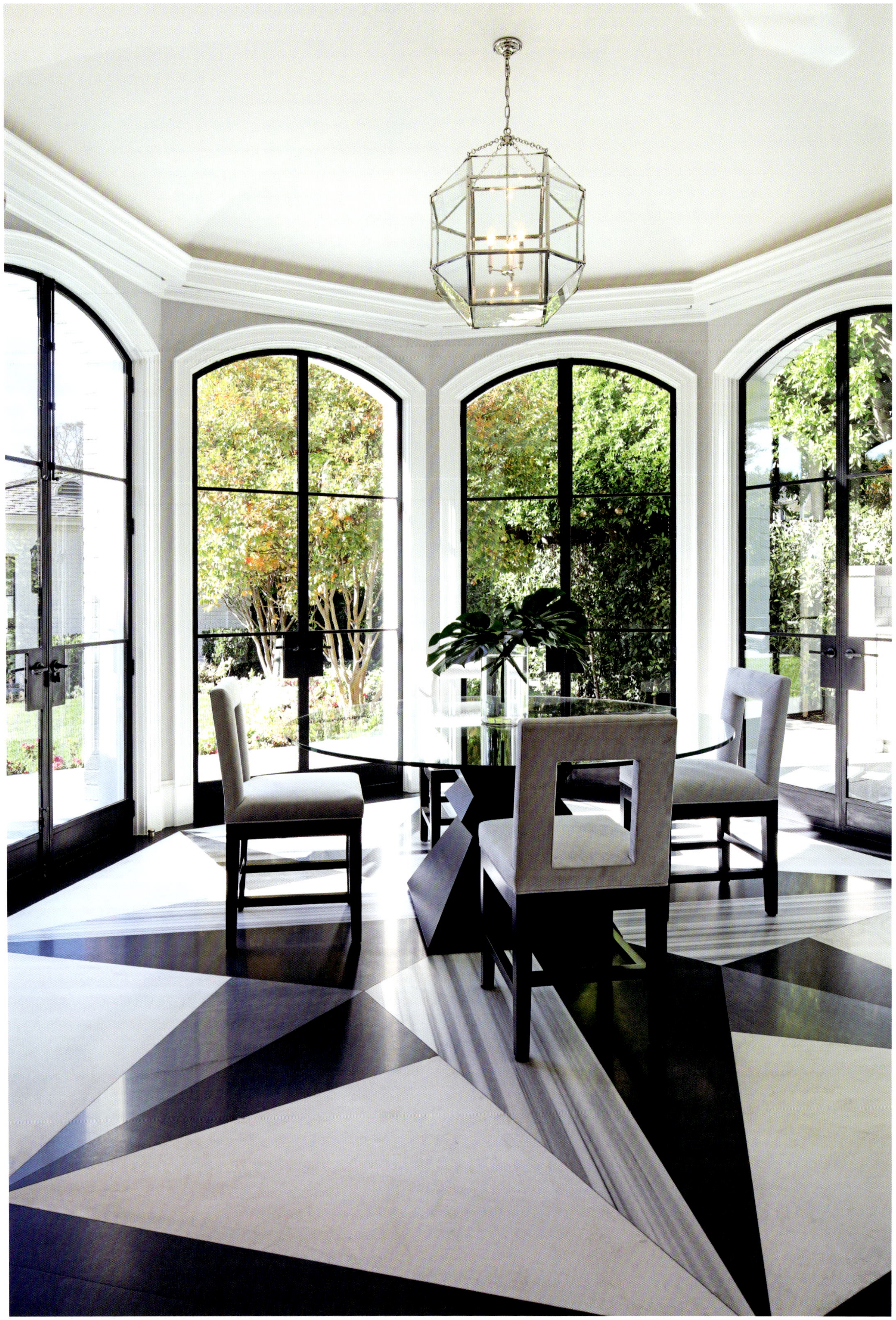

LEFT: *The octagonal breakfast room is defined by sets of steel-framed French doors that open to the garden, a vaulted ceiling, and the David Adler-inspired compass rose floor in four varieties of marble. An octagonal nickel-and-glass lantern hangs over the pedestal table.*

OPPOSITE: *Located at the sunny southwest corner of the second floor, the master bedroom has warm ivory-colored walls that contrast with the dark walnut herringbone floors; the overall effect is relaxing and calm.*

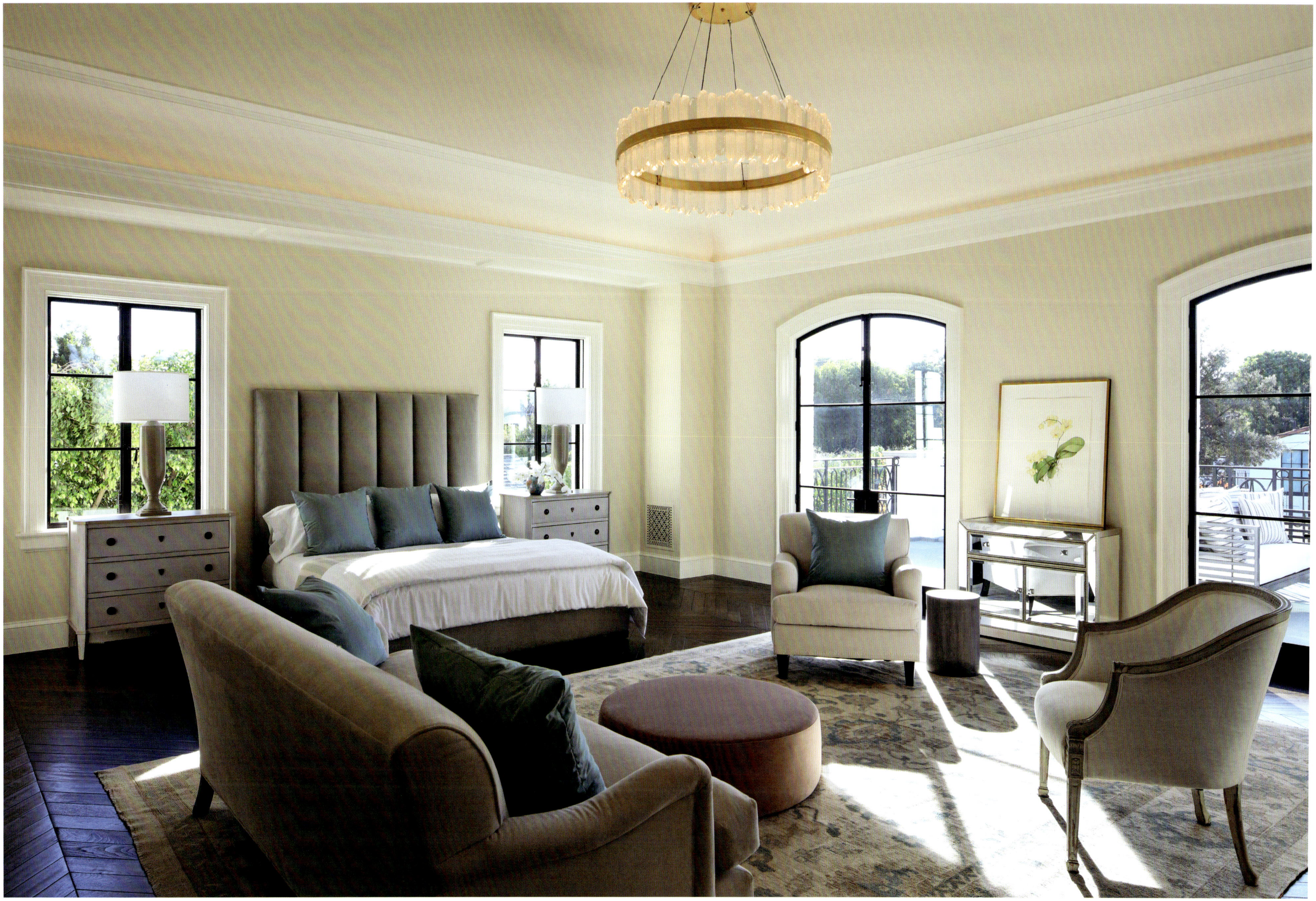

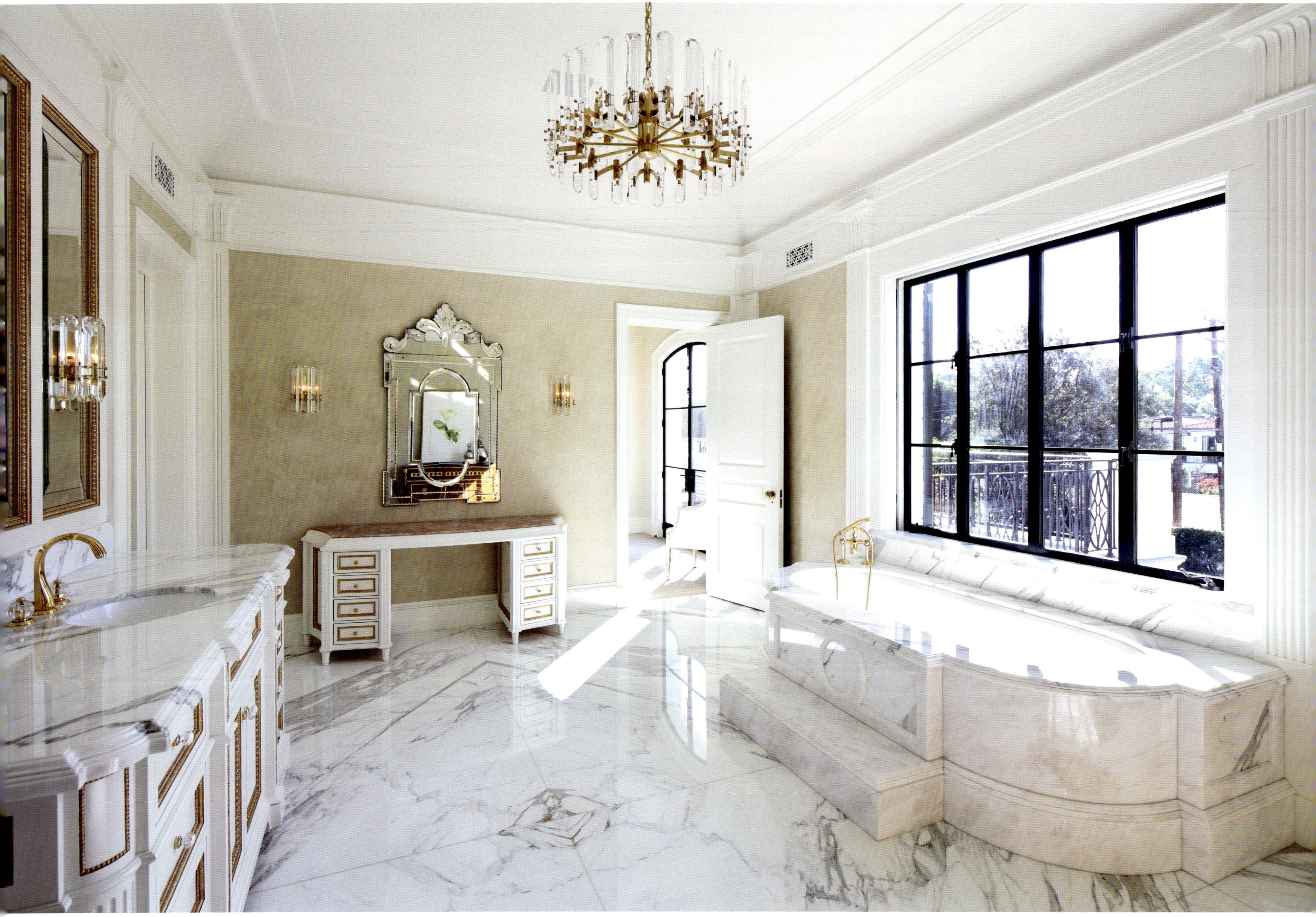

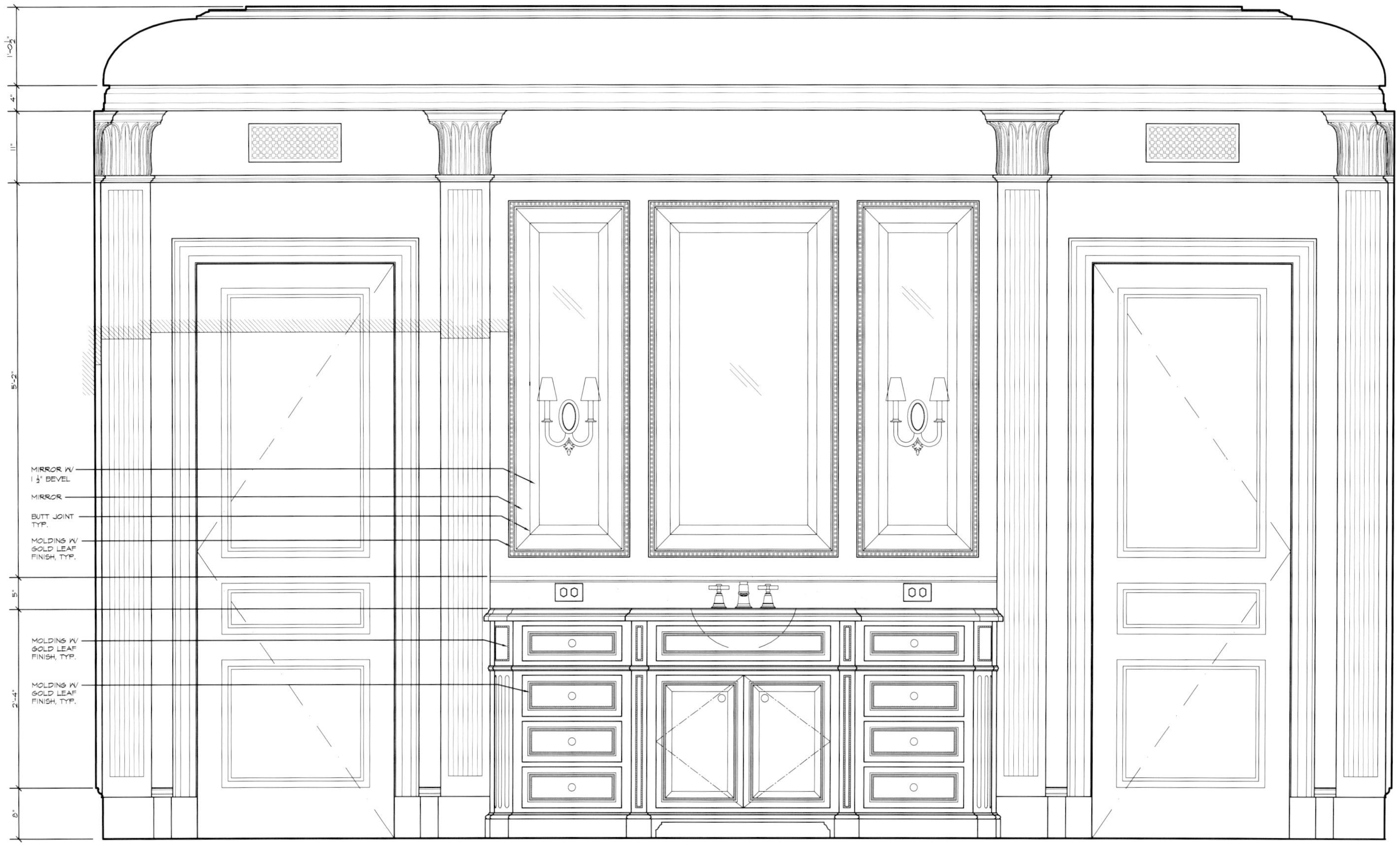

OPPOSITE: *The wife's bathroom is exceptionally light and bright, with walls in Venetian plaster accented by pilasters, the floor in slabs of book-matched Calacatta Gold marble, and dressing table with rose quartz top. The plumbing fixtures are 24-karat gold, and the custom cabinets have gold-leaf accents and knobs.*

ABOVE: *Drawing of the Neoclassical pilasters in the wife's bath.*

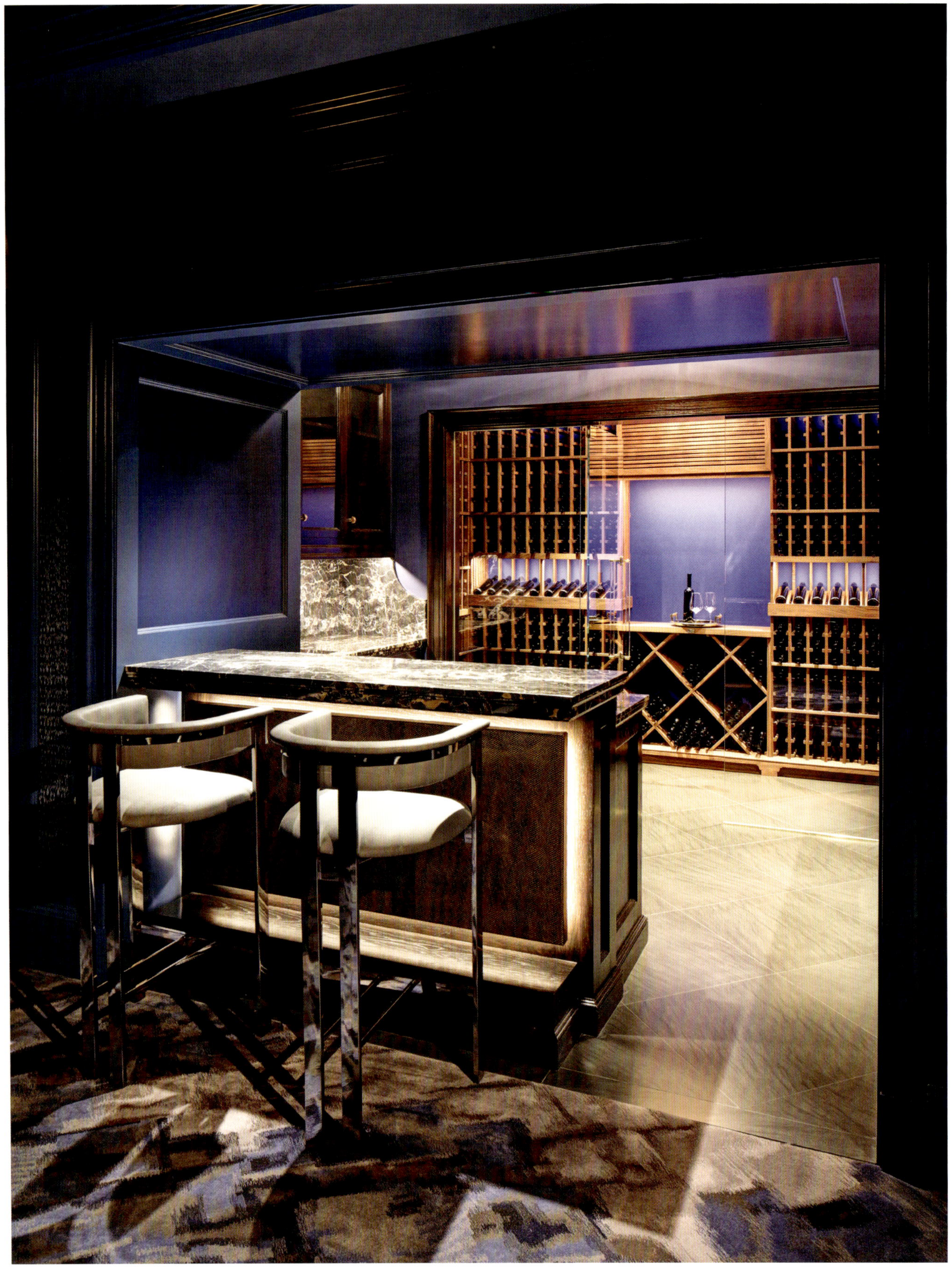

LEFT: The theater bar is Yves Klein blue, which forms the backdrop for the walnut wine racks in the wine cellar. The bar itself has a raised backlit panel clad in gilded snakeskin-patterned leather. The contemporary barstools are in polished nickel and ivory ostrich leather. Floor is of flamed Black Absolute granite.

OPPOSITE: The basement theater looks to Egyptian Revival/Art Deco motifs in its use of parcel-gilt pilasters and Streamline Moderne brass wall sconces. Wall panels upholstered in handwoven blue Ikat fabric surround the black leather reclining sofa and chairs; the custom carpet in shades of black, gray, and lapis.

FOLLOWING PAGES, LEFT: The pool house is an architectural gem, a temple-like pedimented pavilion that is reflected in the pool. RIGHT: The asymmetrical rear façade is dominated by the loggia with columns, the capitals of which were inspired by the Tower of the Winds in Athens.

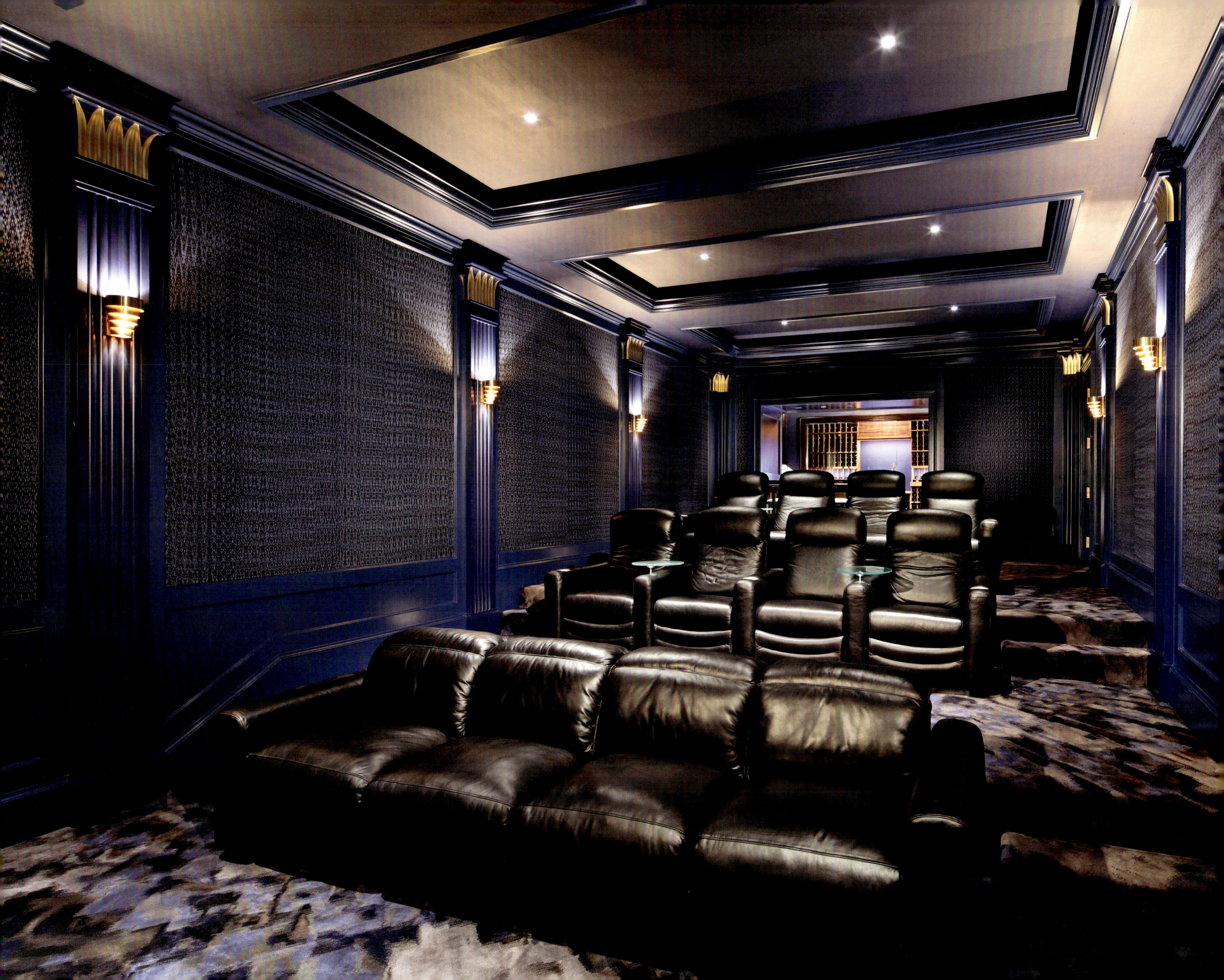

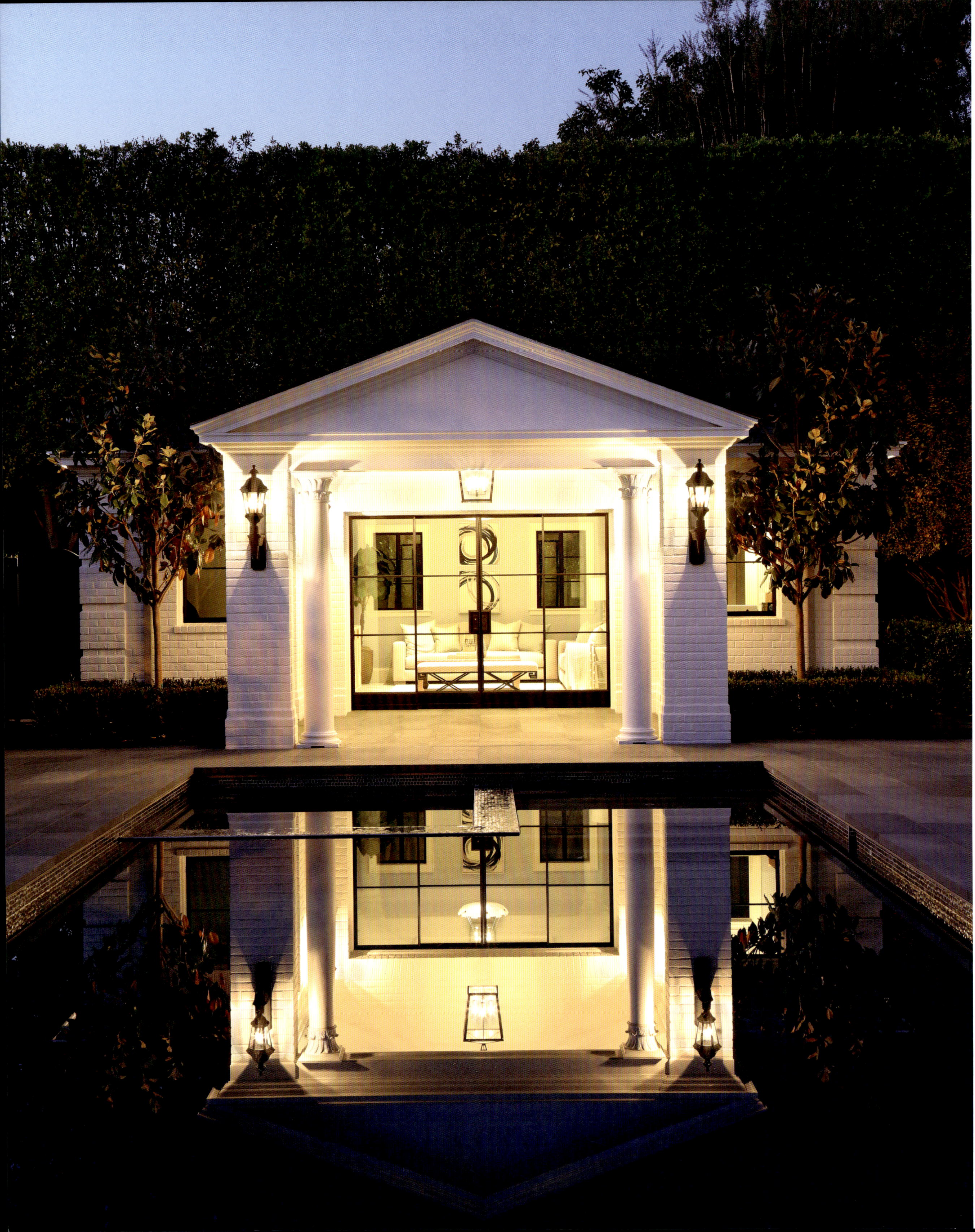
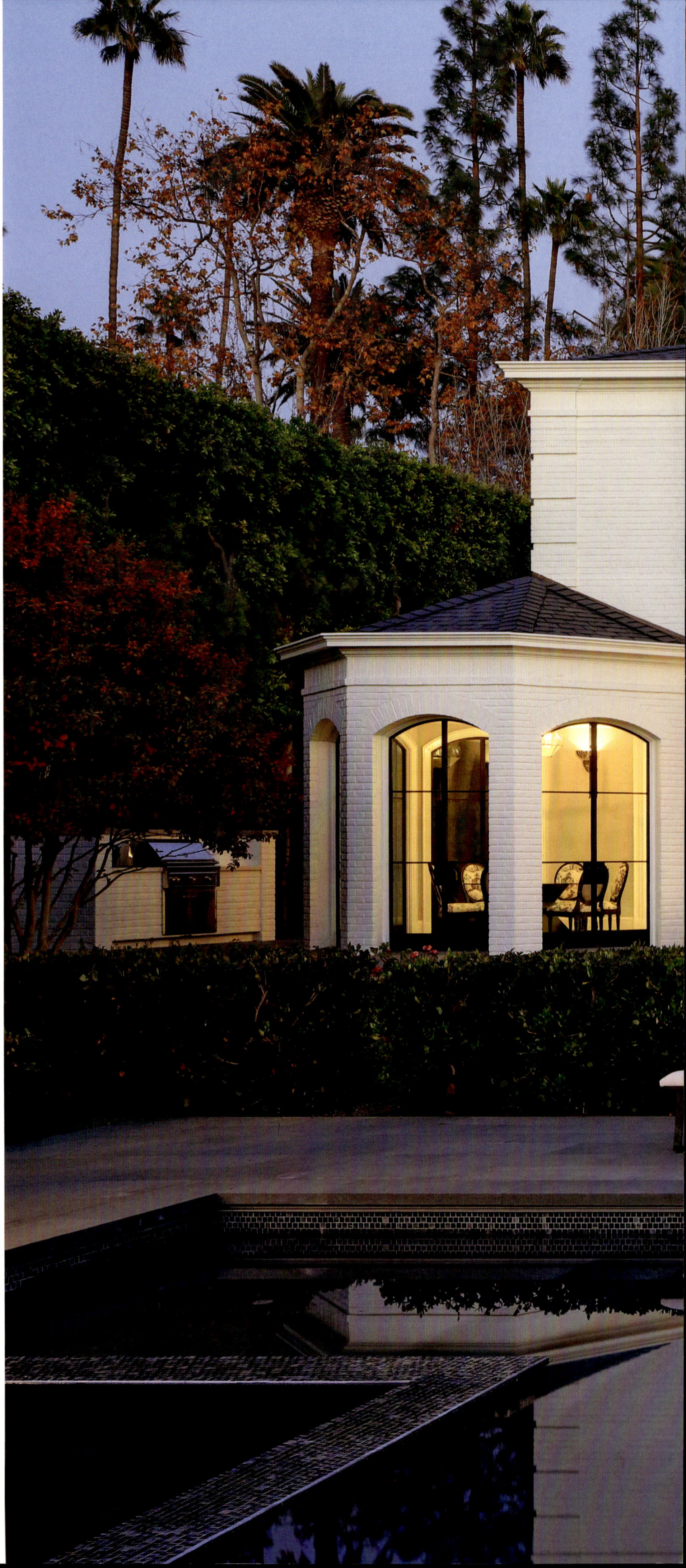

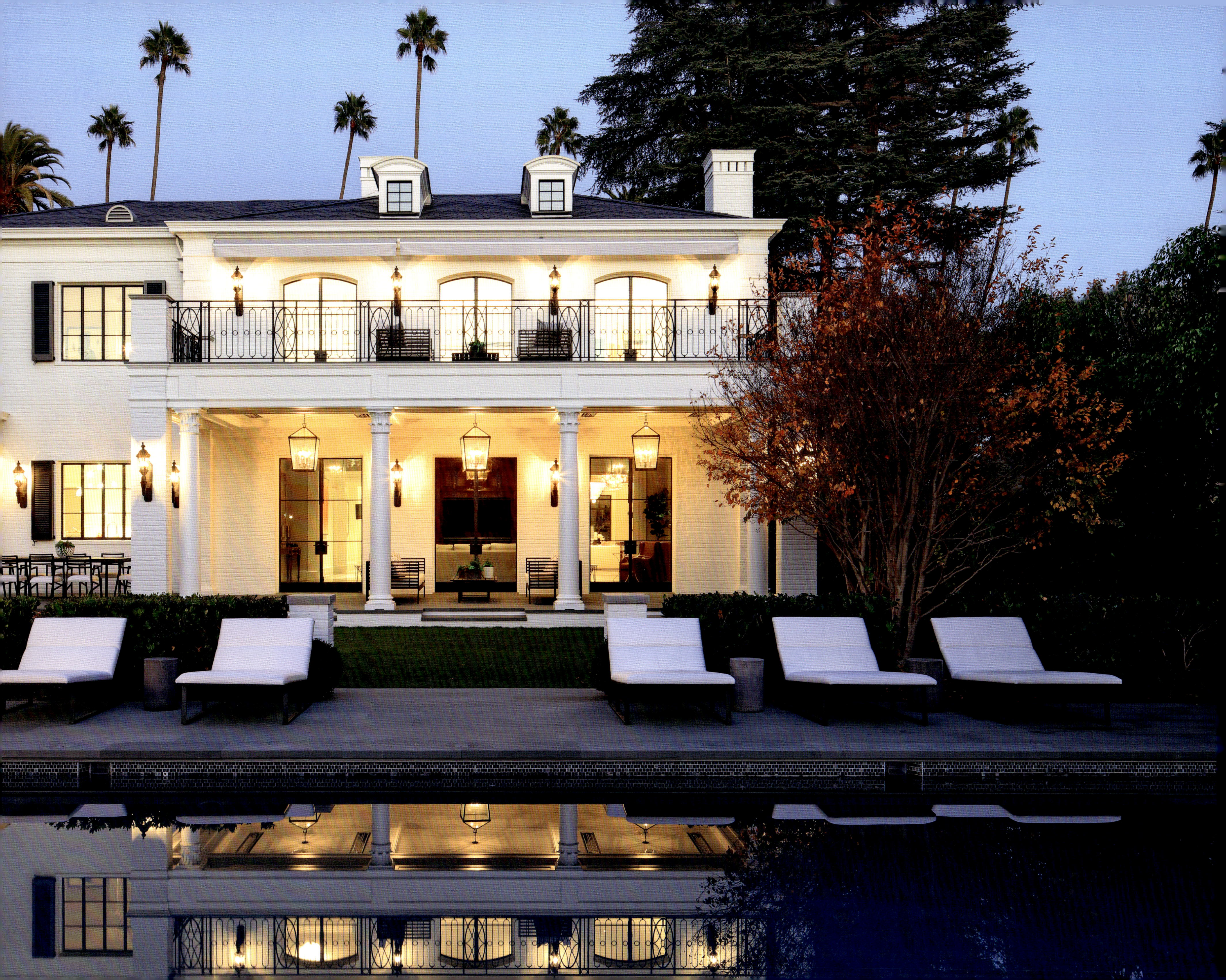

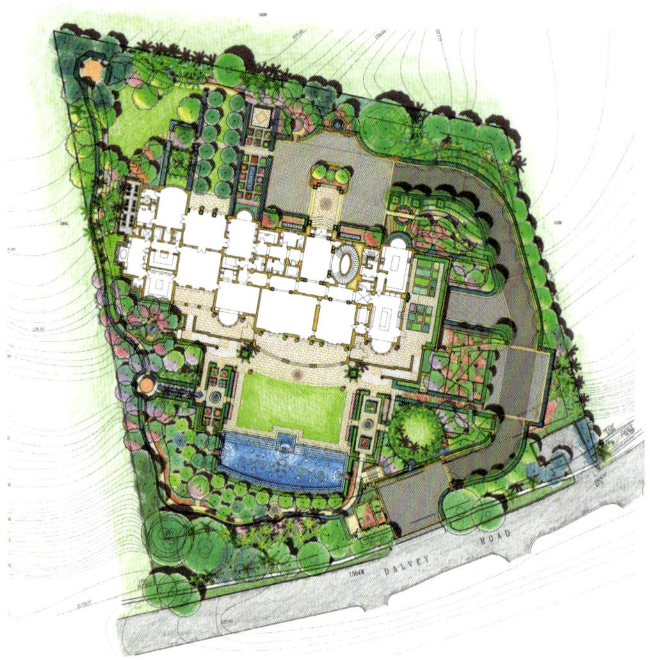
DALVEY ROAD

CHÂTEAU DE LA LUMIÈRE

Singapore

Nestled in Singapore's verdant Botanic Gardens district, Château de la Lumière is an ode to eighteenth-century French architecture. Built for a prominent family and perched on a cascading hillside, the house was designed for grand entertainment and comfortable family living as an essay in modern French design adapted for a unique tropical setting.

From the entry arrival court at street level, the lengthy driveway winds along the property past the lower garden and parking level, and then continues its rise up to the main level, so when you approach the house from the front it looks like a stately two-story residence even though it's actually four. The house is truly a family residence with the first floor featuring formal and family entertainment and living rooms with terraces, and separate family apartments at the second- and third-floor levels. Behind the poolside outdoor loggia at the rear garden level, the basement has a ballroom, wine cellar, and a spa connected to the main terrace by two grand staircases.

Due to programmatic requirements and the hillside topography, this was a complex house to plan—like designing a small boutique hotel. With Singapore lying on the equator, it didn't matter which orientation the house faced as the sun exposure was equal for the north and south sides. It's one of the few places I've worked in the world where the sun moves from one side to the other. Singapore's extremely wet tropical climate and heavy rains necessitated a porte-cochère at the entry. The heat and humidity also meant that much of the entertaining occurs indoors, especially for formal affairs, and so the loggia has glass partitions that can be installed for dinners and events.

With construction in Singapore in concrete, for economy and termite resistance, walls and architectural details were made entirely in plaster. Every element of feng shui was taken into account in our planning of the layout and room flow. With the interiors, our clients liked the idea of a more modern take on classic French interiors, something that would work with their contemporary art and sculpture collections. They loved many of the early-twentieth-century hotels in France, such as the Ritz and George V, and Neoclassical châteaux and *hôtels particuliers*, and we incorporated a lot of vaulting, moldings, paneled walls, plaster bas-relief, and decorative work. The first-floor master suite provides a convenient location to be close to the major entertainment and family spaces while enabling direct access to private gardens. The master suite includes a skylit conservatory where our clients can enjoy views of the garden and fountains.

John Wong of the SWA Group brought in fully mature landscaping for the grounds and sloping hillside gardens to make them look like a botanic garden, in keeping with the neighborhood. To the left of the pool are steps leading up to a hilltop *tempietto* that anchors the garden at the master level and offers a view of the distant business district high-rises. The garden wraps around this private side of the house, terminating at the conservatory. The grounds are punctuated throughout by our clients' distinctive collection of contemporary garden sculpture, bringing art into the lush tropical landscape.

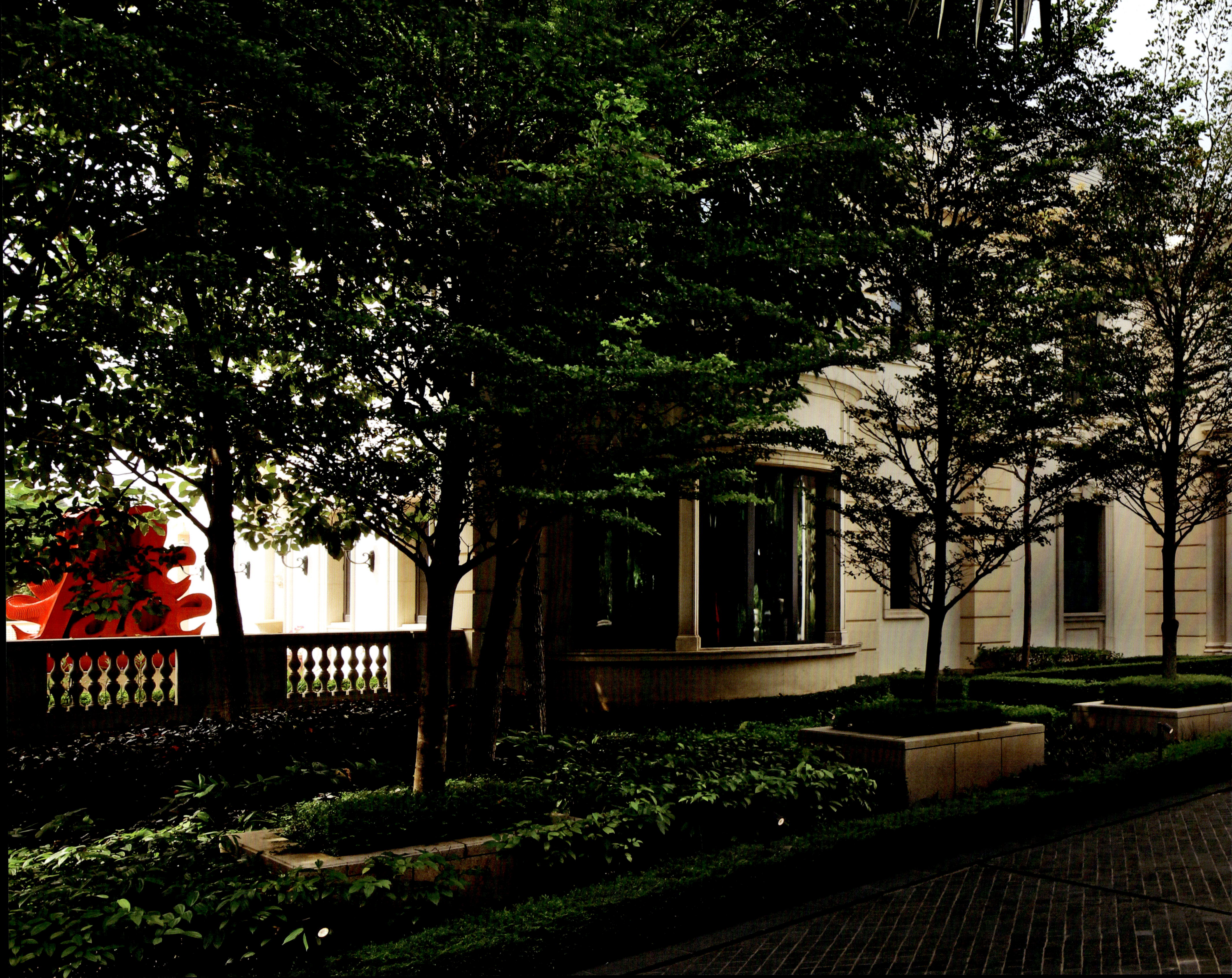

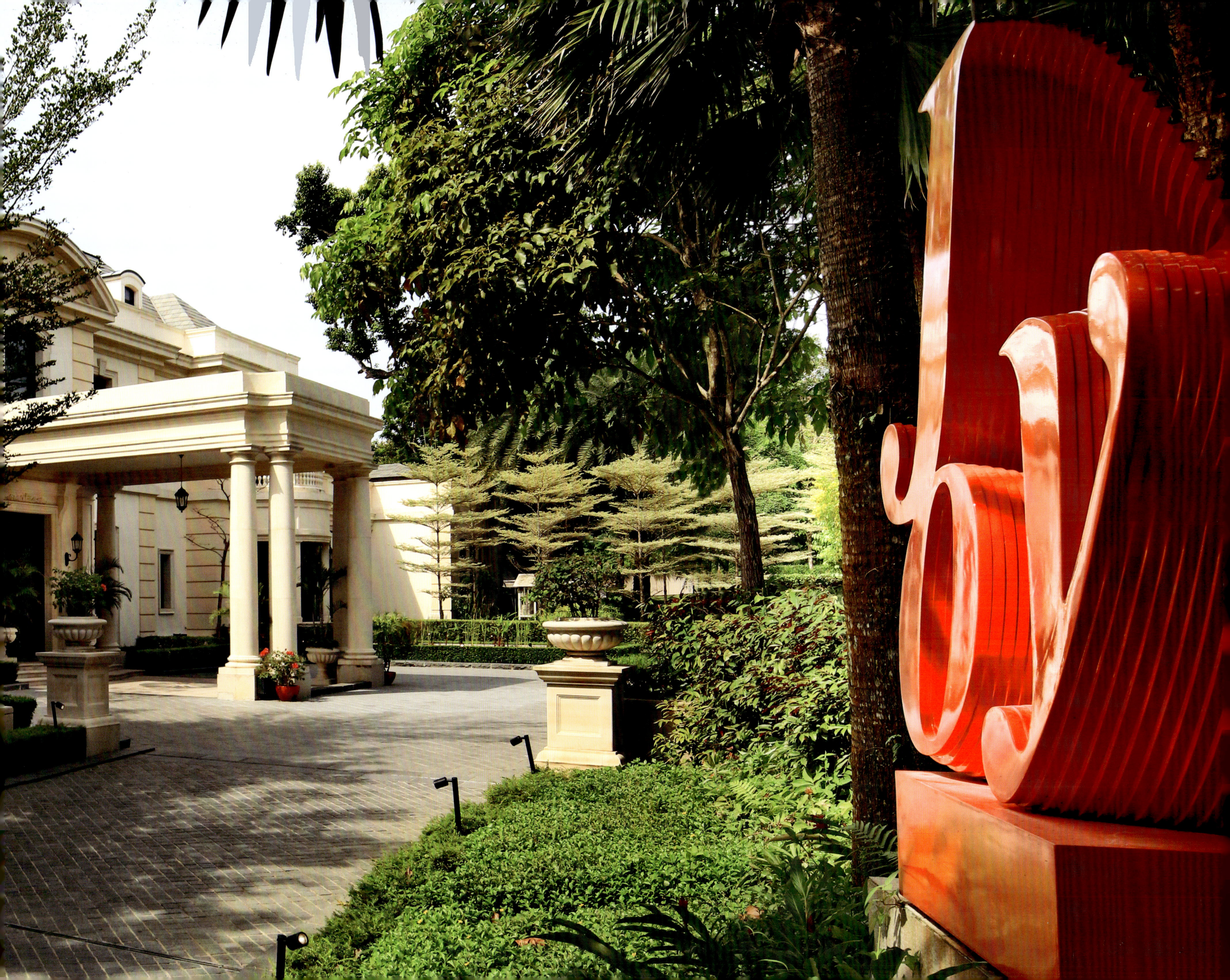

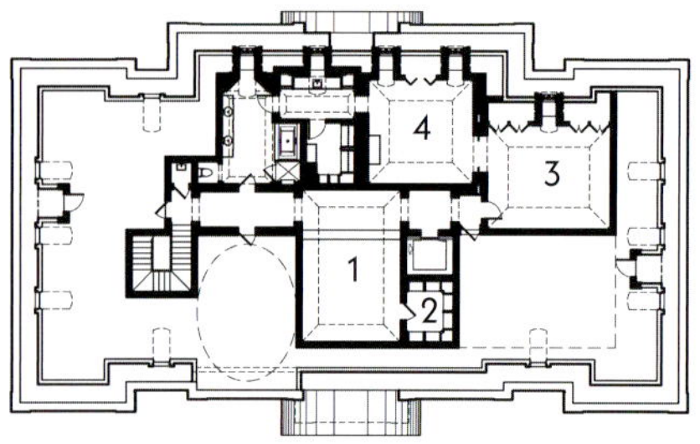

THIRD-FLOOR PLAN

1 Playroom
2 Toys area
3 Guest living room
4 Guest bedroom

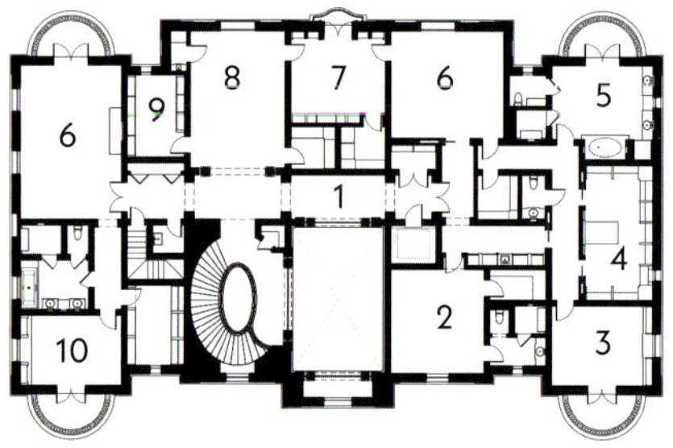

SECOND-FLOOR PLAN

1 Gallery
2 Nursery
3 His study
4 Closet
5 Bath
6 Bedroom
7 Her study
8 Family sitting room
9 Toys area
10 Library

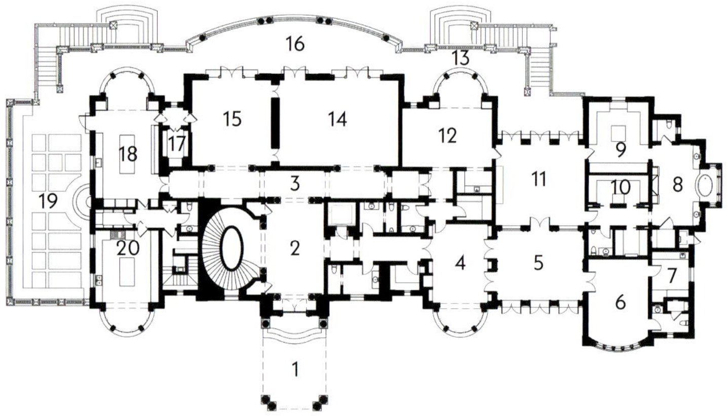

FIRST-FLOOR PLAN

1 Porte-cochère
2 Reception hall
3 Gallery
4 Library
5 Conservatory
6 Office
7 Study
8 Master bath
9 Her closet
10 His closet
11 Master bedroom
12 Master sitting room
13 Master terrace
14 Formal living room
15 Formal dining room
16 Master terrace
17 China
18 Family kitchen
19 Garden terrace
20 Wet kitchen

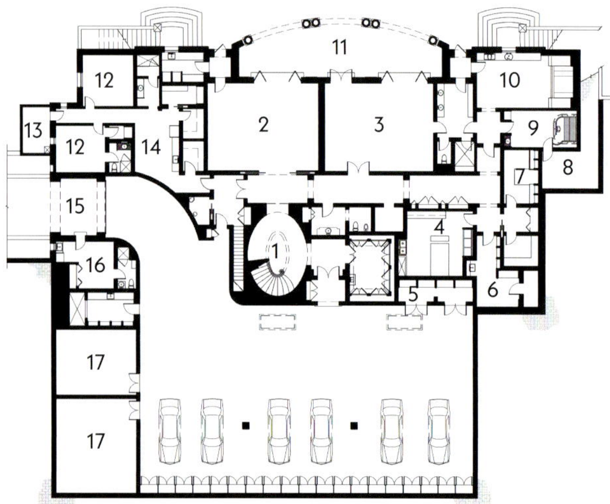

BASEMENT FLOOR PLAN

1 Lower grand stair hall
2 Media/prayer room
3 Gym
4 Laundry
5 Family storage
6 Luggage area
7 Gift-wrapping area
8 Mechanical room
9 Massage/sauna room
10 Spa lounge
11 Garden loggia
12 Staff bed room
13 Staff yard
14 Staff lounge
15 Portal
16 Driver's lounge
17 Mechanical/electrical room
18 Car park

0 8 16 32 ft

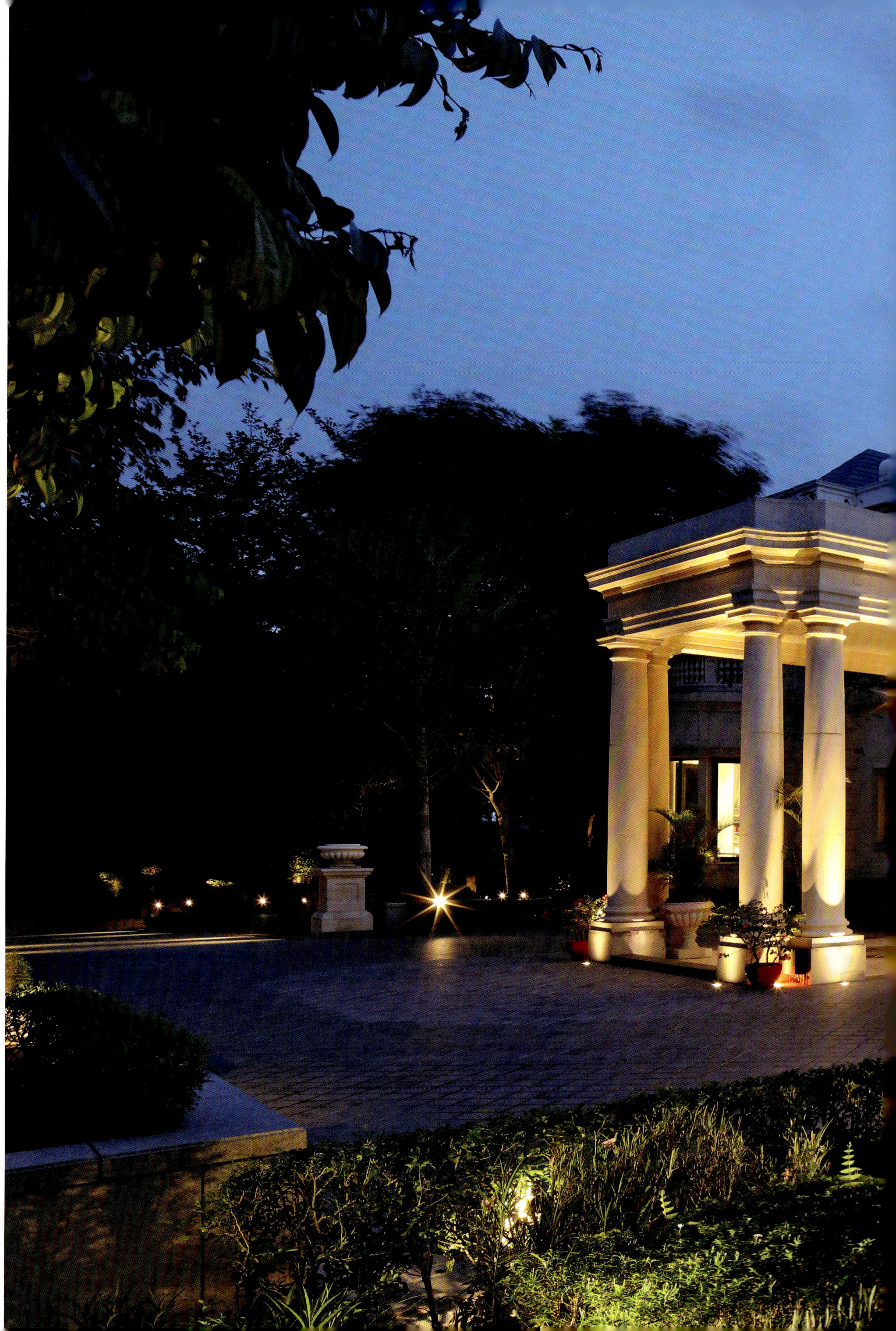

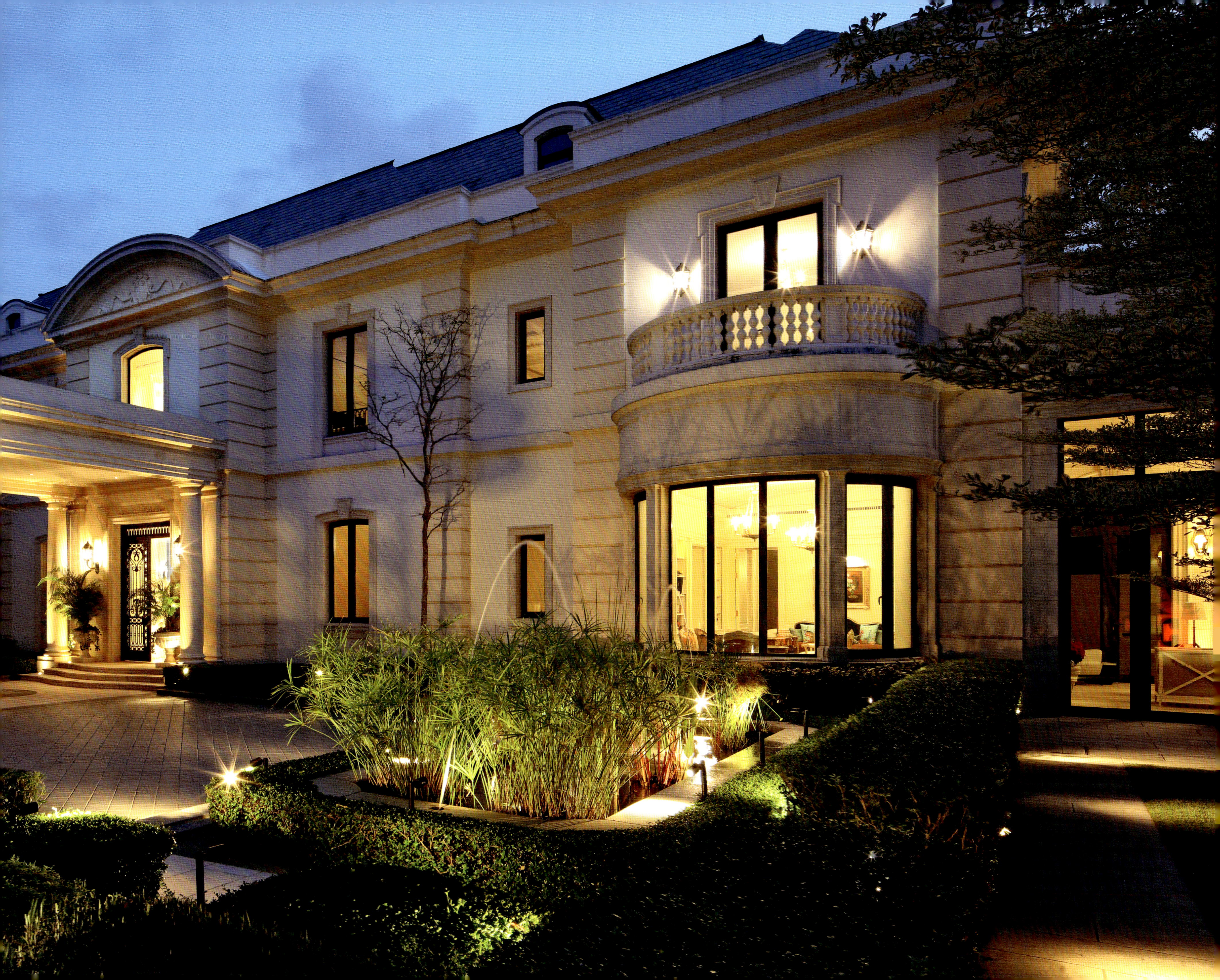

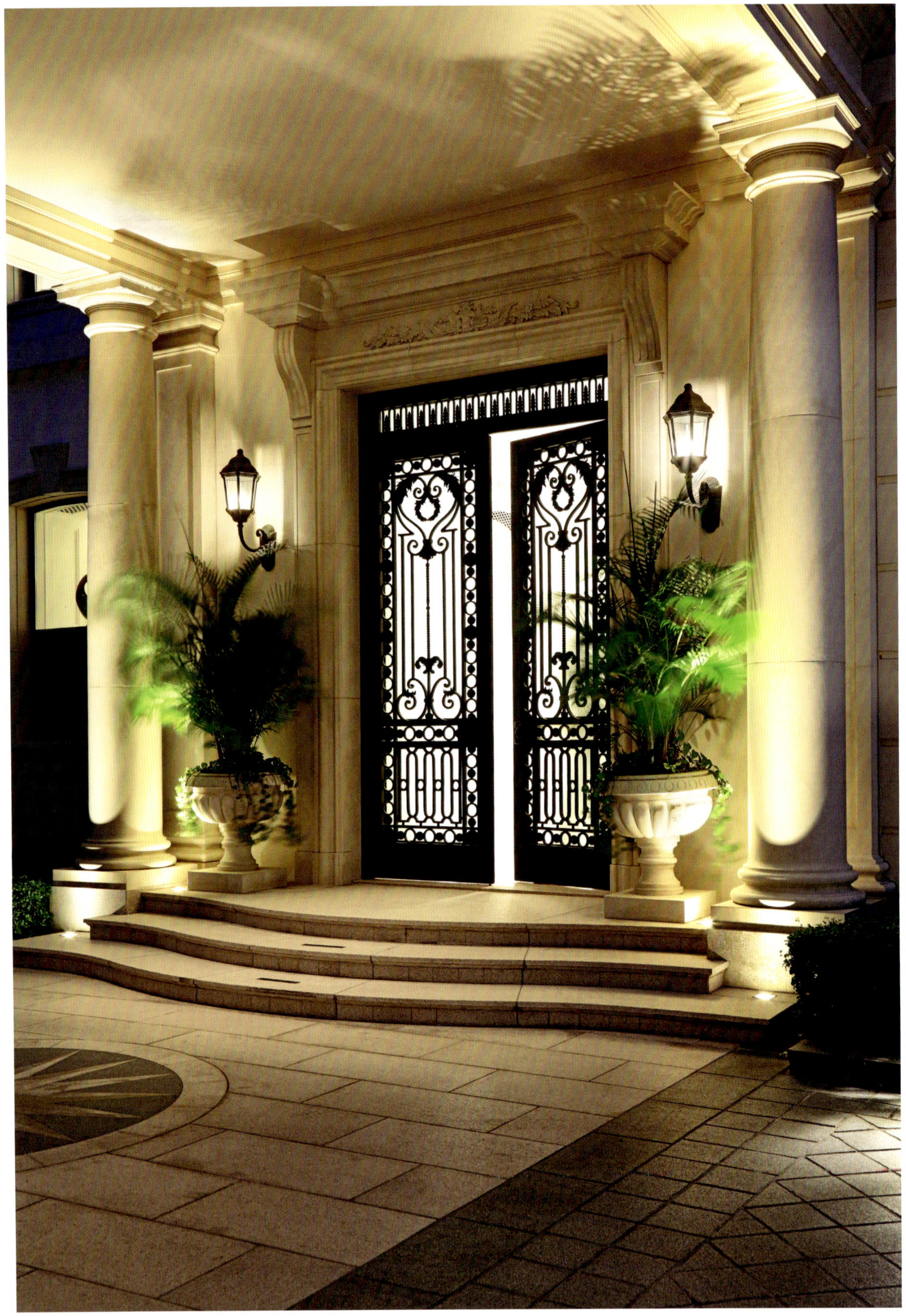

PAGES 244–245: *The Neoclassical* particuliers *of Paris and its early-twentieth-century hotels were the precedents for this traditional villa set in Singapore's lush Botanic Gardens district.*

PREVIOUS PAGES: *The entry motor court at night. Due to the humid climate of Singapore and for longevity, the primary construction materials are concrete, stone, and plaster.*

LEFT: *Since the climate is so tropical with heavy rains year-round, a covered porte-cochère to protect arriving guests was a necessity. The front doors are an intricate iron-and-glass design.*

OPPOSITE: *The two-story foyer and gallery run perpendicular to the front doors. All the walls are plaster, the floor is a classic marble pattern with cabochons, and the furnishings are a blend of Louis XVI style with a contemporary Fernando Botero horse sculpture in marble.*

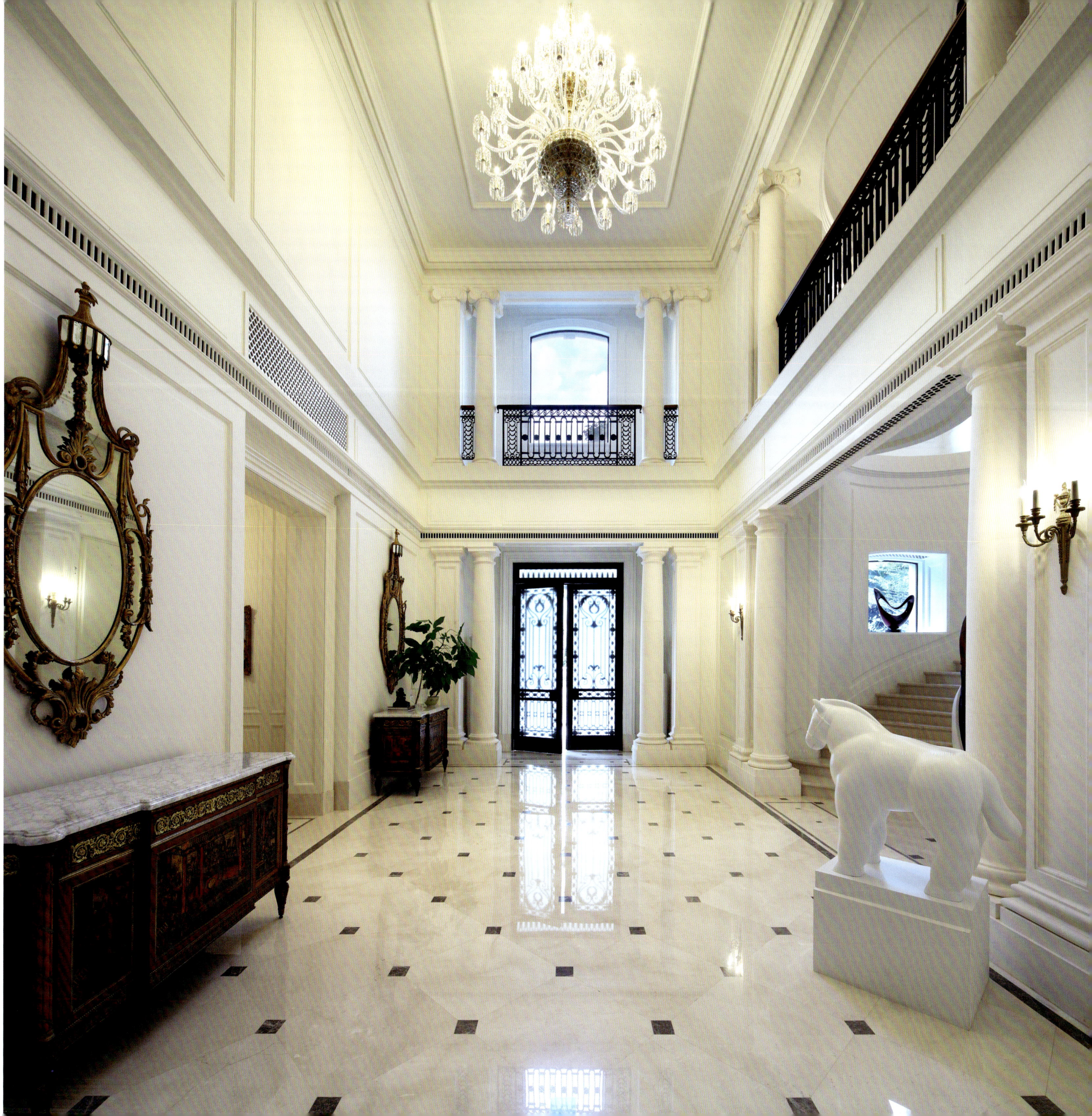

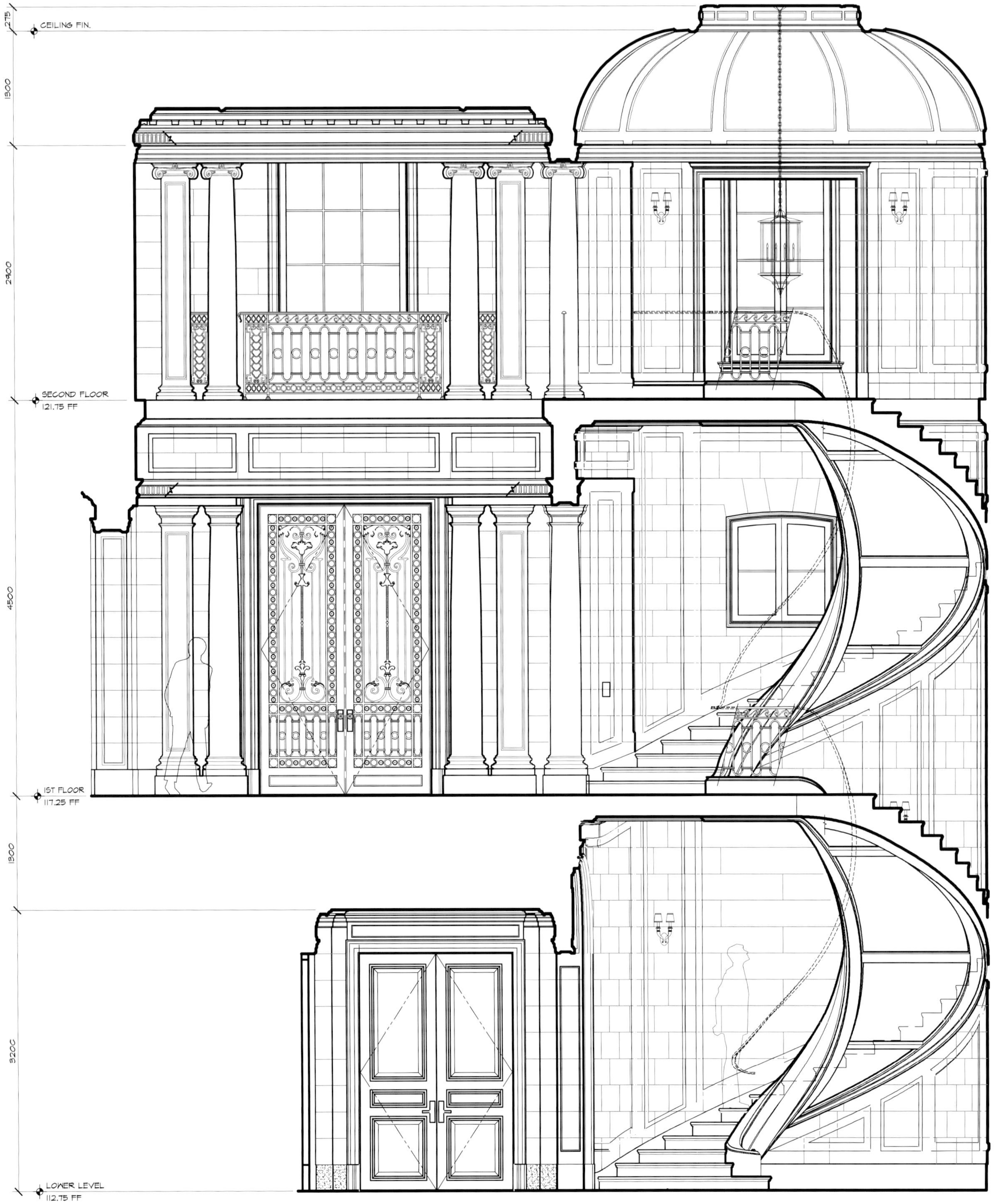

275
CEILING FIN.
1300
2900
SECOND FLOOR
121.75 FF
4500
1ST FLOOR
117.25 FF
1300
3200
LOWER LEVEL
112.75 FF

OPPOSITE: *Drawing of the foyer and main stair.*

RIGHT: *The complex oval staircase, defined by plaster columns and delicate ironwork and topped by a skylight, is placed off to one side in keeping with the feng shui practice of placing the stairs away from the direction of the front door.*

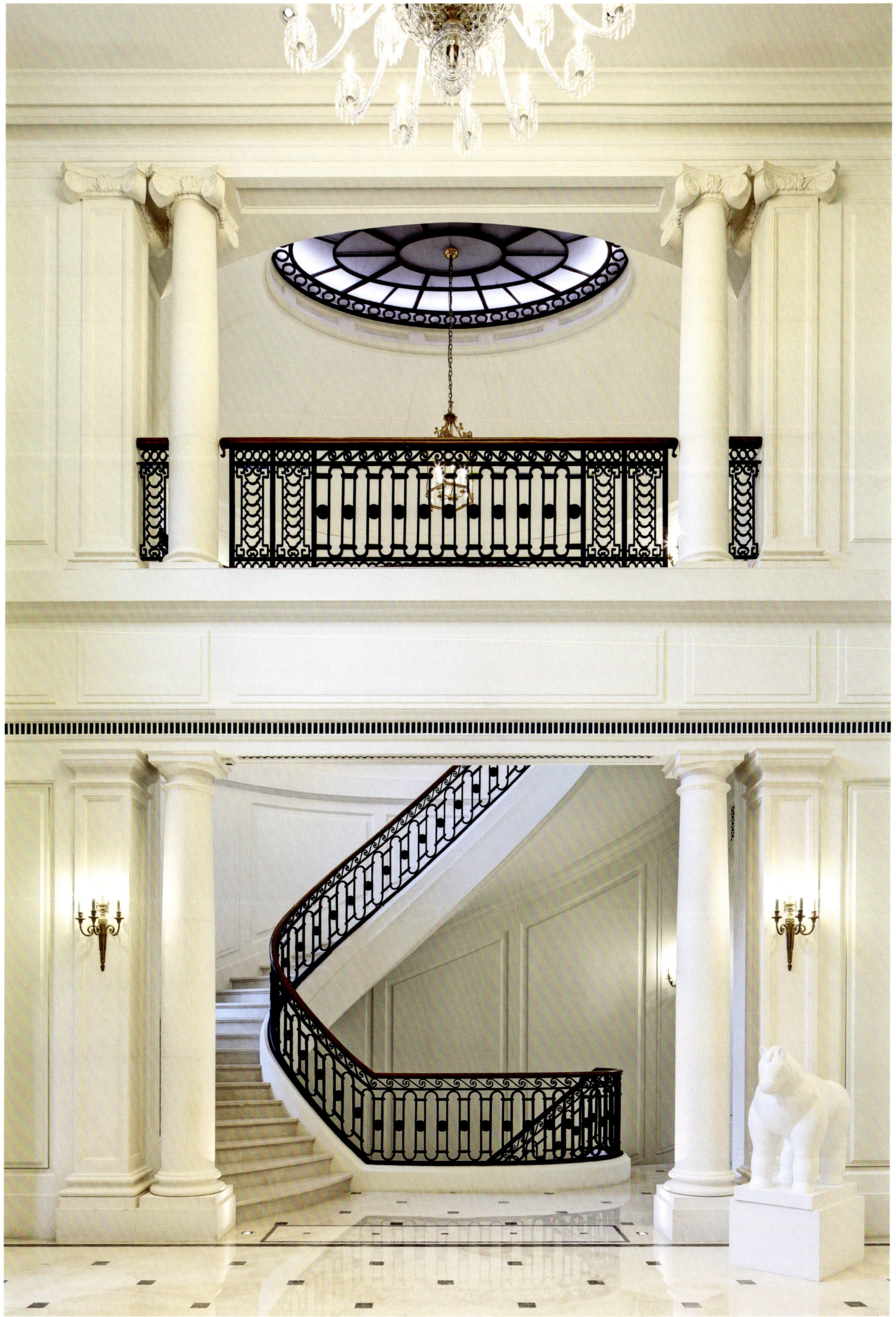

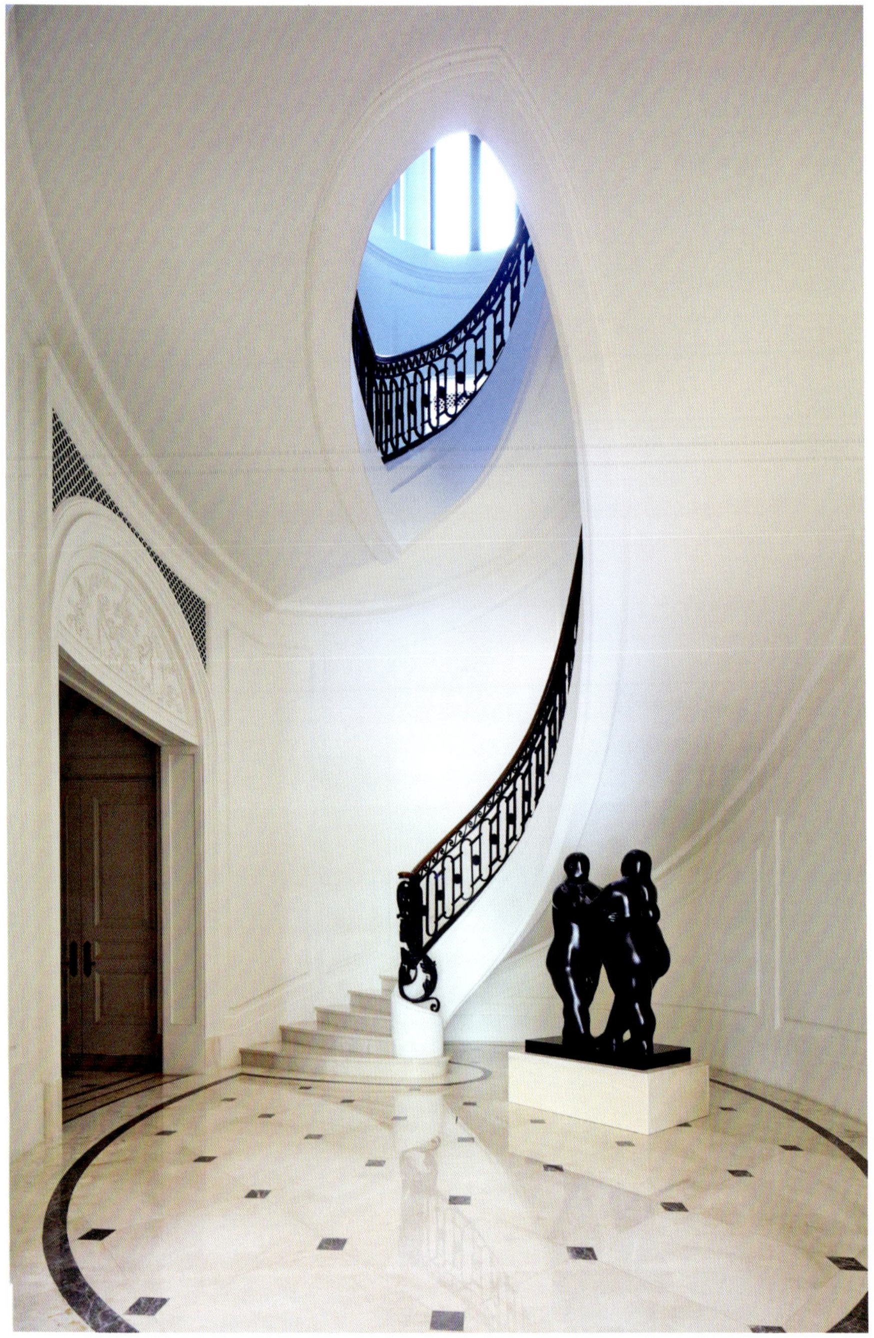

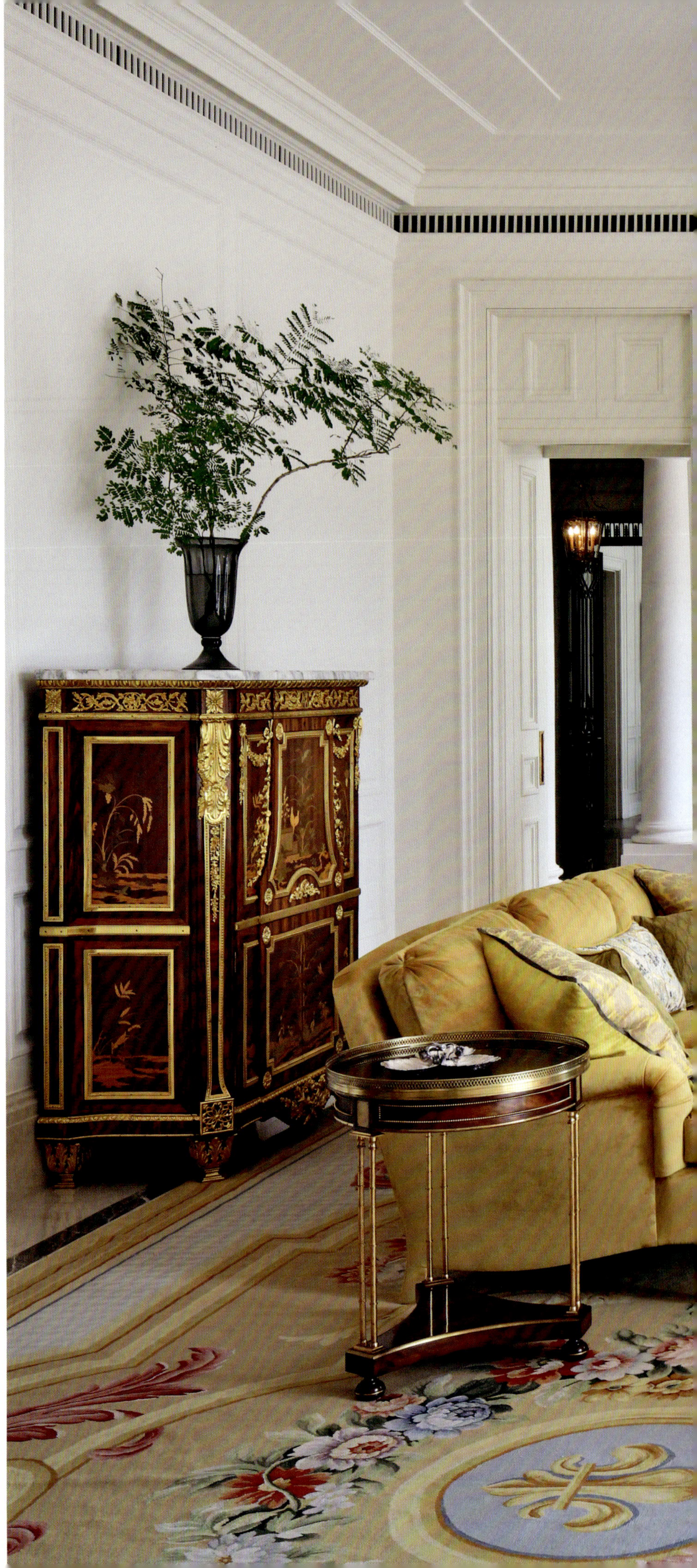

ABOVE: *At the bottom of the staircase in the basement level stands Botero's* Dancers *in bronze.*

RIGHT: *A variety of paneling, moldings, columns, and decorative plasterwork was used in the formal living room, which is anchored by a custom-woven Aubusson rug.*

FOLLOWING PAGES, LEFT: *Interior designer David Desmond took the colors of Hubert de Givenchy's Paris apartment as his inspiration for the living room. The green velvet sofa was based on a Renzo Mongiardino design. Artwork is by Tay Bak Chiang.* RIGHT: *Hand-painted wallpaper panels by Paul Montgomery, a Russian Neoclassical chandelier, and English parcel-gilt chairs highlight the dining room.*

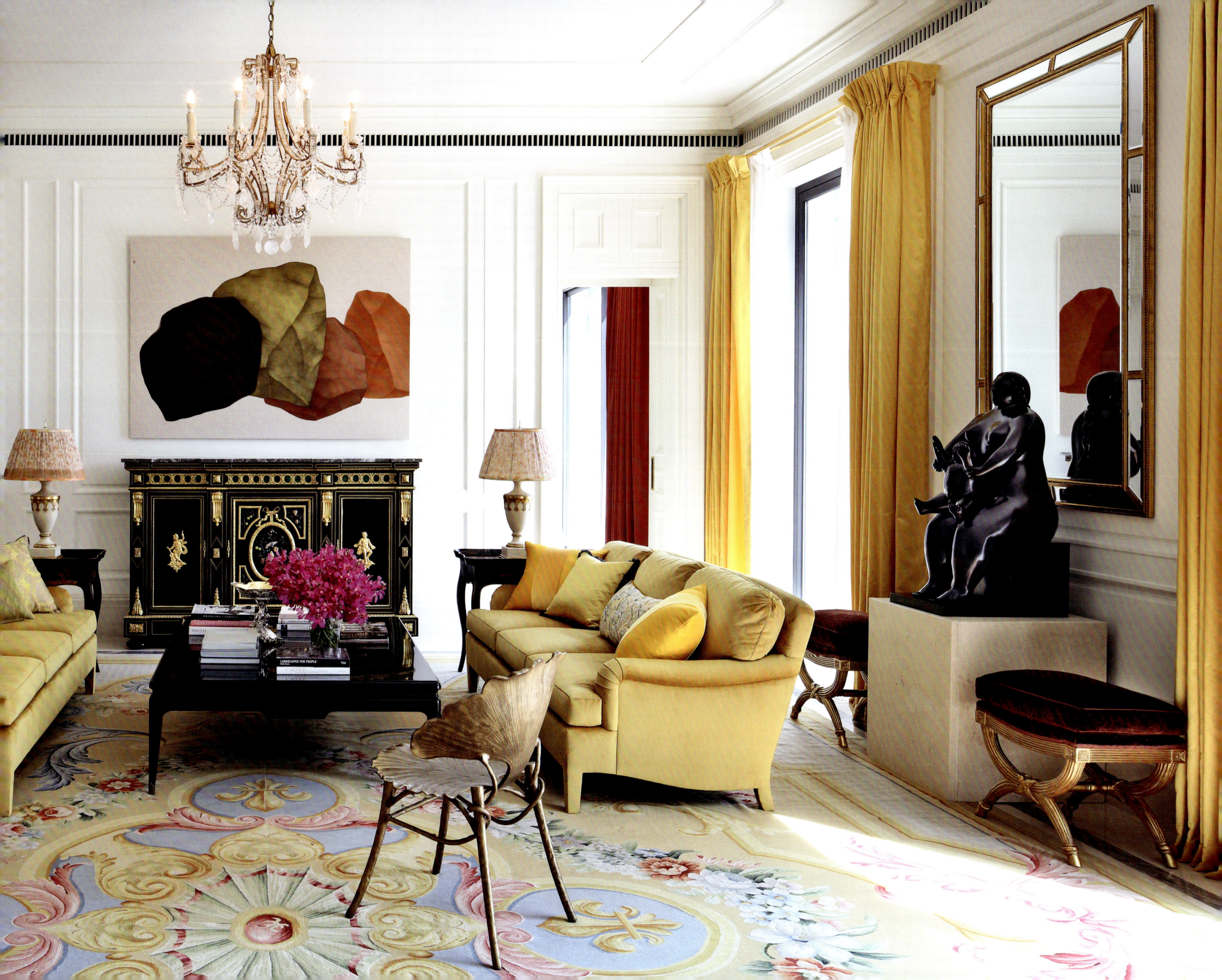
LANDSCAPES FOR PEOPLE
CARTIER

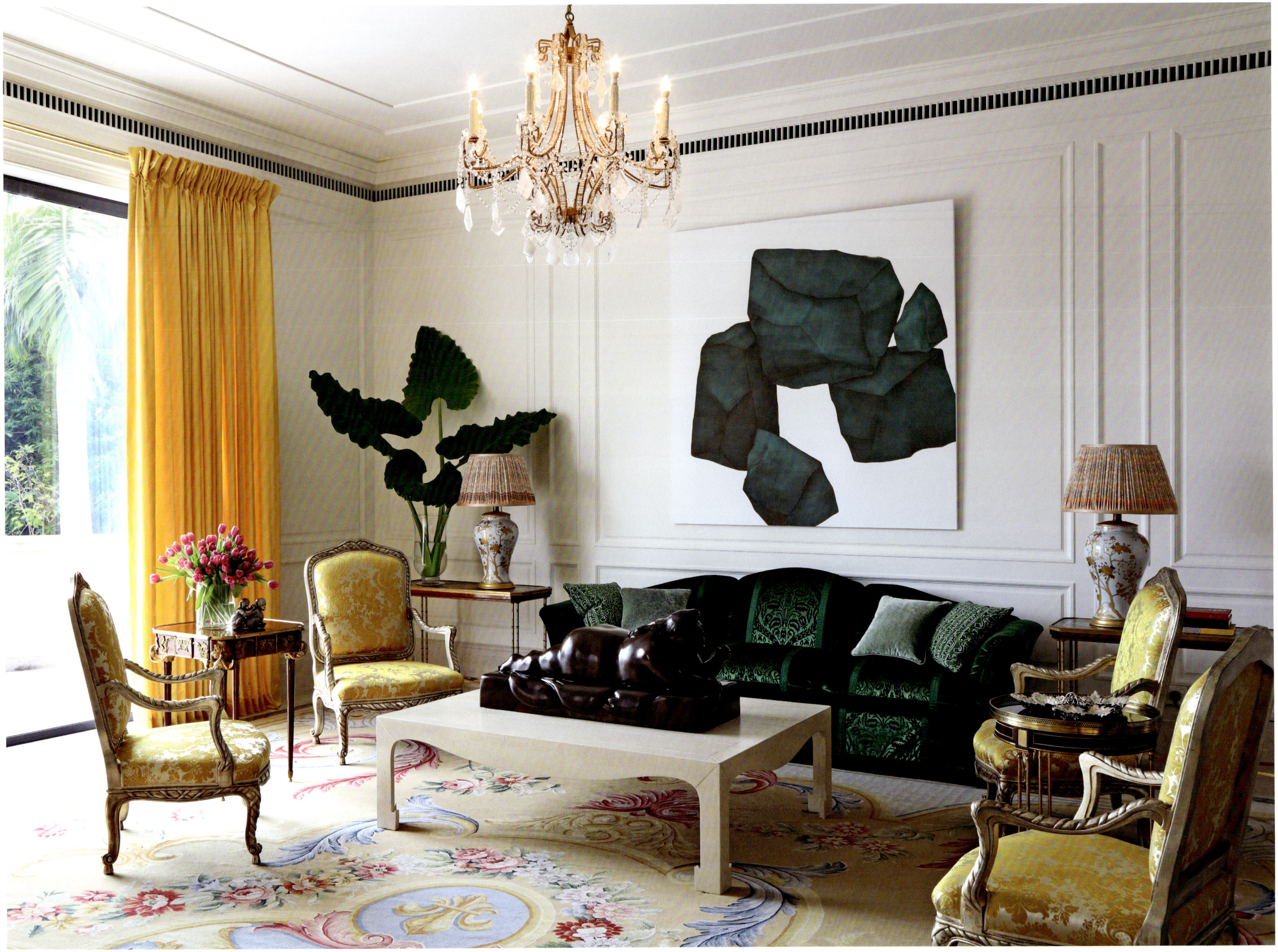

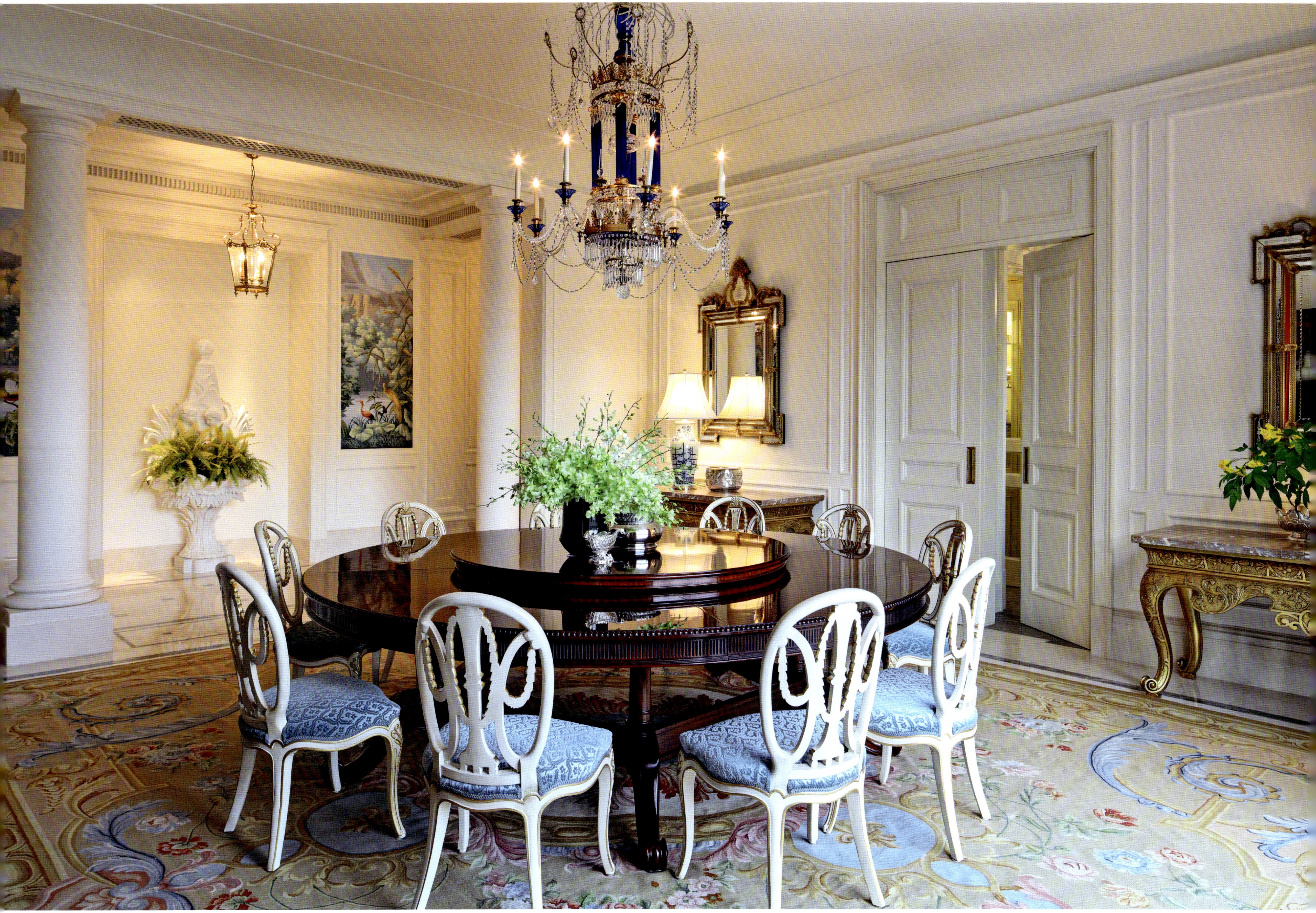

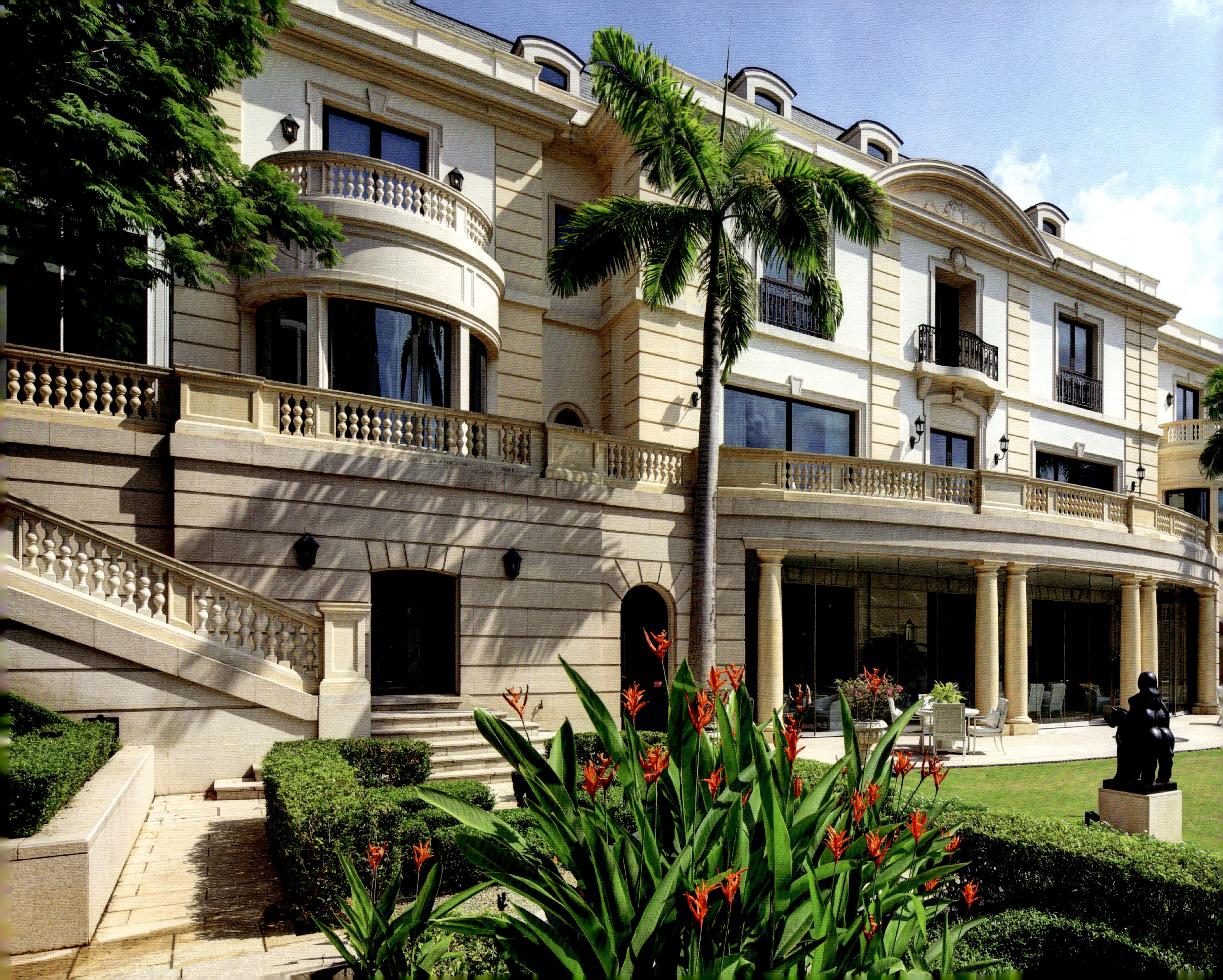

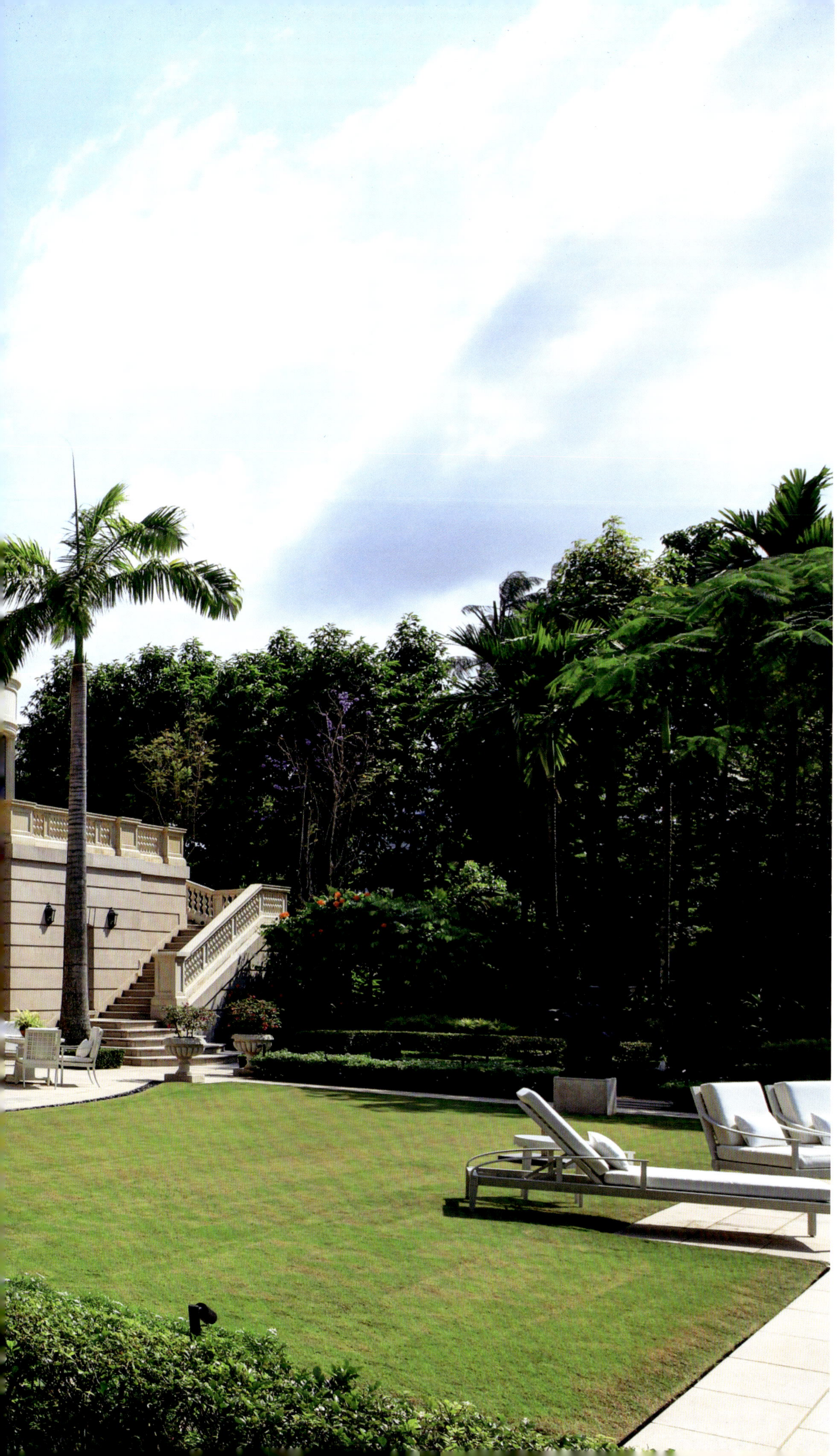

LEFT: *The rear façade is defined by a long balustraded terrace and two staircases that descend from the main living level to the loggia and gardens. Behind the loggia, which can be enclosed with glass partitions for dinner parties, is a ballroom for formal events.*

FOLLOWING PAGES, LEFT: *Adjacent to the master suite on the main level is a glass-roofed conservatory that overlooks the private master garden with a direct view toward Robert Indiana's* Hope *sculpture.* RIGHT: *Dotting the grounds is a collection of distinctive contemporary sculpture.*

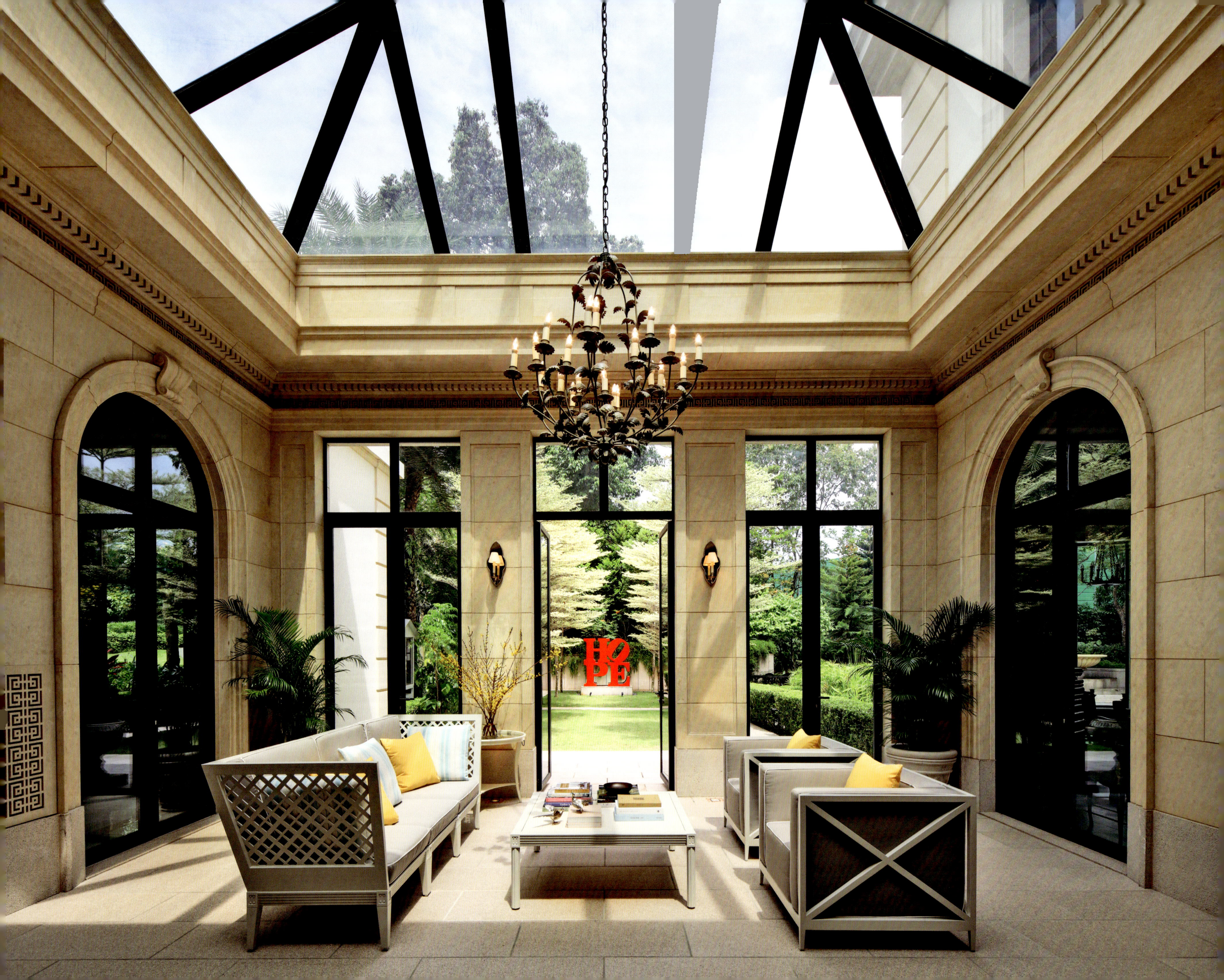
HOPE

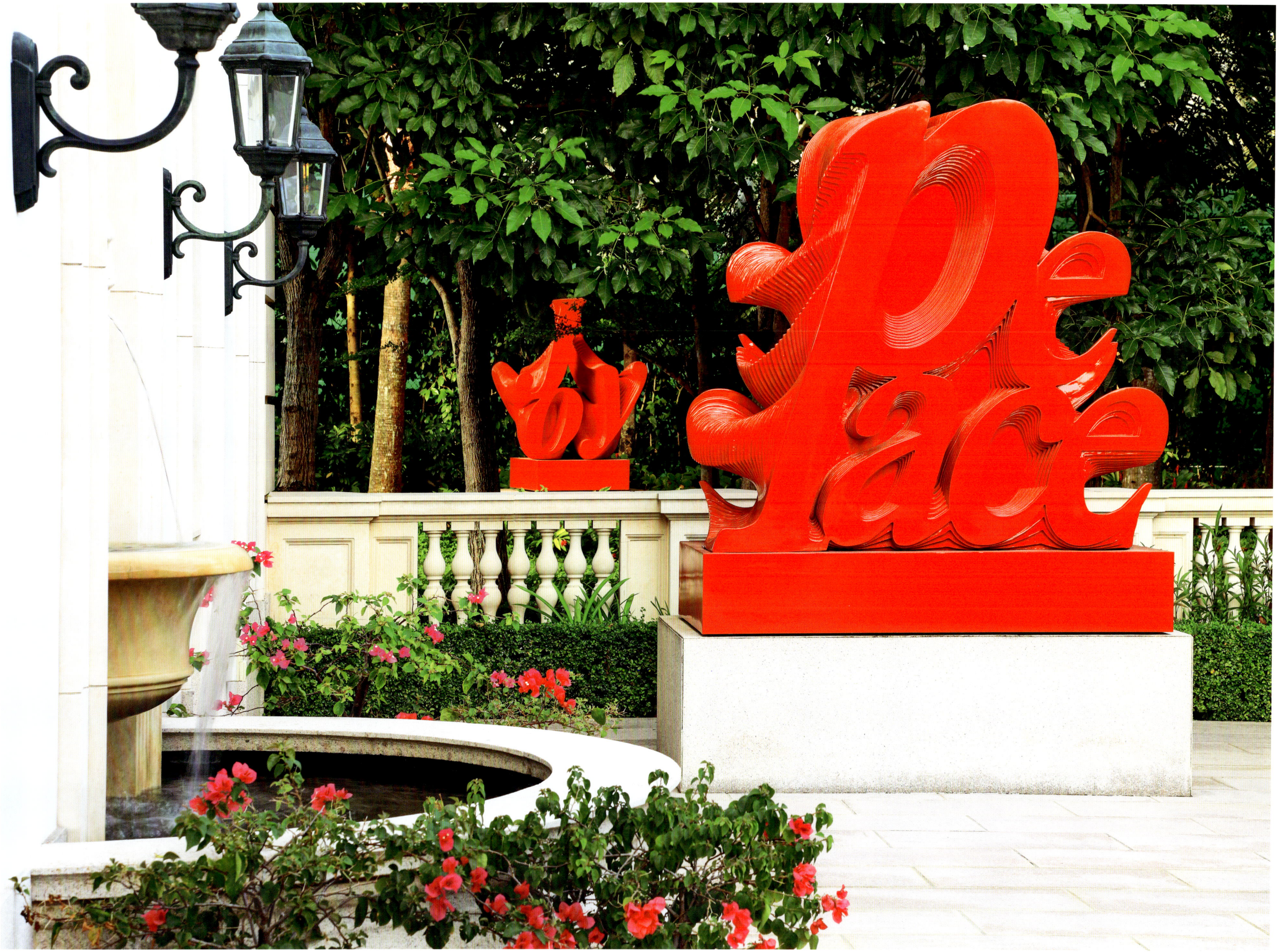
Peace

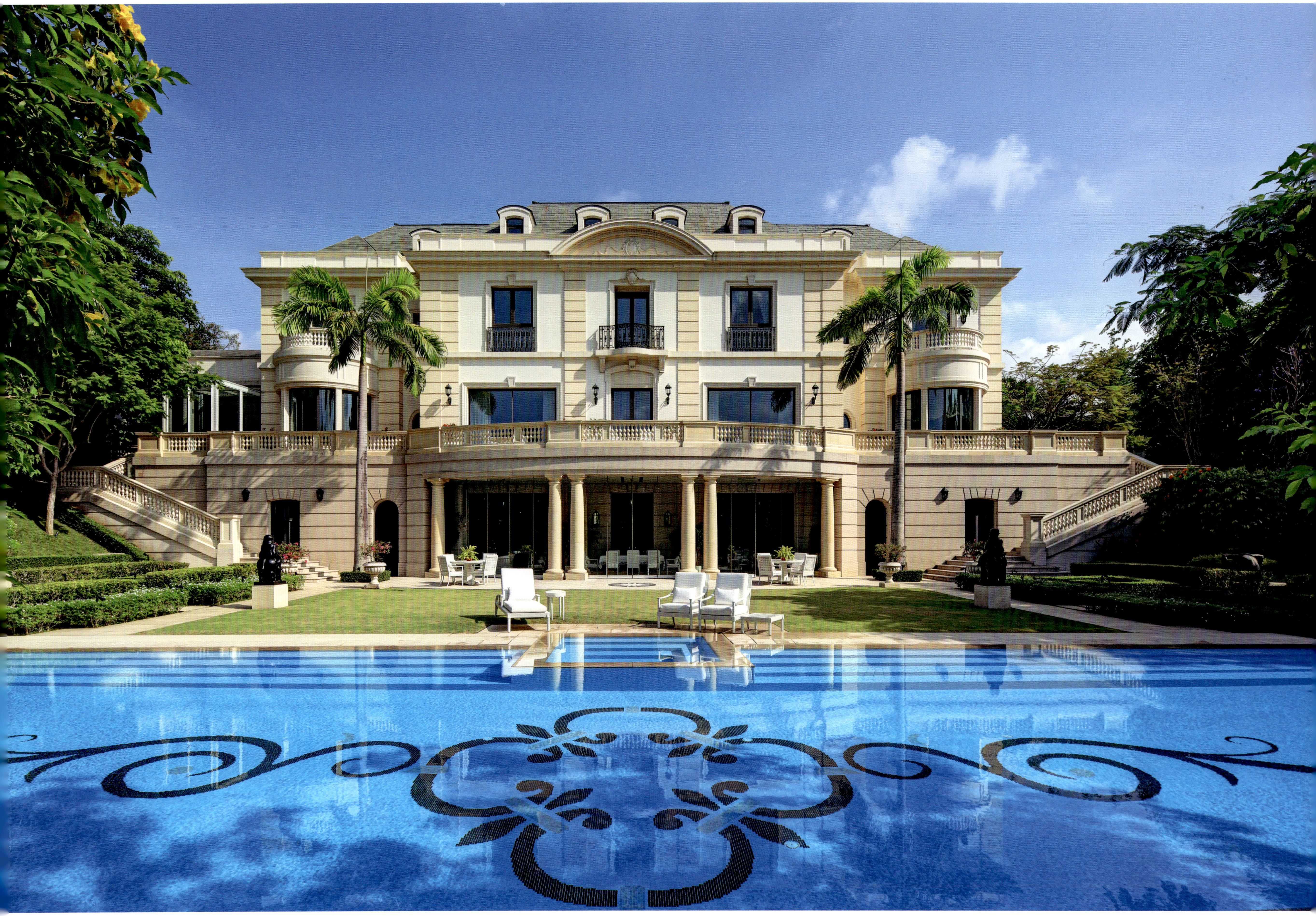

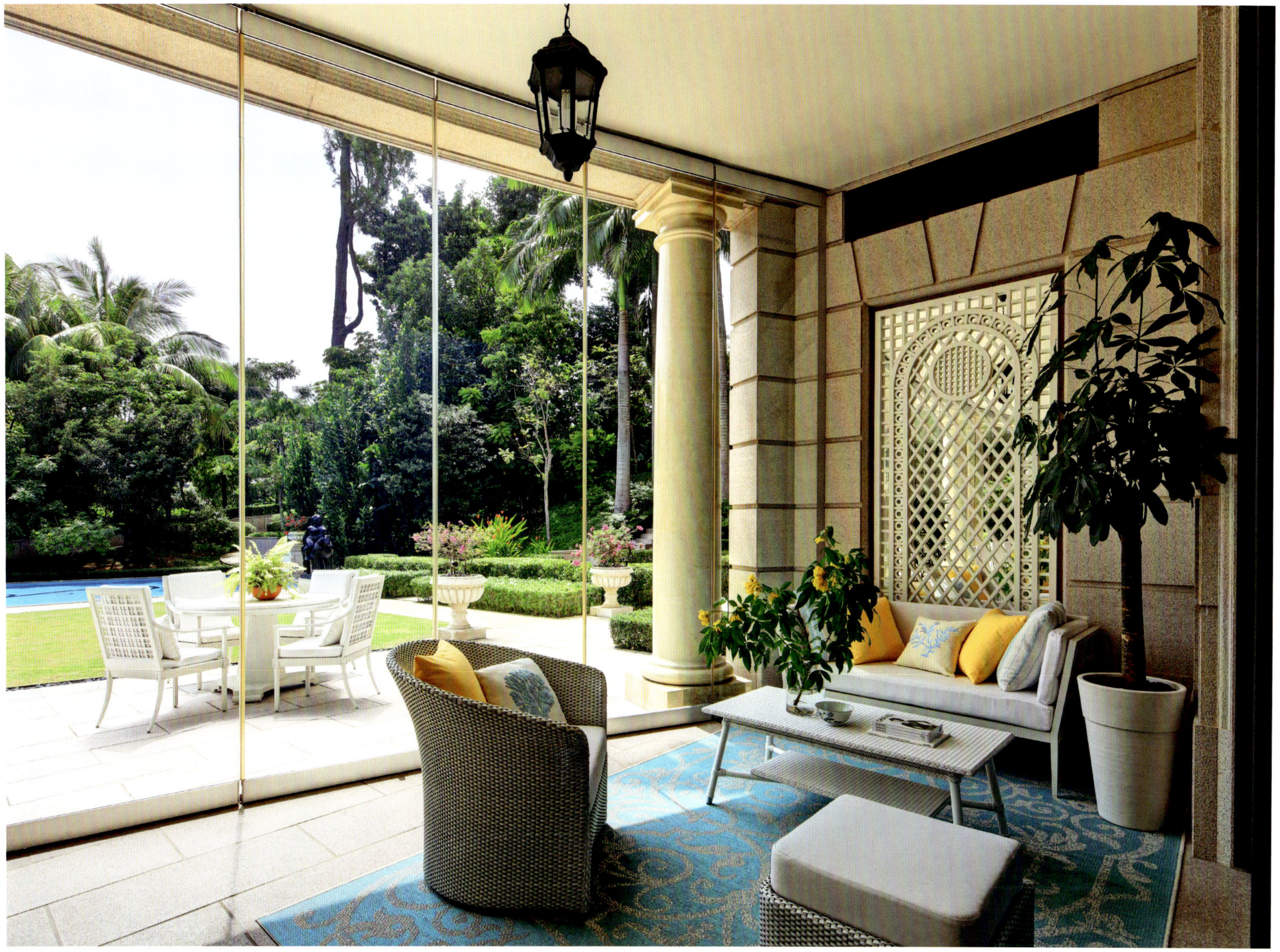

OPPOSITE: *The full rear façade reveals the pool with a mosaic tile pattern, a pair of Botero sculptures, and the four-story house.*

ABOVE: *The loggia, with the glass partitions installed, has rusticated stone floors and walls, and a trellis wall panel backed by an antique mirror. The white wicker furniture and turquoise and canary yellow accents add to the relaxed ambiance.*

FOLLOWING PAGES, LEFT: *The pool and fountain, which quiets any ambient sounds, lit at night with the lush, mature landscaping as a backdrop.* RIGHT: *Steps to the left of the pool lead up to a hilltop* tempietto*, a small, circular, temple-like structure that anchors the garden at the master suite level.*

PAGE 264: *A night-time view of the swimming pool and the steps that lead up to the hillside* tempietto*, which offers views of the city's high-rises. The grounds were planted with fully mature tropical landscaping to emulate the surrounding Botanic Gardens district.*

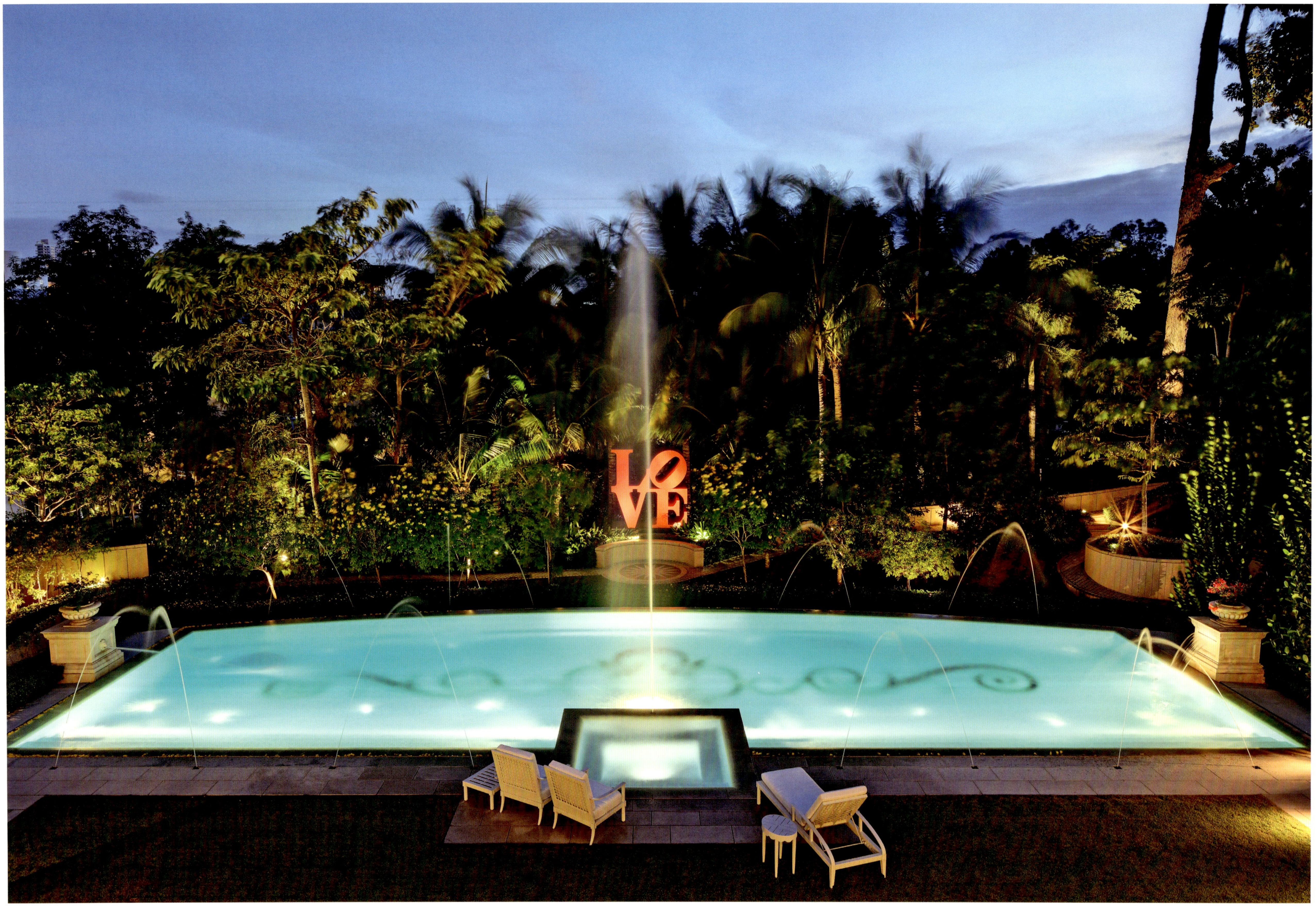
LOVE

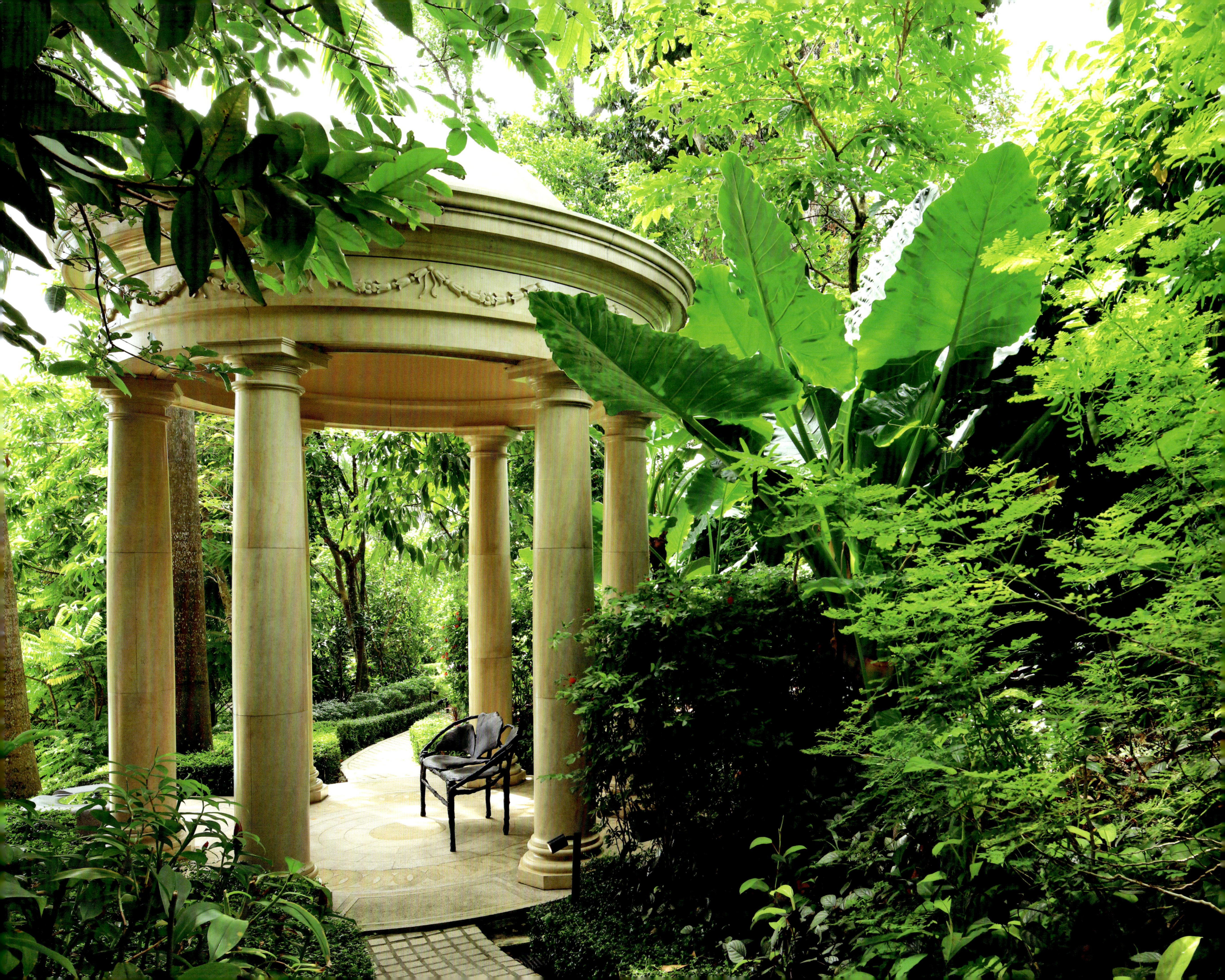

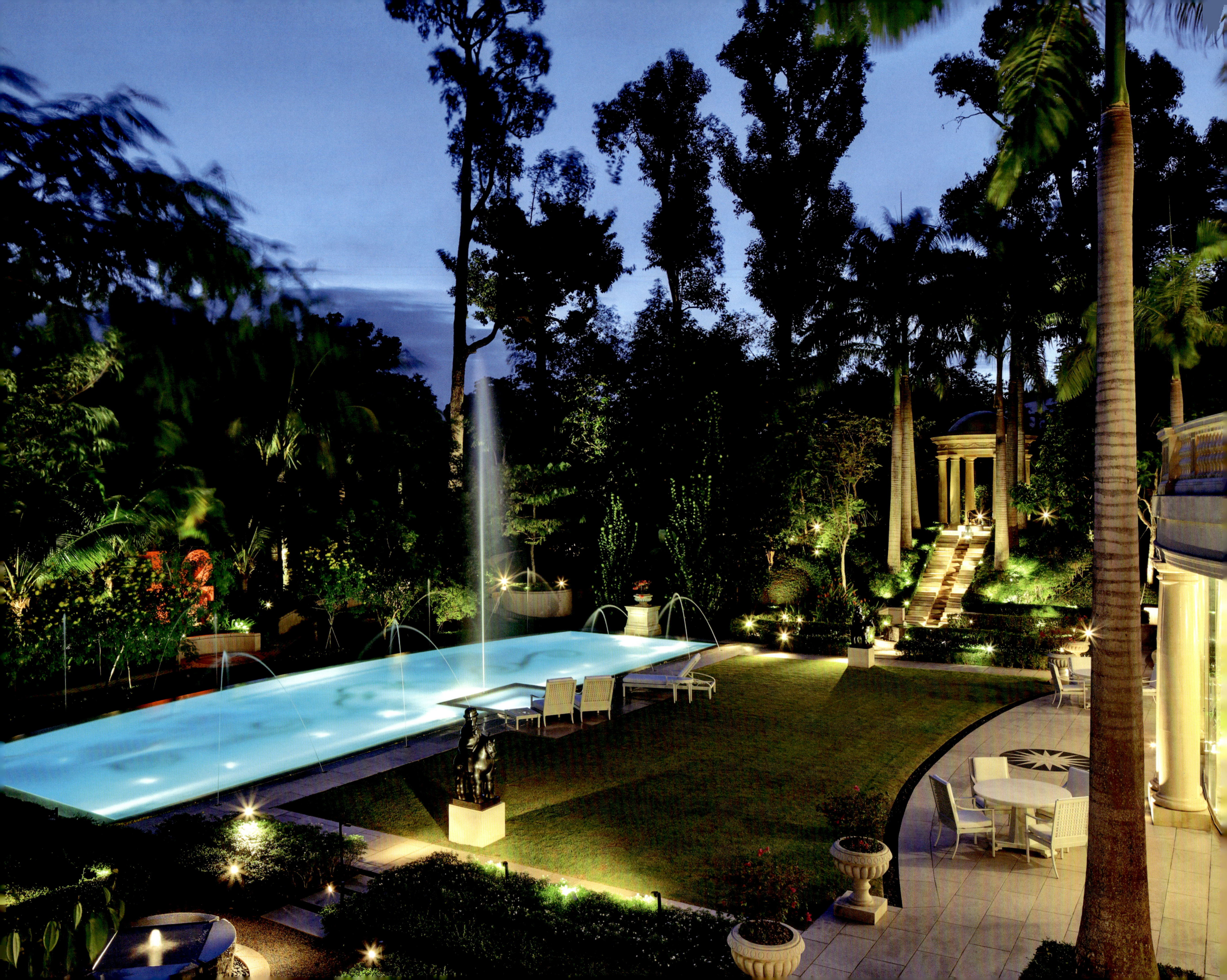

WORKS IN PROGRESS

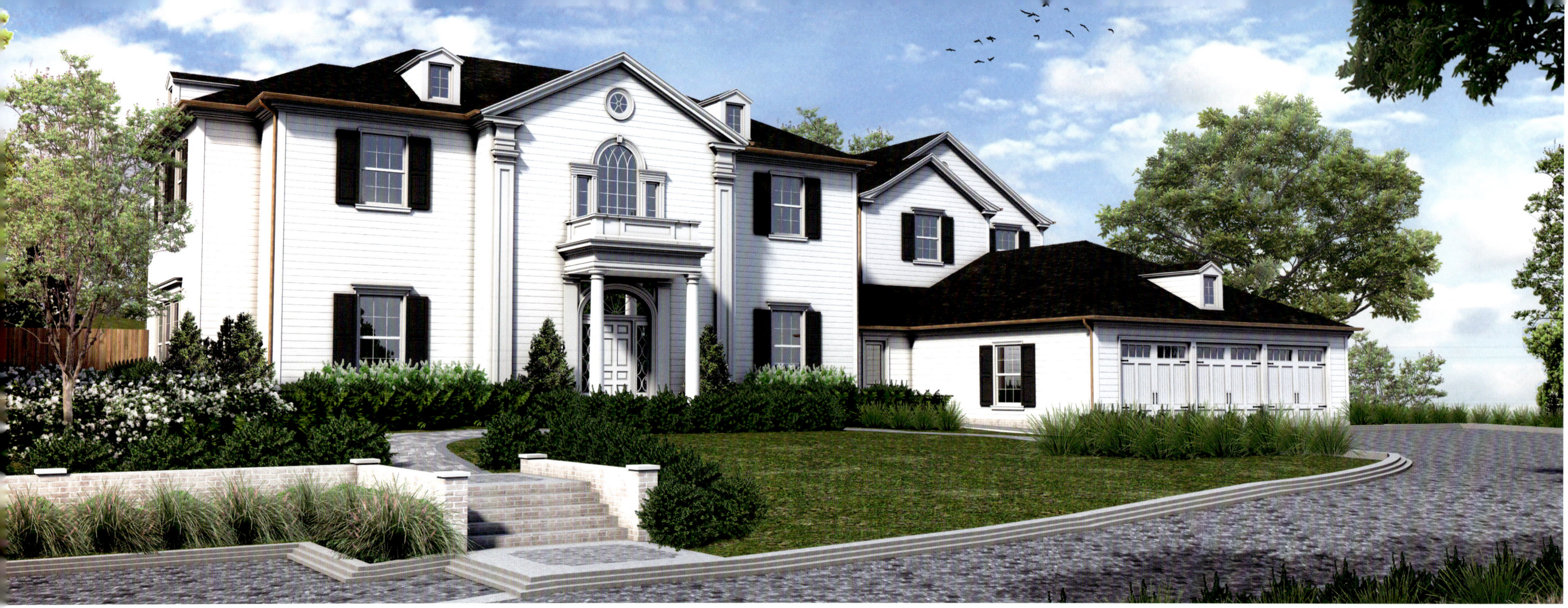

OAK GROVE

Bay Area

This new residence nestled in an oak grove in the San Francisco Bay Area evokes the Shingle and Cape Cod styles of the East Coast. Picturesque massing, with classically inspired architectural details and materials of white brick and wood clapboards, define the exterior design. Interiors will incorporate classical details and paneled rooms in the Colonial Revival tradition.

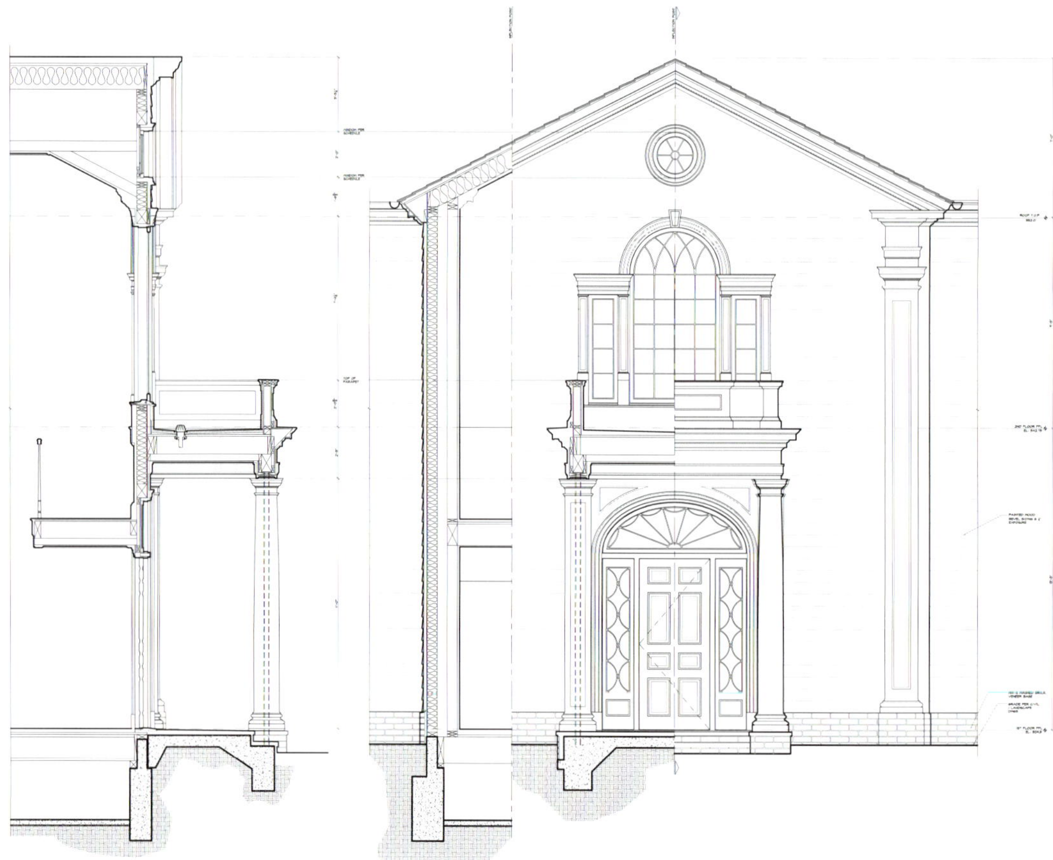

Interior Designer: David Desmond
Landscape Architect: Hoffman and Ospina

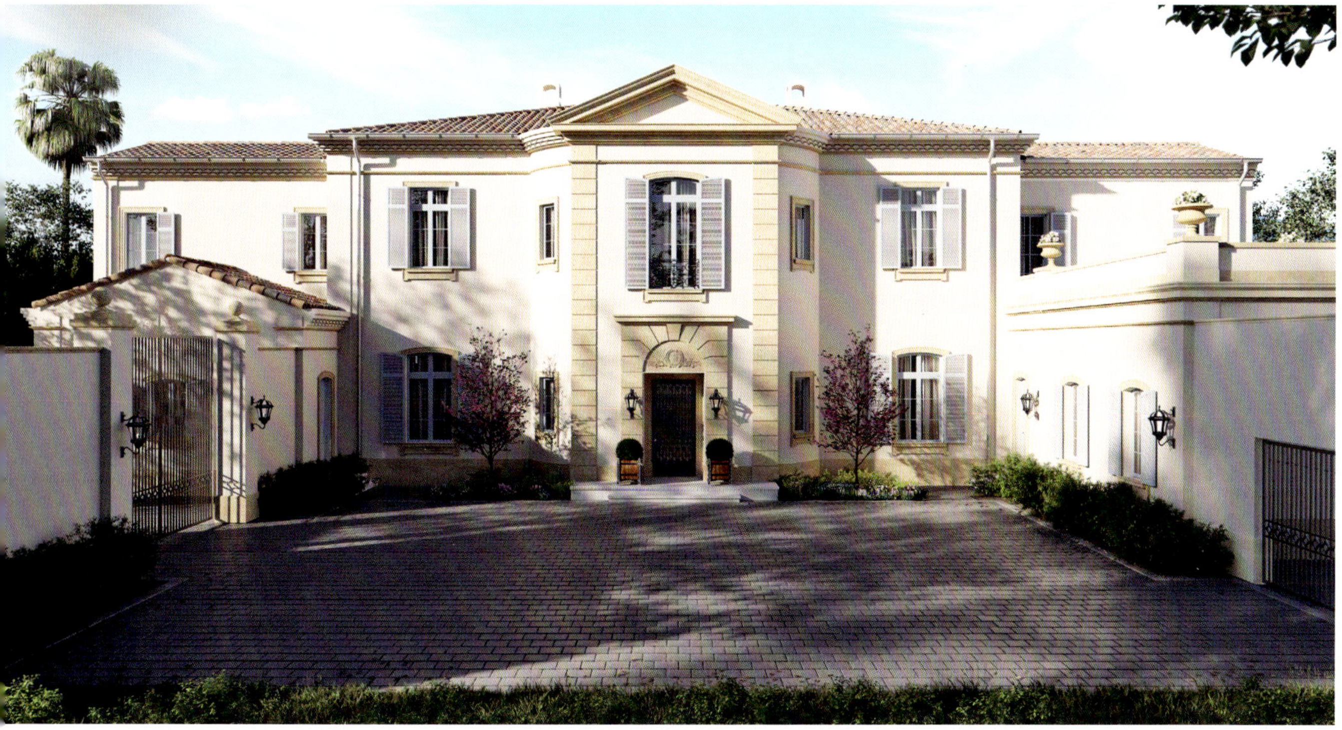

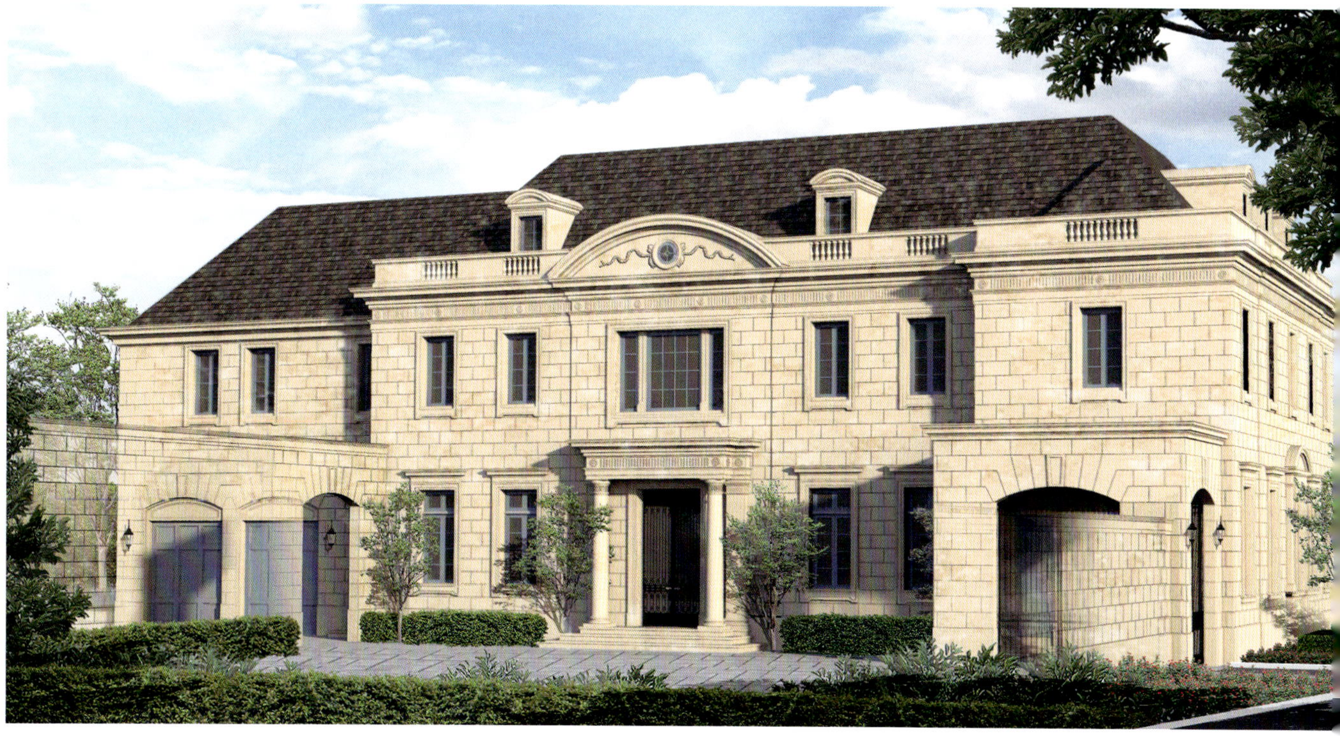

LA COLOMBE

Bel-Air

Located in the Los Angeles foothills, this house evokes the great French Riviera tradition of uniting the heritage of Parisian maisons, with their formal massing and classical details, with the warm character of Provence to create a modern Mediterranean villa for a young family. Walls of straw-colored plaster, golden French limestone trim, shuttered opening accents, and the classic Genoise eave and tile roof combine to bring the romance of southern France to California.

CHÂTEAU D'OR

Beijing

Set within the new luxury gated community of Beijing Huariou, this French-inspired residence incorporates gracious details from châteaux built in the Paris region in the late seventeenth and early eighteenth centuries as well as their nineteenth-century American counterparts. The villa's limestone exteriors have classical columns and details, and the black slate roof has traditional French dormers. A loggia at the rear serves as outdoor living and dining areas during the warmer months. Complete with every amenity, the interiors will encompass a classical environment of fine detailing inspired by the great houses of Europe and America.

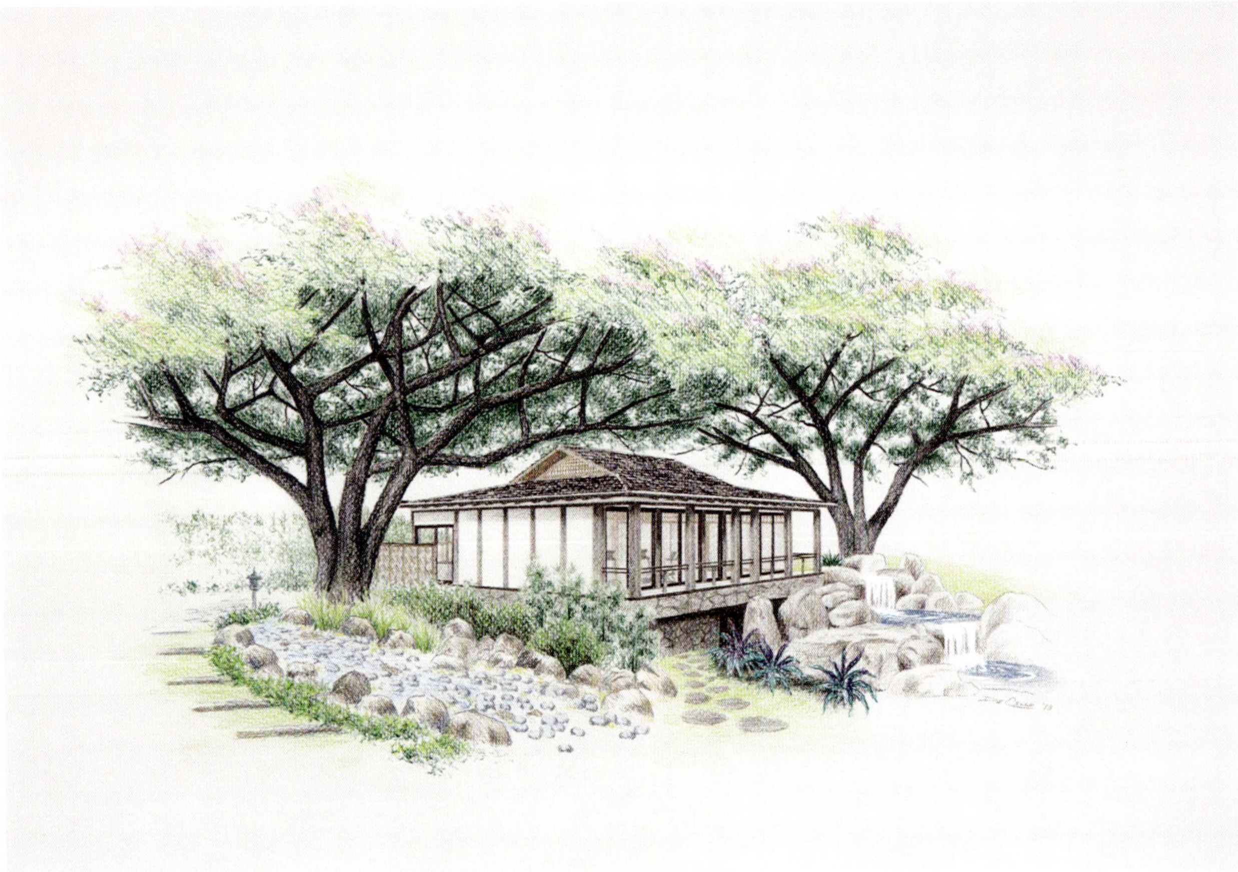

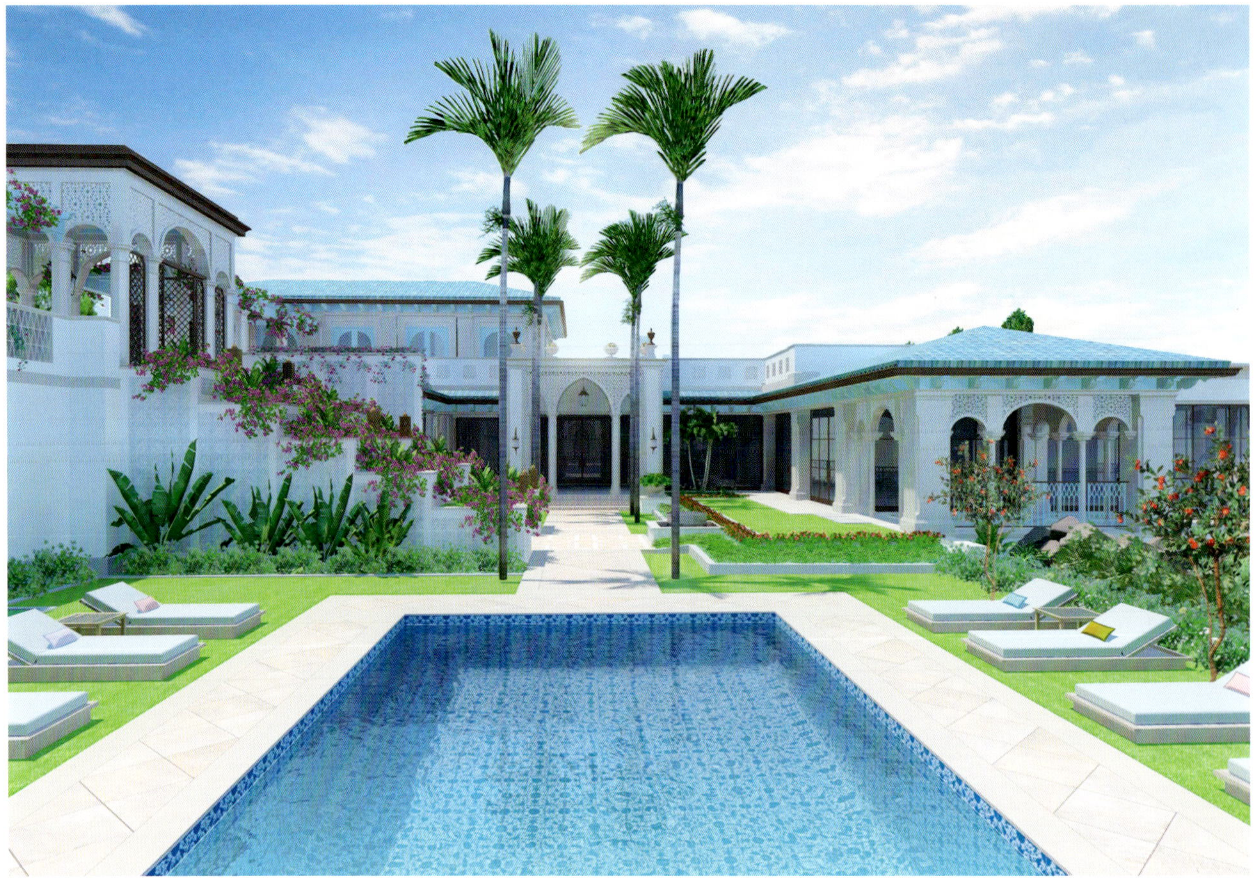

SPA AND BATHHOUSE

Hawai'i

This interpretation of a Japanese-inspired spa building provides a gym, spa and *ofuro* bathing facility under the shade of two giant monkey pod trees above a waterfall that cascades down to the bay below.

DAR MAROC

Hawai'i

Floating alongside Maunalua Bay with panoramic views of Diamond Head, this Moroccan-inspired waterside estate cascades down four levels from an arrival pavilion and roof terrace to a private boat basin. Drawing on the Moroccan and Orientalist aesthetics of such estates as Doris Duke's Shangri-La, Villa Oasis, and Majorelle (the Moroccan home and garden of Yves Saint Laurent) and the distinctive La Mamounia hotel in Marrakech, the estate's architecture features arched pavilions and extensive use of plaster relief, tile, and marble on the exterior and interiors, with expansive gardens and water features.

Interior Designer: David Desmond
Landscape Architect: Steve Mechler

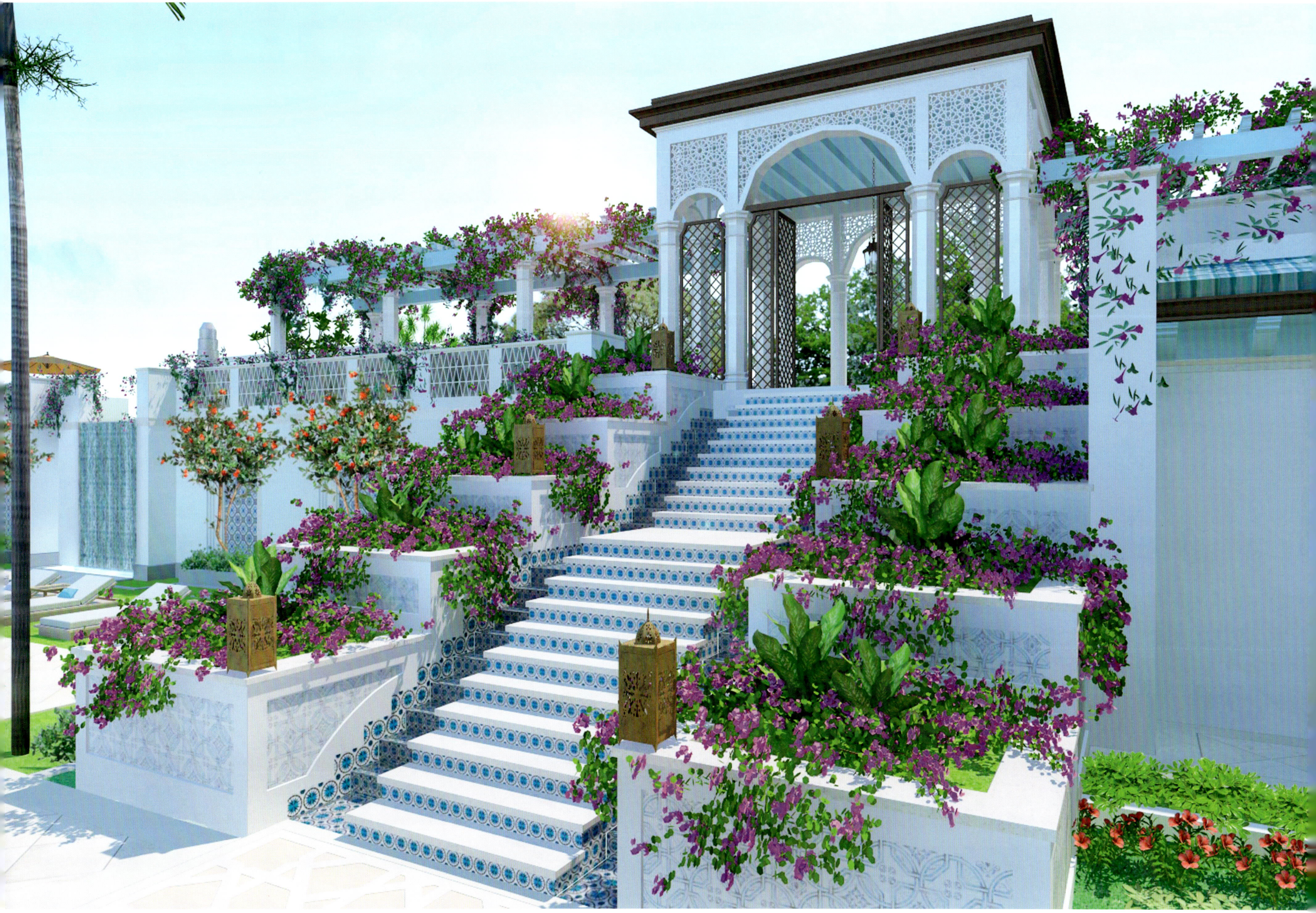

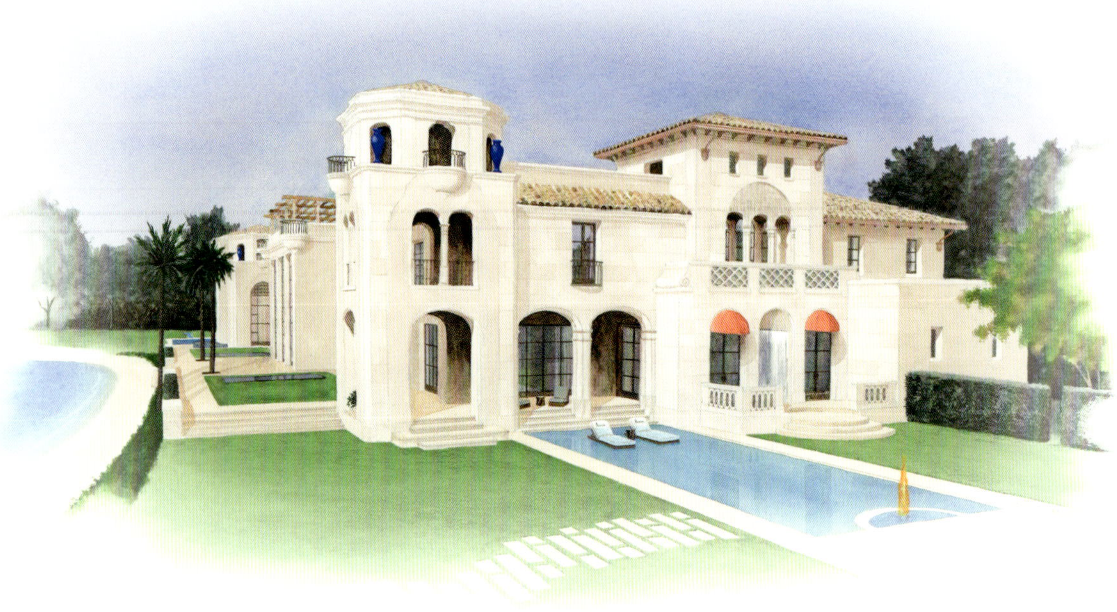

COCONUT ISLAND VILLA

Abu Dhabi

Located on a private island development in the UAE, this streamlined villa evokes the spirit of a Mediterranean-inspired resort infused with subtle Arabic cultural influences. The front façade relates to the formality of the street front while the more casual and dramatic rear façade responds to the space of the great lawn, private beach and picturesque views of the adjacent waterways and nearby islands.

Interior Designer: Joan Behnke
Landscape Architect: Robert Truskowski

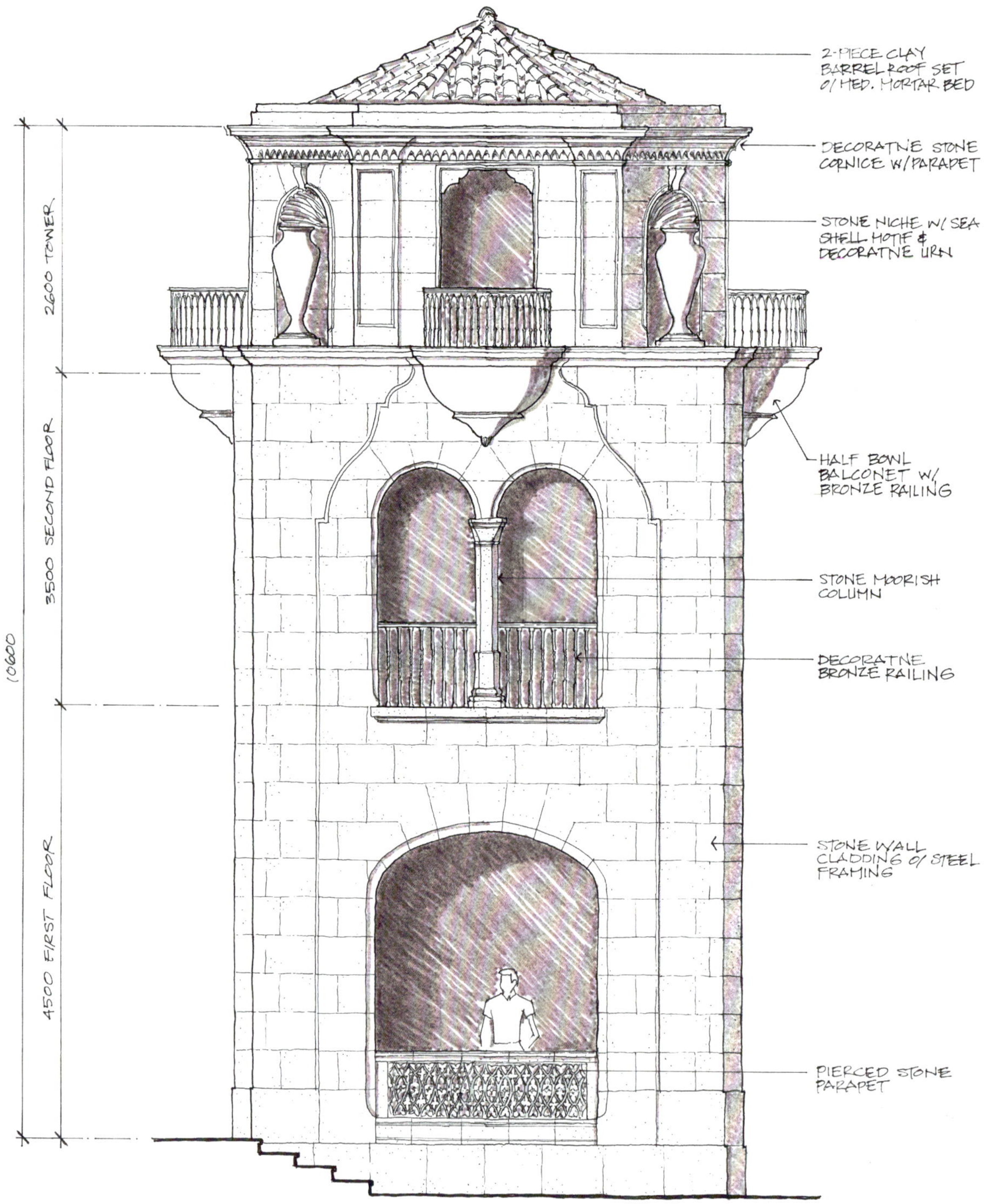

SEA SIDE TOWER - EAST

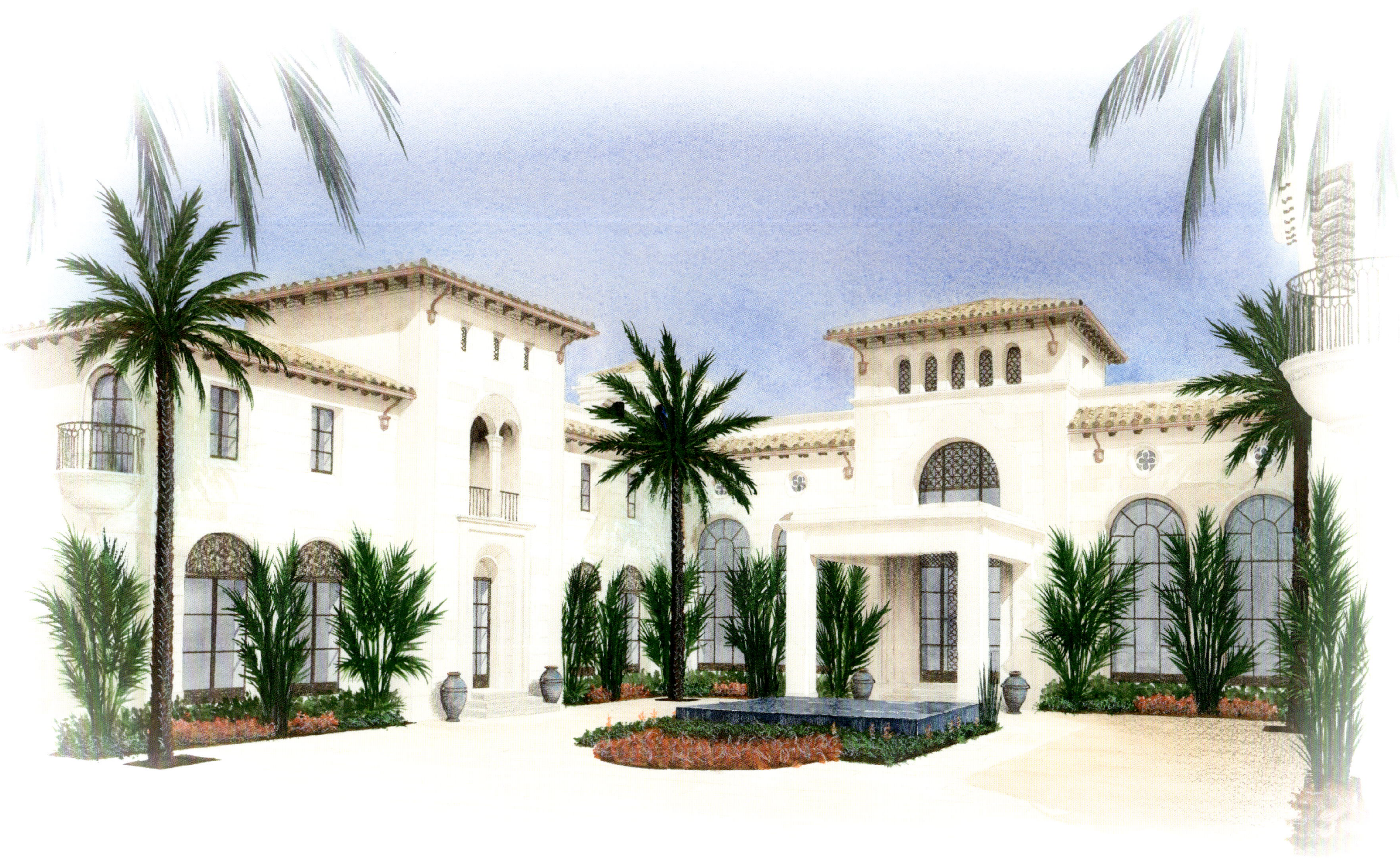

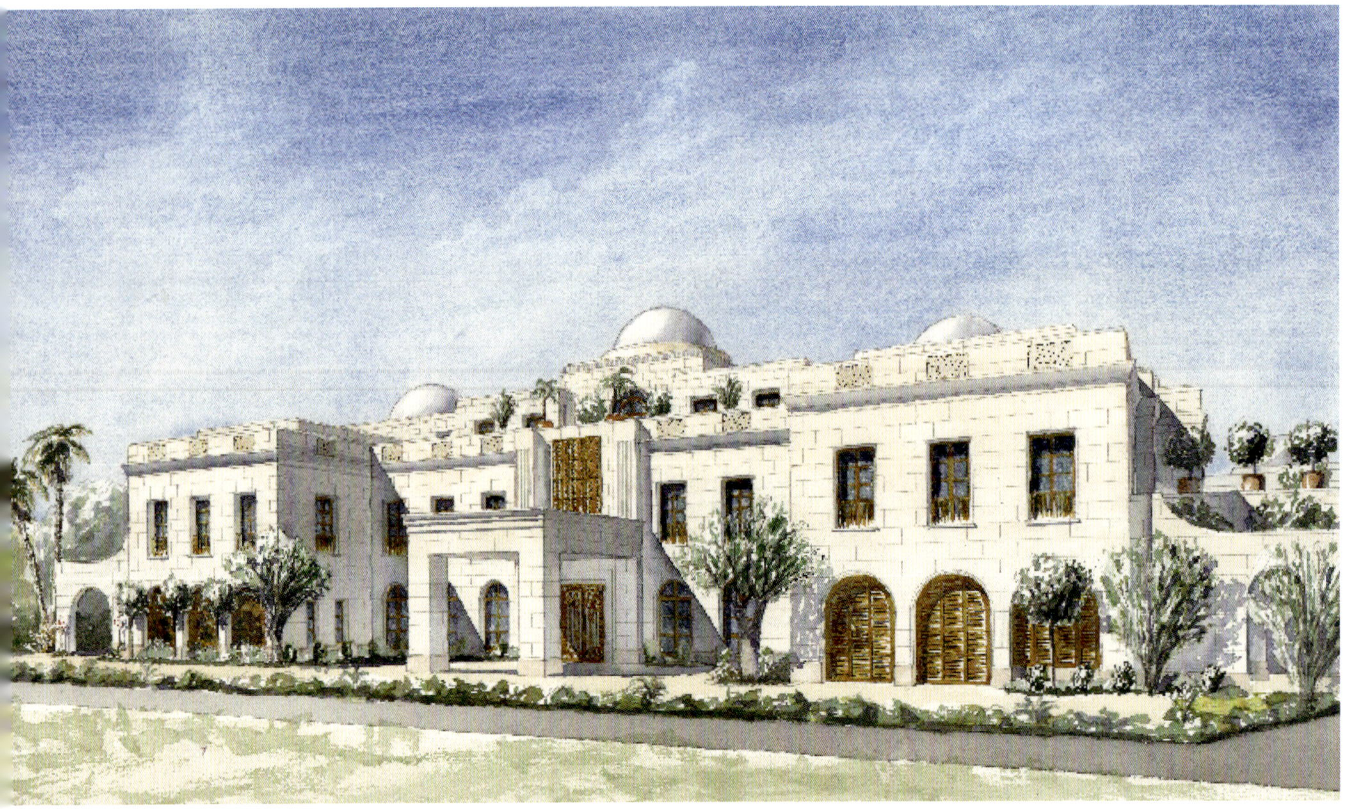

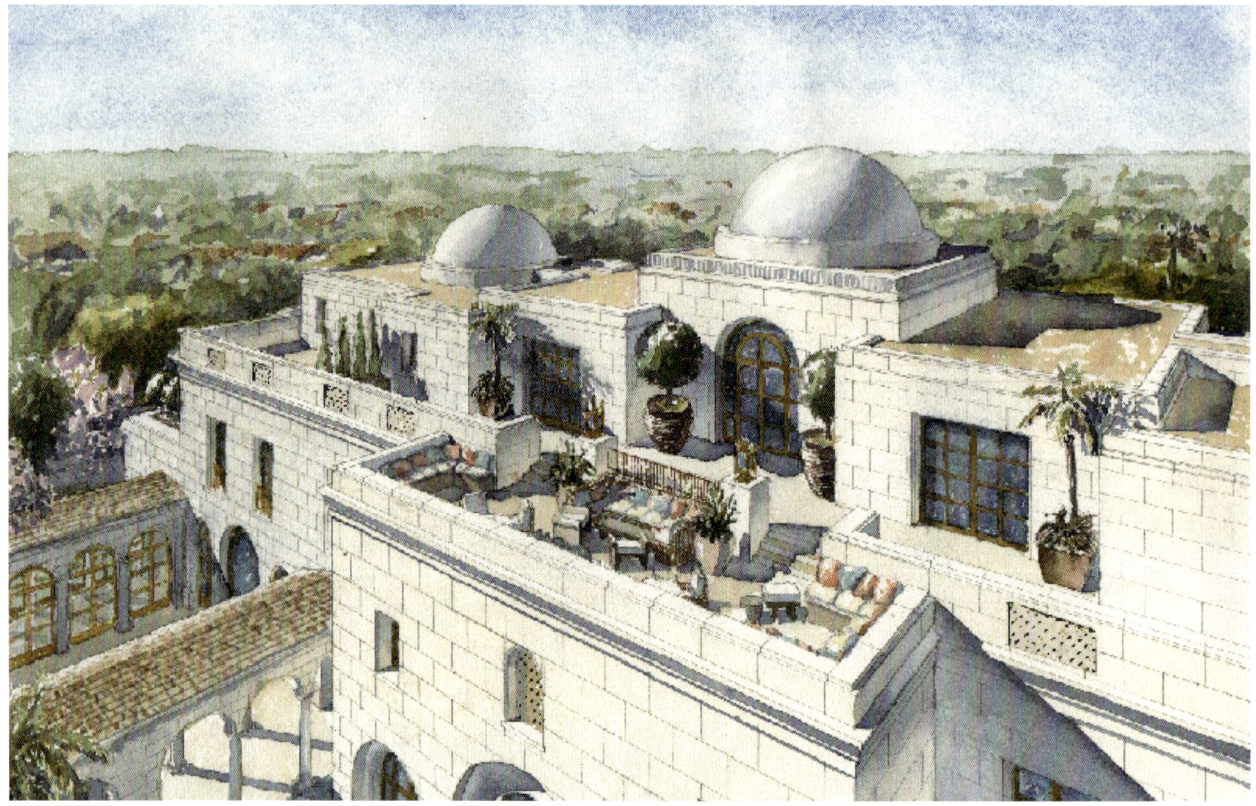

ARABIAN VILLA

Abu Dhabi

Located in a suburban setting, this new residence is designed to blend influences of classical and Mediterranean architecture with modern Arabic details to unite the cultures of the Middle East and the West. Organized around courtyard gardens with water elements, lawns and terraces, the villa provides distinct public and private realms for the requirements of family, friends, and guests. The uppermost floor commands a view across town to the Persian Gulf and features a rooftop entertainment retreat.

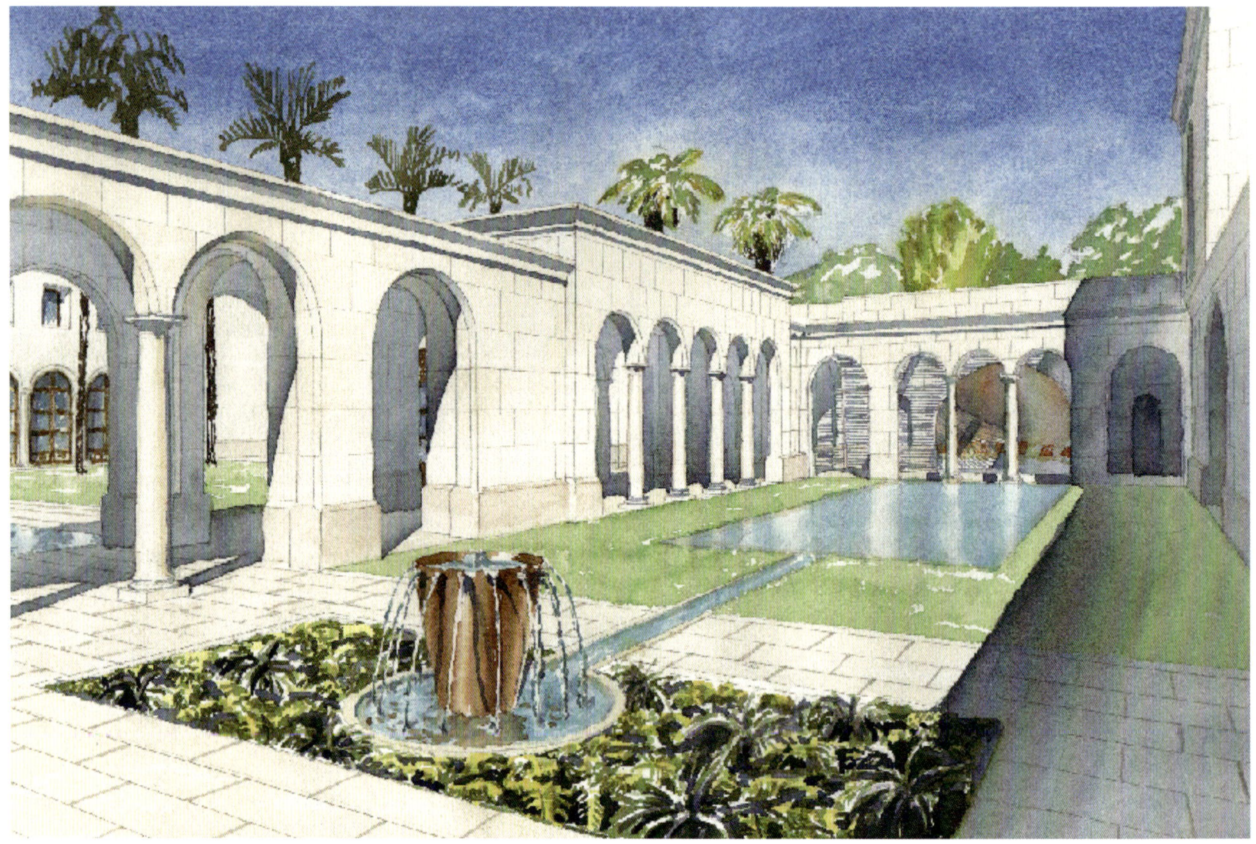

Interior Designer: Joan Behnke
Landscape Architect: Robert Truskowski

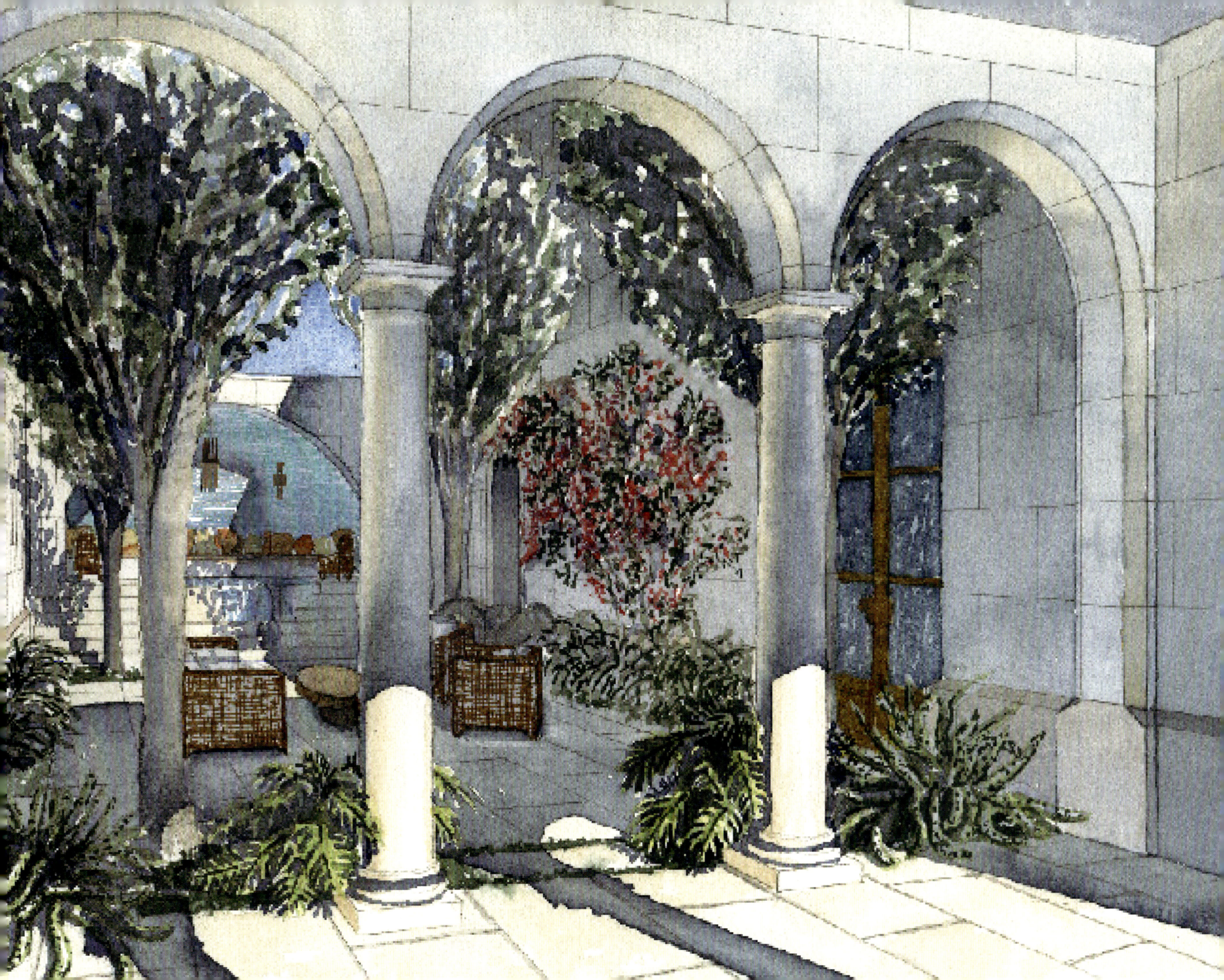

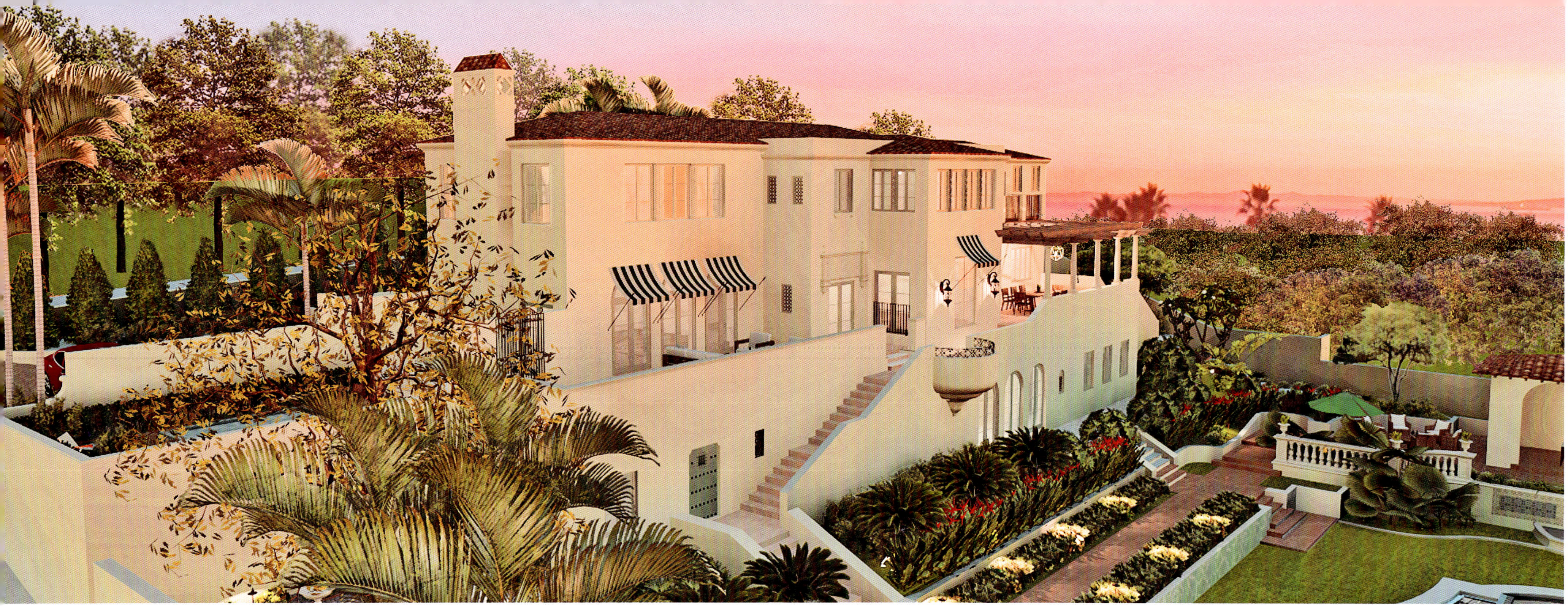

CASA FONTANA

Los Feliz

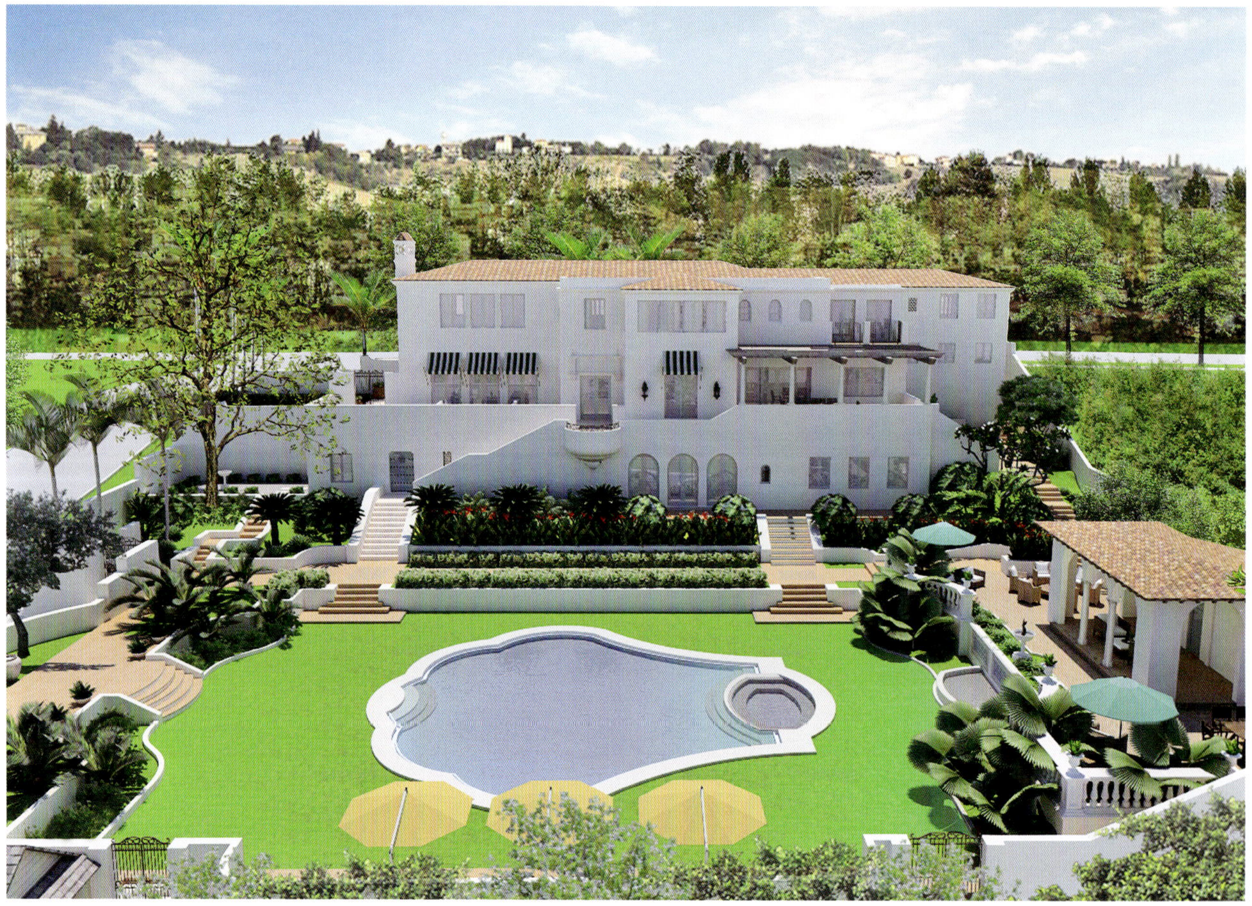

A 1921 villa in the historic Los Feliz neighborhood is an understated interpretation of an Andalusian farmhouse adapted to Southern California living. Our renovation will respect the original design while removing insensitive additions. We are restoring the estate, along with the gardens and their multiple fountains, to its original splendor while incorporating fresh interiors, new family rooms, and basement.

Interior Designer: David Phoenix
Landscape Architect: Scott Shrader

PROJECT CREDITS

VILLA MONTAGNE AL MARE

Project Manager: Denise Dejean
Job Captain: Mary Seed
Project Assistants: Robert Blosfield, Andrew Mitchell
Interior Design: Atelier AM
Landscape Design: Leyva & Wilde
General Contractor: Richard Holz Construction

HOLMBY HOUSE

Project Manager: Marcelo Ciccone
Job Captains: Andrew Mitchell, Katherine Yi
Project Assistants: Edgard Cervantes, Abigail Chen, George Mendez
Interior Design: SFA Design
Landscape Design: Leyva & Wilde
General Contractor: JRC Group

SEASIDE

Project Manager: Robert Meiklejohn
Job Captain: Adrian Rakowicz
Project Assistants: Robert Blosfield, Denise Dejean, Lilian Hun, Matt Silberstein, Katherine Yi
Interior Design: Atelier AM
Landscape Architect: Mark Beall
General Contractor: Richard Holz Construction

VILLA MEZZALUNA

Project Manager: Denise Dejean
Job Captain: Mahshid Katouzian
Project Assistant: Kaiji Yan
Interior Design: Trevor Howells
Landscape Architect: Robert E. Truskowski
General Contractor: JRC Group

RUTHERFORD HOUSE

VP/Senior Associate: Victor Salas
Project Manager: Lilian Hun
Job Captains: Erika Pisca, Katherine Yi
Project Assistants: Keyur Maru, George Mendez, Matt Silberstein, Elizabeth Slaski
Interior Design: David Desmond
Landscape Architecture: Daniel Busbin
General Contractor: JRC Group

COLONIAL REVIVAL POOL HOUSE

VP/Senior Associate: Dave Hogan
Project Manager: Denise Dejean
Job Captain: Robert Blosfield
Interior Design: Nancy Corzine
Landscape Design: Daniel Busbin
General Contractor: JRC Group

KAISER ESTATE

VP/Senior Associate: Dave Hogan
Project Managers: Richard Giesbret, Robert Meiklejohn
Job Captains: Denise Dejean, Lilian Hun, Erika Pisca, Heath Speakman
Project Assistants: Behnoosh Ashtari, Robert Blosfield, Doug Hinrichs, George Mendez, Matt Silberstein
Interior Design: David Desmond
Landscape Architecture: Steve Mechler
General Contractor: Dwight Burdick Construction

CASA CALIFORNIA

Project Manager: Denise Dejean
Project Assistants: Jose Sosa, Katherine Yi
Interior Design: Melissa Partridge
Landscape Design: Leyva & Wilde
General Contractor: Heltzer Development

MAISON DUNAND

Project Manager: Marcelo Ciccone
Job Captain: Adrian Rakowicz
Project Assistants: Doug Hinrichs, Keyur Maru, George Mendez, Andrew Mitchell, Elizabeth Slaski
Interior Design: Dory Novian
Landscape Design: Leyva & Wilde
General Contractor: Tekne Construction

COLLINE D'OR

Project Manager: Robert Meiklejohn
Job Captains: Dudley Emick III, Marie Milat
Project Assistants: Mynor Fahrenreich, Marcelo Goncalves, Claes Hodnett, Yoram LePair, Fariba Yazdani
Interior Design: David Desmond
Landscape Design: Thomas Klope
General Contractor: Swinerton Builders

BUCKHEAD

VP/Senior Associate: Dave Hogan
Project Manager: Robert Fry
Job Captain: Levon Farra
Project Assistants: Behnoosh Ashtari, Denise Dejean, Lilian Hun, Jose Sosa
Interior Design: David Desmond
Landscape Design: Leyva & Wilde
General Contractor: Gordon Gibson Construction

ROSE GARDEN VILLAS

VP/Senior Associate: Victor Salas
Job Captain: Erika Pisca
Project Assistants: Denise Dejean, Adrian Rakowicz, Jose Sosa, Katherine Yi
Interior Design: David Desmond
Landscape Architecture: Mario Nievera
General Contractor: Shanghai Greentown Group

MAGNOLIA

Project Manager: Denise Dejean
Job Captains: Marcelo Ciccone, Katherine Yi
Project Assistants: Abigail Chen, Doug Hinrichs, Keyur Maru
Interior Design: David Desmond
Landscape Design: Leyva & Wilde
General Contractor: JRC Group

CHÂTEAU DE LA LUMIÈRE

VP/Senior Associate: Victor Salas
Project Manager: Lilian Hun
Job Captain: Erika Pisca
Project Assistants: Abigail Chen, Denise Dejean, Jing Liu, Jennifer McAdam, Adrian Rakowicz, Matt Silberstein, Elizabeth Slaski, Katherine Yi
Interior Design: David Desmond
Landscape Design: SWA Group
General Contractor: Actus Builders Pte Ltd

Published in Australia in 2020 by
The Images Publishing Group Pty Ltd
ABN 89 059 734 431

Offices

Melbourne
6 Bastow Place
Mulgrave, Victoria 3170
Australia
Tel: +61 3 9561 5544

New York
6 West 18th Street 4B
New York, NY 10011
United States
Tel: +1 212 645 1111

Shanghai
6F, Building C, 838 Guangji Road
Hongkou District, Shanghai 200434 China
Tel: +86 021 31260822

books@imagespublishing.com
www.imagespublishing.com

The Images Publishing Group Reference Number: 1543

Principal photography is by Erhard Pfeiffer, and all plans, renderings, and illustrations are supplied courtesy of Richard Manion Architecture, with the following exceptions:
Roger Davies: pages 4, 78–79, 80, 81, 82, 84, 85, 86, 87, 88, 89, 90, 91, 92, 93, 94–95, 96–97; Karyn R. Millet: pages 12, 41, 57; David Desmond: page 229; Mario Nievera: page 210; Shanghai Greentown Group: pages 213, 214, 217, 218, 220, 221, 222, 223; Margo Ternstrom and Rhona Conley: interior renderings

NATIONAL LIBRARY OF AUSTRALIA
A catalogue record for this book is available from the National Library of Australia

Title: Richard Manion Architecture: Streamlined // Text by Adele Cygelman; Principal photography by Erhard Pfeiffer
ISBN: 9781864708578

This title was commissioned in IMAGES' Melbourne office and produced as follows: *Editorial* Georgia (Gina) Tsarouhas, *Art direction/production* Nicole Boehringer

Printed by Artron Art Printing (HK) Limited, on 157gsm Chinese OJI matt art paper

FSC www.fsc.org MIX Paper from responsible sources FSC® C019910